CONTROVERSIAL REASONING IN INDIAN PHILOSOPHY

Also available from Bloomsbury

Indian Epistemology and Metaphysics
Edited by Joerg Tuske

Jewel of Reflection on the Truth about Epistemology
Stephen Phillips

Language, Meaning, and Use in Indian Philosophy
Malcolm Keating

The Bloomsbury Research Handbook of Indian Philosophy and Gender
Edited by Veena R. Howard

The Bloomsbury Research Handbook of Indian Philosophy of Language
Edited by Alessandro Graheli

The Philosophy of Sri Aurobindo
Edited by Debidatta Aurobinda Mahapatra

CONTROVERSIAL REASONING IN INDIAN PHILOSOPHY

MAJOR TEXTS AND ARGUMENTS ON *ARTHÂPATTI*

Edited by Malcolm Keating

BLOOMSBURY
NEW DELHI • LONDON • OXFORD • NEW YORK • SYDNEY

Bloomsbury Publishing India
DDA Complex, LSC Building No. 4 Second Floor, Pocket C – 6 & 7,
Vasant Kunj , New Delhi 110070

BLOOMSBURY, Bloomsbury Academic India and the Diana
logo are trademarks of Bloomsbury Publishing Plc

First published in India 2024
First published in Great Britain 2020
This paperback edition published in 2023

Cover design by Louise Dugdale
Cover image © Gameigo Gameigo / EyeEm / Getty Images

This edition is published with permission from Bloomsbury Publishing Plc.
50 Bedford Square, London WC1B3DP

A catalog record for this book is available from the Library of Congress.
A catalogue record for this book is available from the British Library.

ISBN: 978-93-61314-40-7
For sale in the Indian subcontinent only

Exclusively distributed in the Indian subcontinent by
Manohar Publishers & Distributors
4753/23, Ansari Road
Darya Ganj, New Delhi 110002
Tel.: 23284848, 23289100
Email: sales@manoharbooks.com, manoharbooks@gmail.com

Typeset by RefineCatch Limited, Bungay, Suffolk
Printed and bound in India by Replika Press Pvt. Ltd
To find out more about our authors and books visit
www.bloomsbury.com and sign up for our newsletters.

CONTENTS

LIST OF FIGURES AND TABLES

FIGURE

TABLES

NOTES ON CONTRIBUTORS

Nilanjan Das is Associate Professor of Philosophy at the University of Toronto. He mainly works on epistemology and classical Indian philosophy in Sanskrit (especially later Nyāya). His articles have been published in the *Journal of Indian Philosophy, Noûs, the Review of Symbolic Logic,* and *Ratio.*

Elisa Freschi is Assistant Professor of South Asian Philosophy in the Department of Philosophy, University of Toronto. Her main field of research is South Asian philosophy, especially deontic logic, epistemology, and philosophy of language and of religion in the Mīmāṃsā and Viśiṣṭādvaita Vedānta schools. She is the author of two books: *Duty, Language and Exegesis in Prābhākara Mīmāṃsā* (2012) and, with Tiziana Pontillo, *Rule-extension Strategies in Ancient India* (2013). She has edited several volumes, most recently, with Elise Coquereau-Saouma, *The Challenge of Postcolonial Philosophy in India* (2018). Elisa's research for this section has been supported by the WWTF fund MA 16_024.

Alessandro Graheli is Assistant Professor at the Department of Historical Studies, University of Toronto Mississauga, Canada. He is the author of *History and Transmission of the Nyāyamañjarī: Critical Edition of the Section on the Sphota* (2015) and numerous other publications, in his research areas of Nyāya, textual criticism, philosophy of language, theories of knowledge, hermeneutics, aesthetics, and medieval bhakti.

Malcolm Keating is Associate Professor of Philosophy at Yale-NUS College, Singapore. His research focuses on language and epistemology in Indian philosophy. He is the author of *Language, Meaning, and Use in Indian Philosophy: An Introduction to Mukula's "Fundamentals of the Communicative Function"* (2019) and articles in journals such as the *History of Philosophy Quarterly*, the *Journal of Indian Philosophy*, the *Journal of Pragmatics*, and *Philosophy East & West.*

Andrew Ollett is Assistant Professor of South Asian Humanities at the University of Chicago. He works on the literary and intellectual traditions of South Asia, including works composed in Sanskrit, Prakrit, Apabhramsha, and Kannada. His publications include *Language of the Snakes: Prakrit, Sanskrit, and the Language Order of Premodern India* (2017) as well as papers published in the *Journal of Indian Philosophy*, *History and Philosophy of Logic*, and the *Journal of the International Association of Buddhist Studies.*

Stephen Phillips is Professor Emeritus of Philosophy and Asian studies at the University of Texas at Austin and has been a visiting professor of philosophy at the University of Hawai'i, Mānoa and Jadavpur University, Kolkata. He has published numerous papers in scholarly journals and is author or co-author of twelve books, including *Yoga, Karma, and Rebirth: A Brief History and Philosophy* (2009); *Classical Indian Epistemology: The Knowledge Sources of the Nyāya School* (2012); with N. S. Ramanuja Tatacharya, the perception chapter of Gaṅgeśa's fourteenth-century *Tattva-cintā-maṇi* (2008); with Matthew Dasti, *The Nyāya-sūtra: Selections with Early Commentaries* (2017), and a three-volume translation of the *Tattva-cintā-maṇi, Jewel of Reflection on the Truth about Epistemology* (2020).

Mark Siderits teaches analytic Asian philosophy, having retired from Seoul National University in 2012, but is now lecturing regularly at Kyoto University. His research interests lie in the intersection between classical Indian philosophy on the one hand, and analytic metaphysics and philosophy of language on the other. His more recent publications include *Personal Identity and Buddhist Philosophy: Empty Persons*, 2nd edition (2015) and, together with Shōryū Katsura, *Nāgārjuna's Middle Way: Mūlamadhyamakakārikā* (2013). A collection of his papers on Buddhist philosophy, *Studies in Buddhist Philosophy*, was published in 2016.

Anand Vaidya is Professor of Philosophy at San Jose State University. From 1995 to 2005 he was trained as an analytic philosopher, encompassing the philosophy of language and logic, metaphysics, meta-ethics, normative-ethics, applied-ethics, epistemology, philosophy of mind, and the history of Western philosophy. While he continues to work on the epistemology of modality, essence, and grounding, since 2010 he has expanded his interests to the cross-cultural (especially Indian philosophy and Anglo-Analytic philosophy) and multi-disciplinary (especially cognitive science and psychology) study of the mind, the ways of knowing about reality, and critical thinking. He is also interested in the capabilities approach to justice, and core topics in social justice, such as mass incarceration and disability rights.

Kiyotaka Yoshimizu is a research fellow at Toyo Bunko (the Oriental Library) and a former professor at Tohoku University and his main field of research is Mīmāmsā and its related fields. Some of his recent publications include *Der "Organismus" des urheberlosen Veda. Eine Studie der Niyoga-Lehre Prabhākaras mit ausgewählten Übersetzungen der Bṛhatī* (1997); *Kumārila niyoru Shūkyō to shiteno Bukkyō Hihan* (Kumārila's Denunciation of Buddhism as a "Heresy" from the Viewpoint of the Sources of Dharma) (2015); "Tolerance and Intolerance in Kumārila's Views on the Vedic *śākhā*" (2016); "Tradition and Reflection in Kumārila's Last Stand against the Grammarians' Theories of Verbal Denotation" (2012); and "Kumārila's Reevaluation of the Sacrifice and the Veda from a Vedānta Perspective" (2007).

PREFACE

This book is designed to introduce readers to a controversy in Indian philosophy over reasoning. It starts with one side, the Mīmāṃsakas, follows their arguments through time, and then moves to the other side, the Naiyāyikas, with the same chronological approach. That discussion then continues in the essays which draw on the Sanskrit source materials and, with them, engage in constructive philosophical work. Thus, for readers new to Indian philosophy and its dialectics, begin with the Introduction which will give you relevant conceptual context for entering into the discussion. From there, depending on your interests, you can move into the source material directly or begin by reading the essays which examine the philosophical implications of the debate.

Readers interested in the historical development of *arthâpatti* might wish to read some essays and translations together. For instance, Andrew Ollett and Elisa Freschi's translation of Kumārila Bhaṭṭa's *Śloka-vārttika* can be read with Kiyotaka Yoshimizu's essay, "The Physical Existence of a Living Being and Kumārila's Theory of *Arthâpatti*," as the essay develops a philosophical interpretation of Kumārila, employing modern logic. Likewise, Stephen Phillips' translation of Gaṅgeśa's *Tattva-cintā-maṇi* connects to Nilanjan Das's "Raghunātha on *Arthâpatti*," as the essay explains a later Nyāya argument against Gaṅgeśa.

For readers with a background in analytic philosophy, Mark Siderits' and Anand Vaidya's contributions are accessible introductions to the philosophical issues at stake, which might prove a useful starting-point for then returning to some of the specific texts for further investigation. The appended glossaries should be helpful for the technical vocabulary involved in the debate. If you want to reader further, the end of the Introduction includes a discussion of contemporary work on *arthâpatti*.

Readers entering into Sanskrit philosophy for the first time should note something important about its style: it tends to label interlocutors, known as *pūrva-pakṣin*s, and to move through their possible positions, typically from least good until the final, settled view of the philosopher speaking, the *siddhânta* (the one who holds this view is a *siddhāntin*). Translators often identify the interlocutors by which tradition they represent (Bhāṭṭa, Nyāya, and so on), and while this is sometimes explicit in the text, it may not be. And it is a question for scholars how closely the representation actually tracks the traditions, something readers may notice themselves. Further, early Sanskrit philosophers (e.g. Akṣapāda Gautama) wrote in short, memorable statements (*sūtra*s) as well as verse form (as in Kumārila Bhaṭṭa's work), lending themselves to memorization and recitation. These compact works need explication by commentators to be intelligible, and so we have incorporated *sūtra* text and commentary together, both earlier Sanskrit commentary and our modern translators' English commentaries. These remarks are indented from the main text.

Finally, we expect that readers competent in Sanskrit will read the translations along with their own Sanskrit editions, but our translators have also made select new transliterations available on Bloomsbury's website (www.bloomsbury.com/controversial-reasoning-in-indian-philosophy). See the "Notes on Transliteration Conventions and Pronunciation" for discussion of the particular approach used in this volume.

ACKNOWLEDGMENTS

Such a significant project could not have happened without the help of many people. In particular, I'd like to thank all of the contributors to the book for their participation and collaboration—at our workshop in Singapore and throughout the entire project. Thanks also to Yale-NUS College and Singapore's Ministry of Education for funding this project with grant IG16-LR104. Their funding enabled our collaboration to happen in person, which greatly improved the book. Finally, thanks to the team at Bloomsbury for supporting this project.

A NOTE ON TRANSLITERATION CONVENTIONS AND PRONUNCIATION

Throughout the book, Sanskrit words and phrases are printed in italics, transliterated according to the International Alphabet of Sanskrit Transliteration (IAST). Long passages of Sanskrit, such as footnotes, are printed in roman text to facilitate reading. With the exception of proper names, we break words within compounds using hyphens, and mark vowels joined across word boundaries with a circumflex, for example the conjunction of *artha* + *āpatti* is written as *arthâpatti*. Vowel changes are not restored, for example *arthâpatti* + *ābhāsa* is written as *arthâpatty-ābhāsa*. Dropped vowels are represented with a single quotation mark, for example *jñāne api* is written as *jñāne'pi*. Readers should note that, because transliteration conventions vary across genres and geographical regions, the main subject of this book is transliterated in print elsewhere both as *arthâpatti* and as *arthāpatti*.

For readers unfamiliar with Sanskrit, a few words on the above transliteration style is in order, along with a few other conventions. One of the remarkable aspects of the Sanskrit language is its capacity for very long compounds. For instance, in his *Jewel of Reflection on the Truth about Epistemology*, Gaṅgésa writes,

> *vyāptapakṣadharmatājñānajanyatāniyamāt*

with that phrase giving a reason,

> ... because inferential knowledge by its rule-bound nature is generated by knowledge of the inferential mark's being a property of the inferential subject ... as well as of its being pervaded [by the property to be proven].
>
> —See page 215, Phillips

Since the translations and essays in this book are intended for an audience with a wide range of familiarity with Sanskrit (from none to expertise), the editor has elected to indicate word-breaks within compounds using hyphens, so that the phrase above would be written

> *vyāpta-pakṣa-dharmatā-jñāna-janyatā-niyamāt*.

This allows readers, even those who do not know Sanskrit, to identify the component parts of the compound, and begin to learn important terms as they appear throughout the text. For experts who can read Sanskrit without such breaks, it makes transparent the interpretive choices when phonological change, *saṃdhi*, is ambiguous. While this requires some potentially controversial decisions about what parts of speech count as a word, as a general principle, we break according to entries which are discrete words in common Sanskrit dictionaries. The transliterations which Bloomsbury Academic has graciously agreed to host on their website (www.

bloomsbury.com/controversial-reasoning-in-indian-philosophy) are the work of the respective translators and follow their own conventions.

Another convention in this book is the use of brackets, [ ], as in the excerpt of Gaṅgeśa above. While translators have tried to be sparing in their use, sometimes the syntax of Sanskrit strongly implies, but does not directly express, a meaning which English syntax must have explicit, on pain of incomprehensibility. Parentheses, ( ), surround interpolations that are not so indicated by the syntax, but mark content the translator finds useful for explicating an otherwise terse meaning, or they enclose key Sanskrit terms.

Finally, while it is not standard practice everywhere, we have also translated the titles of the Sanskrit works in this volume, save for those which are already well known in Sanskrit (e.g. *Mahā-bhārata*, *Nyāya-sūtra*). Readers should also recognize that these translations may not be widespread, so that existing work on Kumārila's *Extensive Commentary in Verse* likely refers to it as the *Śloka-vārttika* (with or without a hyphen).

Extensive guides to Sanskrit pronunciation are found elsewhere, for instance at the Cambridge University Press website for Ruppel's (2017) textbook and print Sanskrit textbooks such as Goldman and Goldman (2004). Below are a few helpful hints for newcomers to the language:

1. The macron over a vowel (*ā*, *ī*, *ū*) indicates doubled vowel length, so that while *a* is pronounced as the u in "tub," *ā* is pronounced like a in "father" and held longer. Other vowels are roughly like their English counterparts.
2. An *h* after a consonant indicates aspiration, so that *th* is pronounced as the th in "warthog" and not as in "the."
3. There are three different Sanskrit sibilants, *ś*, *ṣ*, and *s*. The first is pronounced with the back of the tongue pressed against the soft palate, while the second involves the tip of the tongue pressed against the roof of the mouth. Both are roughly a *sh* sound as in "wish," while *s* is like "so."
4. The letter *ṛ* is pronounced like the r in "Rita" or "fiber," with the tongue rolled slightly back.
5. The letter *ṃ* is a nasalized sound, roughly as the n in "hang."
6. There are no accents in classical Sanskrit, but the penultimate syllable is typically stressed: "Vedānta." When the penultimate syllable is not long, the stress falls on the preceding long syllable: "Himālaya."

REFERENCES

Goldman, Robert P. and Sally J. Sutherland Goldman (2004), *Devavāṇīpraveśikā: An Introduction to the Sanskrit Language*, Berkeley: Center for South and Southeast Asia Studies, University of California, Berkeley.

Ruppel, A. M. (2017), *The Cambridge Introduction to Sanskrit*, Cambridge: Cambridge University Press.

LIST OF ABBREVIATIONS

B	*Bṛhatī* (*Long Explanation*) of Prabhākara Miśra
BT	*Bṛhaṭ-ṭīkā* (*Long Remarks*) of Kumārila Bhāṭṭa
D	*Dīdhiti* (*Splendour*) of Raghunātha (on the *Tattva-cintā-maṇi*)
GBh	*Granthi-bhaṅga* (*Splitting the Knot*) of Cakradhara (on the *Nyāya-mañjarī*)
K	*Kāśikā* of Sucarita Miśra
MM	*Māna-meyôdaya* (*Elucidation on Epistemic Instruments and Their Objects*) of Nāryāyaṇa Bhaṭṭa and Nāryāyaṇa Paṇḍita
MS	*Mīmāṃsā-sūtra* of Jaimini
NBh	*Nyāya-bhāṣya* (on the *Nyāya-sūtra*) of Vātsyāyana
NK	*Nyāya-kusumâñjali* (*The Flower-Offering of Reason*) of Udayana Ācārya
NM	*Nyāya-mañjarī* (*Flower Garland of Reason*) of Jayanta Bhaṭṭa
NR	*Nyāya-ratnâkara* of Pārthasārathi Miśra
NS	*Nyāya-sūtra* of Akṣapāda Gautama
NV	*Nyāya-vārttika* (on the *Nyāya-sūtra*) of Uddyotakara
NVTṬ	*Nyāya-vārttika-tātparya-ṭīkā* (on the *Nyāya-sūtra*) of Vācaspati Miśra
PATN	*Padârtha-tattva-nirūpaṇa* (*A Demonstration of the True Nature of Things to Which Words Refer*) of Raghunātha Śiromaṇi
PP	*Prakaraṇa-pañcikā* (*Collected Essays*) of Śālikanātha Miśra
PS	*Pramāṇa-samuccaya* (*Compendium of Epistemic Instruments*) of Diṅnāga
PV	*Pramāṇa-vārttika* (*Explanation of Epistemology*) of Dharmakīrti
PVSV	*Pramāṇa-vārttika-sva vṛtti* (*Auto-Commentary on the Explanation of Epistemology*) of Dharmakīrti
RP	*Ṛju-vimalā Pañcikā* (*Straightforward and Lucid Gloss*) of Śālikanātha Miśra
ŚBh	*Śābara-bhāṣya* (*Śabara's Commentary*) of Śabara Miśra
ŚV	*Śloka-vārttika* (*Explanation in Verse*) of Kumārila Bhaṭṭa.
TCM	*Tattva-cintā-maṇi* (*Jewel of Reflection on the Truth about Epistemology*) of Gaṅgeśa
TR	*Tantra-rahasya* (*Secret of the System*) of Rāmānuja Ācārya
TS	*Tattva-saṃgraha* (*Compendium of Truth*) of Śāntarakṣita
TSP	*Tattva-saṃgraha-pañjikā* (*Comprehensive Commentary on the Compendium of Truth*) of Kamalaśīla
TṬ	*Tātparya-ṭīkā* of Umbeka Bhaṭṭa
TV	*Tantra-vārttika* (*Explanation of the System*) of Kumārila Bhaṭṭa
VP	*Vākya padīya* (*About Sentences and Words*) of Bhartṛhari

Introduction

Human knowledge has many sources. For instance, sometimes we use perception: we see that there is an apple on the table. Sometimes we use reasoning: if there is smoke present on a distant hill, then we conclude there is also fire present there, since fire causes smoke. Sometimes we rely on other people's testimony: a friend tells us that our lost book is on the table in the other room, though we don't see it ourselves. Philosophers have long inquired into the different ways people come to know, the necessary conditions for knowing to occur, and the objects (and limits) of our knowledge. Thinkers on the Indian subcontinent have studied these questions for millennia, giving rise to rich textual traditions whose sophisticated inquiry centers on epistemology, logic, language, and their intersections. One question they raised in this context is how to account for knowledge-acquisition which arises to resolve a problem, address an apparent contradiction, or to remove a doubt about knowledge we previously thought firm. This way of knowing is pervasive and ordinary. For instance, entering a room behind someone with my hands full, I may shout "Door, door!" in order to convey that I want them to keep the door open. They understand this despite my not uttering the word "open." Or, arriving at my friend's home, a friend who I have every reason to think is alive, I find their place empty. I think to myself that they must be outside (and still very much alive). These are examples, to which we will return later, of a way of knowing called *arthâpatti*. Indian philosophical debates over its nature and its relationship to other ways of knowing not only tell us about the history of Indian philosophy, but also about the character of knowledge and the structure of reasoning.

This book is both a sourcebook and a selection of essays. It introduces the reader to the intellectual context in which debate over *arthâpatti* occurs, presents a selection of major Sanskrit works in readable translations with critical notes, and, on the basis of those texts, explores the ramifications of this debate through a set of philosophical essays. These essays illuminate the historical debates, extending discussion beyond them to implications in contemporary Anglo-European, as well as classical Indian, philosophy. However, this book is not a comprehensive treatment of topics in Indian epistemology, language, and logic, nor is it even a comprehensive treatment of *arthâpatti*. Because the debate over *arthâpatti* occurs primarily between two traditions of Indian philosophy, Nyāya and Mīmāṃsā, we take selections from important Naiyāyikas and Mīmāṃsakas.[1] However, just as Indian philosophy itself

[1] The ending in Sanskrit, "-ika" or "+-aka," with vowel lengthening in the first syllable, has the effect in English of adding "-ist" or "-an" to the end, as in "empiricist" or "Fregean." Thus the term "Naiyāyika" refers to Nyāya philosophers and "Mīmāṃsaka" to Mīmāṃsā philosophers.

is vast, so, too, the topic of *arthâpatti* is broad, and a complete treatment of it is beyond the scope of any single book. What this book aims to do is provide important texts in English translation, some for the first time, to allow further inquiry into *arthâpatti* and related topics. By engaging with these texts, a range of philosophical questions present themselves.

First, we want to know, what is the precise nature of *arthâpatti*? The Sanskrit term *arthâpatti* is variously translated into English as "postulation," "presumption," "implication"—terms which allude to its status as a kind of reasoning. In the Sanskrit context, there is a question as to whether *arthâpatti* is a kind of reasoning known as *anumāna*, often translated as "inference." For classical Indian philosophers, *anumāna*, the term we will use in this book rather than "inference," is a way of knowing that requires also knowing that two entities have a particular relationship known as "pervasion" (*vyāpti*) or "invariable concomittance" (*avinâbhāva*). For instance, we know that smoke is pervaded by fire, that is, all cases of smoke's presence are cases where fire can also be found. Or, we know that being-an-oak is pervaded by being-a-tree, as all cases of being-an-oak are cases where being-a-tree also occurs. The pervasion relationship enables *anumāna* to occur from seeing the pervaded thing (e.g. smoke) in a location (e.g. a mountain). As a result, an agent comes to know the pervader's presence in the same location (e.g. fire on the mountain). Notably, *anumāna* and *arthâpatti* are understood as knowing-events, or cognitions which occur in an individual thinker at a particular time.

Thus for Indian philosophers, another central question is whether *arthâpatti* is a kind of reasoning which also requires knowledge of a pervasion relationship? If so, how do we characterize this relationship? For instance, in the case of our absent friend, do we reason on the basis of knowing that people are spatio-temporally located, and that absence from one place *x* is necessarily connected to presence in some other place, not *x*? This question points to phenomenological concerns in explaining knowledge-acquisition. The fact that people are spatio-temporally located is not at issue—instead, at issue is whether, and how, an agent uses that information in their reasoning. For contemporary philosophers familiar with the categories of deductive, inductive, and abductive reasoning, there may be a further question: can we understand *arthâpatti* as any one of these varieties? If so, does that tell us anything about its relationship to *anumāna*?

Suppose we were to accept that *arthâpatti* is a variety of *anumāna*—what would that entail? This position, put forward by Naiyāyikas against Mīmāṃsakas, might be characterized as epistemic reductionism. As a rough start, we might say that epistemic reduction is when one putative way of knowing can be entirely accounted for by another way of knowing. In the language of Indian philosophy, a way of knowing is a *pramāṇa*, or epistemic instrument. Perception (*pratyakṣa*) is a commonly-accepted epistemic instrument, as is the aforementioned *anumāna*. But it was controversial how to distinguish different epistemic instruments. For instance, when I believe that my missing book is on the table, in virtue of a friend's telling me so, should this be be added to our stock of epistemic instruments as testimony (*śabda*)? Or is it an *anumāna*, because I reason to the truth of my friend's statement on the consideration that my friend is trustworthy, reliable, and in a position to know about the book?

At this point, we might wonder, why does this debate about *arthâpatti* matter? There is probably some truth to the view that the thinkers in this book were simply interested in doing good philosophy. They wanted to get right the ways in which humans engage with their environment as knowers. Further, if *arthâpatti* can bring about knowing without a knower's having awareness of a pervasion relationship, perhaps it can have as its content objects which *anumāna* cannot. There may be some practical implications, as well. When our knowledge is challenged, or we come to doubt that we genuinely know what we thought we knew, we engage in reflective investigation of our knowledge process. In a case of dubious perception, I might get my eyesight tested or check the lighting conditions. In a case of dubious *anumāna*, I might investigate the pervasion relationship for any exceptions which would vitiate my conclusion. If *arthâpatti* is a kind of *anumāna*, then our investigation in light of doubt will go in certain directions. However, if it is its own independent epistemic instrument, then I should not test it as I would an *anumāna*. Thus how to define *arthâpatti* in relationship to *anumāna* is not a mere taxonomical curiosity, but impacts how we function in the world as good knowers.

Like contemporary analytic philosophy (meaning the broadly Anglo-European-indebted tradition of philosophical inquiry with roots in the work of Russell and Frege), Indian philosophers typically work with a stock set of cases which are the basis for inquiry, and which are shared as common starting-points even among disagreeing camps. So the case of the absent friend at home is a paradigmatic example of *arthâpatti*, even if Nyāya philosophers think it should be explained as *anumāna* and Mīmāṃsā philosophers do not. There are a number of different cases which exemplify *arthâpatti*. These cases lead us to ask if they all share the same underlying structure. For instance, from a piece of language (spoken or written), *arthâpatti* results in the knowledge of something (possibly propositional or possibly linguistic) which is not explicitly stated. As the initial linguistic material could either be a complete sentence or a sentence fragment, the resultant object seems to have two varieties: in the first case, something like an implicature or presupposition and in the second case, some kind of elliptical completion. Should these both be explained by *arthâpatti*?

In addition to cases involving linguistic comprehension, there are those involving what appear to be explanation. For instance, from the knowledge that the sun moves across the sky (known by *anumāna* due to seeing its different positions), one uses *arthâpatti* to conclude that the sun has the capacity for self-movement. Or, in a more complex case discussed by the Mīmāṃsā philosopher Kumārila, from the existence of a certain text with particular properties (being knowledge-conducive, conveying knowledge of one's ethical duties), one uses *arthâpatti* to conclude that the text draws on a now-lost text which is itself a perfect epistemic instrument of ethical duty. Similarities among these cases have led some contemporary scholars such as Arnold (2014) to consider *arthâpatti* a kind of ampliative reasoning, perhaps equivalent to, or closely related to, inference to the best explanation (IBE).[2] But IBE

[2] Arnold (2014) says, "it is perhaps that *arthâpatti* will not as readily admit of formalization; this represents, then, something more like inference to the best explanation—the presumption or 'positing' (*kalpanā*) of something without which some explanandum would not make sense."

is typically considered to have a probabilistic or hypothetical status—it does not deliver knowledge in the same way that, for instance, perception does. The outcome of *arthâpatti* is not a hypothesis, but a veridical cognition. So what is the relationship between *arthâpatti* and IBE? Does it depend upon whether *arthâpatti* is reducible to *anumāna*? What should we say about *arthâpatti* and explanation?

Finally, investigation into *arthâpatti* raises questions about how we revise our beliefs and the role of concepts in our everyday thinking. Some philosophers argue that *arthâpatti* involves resolving two apparently contradictory beliefs. However, a genuine logical contradiction cannot be resolved simply by adding a new claim. (The contradiction between "The cat is alive" and "The cat is not alive" cannot be repaired by adding, "The cat is a zombie." Instead, we must understand "alive" in two different senses or make some other revision to the original claims.) So if the initial beliefs about our living friend absent from home are not genuinely contradictory, what is going on in *arthâpatti*? What triggers a new belief? Is that belief genuinely new, or is it simply making explicit something we already believed (being not at home is, in fact, being outside)? Perhaps *arthâpatti* is a matter of making explicit what is involved in our concepts, such as being alive, being at home, being a moving thing. But if this is so, are we coming to acquire new knowledge? Further, although Mīmāṃsā philosophers agree that *arthâpatti* should not be reduced to *anumāna*, they disagree over how to characterize it. Some accept the apparent contradiction approach, others argue that *arthâpatti* resolves a doubt. That is, when we come to know that our friend is not at home, we doubt our previous belief that she is alive. On this view, then, by presuming or concluding that she is outside of the home and also alive, we can remove the doubt. However, this raises questions about why we are entitled to claim that we know our friend is outside and alive, if being alive was in doubt. What sorts of additions and revisions to our beliefs are appropriate in the face of new information?

All of these questions, and more, are involved in the discussion of *arthâpatti* in Indian philosophy, whose understanding has implications for human knowledge, language, and reasoning.

EPISTEMOLOGY, LOGIC, AND LANGUAGE IN INDIAN PHILOSOPHY

The interrelated areas discussed above—epistemology, logic, and language—have been the subject of sustained, careful, and sometimes quite technical, analysis in the Indian philosophical traditions. The traditions of India energetically investigated the above questions in what is known as its "classical" period (from roughly the third to twelfth centuries CE), although philosophical inquiry pre-dates this time and continues into what are often called the "medieval" and "early modern" periods. Our concern in this book is largely the classical period. It is a time characterized by the proliferation of commentaries on earlier foundational texts, *sūtra*s, and intense debate among—and within—traditions that align themselves with one or another such foundational texts. Within their inquiry into epistemology, Indian thinkers, typically but not always writing in Sanskrit, took up what we today would call "logic" and the "philosophy of language."

The latter is an especially important topic for Indian intellectuals. As many have observed, the discipline (*śāstra*) of grammar is foundational for them in a way that is unrivaled in other cultures—it plays a role like geometry to ancient Greeks. Theories of word reference, sentence unity, and pragmatics are brought together with considerations about testimonial justification, speaker reliability and authority, and other epistemological concepts. Just as language and epistemology are brought together, so are logic and epistemology, as we will see. In what follows, we will set out the major contours of the discussion over *arthâpatti*, identifying the central positions of two Indian brahminical traditions where the debate was primarily found. First, though, we must understand the classical Indian theory of epistemic instruments, *pramāṇa-vāda*.

Introduction to pramāṇa *theory*

While Indian philosophy is often characterized in terms of "schools," "systems," or "traditions," which are indebted to an originary aphoristic root text (*sūtra*), the distinction between textual traditions is not hard and fast, and such a characterization can overlook unifying themes and methods running throughout multiple traditions. One of these themes which shares a method is known as *pramāṇa-vāda*, the Epistemological School, or *pramāṇa* theory—the theory of epistemic instruments, *pramāṇa*.[3] Despite the philosophical distance, for instance, between Buddhists (who deny the existence of a substantial self) and Naiyāyikas (who argue for it), those Buddhists and Naiyāyikas who are part of the intertextual discourse known as *pramāṇa* theory have much in common, perhaps more so than is shared between two Buddhist thinkers when one of them is engaged in *pramāṇa* theory and the other is not.

An early systematic approach to *pramāṇa* theory is found in the Nyāya ("logic" or "reasoning") tradition of philosophy, in Akṣapāda Gautama's second-century CE *Nyāya-sūtra* and his commentator Vātsyāyana.[4] Here, Gautama identifies four epistemic instruments: perception, *anumāna*, comparison, and testimony (more on which below), and Vātsyāyana explains what an epistemic instrument is using grammatical analysis:

> That the epistemic instruments, *pramāṇa*, are causes of veridical cognition can be understood from etymology: *pramīyate'nena*, "It is known by means of this." For the word *pramāṇa* designates something that is an instrumental cause.
>
> —Adapted from Dasti and Phillips 2017: 18

Vātsyāyana uses the vocabulary of grammatical analysis of action words to explicate the structure of *pramāṇa*, in particular analysis involving an action's contributors (*kāraka*s, the "doers," "performers"). In theoretical study of Sanskrit grammar going

---

[3] While titles using the term *nyāya* are translated "logic" in this volume, following a general trend in broader scholarship, it is important to recognize that Sanskrit philosophers are concerned with "logic" in the broad sense of principles of reasoning, and not in the narrower sense of formal methods of representing arguments.

[4] In this book, we will translate Sanskrit titles into English unless they are already widely known in Sanskrit (e.g. the *Mahā-bhārata*, the *Nyāya-sūtra*).

back to Pāṇini's *Eight Chapters* (*Aṣṭâdhyāyī*), the case-endings of Sanskrit nouns express these contributors, although there is not a one-to-one correspondence between case and contributor. In this analysis, any action has six contributors: agent, object/patient, instrument, destination, source, and locus. Since it is widely accepted that the word *pramāṇa* designates the instrument, we can use the structure of grammatical analysis to understand there is an agent (*pramātṛ*) and an object (*prameya*) involved in the action of knowing (*pramiti*, *pramā*). This analysis emphasizes the nature of knowing as an action involving a knowing agent, rather than a disposition, belief, etc., which is more common in modern epistemology. Knowledge is discussed in terms of cognitions (*jñāna*s), which are knowledge episodes located in a knower: a knowing agent *S* knows that *p* at a particular time *t*.

Now, although *pramāṇa* theorists share this framework—and common vocabulary—for knowledge, they disagree over the details of analysis. The most obvious disagreement, perhaps, is in the different enumerations of epistemic instruments. We have seen the Naiyāyika, Gautama, list four (perception, *anumāna*, comparison, and testimony), but Buddhists typically exclude comparison and testimony from that list, preferring to reduce them to *anumāna*. In the other direction, Bhāṭṭa Mīmāṃsā thinkers admit six distinct epistemic instruments (perception, *anumāna*, comparison, testimony, *arthâpatti*, and knowledge of absences).[5] This debate, which occurs within and between the textual traditions, is over the individuation and structure of epistemic instruments: the focal point is whether epistemic instrument *x* can be reduced in its structure to another epistemic instrument *y*. In the *kāraka* terms above, this is a question about the instrument of knowing. A common analogy to explain this way of understanding *pramāṇa* is with the action of chopping down a tree: the person chopping and the object being chopped are so identified in virtue of their relationship with the instrument used—something that chops, like an axe. However, if we change the instrument to a saw, then while the object and agent may remain the same, they are no longer "chopping" and "being chopped."

Major pramāṇas *in Indian thought*

The debate about *arthâpatti* is situated within this larger intertextual discourse of *pramāṇa* theory. Because one of the central debates is about whether it can be reduced to another epistemic instrument, let us survey the major *pramāṇa*s, with the caveat that this can only be a broad overview—the details will vary among thinkers.

Perception (*pratyakṣa*) is the epistemic instrument most commonly agreed upon by Indian thinkers. Setting aside the skeptical Cārvāka thinkers—of whose work not much is extant—every Indian philosopher accepts perception as an authoritative instrument of knowing, although the nature of its object and the grounds for its authority (or validity) are two contentious topics. While "perception" is an adequate

[5] While we can make broad generalizations about traditions like Nyāya, Buddhism, and so on, in what follows, we will mostly talk about particular thinkers belonging to a tradition. Just as it would be overly broad to talk about what "empiricists" believe in the contemporary analytic context, without reference to particular empiricists, so too in the Indian context, despite the existence of root texts and a commentarial tradition.

translation for the Sanskrit term, Indian philosophers add one more to the external sensory capacities (sight, hearing, touch, taste, smell) familiar to modern philosophers: the internal capacity of mind (*manas*). Perception is typically taken as a basic epistemic instrument in some manner—it is the input to *anumāna*, for instance, and it is direct, usually a kind of contact through sense organs with reality. One question that occupies philosophers about perception is whether its content is conceptual (*vikalpaka*) or devoid of conceptual content (*nirvikalpaka*).

Anumāna is etymologically characterized by Naiyāikas as being an instrument (*māna*) that works after (*anu-*) perception. With *anumāna*, we can gain knowledge of things beyond perception. It is the other epistemic instrument that Indian thinkers tend to agree upon as being authoritative and *sui generis*—again, setting aside Cārvāka. However, there is significant disagreement over its structure. The most basic parts of *anumāna* are exemplified in a paradigmatic case:[6]

Thesis: That mountain (*site*) has fire (*property to be proven*)

Reason: because there is smoke (*reason property*),

Example: and wherever there is smoke there is fire (*pervasion relationship*), just like the kitchen hearth (*positive example*) and unlike the lake (*negative example*).

Again, it should be emphasized that there is always an agent who is engaging in *anumāna*—further, the content of an *anumāna* must be true for it to constitute a genuine epistemic instrument, so that, strictly speaking, there is no formally valid but unsound *anumāna*. And yet there is a structure in virtue of which an *anumāna* can be knowledge-conducive or fallacious, and these fallacies receive significant attention, especially in Nyāya. Key to a successful *anumāna* is the co-location of two properties in a subject (*pakṣa*). Here, the mountain is the place in which the agent wishes to know if there is fire, and she can know this in virtue of (1) knowledge of the property's presence there, that is, smoke; and (2) knowledge of the relationship between smoke and fire. While in this case, knowledge of smoke is perceptual, *anumāna* can function on any knowledge cognition, whether it originates from testimony, comparison, and so on (though these sources tend to be traced back to some perceptual input at some point in their causal history). The pervasion relationship is so called because there is a directionality involved: the presence of smoke is pervaded by fire (it is invariable in this direction) whereas the presence of fire is not pervaded by smoke (it is not invariable, as one can have non-smoky fire in a hot ball of iron). Typically, repeated observations are necessary for ascertaining the pervasion relationship, although this, too, is a point of controversy—especially when it comes to relationships between properties which are not observable.

[6] These three parts of the inference are the most broadly agreed upon, although there is debate about whether two further aspects should be added: a sentence confirming that the current case is like the example(s) adduced and a conclusion which restates the thesis in light of what has just been said. These two statements are included by Naiyāyikas in what is known as inference-for-another, or inferences which are given in order to convince another person (or explicitly stated for oneself) in contrast to inference-for-onself, which may have only the first three elements and which need not be explicitly stated. Not all philosophers accept the distinction between inference-for-onself and inference-for-another.

The *anumāna* above is called positive and negative (*anvaya-vyatireka*), as its evidence supports the pervasion relationship in its two directions: when the property to be proven is present and absent. However, while the paradigmatic case admits of both positive and negative supporting examples, there are two other kinds (putatively at least—not all thinkers accept all three) which have only a positive and only a negative example:[7]

Positive-only (*kevalânvaya*)
Sound (*subject*) has impermanence (*property to be proven*) because it can be perceived (*reason property*), and wherever there is perceptibility there is impermanence (*pervasion relationship*), just like a pot (*positive example*).

Negative-only (*kevala-vyatireka*)
A living body (*subject*) has the property of not-lacking-a-self (*property to be proven*) because it is alive (*reason property*), and wherever there is being-alive there is not-lacking-a-self (*pervasion relationship*), unlike a pot (*negative example*).

In the positive-only *anumāna*, because of the nature of the reason property, there is no way to adduce any negative examples. We cannot perceive something imperceptible and thereby use that as evidence that the imperceptible lacks impermanence (i.e., is permanent). In contrast, the negative-only *anumāna* cannot have any positive example on pain of circularity. The only place where not-lacking-a-self occurs is thought to be living bodies. Unlike the case of the fiery and smoky mountain, where we can observe a kitchen hearth and see the same causal relationship as on the mountain, in the case of the self, all we have for evidence are other living bodies. Thus the evidence can only be negative. Of course, this type of *anumāna* is controversial, as it seems to enable us to demonstrate anything, so long as we can find a single example where the putative property fails to be found. This sort of *anumāna* is often reserved for conceptual definitions—such as the relationship between being a tree and being an oak, where we infer that an oak is a tree because things that aren't trees, like lotus flowers, are also not oaks. This type is also crucial in the discussion about *arthâpatti*, since some Nyāya philosophers and some Buddhists wish to argue that *arthâpatti* is in reality this same kind of *anumāna*, as it relies on negative examples (see section 3 below).

Testimony (*śabda*) is for some thinkers reducible to *anumāna*, but for others it is *sui generis*. The category of testimony is important in both ordinary and religious/scriptural contexts, as both brahminical thinkers and those outside of brahminical orthopraxy such as Buddhists have scriptural traditions. Like *anumāna*, testimony enables us to go beyond the bounds of our perceptual cabilities, whether this is in virtue of the words of the Vedas or the Buddha or simply our trustworthy next-door neighbor. For those who think testimony is simply a kind of *anumāna*, the necessity of an authoritative and trustworthy speaker is telling: we must not merely understand the testimonial utterance, but also take a further step of reasoning to what we

[7] Both examples are paradigmatic for Nyāya philosophers. Different philosophers use different examples depending upon their commitments.

understand is true, in virtue of the speaker's nature (not wanting to mislead and having relevant expertise). Against this position, some thinkers, especially Bhāṭṭa Mīmāṃsā thinkers (part of a tradition focused on developing interpretive rules for Vedic texts that describe ritual praxis), argue that testimony is authoritative in virtue of its nature as testimony. No *anumāna* based on a speaker's nature is necessary—for an ordinary case we might think of asking a stranger for directions in an unknown city, when we have no knowledge of their character. In the special context of Vedic ritual praxis, given that the origins of these texts (orally transmitted for a millennium) are lost in time, there is additional impetus to consider speech itself the epistemic instrument, and not some pervasion relationship between a speaker and the speech, as would be the case in *anumāna*. Sometimes, though, speech is incomplete or open-ended, and then a further kind of reasoning is necessary. For some thinkers—again Mīmāṃsā is one important case—*arthâpatti* is closely connected with these types of testimony. It enables completion of ellipsis—someone saying, "the door, the door," and thereby meaning "close the door, close the door"—as well as understanding of things implied by complete sentences, for example "stout Devadatta does not eat during the day," from which we understand that he eats at night. Again, though, the question arises whether *anumāna* might not be a better explanation of this process.

There are other putative epistemic instruments, such as comparison (*upamāna*) and perception of absences (*abhāva*, *anupalabdhi*), as well as omniscience/yogic perception (*yaugika-pratyakṣa*), which space does not permit us to discuss.[8] The debates about these instances, however, follow the general structure of what has been laid out already.

ARTHÂPATTI IN NYĀYA AND MĪMĀṂSĀ

While *arthâpatti* is discussed in other places than the two traditions of Nyāya and Mīmāṃsā, much of the debate occurs between them, and thus they are the primary focus of this volume. As we will see, Naiyāyikas tend to prefer a reductionist account, in which *arthâpatti* is a kind of *anumāna* as described above, while Mīmāṃsakas wish to carve out a place for it to stand on its own. Just what kind of *anumāna* an *arthâpatti* would constitute is an internal debate within Nyāya, and within Mīmāṃsā there are competing theories about the structure of the epistemic instrument. Before moving on to the specifics of these debates, though, let us explain *arthâpatti* in its most basic contours.

1. *What is* arthâpatti?

The Sanskrit term *arthâpatti* is a compound, comprised of two words: *artha* and *āpatti*. Trying to gloss the compound, as a whole or in parts, is difficult, since each

[8] In particular, *abhāva* or *anupalabdhi* is important for *arthâpatti*, since the latter seems to often involve reasoning based on something's being missing (a bit of language from an utterance, a person from a house). Das's essay (see p. 255) explains this connection further.

word's meaning is ambiguous, as is their relationship.[9] We will see that the ambiguity in *artha* is a point of contention internal to Mīmāṃsā: it can refer to a word-meaning or to an object in general. As for *āpatti*, it is derived from a verb (*ā-pad*) and can simply mean "obtain," so that *arthâpatti* is the obtaining of a meaning or an object.[10] On the other hand, it could also mean "get into trouble," which makes *arthâpatti* the case of a meaning or an object being threatened—for instance, by a contradiction, or a doubt. Semantic analysis is not going to tell us what *arthâpatti* is—for this we will need to investigate the positions of various thinkers. Thankfully they also give us multiple cases to illustrate *arthâpatti*, which are then subjected to analysis. One of the earliest examples is found in the *Treatise on Material and Political Aims* (*Artha-śāstra*) of Kauṭīlya, who includes *arthâpatti* in his enumeration of methodological principles (*tantra-yukti*):

> What naturally follows from a statement of facts, though not spoken of in plain terms, is *arthâpatti*; for example, "Whoever has full experience of the affairs of this world should, through the medium of the courtiers and other friends, win the favour of a king who is of good character and a worthy sovereign. It follows from this that no one should seek the favour of a king through the medium of the king's enemies."
>
> — Kauṭīlya's *Artha-śāstra*, transl. Shamasastry 1929

This illustration emphasizes the linguistic role of *arthâpatti*, but, as we will see, it is understood in philosophical texts as a more broadly applicable epistemic instrument—although we do not know with certainty whether this is an extension from an original more limited use or if Kauṭīlya is using an already broad concept in a limited sense here. Either way, the debate over *arthâpatti* includes its scope (does it include linguistic knowledge?) as well as its structure (is it reducible to *anumāna* or other epistemic instruments?). In what follows, we start with Mīmāṃsakas, who take *arthâpatti* to be an independent epistemic instrument, distinct from *anumāna*. Their approach to *arthâpatti* is informed by their willingness to use it in Vedic exegesis, although we will see that they do not limit its role to this context alone. Naiyāyika philosophers find no need for another epistemic instrument, arguing that *anumāna* alone (or *anumāna* with hypothetical reasoning, *tarka*) will suffice in accomplishing the aims attributed to *arthâpatti*.

---

[9] Further, translating *arthâpatti* into English poses a challenge. The typical options include "implication," "presumption," and "postulation." The first option is a technical term in Anglo-European philosophy of language and logic. If taken in the logical sense, "implication" might suggest that *arthâpatti* is a matter of deductive reasoning—close to the Nyāya viewpoint, but this leaves out the possibility that it is something else. If taken in the linguistic sense, this might foreclose the broader view, on which *arthâpatti* also "implies" things (and for that, see the logical sense). The term "presumption" connotes probabilistic and sometimes even unwarranted reasoning, which could undermine the idea that *arthâpatti* is a genuine epistemic instrument. Finally, "postulation" strikes an axiomatic tone—making *arthâpatti* a matter of something provisionally accepted until further inquiry, which is rather more like *tarka* (though we will see that Gaṅgeśa sees the two as being related).

[10] For discussion of early uses of the term in Mīmāṃsā, see Yoshimizu (2000), which argues it was not originally taken as a *pramāṇa*, and Freschi (forthcoming).

Mīmāṃsā: arthâpatti *is an independent* pramāṇa

As with Kauṭīlya's example, in which *arthâpatti* involves sentences, the earliest treatment of the topic in Mīmāṃsā is as an interpretive-exegetical tool, in Jaimini's maybe second to fourth-century BCE *Mīmāṃsā-sūtra* (at 7.4.16, 7.4.18, and so on). Again, though, as with Kauṭīlya, it's unclear whether this is because *arthâpatti* is originally so concerned, or if it is simply due to the context—Mīmāṃsā, as indicated by its name ("investigation," "examination,") is an investigation into the ancient, orally transmitted scriptures known as the Vedas, especially the ritual instructional texts known as the *Brāhmaṇa*s. They are motivated by a desire to know not only what these scriptures mean, but to formulate precise principles for their interpretation, centering on ritual injunctions (*vidhi*). Thus *arthâpatti* is an important tool for understanding what is beyond the direct sense of the text—crucial when "filling in" the gaps of elliptical statements or incomplete descriptions of ritual practices. However, Jaimini's commentator, Śabara, in the roughly third-century CE *Commentary on the Mīmāṃsā Sūtra* (*Mīmāṃsā-sūtra-bhāṣya* or *Śābara-bhāṣya*), defines *arthâpatti* in this manner:

> Also *arthâpatti*, that is, the postulation of a thing when another thing that is seen or heard does not make sense otherwise.
>
> —see Ollett and Freschi, p. 43

The diverging groups within Mīmāṃsā—a split which comes after Śabara—will subject the term "seen or heard" to much analysis, focusing on whether the "or" here is exclusive of two options or simply a restatement of the ways in which we come to know things. The first option—exclusive or—is found in Śabara's seventh-century CE commentator, Kumārila Bhaṭṭa, whose title, *bhaṭṭa*, comes to metonymically refer to his followers, Bhāṭṭa Mīmāṃsakas. Kumārila argues that *arthâpatti* comes in two varieties—based on what is known by testimony ("heard," *śruta*) and based on what is known by the other epistemic instruments, such as perception, *anumāna*, and so on ("seen," *dṛṣṭa*), though how precisely Kumārila understands these two varieties is a point of contention for his commentators. As we will see below, Prābhākara Mīmāṃsakas (long ā indicating their naming after the seventh-century Prabhākara Miśra) disagree, arguing that the cases of testimony are no different in kind than the cases like seeing that Devadatta is not at home. For them, "heard or seen" is not a reference to two distinct kinds of knowledge-conducive processes, but to knowing in general.

To understand the debate within Mīmāṃsā (as well as the external one with Nyāya), it is important to understand some of the major commitments that characterize this tradition. The aforementioned focus on injunctions is embedded within a concern about knowing *dharma*: which means for them particularly the performance of Vedic rituals, but also the broader sense of an ethically ordered life grounded in the order of the universe (the verbal root of *dharma*, *dhṛ*, which means "to hold up," "to sustain," is a source of this semantic range). Also known as the science of sentences (*vākya-śāstra*), Mīmāṃsakas are all, regardless of sectarian distinctions, interested in articulating how Vedic sentences hang together as parts of a whole to communicate *dharma*. This communicative efficacy makes the Vedas testimony, but not in the same way as the ordinary testimony of human beings, with their propensity for cognitive errors. Rather, for Mīmāṃsakas, the Vedas are unauthored sentences whose meanings are understood through a variety of technical tools that attend to syntactical and semantic features of the sentences. It is perhaps given the importance of *arthâpatti* as a support for Vedic testimony that Mīmāṃsakas prefer to keep it as an independent epistemic instrument, rather than one reducible to *anumāna*, since the latter requires a pervasion relationship difficult to secure in the case of authorless testimony. Yet the fact that paradigmatic examples of *arthâpatti* which come to be discussed in Mīmāṃsā go beyond (though never leave behind—see the late *Māna-meyôdaya* in this volume) Vedic language demonstrates the broader philosophical concern of Mīmāṃsā in their attempt to carve out space for a kind of reasoning which is not *anumāna* but yet is knowledge-conducive.

Bhāṭṭa Mīmāṃsā

Kumārila Bhaṭṭa (*c.* seventh century CE) treats the topic of *arthâpatti* most directly in his *Explanation in Verse* (*Śloka-vārttika*). This commentary (really a subcommentary, as it remarks on Śabara's commentary) is difficult and compact, written in verses that later commentators have to unpack. We include excerpts from three of these commentaries: Umbeka (or Uṃveka) Bhaṭṭa, *c.* eighth century CE; Sucarita Miśra, *c.* tenth century CE; and Pārthasārathi Miśra, *c.* eleventh century CE. In writing his *Explanation in Verse*, Kumārila has within his sights the rise of the so-called "heteroprax" traditions such as Buddhism, which deny the Vedas their central organizing principle in religious and social life. Buddhists in particular receive much attention—directly or indirectly—in Kumārila's work, not only for their Veda-denying position, but their interrelated epistemological and metaphysical views. They are aggressively reductionist about most of the epistemic instruments that Mīmāṃsakas accept, and they find *arthâpatti* theoretically unnecessary. Likewise for Naiyāyikas, although they are within the fold of "orthopraxy," disagreeing with Mīmāṃsā on the authorship but not the importance of Vedic scripture (they prefer a divine origin). Kumārila writes the section on *arthâpatti* with the aim of showing that it must be distinguished from *anumāna*, and in so doing focuses on two paradigmatic cases of the former, which he submits to interrogation through the voice of a "first objector" (*pūrva-pakṣin*).

Before discussing these two cases and making some general observations about the Bhāṭṭa view of *arthâpatti* as understood through Kumārila's commentators and later thinkers, let us see Kumārila's definition of the concept, with several examples. He says

> When a thing that is known from one of the six instruments of knowledge does not make sense otherwise and causes one to postulate something that is not known, that is *arthâpatti* . . .
>
> —see Ollett and Freschi, p. 45

Bhāṭṭa Mīmāṃsakas adduce six epistemic instruments in total, and each example Kumārila gives of *arthâpatti* involves one of these—including *arthâpatti* itself, demonstrating the possibility of iterative "stacking" of epistemic instruments.[11] For instance, based on the perception of a fire burning some object, one postulates through *arthâpatti* that fire has a capacity for burning. A similar kind of reasoning, to unperceived causal capacities, occurs when one reasons by *anumāna* that the sun moves—since the movement is too slow to be directly perceived—and then postulates that the sun has a capacity for movement. These examples continue (see Ollett and Freschi, p. 46), but Kumārila selects for most sustained inquiry two cases which will also guide much later discussion: the postulation of Caitra's being alive and outside, discussed earlier, and the postulation that Devadatta eats at night based on hearing testimony that he is stout and does not eat during the day.[12]

In both of these cases, Kumārila attempts to show that there is no good *anumāna* from which to draw these conclusions. As we saw above, *anumāna* requires that there is an observed property whose invariable pervasion with the target property warrants the conclusion that the target property is present where the observed property is. However, in the case of Caitra who is not at home, what we perceive is an absence from home—and an absence from home is not invariably associated with a living presence in a particular place. The case of stout Devadatta isn't subjected to analysis in terms of *anumāna*, but rather with regard to testimony. Here the worry is that if *arthâpatti* is involved in understanding Vedic sentences—as we have seen, completing what is incomplete—then, if it is something other than (sentential or linguistic) knowledge, it would not be of a piece with the Vedas. This would threaten the hermeneutic enterprise of Mīmāṃsā, since so much content necessary for knowing *dharma* is implicit.

The introduction and commentarial essay included with our translation of *Explanation in Verse* elaborates on the major themes above in detail, as well as others. For instance, Kumārila's epistemology is known for its position that the results of epistemic instruments, cognitions, should be taken as intrinsically *valid* in virtue of their arising from such epistemic instruments, and not after a further cognition that verifies the first. Naiyāyikas and Buddhists both challenge this position known as "intrinsic validity" (*svataḥprāmāṇya*), and Kumārila's commentators take *arthâpatti* as a place to stake out their defenses of the position as well as their own particular understandings of its subtleties. As well, at least one commentator, Sucarita, uses the opportunity to argue against the Prābhākra account of *arthâpatti*, in particular their account of what triggers the process. Kumārila is explicit that there is something known which is incongruous or "does not make sense" otherwise (*anyathânupapatti*) and this is the cause of *arthâpatti*. Some Prābhākara thinkers challenge this role for incongruity, arguing that, instead, the trigger is doubt about the first thing which was known until the acquisition of a second piece of knowledge. In response, Sucarita spells out Kumārila's notion of not making sense otherwise in terms of a potential conflict (*virodha*) between two cognitions. Otherwise, the *Explanation in Verse* and its subsequent commentators

---

[11] The full list includes perception, *anumāna*, testimony, comparison, *arthâpatti*, and perception of absences.

[12] For the sake of clarity, in the Introduction we will keep Caitra and Devadatta distinctly paired with their respective examples, but in actuality, the names associated with the cases are variable (Caitra or Devadatta for either) as these are just common placeholder names like "John Doe" and "Jane Doe" used to be in English.

focus mainly on defending the independence of *arthâpatti* and explicating its structure.

We also include a later Bhāṭṭa Mīmāṃsaka: Nārāyaṇa Bhaṭṭa (seventeenth century). By this time, the polemic around *arthâpatti* shifts to focus primarily on Nyāya and Prābhākara Mīmāṃsā, with no reference to Buddhists at all. (This makes sense, given the irrelevance of Buddhists since roughly the thirteenth century CE as living interlocutors to Mīmāṃsā.) The seventeenth-century *Elucidation of Epistemic Instruments and Knowledge Objects* (*Māna-meyôdaya*) is a primer for students and useful as a condensed summary of generally accepted positions. Around half of this short section—which forms part of the section on epistemic instruments written by Nārāyaṇa Bhaṭṭa—is focused on Prābhākara Mīmāṃsā. Among other criticisms, Nārāyaṇa charges that if Prābhākaras allow doubt to be a knowledge-generator, it will go too far and prove anything. This discussion also makes explicit the role of *arthâpatti* in Vedic exegesis. Nārāyaṇa echoes Śabara (*Commentary* on MS 4.3.11) in using the example of the phrase "door, door" as a case where *arthâpatti*—of the linguistic variety, *śruta*—is used to understand what is missing, in this case a word which communicates the meaning *close*. As well, he argues *arthâpatti* of this type is used for modifying *mantra*s to fit new contexts (a process known as modification or *ūha*), where an adapted sentence is actually uttered. This, he says, gives further evidence that there is a distinct kind of *arthâpatti* which the Prābhākara reject, as they claim that only a meaning, not anything linguistic, is postulated. As we will now see, Prābhākara thinkers argue that their competing position is not only equally useful for Vedic exegesis, but it has added virtues, both intrinsic to the theory and as against Nyāya reductionists.

Prābhākara Mīmāṃsā

The Prābhākara tradition of Mīmāṃsā originates at roughly the same time as the Bhāṭṭa school, *c.* seventh century CE, with a commentarial tradition diverging from Kumārila's, based on Prabhākara Miśra's *Long Commentary* (*Bhṛhatī*). The relative chronology of these two important thinkers is contentious, and neither directly refers to the other. While Prabhākara's position is, like Kumārila, that the Vedas are a testimonial epistemic instrument, conveying *dharma*, he differs in his epistemology and metaphysics and in how to account for the communication of *dharma*, as well as the structure of human motivation for engaging in ritual acts. Many of these differences do not directly concern us here, although to understand why this tradition diverges in its analysis of *arthâpatti*, some general remarks are useful. These are based primarily on Prabhākara's commentator, Śālikanātha (*c.* tenth century CE), who systematically lays out the Prābhākara position in his *Straightforward and Lucid Gloss* (*Ṛju-vimalā-pañcikā*). While Śālikanātha comes to stand in for the entirety of the tradition in the eyes of many later thinkers, we see internal debate among Prābhākaras in his own text (see discussion Ollett and Freschi, p. 105), showing that the tradition is not univocal. Unfortunately, many Prābhākara texts are lost to us and we have fewer representatives of this aspect of Mīmāṃsā than of Bhāṭṭa.

There are two major points of contention between Prābhākaras and Bhāṭṭas on *arthâpatti*: the trigger (*gamaka*) of the process and the division into two kinds, heard (*śruta*) and experienced/observed (*dṛṣṭa*). In fact, the first point of contention is subtle, since Śālikanātha himself seems to accept the Bhāṭṭa perspective in a sense, which is that the trigger of *arthâpatti* involves tension between two competing deliverances from genuine epistemic instruments. However, Śālikanātha argues that this tension—whether it rises to the level of a contradiction or not is an open question—is only understood through a single primary trigger. In the case of Caitra's being absent from the home, it is his mere absence (understood by *anumāna*). We will see Naiyāyikas as well as Bhāṭṭas subject this claim to ridicule, arguing that it overgenerates—we could come to "know" that Caitra is dead from this, too! Here we also see some Prābhākara disagreement, since Śālikanātha presents some of his own cohort arguing that Caitra's being alive is the trigger, perhaps, as Ollett and Freschi (p. 106) suggest, because Prābhākaras worry about reifying absences as an object of knowledge. In either case, Prābhākaras argue that it is doubt about something's status as knowledge, not a tension between two epistemic instruments, that leads to *arthâpatti*.

The other point of contention is whether to admit two different kinds of *arthâpatti*. Śālikanātha argues that the case of stout Devadatta is one where we postulate a state of affairs, which is the referent of a word (*padârtha*), since it is only this which removes the difficulty with the first sentence. After all, even after positing the phrase "Devadatta eats at night," we must still understand its *artha*, referential object or meaning. In his discussion of this case, Śālikanātha also answers the Bhāṭṭa worry about modifying Vedic sentences. Even for *mantra*s and other cases of Vedic language, Śālikanātha argues that what doesn't make sense is the meaning or state of affairs, not merely the linguistic expression. So incomplete sentences are incomplete in virtue of an *artha* and it is an *artha* (which is the content of the putative *dṛṣṭârthâpatti*) that must be understood. Here we should also note an important difference between Bhāṭṭas and Prābhākaras. For the latter, the Vedic testimonial capacity is different in kind from ordinary human speech, the latter being authoritative in virtue of its being reducible to *anumāna*. Only Vedic speech, authorless and perfect, has the elevated status of directly informing without recourse to knowing speaker intention. When human beings speak, we understand their meaning (through comprehension of the sentence) but must infer whether they are representing the world accurately, based on the speaker's epistemic virtues. Thus even if *arthâpatti* is involved in completing incomplete speech of both Vedic and ordinary varieties, for the latter, there is a further cognitive step necessary for it to be judged as knowledge. In contrast, Bhāṭṭas do not distinguish between what grounds the knowledge-conducive nature of Vedic and ordinary speech—neither one of them are *anumāna*—although they do distinguish between them in other ways, most importantly in that Vedic speech is authorless, without an original "speaker."

There are a few other differences between Śālikanātha and Bhāṭṭa thinkers which may shed light on his approach to *arthâpatti*. First, Śālikanātha rejects the Bhāṭṭa position that perceptions of absences constitute a *sui generis* epistemic instrument. He prefers to countenance only awareness of positive entities. So when considering the case of Caitra, who is absent from home, we know that Caitra is absent not through a special epistemic instrument, perception of absences (*anupalabdhi* or *abhāva*), but through directly perceiving the empty house, remembering times when Caitra was there with the house, and then inferring that Caitra is absent from the home. However, it is not just that Prābhākara thinkers prefer fewer epistemic instruments—they also have a different conception of what makes epistemic instruments authoritative (*prāmāṇya*). In contrast to the "intrinsic validity" view of Bhāṭṭa, Śālikanātha emphasizes the role of a (valid/veridical) cognition's conformity to its object, insofar as it has a direct grasping of the entity. This, coupled with a metaphysical distaste for negative entities, motivates their construal of the Caitra case.

Second, Śālikanātha's view of *anumāna* differs from Kumārila, which perhaps impacts how he analyses the reconstruction of *arthâpatti* into putative cases of *anumāna*—although he spills less ink on this subject and instead focuses on the trigger of *arthâpatti*, on which more below. Śabara distinguishes between two kinds of *anumāna*, which are then explained differently by later Mīmāṃsakas. There is (1) *anumāna* which depends on the relationship between something unseen and something seen (*pratyakṣato-dṛṣṭa-sambandha*); and (2) *anumāna* which depends on the relationship between something unseen and a general character or universal (*sāmānyato-dṛṣṭa-sambandha*). Kumārila understands the first kind as being between two particulars: from seeing the rise of one star in the evening sky, we can infer the rise of another star will happen, since we've seen them both appearing together many evenings. He explains the second with our paradigmatic smoke–fire case, because it is in virtue of smoke's general character, its universal nature as something which causes fire, that we are licensed to know that there is fire when we see smoke. Śālikanātha instead argues that the first kind of *anumāna* involves cases where previously observed cases underwrite the *anumāna* of something we can observe—like when we have seen earlier cases of fire and smoke together and can reason to the unseen fire based on the observed smoke. The focus is not on individuals in contrast to particulars, but on whether the thing known by *anumāna* is capable of being observed. Thus the second kind, on his view, is exemplified by the *anumāna* to the sun's (in principle) unobservable movement, on the basis of observation of its previous positions in the sky. However, this observation also involves generalization.

A further difference between the thinkers has to do with negative examples. On Kumārila's view, set out in the "Chapter on *anumāna*" in his *Explanation in Verse*, *anumāna* involves apprehension of an inferential property (*dharma*) in a particular place (*pakṣa*) and a pervasion relationship (*vyāpti*) which lacks deviation, supported by examples which can be both positive and negative. The ascertainment of the pervasion relationship is a contentious topic, and while Kumārila emphasizes the repeated perception of the two properties (presence of smoke entails presence of fire), his commentator Umbeka argues that *arthâpatti* is involved in making the connection that there is a pervasion relationship, on which see Pandurangi (2006). Śālikanātha, who is probably engaging with Umbeka, argues that *arthâpatti* can establish a negative pervasion relationship (the lack of smoke entails the lack of fire) once a positive relationship has been understood. For him, positive pervasions are understood through repeated observations, as well, though with the caveat that the connection between smoke and fire is apprehended timelessly, as a constant.

Finally, Bhāṭṭa and Prābhākara thinkers hold different views on how sentence meaning is understood. Śālikanātha's position is that sentences are composed of related word meanings in a particular context. Roughly, this means that words do not denote independently, but only within a context and in sentential relationship to another word. In contrast, the Bhāṭṭa hold the view that words first denote independently— "cow" denotes a universal, Cowhood—and then a second operation, assisted by grammatical strictures and semantic content, determines the contextual meaning—from Cowhood we understand a particular cow. Śālikanātha argues that the first denotation is unnecessary and that grammatical strictures and semantic content together enable words to denote in relationship: "cow" means a particular cow, given an appropriate context of utterance. Against these competing linguistic theories, Prābhākara and Bhāṭṭa differently analyze the case of "stout Devadatta" who does not eat during the day, as well as the case of "door, door," which is elliptical. The stage of determining the particular context-sensitive meaning involves *arthâpatti* for Bhāṭṭas, but Prābhākaras can do without this, and thus *arthâpatti* may be less crucial for interpretive gap-filling than for the Bhāṭṭa.

Despite these differences in understanding the nature of *arthâpatti*, Bhāṭṭa and Prābhākara thinkers stand united against Naiyāyikas and Buddhists who argue that it is reducible to *anumāna*. We turn to Nyāya next, leaving Buddhism for the end, as we will see that *arthâpatti* is largely not thematized there to the same degree, perhaps because it lacks the shared Vedic context which drives much of its importance for their brahminical interlocutors.

NYĀYA: *ARTHÂPATTI* IS A KIND OF *ANUMĀNA*

Sharing with Mīmāṃsā the broader Vedic worldview, Nyāya is a philosophical tradition whose name means "rule" or "reasoning" (sometimes translated as "logic"). As with other Indian textual traditions, it originates with a *sūtra*-writer, Akṣapāda Gautama, whose *Nyāya-sūtra* can't be dated with complete certainty, but is probably written down roughly in 150 CE based on an oral tradition preceding him. While aligned with Mīmāṃsā against naysayers (*nāstikas*) who repudiate the Vedic scriptures as authoritative sources, Nyāya engages in significant philosophical argumentation with its orthoprax peers, taking on Mīmāṃsā metaphysics and epistemology. The topic of *arthâpatti* is discussed in Gautama's original *sūtra* text and taken up with increasing sophistication by later commentators. Their basic position can be stated simply: *arthâpatti* is indeed a epistemic instrument, but it is not *sui generis*, rather, it is a kind of *anumāna*. Precisely what kind of *anumāna* it is will occupy generations of Naiyāyikas, and some of them (especially Gaṅgeśa) will also involve a method of reasoning which is not knowledge-conducive in itself, but which supplements *anumāna*—that is, hypothetical reasoning (*tarka*). While not a hard-and-fast distinction, we can carve Nyāya history into early or classical Nyāya thinkers up to Udayana in the eleventh century CE, and "new" or *navya* Nyaya, after Gaṅgeśa in the early fourteenth century CE.

Early Nyāya

Gautama's *Nyāya-sūtra* treats *arthâpatti* under the question of how many epistemic instruments there are (NS 2.2.1–6). While he does not identify who—this will wait for the later Vācaspati Miśra and Jayanta Bhaṭṭa—he notes that some people think that *arthâpatti* are distinct from *anumāna*. The earliest extant commentary we have, the *Commentary on Nyāya* (*Nyāya-bhāṣya*) of Vātsyāyana (*c.* 450 CE), cites the already-discussed cases of stout Devadatta and also adds a new one. This is the statement that "When there are no clouds, there is no rain" which (opponents argue) brings about the postulation through *arthâpatti* that "When there is rain, there are clouds," which contemporary philosophers might call the contrapositive of a conditional (see Keating, p. 131).

The dialectic within the NS and later commentators involves several players. First, there are those who think that *arthâpatti* should be an independent epistemic instrument (Mīmāṃsakas as we have seen). Second, there are those who think *arthâpatti* is not really a reliable epistemic instrument at all. Finally, there is the established position of the Nyāya that *arthâpatti* is reliable, but a kind of *anumāna*, and not *sui generis*.

Against the idea that *arthâpatti* is its own kind of epistemic instrument, Vātsyāyana puts things first in terms of sentences (yet further suggestion that its role was originally primarily about testimony and not other kinds of reasoning). He argues that when we understand a sentence meaning, then through opposition (*pratyanīka*), we come to understand something that is not part of the original sentence meaning. Uddyotakara, in his *Explanation of the Nyāya System* (*Nyāya-vārttika*), is the one who applies a specific technical term to the *anumāna* involved: it is known as *sāmānyato-dṛṣṭa* or *anumāna* through observation (*dṛṣṭa*) based on a common characteristic (*sāmānyataḥ*), discussed under NS 1.1.5. Vātsyāyana and Uddyotakara have different positions on the nature of this kind of *anumāna*, although it seems they both want to subsume *arthâpatti* under it. Vātsyāyana thinks that we use it to conclude (1) that the sun is moving based on seeing it one place in the morning and another place at night, and (2) that there is a self based on the presence of desire, which is a property, given that properties always inhere in a substance (the self). For Vātsyāyana, in both of these cases, we cannot perceive the relationship between the sign (*liṅga*) and the thing to be proven (*sādhya*).

But Uddyotakara raises the problem of what it means to say that we cannot perceive this relationship—is it imperceptible in principle or simply at the time of the *anumāna*? Neither will work (the second isn't unique to *sāmānyato-dṛṣṭa* and the first fails to ground *anumāna*). So he argues that *sāmānyato-dṛṣṭa* is an *anumāna* where a particular property is perceived, and based on that property, one infers another property in its general nature. In Uddyotakara's discussion of *sāmānyato-dṛṣṭa* we can see the origins of Gaṅgeśa's insistence that a supplementary form of reasoning is involved. Suppose we observe desire and we want to know that it belongs to something, that is, that desire has the relationship of qualifier to a qualified thing. If we want to conclude that it is the self which is qualified by desire—as opposed to another substance—we must eliminate other alternatives, according to Uddyotakara. Gaṅgeśa will later argue that this eliminative capacity is due to hypothetical reasoning, *tarka*.

So Uddyotakara argues that the case of stout Devadatta fits the pattern of *sāmānyato-dṛṣṭa*: one understands the denial of Devadatta's eating at a particular time (through testimony) and this is the basis for knowing by *anumāna* his eating at another time. Eating has the general character of occurring at a particular time, and since it has been denied during the day, it must be affirmed as occurring at night.

The arguments of the second group, deniers of *arthâpatti*'s authority, are put forward by Vātsyāyana as well as Uddyotakara. These possibly Buddhist skeptics regarding *arthâpatti* note that the putative case of *arthâpatti* involving rain and clouds is unreliable—in fact, despite the presence of clouds, there can fail to be be rain. However, Vātsyāyana and Uddyotakara argue that this does not really get at what *arthâpatti* is concluding in such a case, which is that when some cause is present, so is its effect. They note that while clouds are a necessary causal condition for rain, they are not a sufficient causal condition, so high winds, for instance, could prevent rain from occurring. But the postulated conclusion still holds, which is that when a cause is present, so is its associated effect.

In his *Subcommentary on the Meaning of the Explanation of Nyāya* (*Nyāya-vārṭika-tātparya-ṭīkā*), Vācaspati Miśra (*c.* tenth century CE) takes up a Mīmāṃsā interlocutor for the first time in some detail, explicitly identifying them and making explicit what the pervasion relationship might be in the putative cases of *arthâpatti*. Vācaspati argues that we can use self-knowledge to formulate the basis for a pervasion relationship in the case of Caitra's absence: just like myself, when I am absent in one place, I am present in some other place (which is not that first place). So since Caitra is not at home, we can conclude that he is present in some other place—given the background knowledge that he is alive. Here Vācaspati makes use of a technical term which is important in his and later Nyāya philosophy: a delimiter (*avacchedaka*). To the Mīmāṃsā worry that, seeing Caitra's absence, we should doubt whether he is alive, Vācaspati notes that his absence is delimited by the house, so it shouldn't touch the claim that he is alive. He's simply not at home, and alive elsewhere.

Somewhere around the end of the ninth century CE, the Naiyāyika thinker Jayanta Bhaṭṭa writes the *Flowers of Reason* (*Nyāya-mañjarī*). This text is a major contribution to Nyāya philosophy, not only for its advancing Nyāya positions, but for its careful representation of the views of their interlocutors. In this text we find even more detailed discussion of *arthâpatti* from the Mīmāṃsā point of view than in Vācaspati's, as Jayanta thoroughly develops the competing perspectives within that tradition. Along with analysis of the Caitra and Devadatta cases, Jayanta spends a great deal of time on two other topics: the use of *arthâpatti* to postulate an unseen causal capacity (*śakti*) and to postulate completions for incomplete expressions. On the first issue, Jayanta argues that Mīmāṃsakas are guilty of bloating the necessary explanatory mechanisms for causation (see Graheli, p. 148). He appeals to the principle of parsimony (*laghutā*) to argue that an unseen causal capacity is superfluous when one can simply appeal to (visible) conditions which, taken together, result in an effect.

Jayanta's discussion of elliptical language is lengthy, and involves discussion of Vedic injunctions as well as ordinary cases of language. His main point is that there are cases where unuttered parts of an expression contribute to its meaning, and so there is no need for *arthâpatti* to supplement what the uttered parts contribute (see Graheli, p. 177). He appeals to syntax: in Sanskrit compounds, we do not hear the case-endings but yet we understand them. For instance, the compound "king-man" (*rāja-puruṣaḥ*) means "the king's man" (*rājasya puruṣaḥ*), but the ending *-sya* which signifies the genitive case is not heard. However, according to syntactical principles, that case-ending was present and then is elided—and it is this unarticulated constituent which communicates the possessive nature of the relationship. Likewise, in a paradigmatic Vedic case frequently discussed by Mīmāṃsakas, "The one desirous of heaven should sacrifice," what is understood is "The one desirous of heaven should *bring heaven into existence through* sacrifice." However, the instrumental ending (corresponding to "*through* sacrifice") and the accusative ending (corresponding to "*bring heaven into existence*") are not uttered.

Jayanta also intervenes in the dispute between Bhāṭṭa and Prābhākara Mīmāṃsākas over sentence meaning, which involves *arthâpatti* for Bhāṭṭa Mīmāṃsākas. Because the primary meaning of a word (a universal) does not make sense otherwise than in a given context, it will shift to a contextually-suitable meaning (viz, a particular) through a capacity known as *lakṣaṇā*, "secondary meaning." Secondary meaning is involved in various metonymical shiftings through relationships such as contiguity, association, etc., and for the Bhāṭṭa Mīmāṃsākas it involves *arthâpatti* (on which see below). However, as we have seen, Prābhākara Mīmāṃsākas reject the idea that the primary word-meaning is a universal, arguing instead that words denote their meanings only in combination with other words in particular sentence contexts. Jayanta, who elsewhere gives his own opinion on this debate, lays out the dialectic between the two, and seems to prefer the Prābhākara against the Bhāṭṭa, although his own view is distinct from both. He concludes by taking up another interlocutor, briefly, merely to dismiss their view as confused—this is probably the poetic/aesthetic theorist Ānandavardhana, who would add a new linguistic capacity to the primary and secondary, one known as "suggestion" or "resonance" (*dhvani*). Jayanta simply rejects him as being a "self-fancied scholar" (*paṇḍitaṃ-manya*). Neither suggestion nor *arthâpatti* are necessary to explain the full range of linguistic meaning for Jayanta given other conceptual tools such as *anumāna*.

After Jayanta, Udayana writes *The Flower-Offering of Reason* (*Nyāya-kusumâñjali*) in the late tenth century CE. In this text we see that Udayana focuses on the notion of *anyathânupapatti* or "incongruity-otherwise" as central to his reductionist arguments about *arthâpatti*. Udayana has more than just strictly epistemological issues in his sights with this argument. His concern with *arthâpatti* is also to repudiate the Mīmāṃsā argument against the existence of God, on which the Veda's existence is incongruous unless we posit God's non-existence (see Das, p. 183). It is in this context that the theist Naiyāyika Udayana focuses on *arthâpatti* and incongruity-otherwise, after previously having shown that *anumāna* is unable to prove God's non-existence. If *arthâpatti* is nothing other than *anumāna*, the theist has won the day.

In addition to elaborating on some by-now standard Nyāya arguments against the independent status of *arthâpatti*, Udayana contends that Bhāṭṭa Mīmāṃsakas must accept awareness of incongruity-otherwise as necessary for *arthâpatti*. While this initially seems harmless, one implication is that if they do accept such awareness, they are in danger of accepting awareness of a pervasion relationship (*vyāpti*) which lands them in the territory of *anumāna*. But if they reject the awareness of incongruity-otherwise as necessary, then they are unable to explain the distinction between good and bad, or pseudo, cases of *arthâpatti*. As well, Udayana expands on the concept of conflict (*virodha*) initially mentioned in Vācaspati's work, though not developed there. His Mīmāṃsaka interlocutor characterizes *arthâpatti* as "When two means of knowing conflict with each other, *arthâpatti* is what demonstrates that there is no such conflict (*avirodhôpapādika*)" (see Das, p. 192). In reply, Udayana argues that a genuine conflict would block knowledge, not lead to it, and that if there is a genuine conflict, the initial cognitions could not constitute genuine knowledge. Further, he argues that if we understand incongruity as a conflict, this would result in the unacceptable consequence that *anumāna* is reduced to *arthâpatti*. This is because we could understand the absence of fire on a visible part of a mountain as being incongruous with, or in conflict with, the observation of smoke on the visible part of the mountain (since we already know that where there is smoke there is fire). Positing that there is fire on the unobservable part would resolve the conflict. But not even a Mīmāṃsaka wants to reduce *anumāna* to *arthâpatti*. As we have seen, these last two arguments—about conflict and *arthâpatti* threatening *anumāna*—emerge again later, in the Mīmāṃsaka Nārāyaṇa Bhaṭṭa, who raises and objects to them in his *Elucidations*.

New (navya) Nyāya

By the fourteenth century CE, a self-described "new" (*navya*) Nyāya thinker distinguishes his views as differeing in some ways from those who come before him. Gaṅgeśa writes the *Jewel of Reflection on the Truth about Epistemology* (*Tattva-cintā-maṇi*), which is not a commentary on the NS, but rather a treatise which draws on previous Nyāya thought as well as breaks with it. This major work is influential for the emergence of Navya-Nyāya philosophers, especially in its discussion of *anumāna*, which is the subject of one of its four chapters—each chapter focusing on a different epistemic instrument. The section in our text on *arthâpatti* (which has not been translated previously) occurs within this chapter on *anumāna*, as Gaṅgeśa argues that *arthâpatti* is a kind of *anumāna* known as "negative-only *anumāna*" (*kevala-vyatireky-anumāna*), assisted by a subsidiary reasoning process known as "hypothetical reasoning," *tarka*—which is not an epistemic instrument, though it is an auxiliary to them.

As we saw above, negative-only *anumāna* is exemplified by the paradigmatic case where one reasons without a substantiating positive example (*sapakṣa*) but only with a negative example (*vipakṣa*). Taking the case of Caitra being outside, we might think that it is a case of *anumāna* in this way:

Thesis: Caitra (*subject*) has being-alive-and-being-outside (*property to be proven*)

Reason: because he has absence-from-home (*reason property*),

Example: and wherever there is absence-from-home there is being-alive-and-being-outside (*pervasion relationship*), unlike the person living at home (*negative example*).

Gaṅgeśa's position about *arthâpatti* is more complex, however, since he also explains that *arthâpatti* occurs by *anumāna* through observation of a common characteristic (*sāmānyato-dṛṣṭa*), coupled with *tarka*. Gaṅgeśa's account of Caitra and his home makes explicit the epistemic instruments involved:

1. **Aging rule.** There is a rule that 100-year-old people stay at home towards the end of their lives.
2. **Astrological prediction.** There is knowledge through astrology that Caitra will live to be 100 (and we assume he is 99 currently).

3. **Perception of absence.** There is the perception of Caitra's absence from his home—which we can say is through *anumāna* or perception of absence, *anupalabdhi*, depending on your preferred epistemological stance.

Now, the **aging rule** seems to be in conflict with the **astrological prediction**, in the specific case when there is also a **perception of absence.** This is because the first would have us expect Caitra to be alive and at home, whereas the second, together with the third, makes us think Caitra is alive and elsewhere.

What Gaṅgeśa says is that one of these two (the **aging rule** or the **astrological prediction**) must be defeated. This happens through *sāmānyato-dṛṣṭa* along with *tarka*, or hypothetical reasoning (which he has explained prior to our excerpt, in the same chapter) which is prompted by doubt. In particular, Gaṅgeśa says that hypothetical reasoning involves doubt in the form, "Is *x* an F (or a G)?" This doubt, for instance, can apply to the pervasion relationship between smoke and fire: we might wonder "Is smoke caused by fire (or something else)?" When faced with this doubt, we reason counterfactually, considering how things would be if *x* were an F or a G. So in the case of Caitra and the conflicting rules, hypothetical reasoning tells us what would happen were we to take a position on either **astrological prediction** or the **aging rule.** However, we are then able to reason using Caitra's being alive as a reason property:

> Caitra (*subject*) has being-outside (*property to be proven*) because he has being-alive and non-perception-at-home (*reason property*), and wherever there is being-alive and non-perception-at-*x* there is being-alive-and-being-at-not-*x* (*pervasion relationship*), like myself (*positive example*).

Here we see that the kind of reasoning involved takes the specific case of Caitra's not being perceived as present in his home as an exemplification of a more general rule about (living) people who are not in one place—and thus must be in another. Gaṅgeśa's point is that we can only engage in this kind of *anumāna* if we are able to take Caitra's being alive as evidence for our reasoning. And the only way we can do that is if we engage in hypothetical reasoning. Later on, though, Gaṅgeśa identifies the *sāmānyato-dṛṣṭa anumāna* as being the specific application of a general rule about living creatures to Caitra. This is consistent with negative-only *anumāna* since there are multiple levels of *anumāna* and there are multiple places where we have or lack supporting examples. The positive example which we lack—and in its place have a negative example—is Caitra's absence in the house corresponding to (being the counterpositive of) his presence outside of the home. By its very nature, we cannot observe the correlation of Caitra's being absent in the home and (simultaneously) present outside.

Although most of Gaṅgeśa's discussion is taken up with the example of Caitra in the home, he does touch on linguistic issues towards the end of his discussion, introducing a new (putative) example of linguistic *arthâpatti*, "The peacock does not dance on anything other than a mountain, and he is dancing," from which we understand—again, for Gaṅgeśa through *anumāna*—that the peacock is dancing on the mountain (see Phillips, p. 218). Gaṅgeśa, throughout his discussion, shows sophisticated awareness of debates within Mīmāṃsā, and he concludes with a discussion, from the Prābhākara point of view, of the importance of *arthâpatti* for understanding Vedic sentences.

ARTHÂPATTI IN BUDDHISM

So far, we have focused primarily on Mīmāṃsā and Nyāya, although especially in early Mīmāṃsā we saw that Buddhists were part of the dialectic. Given the important polemical role of Buddhists in the development of Mīmāṃsaka and Naiyāyika views about *arthâpatti*, in what follows, we will make a few observations and raise some questions for further reflection.[13]

Buddhism in India began roughly in the fifth century BCE, with the historical person of Siddhārtha Gautama, who comes to be known as "the Buddha," the awakened or enlightened one, after he leaves behind his life of princely comfort to search out the cause of, and solution to, suffering. His teachings form the basis of a movement which rejects Vedic orthopraxy in favor of the cluster of claims taught by the Buddha: the Four Noble Truths. These claims are shared by Buddhists of all kinds, although quickly within India a variety of divisions arise, motivated by philosophical as well as sociological disagreements (not to mention the varieties which arise beyond India in Tibet, China, Japan, and so on). Buddhists think that (1) life is characterized by suffering *(duḥkha)*, (2) this suffering has a cause, (3) this suffering can be ended, and (4) the way to end suffering is to follow a way of life known as the Eightfold Path, a way which includes ethical living, meditative practices, etc.—but not Vedic rituals. One of the central causes of suffering—which is understood not merely in the sense of painful experiences, but the existential angst caused by awareness of pain, by dissatisfaction with life, and so on—is the mistaken view that human beings have an unchanging self (*ātman*). Here is one direct challenge to the philosophical position of brahminical thinkers, who argue for a self as an unchanging substratum for qualities, although the range of views about the self in brahminical thought is immense. This anti-essentialism about the self becomes a broader anti-essentialism, spun out in a number of philosophically interesting ways.

In the context of epistemology, what is relevant for thinking about *arthâpatti* in the Buddhist context is their generally minimalist approach to epistemic instruments, of which they typically admit two to four: perception and *anumāna*, and sometimes also testimony and comparison. Further, those Buddhists such as Diṅnāga (*c.* 500 CE) and Dharmakīrti (*c.* 700 CE) who focused heavily on epistemology—part of the intertextual *pramāṇa-vāda* discussed earlier—engaged in sophisticated polemics with brahminical thinkers, at least up until the near-disappearance of Buddhism in India towards the thirteenth century CE. As they are not committed to real universals or repeatable property types, Buddhists must explain the underpinnings of *anumāna*—in virtue of what can a pervasion relationship between smoke and fire be said to exist, if not universals?—and the content of our perception—when we perceive colors, for instance, what do we perceive, if not a repeatable property?

---

[13] More could also be said about thinkers within the realm of Vedic orthopraxy, such as Vedāntins (Uttara-Mīmāṃsakas), who joined Mīmāṃsakas (Pūrva-Mīmāṃsakas) in defending *arthâpatti* as a epistemic instrument. There are also interesting questions about the relationship between the Jaina conception of *anyathânupapatti*, "inexplicability otherwise," and *arthâpatti*. However, these are best explored in another context. For discussion of Vedānta on *arthâpatti*, see Kasturirangan et al. (2010), Simha (1991). For discussion of Jainas on *anyathânupapatti*, see Balcerowicz (2003).

Unlike Nyāya and Mīmāṃsā thinkers, who take up *arthâpatti* as a topic of its own within discussion of epistemic instruments, Buddhists (on the whole) seem content to mention it in passing—with some important exceptions. However, it is possible that there are earlier Buddhists who discussed it in more detail whose work we do not have. Tucci (1929) suggests that a lost Buddhist work, known as the *Science of Reasoning* (*Tarka-śāstra*), may have included skepticism about *arthâpatti* as an epistemic instrument at all—which would be the view to which Vātsyāyana refers in his commentary.[14] However, just because Buddhists do not focus on *arthâpatti* as an independent problem, we cannot conclude that it plays no role in their thinking. In fact, it appears in some crucial places, primarily concerned with linguistic reasoning. For instance, Diṅnāga and Dharmakīrti both talk about *arthâpatti* as they explicate *anumāna* more generally.

Diṅnāga, in his *Compendium on Epistemology* and his *Commentary* thereon (*Pramāṇa-samuccaya* and *-vṛtti*), argues that, when making an *anumāna*, *arthâpatti* allows us to generate a negative form of the pervasion relationship from a positive one or vice versa.[15] Thus, if I understand "Where there is smoke, there is fire," it is *arthâpatti* which enables me to formulate the contrapositive: "Where there is no fire, there is no smoke." I do not need to state them both. Relatedly, Dharmakīrti uses the same principle—that *arthâpatti* allows us to understand something unstated yet connected to what is stated—to argue that the thesis statement in an *anumāna*-for-another is unnecessary. (Of course, what he means by *arthâpatti* is an important question, as we have seen that the term in early use refers to a few things.) So there is no need to say "There is fire on the mountain." In contrast to Naiyāyikas, who think the thesis statement is necessary at the outset and again at the close of an *anumāna*-for-another, Dharmakīrti argues that the thesis statement accomplishes nothing, epistemologically speaking. Rather, if we are told (1) a property q is present in a particular locus l and (2) when property q is present, so also is property p, we can use *arthâpatti* to understand what is at stake: (3) the point of these two statements is to prove that property p is in locus l (Tillemans 1999: 72–3). Interestingly, Dharmakīrti uses a range of different terms to describe this process: *arthāpattyā* (by *arthâpatti*) as well as *sāmarthyāt* (from the semantic capacity/the sense of things) and *arthāt* (from implication, from the meaning). These terms emphasize the

[14] "There is in *Nyaya-sutras*, ii, 2.3, an allusion to some logicians who denied any validity to *arthāpatti*, as being inconclusive. Vātsyāyana, commenting upon this *sūtra*, writes, asatsu megheṣu vṛṣtir na bhavatiti satsu bhavatity etad arthad apadyate, satsv api caikada na bhavati seyam arthâpattir apramāṇnam iti. Now we have in the second section of the *Tarka-śātra* referred to the following passage: 可顯物者。有二種有義至有非義至。 義至者若有 雨必有雲若有雲則不定或有雨或無雨, which can be translated into Sanscrit thus: yad abhivyaktam dvi-vidham, arthāpattir anarthāpattis ca. yadi vṛṣtir bhavati tada meghenâpi bhavitavyam, meghe saty api tukadacid vṛṣṭir bhavati, kadacin na bhavatity anaikāntikata. The correspondence is almost perfect; so we should be inclined to think that Vātsyāyana and even the final redactor of the *Nyāya-sātras* knew, if not this same text, then another of those *Tarka-śāstras* which seem to have existed long before Diṅnaga and in which the criticism of arthapatti was already formulated" (Tucci 1929: 485–7).

[15] Dunne (2004: 146) has a relevant footnote (fn. 6): "Diṅnāga (PSV:40a2ff *ad* PS 2.49) specifically discusses presumption (*arthâpatti*), and he argues that some forms of presumption are actually anumānas." See also PSV 150b5, arthāpattyā vânyatareṇôbhayapradarśanāt (Katsura 1983–4).

linguistic capacity of *arthâpatti*, as it is a term which can be used more broadly just to mean "based on context" or "based on the sense of the sentence."[16]

Another important, relatively early place, where *arthâpatti* occurs is in Avalokitavrata's commentary (*c.* 700 CE) on Bhāviveka's *Elucidation of Wisdom* (*Prajña-pradīpa*), a commentary on Nāgārjuna's *Verses on the Foundations of the Middle Way* (*Mūla-madhyamaka-kārikā*), where Avalokitavrata talks about an important kind of negation known as *paryudāsa*. In this kind of negation, one denies the existence of some *p* and in so doing also commits oneself to the existence of something positive that is not-*p*. What Avalokitavrata says is that this kind of negation communicates through *arthâpatti*, or the implication of something which is not itself stated. So, for instance, one might say "Devadatta is not a brahmin" and in denying that, through *arthâpatti* commit oneself to the fact that Devadatta is a warrior (*kṣatriya*). What's important for Avalokitavrata (and other Buddhists) is that there is another kind of negation that does not involve *arthâpatti*, so one is not committed to a positive entity.[17] Since many Buddhists—in this context it is Nāgārjuna—wish to deny the existence of things like universals, properties, and so on, but not thereby commit themselves to another problematic class of entities, having this non-implicative conceptual tool is important.

Finally, in the work of two Buddhist monks—Śāntarakṣita (725–88 CE) and his disciple, Kamalaśīla (740–95 CE)—we find an extended engagement with the brahminical tradition on *arthâpatti*. In fact, Śāntarakṣita's text, the *Compendium of Truth* (*Tattva-saṃgraha*), develops its discussion by quoting Kumārila extensively, and his disciple's commentary, the *Comprehensive Commentary on the Compendium of Truth* (*Tattva-saṃgraha-pañjikā*), quotes Kumārila and Śabara, along the way referring to Nyāya positions on *arthâpatti*. Only after extensively setting forth the first objector do the Buddhists engage in criticism, which has a different flavor than the typical Naiyāyika reduction of *arthâpatti* to *anumāna*, although it overlaps with some of Jayanta Bhaṭṭa's concerns. Śāntarakṣita and Kamalaśīla have two major problems with the putative epistemic instrument: first, it is often used to conclude that there is some unseen causal capacity (*śakti*), which is the sort of entity Buddhists reject, and second, when it is not used in this manner, it should simply be understood as *anumāna*. Thus, rather than going straight to the reductionist rebuttal (which involves the standard cases of stout Devadatta and absent Caitra), Śāntarakṣita and Kamalaśīla take issue with the way that *arthâpatti* is used to justify a bloated metaphysics, involving fire having a burning power, or the sun having a moving power. We simply perceive fire or the sun, which is itself the cause, and thus in these cases, there is no need for *arthâpatti*—which is, in fact, a faulty basis to conclude that such independent causal capacities exist. However, their arguments, for which see Mark Siderits's discusssion in this book (see p. 289), also take up the usual

[16] See Dharmakīrti's PVSV: tenaiva jñāta-sambandhe dvayor anyatarôktitaḥ | arthâpattyā dvitīye api smṛtiḥ samupajāyate ‖ 28 ‖ yad āha arthâpattyā vā anyatareṇôbhaya-pradarśanād iti | tatra api dṛṣṭântena tad-bhāva-hetu-bhāva-pradarśanaṃ manyamāno'rthāpattyâika-vacanena dvitīya-siddhim āha | tathā hi yat-kṛtakaṃ tad-anitya ity-ukte anarthântara-bhāve vyaktam ayam asya svabhāvas tan-mātra-anubandhī pramāṇa-dṛṣṭas tad-bhāva-niyamād iti | jñāta-tad-bhāvasya arthâpattyā anityatva-abhāve kṛtakatvaṃ na bhavati iti | (Pandeya 1989: 187).

[17] Avalokitavrata quoted in Kajiyama (1973: 170).

reductionist line, echoing Nyāya objections that we can indeed identify a pervasion relationship in cases such as Caitra's being alive and not in his house.

Although Buddhists were not typically engaging directly in the in-house reductionist debate between Mīmāṃsakas and Naiyāyikas, they were certainly aware of it, and employed technical terminology resonating with *arthâpatti* in a number of places. For instance, Kei Kataoka (2005) has traced connections between Kumārila's arguments against the validity (*prāmāṇya*) of the Buddha's words in the *Tantravārttika* and Dharmakīrti's argument that the Buddha's words are a valid epistemic instrument. While Kumārila argues that we can explain the Buddha's words by appeal to greed or a desire to deceive, Dharmakīrti argues that there is no other explanation for the Buddha's words, other than its being an epistemic instrument. Kataoka argues that Dharmakīrti's notion of there being "no other way" (*agatyā*) is logically equivalent to *anyathânupapatti*, or something's "not making sense otherwise," which Kumārila takes as trigger for an *arthâpatti*. However, does this make Kumārila's and Dharmakīrti's arguments equally cases of inference to the best explanation? (Kataoka suggests in a final footnote that Dharmakīrti's reasoning here may be "hypothetical," but in what sense?) Or should we, with Yoshimizu (forthcoming), take this as a kind of (deductively valid) exhaustive elimination of possible cases? We might also wonder why Dharmakīrti does not appeal to *anumāna* in his justification for the Buddha's words, if he takes *arthâpatti* to simply be *anumāna*. What is the relationship between the two for him and other Buddhists like Diṅnāga, who do not explicitly take up the reductionist debate? From historical and philosophical standpoints, it is worth inquiring further into how Buddhists use *arthâpatti* and associated concepts—and much more work is left to do.

At this point, we can summarize the various positions on *arthâpatti* with a concept map (see Figure 1).

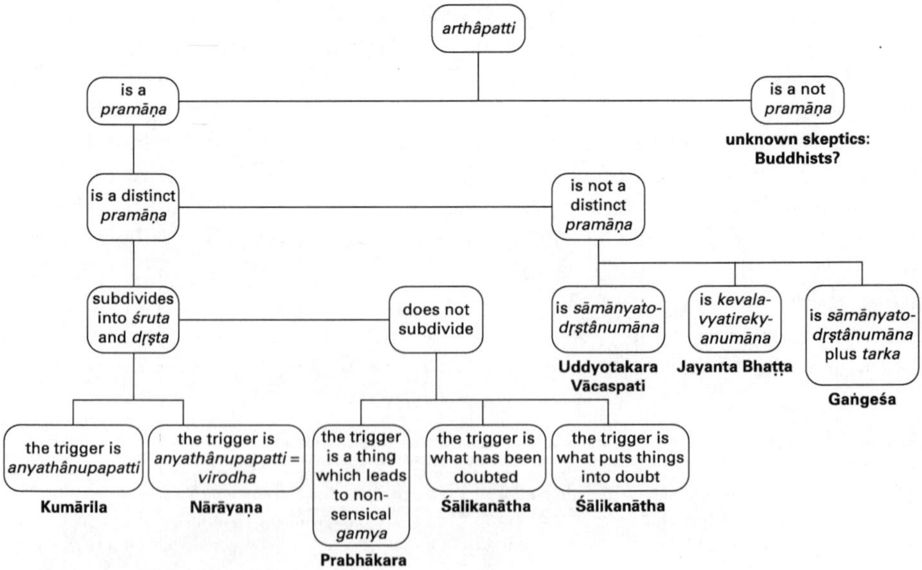

FIGURE 1: Summary of Positions on *Arthâpatti*.

Arthâpatti *in modern thought*

In the twentieth century and later, with the increasing connections between Indian philosophy and Anglo-European philosophy being made by thinkers like B. K. Matilal and J. N. Mohanty, the study of Indian epistemology, logic, and language has taken central focus. This has led to much discussion of three important *pramāṇa*s in particular: perception, *anumāna*, and testimony. Yet while this emphasis is in many ways motivated by emphasis within Indian thinkers themselves, discussion of *arthâpatti* has received little attention, despite its importance in the traditions. As it is part of this volume's thesis that *arthâpatti* merits focus as an interesting topic within the Sanskrit literature on epistemic instruments, and that it has not yet received such focus, what follows is a brief tour of the most important works to date on *arthâpatti*. The relatively small number of such contributions makes it possible for this to be a fairly extensive—though by no means comprehensive—discussion. We hope that this discussion will help orient readers to the secondary literature available already, in conjunction with our set of philosophical essays.

Logic Some discussions of *arthâpatti* occur within textbooks on "Indian logic," although as we have seen, our thinkers do not explicitly engage in a discipline known as logic, distinct from epistemology. The first significant English-language discussion of *arthâpatti* is Randle (1930), a work which focuses on logic until the time of Vācaspati Miśra. In his treatment of the Nyāya-Mīmāṃsā controversy, Randle claims that Vātsyāyana is analyzing *arthâpatti*, which he calls "implication," in the same way that contemporary logicians understand immediate inference through opposing propositions, although there is no Indian square of opposition as such. (Immediate inference is an inference from one premise to a conclusion, such as from "All durians are tasty" to "Some durians are tasty.") In his analysis, immediate inference is related to *arthâpatti* because "all implication is within a system, and therefore relational" (322). Such relations may be cause–effect, here–elsewhere, or now–later (depending upon which philosopher one reads), but they are all opposed binary pairs of a negation and a positive. He concludes with some comparative comments about the relationship between "the Western syllogism," *arthâpatti*, and *anumāna*, arguing that Western philosophy cannot give a syllogistic analysis of relational inferences such as "A is to the right of B, and B to the right of C, therefore A is to the right of C" (325). On his view, inferences that resist such analysis fall under *arthâpatti*, which he characterizes as "inadequate" in the Indian treatment but "still a valuable suggestion" (325).

In general, however, a survey of books that are treatments of Indian logic turns up very little focus on *arthâpatti*—so a newcomer to the topic would be excused for thinking the subject is minor. B. K. Matilal's *The Character of Logic in India* (1970) states only that *arthâpatti* (he calls it "presumption") "is an inference based on negative evidence—the conclusion is presumed because no other alternative explanation is available," and goes on to give an example of how *arthâpatti* can be used as a rebuttal to an *anumāna* (70). Collections such as Ganeri's *Indian Logic: A Reader* (2013), Perrett's *Indian Philosophy: Logic and Philosophy of Language* (2001), and Staal's *Universals: Studies in Indian Logic and Linguistics* (1988) lack papers devoted to the topic. Typically, if it is mentioned, it is in a manner that presents discussion as closed, as in Perrett (2001: 413): "*arthāpatti*, Presumption or Implication, the stock example of which is just a disjunctive syllogism."[18] Vattanky's *A System of Indian Logic: The Nyāya Theory of Inference* (2003) is an exception, as it includes a translation of important commentaries on Gaṅgeśa's *Jewel* which discusses *arthâpatti*. However, this reference book is for philosophers and scholars working with Sanskrit sources, and is not an attempt to analyse *arthâpatti* philosophically.

S. S. Barlingay's *A Modern Introduction to Indian Logic* (1965) and V. Bharadwaja's *Form and Validity in Indian Logic* (1990) are such attempts. Barlingay argues that *arthâpatti* is "semantic implication," while Bharadwaja thinks it should be understood as "contextual interpretation." Barlingay disagrees with the Nyāya reduction to *anumāna*, characterizing *arthâpatti* as "a case where two basic truth-functions, implication and disjunction, are combined for drawing an inference" (20). Barlingay further gives a possible formal representation of *arthâpatti* (90):

$[p \cdot (p \supset (q \vee r)) \cdot \neg q] \supset r$
p = "Devadatta is fat"; q = "He must be eating by day time," r = "He is eating by night time."

Still, since the inference depends on the meaning of the statements involved, Barlingay argues that it is semantic implication, and not purely formal. In contrast, Bharadwaja argues that we should not think of *arthâpatti* as a deductive inference in which, if the premises are true and the argument form valid, the conclusion necessarily follows. (This is related to his broader thesis that it is misplaced to think of Indian philosophers as engaging in "logic" *vis a vis* conceptions of formal validity.) After looking at seven major examples (due to Mīmāṃsā, Nyāya, and Vedānta), he concludes that *arthâpatti* is a matter of removing inconsistency or unclarity to interpret linguistic expressions. On his analysis, then, *arthâpatti* fails to be an epistemic instrument at all. However, among other flaws, his analysis fails to address the contention between Prābhākara and Bhāṭṭa over the two kinds of *arthâpatti*—he merely asserts that the case of Caitra's going out is one where linguistic expressions are involved.

A number of relatively recent articles have taken on the putative logical form of *arthâpatti*: Yoshimizu (2007), Das (2011), Guha (2012) and (2015), as well as this editor's own (2013a and 2013b). The debate between Das and Guha belongs more properly to discussion of epistemology, but a few remarks on Yoshimizu (2007) are relevant to his contribution in this book (see Yoshimizu, p. 225). Yoshimizu defends a view on which Kumārila's notion of *arthâpatti* can be characterized as "propositional derivation without pervasion," and as possibly motivated by a reticence (perhaps grounded in his orthodox brahminism) to assert too many universal rules, given the limitations of human reason. Whatever the historical and philosophical motivation,

[18] This quote is in fact the aforementioned Randle, whose "A Note on the Indian Syllogism" (1924) is collected in the volume—no other paper in the collection, ranging seventy-five years since that publication, takes up *arthâpatti*.

Kumārila's *arthâpatti*, according to Yoshimizu, can be understood through the tools of natural deduction. To summarize (the full proof is found in the 2007 paper):

1. There is the presupposition that if Caitra is alive (A), he is either at home (H) or outside (O).

   $A \supset (H \vee O)$

2. There is the knowledge that Caitra is alive and he is not at home.

   $A \wedge \neg H$

3. From (1) and (2) we can infer that if Caitra is alive and not at home, then he is outside.

   $(A \wedge \neg H) \supset O$

Yoshimizu argues that what is involved in *arthâpatti* is sentential—in the sense that we are not working with predicates and properties, such as is the case in *anumāna*, when we consider the property of smoke and fire as occurring in a particular locus. However, this does not mean that the process is only "contextual interpretation," as Bharadwaja (1990) argues, rather that the propositions involved are not broken down into their constituent parts for analysis.

Epistemology Books and articles focusing on epistemology are another context in which modern discussion of *arthâpatti* occurs. An early discussion is D. M. Datta's now-classic *Six Ways of Knowing* (1932), which devotes a chapter to *arthâpatti* (he translates it as "postulation"). His focus is Vedānta epistemology and its six epistemic instruments, and in particular, bringing them within the purview of modern Anglo-European philosophical methods of analysis through comparative modes of explication as well as criticism. Thus when he arrives at *arthâpatti*, he makes use of concepts in contemporary logic, arguing that the epistemic instrument can be reduced to the "disjunctive-categorical syllogism" and that the Nyāya attempt to reduce *arthâpatti* to *anumāna* is vitiated by *petitio principii* (203). Interestingly, he takes up the converse of the Nyāya reduction as a point of investigation: could we take all cases of *anumāna* and understand them as *arthâpatti*? For instance, we might think that the paradigmatic *anumāna* from smoke to fire on the mountain could be put this way: "the mountain smokes, and smoking cannot be explained except on the supposition that there is fire; therefore the mountain is fiery" (204).

Datta concludes that the reduction fails, since although the above reformulation may work, we cannot admit the formulation to lead to knowledge unless we know the pervasion relationship between smoke and fire—and this, he says, is known itself by *anumāna* on the Vedāntin's view. He concludes by trying to formulate points of contact between *arthâpatti* and "Western" epistemology and logic, identifying two potential analogs: hypothesis and Kantian transcendental proof. He notes, though, that a hypothesis is not conclusive knowledge—as *arthâpatti* is in the Indian tradition. Still, we have seen both that there were skeptics about its reliability and that some Naiyāyikas thought that hypothetical reasoning, which does not lead to conclusive knowledge, is involved in it (though neither conception is obviously and directly equivalent to a scientific hypothesis). Datta thinks that Kant's transcendental proof for the *a priori* intuition of space and time in the *Critique of Pure Reason* could be regarded as "an instance of *arthâpatti*," since Kant's reasoning is triggered by an incongruity to look for the only postulated thing (e.g. *a priori* intuition) that would resolve it (314).

Another early discussion of *arthâpatti* is again by a modern Indian thinker engaging with Western literature—H. P. Maiti. However, unlike Datta whose academic home was in a philosophy department, Maiti was a psychologist by training. In opening his analysis of *arthâpatti*, Maiti observes that in Indian thought, "the distinction between psychology, epistemology, and logic is not so rigidly drawn as in [W]estern philosophy" (1939: 314). He goes on to analyze the "psychology of doubt," which motivates his exploration of the Prābhākara approach to *arthâpatti*, as it involves doubt as a trigger. Throughout his paper, he engages with Datta and Randle, agreeing that *arthâpatti* is not reducible to *anumāna*, and speculating some on the reasoning processes of Descartes, Kant, Hegel, and Hume and as they might relate to *arthâpatti*. The paper's main contribution beyond its summary of Datta and Randle is to outline some aspects of doubt, in broad contours.

We find similar emphasis on what we might call the phenomenology of *arthâpatti* in the aptly titled "Indian cognitivism and the phenomenology of conceptualization." In this relatively recent paper (2010), Kasturirangan et al. argue that argue that *arthâpatti* draws consequences from conceptual structures (like the concept of being located), but without requiring concepts to be understood purely formally or purely phenomenologically (285). Thus both epistemology and phenomenology are implicated in *arthâpatti*. Focusing on the Advaita Vedānta contribution to the debate, which they note (291) is drawn from Śabara's ŚBh, they argue that while it resembles abductive reasoning (which they equate with inference to the best explanation), it is not the same. For them, an inferred best explanation explains some set of observations according to a particular theory if that explanation is consistent with the theory and if those events are a consequence of the explanation. In contrast, *arthâpatti* requires inexplicability, which they argue is an intuition that is conceptually basic and not itself able to be explained (290). Further, they argue that *anumāna* requires prior observation (to inductively establish the pervasion relationship), but that, due to inexplicability-otherwise, *arthâpatti* does not.

In a manner echoing Randle's claim that *arthâpatti* operates on a relational system of oppositional binary pairs, Kasturirangan et al. argue that the process involves "cognitive mapping" which is not analytic in nature but rather grounded in the general "scenario" or mental representation of our world. That is, they say that it isn't in virtue of being contained in the meaning of "Devadatta is not home" that one postulates "Devadatta is somewhere else," but rather it is a consequence of our understanding of the nature of the world (291). So *arthâpatti* isn't semantic implication, per Barlingay—but neither is it reducible to formal logic alone, as they see it containing both deductive and phenomenological aspects (the incongruity or inexplicability adduced by Vedānta is not a logical but a phenomenological one, in their view).

While Kasturirangan et al. see the dual aspect of *arthâpatti* as an important part of its nature, others, such as Tulsi Ram Kanaujia, argue that the dual aspect—and indeed, much of the debate over its nature—is a result of confusion over the multiplicity of concepts characterized by the single term, *arthâpatti*. In his 1992 paper, Kanaujia argues that there are several kinds of *arthâpatti* which have been lumped together, and that only some of these kinds constitue genuine epistemic instruments. These kinds are distinguished depending on the sort of "unintelligibility" (*anyathânupapatti*) at issue: linguistic, factual (with subtypes explanatory, psychological), and belonging to a contradiction.

He argues that only *arthâpatti* arising from factual intelligibility is an epistemic instrument, but it could be either *anumāna* (if the intelligibility is explanatory) or *arthâpatti* as something independent (if the intelligibility is psychological). From this taxonomy Kanaujia explains why Bharadwaja thinks *arthâpatti* is not an epistemic instrument and is merely contextual interpretation—this is because he is focusing on linguistic unintelligibility. Likewise, the debate over whether *arthâpatti* is reducible to *anumāna* or not is misguided, as it fails to distinguish between explanatory or psychological intelligibility. His paper's method is to focus on the differing definitions of *arthâpatti* and investigate examples in light of those (in contrast to merely collecting examples), and in the article he cites Mīmāṃsā, Vedānta, and Nyāya texts. However, Kanaujia's approach, to argue from the heterogeneity of discussions in different context to the heterogeneity of *arthâpatti* itself, is suspect. For instance, he identifies the case of stout Devadatta as grammatically acceptable and thus a matter of factual unintelligibility. But, this claim would be disputed by the Bhāṭṭa Mīmāṃsakas who take pains to explain in virtue of what semantic features the sentence is unintelligible (see Ollett and Freschi, p. 69ff) in contrast to Gaṅgeśa (see Phillips, p. 220), as we will see next. His argument, while it correctly identifies heterogeneity that could stand to be examined (hence this volume), misses the point that these differences are due to disagreements among thinkers, and that the treatments of various examples differ because of a complex of philosophical commitments beyond those pertaining just to *arthâpatti*.

Language As we have seen, especially according to Bhāṭṭa Mīmāṃsakas, *arthâpatti* is tied up with linguistic comprehension, at least in some cases. Precisely how is the subject of some discussion in modern reflection on *arthâpatti*. K. K. Raja gives attention to this question in his important *Indian Theories of Meaning* (1969), taking up the topic in his discussion of the factors necessary for complete sentences (171–3). He mainly focuses on presentation of the historical views on the relationship between *arthâpatti* and elliptical sentences—as historical introduction is the primary focus of the text. More recently, Keating (2017) focuses on this same topic, but as found in Kumārila, his early commentators, and the MM. In another place, Raja (1994) takes up the relationship between *arthâpatti* and secondary meaning or *lakṣaṇā*, a semantic process which, for Bhāṭṭa Mīmāṃsakas, shifts word meaning from its primary general sense (e.g. Cowhood) to its contextual specific sense (e.g. a particular cow). Raja argues that in his *Jewel*, Gaṅgeśa makes a mistake in distinguishing this Bhāṭṭa view from the view of Maṇḍana Miśra (who uses the Sanskrit term *ākṣepa* for this process), and that it is based on this (faulty) distinction that later authors, including modern ones such as B. K. Matilal, think that there are three distinct processes: *ākṣepa*, *arthâpatti*, and *lakṣaṇā*, when they are actually identified as the same in Mīmāṃsā.

In the last ten years, discussion on this same topic—the relationship between *lakṣaṇā* and *arthâpatti*—has occurred among Das, Guha, and the editor of this book. The impetus for the debate's revival came from Das (2011), who argues that there is an internal tension in Gaṅgeśa's treatment of *anumāna* and secondary meaning. We have already seen that Gaṅgeśa, like other Naiyāyikas, prefers to reduce *arthâpatti* to *anumāna*. On the other hand, he explains secondary meaning (*lakṣaṇā*) as involving a kind of sentential connection which has inexplicability (*anyathânupapatti*) requiring a certain solution. Thus, when someone says, "The village is on the Ganges," on pain of inexplicability (the village being in the river's currents), we understand it to mean "The village is on the *bank of* the Ganges." He also gives the example of "Close with the cloth," when what is meant is "Close *the door* with the cloth." These are cases which seem like instances of *arthâpatti* of what is heard. However, Das reasons that since these utterances are cases of testimony, if they are understood through *arthâpatti*, then that makes testimony a matter of *arthâpatti*—which for Gaṅgeśa is *anumāna*. Yet Gaṅgeśa is committed to the claim that testimony is not reducible to *anumāna*.

Guha's (2012) rejoinder focuses on blocking the reduction of secondary meaning to *anumāna*, arguing that secondary meaning, unlike *anumāna*, does not rely on prior observations (which requires a pervasion relationship underwritten by induction), and that secondary meaning is a tool of last resort, unlike *anumāna*. His discussion of *arthâpatti* takes up the possible way in which an elliptical utterance like "close" might, in Gaṅgeśa's view, be reduced to an *anumāna* involving observation—such as observing that the door is the only thing open and knowing already that "close" is a verb which takes as its subject things that are open, although he notes (499) that Gaṅgeśa does not take such an approach. What Gaṅgeśa does do—and in this he is anticipating the distinction we saw in Kanaujia between kinds of linguistic incompatibility—is to claim that the case of stout Devadatta is unlike the case of the village on the Ganges in its incompatibility. The first is comprehensible as a sentence, but causes problems if we consider the state of affairs it represents. The second has a failure of "semantic fit" (*yogyatā*) and thus requires secondary meaning to repair it. Thus, Gaṅgeśa distinguishes between secondary meaning and *arthâpatti*.

Yet in the work of Mukula Bhaṭṭa, a tenth-century Kashmiri thinker whose work brings together philosophy, grammar, and poetic/aesthetic theory, we see the broadening of the notion of incongruity in such a way as to include more than simply failure of sentence composition. In a partial response to Guha, I argue (2013a) that by including the stout Devadatta case as an example of secondary meaning in his text, Mukula is commiting himself to the view that *arthâpatti* underwrites secondary meaning. I argue that this structure is parallel to points one and two in H. P. Grice's description of conversational implicture, in which S conversationally implicates that q in saying that p iff S implicates q when:

1. S is presumed to be observing the conversational maxims
2. The supposition that S thinks that q is required to make saying that p consistent with the presumption 1,
3. S thinks, and expects H to think that S thinks, the hearer can work out, or grasp intuitively, that the supposition that Q is required.[19]

---

[19] This point of connection was also observed by Hota (2014), a paper which I did not encounter until late 2017. However, Hota's paper focuses on *arthâpatti* as a figure of speech (one of a number named after epistemic instruments), citing Ruyyaka on the topic.

Drawing to an extent on contemporary linguistic formalizations of ambiguity resolution, the paper distinguishes between "semantic" and "pragmatic" secondary meaning, arguing that the first is a matter of sentence-internal elements while the latter is a matter of contextual cues, but that both are broadly patterned on, and in fact involve, *arthâpatti*.

This analysis is corrected and developed further in Keating (2019), which also partly responds to another discussion of *arthâpatti* by Guha—one which focuses primarily on Śrī Harṣa's (Advaita Vedāntin) account of the epistemic instrument. Like earlier philosophers, Guha (2016) takes Sanskrit sources as a starting-point for broader philosophical thinking. In particular, Guha distinguishes between *arthâpatti*, abduction, and hypothetical reasoning (*tarka*), further arguing that *arthâpatti* is not necessary for secondary meaning. He argues that we can distinguish between secondary meaning's trigger, which is the "indicative power" (*lākṣaṇika-vyāpāra*), and its resolution (which may be *anumāna*, *arthâpatti*, or something else). However, Guha (2016: 771) admits that the case of "door, door" seems like inference to the best explanation (IBE) and that abduction seems to be a *tarka*, which puts his analysis in a difficult situation (at least if abduction and IBE are the same for him, though they are not for all philosophers). This debate, it seems, is only getting started, and can benefit from further attention on specific cases and their contexts, such those found in this book.

REMARKS ABOUT THIS VOLUME

In order to make progress in the issues just described, this book includes both translations and philosophical essays. We have seen that it is important to pay attention to the details of the philosophical context in which thinkers discuss *arthâpatti*. There is no "Bhāṭṭa" or "Nyāya" view, except in broad generalizations drawn from individual thinkers. Thus, if we want philosophers not trained in Sanskrit to engage with these ideas in a historically responsible manner, we need accessible and accurate translations. On the other hand, we are not only interested in a historical exegesis of Kumārila or Gaṅgeśa on *arthâpatti*. We want to know whether *arthâpatti* is a genuine way to attain knowledge, and if so, how. To understand *arthâpatti*, we need to evaluate arguments and conceptual distinctions in the Sanskrit texts, and we may be helped in our reflection by drawing on resources from other philosophical traditions. Thus, we need to continue first-order philosophical work along with the historical.

Organization

The volume is divided into two sections: primary sources in translation and philosophical essays. As noted above in our discussion of Buddhist contributions to *arthâpatti*, it would have been possible to include a number of other primary sources in this book. The choice of focusing on the Nyāya–Mīmāṃsā debate is motivated by a desire to provide an introduction to the topic, with the hope that future works will take up other thinkers in more detail. Each translation includes a translator's introduction situating the text in its historical context and giving an overview of its major arguments. These translations are interspersed with commentary, typeset in a manner which enables readers to easily distinguish the primary text and modern comments. A word on this choice: while there is merit in presenting the original text alone in it its entirety, so that the reader may engage it in an uninterrupted manner, given the difficulty of these texts, we have decided to incorporate commentary throughout. In a sense, this is to continue in the Indian commentarial tradition, which interprets earlier texts in light of the concerns of the commentator's audience.

Section One addresses arguments for the *sui generis* nature of *arthâpatti* as a knowledge source, beginning with the *Explanation in Verse* of Kumārila Bhaṭṭa, which is translated along with portions of his later commentators. In this translation, Andrew Ollett and Elisa Freschi weave together their remarks with discussion of, and sometimes translations from, three early commentarial works, since Kumārila's compressed original text is difficult to understand on its own. They have chosen to incorporate excerpts from Umbeka (early eighth century CE), Sucārita Miśra (middle tenth century), and Pārthasārathi Miśra (early eleventh century). Although sections of Pārthasārathi and Sucarita's commentaries have been summarized previously in Jha's 1906 translation of the *Śloka-vārttika*, Ollett and Freschi's careful treatment of Umbeka and Sucārita Miśra makes the discussion among all three thinkers available to English readers for the first time. In addition to Kumārila's own objections to reducing *arthâpatti* to *anumāna*, in this translation, we are given analysis of the very important concept of "does not make sense otherwise," or *anyathânupapatti*, as well as the distinction between *arthâpatti* which is "seen or heard." This latter distinction is a significant point of disagreement between Bhāṭṭas and Prābhākaras.

The Prābhākara tradition is then represented through three texts: the *Long Commentary* of Prabhākara on the MS and Śālikanātha Miśra's commentary thereon, *The Straightforward and Lucid Gloss*, and his *Collected Essays*, all also translated by Andrew Ollett and Elisa Freschi. In Prabhākara's text, we see his disagreement with Kumārila about the nature of *arthâpatti*. In particular, he rejects Kumārila's distinction between two discrete types corresponding to *arthâpatti* which is "seen or heard" and he disagrees with Kumārila that what "does not make sense otherwise," or *anyathânupapatti,* is the trigger for *arthâpatti*. Ollett and Freschi show how Śālikanātha Miśra's commentary interprets Prabhākara's text in some creative ways in order to support the former's own, distinct, analysis of *anyathânupapatti*. Further, Śālikanātha, unlike Prabhākara, actually mentions the putative sub-type of *arthâpatti*, *śrutârthâpatti*, or *arthâpatti* on the basis of what is heard, in order to repudiate the Bhāṭṭa's acceptance of it.

One further Mimamsa text, Nārāyaṇa Bhaṭṭa's *Elucidation of Epistemic Instruments and Their Objects*, translated by the editor, bring us up to the seventeenth century, though it mostly draws on a longer fourteenth-century text. The *Elucidation* is written as a primer for students, and by this time we see *arthâpatti* characterized in terms of opposition or conflict (*virodha*), a term not emphasized in early Bhāṭṭa discussion. We also see an emphasis on the role of *arthâpatti* in Vedic interpretation, in particular, of revising utterances to fit new contexts, an application not explicitly mentioned by Kumārila in his discussion, but discussed by his commentators and Nyāya thinkers like Jayanta. This text shows how later Bhāṭṭa thinkers integrated discussion of doubt and conflict, originally solely a Prābhākara approach, into their own analysis, and forms a lucid introduction to the topic as a whole, more accessible than the depths of Kumārila and the rest.

In Section Two, the Nyāya arguments for *arthâpatti* as a form of *anumāna* are represented by selections beginning with Gautama's NS and early commentators Uddyotakara, Vātsyāyana, and Vācaspati, also translated by the editor. It is in Vācaspati's work, here translated in English for the first time, that we see first explicit mention of Mīmāṃsā views on *arthâpatti*, along with mention of conflict (*virodha*). These texts give a sense of the refining developments within early Nyāya on this topic.

Later, in Jayanta Bhaṭṭa's *Flowers of Reasoning*, translated by Alessandro Graheli, we get very detailed analysis of both schools of Mīmāṃsā thought, in which Jayanta not only engages with the cases of stout Devadatta and absent Caitra, but in a detailed manner with linguistic philosophy relevant to Vedic interpretation as well as poetic analysis. Graheli's contribution, in addition to a running commentary by the translator, includes excerpts from, and discussions of, Cakradhara's untranslated commentary *Splitting the Knot* (*Granthi-bhaṅga*) on Jayanta's text (*c.* 1050 CE). Jayanta not only argues against *arthâpatti* on grounds familiar to his Nyāya predecessors, but he entertains a Prābhākara position temporarily in order to argue from their perspective against *śrutârthâpatti*, *arthâpatti* on the basis of what is heard. This facility with, and careful representation of, his interlocutor's views makes Jayanta's text invaluable for understanding not only early Nyāya, but Mīmāṃsā thought.

Shortly after Jayanta Bhaṭṭa, Udayana's *The Flower-Offering of Reason* continues the reductionist Nyāya arguments. In his translation and comments, Nilanjan Das situates Udayana's arguments in its larger context, both in terms of how he argues in other texts and what implications the denial of *arthâpatti* has for other Nyāya arguments, such as the existence of God. An important Naiyāyika who is a kind of transitional figure from classical to new or *navya* Nyāya, Udayana rehearses previous arguments familiar from Jayanta and his predecessors, but adds his own, notably ones which pick up on the theme of conflict (*virodha*) and on whether awareness of incongruity or not-making sense (*anupapatti*) is necessary for *arthâpatti*.

Concluding this section is another new translation: Gaṅgeśa's discussion of *arthâpatti* in his *Jewel of Reflection on the Truth about Epistemology*, with Stephen Phillips' remarks interspersed throughout the translation. Unlike previous Naiyāyikas, Gaṅgeśa argues that *arthâpatti* should be reduced to *anumāna* (of the *sāmānyato-dṛṣṭa* kind) along with *tarka* or hypothetical reasoning. Engaging largely with a Mīmāṃsaka interlocutor, possibly Śālikanātha Miśra, Gaṅgeśa also focuses on problems with doubt as a trigger for knowledge, and on the problem of *arthâpatti* as a means to know invisible powers (*śakti*s). These sections, though picking up on earlier threads in Nyāya thought, are developed further in Gaṅgeśa, who also employs his sophisticated account of absences and their counterparts (*pratiyogin*s) in order to account for *arthâpatti*'s structure.

Section Three brings together four philosophical essays on the topic of *arthâpatti*. Two directly engage with the texts in Sections One and Two, while two explore the implications of *arthâpatti* in other contexts: Buddhism and contemporary Anglo-

European philosophy. Engaging directly with Kumārila's *Explanation in Verse*, Kiyotaka Yoshimizu's paper argues that *arthâpatti* can be understood as a kind of deductively valid reasoning which does not rely on an expression of universal quantification, which is a reason why it cannot be understood as *anumāna*. He uses Lemmon's system to construct deductively valid proofs that correspond to *arthâpatti* as Kumārila understands it—which updates his 2007 paper and further argues that the controversial "not making sense otherwise" (*anyathânupapatti*) corresponds to *modus tollens*. This paper illustrates a way to think both exegetically and philosophically about Kumārila's epistemology and logic with the help of contemporary models, and can be read in tandem with Ollett and Freschi's translation.

Nilanjan Das's paper, on the other hand, takes up Nyāya arguments about *arthâpatti*, in particular those found in Gaṅgeśa and Raghunātha Śiromaṇi (fourteenth and fifteenth centuries CE, respectively). He argues not only that previous work on *arthâpatti* has mischaracterized the tradition insofar as discussions present Nyāya reductionism as univocal, but also that some Naiyāyikas, such as Raghunātha, are not reductionist at all. The paper takes up the problem of how a negative pervasion relationship can be known—e.g. that the absence of smoke is pervaded by the absence of fire—and how apprehension of negative and positive pervasion functions, causally and phenomenologically. For Raghunātha, *arthâpatti* is a special means for coming to know a negative pervasion, one which cannot be reduced to *anumāna*. In contrast, although Gaṅgeśa thinks that *arthâpatti* is reducible to *anumāna*, he disagrees that it requires apprehending a negative pervasion. Das's paper, which introduces readers to Nyāya thinking on *arthâpatti* and *anumāna*, is fruitfully read along with Phillips' translation of Gaṅgeśa as well as Graheli's translation of Jayanta.

Mark Siderits' paper focuses on the Buddhist thinkers Śāntarakṣīta and Kamalaśīla, who argue that *arthâpatti* is reducible to *anumāna*. Siderits argues that their arguments fail, and that Kumārila is right—although here Siderits interprets him differently than Yoshimizu, understanding the Bhāṭṭa Mimamsaka's *arthâpatti* to be a kind of ampliative inference, that is, an inference to the best explanation. Siderits argues that the distinction from *anumāna* is at least partly about the phenomenology of *arthâpatti*, insofar as the latter does not require cognition of a pervasion relationship, even if reconstruction into a logical form including universal quantification is possible. This paper draws connections among Indian philosophers (Buddhist and Mīmāṃsā) as well as with contemporary philosophy of mind. Siderits argues that Kumārila holds a view known in analytic philosophy as a higher-order thought (HOT) account of meta-cognition, that we infer our cognitions as occurring because "the object's cognizedness would otherwise be inexplicable" (Siderits, p. 305). Taking this argument against mental transparency (and for mental opacity) to be an *arthâpatti*, Siderits argues further that we cannot know a pervasion relationship between an object we cognize (such as a doorknob) and the fact of that doorknob's being cognized. Lacking such a pervasion, only *arthâpatti* can generate knowledge of our cognitions, pace Yogācāra Buddhist commitments to mental transparency. Siderits concludes with remarks about why a Madhyamaka Buddhist might wish to admit *arthâpatti* into their epistemological toolkit, both to argue for opacity and for other purposes.

Finally, Anand Vaidya's contribution considers why *arthâpatti* is important for a different set of thinkers than Naiyāyikas, Mīmāṃsakas, or Buddhists, as part of a method he calls "cross-cultural conceptual engineering." In this paper, Vaidya focuses on the question of *arthâpatti*'s reducibility to *anumāna* in order to also think about a contemporary question in analytic epistemology: whether inference to the best explanation is epistemically reducible to enumerative induction. He argues for a distinction between the fundamentality of epistemic instruments and their independence, and so that even if enumerative induction is rationally more fundamental than IBE, it need not entail that inference to the best explanation is thereby reducible to IBE. This idea comes about by considering the causal cognitive processes at play in epistemic instruments and their "epistemic grounding." Vaidya's paper engages with each of the three papers preceding it, reflecting on their content and methodology as he builds both a first-order philosophical argument (about IBE and enumerative induction) and suggests a second-order methodological argument (about how to do cross-cultural philosophy). Given this book's aim, Vaidya's paper is a fitting conclusion as one example of how contemporary philosophers could think along with premodern Indian philosophers.

Translation conventions

This volume aims for fidelity to its historical sources while simultaneously opening up those sources to a broader audience than specialists in Indian philosophy and the Sanskrit language. Thus we have tried to minimize the number of untranslated Sanskrit terms, in order to ease the cognitive load for readers. At the same time, there are certain terms best left untranslated to act as technical terms: in this context, *arthâpatti* and *anumāna* are typically left untranslated throughout the book since their understanding is the question under discussion. Translators have made their own choices for key terms which they leave untranslated or insert in parentheses after translations as a guide to readers. Given the substantive philosophical differences among our thinkers, sometimes it would be misleading to translate the same Sanskrit term across different texts (or even at different points within the same text). However, to help readers in making semantic and conceptual connections, we have included a glossary of Sanskrit terms and their varying translations. We have also included a chronology of key texts and thinkers.

REFERENCES

Arnold, D. (2014), "Kumārila," in E. Zalta (ed.), *The Stanford Encyclopedia of Philosophy* (Winter 2014 Edition), https://plato.stanford.edu/archives/win2014/entries/kumaarila/.

Balcerowicz, P. (2003), "Is 'Inexplicability Otherwise' (*Anyathânupapatti*) Otherwise Inexplicable?" *Journal of Indian Philosophy* 31: 343–80.

Banerjee, N. (2015), "Anumāna-vibhāga and the Two Warring Schools of the Pūrva Mīmāṃsā," in S. C. Gowsami (ed.), *Nature of Anumāna*, Kolkata: Asiatic Society.

Barlingay, S. S. (1965), *A Modern Introduction to Indian Logic*, Delhi: National Publishing House.

Bharadwaja, V. (1990), *Form and Validity in Indian Logic*, New Delhi: Indian Institute of Advanced Study, Simla, in association with Munshiram Manoharlal Publishers.

Bronkhorst, J., ed. (2007), *Mīmāṃsā and Vedānta: Interaction and Continuity*, Delhi: Motilal Banarsidass.

Das, N. (2011), "Lakṣaṇā as Inference," *Journal of Indian Philosophy* 39: 353–66.

Dasti, M. and S. Phillips, eds. and trans. (2017), *The Nyāya-sūtra: Selections with Early Commentaries*, Indianapolis: Hackett.

Datta, D. M. (1932), *The Six Ways of Knowing*, Calcutta: University of Calcutta.

Dunne, J. (2004), *Foundations of Dharmakīrti's Philosophy*, Boston: Wisdom Publications.

Freschi, E. (forthcoming), "*Arthāpatti* in early Mīmāṃsā and until Pārthasārathi Miśra," in V. Eltschinger, Birgit Kellner, Ethan Mills (eds), *A Road Less Travelled—Contributions to the Study of Indian Philosophy in Honour of John Taber.*

Ganeri, J. (2013), *Indian Logic: A Reader*, New York: Routledge.

Guha (2012), "*Lakṣaṇā* as a Creative Function of Language," *Journal of Indian Philosophy* 40, no. 5: 489–509.

Guha, N. (2016), "On *Arthāpatti*," *Journal of Indian Philosophy* 44, no. 4: 757–76.

Hota, K. N. (2014), "Implicature and *arthāpatti*," in B. K. Dalai and R. A. Muley (eds.), *Introduction to Indian Poetics and Aesthetics*, Pune: Centre of Advanced Study in Sanskrit.

Jha, G., trans. (1906) *Ślokavārttika*, Biblioteca Indica, Calcutta: Asiatic Society.

Kajiyama, Y. (1973), "Three kinds of affirmation and two kinds of negation in Buddhist philosophy," *Wiener Zeitschrift für die Kunde Südasiens/Vienna Journal of South Asian Studies* 17: 161–75.

Kanaujia, T. R. (1992), "Heterogeneity of *arthāpatti*," in G. Roth and H. S. Prasad (eds.), *Philosophy, Grammar, and Indology: Essays in Honour of Professor Gustav Roth*, 165–84, Delhi: Sri Satguru Publications.

Kasturirangan, R., N. Guha, and C. Ram-Prasad (2010), "Indian cognitivism and the phenomenology of conceptualization," *Phenomenology and the Cognitive Sciences* 10: 277–96.

Kataoka, K. (2005), "Manu and the Buddha for Kumārila and Dharmakīrti," *Religion and Logic in Buddhist Philosophical Analysis, Proceedings of the Fourth International Dharmakirti Conference Vienna, August 23–27*, 255–69, Vienna: Austrian Academy of Sciences Press.

Katsura, S. (1983–4), "Diṅnāga on Trairūpya," *Journal of Indian and Buddhist Studies (Indogaku Bukkyogaku Kenkyu)* 32, no. 1: 538–44.

Keating, M. (2013a), "Mukulabhaṭṭa's Defense of *Lakṣaṇā*: How We Use Words to Mean Something Else, but Not Everything Else," *Journal of Indian Philosophy* 41, no. 4: 439–61.

Keating, M. (2013b), "The Cow is to Be Tied Up: Sort-Shifting in Classical Indian Philosophy," *History of Philosophy Quarterly* 30, no. 4: 331–2.

Keating, M. (2017), "(Close) the Door; the King (is Going): The Development of Elliptical Resolution in Bhāṭṭa Mīmāṃsā," *Journal of Indian Philosophy* 45, no. 5: 911–38.

Keating, M. (2019), *Language, Meaning and Use in Indian Philosophy: An Introduction to Mukula's "Fundamentals of the Communicative Function,"* London: Bloomsbury.

Maiti, H. P. (1939), "Arthapatti [sic.] and Epistemological Possibilities of Doubt," *Philosophical Quarterly*: 314–21.

Matilal, B. K. (1998), *The Character of Logic in India*, ed. Jonardon Ganeri and Heeraman Tiwari, Albany: State University of New York Press.

Pandeya, R. C., ed. (1989), *The Pramāṇavārttikam of Ācārya Dharmakīrti with the Commentaries Svopajñāvṛtti of the Author and Pramāṇavārttikavṛtti of Manorathanandin*, Delhi: Motilal Banarsidass.

Pandurangi, K. T. (2006), *The Epistemology of Pūrvamīmāṃsā*, Vol. 2, Part 6, in K. T. Pandurangi, *Pūrvamīmāṃsā from an Interdisciplinary Point of View*, 53–100, Delhi: PHISPC Centre for Studies in Civilizations.

Perrett, R. (2001), *Indian Philosophy: Logic and Philosophy of Language*, New York: Routledge.

Raja, K. K. (1969) *Indian Theories of Meaning, Second Edition*, n.p.p.: Theosophical Publishing House.

Raja, K. K. (1994), "Ākṣepa, Arthāpatti and Lakṣaṇā," in Viśvanātha Devaśarmā et al. (eds.), *Cultura Indica: Tributes to an Indologist Professor Dr. Asoke Chatterjee Sastri*, 103–6, Delhi: Sarada Publishing House.

Randle, H. N. (1930), *Indian Logic in the Early Schools*, Oxford: Oxford University Press.

Sadhukhan, S. K. (2015), "The Characteristics of *Sāmānyato-dṛṣṭa Anumāna* in the Nyāya System of Philosophy," in S. C. Goswami (ed.), *Nature of Anumāna*, 115–23, Kolkata: Asiatic Society.

Shamasastry, R., trans. (1929), *Kautilya's Arthasastra*, Mysore: Wesleyan Mission Press.

Simha, G. P. (1991), *Arthāpatti: A Critical and Comparative Study of the Views of Pūrva Mīmāṃsā, Advaita Vedānta, and Nyāya-Vaiśeṣika Systems*, Tirupat: Sri Venkateswara University.

Staal, F. (1988), *Universals: Studies in Indian Logic and Linguistics*, Chicago: University of Chicago Press.

Tillemans, T. (1999), *Scripture, Logic, and Language: Essays on Dharmakīrti and His Tibetan Successors*, New York: Simon & Schuster.

Tucci, G. (1929), "Buddhist Logic before Diṅnāga," *Journal of the Royal Asiatic Society of Great Britain and Ireland* 7: 451–88.

Vattanky, J. (2003), *The Nyāya Theory of Inference: Analysis, Text, Translation and Interpretation of the Anumāna Section of Kārikāvalī, Muktāvali and Dinakarī*, New York: Routledge Curzon.

Yoshimizu K. (2000), "Mīmāṃsāsūtra ni okeru arthâpatti to Anumāna (arthâpatti and Anumāna in the Mīmāṃsāsūtra), *Journal of Indian and Buddhist Studies* 48, no. 2: 1109–15.

Yoshimizu, K. (2007), "Kumārila's Propositional Derivation (*arthāpatti*) without Pervasion (*vyāpti*)," in K. Preisendanz (ed.), *Expanding and Merging Horizons: Contributions to South Asian and Cross-Cultural Studies in Commemoration of Wilhelm Halbfass*, 315–35, Vienna: Austrian Academy of Sciences Press.

Yoshimizu, K. (forthcoming), "Arthâpatti in Kumārila's *Tantravārttika*," in P. M. Scharf (ed.), *Festschrift to Cardona*.

SECTION ONE

CHAPTER ONE

Kumārila Bhaṭṭa's *Explanation in Verse*

Translated by ANDREW OLLETT and ELISA FRESCHI

This chapter contains a translation of the section on *arthâpatti* in Kumārila Bhaṭṭa's *Explanation in Verse* (*Śloka-vārttika*). This work, dating to the sixth or seventh century, is what it sounds like: an explanation, written entirely in verse, on Śabara's *Commentary* (*Bhāṣya*) on the Mīmāṃsā system, which was composed a few centuries prior. Kumārila's *Explanation*, which provided detailed philosophical arguments for his reading of the Mīmāṃsā system, proved to be one of the most influential works in South Asian philosophy.

The discussion of *arthâpatti* in Śabara's *Commentary* actually forms part of a long quotation of an earlier commentator, who is known only as "the author of the *Vṛtti*" or *Vṛtti-kāra*. The *Vṛtti-kāra* provided definitions of the six epistemic instruments (*pramāṇa*; see p. 2 in the Introduction to this volume) that would be accepted as valid and independent in the Mīmāṃsā system. About *arthâpatti*, the *Vṛtti-kāra* had provided the following definition, which has since formed the starting-point of all discussions of *arthâpatti* in Mīmāṃsā:

> Also *arthâpatti*, that is, the postulation of a thing when another thing that is seen or heard does not make sense otherwise.

Kumārila's main task in this eighty-eight-verse section of the *Explanation* is to argue against the reduction of *arthâpatti* to inference. Thus, after applying the *Vṛtti-kāra*'s definitions to various types of cognitions (vv. 1–9)—with the exception of linguistic cognitions, to which he will return—Kumārila devotes forty-one verses (vv. 10–50) to anti-reductionist arguments. He uses a single example throughout this section: "A certain man named Caitra, who is known to be alive, is not at home; therefore he must be outside." While he does not associate the reductionist position with any specific philosophical system, the understanding of inference that he takes for granted, and imputes to his opponents as well, follows that of the Buddhist philosopher Diṅnāga. He demonstrates, in several ways, that the pattern of reasoning Mīmāṃsā authors call *arthâpatti* necessarily takes a different *form* than the pattern of reasoning that South Asian philosophers, following Diṅnāga, call inference (*anumāna*). This point is perhaps made most clearly in verse 22, where Kumārila shows that the two premises, Caitra's being alive and Caitra's absence from home, guarantee the conclusion, Caitra's presence outside, immediately and independently of the formal relations between the premises and conclusions that are required for inference.

Kumārila then (vv. 51–78) discusses another type of *arthâpatti*, "*arthâpatti* on the basis of what is heard." His motivation for arguing that this type is qualitatively different from the preceding type seems to come from the need to invest the cognitions produced through this type of *arthâpatti*, when applied to Vedic texts, with the same authority of the Vedic texts themselves. But the distinction between "*arthâpatti* on the basis of what is seen" and "*arthâpatti* on the basis of what is heard" would come to distinguish Kumārila's theory of *arthâpatti* from that of Prabhākara (see the following chapter, p. 89). Kumārila then "zooms out" and argues that his account of *arthâpatti* is consonant with a broader epistemological theory in which the relations that *cause* valid cognitions need not be known at the moment of cognition (vv. 79–86). He concludes with a discussion of the applications of *arthâpatti* (vv. 87–8).

Three commentaries are available on this section of Kumārila's *Explanation*: those of Umbeka (early eighth century), Sucaritamiśra (middle of the tenth century?), and Pārthasārathimiśra (early eleventh century).[1] Our reading of the *Explanation* is deeply informed by these commentaries, and we have given summaries and extracts of them throughout.[2]

ARTHÂPATTI: DEFINITION AND EXAMPLES

According to UMBEKA, there are two potential sources of confusion in the definition quoted by Śabara. The first is the use of the phrase "seen or heard." The word "seen," by itself, could potentially refer to three domains: that which is literally *seen* with the organs of sight; that which is *perceived* in general (including what is heard, touched, smelled, and tasted in addition to what is seen); and that which is *apprehended* in general (including inferential, analogical, testimonial, and suppositional cognitions in addition to perceptual cognitions). The first and second senses are too narrow, as we will want to include cases of *arthâpatti* that start from inferential cognitions. The second and third senses make the separate mention of something "heard" redundant, since hearing is covered by both perception in general and apprehension in general. SUCARITAMIŚRA mentions a fourth possibility, according to which "seen or heard" does not refer to different things, but is an idiomatic way of saying "anything apprehended in general." This was how Prabhākara and Śālikanātha understood the text (see the following chapter, p. 89).

The second potential source of confusion is the use of the phrase "does not make sense otherwise," (*anyathânupapatti*) which will turn out to be a crucial component

[1] For these dates, see Kataoka 2011: 112. These commentators have different agendas and styles, and in particular, Sucaritamiśra—and Pārthasārathimiśra after him—have tried to defend Kumārila's positions against the arguments of Prabhākara and Śālikanātha. See also Freschi (forthcoming).

[2] Editor's note: Because of the need for significant commentary on Kumārila's concise verses, the main text in this chapter is indented, surrounded by the translators' comments, unlike other translations. The names of classical commentators are in small caps to draw attention to their remarks translated or paraphrased in the comments.

of *arthâpatti* in all of its varieties. It is not immediately obvious why something that does not make sense should cause us to postulate something in virtue of which it comes to make sense. After all, UMBEKA claims, if I imagine a hundred herds of elephants on the tip of my finger, this clearly does not make sense, but I don't go postulating something else in virtue of which it comes to make sense; I simply give up the imagined idea.

Kumārila addresses both questions in his commentary:

> **1.** When a thing that is known from one of the six epistemic instruments does not make sense otherwise[3] and causes one to postulate (*kalpayet*) something that is not known, that is *arthâpatti*. Examples of it follow.

In this way, Kumārila makes it clear that the word "seen" in Śabara's commentary is to be understood in the third sense, namely, "apprehended" in general, and furthermore, that it is apprehended through one of the six well-known epistemic instruments. Hence *arthâpatti* does not start from any cognition at all—which would include bogus cognitions of the elephants-on-the-fingertip type—but only from *valid* cognitions.

Since the problem of redundancy still remains in this interpretation—that is, "heard" is surely included within "seen" if the latter really means "apprehended" in general—Kumārila provides a justification for mentioning a type of *arthâpatti* that begins from what is "heard" separately from the more general case of *arthâpatti* that begins from what is apprehended:

> **2.** "Seen" means cognized through the five other epistemic instruments. The type that starts from what is "heard" is mentioned separately, because it is different from the previous type, insofar as it encompasses an epistemic instrument.

This verse establishes that there are two qualitatively-distinct kinds of *arthâpatti*, namely, *arthâpatti* on the basis of what is seen (*dṛṣṭârthâpatti*) and *arthâpatti* on the basis of what is heard (*śrutârthâpatti*). Whereas the content of the first type is a thing, the content of the second type is another epistemic instrument, namely, a linguistic expression. Kumārila returns to this distinction in verse 58*cd*.

PĀRTHASĀRATHIMIŚRA explains the choice of words by referring to the principle of the cows-and-bulls (*go-balī varda-nyāya*): just as the word "cow" can refer to a male or female, but when used in conjunction with the word "bull" it most naturally refers to the complement of "bull," namely female cows, in the same way the word "seen" can refer to something that is cognized through any epistemic instrument, but when used in conjunction with the word "heard" it most naturally refers to the complement of "heard," namely, something cognized through the five epistemic instruments apart from language. This principle is actually taken from one of Pārthasārathimiśra's opponents, Śālikanātha, who invokes it in his discussion of the same passage from Śabara (see p. 102 in our translation of Śālikanātha's *Straightforward and Lucid Gloss* below).

---

[3] *bhavet* Su, Pā; *bhavan* U. The reading of the Umbeka MS is a *lectio facilior* insofar as it solves the slight syntactic problem of two unlinked verbs (*bhavet*, *kalpayet*).

Kumārila now exemplifies different kinds of *arthâpatti* based on the five epistemic instruments, excluding testimony. All of them involve (a) a starting cognition, which is the result of any of the five epistemic instruments; (b) some problem that afflicts the starting cognition; (c) a final cognition, the result of *arthâpatti*, which resolves the aforementioned problem. Kumārila's examples are very compressed, and in particular, he does not tell us why the starting cognition does not make sense without the additional cognition supplied by *arthâpatti*.

> **3ab.** Among the six varieties, it is on the basis of *perception* that we cognize burning, and from this we get that a fire has the capacity to burn.

The perceptual cognition is the feeling of being burned by fire. Since we cannot make sense of the fact that fire burns without also supposing that fire has an inherent capacity to burn, we postulate the latter.

> **3cd.** It is on the basis of *inference* (*anumāna*) that we cognize the sun's movement, and from this we get that the sun has the capacity to move.

According to Kumārila, the fact that the sun has moved *on its own* (as opposed to having been moved by something else) is an inference from the fact that it has changed its position in the sky over the course of the day. The sun's movement, thus established inferentially, would not make sense unless the sun had the capacity to move, and hence the capacity is understood through *arthâpatti*.

> **4ab.** *Arthâpatti* on the basis of what is heard will be discussed later on in this section.

See verses 51ff. "What is heard" refers to language, which the Mīmāṃsakas accept as a distinct epistemic instrument.

> **4cd.** When we cognize a cow on the basis of *comparison* with the gayal, the possibility of the cognition of the cow being included in that cognition is admitted on the basis of *arthâpatti*.[4]

Comparison (*upamāna*) is a relatively marginal epistemic instrument, and the cow–gayal example is the only one that is commonly cited.

A cow can be cognized on the basis of perception, that is, by looking at a cow. But the Mīmāṃsakas admit that a cow can also be cognized on the basis of comparison. For it is a characteristic of Kumārila's treatment of comparison that once a similarity between two terms has been established, the perceptual cognition of one introduces an analogical cognition of the other.[5] When one sees a gayal, one has the cognition, "a cow is similar to a gayal." Yet there is apparently nothing in the gayal that would provoke such a cognition. According to Sucaritamiśra, if the analogical cognition of the cow was caused simply by the gayal, then we would have that cognition whenever we see the gayal, even if we had never seen a cow before. There must therefore be another cause of the cognition. "There must," he says, "be some special property of

[4] gavayopamitāyā gos tajjñānagrāhyatā matā U, Su; gavayopamitā yā gauḥ tajjñānagrāhyatā matā Pā.

[5] See *Explanation in Verse*, section on comparison (*upamāna*), v. 46.

the cow which, once it becomes manifested by the perception of its correlate, generates the cognition of its similarity to the gayal."

> **5.** We have to rely on *arthâpatti* to understand the power of linguistic expressions to convey their meanings, in order that their function of expression can be established, and on this basis, we rely on *arthâpatti* once again to understand that those linguistic expressions as fixed.

The cognition that linguistic expressions have a power to denote a meaning is based on *arthâpatti*. That is to say, we know that linguistic expressions bring about the cognition of a meaning, and in order to account for this process, we suppose that linguistic expressions have an inherent power to communicate their meanings. Apart from this power, it would be impossible to otherwise account for the specific kind of connection that exists between linguistic expressions and their meanings (a particular characteristic of which is, for example, that linguistic expressions only bring about a cognition of their meanings for somebody who has learned those meanings). As SUCARITAMIŚRA notes, no other kind of connection between expressions and their meanings exists, least of all an ontological connection (e.g., physical contact). Mīmāṃsakas further maintain that it is impossible to account for the power of linguistic expressions to denote their proper meanings so long as the relationship between linguistic expressions and meanings is arbitrary, and hence we appeal to *arthâpatti* once again in order to conclude that linguistic expressions are fixed.

Kumārila explains the example of *arthâpatti* based on *arthâpatti* in greater detail:

> **6–7.** Expression cannot be established otherwise, hence we understand on the basis of *arthâpatti* that linguistic expressions have a power to express meanings. And because there is no other way, by means of yet another *arthâpatti* we conclude that linguistic expressions are fixed. This will be said in the commentary to the *sūtra* "because its appearance is for the sake of others." (MS 1.1.18)
>
> **8–9ab.** The final type of *arthâpatti* is the one based on absence (*abhāva*), which Śabara has adduced as an example:[6] we can establish that Caitra is outside on the basis of his house, which is qualified by Caitra's absence, which is itself ascertained on the basis of the epistemic instrument known as absence.
>
> **9cd.** Other examples can be found in the discussion of the faults of the locus (*pakṣa-doṣa*).

See the commentary on *Mīmāṃsā Sūtra* 1.1.18 (*Explanation in Verse*, section on the fixity of the relation between words and their meanings, vv. 237ff.) and see *Explanation in Verse*, section on inference, vv. 68ff.

ARTHÂPATTI IS DIFFERENT FROM INFERENCE

Now Kumārila shows that *arthâpatti* is a qualitatively different epistemic instrument than inference:

---

[6] *udāharat* Su, U; *udāharet* Pā.

10. The suggestion of Caitra's being outside, on the basis of perceiving that Caitra is absent, is completely different[7] from inference, since it does not have all of the necessary components (*aṅga*) of an inference, such as "being a property of the locus."

The purported inferential reason cannot be a property of the locus

A well-formed inference has certain formal properties. An inference will always have a thesis (*pratijñā*), which attributes an inferred property (*sādhya*) to a given locus (*pakṣa*), and an inferential reason (*hetu*). For example, in the standard example, the thesis, "there is fire on the mountain" expresses an inferred property (fire) present in a given locus (the mountain), and "because there is smoke" is the inferential reason. One of Kumārila's most important influences is the Buddhist logician Diṅnāga, who argued that an inference of this form will only be valid if it meets three additional criteria. (1) The inferential reason must be a property of the locus. In the standard example, since we are trying to infer the presence of fire *on the mountain*, the inferential reason, smoke, must also be present on the mountain. (2) The inferential reason is present in at least one co-locus, that is, another locus in which the inferred property is present. In the standard example, the co-loci are defined by the presence of fire. The inferential reason, smoke, is indeed present in many but not all of the cases where fire is also present. (3) The inferential reason is absent in all of the counter-loci, that is, loci in which the inferred property is absent. Since there is no non-locus, i.e., a situation in which fire is absent, where smoke is *not* absent, the standard example also meets this third criterion.

Kumārila now explains what it means to say that the criterion of "being a property of the locus" is not satisfied in the case of *arthâpatti*:

11. How can absence from home be a property of the locus? It would have to belong to either something qualified by someplace outside, or someplace outside qualified by it.

If we were to try to model the example of *arthâpatti* on an inference, we would have to say, "Caitra is outside (thesis), because he is absent from home (reason)." As we have seen, however, the thesis must be formulated as a relationship between an inferred property and a given locus. We have two options in this case: we could either say that *Caitra* is the locus, and that he is qualified by being outside, or we could say that *outside* is the locus, and that this is qualified by Caitra. As for the inferential reason, we see that it is "absence from home" in both cases.

But how, exactly, do we understand this phrase, absence from home? SUCARITAMIŚRA mentions the possibility that the inferential reason is absence itself, but quickly rejects it on the grounds that *anything's* absence can do nothing to establish that *Caitra* is outside. This reason, therefore, would be inconclusive (*anaikāntika*). He mentions an additional possibility that the inferential reason is absence qualified by the house, but he rejects this as well, on the grounds that the qualifier should be

---

[7] *bhinnaiṣā-* U; *bhinnaivā-* Su, Pā.

dependent on what it qualifies, and the house, being a substance, should be said to be qualified by absence, rather than the other way around. As UMBEKA points out, we have two more realistic possibilities for the inferential reason: the house, qualified by absence, or Caitra, also qualified by absence. Kumārila rejects both:

> **12–13ab.** On the one hand, a house qualified by somebody's absence is not a property of anything. On the other hand, Caitra, qualified by absence from the house, is not understood at that time. What we understand is the house, and Caitra is not understood there.

"Anything," or more specifically, the two possibilities of the locus that were mentioned in verse 11: Caitra, or outside. Kumārila will take for granted, however, that the locus of the proposed inference is Caitra, rather than outside, in the subsequent verses.

Verse 11 introduces the main formal problem with the proposed inference. In order for something to be a suitable inferential reason, it needs *both* to be cognized—for one cannot reason on the basis of what one does not know—*and* to be a property of the locus. If the inferential reason is "a house qualified by absence," the first condition is met, but not the second: we do in fact cognize the house, but the house is not a property of whatever it is we are trying to produce inferential knowledge about (e.g., Caitra). If the inferential reason is "Caitra qualified by absence from home," the second condition is met, insofar as it is Caitra's being outside that we are trying to establish inferentially, but the first is not.

SUCARITAMIŚRA would claim that the second condition, being a property of the locus, is not met in this case either. He says that a test for something's being a property of the locus is that it is cognized when one cognizes the locus. We cognize smoke when we cognize the mountain. However, in this example, given the cognition of the supposed inferential reason (Caitra qualified by absence from his house), we do not cognize the locus (Caitra). There can be no cognition of a property of something, if we have not cognized the property-possessor in the first place. In this case, we cannot have a cognition of a property of Caitra—such as his absence from home—given the fact that we have not cognized Caitra himself.

The problem with understanding the inferential reason as "Caitra qualified by absence from home," according to Kumārila, is that Caitra is not directly cognized. As PĀRTHASĀRATHIMIŚRA says, we only cognize Caitra indirectly. He cannot be perceived. Nor, according to SUCARITAMIŚRA, can he be inferred, since such an inference would contradict his observed absence.

Kumārila has now eliminated all of the possibilities of understanding the example as a formal inference. To review these possibilities, we have two potential loci, Caitra (C) and Outside (O), corresponding to two slightly different (but practically the same) theses, Caitra qualified by Outside, and Outside qualified by Caitra, which we can represent as *C(O)* and *O(C)*. We also have two potential inferential reasons, the house qualified by Caitra's absence, and Caitra qualified by his absence from his house, which we can represent as *H(A)* and *C(A)*. We therefore have the following:

$H(A) \rightarrow O(C)$, fails because *H(A)* is not a property of *O(C)*
$H(A) \rightarrow C(O)$, fails because *H(A)* is not a property of *C(O)*

C(A) → *O(C)*, fails because C is not cognized
C(A) → *C(O)*, fails because C is not cognized

The opponent might argue that we can in fact cognize the purported inferential reason, Caitra's absence from home. Since the opponent is a "reductionist," who wants to reduce both *arthâpatti* and absence to inference, he will argue that this cognition is produced on the basis of inference rather than on the basis of absence as an independent epistemic instrument. According to Kumārila, however, we cannot infer the absence of a thing simply from the fact that we do not apprehend it. See *Explanation in Verse*, section on absence, vv. 29–53.

> **13cd–14ab.** Not seeing someone in a certain place can never be an inferential reason, as will be explained in the section on absence. Therefore, you cannot suppose that the inferential reason is the fact that he has not been seen in the house.

The opponent now faces two problems. What he wants to infer is Caitra's being outside, on the basis of Caitra's not being apprehended at home. In actual fact, however, this inference would need to be split into two smaller inferences:

> The preliminary inference, Caitra is absent from home because he is not apprehended there.
>
> The replacement inference, Caitra is outside because he is absent from home.

The preliminary inference fails because it lacks a suitable inferential reason, as Kumārila had just explained in verse 13*cd*–14*ab*. Therefore, the replacement inference will fail because it lacks the step needed to establish Caitra's absence from home. And any attempt to skip the first step, and infer Caitra's being outside directly out of not apprehending him at home, will fail for the same reason that the preliminary inference fails.

> **14cd–15ab.** It is only if the absence of what is to be known could be ascertained on the basis of not apprehending him that there could be an inferential cognition of his being outside, and hence not apprehending him is not a reason for that cognition.

"The absence of what is to be known," namely, the absence of Caitra himself. SUCARITAMIŚRA: "It is only when the non-apprehension of Caitra has been completely used up (*upakṣīṇa*) in ascertaining Caitra's absence that the cognition of his being outside arises." PĀRTHASĀRATHIMIŚRA: "Given that absence is understood first, on the basis of not apprehending Caitra, and subsequently a cognition of his being outside arises, it follows that this latter cognition cannot have not seeing Caitra as its immediate cause."

SUCARITAMIŚRA understands the verse to be directed against the possibility of inferring that Caitra is outside *directly* out of the fact that he is not apprehended at home. He says that this inference is not possible because the reason (not apprehending Caitra at home) would be "used up" in a preliminary inference of Caitra's absence. Both commentators agree that there is a gap between not seeing Caitra and the cognition of his being outside, such that the former cannot be the immediate cause (PĀRTHASĀRATHIMIŚRA calls it a *nimitta*) of the latter.

As noted above (vv. 13*cd*–14*ab*), the opponent is a "reductionist." Thus, although a non-reductionist, like a Mīmāṃsaka, may be able to cognize Caitra's absence from home directly, on the basis of absence as a distinct epistemic instrument, this possibility is not open to the opponent. He needs to reduce the cognition of Caitra's absence from home to an inferential cognition, and this ends up being impossible. Kumārila does not address the objection that a Mīmāṃsaka might raise, namely, that Caitra's absence from home is cognized directly, and hence this can serve as the reason for the inference of Caitra's being outside. This objection would be more difficult to counter.

Kumārila concludes the discussion of this formal defect of the proposed inference, namely that its reason is not a property of the locus, with the following half-verse:

> **15cd.** It is claimed that Caitra's absence is an inferential reason. The locus of that absence, however, is his house.

We had been assuming that the purported inferential reason, Caitra's absence from home, can be a property of the locus because it is a property of Caitra. In fact, Kumārila says, the locus of this absence is not really Caitra, but Caitra's house. If it is a property of the house, then it cannot be a property of the locus of the inference, namely Caitra. The opponent's attempts to make Caitra's absence from home a legitimate inferential reason, insofar as it is a property of the same Caitra whose presence outside we are trying to establish, are therefore moot, since the locus of Caitra's absence from home and the locus of his presence outside are different.

The purported locus is not previously cognized Now Kumārila moves onto a different argument. The two loci that have been proposed, namely, Caitra himself and outside, are not valid loci for an inference, because the locus of an inference needs to be something that has been previously cognized.

> **16.** When a locus has not been cognized previously it cannot be the subject of an inference. In this case, neither outside nor Caitra himself has been cognized previously.

At this point, Kumārila has an opponent raise an objection: if it is really necessary for us to have previously cognized a locus in order to make inferences about it, then many of the inferences that we commonly accept as valid will suddenly become invalid. One example is as follows: there has been a rain upstream, because the river is flooded. Here, the locus of the inference is a place upstream, which we don't need to have cognized prior to seeing the flooded river and making the inference.

> **17.** What about the presence of rain somewhere upstream that is cognized on the basis of a flooded river? Surely being a property of the locus is impossible in this case, since the locus is not cognized!

Kumārila responds to this challenge in two ways. On the first pass, Kumārila says that the actual locus of the inference is not somewhere upstream, which is not previously cognized, but the very place where flooding has occurred:

> **18abc.** What people cognize is that the place where there is flooding is preceded by a place where it has rained.

The inference would therefore run as follows: this place, where flooding has occurred, is connected with some other place where rain has fallen, since the river is flooded in this place (and wherever there is flooding, there is a particular geographic connection with a place where rain has fallen). As the commentators note, however, this is rather far-fetched. When people engage in reasoning like this, they actually believe that they are reasoning about the place upstream, not the place where the river is flooded. Hence Kumārila takes another pass at the problem, and suggests that this purported inference is actually an example of *arthâpatti*:

> **18d.** Alternatively, this too is an *arthâpatti.*

Both SUCARITAMIŚRA and PĀRTHASĀRATHIMIŚRA, however, insist that this example is not really an *arthâpatti*, but simply an inference, and that this statement of Kumārila's is a "concession" to the way that the layperson might describe his or her own reasoning. The challenge is understanding why the flooding example should be an inference while the Caitra example should not be, despite the fact that both examples involve reasoning about something that is not cognized previously. In the case of the flooding example, we might plausibly be reasoning about a single locus, namely the river, throughout; in the case of the Devadatta example, it clearer that there are two loci—the place where Devadatta is observed to be absent, and the place where he is postulated to be present—and therefore it does not seem to be a canonical inference.

The purported inferential reason is not probative of the conclusion

Kumārila has now established (vv. 11–15) that the purported inferential reason, Caitra's absence from home, fails to be legitimate from a purely formal perspective, that is, it is not a property of the locus. Now he will argue that it fails to actually prove the conclusion. That is, however we understand "absence from home," there is no sense in which it would yield the knowledge of "presence outside" through a valid inference. Either it is not independent from the conclusion, in which case we have a *petitio principii*, or it is, in which case it is inconclusive.

Let us suppose, to begin with, that the inferential reason is "a living person's absence from home," as in the Vṛtti-kāra's formulation. According to Kumārila, this cannot function as an inferential reason, because we do not cognize it before the conclusion.

> **19.** In the case under consideration, the property of the locus that is posited is a living person's absence from home. But that cognition does not arise without the awareness that that person is outside.

In other words, we only know that the absence from home that we cognize to begin with belongs to somebody who is alive if we cognize, simultaneously, that the person is outside. This is SUCARITAMIŚRA's interpretation, which recalls the Prābhākara position that the starting cognition is "thrown into doubt" that is only resolved by *arthâpatti*.

In contrast to this case, Kumārila adduces the familiar example of inference, and shows that the inferential reason (the fact of possessing smoke) is cognized independently of the conclusion (the fact of possessing fire).

> **20.** By contrast, the fact that something possesses smoke is understood independently of the fact that something possesses fire. At the moment that one grasps the former, there is nothing that depends on fire.

"Nothing" likely means that both the inferential reason (the fact of possessing smoke) and the locus (the mountain) can be cognized without cognizing fire.

Now we might attempt to avoid the sequential problem that Kumārila raises by maintaining that the inferential reason is not "a living person's absence from home," as was supposed earlier (v. 19), but simply "absence from home." This modification does avoid the problem of dependency, insofar as "absence from home" does not depend on "being outside." But now we have a different problem: the purported reason, "absence from home," is not invariably concomitant with the conclusion (in Sanskrit: the conclusion is not "pervaded by," *vyāpta*, the reason), "being outside," in the sense that there might be people who are absent from home who are nevertheless not outside. The inference now becomes, as SUCARITAMIŚRA says, "inconclusive":

> **21.** Sheer absence from home, apart from his being alive, cannot establish being outside, since that is also observed in people who are dead.

Now Kumārila has his opponent in a corner. The purported inferential reason, "absence from home," has to take one of two forms. Either it is conjoined with the cognition of a person's continued existence, in which case the cognition that he exists outside (the purported conclusion) is given already in the premises (namely, his being absent from home and his continued existence), without having to be inferred. Alternatively, it is not conjoined with any such cognition, in which case it does not lead us to infer that anyone in particular is outside, if indeed it leads us to infer anything at all. Thus the purported inferential reason either gives us to know too much, or too little, to have a valid inference. This will be argued more explicitly in verses 27–9.

Kumārila now explains the first part of the dilemma in greater detail. The key here is that the starting cognition of Caitra's absence from home, if it does include the fact that Caitra is in fact alive, already includes his being outside: for once the house is excluded (*utkālita*) as a locus of Caitra's presence, there is nowhere else for him to be.

> **22.** Through the cognition of an absence from home that is conjoined with being alive, Caitra, being excluded from his house, has to exist outside.
>
> **23.** But as for the sheer absence from home that is cognized independently, that alone will not allow us to ascertain that a particular person, Caitra, is somewhere else.

In these two verses, SUCARITAMIŚRA notes that the absence involved in the postulation of Caitra's presence outside is an absence of a special kind: it is qualified by Caitra's continued existence. Thus the qualifier, Caitra's continued existence, must be understood in the cognition of what it qualifies, namely, Caitra's absence from home. But it is not possible to cognize Caitra's continued existence without assigning it a substrate. Since the house is excluded from being such a substrate, we conclude by elimination (*pāriśeṣyād*) that the substrate must be "outside."

PĀRTHASĀRATHIMIŚRA notes that if you start from Caitra's being alive and his absence from home, the only possible way to connect these cognitions is in the cognition that Caitra is outside. "For one does not think: 'Caitra is absent from home, but he exists, either at home or outside.'" If you only start from Caitra's being alive, however, and a general cognition of somebody's (not necessarily Caitra's) absence from home, you would only cognize "there is nobody at this house," and that would never lead you to the cognition of Caitra's being outside.

Note that in contrast to SUCARITAMIŚRA, who comments on verses 22 and 23 together, UMBEKA comments on verses 23 and 24 together. UMBEKA notes that the "sheer absence" in this verse has a different consequence than the "sheer absence" mentioned in verse 21: in that verse, it was too broad, allowing us to incorrectly infer that *anyone* who is absent from home is present outside, even dead people or people who have not yet been born; in this verse, however, what we infer is is that *somebody* (e.g., Devadatta) is present outside if *somebody* (e.g., Caitra) is absent from home, which is insufficient for cognizing that the some person who is absent from home is present outside. Thus the purported inferential reason needs to have two qualifiers: it needs to relate to a particular person (e.g., Caitra), and the person who it relates to needs to be alive.

The next verse closely recalls verse 22, which established that Caitra's being outside followed as an automatic consequence of adding the fact of Caitra's being alive to the fact of his absence from his house:

> **24.** It is only when Caitra's existence has been established that the cognition of his absence from home leads us to believe that his existence, having been excluded from his house, is now located outside.

According to SUCARITAMIŚRA, this statement is directed against the followers of Prabhākara who would maintain that Caitra's existence is rendered "doubtful" by seeing that he is not at home (see the chapters on Prabhākara and Śālikanātha in this volume, p. 89). If such a doubt as to Caitra's existence really did arise, then simply postulating that he is outside would not put the doubt to rest. Rather, in SUCARITAMIŚRA's interpretation, Kumārila says we cognize that Caitra is outside when we have determined Caitra is actually alive (which is to say, from Kumārila's epistemological perspective, that neither a doubt nor a contrary cognition regarding Caitra's continued existence has arisen).

SUCARITAMIŚRA's interpretation hangs on the word "established" (*siddhe*), and it is possible that the word does not have the sense of being "free from doubt" that Sucaritamiśra assigns to it. If we do not follow Sucaritamiśra's interpretation, however, it is difficult to make sense of the apparent repetition of the ideas of verse 22: Umbeka considers that verse 24 restates the same problem as verse 22, but with an additional qualifier (not just "being alive," but "Caitra's being alive"). In any case, the verse emphasizes that the cognition of Caitra's being outside is qualitatively different from inference, insofar as Caitra's existence is "automatically" said to be outside when his absence from home is cognized against the assumption of his continued existence. There is, as PĀRTHASĀRATHIMIŚRA says, "nothing left to infer."

The next verse restates the double bind that the proponent of a "reduction to inference" has been placed in:

> **25.** Therefore,[8] in this case, if on the one hand the reason makes no reference to Caitra's being alive, then it will not be invariably concomitant with the conclusion, in case he is dead or not yet born. If, on the other hand, the reason is invariably concomitant with the conclusion, nothing apart from it is apprehended.

The purported inferential reason, absence from home, has two forms: in its "sheer" form, it is not invariably concomitant with its conclusion, in the sense that somebody who is absent from home is not necessarily outside if he is dead; in its "qualified" form—that is, the absence from home of a particular person who is known to be alive—it is invariably concomitant with the conclusion, but in that case the conclusion does not tell us anything that is not already there in the inferential reason.

UMBEKA expands on this verse according to his understanding that "absence from home" needs not one but two qualifiers: "The reason, absence from home, qualified only by Caitra will not lead one to infer that he is outside, since it would also apply to Caitra if he were dead. Nor would the reason qualified only by *somebody's* being alive, since that is the case when, say, Devadatta is outside, and Caitra is not. Rather, only when absence from home is qualified by both of them does it lead one to infer that Caitra is outside. But this is possible only insofar as it already includes the understanding that he is outside, so it cannot be an inferential reason for that understanding."

According to PĀRTHASĀRATHIMIŚRA, the following verse anticipates an objection: how can we say that nothing new is apprehended from the qualified inferential reason, given that being outside is surely different from being alive and being absent from home?

> **26.** Therefore, when the house is cognized through perception, and Caitra's absence is cognized through absence, what is outside is nothing other than the cognition of Caitra's existence.

PĀRTHASĀRATHIMIŚRA: "Even though being outside is something different, nevertheless, as for the cognition of being alive, the fact of being alive that is the content of the cognition cannot be combined with absence from the house without assigning it to a locus outside,[9] and so in order to conjoin being alive with absence from home, it 'is located outside,' that is to say, it places the fact of being alive outside. There is not, however, an additional cognition that is produced by it."

---

[8] *tenātra* U, *tenāsya* Su, Pā.

[9] Read *bahiṣṭhānam asthāpya* for the editions' *bahiṣṭhānavasthāpya*. The change of *ma* to *va* could be conditioned by the similarity of these characters in southern scripts, and reinforced by the commonness of the prefixed root *ava-sthā*.

PĀRTHASĀRATHIMIŚRA explains the slightly odd expression in the verse, "what is outside is nothing other than the cognition of Caitra's existence," as a condensed way of saying that Caitra's being outside is given in the cognition of Caitra's continued existence. SUCARITAMIŚRA, however, understands the expression differently: "the cognition of Caitra's existence is outside," namely, outside of inference, or distinct from inference. The use of the equational sentence ("nothing other than") speaks in favor of PĀRTHASĀRATHIMIŚRA's interpretation, as does the fact that in this discussion Kumārila otherwise uses "outside" only to speak of Caitra's position. UMBEKA reads verses 26 and 27 together as a summary of why the cognition of Caitra's being outside, given his absence from home, is distinct from inference.

In the following two verses, Kumārila explains exactly why it is unacceptable to regard the present case as an inference:

> **27.** In order for absence from home to be a property of the locus, the fact of being outside is introduced. Something qualified by being outside would be precisely what we sought to infer on the basis of co-presence and so on with the property of the locus.

"And so on" means that the fact of the locus (here Caitra) possessing a particular property (here being outside) is, in the standard case of inference, established on the basis of the inferential reason, and in particular, its (1) being a property of the locus; (2) being co-present with the property to be proven in similar loci; and (3) being co-absent in all counter-loci of the property to be proven. These, in any case, are the conditions accepted by Kumārila's reductionist opponents.

PĀRTHASĀRATHIMIŚRA then explains the problem as follows: "What we seek to infer is Caitra, qualified by being outside. But 'being outside' is introduced only at the moment of apprehending his absence from home, in order for this absence to be considered to be a property of the locus, which is the living Caitra."

> **28.** If the cognition of the property of the locus and so on is based on the awareness of his being outside, then because that awareness is based on those cognitions, we will certainly be involved in circular reasoning.

The problem is as follows. To start with, we observe only Caitra's absence from his house. At this moment, we do not know whether Caitra is dead or alive; thus we do not know whether the property we have observed, namely Caitra's absence from his house, is indeed a property of the locus, namely the living Caitra. If we assume that Caitra is somewhere else, in order to provide a locus for his observed absence, then we are reasoning in a circle: for the locus, Caitra, qualified by being somewhere else, is precisely what we are supposed to infer in the first place.

As a conclusion to this discussion of the failure of "absence from home" to be a probative inferential reason, Kumārila anticipates the objection that all of the same faults that he had identified in the purported inference—above all, the introduction of the conclusion into the premises and the attendant fault of circular reasoning—would also apply to the Caitra example considered as an *arthâpatti*. In his answer, Kumārila insists that what would be a fault in an inference is not a fault in *arthâpatti*:

29. When something does not otherwise make sense, however, the introduction of the conclusion into the premises does not appear to us to be a fault,[10] because of the cognition having precisely that form.

As Yoshimizu (2007: 323) notes, "Kumārila includes Caitra's existence in the premise of the *arthâpatti* without discussing how it should be confirmed." This short verse moves the Caitra example away from the model of inference and towards the model of a distinct epistemic instrument that has, as SUCARITAMIŚRA and PĀRTHASĀRATHIMIŚRA both say, "distinct components." It is the closest Kumārila comes to an explanation of *arthâpatti* as such, in contradistinction to inference, and hence the three commentaries have attempted to expand on it. Rather than talking about inferential reasons, properties of the locus, and all of the other distinctive terminology of inference, Kumārila here uses the distinctive terminology of *arthâpatti*: "not making sense otherwise," and possibly "clash."

We say "possibly" because there are two different readings in the last part of the verse. One is the relatively banal "appears to us" (*pratibhāti naḥ*), which was possibly read by UMBEKA (he remains silent on this point) and definitely by SUCARITAMIŚRA, and the other "of what possesses a clash" (*pratighātinaḥ*), which was read by PĀRTHASĀRATHIMIŚRA. According to the latter, *arthâpatti* is the epistemic instrument that "possesses a clash," because it is generated by the clash between two other epistemic instruments. He gives exactly the same account of *arthâpatti* in his commentary (*Śāstra-dīpikā*) on *Mīmāṃsā Sūtra* 1.1.5. *Arthâpatti* works by postulating a further piece of information that resolves the clash, and in this way, according to PĀRTHASĀRATHIMIŚRA, it differs from inference.

There is another substantial disagreement in the commentaries on this verse. "Having precisely that form" is understood by SUCARITAMIŚRA and PĀRTHASĀRATHIMIŚRA to mean that the appearance of the conclusion in the premises is a distinctive feature of *arthâpatti* that characterizes it in contrast to inference. According to UMBEKA, however, it means that the cognition that *arthâpatti* results in "takes the form of" the cognition that it begins with, in the sense that it is what allows the original cognition to make sense.

SUCARITAMIŚRA: "suppose one objects as follows: 'In *arthâpatti*, too, the conclusion is introduced into the premises. For how can Caitra's absence from his house, which does not make sense as a result of another cognition and is therefore undetermined, lead us to cognize that he is outside?' This is the question that Kumārila responds to. For something can 'not make sense' in two ways. First, something does not make sense if there is no way at all for it to make sense. But something can also not make sense so long as something else is not postulated. Among these two, we do not need to be concerned about the first, something that does not make sense at all. But when something makes sense when something else is postulated, and does not make sense otherwise, it is possible to determine that it does indeed make sense by postulating that other thing. For this is precisely how everyone reasons, both laypeople and

[10] *pratibhāti naḥ* Pā (however the commentary clearly presupposes the reading *pratighātinaḥ*), Su (corroborated by his commentary); *pratighātinaḥ* U (he does not, however, comment on this part of the verse).

experts. Nor do we see that it is controverted in other places and so on. Therefore this is an instrument of valid knowledge. And just as, in inference, it is an inferential sign that has already been ascertained that leads to the conclusion, in the same way, in this case, it is something that has been understood on the basis of one cognition, and further consideration (*vitarka*) about it has been introduced by another."

SUCARITAMIŚRA, with a Prābhākara opponent in mind, hastens to refute the possibility that we actually doubt one of the two cognitions. To do so, he uses an example from Vedic ritual which would have been familiar to his audience (*Mīmāṃsā Sūtra* 2.4.26). The issue is that one recension of the Vedas enjoins the use of a *ṣoḍaśin* cup during the *Atirātra* sacrifice, while another prohibits it: "Nor do we doubt that one or the other cognitions is valid. Rather, there is simply a need to corroborate the two cognitions whose validity has already been ascertained, by saying, 'how does it make sense for both to be the case simultaneously?' It is similar to the case of the *ṣoḍaśin*, when there is one text that says to take it up, and another that says not to take it up. Therefore, just as in that case, given that there is a requirement for both options to make sense simultaneously, we find that there is such a way, namely, by distinct performances, in this case as well, two things which are accepted on the basis of a valid cognition, and whose validity has been ascertained, can be corroborated by postulating something else."

The impossibility of establishing an invariable concomitance

According to PĀRTHASĀRATHIMIŚRA, Kumārila has now concluded his point that in *arthâpatti* there is no "property of the locus" that provides the inferential reason in a well-formed inference. Now he moves onto a different argument: inference consists in cognizing one thing based on its invariable concomitance with something else, but such a cognition is impossible in the case of *arthâpatti*.

Kumārila says that an invariable concomitance between the two properties, absence from home and presence outside, can only ever be known *a posteriori*:

> 30. A relationship of inseparability in the case under consideration may be presumed only at that point. It is not determined before. Therefore, although this is present,[11] it cannot be a cause for the cognition itself.

We understand that in this section Kumārila uses the words "inseparable" and "concomitant" synonymously to refer to an invariable concomitance.

UMBEKA: "Although it is the case here that two things are inseparable, nevertheless it is not an inference, because only one who has previously grasped this inseparability can make the inference."

The point is not that there is no inseparability between absence from home and being outside (in fact, Kumārila does seem to admit that these qualities are inseparably connected, especially if the reading adopted here is taken), nor is it that their

[11] *saty apy eṣā* Pā, U (seemingly corroborated by their commentaries); *anyathaiṣā* (which would mean "unless it has been determined previously") Su (his commentary, however, does not corroborate this reading and actually hints at the other reading).

inseparability cannot ever be determined (in fact, Kumārila argues below, vv. 31–2, that it can be determined through *arthâpatti*). The point is rather that our cognition does not require that we have previously determined their inseparability. This is absolutely unlike the case of inference, which requires knowledge of the connection between the two terms to begin with. To emphasize the difference, SUCARITAMIŚRA mentions a definition of inference, namely "inference is the cognition of something inseparable for one who knows it," that is, the cognition is only an inference if one already knows that one term is inseparably connected with the other term. A very similar definition is discussed also in the *Explanation of the Nyāya System* of Uddyotakara.[12]

Kumārila says this in the following verses:

> **31–2.** Absence from home and presence outside are not necessarily observed together. Rather, there is no other way to cognize their concomitance.[13] For it is only on the basis of not making sense otherwise that we understand one from the other. That is to say, we do not understand their concomitance unless we postulate it.

That is, although they are not necessarily cognized together, when they are, we have nothing to thank besides *arthâpatti* for this cognition. Kumārila is perfectly fine with saying that we infer one thing from another thing *afterwards*, that is, after we have cognized their co-presence on the basis of *arthâpatti*:

> **33.** Therefore, at the moment of cognizing the relation, we have to cognize the other correlates through *arthâpatti*. Afterwards, it may well be[14] an inference.

That is, after cognizing the relation between the correlates (absence from home and presence outside) through *arthâpatti*, we can forever afterwards use inference to cognize one of the correlates given the other; this inference, however, will always be based on an original *arthâpatti*. Neither Kumārila nor his commentators explicitly say whether we can use such a cognition only in the case of Caitra's absence from home, or in any case where a person is absent from home.

Note that the relation of entailment between being present in one place and being absent in another place is the missing theorem that Yoshimizu (2007) noted in his discussion of the attempt, on the part of Kumārila's opponent, to reduce *arthâpatti* to inference. Where A means "Caitra's presence at home" and B means "Caitra's presence outside," the concomitance can be stated as $((A \vee B) \wedge \neg A) \rightarrow B$.

Even when concomitance is observed no valid inference is possible At this point someone objects, and says that it is indeed possible to cognize the two correlates of the relation as concomitant:

---

[12] On *Nyāya-sūtra* 1.1.5, p. 161 of Taranatha and Amarendramohan's edition. See p. 127, this volume, for translation.

[13] *sāhitye tu* U, Su; *sāhitye'pi* Pā.

[14] *astv* U (corroborated by his gloss *bhavatv*); *asty* Pā (although he glosses it as *bhavatu*), Su (although the editor conjectures *astv*).

> **34.** But somebody who has stood at the door of the house might suppose that Caitra is outside: When he is in one place, then he is not somewhere else.

Kumārila now shifts from the example that the Vṛtti-kāra discussed, the cognition that Caitra is outside given his absence from home, to a different example. Here, somebody comes to Caitra's house and, while standing in the doorway, has two cognitions more or less simultaneously: he observes that Caitra is not in his house, but he also observes that Caitra is somewhere nearby. (UMBEKA imagines that Caitra is observed to be "in the *romaśā*," a rare word that might refer to a garden.) In this sense, there is a "concomitance" of Caitra's absence from home and his presence outside.

Is this, however, the kind of concomitance which can serve as the basis of an inference? The discussion now revolves around whether our joint cognition of Caitra's absence from home and presence outside, which occurs to us as we stand in the doorway, can ever be, or be transformed into, the cognition of an invariable concomitance (*avinâbhāva*), *without* appealing to *arthâpatti*. What would need to be the case in order for these cognitions to yield an invariable concomitance, such that whenever we are given one of the correlates, we can infer the other? Kumārila will argue that, despite the existence of a real invariable concomitance between Caitra's absence from home and his presence outside, we can never *cognize* such a relation without *arthâpatti*, and hence every attempt to reduce *arthâpatti* to inference must fail. The "reductionist" argument that will be discussed in the following verses has a tripartite structure:

> Somebody stands in the doorway of Caitra's house, and cognizes both his absence from home (through the epistemic instrument known as absence) and his presence outside (through perception).
>
> Next, that person combines these cognitions into a cognition of the invariable concomitance between absence from home and presence outside *without* using *arthâpatti*.
>
> Finally, that person is able to apply the cognition of the invariable concomitance in an inference.

This tripartite structure can be discerned in verse 34: somebody stands at the doorway of the house; the same person attempts to combine his cognitions into a cognition of an invariable concomitance ("when he is in one place, then he is not somewhere else"); finally, he is able to "suppose" (*prakalpayet*), that is to say infer, that Caitra is outside when he finds that Caitra is not at home, because he knows that "not being somewhere" is invariably concomitant with "being somewhere else."

The last part of the verse, which expresses the cognition of the invariable concomitance, can actually be read in two different ways: "whenever he is not in one place, then he is somewhere else," and "whenever he is in one place, then he is not somewhere else." It seems that Kumārila treats both of these formulations as logically equivalent, and perhaps we are even meant to understand the text in both ways simultaneously. In the following verses, however, it is clear that the invariable concomitance that has been put forward is between "being in one place" and "not being somewhere else." Why does Kumārila, or rather the opponent that he introduces, use *this* version? It may be that, although Kumārila treats them as equivalent, he knows that one version is easier to refute than the other: in particular, "whenever he is not in one place, then he is somewhere else" does not necessarily involve a quantification, whereas "whenever he is in one place, then he is not somewhere else" involves a quantification over all other places besides the place where Caitra is, and this quantification is precisely what Kumārila will attack.

Kumārila now criticizes the reductionist argument of verse 34: the cognition of the invariable concomitance is problematic, because it relates Caitra's presence in one place with his absence from *every* other place.

> **35ab.** But even then, the person's absence from *every* place is not understood.

PĀRTHASĀRATHIMIŚRA: "Now to the person who says that not being at home and being outside can be grasped at the same time even without *arthâpatti*, provided that one stands in the doorway of the house, the following reply can be made: this is indeed the case, but what is at issue here is the absence in *every* other place on the part of a person who exists in a single place, and since those two attributes (namely, being in one place, and not being in every other place) cannot be grasped at the same time, no inference is possible."

What the reductionist has observed is Caitra's presence in *one* place and his absence from *one* place. What he wants to be entitled to say, however, is that Caitra's presence in one place is invariably concomitant with his absence in *every* other place. Only if we know that his absence from *every* other place is concomitant with his presence in one place can we infer, on the basis of Caitra's absence from *any* place whatsoever, that he is present somewhere else. By contrast, if we only knew that his absence from *one* place was concomitant with his presence in one other place, then we could have to observe Caitra's absence from the *same* place in order to be able to infer his presence somewhere else.

Kumārila claims that one term of this relation—Caitra's absence from *every* place other than the one where he is—cannot be cognized. Thus it can't be cognized as concomitant with Caitra's presence in one place. And thus there can be no knowledge of the invariable concomitance.

Why can't Caitra's absence from every place, other than the one where he in fact is, be cognized? One could claim that it can be cognized, either on the basis of inference, or on the basis of non-apprehension. To begin with inference, we might reason as follows: "Caitra is not in any other place, because he is in a particular place, such as his garden." In this case, the inferential reason is Caitra's being in a particular place. Kumārila denies that this strategy is viable:

> **35cd.** Nor can there be an invariable concomitance of the inferential reason on account of the person's not being in one place.

The suggested inference ("Caitra is not in any other place, because he is in a particular place") fails because the reason, namely his being in a particular place, is not invariably concomitant with the property to be proven, namely his not being in any other place. The reason is limited to a single locus, whereas the property to be proven encompasses infinitely many. The opponent can appeal to the concomitance previously established between Caitra's presence in one place, such as his garden, and his absence in another place, such as his house, but such an appeal is in vain: the concomitance between Caitra's presence in one place and his absence in *one* other place is insufficient to establish a concomitance between Caitra's presence in one place and his absence in *every* other place.

SUCARITAMIŚRA admits that it would be possible to infer being outside on the basis of absence from home, provided that one has grasped an invariable concomitance between them. But besides the fact that it is actually impossible to grasp this invariable concomitance ("it is not possible to establish the invariable concomitance of the inferential reason with absence from the three worlds, simply on account of somebody's being in a certain place"), SUCARITAMIŚRA mentions another objection: people do not actually reason this way, "since even people who have not grasped the connection (between absence from home and being outside) can cognize Caitra's being outside."

The opponent now suggests that there is another way of establishing an invariable concomitance between being in one place and being absent everywhere else, namely, by using the non-apprehension of Caitra as a reason for inferring his absence:

> **36.** One might object that the absence in the case under consideration could be known through non-apprehension. And because no special effort is required to establish it, that will work for a person who is in a single place.

"For a person who is in a single place": the objector states that non-apprehension is an "easy" way to establish that Caitra is absent everywhere else, since a person who is in a single place will not apprehend Caitra's presence elsewhere. This is the sense that UMBEKA and SUCARITAMIŚRA give to the phrase. Another interpretation, however, is possible: the objector could be saying that the non-apprehension "*of* a person who is in a single place," that is, of Caitra, will be established easily enough.

According to PĀRTHASĀRATHIMIŚRA, the sense of this objection is that we do not need to *infer* that Caitra is absent from all of the places in which we do not observe him; this is something we can cognize directly, through non-apprehension. In the same way that non-apprehension secures for us the cognition that Caitra is not in a particular place, it can also secure for us the cognition that he is not anywhere else. And again, if we can legitimately cognize that there is an invariable concomitance between a person's being in one place (established on the basis of perception) and his not being anywhere else (established on the basis of non-apprehension), then this might allow us to infer that Caitra is outside given his absence from home.

According to both UMBEKA and SUCARITAMIŚRA, however, inference still has a role to play in establishing the invariable concomitance in the opponent's view: that is, we can use non-apprehension as a reason to inferentially establish that Caitra is absent everywhere else. Since we do not apprehend Caitra everywhere else, we conclude that he is absent everywhere else. This recalls the reductionist opponent's strategy in vv. 14*cd*–15*ab*.

An answer to the previous objection:

> **37.** It is not the case that through non-apprehension the absence of a thing is understood, because one has not gone to those places. For non-apprehension

operates in regard to things which, although they are not in front of us, nevertheless exist.

"Because one has not gone to those places": because one cannot possibly go to all of the places where a thing might be observed not to be present. The sense here is that non-apprehension only yields locatival predicates ("the pot is not *on the ground*"), and never existential predicates ("the pot *is not*"). Thus the knowledge produced by non-apprehension is necessarily qualified by the particular locus in which something is not apprehended.

"Absence of a thing" is a somewhat confusing turn of phrase, since the opponent is not seeking to cognize Caitra's absence, in the sense of his non-existence, but rather his absence from every place in the universe except for one. Kumārila's point, however, is that the opponent is not entitled to this cognition for precisely the same reason that we are not entitled to use non-apprehension to cognize the absence of a thing in general. Given that we can never be in a position to apprehend the absence of Caitra from every possible place, we cannot use non-apprehension to arrive at the conclusion that he is absent everywhere besides the place he in fact is. Under what circumstances can non-apprehension lead to the cognition of something's absence everywhere?

38. But if you do not apprehend a thing after going to all of those places, then, when there is no longer any other reason, you can understand that it does not exist.

"No longer any reason," that is, for its non-apprehension. Thus what the opponent said, "no special effort is required," is only half true: once we are in a place, the non-apprehension of a thing there is easy. But putting ourselves in a position to have similar cognitions about every place is impossible.

With these conditions, Kumārila has made it nearly impossible to cognize the non-existence of something through non-apprehension. This is a problem from the point of view of establishing a negative concomitance, for example, whenever fire is absent, smoke is also absent. Stated otherwise, smoke should be absent in *all* of the counter-loci of fire, or loci in which fire is absent. Buddhist philosophers, namely Diṅnāga and his followers, have put forward this negative concomitance as one of the conditions of a well-formed inference. Generally, such a negative concomitance is established on the basis of a joint non-apprehension, that is, when we do not apprehend fire in a locus (which is thereby a counter-locus of fire), we do not apprehend smoke in it, either. But Kumārila would seemingly require us to personally inspect every single possible counter-locus of fire to ensure that there really isn't *one* thing out there that possesses smoke but not fire.

39. One might object that, even in the absence of fire and so on, an obvious co-absence of negative concomitants such as smoke could not be established, since we do not go to those places.

"Those places" refers to every locus of the absence of fire, i.e., every place where there is no fire. Kumārila's response is slightly flippant:

40. That is indeed a problem for somebody who needs to know that the reason is absent from other loci. But as for me, just on the basis of not observing, one thing can trigger the cognition of its correlate.

"On the basis of not observing," i.e., not observing any cases where the reason is present in a counter-locus.

SUCARITAMIŚRA identifies the "somebody" here as a Buddhist, who insists that a valid inference requires us to know that the inferential reason is absent from every single counter-locus (in which the property to be proven is absent). Kumārila, by contrast, adopts the view that cognitions are valid unless proven otherwise. Thus something can cause us to infer its correlate, so long as we do not observe a contrary case. SUCARITAMIŚRA and PĀRTHASĀRATHIMIŚRA say that a concomitance between two things can be established on the basis of a handful of positive instances (in which, e.g., fire is present where smoke is present). The negative instances (in which, e.g., smoke is absent where fire is absent) do not need to be known *per se*, for which see Taber (1992).

If it is so easy to arrive at the cognition of an invariable concomitance in the case of smoke and fire—since, as Kumārila says, all we need to do is *not* observe a case in which smoke is present but fire is absent—then why is it so hard to arrive at the cognition of an invariable concomitance in the Caitra example? After all, we do not observe a case in which Caitra is present in one place and *not* absent in another place:

> **41.** One might object that, if this is so, then in the other case as well, the relation of Caitra's absence, which is based on non-apprehension, with his presence, would stand to reason, because it is observed.

"In the other case as well": this could refer to the example of Caitra being observed to be in one place and not in another place, introduced in verse 34, or alternatively to the original example of Caitra being absent from home. The "relation" is between Caitra's being in one place and his not being in any other place. Kumārila responds to this criticism as follows:

> **42.** And since the concomitance of smoke and fire is well-established on the basis of their both occupying a a limited space, and hence no separation is seen, we suppose that smoke can lead to the cognition of fire.

This verse indicates an important difference between *arthâpatti* and inference that pertains to the different role of *universals* and *particulars* in each kind of reasoning, and thus also to the different role of *quantification*. Partly on the basis of this verse, Kiyotaka Yoshimizu has argued (2007 and in this book) that, in Kumārila's view, inference always involves universal quantification over a particular locus, whereas *arthâpatti* operates in cases where universal quantification is impossible.

One reason why the invariable concomitance between smoke and fire is easy to establish, in contrast to the invariable concomitance between Caitra's presence outside and his absence from home, is the fact that smoke and fire both occupy a "limited space," which in turn explains why "no separation is seen." According to UMBEKA, fire and smoke are each found in a a limited space and hence they can each be apprehended as a whole. SUCARITAMIŚRA and PĀRTHASĀRATHIMIŚRA explain further that, although inference concerns universals, the universals inhere completely in particulars. Thus through any particular instance of a universal, the entire universal can be apprehended, as can its concomitance with another universal.Thus, if smoke were not invariably concomitant with fire, then we would have noted it after a few observations, since each observation apprehends the entire locus and hence also the entirety of the relevant property (e.g., the fact of possessing smoke, or the fact of possessing fire). The fact that we do not observe any exceptions to this invariable concomitance is strong evidence that there are no exceptions. In this verse, "suppose" (*prakalpyate*) is used as an equivalent of "accept" (similar to verse 34). UMBEKA explicitly, and the other commentators implicitly, understands "separation" as the lack of invariable concomitance.

The case of the concomitance of Caitra's presence in one place with his absence everywhere else is different:

> **43.** In the case under consideration, this concomitance does not stand to reason, since one of the concomitants is present in an infinite number of loci.

Unlike the case of smoke and fire, Caitra's presence in one place and his absence from another place never have the same locus; indeed, his absence from "another place" really means his absence from every place apart from the one in which he is observed to be present, and hence there is an infinite number of loci of Caitra's absence. Thus, whereas it would have been possible to find an exception to the invariable concomitance of smoke with fire, had there been any such exceptions, given the fact that both properties (possessing smoke and possessing fire) inhere in spatially-delimited loci that can be apprehended as a whole, this cannot happen in the present case, because Caitra's absence is from an infinite number of places, and therefore we cannot apprehend it as a whole.

The opponent has failed to ground the invariable concomitance noted in verse 34, namely when one is in one place, he is not somewhere else, because the invariably concomitant property of "not being somewhere else" has an infinite number of loci, which cannot be checked individually. He now attempts to ground it in another way: the locus of Caitra's absence has a particular property, namely, being distinct from the locus of Caitra's presence. If we know that Caitra's being in one place is invariably concomitant with his *not* being in a different place, then once we know that Caitra is not in one place, we can infer that Caitra really is in another place. Thus one does not have to actually establish Caitra's absence from an infinite number of loci, but only the property of being distinct from the locus of Caitra's presence. From this, the opponent argues, we can establish his absence from all other places.

> **44.** One might object that what is understood in this way is that Caitra is absent from some other place, since it is distinct from the place where Caitra is, just like someplace nearby.

According to UMBEKA and SUCARITAMIŚRA, what the opponent needs to establish is Caitra's absence from *all other places* besides the place where he in fact is, and hence the "other place" that is the locus of this inference is any place within that set of "all other places." This inference may, however, be open to the objection that Kumārila had just made, namely that the opponent is attempting to reason about an infinite number of loci.

According to PĀRTHASĀRATHI, the opponent is able to establish the required invariable concomitance at a slightly lesser cost: we only need to establish that Caitra is absent in *one other place*. Once we know that this place is distinct from the place where Caitra in fact is, we can infer Caitra's absence, on the basis of an observed concomitance between Caitra's presence in one place (his garden) and his absence from a place nearby (his house).

Kumārila responds to the objection by turning the opponent's reasoning on its head:

> **45.** However, in the same way we could also know that "Caitra is in that very place, since that place is distinct from someplace nearby, just like the place where Caitra is." And hence the invariable concomitance is contradicted.

About the "other place" that the opponent had tried to claim was a locus of Caitra's absence, we could just as easily reach the opposite conclusion, namely, that it is a locus of Caitra's presence. Hence, as Kumārila says, the "invariable concomitance" established by the opponent's inference is itself contradicted. How can that be so?

From the way that the commentators have explained these pair of inferences, it is clear that the problem lies in a single locus being susceptible to two contradictory conclusions on account of two contrary but, at first sight, equally valid inferential reasons. The opponent had given the reason that x is different from a locus of Caitra's presence ($x \neq a$, where $L(C,a)$), and Kumārila reasons that x is also different from a locus of Caitra's absence ($x \neq b$, where $\neg L(C,b)$). If "another place" really means "all other places," then Kumārila's response here has the additional character of a *reductio ad absurdum*, since it would be absurd to say that Caitra is present *everywhere* except for the putative locus of his absence.

According to Pārthasārathimiśra, the idea is that it is impossible to establish that Caitra is present or absent in an arbitrary locus (x) simply on the basis of this locus being different from another locus, where Caitra is presupposed to be absent or present, since this difference is precisely what is in doubt: is x the same, or different, from the locus of Caitra's presence? But the opponent might say that Kumārila's response, especially in Pārthasārathimiśra's formulation, misses the point. The opponent takes for granted that Caitra's presence in a given locus is known (e.g., $L(C,a)$). And it appears that once we are in a position to know this, then we can easily know that there is another place, x, where Caitra is absent. In Kumārila's inference, by contrast, we are also given to know that Caitra is present in a and absent in b, but we wrongly infer that Caitra is present in x simply because x shares with a (Caitra's garden) the property of being different from b (Caitra's house). This countervailing inference is wrong, but for a further reason that has not yet been introduced: Caitra cannot be in several places at the same time. Although Kumārila merely suggests it in the next verse, his commentators are more explicit about the fact that the impossibility of Caitra being in different places at the same time is one of the factors in our postulation, by *arthâpatti*, of his not being anywhere else in the world.

In the next verse, Kumārila says that the only way to ground the invariable concomitance between presence in one place and absence everywhere else is through *arthâpatti*:

> **46.** But the apprehension in one place of a person as a whole would not be established otherwise, and this accounts for his absence from other places.

The core of this argument is that Caitra's absence from other places is not something that we arrive at by perception, inference, or non-apprehension, but something that we postulate in order to account for the fact that we are able to cognize Caitra "as a whole" (*kārtsnyena*) in one place. UMBEKA explains that "the fact that the grasping of all of the parts of an individual that has parts would not make sense otherwise is evidence for its absence elsewhere."

SUCARITAMIŚRA explains the shape that *arthâpatti* takes here: we know that when we apprehend Caitra, we apprehend him as a whole; we are not missing a part of him that is in some other place. Yet this apprehension would not make sense if Caitra were actually in any other place. If we really need to, we can exclude the possibility that Caitra is "all-pervading" (*vibhu*). Thus the cognition of his being absent everywhere else comes to be included in the cognition that he is apprehended as a whole.

In their long discussions of this verse, both SUCARITAMIŚRA and PĀRTHASĀRATHIMIŚRA begin by rejecting what we would call an argument from analogy. One might claim that, on the basis of one's own experience, one can know one's own absence from places other than the place where one in fact is, and similarly, one might claim that Caitra's presence in one place guarantees his absence from other places. But both commentators insist that Caitra's absence from other places can only be known through *arthâpatti*. SUCARITAMIŚRA in fact denies that one can establish an invariable concomitance between "being in one place" and "not being in any other place" in one's own case, since the latter can never be observed. PĀRTHASĀRATHIMIŚRA reasons somewhat differently, saying that what we know on the basis of our perceptual experience of ourselves is that one cannot be in contact with multiple places at the same time. In both cases, however, they speak of a "clash"—an idea that was introduced, in one reading of the text, in verse 29—that would cause the original cognition, namely Caitra's presence in one place, to not make sense unless the conclusion, his absence from other places, were postulated. Both commentators thus seem to conceive of *arthâpatti* as an epistemic instrument that is called upon, not to adjudicate a conflict between cognitions (for that is ŚĀLIKANĀTHA'S position, which SUCARITAMIŚRA explicitly argues against), but to prevent such a conflict from arising.

According to SUCARITAMIŚRA, the potential conflict is between the countervailing inferences that Kumārila had introduced in verse 45, namely, the fact that from his presence in one place, we could infer either his absence from some other place, or his presence in another place. But if we are to understand our apprehension of Caitra in a given place as a *total* apprehension, and thus to exclude the possibility that he is all-pervading, the cognition of his absence elsewhere must be included, by *arthâpatti*, in the cognition of his presence in a given place. Hence the countervailing inference, leading to Caitra's presence in some other place, is defeated.

According to PĀRTHASĀRATHIMIŚRA, the potential conflict is rather between the fact of Caitra's not being in multiple places at a given time (which PĀRTHASĀRATHIMIŚRA, in contrast to SUCARITAMIŚRA, believes it is possible to infer) and the fact of Caitra's being in one place at a given time (which is known through perception). The latter is compatible both with the former and its negation. In this case, *arthâpatti* plays its usual role in rendering the two cognitions compatible by adding a third cognition, namely, Caitra's absence from other places.

Given that our knowledge of the concomitance between Caitra's being in one place and his not being anywhere else can only be due to *arthâpatti*, any inference that is based on the knowledge of this concomitance—such as seeing Caitra's absence from home and inferring that he is outside—will ultimately be based on *arthâpatti*:

47a. Therefore it is based on an *arthâpatti* in the case under consideration.

"The case under consideration" refers to the example set out in verse 34, where somebody purports to infer Caitra's being outside on the basis of a previously-cognized concomitance between his presence in one place and his absence everywhere else.

Other types of arthâpatti are also not reducible to inference

Kumārila, having concluded his discussion of the Caitra examples, now discusses other examples of *arthâpatti*, notably those based on perception. This kind of reasoning is often applied in Mīmāṃsā in the postulation of "capacities."

47bcd. And wherever the existence of a capacity is understood on the basis of observing[15] an effect, given a cause.

The original reading of the verse seems to have been "on the basis of observing an effect," read by UMBEKA and SUCARITAMIŚRA. "On the basis of not observing an effect" might have been introduced later, under the influence of the following discussion (which revolves around the need for *arthâpatti*, instead of simply inference, given that the presence of the cause does not always guarantee the presence of the effect).

48a. One might object that the effect is the reason.

That is, a capacity is not postulated, but inferred on the basis of the effect. Kumārila answers the objection:

48b. That is wrong, because there is no requirement for a relation.

Arthâpatti, unlike inference, works in the absence of the knowledge of an invariable concomitance. This is important, because an invariable concomitance can only be known if the concomitant elements themselves are known. Kumārila uses the word "requirement" here, as well as in v. 81, in a specific sense: the requirement that the cognizing subject should have already cognized the relation between two things in order to have the relevant cognition.

Because it is impossible to know a capacity, which is by nature imperceptible, independently of its concomitance with an effect, the concomitance can't be established inferentially:

[15] *kāryadarśanataḥ* Su (corroborated by his commentary); *kāryādarśanataḥ* U (although his commentary presupposes *kāryadarśanataḥ*), Pā.

> **48cd–49.** And this capacity could be understood after having observed that it is a correlate of something else, but not otherwise. And because at that time it is impossible for perception and so on to observe it, *arthâpatti* should be its epistemic instrument, since there are not the three characteristics of inference.

The relevant background to this discussion is given by SUCARITAMIŚRA. Once we understand a concomitance between two things, we might understand a relationship of cause and effect: a seed, for instance, is the cause of a sprout. Sometimes, however, we do not observe the effect when we observe the cause. Sometimes a seed does not put forth a sprout. Thus we have a set of arguments for the seed being the cause of the sprout, based on the seed being a necessary condition for the sprout, but we have a second set of arguments for the seed *not* being the cause of the sprout, based on the seed *not* being a sufficient condition for the sprout. In order to reconcile these two positions—or rather, as SUCARITAMIŚRA would say, in order to decide in favor of the seed being the cause—we have to postulate a capacity that needs to be present in the seed when the sprout is produced. This capacity is not accessible to perception or inference.

Because the whole point of discussing *arthâpatti* separately from inference is that it is a distinct epistemic instrument, with different conditions of validity, it is important to avoid adducing examples of *arthâpatti* that are in fact reducible to inference. According to all of the commentaries, another commentator had adduced the example of the snake and the mongoose, but Śabara did not, precisely because that example is reducible to inference:

> **50.** As for victory and defeat in cases like the snake and mongoose, on the basis of their being predator and prey, they have not been discussed because they are not different from inference.

The example must have been as follows: you see the bloody corpse of a snake, and you postulate that it must have been killed by a mongoose, on the basis of the fact that the mongoose and the snake are natural enemies, and if one has been defeated, the other must have been victorious. This is not a good example of *arthâpatti* because it can be reduced to an inference for someone who is aware of the invariable concomitance between victory and defeat, on the one hand, and the fact that mongooses are the only natural predators of snakes. This example was discussed by Diṅnāga in his *Compendium of the Epistemic Instruments.*[16]

ARTHÂPATTI ON THE BASIS OF WHAT IS HEARD

Now Kumārila turns to the topic that he announced in verse 4, when *arthâpatti* based on the various epistemic instruments was discussed:

> **51.** "The stout man doesn't eat during the day": when you hear a statement like that, and cognize that he eats at night, that is what is called "*arthâpatti* on the basis of what is heard."

---

[16] See Chapter 2, beginning of the section on Sāṅkhya. See also Freschi (forthcoming).

> **52.** Some people suppose that its content is a *meaning* (*artha*). Others, that its content is a *linguistic expression*. But people agree that this kind of *arthâpatti* is not different from linguistic communication.

There has been a debate about whether this type of *arthâpatti* results in the cognition of meaning or of a linguistic expression. Both sides, however, agree that whatever *arthâpatti* produces should be viewed as identical to linguistic communication, which is to say, it has the same epistemic authority as linguistic communication. Why should this type of *arthâpatti* be considered to be the same as linguistic communication?

> **53.** It is through this kind of *arthâpatti* that a procedure in the Veda is generally settled. If it were different from linguistic communication, then it would follow that such procedures were no longer Vedic.

The key question here is one of authority. If I am a Mīmāṃsaka, and I find that the prescriptions pertaining to a particular ritual do not establish what the result of the ritual is, I need to postulate one of two things: either I postulate a meaning, e.g., that the ritual has heaven as its particular result, or I postulate a linguistic expression, namely "one who desires heaven should perform this sacrifice."[17] In either case, the whole point of introducing this additional piece of information is to make sense of a set of existing statements in the Vedas, so we want the additional information to be equal in authority to the Vedas, as if it were an "extension" to the Vedas (or, to use the metaphor that Kumārila uses in verse 54, an "overflow" of the Vedas). If this kind of *arthâpatti* produced cognitions that were qualitatively different from those produced by the Vedic texts, then it is at least unclear why the deliberations of Mīmāṃsakas regarding this additional information should be accepted and followed as equal in authority to Vedic prescriptions themselves, rather than dismissed as speculative.

Among those who accept that this type of *arthâpatti* is identical to linguistic communication, there are two positions:

> **54.** Some people accept that the meaning belongs to the very same statement that has been heard. Other people want it to be the meaning of another sentence, which is in turn an overflow of the meaning of the first.

In the case of the sentence "the stout man does not eat during the day," is the additional meaning of eating at night conveyed by the very same sentence, or is it conveyed by a different sentence, namely, "he eats at night"? UMBEKA says that the "overflow" sentence is one that is brought into consideration by the sentence that is actually heard. In the following, Kumārila will refer to these two sentences as "the day-sentence" (i.e., "the stout man does not eat during the day") and "the night-sentence" (i.e., "he eats at night").

---

[17] The *viśvajit* principle (*Mīmāṃsā-sūtra* 4.3.15) says that the result of any ritual whose result is left unspecified is understood to be heaven.

The meaning belongs to an overflow sentence and not to the sentence that is heard

Kumārila concludes by taking the second position, namely, that one cognizes eating at night as the meaning of the night-sentence, which is itself an "overflow" of the meaning of the day-sentence. He reaches this conclusion by an argument from elimination (*pāriśeṣya*), by showing that the first position, namely, that one cognizes eating at night directly from the day-sentence, is impossible.

> **55.** Now we do not accept that this meaning belongs to the statement that is heard. For it would not be appropriate for a sentence to have multiple meanings, or for a sentence to be what conveys meaning at all.

There are two problems with the suggestion that eating at night belongs to the day-sentence as its meaning. As Umbeka notes, it conflicts with more general features of Kumārila's philosophy. First, we would have to entertain that a single sentence is expressive of more than one meaning. We have here two meanings, namely not eating during the day and eating at night. To ascribe both of them to a single sentence would entail that any sentence might have the possibility of multiple meanings. This violates the Mīmāṃsā principle of postulating entities, including expressive capacities, only when they are absolutely needed, as Umbeka points out.

Second, we would have to account for why it is that a single sentence is expressive of more than one meaning. And if we say that the sentence itself expresses those meanings directly, we will have an additional problem: as Sucaritamiśra and Pārthasārathimiśra point out, in Kumārila's view it is the words rather than the sentence which are the actual expressive units of language.

Thus Kumārila rejects the first alternative because it is incompatible with the theory of meaning that he has argued for elsewhere in the *Verse Explanation* (section on sentence): a particular sentence is not an expressive element, and even if it were, then it would be problematic for it to express multiple meanings simultaneously. If a sentence is not expressive of a meaning, then how do we arrive at the meaning of a sentence?

> **56ab.** For the meaning of a sentence is understood in the form of a complex of word meanings.

This verse summarizes Kumārila's theory of sentential meaning, which later authors would designate as *abhihitânvaya*, "the relation of expressed meanings," in contrast to Prabhākara's theory of *anvitâbhidhāna*, "the expression of relational word meaning." According to Kumārila's view, the words in a sentence first denote their proper meanings, and these meanings are then incorporated into a relational complex. In Prabhākara's theory, the word meanings are already related to each other at the moment that they are expressed.

Kumārila will now proceed to show that there is no way of arriving at the meaning of the night-sentence from the day-sentence. First of all, none of the constituent word-meanings of the night-sentence are expressed by the day-sentence:

> **56cd.** And the meanings of the words "night" and so on are not understood from the day-sentence.

Secondly, one cannot arrive at the meaning of the night-sentence by considering it to be a kind of overall sentence-meaning of the day-sentence:

> **57.** Eating at night is not a combination (*saṃsarga*) of the meanings of the words "day" and so on. There is no mutual exclusion (*bheda*), on account of which that sentence should convey that meaning.

"On account of which . . .": on account of which the day-sentence (or rather the meaning of the words therein) produces the meaning of the night-sentence.

Kumārila mentions two theories of sentence-meaning that were proposed by ancient Indian grammarians. The first, associated with Vājapyāyana, holds that the sentence-meaning is a combination of the word-meanings; the other, associated with Vyāḍi, holds that the sentence-meaning results from the mutual exclusion of the words in a given sentence from other possible referents, for which see Kunjunni Raja (1969: 192). In either theory, there is nothing in the day-sentence that would lead us to the meaning of the night-sentence.

According to SUCARITAMIŚRA, Kumārila now elaborates upon the point raised in verse 55, namely that sentences do not have multiple meanings, by explaining how multiple meanings cannot be produced on the level of the word:

> **58ab.** And because they have already operated in regard to one meaning, there is no postulation of a second meaning.

Kumārila does not brook the possibility that the word-meanings in the day-sentence can first denote their proper meanings, which are then assembled into a complex that conveys the meaning of the day-sentence, and then the denotative process can begin all over again to yield the "night" meaning. Once a word denotes its meaning, the process stops, as Śabara has said (at MS 1.1.25). According to PĀRTHASĀRATHIMIŚRA, even though a linguistic expression might have multiple meanings, if it has been used in a sentence in a given meaning, it cannot mean something else in the same sentence.

One might also add that it is not possible to understand the meaning of the night-sentence as a secondary meaning of the day-sentence, because, according to Kumārila, one only resorts to secondary meaning when the primary meaning of a sentence fails to make sense. Kumārila's conclusion is that the state of affairs of eating at night has to be cognized from the night-sentence, which is not directly heard, but is rather present in the intellect:

> **58cd.** Therefore eating at night is understood by means of another sentence that arises in the intellect.

Arthâpatti *is the only acceptable epistemic instrument for the overflow sentence*

Having established on the basis of elimination that we can only understand the meaning of the night-sentence from the night-sentence itself, Kumārila will now use another argument from elimination to establish that we owe our cognition of the night-sentence to *arthâpatti* and not to any other epistemic instrument.

> **59.** As for the sentence that is understood, even if this was based on a statement, one should say which among the six is the epistemic instrument for it.

Which of the six epistemic instruments (perception, inference, comparison, language, *arthâpatti*, and absence) has the night-sentence as its content? In the next verse, he begins with perception:

> **60ab.** But perception is not acceptable in the case of a sentence that has not been pronounced.

Perception, namely auditory perception, cannot be the means by which we know the sentence "he eats at night," since that sentence is not actually pronounced. Since inference is a more plausible candidate, the argument against inference is more extensive. Kumārila begins by denying that the knowledge of an invariable concomitance between two things, which is required for an inference, is necessary in this case:

> **60cd.** Nor is inference.[18] For this is not observed to be concomitant with that anywhere.

Inference requires knowledge of an invariable concomitance between the reason and the property to be inferred, which would mean that the day-sentence has to be observed to be invariably concomitant with the night-sentence. For it is not the case that we first observe a relationship between these two sentences, and then at a later point we use one to infer the other; rather, what happens is that we cognize the night-sentence more or less directly out of the day-sentence. This discussion recalls the impossibility of reducing *arthâpatti* on the basis of what is seen to inference, which also turns on the lack of an invariable concomitance.

One might claim that the day-sentence could allow one to infer the night-sentence even in the absence of a previously-established concomitance between the two.

> **61.** And if one accepts that something can be an inferential reason even if the relation between two things has not been apprehended, then the result would be that any sentence whatsoever could be cognized[19] as soon as that sentence is pronounced.

The problem is that unless there is a way of accounting for the understanding of a particular sentence given another particular sentence, then we will have two bad options: first, as Umbeka and Sucaritamiśra note, we might only understand that one sentence (say the day-sentence) is connected with another sentence in general, but we would be unable to know exactly what that sentence is; second, if we were able to cognize a particular sentence, it could be any particular sentence whatsoever.

One might claim that in this case one could first grasp a concomitance between the two sentences and then infer one from the other, just as an opponent attempted

---

[18] *na tv* U (corroborated by his commentary); *na hy* Su (corroborated by his commentary), Pā.

[19] *mitir* U, Su, Pā (Chaukhambhā); *matir* Pā (Ratna ed.), a *lectio facilior* and probably an error for *mitir* (given that the Ratna edition otherwise follows the Chaukhambhā edition closely).

to do in the previous example (verse 34). But Kumārila's point is precisely that we do not need to do this:

> **62.** It is not the case that we encounter all those sentences that we know on the basis of *arthâpatti* as already standing in a relation to all of their correlates, such that, when those correlates are present, an inference is possible.

Although it is possible to know the relation between two sentences beforehand, this is not the case with all of the sentences that are known through *arthâpatti*. Given any sentence that "does not make sense otherwise," we can easily arrive at the corresponding "overflow" sentence, even without knowing the relation between them beforehand.

UMBEKA provides some exegetical background for this point. It is very often the case that, in the course of attempting to determine the hierarchical relations between different elements in a ritual, a particular sentence acts as an "indicator" (*liṅga*) of that relation. Hence we might suspect that the day-sentence might similarly function as an indicator—or, to use the language of inference, an inferential reason (*liṅga*)—of the night-sentence. The difference, however, is that in the exegetical case, all of the sentences involved are known through direct perception, and all we need to determine inferentially is how they relate to each other, whereas in this case, we do not have anything besides *arthâpatti* to make us aware of the night-sentence.

Kumārila adduces another argument against the role of inference in cognizing the night-sentence: inference draws a connection between two generic properties (e.g., the property of possessing smoke, and the property of possessing fire), whereas what one cognizes in this case is qualitatively different: it is the existence of a particular sentence. Neither the "existence" of anything nor a "particular" are admitted to be objects of inference. For more on this qualitative difference, see Yoshimizu in this volume, p. 225.

> **63.** And neither existence, nor a particular, is inferred through inference. Yet here what one understands is the very existence of a particular sentence.

UMBEKA: "Neither existence nor a particular can be inferred. Existence cannot be inferred because there can be no valid inferential reason for it: given that we want to infer the existence of something, if the reason were a property of an existing thing, it would be unestablished (because it is existence we are trying to prove, and if you start with something already existing, you are begging the question); if it were a property of a non-existing thing it would be contradictory, and if it were a property of both it would be inconclusive (because it could be used to infer both conclusions)."

An inference also has a standard form, wherein one infers that a property-possessor is qualified by a property, where these two are epistemically independent from each other (i.e., one knows the property-possessor independently of the property that is inferred). See verse 20. Once again, this cannot be said of the current case, since we do not infer the night-sentence as the property of an independent property-possessor:

64. In this case, we do not cognize what is inferred, namely, a previously-established and independent thing that is qualified by something independent, that is to say, a property-possessor qualified by a property.[20]

Kumārila anticipates another attempt to salvage the inferential framework: instead of inferring the night-sentence directly, we might infer, rather, that the day-sentence is qualified by the night-sentence. In this case, the day-sentence will be the locus of the inference.

65. One could object that what is inferred is the fact that the sentence we have heard is qualified by the night-sentence. But then, we would have to agree that locus would be qualified by something that is unestablished.

We can only inferentially attribute to a locus properties that are independently established, that is to say, known in some form already before the inference in question, just like fire is known to us before we infer its presence on the hill. If we do not know the night-sentence before hearing the day-sentence, how can we use the night-sentence as a property of the day-sentence in an inference?

Besides the fact that the inferred property is not previously established, there is another problem with the opponent's suggestion: if the day-sentence is the locus, and the night-sentence is the property to be inferred, then there is nothing left to be the inferential reason. In that case, we might end up in a situation where the same thing serves as the inferential reason and the locus. And this is a major fault in an inference, called "introduction of the conclusion into the premises" (*pratijñârthâika deśa*; see also verse 29).

66. Moreover, since there is no other reason, if this were to be the reason, then what would follow is the fault of the introduction of the conclusion into the premises, just as in the case of language.

Someone who wanted to reduce linguistic communication to inference might suggest that the word-meaning is inferred out of the word, but in that case, the word would act as both the inferential reason and the locus, which is unacceptable. In the same way, the day-sentence cannot function as both the inferential reason and the locus for inferring the night-sentence.[21]

In the following verse, according to UMBEKA's and SUCARITAMIŚRA's interpretation, Kumārila has another configuration in mind, according to which the day-sentence is the inferential reason, and the night-sentence is the locus. This will not work, either:

67. In precisely the same way we must reject[22] the relation of property and property-possessor between the two sentences.[23] For if the one is not grasped, the other cannot be a property of it, and if it is grasped, there is nothing to be inferred.

---

[20] *dharmī dharmaviśiṣṭo* Su (corroborated by his commentary, and suggested by Pārthasārathimiśra's commentary); *dharmādharmaviśiṣṭo* U, Pā, which could be translated as "qualified by a property or the absence of that property."

[21] See the section on language, verses 62*cd*–63*ab*, and the section on the sentence, verse 232.

[22] *nivāryātra* U; *nirākāryā* Su (supported by his commentary), Pā (cf. Umbeka's *nirākartavya*).

[23] *vacasor* Su (supported by Sucaritamiśra's and Umbeka's commentary); *vacaso* U, Pā.

In the same way as we must reject the same relation between words and their meanings: if a meaning is not grasped, then a word cannot be a property of it; if it is, then the inference is pointless. In this case, too, if the night-sentence is not understood, the day-sentence cannot be understood as its property, and if it is, then there is nothing left to infer.

Kumārila has so far been addressing a formal problem: if we use the day-sentence as a reason to infer either the night-sentence or the day-sentence qualified by the night-sentence, the inference will fail, because the reason is not a property of the locus in the first case, and because the locus is qualified by something unestablished in the second case. He now steps back from the formal problems, and addresses the real impossibility of any relation between the day- and night-sentence, such that the one might be a property of the other.

> **68ab.** One sentence cannot be a property of another in the absence of a relation of action and factor of action between the two of them.

The only way for two sentences to be "related" to each other is through the relation of an action and its factors, and Kumārila denies that such a relation subsists between the two sentences at the time that the night-sentence is cognized. Umbeka and Sucaritamiśra claim that the same applies to the case of words and their meanings, which also do not stand in this kind of relationship.

There is, however, a difference between the case of words and their meanings, on the one hand, and the case of the two sentences, on the other. In the case of words, there is a relation of expressor and expressed insofar as the words denote a meaning. But this is ostensibly not the case in the case of the day-sentence and night-sentence.

> **68cd.** Since the day-sentence cannot express the night-sentence, the latter cannot be a property of the former in the sense of being its content.

Pārthasārathimiśra suggests that at this point an objector might contend that the night-sentence is indeed the content of the day-sentence and that the latter does indeed express the former. After all, we cognize the latter upon hearing the former.

> **69ab.** If you say that the day-sentence does express the night-sentence, because we do understand the latter out of the former, then it would follow that the same sentence has multiple expressive capacities.

One might argue that, given that we need to postulate something—either the night-sentence itself, or a capacity, on the part of the day-sentence, to express the night-sentence—there is no reason to prefer the former to the latter. But we already have to postulate the day-sentence's capacity to express its proper meaning. Nobody disputes that the day-sentence expresses its meaning, and is able to do so on account of an inherent capacity. Thus, if we postulate an additional expressive capacity for the day-sentence, we will end up in the situation where a single linguistic expression has more than one expressive capacity. And this is a problem for Mīmāṃsakas (as noted in the commentary to verse 55) because it would destroy the one-to-one correspondence between linguistic expressions and their meanings.

One might propose, as a last resort, that the day-sentence is a property of the night-sentence in the following way: the day-sentence is the inferential reason for the night-sentence, and it is therefore a property of the night-sentence thanks to its role in the inferential cognition of the latter.

> **69cd.** If[24] you say that one could infer that the night-sentence is a property of the day-sentence, then the fact of being such a property would be useless.

PĀRTHASĀRATHIMIŚRA: "If we only know that it is a property of the locus *after* we perform the inference, then the fact of being a property of the locus can't be a component of the inference." For the word "component," which has the sense of a precondition, see verse 10.

At this point, Kumārila has proven that the day-sentence cannot by itself give rise to an inferential cognition of the night-sentence. But the opponent now tries a different strategy: what if it is the individual word-meanings of the day-sentence that give rise to an inferential cognition of the night-sentence? Kumārila will argue elsewhere that we do not need to grasp the relationship between the individual word-meanings and a sentence-meaning in order to cognize the latter. So why shouldn't the same be the case here, namely, that from the individual word-meanings of the day-sentence we directly cognize the night-sentence?

> **70ab.** That sentence is not understood from the word meanings, either, because there is no relation. For universals communicate a particular because they are not possible without it.

We understand that the word-meanings, which are universals, lead us to the cognition of a sentence meaning, which is a particular. This is because universals do not exist without their corresponding particulars. Specifically, universals, in the form of word-meanings, could not generate a linguistic cognition unless they conveyed a particular, in the form of the sentence-meaning.

The word-meanings do in fact convey something beyond themselves, a particular sentence-meaning, but they only convey the particular sentence-meaning in which they are present as universals. They don't convey another particular sentence-meaning. But this is not the case for the cognition of the night-sentence.

> **71ab.** By contrast, it is not the case that the word-meanings of the day-sentence cannot produce a linguistic cognition without the other sentence.

The words in the day-sentence can convey their meanings even without conveying the particular sentence-meaning of the night-sentence. Kumārila now denies that there is any other way to imagine a relation of the word-meanings of the day-sentence with the night-sentence:

> **71cd.** Nor is there any other alternative for a relation with the night-sentence.

According to UMBEKA, the only conceivable alternatives are not making sense otherwise (which has been disproven above, v. 71) and inference (which is not even raised as a possibility because of the lack of a relation). According to PĀRTHASĀRATHIMIŚRA, this verse signals that Kumārila has concluded his argument

---

[24] *ced* U (corroborated by his *pratīka*); *tu* Su, Pā.

that the cognition of the night-sentence cannot be the result of either perception or inference.

Kumārila's opponent now raises another possibility. If neither the day-sentence nor its word-meanings can cause us to cognize the night-sentence, then we might postulate another sentence which does. According to PĀRTHASĀRATHIMIŚRA, this argument addresses the possibility that the night-sentence is not cognized on the basis of perception or inference, but on the basis of language, namely, a sentence which directly conveys it.

> **72–73ab.** Well then, another sentence might be postulated to express that sentence. But if that were so, we would still be far from avoiding the aforementioned undesirable consequence, since there would still be no relation. Therefore, it is better to know it just from the first sentence, since any other sentence will lack a relation to it.

Any additional sentence that the opponent might postulate to express the night-sentence would have precisely the same problem, namely, the lack of a relation between it and the day-sentence. Hence it seems better to postulate the night-sentence in the first instance, without any intermediate steps. SUCARITAMIŚRA adds to this the point that, whatever sentence we postulate, it will fail to express the night-sentence because it will inevitably lack a relation with it, and hence we will keep on postulating sentences endlessly.

The next half-verse discusses the inapplicability of co-presence and co-absence (*anvaya-vyatireka*) for determining a relation between the day-sentence and the night-sentence.

> **73cd.** And co-presence and co-absence cannot be applied here, as they can be in the case of words.

As noted by PĀRTHASĀRATHIMIŚRA, this argument, too, concerns the possibility of cognizing the night-sentence using language as an epistemic instrument. The decisive argument in favor of language as a distinct epistemic instrument is that words have a fixed relation with meanings that is not established on the basis of inference, but is rather observed from co-presence and co-absence: when we hear the sentence "bring a cow" and see someone bringing a cow, and then when we hear the sentence "bring a horse" and see someone bringing a horse, we can form the idea that the linguistic expression "cow" is linked to the meaning of a cow, and that the linguistic expression "horse" is linked to the meaning of a horse. In contrast, no co-presence or co-absence obtains between the day-sentence and the night-sentence, or between their respective meanings.

SUCARITAMIŚRA makes this point clear: "For it is not the case that there is a co-presence and co-absence, such that the day-sentence is only present when the night-sentence is present, and absent when it is not, because of the lack of a connection such as having the same place or the same time." One might object: it is in fact possible to have the cognition of the night-sentence at the same time as the cognition of the day-sentence. In fact, that is the very phenomenon that *arthâpatti* is introduced to explain. But SUCARITAMIŚRA argues against this as well: "Nor is there a co-presence of their cognitions, since there is a cognition of the day-sentence on the part of one who has learned the language even if there is no corresponding cognition of the night-sentence, and because co-presence and co-absence, which arise subsequent to the time of the cognitions, are of no use in cognizing the night-sentence in the first place. Hence it is like the case of words and word-meanings." The now-familiar point is that the relation between the sentences can only be established *a posteriori*.

Now Kumārila attacks the next epistemic instrument in the list, comparison, as the source of the cognition of the night-sentence:

> **74.** There is no similarity at all between the sentence that we have heard and the one we haven't. Therefore it is not comparison. Nor is the meaning of the day-sentence similar to the night-sentence.

Since there is no similarity between the day-sentence and the night-sentence, or between the former's meaning and the latter: the hallmark of comparison as an epistemic instrument is absent.

> **75ab.** Both the possibility of comparison and an inferential reason[25] have been refuted in reference to the night-sentence. Precisely the same is true in reference to its meaning.

We have already established that neither the day-sentence nor its meaning can cause the cognition of the night-sentence through comparison or and inference; now we are also rejecting the possibility that the two of these can cause the cognition of the *meaning* of eating at night. By this point, Kumārila has reached the conclusion of the argument from elimination:

> **75cd.** Therefore it is impossible in the case of the preceding epistemic instruments.

What is impossible is the cognition of the night-sentence. The epistemic instruments that precede *arthâpatti* in the list accepted by Mīmāṃsakas are perception (60*ab*), inference (60*cd*–71), language (72–3), and comparison (74–5).

> **76.** Therefore this is what we accept: the meaning that the sentence we have heard conveys could not come into being without it.

That is, without the sentence that is known through *arthâpatti*. In this example, the meaning of the day-sentence does not make sense as such unless we postulate the night-sentence. Hence *arthâpatti* is the only epistemic instrument available for our cognition of the night-sentence.

SUCARITAMIŚRA notes that there must be a clash (*pratighāta*) between two sets of cognitions, namely stoutness (which SUCARITAMIŚRA claims is perceptually experienced, although that seems not to be a requirement in this example) and the lack of eating during the day. Once again, PĀRTHASĀRATHIMIŚRA summarizes the point nicely: "The night-sentence is postulated as a supplement (*śeṣa*), in order for the stoutness and the lack of eating, which are mutually contradictory (*pratiṣedha*) and would not otherwise make sense in the same sentence, to make sense."

---

[25] *liṅgatve* Pā (Ratna, and corroborated by Umbeka's commentary); *liṅgena* Su, U, Pā (Chaukhambhā).

Arthâpatti *on the basis of what is heard has a linguistic expression as its content*

The following verse introduces two objections. The first returns to the question of whether *arthâpatti* in this case results in the cognition of a meaning, or in the cognition of a linguistic expression from which, in turn, a meaning is cognized. Kumārila had maintained the latter view. But the explanation that Kumārila put forward in verse 76, that the meaning of the sentence that we actually hear "could not come into being without it," raises once again the question of what, precisely, is lacking in order for this meaning to come into being. Why is it the case that we need a linguistic expression rather than its meaning?

> **77ab.** When something cannot exist without something else—namely, a meaning—why not postulate that meaning directly?

In the example in question, why should we postulate the sentence "he eats at night" rather than the meaning expressed by that sentence, when the latter would solve the difficulty equally well?

As UMBEKA imagines it, the opponent claims that this objection does no harm to the principles of Mīmāṃsā in general. First, if the meaning that we understand is something that we wouldn't have understood without the Vedas, then the cognition of this meaning has the same status as the cognition of Vedic sentences, even without postulating an additional sentence. Second, Mīmāṃsakas maintain that, when there are several kinds of evidence for understanding a hierarchical relationship between two things (these forms of evidence being called *viniyoga-pramāṇa*), we choose the type of evidence that is closest to the textual statement. Since a meaning that we postulate on the basis of a textual statement is closer to that statement than a sentence which would express that meaning, we should postulate the meaning directly. The objector, in UMBEKA'S understanding, could have also used Kumārila's own words against him: for he had stated in verse 51 that an example of *arthâpatti* on the basis of what is heard is "the cognition of eating at night," and not of the sentence "he eats at night."

This objection seems similar to the arguments of Prabhākara, who claimed that the content of *arthâpatti* should always be a meaning and not a linguistic expression. Kumārila was most probably older than Prabhākara, and thus not aware of the arguments about *arthâpatti* that Prabhākara presented in the *Long Explanation*, but Umbeka does seem to refer to them.

> **77cd.** Why can't we understand it as a meaning communicated by language, just like sentence meaning?

Whereas UMBEKA understands the phrase "just like sentence-meaning" to mean that the postulated meaning is said to belong to the sentence (e.g., "the stout man does not eat during the day") in the same way as the non-postulated meaning of the same sentence, PĀRTHASĀRATHIMIŚRA and SUCARITAMIŚRA interpret it in the light of an overall theory of sentence-meaning called "the relation of expressed word-meanings" (see verse 56). The fact that UMBEKA does not do so might hint that this theory had not yet been systematized as such.

The sense of this objection, in SUCARITAMIŚRA and PĀRTHASĀRATHIMIŚRA's interpretation, is the following. A general condition on a cognition's being "based on language" is that the cognition arises immediately upon the cognition of a linguistic expression. Yet Kumārila himself had admitted that there is one important case where we consider a cognition to be "based on language" even if it does not arise from the cognition of a linguistic expression: namely, the case of sentence-meaning. In Kumārila's theory of language, at least as SUCARITAMIŚRA and PĀRTHASĀRATHIMIŚRA understand it, what we directly understand from linguistic expressions are word-meanings, which are subsequently assembled into sentence-meanings by secondary cognitive processes. Our cognition of the meaning of the night-sentence might be "based on language" in the same way, since it arises ultimately, if indirectly, from our cognition of the meanings of the words in the day-sentence.

From Kumārila's response to this objection, in verse 78*cd* it seems that the phrase "a meaning communicated by language" could also mean "the purpose of linguistic communication." Kumārila responds to these two objections in a single verse. His response has occasioned an enormous amount of discussion by the three commentators. To begin with, he responds to the first objection (v. 77*ab*):

> **78ab.** What we understand first, through conceptual cognitions (*savikalpaka-vijñāna*), is a linguistic expression.

UMBEKA finds this response to be wrong, because it seems very close to the position of Bhartṛhari, who had argued that "every cognition appears as if permeated by language." This is at odds with Kumārila's own position, according to which the objects of language as an epistemic instrument and the objects of perceptual cognition are separate.[26] We do recall linguistic expressions whenever we experience conceptual cognitions, but the expressions are, precisely, "recalled"; they do not figure as crucial ingredients in the cognitions themselves.

UMBEKA proposes an alternative response that is more closely aligned with the principles of Kumārila's system. What we understand from a linguistic expression is a sentence-meaning in the form of the actualization, or bringing-into-being (*bhāvanā*), of a particular result.[27] UMBEKA notes that the actualization is only properly conveyed by (1) a linguistic expression conveying the impelling of the agent (i.e., the optative affix); in conjunction with (2) a linguistic expression conveying the agent himself (who is impelled), and (3) a linguistic expression conveying the content of the action. He says that one actually needs the *linguistic expressions themselves* to come to a complete understanding of the actualization. Therefore when we hear a statement that "doesn't make sense," like "the stout man does not eat during the day," we actually only hear a part of a statement that would,

---

[26] See the perception section of the *Explanation in Verse*, v. 230, which Umbeka refers to. The verse of Bhartṛhari quoted here (*anuviddham iva jñānaṃ sarvaṃ śabdena bhāsate*) is from *About Sentences and Words* (*Vākyapadīya*) 1.115.

[27] See Kumārila's *Explanation of the System*, p. 445: "it is the actualization that is the sentence-meaning" (*bhāvanâiva ca vākyârthaḥ*). On actualization, which is a technical term of Mīmāṃsā, see Frauwallner (1938).

if it were to be given to us in full, be an instance of language as an epistemic instrument. It is in order to complete the actualization of this statement that we postulate the missing portion of it. Hence, what we are postulating is not an entirely separate statement, but just enough to complete the sentence we are given. This accounts for the qualitative difference between *arthâpatti* on the basis of what is heard, on the one hand, and *arthâpatti* on the basis of what is observed, on the other: there is nothing incomplete in the starting cognitions of the latter.

SUCARITAMIŚRA and PĀRTHASĀRATHIMIŚRA also raise a similar problem: if Kumārila really means that language is the ultimate object of all conceptual cognitions *per se*, then he will have a difficult time explaining why perception and inference, although conceptual in his own view, should not also have linguistic expressions as their objects. Indeed, Kumārila had explicitly argued that the objects of perception, inference, and language are different. PĀRTHASĀRATHIMIŚRA notes that the object of *arthâpatti* is whatever causes the starting cognition to "make sense." In the case of *arthâpatti* on the basis of what is observed, this is always a thing, or a state of affairs (e.g., Caitra's being outside). In the case of *arthâpatti* on the basis of what is heard, this is always a linguistic expression.

Why should it be the case that the "not making sense" of the starting cognition is repaired by a linguistic expression, rather than by a meaning? SUCARITAMIŚRA, and PĀRTHASĀRATHIMIŚRA following him, argue that this is because the specific form of "not making sense" that happens when we hear a sentence such as "the stout man does not eat during the day" is a kind of "expectancy" (*ākāṅkṣā*) that can only be satisfied by a further linguistic expression.[28] SUCARITAMIŚRA in particular is concerned to justify his explanation by an appeal to the widespread practice, in Mīmāṃsā, of completing a Vedic sentence with further linguistic expressions. He mentions several examples: the modification (*ūha*), which occurs in an ectypal ritual, of a *mantra* that is prescribed in its archetype; the completion (*adhyāhāra*) of a *mantra* by means of the syntactically-required word; the extension (*anuṣaṅga*) of a word to subsequent sentences in a ritual context. In all of these cases, the expectancy is only satisfied when a linguistic expression is supplied. SUCARITAMIŚRA cites a passage from the *Mīmāṃsā-sūtra*s to this effect (2.1.40). In perception and inference, there is no such expectancy; what is grasped in those cognitions is a state of affairs. If one attaches a linguistic expression to that state of affairs, SUCARITAMIŚRA says, then that is fine, but it is "just there" (*sanmātra*): it doesn't make an essential contribution to the cognition. In the case of *arthâpatti* on the basis of what is heard, by contrast, it is "satisfied" by a linguistic expression and hence the resulting cognition does not need to go "as far as the meaning" of that expression, to use PĀRTHASĀRATHIMIŚRA's terminology.

SUCARITAMIŚRA complements his argument that perception and inference have expectancy for linguistic expressions by means of pointing out that animals, which have no language, nevertheless have perception and inference, but not

[28] In the Mīmāṃsā theory of sentence-meaning, expectancy is one of the three criteria for a sound sentence, together with compatibility (*yogyatā*) and proximity (*sannidhi*). It is described as the relation which obtains between the action expressed by the verb and the factors of action (such as agent, patient, and so on) which are expressed by nouns.

arthâpatti on the basis of what is heard. Indeed, even human beings who have not properly learned a language cannot avail themselves of this kind of *arthâpatti*. He then weakens his claim that the expectancy is satisfied by a linguistic expression alone by claiming that what makes the starting cognition make sense again is a "meaningful linguistic expression, not a meaning alone or a linguistic expression alone." PĀRTHASĀRATHIMIŚRA does not follow him in either of these arguments.

Kumārila addresses the second objection (77*cd*) as follows:

> **78cd.** When a sentence already has a purpose, another one is not based on linguistic cognition for us.

The use of the word "purpose" in this response suggests that the term "meaning" (*artha*) in the objection has the additional sense of the "purpose," as noted above (verse 77*cd*).

The central issue, which SUCARITAMIŚRA and PĀRTHASĀRATHIMIŚRA identify, is when a cognition that originates from a statement "not making sense" should be considered to be the result of language as an epistemic instrument, and when it should be considered to result from *arthâpatti*. This question is indexed to the question of when a linguistic expression can be said to "fulfill its purpose." This is especially important because, as discussed in the previous half-verse (78*ab*), SUCARITAMIŚRA and PĀRTHASĀRATHIMIŚRA claim that what generates *arthâpatti* on the basis of what is heard is an unfulfilled "expectancy" in the original expression. Such an interpretation seems difficult to reconcile with Kumārila's claim here that each sentence, including the day-sentence, is complete in itself.

According to these two commentators, the sentence has not "fulfilled its purpose" until it communicates a sentence meaning that makes sense. Up until this point, any cognitions that we have about the sentence are considered to be the result of language as an epistemic instrument. Once a sentence-meaning has been ascertained, however, any additional cognitions we have from it are not considered to be based on language as an epistemic instrument, but rather on *arthâpatti*.

It is unclear whether the examples that SUCARITAMIŚRA had mentioned in his commentary to verse 78*ab*, such as completion and extension, fall in the first phase (and thus are known through language as an epistemic instrument) or the second phase (and are thus known through *arthâpatti*). Presumably SUCARITAMIŚRA wants them to be examples of *arthâpatti*, but in most of the examples, the original sentence is actually incomplete, unlike the day-sentence.

At this point, SUCARITAMIŚRA pictures an objector who thinks that deciding whether the additional meaning belongs to the statement we have actually heard, or whether it belongs to the statement that we have postulated, is splitting hairs. SUCARITAMIŚRA then explains what difference it makes to ritual practice: if an error takes place during a performance based on an actually heard Vedic text, one will have to perform the corresponding expiation rite. For an error occurring during a performance based on a precept obtained through *arthâpatti*, by contrast, one will need to perform a generic expiation rite.

ARTHÂPATTI DOES NOT REQUIRE A RELATION BETWEEN THE STARTING AND FINAL COGNITIONS

An opponent now tries to attack *arthâpatti* on the grounds of a lack of a relation between the starting cognition and the final cognition. The objection pertains to both varieties of *arthâpatti*, namely on the basis of what is observed and on the basis of what is heard. According to UMBEKA, the opponent expects the cognition to be grounded on a relation of inseparability (see verse 30), which comes in two varieties, according to the theory of inference defended by Dharmakīrti: either x is identical with y, or x is caused by y.

> **79.** One might object that when there is no relation, or when it has not been ascertained, it would turn out that this sentence, from which the cognition arises, would lack an epistemic instrument.

Kumārila responds:

> **80.** Well, is there a royal decree that only a relation can be an epistemic instrument? How would perception be an epistemic instrument in the absence of a relation?

The counter-example to the opponent's claim is perception, which according to Kumārila does not require any kind of relation.

> **81.** If one objects that in that case there is a relation between the sense faculties and the thing perceived, that is wrong, because there is no such requirement. For nobody ascertains that relation at the moment of perception.

For the sense of "requirement" here, see 48*b*. Kumārila shuttles between two senses of the word "relation" in this and the following verses. On the one hand, it has an ontological sense: two things are related if they stand in some relation to each other in the real world. On the other hand, it has an epistemic sense: two things are related if they are always found together in the mind of a cognizing subject. The latter sense can also be reflexive, that is, the subject can be aware that the two things are so related. Hence the latter sense can refer not simply to the relation itself, but also to the cognition of the relation. Kumārila trades on this ambiguity, although SUCARITAMIŚRA clearly distinguishes the two senses: in his commentary on verse 79, he notes that it may be the case that despite a real, ontological relation between the object of cognition and some other thing, this relationship is nevertheless not known to the cognizing subject.

In the case of perception, the sense faculties are related (in the ontological sense) to the external objects that they perceive. But this relation can only ever be known to the cognizing subject (in the epistemic sense) after the fact. As UMBEKA says, "with reference to the visual form, which can only be cognized through the faculty of sight, there can be no grasping of a relation with the faculty of sight itself, which can only be cognized through the visual form."[29]

---

[29] Umbeka goes further and argues that there is no relation in the ontological sense, either. For such a relation, he claims, there would have to be either suitability (presumably, of the sense faculties to intercept and produce perceptual cognitions of certain types of external objects), or contact. He interprets the subsequent two verses as eliminating each of these possible relations, respectively.

82. By contrast, that relation by means of which you might ascertain something after the perceptual experience could not be a component of the epistemic instrument. It is as if it did not exist.

This is the now-familiar argument: that which is only ascertained *a posteriori* cannot be said to lead to the production of a given cognition. We follow SUCARITAMIŚRA's understanding of this verse. PĀRTHASĀRATHIMIŚRA, however, seems to take the verse as referring to a *person* who ascertains the connection, since he comments that a person who has no means of ascertaining the connection would not have this component of the perceptual cognition (and therefore wouldn't have the perceptual cognition at all), which is false.

83. There are those who claim that the faculties of sight and hearing produce valid cognitions without coming into direct contact with their objects. It should be the same in this case.

Kumārila himself accepts a theory of perception in which there is contact between the sense faculties and the external objects they perceive. However, not everyone accepts this theory. Some, whom PĀRTHASĀRATHIMIŚRA identifies as Buddhists, argued that the sense faculties operate without direct contact with their objects. Kumārila says that, for these philosophers, there is not even an ontological relation between the sense faculties and their objects, much less the conscious apprehension of a relation. Yet they still admit the validity of perceptual cognitions. So, too, we should admit the validity of *arthâpatti* even in the absence of a relation.

At the end of this sequence of verses (vv. 79–83), UMBEKA adduces another example of valid cognition in the absence of a predetermined relation, namely, the cognition of the meanings of Vedic sentences. The passage is terse and its meaning not completely clear.

Kumārila summarizes by stating his view that, whatever the cause of a cognition's *arising* may be, the cause of its *validity* is always the absence of a sublating cognition. This is the theory of "intrinsic validity," about which see Taber (1992).

84. Therefore, whether a relation exists or not, for us, any cognition at all that might arise,[30] so long as it is not invalidated, should be valid.

SUCARITAMIŚRA says that a cognition can be invalid on account of three circumstances: not having been produced, being sublated by a subsequent cognition, and being put into doubt. He understands Kumārila's verse in reference to all three: "that might arise" refutes invalidity as a result of a cognition not having been produced, and "so long as it is not invalidated" refutes invalidity as a result of either sublation or doubt.

Now the discussion returns to *arthâpatti* in particular. Kumārila claims that nobody entertains serious doubts regarding the validity of the cognitions it produces, despite their doubts about whether *arthâpatti* or some other epistemic instrument is responsible for producing those cognitions.

[30] *jāyeta* all witnesses, although Su's commentary suggests *jāyate*.

> **85.** And there is nobody who would disagree with the validity of *arthâpatti*. The debate is about its difference from inference, or lack thereof, and we have settled this point.

An objector may interrupt here, disturbed by Kumārila's seemingly flippant disregard for a relation between the starting and final cognitions in the case of *arthâpatti*. If we don't need a relation for *arthâpatti*, then why would we ever need it? Couldn't we infer smoke from fire, even in the absence of a relation, in either the ontological or epistemic senses? As UMBEKA says, "why should we need a relation of inseparability, or the knowledge of such a relation?"

> **86.** By contrast, in those cases where the cognition itself does not arise in the absence of a relation,[31] what is to be done? Even that kind of relation would not be a reason for the cognition's validity.

SUCARITAMIŚRA: "The knowledge of the relation is a component in the production of the cognition. It is not a component of the cognition's validity, which is assured only by the absence of sublating cognitions." Even in the case of inference, its validity is not due to the knowledge of the relation, but is rather intrinsic to the cognition itself.

APPLICATIONS OF *ARTHÂPATTI*

UMBEKA now notes that it was important for Kumārila to state the difference between *arthâpatti* and inference because of the use of *arthâpatti* in the interpretation of the Vedas, which he will now describe:

> **87.** Here, the Vedic statement that is postulated on the basis of traditional texts, and the applicatory statement that is postulated on the basis of indication and the other forms of evidence, and the completion of a Vedic sentence that is postulated on the basis of the result and so on—in none of these is there any hint of a relation.

"Here": in this system, i.e., Mīmāṃsā. The first example is the postulation of a Vedic statement (*śruti*) on the basis of traditional texts (*smṛti*) such as Manu's *Laws*. When the possibility that those texts were composed by human beings has been ruled out, the only possible remaining option is that they were based on Vedic texts that are now lost.

The second example is a Vedic statement that is postulated in the process of "application," which situates all of the elements of a ritual together into a hierarchical unity (see UMBEKA'S comments on verse 62 and 77*ab*). In this process, when it is not explicitly mentioned which element is subordinate to which, Mīmāṃsakas avail themselves of five additional forms of evidence to make the decision. And on the basis of this evidence, they can postulate an additional sentence that makes the relation clear. SUCARITAMIŚRA gives examples for the postulation of sentences on the basis of each of these five forms of evidence. For example, nowhere in the context of the Full- and New-Moon Sacrifices is it explicitly prescribed that the *mantra* "I cut the *barhis*, the seat of the gods" (*barhir deva-sadanaṃ dāmi*) is to be employed

[31] *ṛte* Su, U; *kṛte* Pā.

in the cutting of the *barhis*-grass, although both the *mantra* and the cutting of the grass are so prescribed. But on the basis of a "indication" (*liṅga*) in the *mantra*, we postulate the "applicatory statement" that "one should perform the cutting with that *mantra*." The third example is the postulation of a result in relation to Vedic prescriptions in which the result is not explicitly mentioned. The result is one of required elements of a prescription. Whenever it is not mentioned it has to be supplied, and hence it is brought in from other contexts or postulated. Most commonly the result with which Vedic prescriptions are construed is "heaven." Mīmāṃsakas understand "heaven" very broadly, in the sense of a felicity which every human being desires, as argued in a section of Śabara's commentary on the *Mīmāṃsā-sūtra*s (6.1.1).

> **88.** All of this and more would be invalid, if *arthâpatti* were not different from inference. But if *arthâpatti*, as we have defined it, were to be called inference, then we would be satisfied.

Kumārila thus makes it clear that much of the interpretive enterprise of Mīmāṃsā depends on *arthâpatti*, in the sense that Mīmāṃsakas must postulate texts that are equal in authority to the text of the Veda.

UMBEKA understands the last half of the verse to mean that *arthâpatti* can be called inference in an etymological sense, that is, an "after-cognition" (*anu-māna*), since like inference it occurs subsequent upon another cognition. In the case of *arthâpatti*, it occurs after a cognition of something not making sense; in the case of inference, it occurs after the cognition of an invariable concomitance. As long as the essential differences between inference and *arthâpatti* are maintained, Kumārila has no issue with using the vocabulary of inference to talk about *arthâpatti*. He made a similar concession at the end of the section on language as an epistemic instrument (verse 111).

REFERENCES

Primary sources

Commentary [*Bhāṣya*] (Śabara)
See *Mīmāṃsā Sūtra*.

Compendium of the Epistemic Instruments [*Pramāṇasamuccaya*] (Diṅnāga)
Steinkellner, E., H. Krasser, and H. Lasic, eds. (2005), *Jinendrabuddhi's Viśālāmalavatī Pramāṇasamuccayaṭīkā Chapter 2*, Beijing and Vienna: China Tibetology Publishing House and Austrian Academy of Sciences.

Explanation in Verse [*Ślokavārttika*] (Kumārila)
With the commentary of Umbeka:
Ramanatha Sastri, S. K., ed., revised by K. Kunjunni Raja and R. Thangaswamy (1971), *Slokavartikavyakhya Tatparyatika of Umveka Bhatta*. Madras: University of Madras.
With the commentary of Sucaritamiśra:
Rāmasvāmiśāstrī, Vi. E., ed. (1943), *Kumārilabhaṭṭapraṇītaṃ Mīmāṃsāślokavārtikam Sucaritamiśrapraṇītayā Kāśikākhyayā Vyākhyayā Sametam*, Vol. 3, Anantaśayana [Thiruvananthapuram]: Rājakīyamudraṇayantrālaya.

With the commentary of Pārthasārathimiśra:

Tailanga, Râmaśâstri, ed. (1898–9), *The Mîmânsâ-Śloka-Vârtika of Kumârila Bhatta, With the Commentary called Nyâyaratnâkara by Pârtha Sârathi Miśra*, Benaras [Varanasi]: Vidya Vilas Press.

Explanation of the Nyāya System [*Nyāyavārttika*] (Uddyotakara)

Nyaya-Tarkatirtha, Taranatha and Amarendramohan Tarkatirtha, eds. (1985), *Nyāyadarśanam with Vātsyāyana's Bhāṣya, Uddyotakara's Vārttika, Vācaspati Miśra's Tāt-paryaṭīkā and Viśvanātha's Vṛtti*, New Delhi: Munshiram Manoharlal.

Explanation of the System [*Tantravārttika*] (Kumārila)

See *Mīmāṃsā Sūtra*.

Mīmāṃsa-sūtra (Jaimini)

Subbāśāstrī, ed., vols. (1929–34), *Śrīmajjaiminipraṇīte Mīmāṃsādarśane*, 6 vols., Pune: Ānandāśramamudrālaya. Ānandāśramasaṃskṛtagranthāvaliḥ 97.

Secondary literature

Frauwallner, E. (1938), "Bhāvanā und Vidhi bei Maṇḍanamiśra," *Wiener Zeitschrift für die Kunde des Morgenlandes* 45: 212–52.

Freschi, E. (forthcoming), "*Arthāpatti* in early Mīmāṃsā and until Pārthasārathi Miśra," in V. Eltschinger, B. Kellner and E. Mills (eds.), *A Road Less Travelled—Contributions to the Study of Indian Philosophy in Honour of John Taber*.

Kataoka, K. (2011), *Kumārila on Truth, Omniscience and Killing*, Sitzungsberichte der philosophisch-historischen Klasse, No. 814, Vienna: Verlag der Österreichischen Akademie der Wissenschaften.

Kunjunni Raja, K. (1969), *Indian Theories of Meaning*, Madras: Adyar Library and Research Institute.

Taber, J. (1992), "What did Kumārila Bhaṭṭa mean by *svataḥ prāmāṇya*?" *Journal of the American Oriental Society* 112, no. 2: 204–21.

Yoshimizu, K. (2007), "Kumārila's Propositional Derivation (*Arthāpatti*) without Pervasion (*Vyāpti*)," in K. Preisendanz (ed.), *Expanding and Merging Horizons: Contributions to South Asian and Cross-Cultural Studies in Commemoration of Wilhelm Halbfass*, 315–35, Vienna: Austrian Academy of Sciences Press.

Yoshimizu, K. (1994), "Der Geltungsbereich des *niyoga* bei den Prābhākaras," *Wiener Zeitschrift für die Kunde Südasiens* 38: 485–507.

CHAPTER TWO

Prabhākara's *Long Explanation*

Translated by ANDREW OLLETT and ELISA FRESCHI

Prabhākara was most likely a younger contemporary of Kumārila and might have therefore lived in the seventh century.[1] His only extant work is the *Long Explanation* (*Bṛhatī*) on Śabara's *Commentary* (*Bhāṣya*). Prabhākara's style is quite elliptical, and his ideas are often original and challenging. For these reasons, it is often difficult to follow the thread of his argument. In our translation, we have often followed the commentary of the ninth-century philosopher Śālikanātha, called *Straightforward and Lucid Gloss* (*Ṛjuvimalā*). Indented discussion marked COMMENTS is our explanation also often following him. Śālikanātha, however, is an original thinker in his own right, and in our reading, he sometimes diverges from Prabhākara on key issues. The following chapter (see p. 95) will examine Śālikanātha's original ideas on *arthâpatti*, while in this chapter we have only included a few extracts from his commentary.

Prabhākara's understanding of *arthâpatti* differs sharply from Kumārila's in the following respects:[2]

- The element which does not make sense, according to Kumārila, is the trigger, e.g., the cognition of Devadatta's absence from home, whereas for Prabhākara, it is the thing known, e.g., the cognition of Devadatta's presence elsewhere.
- "Not making sense otherwise" for Kumārila seems to mean a logical impossibility, whereas for Prabhākara, it only means that something *in fact* does not occur apart from something else.
- On whether and how the relation between trigger and the thing known through *arthâpatti* is known, Kumārila insists that the relation is not known beforehand, whereas Prabhākara admits that a relation must be known in general terms.
- On whether "*arthâpatti* on the basis of what is heard" constitutes a distinct type of *arthâpatti*, Kumārila argues at length for this type, while Prabhākara does not even mention it.

[1] See Yoshimizu (1994) for an insightful discussion of the chronology of Kumārila and Prabhākara.

[2] For more on the differences between Kumārila's and Prabhākara's understanding of *arthâpatti*, see Freschi (forthcoming).

THE *PRIMA FACIE* POSITION

> COMMENTS: Prabhākara structures his discussion by first introducing the definition of *arthâpatti* that was provided in Śabara's *Commentary*, and then presenting a *prima facie* position (*pūrva-pakṣa*), according to which *arthâpatti* so defined is no different from inference.

"Also *arthâpatti*, the postulation of a thing when a thing that is seen or heard does not make sense otherwise. For example, on seeing that Devadatta, although alive, is not at home, the postulation of his being outside, which is not seen."

Now, what is this "not making sense otherwise?" If, to begin with, one says that the existence of a thing does not make sense without something else, then that is simply the inference of an effect from the cause, and it is not a distinct epistemic instrument.

> COMMENTS: Note that the sense of "not making sense otherwise" according to this position is very close to the sense that Prabhākara will later give to it: namely, that (the cognition of) one thing simply does not occur without (the cognition of) another thing.
>
> Śālikanātha makes it even clearer that no *logical* inconsistency is involved in "not making sense otherwise": "For the word 'otherwise,' which generally denotes a manner other than the manner under discussion, denotes the absence of what is postulated. And this is also denoted by the phrase 'does not make sense.' So we get this meaning: when we understand that this state of affairs does not obtain in the absence of something postulated, we postulate another state of affairs."

If, instead, one says that the definition of inference is a cognition of something whose relation with something else is *known*, whereas in this case the relation is not known, and for that reason it is a distinct epistemic instrument, that too is incorrect.

> COMMENTS: The definition of inference quoted here is the one that Śabara, too, had given in his *Commentary* to *Mīmāṃsā Sūtra* 1.1.5.

If one has not already known of a relation between two things, how can one understand that one of them does not make sense without the other? For not making sense otherwise is not something that can be apprehended through perception. For that is apprehended on the basis of an invariable concomitance with its effect, and such an invariable concomitance is always established through multiple observations. Therefore, no matter whether something is observed or not, only if its relation with what one perceives is known can one know it on the basis of the fact that what one perceives would not make sense otherwise. Therefore a distinct epistemic instrument is simply a mirage.

> COMMENTS: Śālikanātha takes this opportunity to explain that it is not enough, for *arthâpatti*, that one thing does not occur without another; it must be *cognized* that one thing does not occur without another: "Not making sense otherwise does not lead to an understanding of anything at all if it is not ascertained in the

first place. For Śabara has used the phrase 'does not make sense otherwise,' followed by *iti*, where the word *iti*[3] is commonly understood to refer to a cognition. If not making sense otherwise is not ascertained, then it cannot be the reason for a particular understanding. Therefore it is only when it is understood that not making sense otherwise leads to another understanding."

PRABHĀKARA'S POSITION

COMMENTS: At this point, another speaker—whom we, following Śālikanātha, identify as Prabhākara himself—responds to the *prima facie* position.

That would be true, if that which did not make sense without something else were the trigger. But in this case, what does not make sense is precisely what is known through *arthâpatti*.

COMMENTS: As Śālikanātha explains, "if the trigger for the cognition of something was the thing that does not make sense without it, then this would simply be an inference." In contrast, Prabhākara maintains that it is exactly the thing known through *arthâpatti* which "does not make sense otherwise."

OBJECTION: Now what does not make sense in this example? When a person is observed to be absent from home, provided that he is alive, what does not make sense is his absence from other places. And what follows from this? It is not his absence that is understood, but rather his presence. And it is not the case that his presence does not make sense once we have observed his absence from home.

RESPONSE: Surely it does not make sense. For presence outside does not make sense apart from observing his absence from home.

COMMENTS: Prabhākara's response is that the being outside would indeed not make sense if it were not for one's experience of the absence from home. Thus, he understands "not making sense otherwise" as a factive statement: the cognition of *x* would not take place in the absence of the cognition of *y*. Śālikanātha makes the point explicit when he says that "'Otherwise' means 'without the postulation of the thing that is postulated,' that is, so long as its relation with being outside is not understood." Note, however, that our interpretation of Prabhākara's text differs significantly from Śālikanātha's, which we provide in the following chapter (see p. 95). In the following exchange, Prabhākara addresses an objection to his interpretation of the text of Śabara's *Commentary*. He must be aware that his interpretation is rather strained, from a grammatical point of view.

OBJECTION: In saying "a thing that is seen or heard does not make sense otherwise," Śabara has made it clear that it is the trigger that does not make sense otherwise.

---

[3] In Sanskrit, */iti/* marks the end of an embedded clause and in this context, it marks the end of one part of Śabara's definition, 'when a thing that is seen or heard does not make sense otherwise' (p.90).

Response: God bless you, how little you know the text! Śabara has said, "a thing that is seen or heard is the postulation of a thing." Now what does he mean by "the postulation of a thing"? A thing that is seen or heard is the epistemic instrument for another thing.

Objection: So with what is the phrase "does not make sense otherwise" construed?

Response: "Knowledge," we answer. In bringing about a state of not making sense otherwise, it triggers the cognition of another thing.

> Comments: In other words, in Prabhākara's interpretation, the clause "does not make sense otherwise" in Śabara's commentary is not to be construed with "a thing heard or seen" but rather with an unspoken and implicit word "knowledge." At this point, an objector claims that one needs to know that the trigger is correlated with the thing one is about to know through *arthâpatti* in order for this instrument of knowledge to work. Prabhākara seems to accept that knowledge of a "mere relation" is necessary.

Objection: Isn't there a requirement in this case of being known to be a correlate of something else?

Response: What is required is the knowledge of a mere relation, not the fact of being a correlate. In inference, by contrast, the trigger is the fact of being a correlate itself, and this is suggested by the phrasing of the definition of inference as "the cognition of something whose relation with something else is known."

> Comments: Unfortunately Prabhākara does not elaborate on what it means to be a "mere relation" (*sambandhamātra*). Śālikanātha elaborates as follows: "True, a relation between being alive and a place is required. But absence from home, which is the trigger, is not a correlate (*sambandhin*) of presence outside. Therefore, in *arthâpatti*, what is required for the understanding is the cognition of a mere relation between being alive and a place." In other words, one needs to be aware that being alive is related to being somewhere, but one does not need to know the invariable concomitance linking absence from home and presence outside. If one knew it, the instrument of knowledge used would be inference, not *arthâpatti*.

"A THING THAT IS SEEN OR HEARD"

> Comments: The final topic of Prabhākara's discussion concerns the purpose of the words of "heard" and "seen" in Śabara's definition. The answer is that they are just synonyms and that all is meant is that something has been apprehended. Noteworthy here is the fact that Prabhākara does not mention the existence of a distinct type of *arthâpatti*, "*arthâpatti* on the basis of what is heard" (*śrutârthâpatti*), which occupies so much of Kumārila's discussion.

Objection: Does the mention of seeing and hearing in the definition of *arthâpatti* serve to exclude other causes?

Response: No, we say. It just means something that is apprehended.

Objection: Why, then, is the word "heard" used, when just "seen" should have been used?

Response: It is just a different way of expressing it. "Seen or heard" expresses apprehension.

REFERENCES

Primary sources

Long Explanation [*Bṛhatī*] (Prabhākara)

Ramanatha Sastri, S. K., ed. part 1 and 2, and S. Subrahmanya Sastri, ed. part 3, 4, and 5 (1934–67), *Bṛhatī of Prabhākara Miśra [on the Mīmāṁsāsūtrabhāṣya of Śabarasvāmin] with the Ṛjuvimalāpañcikā of Śālikanātha*, Madras University Sanskrit Series, Nos. 3.1, 3.2, 24, 25, 26, Madras [Chennai]: University of Madras, 110–17.

Straightforward and Lucid Gloss [*Ṛjuvimalā Pañcikā*] (Śālikanātha)

See *Long Explanation*.

Secondary literature

Yoshimizu, K. (1994), "Der Geltungsbereich des *niyoga* bei den Prābhākaras," *Wiener Zeitschrift für die Kunde Südasiens* 38: 485–507.

Freschi, E. (forthcoming), "Reconstructing an episode in the history of philosophy: *arthāpatti* in Kumārila's commentators,"in F. Sferra and V. Vergiani (eds.), *Festschrift for Raffaele Torella*.

CHAPTER THREE

Śālikanātha's *Straightforward and Lucid Gloss; Comprehensive Survey of the Epistemic Instruments*

Translated by ANDREW OLLETT and ELISA FRESCHI

Śālikanātha was an author of the later eighth or ninth century who is best known as the earliest commentator on, and expositor of, the thought of Prabhākara. He is thus one of the earliest representatives of a "Prābhākara Mīmāṃsā" (Mīmāṃsā following Prabhākara), which came to be doxographically opposed to "Bhāṭṭa Mīmāṃsā" (Mīmāṃsā following Kumārila). Śālikanātha wrote widely on Mīmāṃsā topics, besides authoring a commentary—now lost—on an important text of the Vaiśeṣika system (the *Praśasta-pāda-bhāṣya*).

The sections translated below come from two separate works. The first comes from the *Straightforward and Lucid Gloss* (*Ṛju-vimalā Pañcikā*), which is a running commentary on Prabhākara's *Long Explanation*. Since Śālikanātha's commentary is mostly dedicated to explaining Prabhākara's remarks, we have focused on three sections where he offers something above and beyond what Prabhākara discusses. These are (1) his understanding of the crucial condition of "not making sense" which applies in any case of *arthâpatti*; (2) the "summary verses" which he supplies toward the end of Prabhākara's discussion; and (3) his discussion of *arthâpatti* on the basis of what is heard, which Kumārila had taken to be a qualitatively distinct kind of *arthâpatti*. In these selections, the quotations from Prabhākara are in bold.

The second section is the section on *arthâpatti* in an independent essay entitled *Comprehensive Survey of the Epistemic Instruments* (*Pramāṇa-pārāyaṇa*) that Śālikanātha wrote on the six epistemic instruments that Mīmāṃsā authors accepted as valid and distinct: perception, inference, testimony, comparison, *arthâpatti*, and absence. This essay forms part of a collection of essays on Mīmāṃsā topics called *Prakaraṇa-pañcikā* (which might be translated as *Topical Elaborations*).

FROM THE *STRAIGHTFORWARD AND LUCID GLOSS*

What does not make sense in arthâpatti

In response to the proponent of the accepted position, an OBJECTOR (*pūrvapakṣin*) now speaks: **Now what does not make sense in this example? When a person is observed to be absent from home, provided that he is alive, his absence from other places does not make sense.** This is a single passage.

When absence from home on the part of someone who is alive has been observed, the same person's absence anywhere else does not make sense, because that would result in the absence of his being alive. **And what follows from that?** In response to this question, the OBJECTOR makes his own position clear. **It is not his absence that is understood as a result of *arthâpatti*, but rather his presence. And it is not the case that his presence does not make sense once we have observed his absence from home.** What is understood is his presence outside. This is what is called the postulation of something that is not observed, namely, his presence outside. And it is not the case that this does not make sense given his absence from home. By contrast, up until that point, it makes perfect sense. What does not make sense is his absence, but this is not what is understood through *arthâpatti*. Therefore it is not suitable to say that *arth â patti* is the understanding of something that does not make sense.

Now suppose an OPPONENT (*uttarapakṣin*) responds to this objection as follows: True, when we do in fact observe his absence from home, it is not the case that his presence elsewhere does not make sense. But without observing his absence from home, it is indeed the case that his presence outside does not make sense. And the word "otherwise" simply expresses the meaning of the word "without," so what this means is that his presence outside does not make sense without observing his absence from home.

> COMMENTS: In our reading, the critic of the opponent—that is, the *uttarapakṣin*, who does not necessarily side with the proponent of the accepted position (*siddhāntin*)—takes a position very close to Prabhākara's own position. Śālikanātha, however, interprets Prabhākara rather forcedly, and thus his reconstruction of the accepted position (*siddhânta*) differs both from the position defended here (by the *uttarapakṣin*) and from what we understand Prabhākara's own position to have been.

A response from the first OBJECTOR (*pūrvapakṣin*): That would be wrong. For it is not the case that his presence outside does not make sense without observing his absence from home. For even someone who does not see that Devadatta, for example, is absent from home will not experience the slightest glimmer of not making sense with respect to his being outside. Therefore this manner of responding to the objection, too, does not stand to reason.

Now the proponent of the ACCEPTED POSITION (*siddhāntin*) speaks: **Surely it does not make sense.** Here is the idea. It is not the case that we say that his presence outside does not make sense without observing his absence from home, but rather that when we observe his absence from home, his presence does not make sense without being outside.

COMMENTS: As noted above, Śālikanātha identifies Prabhākara's statements with the "accepted position" (*siddhânta*), but he interprets those statements in a rather unnatural way, so effectively Śālikanātha's "accepted position" is different from Prabhākara's.

Therefore observing his absence from home is the cause of his presence not making sense, so long as we have not understood that it is related to being outside. And this state of not making sense is a conflict with another epistemic instrument. When we have observed his absence from home, so long as we have not understood that it is related to being outside, his being alive, which was understood on the basis of another epistemic instrument, is thrown into doubt—"Why isn't he here? Is he alive at all?"—and is then understood to be related to his being outside. Therefore it is precisely his presence that does not make sense here, and it is precisely his presence that is understood through *arthâpatti*. This is the accepted position.

COMMENTS: Śālikanātha understands "not making sense" to be a state of potential or actual conflict with other veridical cognitions, while Prabhākara understood it to refer to a necessary antecedent condition.

For presence outside does not make sense apart from observing his absence from home. The meaning of the text is that, when we have observed his absence from home, his presence does not make sense unless it is outside. The word "surely" expresses that it really doesn't make sense at all.

COMMENTS: Once again, Śālikanātha forcibly construes Prabhākara's text to support his own interpretation of *arthâpatti*. In this case, he construes *vinā* "without" with *bahiḥ* "outside," where a much more natural reading of Prabhākara's text would construe *vinā* with *gṛhâbhāva-darśanena* "observing his absence from home."

Summary verses on arthâpatti

On this topic there are the following verses:

The domain of *arthâpatti* is something
that is postulated because of something else
that would bring about a state of not making sense
if the first thing were not postulated.[1]
For example, being outside is postulated
because if it were not postulated,
a person's absence from home would cause
his being alive to not make sense.
Here the state of not making sense without
the postulation of the result is characterized

[1] A very similar verse is found in Śālikanātha's *Comprehensive Survey of the Epistemic Instruments*, at the beginning of the *arthâpatti* section (p. 272). See our translation on p. 102 in this volume.

by the fact that one ends up with a doubt,
because of a conflict (*virodha*) with another epistemic instrument.
For being alive is never observed without a place.
Because of one's absence from home,
although one's being alive is already established,
it becomes doubtful.
The postulation that arises in order to resolve
that doubt is called *arthâpatti*, because of
the thing (*artha*) that generates (*āpādaka*) the doubt.[2]
In inference, by contrast, what is understood is
that the trigger does not make sense apart from the thing
that is understood through inference,
a condition that is characterized
by absence from all of the counter-loci.

COMMENTS: A "counter-locus" is a locus where the property to be proven (e.g., the presence of "fire" in the inference "there is smoke on the mountain, therefore there is fire on the mountain") is absent. The inferential reason (e.g., the presence of "smoke") must be absent from all such loci, otherwise it will fail to be probative (e.g., if there is smoke in a place where fire is absent, then the invariable concomitance between the two properties does not hold).

Therefore, these two epistemic instruments
called *arthâpatti* and inference are different,
because their components are different.
That is what we have ascertained.

Arthâpatti *on the basis of what is heard*

COMMENTS: In this section, we have identified the OBJECTOR (*pūrva-pakṣin*) as "Bhāṭṭa," that is, a follower of Kumārila's interpretation, and the proponent of the ACCEPTED POSITION (*siddhāntin*) as "Prābhākara," that is, a follower of Prabhākara's interpretation. Śālikanātha does not label them as such. Bear in mind here that the word for "state of affairs" and "meaning" is the same (*artha*).

BHĀṬṬA: Even if what is heard, too, is in fact "apprehended," nevertheless the use of the word "heard" serves to suggest that *arthâpatti* on the basis of what is heard is different insofar as it results in an epistemic instrument.

COMMENTS: Kumārila Bhaṭṭa, *Explanation in Verse*, *arthâpatti* section, verse 2. See our translation on p. 45 in this volume. Note that throughout this discussion, Śālikanātha focuses on Kumārila's claim that *arthâpatti* on the basis of what is

[2] This verse is also found in Śālikanātha's *Comprehensive Survey of the Epistemic Instruments*, *arthâpatti* section (p. 275). See our translation on p. 105 in this volume. It provides an etymological explanation of *arthâpatti*.

heard is qualitatively different from other types of *arthâpatti*, and ignores Kumārila's parallel claim that this kind of *arthâpatti* has important hermeneutical applications.

PRĀBHĀKARA: Also in *arthâpatti* on the basis of what is heard, what is heard, namely the absence of eating during the day, does not make sense, given that Devadatta's being stout does not make sense without eating during the night, and therefore causes us to postulate simply his eating at night, and not the linguistic expression thereof. For it is not the case that a meaning does not make sense without a linguistic expression, but rather only without another meaning.

BHĀṬṬA: That is true. *Arthâpatti* gets started in order to postulate only a meaning. However, because that meaning is grasped by a conceptual cognition, we have to cognize it on the basis of a linguistic expression, and therefore *arthâpatti* stops at the linguistic expression that appears in the first instance. It does not extend up to the meaning. It is the linguistic expression itself, that, once it is understood, puts the meaning in place.

COMMENTS: This explanation closely follows verse 78*ab* of the *arthâpatti* section of Kumārila's *Explanation in Verse*; Pārthasārathimiśra borrows from Śālikanātha's formulation in his commentary on that verse. See our translation on p. 81 in this volume.

PRĀBHĀKARA: If this were the case, then also in the case of perceptual cognitions and so on, conceptual cognition would not grasp a meaning, but would instead stop at the linguistic expression. With regard to comprehension of animals, infants, and other conscious beings not proficient in language use, a comprehension we maintain is non-linguistic, we have concluded that the sense faculties have a capacity exclusively in regard to a state of affairs, that is, a meaning. Therefore in the conceptual stage, too, they should have a capacity for precisely the same object, and not for anything else, because we have already used up the chance to postulate such a capacity.

BHĀṬṬA: *Arthâpatti* on the basis of what is heard, however, never exists among animals, because it depends upon language acquisition, since one who has not learned a language cannot cognize a sentence meaning, which is preceded by linguistic expressions.

PRĀBHĀKARA: In *arthâpatti* on the basis of what is observed, we have concluded that *arthâpatti* has a capacity exclusively in regard to a state of affairs, that is, a meaning, and in this case as well it should have a capacity for precisely the same object.

BHĀṬṬA: That is true, we observe that it has a capacity exclusively for a meaning, but it is insofar as the meaning is what causes something else to make sense. For even the meaning is not understood as such, but rather insofar as it causes something else to make sense. And what is it that makes something else make sense? That upon the understanding of which the state of not making sense disappears. And even as soon as a linguistic expression is pronounced, the state of not making sense disappears, and hence *arthâpatti* on the basis of what is heard operates in regard to the linguistic expression that appears in the first instance. This is what the revered author of the *Explanation* has said:[3]

And it is not the case that one meaning is understood
on the basis of another meaning. By contrast,
the first meaning is concealed,
because it is grasped by a conceptual cognition.

COMMENTS: The following verse appears to be an objection, to which Kumārila responds in the subsequent verse. Kumārila believes that our perceptual and inferential cognitions are conceptual, and if he is claiming that linguistic expressions "conceal" all such conceptual cognitions, then he would be in the absurd position of arguing that, on the one hand, animals have conceptual cognitions, and on the other hand, that these cognitions are "concealed" by linguistic expressions that the animals themselves could never understand.

It is fire that is grasped on the basis
of the sense faculties or of an inferential sign,
not the word "fire."
Similarly, this fire is apprehended by animals, too,
only insofar as it is a state of affairs.
Arthâpatti on the basis of what is heard, however,
is never observed in animals. For the cognition
produced by *arthâpatti* on the basis of what is heard
is considered to arise out of linguistic competence.
It does not arrive at the meaning itself,
insofar as it cognizes other linguistic expressions and stops there.
Thus it necessarily has a sentence as its domain
in the first instance.

COMMENTS: In other words, as soon as one postulates another linguistic expression (e.g. *rātrau bhuṅkte*), one stops there; one does not need to postulate the meaning of this linguistic expression. The meaning would be delivered, as usual, by linguistic communication, as he explains:

In turn, it is the sentence alone that causes
one to know the meaning
because this sentence is what is understood.

---

[3] The following verses come most probably from Kumārila's *Long Remarks* (*Bṛhaṭ-ṭīkā*), as noted by Yoshimizu (1999:6). Very similar ideas are discussed in Sucaritamiśra's commentary on Kumārila's *Explanation in Verse*. See our translation on p. 43 in this volume.

PRĀBHĀKARA: The blessed author of the *Commentary* doesn't stand for any of this. We might answer in accordance with Prabhākara's views as follows. In conceptual cognitions, a linguistic expression is understood in the form of something that delimits a meaning, and a linguistic expression delimits a meaning insofar as it expresses it. Therefore in the cognition (of the word) "cow," we understand a meaning in a particular manner, namely, that 'this is expressed by the linguistic expression "cow."' And it is not the case that a linguistic expression expresses the fact that its meaning is expressed by a linguistic expression. Thus, a linguistic expression does not convey a meaning in reference to this (namely the fact that its meaning is expressed by a linguistic expression). Rather, a linguistic expression appears as specifying what it expresses as being expressed by something that is understood in the discursive practice of adults. Therefore, even though it appears in the first instance, that is not sufficient to dispel the state of not making sense, because it does not set a meaning in place. Therefore it cannot be what is known through *arthâpatti*. And hence, since this too has a meaning as its content, the use of the word "heard" does not have the purpose of pointing out a difference between types of *arthâpatti*.

> COMMENTS: On the next topic, Śālikanātha abandons the back-and-forth dialogue with an adherent of Kumārila's views for a more polemical criticism. It is noteworthy that most of the positions that the opponent held in the above dialogue can be found, in some form, in Kumārila's works, and hence Śālikanātha treats them with respect. The opponent's position in the following section, however, cannot be found in Kumārila's works, and probably represents an elaboration on Kumārila's views by a later follower.

As for those who think that, in the case of the *viśvajit* sacrifice[4] and so on, it is a linguistic expression that does not make sense on account of its being incomplete, and that therefore it is a linguistic expression that is postulated to make sense of it, although those people, who speak nonsense in postulating according to their own judgment, deserve to be ignored, nevertheless beginners pay attention to them, so something may be said for the sake of educating the beginners.

What is it about the linguistic expression that doesn't make sense, above and beyond the meaning not making sense? If you say that it is the fact that it is incomplete, well then, what exactly is incomplete about the linguistic expression? For only a *meaning* can be incomplete when some portion of that meaning is lacking. If you say that the linguistic expression is incomplete because of the incompleteness of the meaning, that is fine, for when something's not making sense depends on something else, then we must accept that it's the latter that ultimately does make sense. Otherwise the linguistic expression would remain incomplete in that stage (i.e., the stage before the meaning of the linguistic expression is understood). Therefore, even when the linguistic expression is incomplete, we only need to postulate a meaning. Nor is it the case that when a meaning does not make sense, the

[4] See n. 17 on p. 70.

linguistic expression does not make sense either, since the linguistic expression and the meaning are different.

Now one might object that when a meaning does not make sense, there is nothing that results from the cognition of a linguistic expression, and hence the fact that the linguistic expression is an epistemic instrument would not make sense at all. That too may be true, but what would not make sense is the fact that a linguistic expression is an epistemic instrument, not the linguistic expression itself. Nor is it the case that this fact, of a linguistic expression's being an epistemic instrument, does not make sense on its own; rather, it does not make sense simply because its meaning does not make sense. If this is the case, then the fact that the underlying meaning does not make sense alone is what puts the *arthâpatti* in place. Moreover, what would render it impossible for a linguistic expression to be an epistemic instrument would be a doubt that there is no object of the cognition, in the absence of a meaning, not the absence of some further linguistic expression, such that one should postulate one. Well, enough of this extended discussion. We have gotten too far from the point, and now we will return.

The meaning of Prabhākara's commentary is that a total apprehension is not communicated by the word "seen" alone, but only when it is combined with the word "heard," and that is why the use of the word "heard" is not pointless. And how, precisely, is the fact of being apprehended communicated by the word "seen" together with the word "heard?" Listen: Although the word "seen" expresses something that has been apprehended in general, nevertheless, because of its proximity with the word "heard," it expresses everything besides what is cognized from language through the principle of the cows-and-bulls. What is the purpose of using this principle of the cows-and-bulls, you might ask? Look. We are worldly people, and in the real world, people are seen to use expressions like this. Nor is there any scope for criticizing such usages in the world, since they have no beginning. Therefore this is simply another way of saying the same thing: an expression that people in the real world understand to mean apprehension in general.

FROM THE *COMPREHENSIVE SURVEY OF THE EPISTEMIC INSTRUMENTS*

The definition of arthâpatti

Now the postulation triggered by an
observed state of affairs which would lead an
unobserved state of affairs to not make sense
in the absence of that postulation
is called *arthâpatti*.[5]

Arthâpatti is the postulation of an additional state of affairs on the basis of an observed state of affairs which would lead to an unobserved state of affairs not

[5] A very similar verse is found in Śālikanātha's *Straightforward and Lucid Gloss*. See our translation on p. 98.

making sense so long as that additional state of affairs is not postulated. For example: on the basis of not seeing Devadatta at his home, although he is alive, we postulate an unobserved state of affairs, namely, his being outside.

Arthâpatti *is distinct from inference*

Objection: The postulation that someone who is alive is outside, on the basis of observing his absence from home, is simply an inference. That is to say: we understand with reference to ourselves that whoever, being alive, is not in one place, is in another place, and hence it makes sense that when we understand, on the basis of someone's absence from one place, that person's existing in another place, which is known to have a necessary connection with it, that is simply an inference.

Thus, existence in once place and absence from another place, being connected in a relation defined by occurring at the same time, are complements belonging to the same time, just as high tides and the rising of the moon are complements belonging to the same time. One can infer through this inferential complex that when Devadatta, being alive, is not at home, he is somewhere else.

Similarly, given Devadatta's absence from one place, his existence elsewhere stands in a relation of necessary connection to this absence that is characterized by inherence in the same thing, on account of his connection with another place, and is thus a complement to this absence, both properties—the absence from one place and the existence elsewhere—being located in Devadatta. Thus all of the elements are available for an inference to take place:

1. Devadatta is in contact with an external place (thesis),
2. because he exists while being absent at home (reason),
3. since whoever exists while being absent from home is somewhere else (invariable concomitance),
4. just as in the case of myself (example).

Response: To start with his being alive, this cannot be an inferential reason, because this is precisely what is put into doubt. For suppose someone has understood Devadatta's existence only in relation to his house. So long as the connection between Devadatta's existence and an external place is not brought in, when such a person sees that Devadatta is not at home, that would bring the fact that he is alive into doubt, even though it previously was understood on the basis of an epistemic instrument: "How can Devadatta be alive," he will think, "if he is not at home?" For once something has been apprehended, understanding a form of it different from the form that had previously been apprehended is sufficient to generate a doubt. And Devadatta's existence was understood only in connection with his house. Hence, when his absence from home is apprehended, it would be rendered doubtful, so long as its connection with an external place is not understood. For this reason his existence, being afflicted by doubt, cannot function as an inferential reason.

One might say that his existence becomes an inferential reason when we come to understand his relation with an external place, and consequently our doubt regarding his existence is dispelled. But that is not the case, since there would be nothing to infer. For it is precisely Devadatta's relation with an external place that we wanted to infer in the first place, and if that is admitted, there is nothing left to be known. This is what the learned author of the *Explanation* has said:

> Therefore, it cannot be an inferential reason,
> since insofar as it is independent
> from what is to be known, it is doubtful.
> At the very moment, however, when it can
> become an inferential reason,
> nothing remains to be inferred.[6]

Therefore his being alive is not capable of producing any further understanding, since it is subject to doubt.

To move on, then, to his absence from home: it does not make sense that his absence from home is the reason that allows us to infer that he is related to an external place. For it is not his absence on its own that we must provisionally admit to be an inferential reason, but rather his absence qualified by his being alive, since absence from home on its own can be accounted for even without being outside, in the case of dead people and people who have not yet been born, as has been said:

> Sheer absence from home, apart from his being alive,
> cannot establish being outside,
> since that is also observed in people who are dead.[7]

Since being alive, which is the qualifier, is rendered doubtful, whatever is qualified by it cannot be an inferential reason.

Therefore it makes sense that the trigger is just absence from home, on its own, which is itself free from any doubt. And there is no epistemic instrument which might render this cognition doubtful.

One might object as follows. If this alone were the trigger, then we would run into the absurd consequence that we understand a dead person, or a person who has not yet been born, to be related with an external place. To this we say: we define the trigger to be something that is capable of throwing something else into doubt so long as the postulation of some other thing does not take place.[8] That is to say, Devadatta's absence from home, which throws his existence into doubt so long as the postulation of his being related to an external place does not occur, is in fact a trigger, whereas the absence from home of dead people, or people who have not yet been born, does not throw anything at all into doubt, and hence it is not a trigger. Therefore the absurd consequence that you mentioned will not occur. Moreover, what is

[6] This verse is probably quoted from Kumārila's *Long Remarks* (*Bṛhaṭ-ṭīkā*).

[7] Kumārila, *Explanation in Verse*, *arthâpatti* chapter, v. 21 (see our translation on p. 53 of this volume).

[8] In this and several following sentences we have both *sasaṃśayam āpad-* and *saṃśayam āpad-*; possibly the first involves an implied *artha-* ("render something doubtful"), but it might also be a misreading (E. Freschi suggests *yas saṃśayam* might have been read as *yasasaṃśayam*). In the following sentence, read *vidyamānatāṃ saṃśayam āpadayan*.

understood in this case is precisely that which, if it is not postulated, a doubt arises, whereas if it is postulated, the doubt subsides.

> COMMENTS: Śālikanātha has used various forms of the verb *ā-pad*, which is present in the name *arthâpatti*, to describe how a cognition is "beset," "afflicted," or "seized" by doubt. Below he will quote a verse from an unknown source—possibly his own—which explains *arthâpatti* in precisely these etymological terms, namely as a cognition that arises when a given state of affairs (*artha*) is beset by (*āpatti*) doubt by another state of affairs.

Now absence is the trigger in this case, but it is nevertheless not an inference, because the way in which the cognition arises is different. When you observe one complement, the cognition that arises thereupon, assisted by the memory of a necessary connection between the two complements, is an inference. By contrast, so long as one does not postulate an external place, absence from home throws Devadatta's existence into doubt, and in order to resolve that doubt, it causes one to postulate his relation with an external place. Therefore it is not possible for this cognition to be an inference. Contrast an inferential reason such as smoke, which does not lead anyone to understand fire by throwing something unto doubt, and thus cannot be an *arthâpatti*. On this topic there is the following verse:

> The postulation that arises in order to resolve
> that doubt is called *arthâpatti*, because of
> the thing (*artha*) that generates (*āpādaka*) the doubt.[9]

> COMMENTS: The position espoused in this verse is that the trigger of *arthâpatti* is the cognition of a state of affairs that puts one's existing knowledge into doubt (in this case, Devadatta's absence from home).

An alternative view of arthâpatti

> COMMENTS: In the following section, Śālikanātha offers a different definition of *arthâpatti*, according to which the trigger is not the cognition that throws an existing cognition into doubt, but the existing cognition itself, which is thrown into doubt. Śālikanātha gives slight preference to this interpretation.

> Some people, however, say that *arthâpatti*
> is the postulation that is so called
> on account of the state of affairs which,
> although previously apprehended,
> would come into doubt without that postulation.

Some people, however, say the following. A state of affairs which, although it has already been known from an epistemic instrument, enters into a condition of not

---

[9] This verse is also found in Śālikanātha's *Straightfoward and Lucid Gloss*. See our translation above, p. 98.

making sense, in the form of a doubt, when a different form of it than was previously encountered has been understood, so long as another state of affairs is not postulated—that *first* state of affairs produces the postulation of that *other* state of affairs, in order to remove the doubt that affects it, and this is *arthâpatti*.

And this is to be preferred because of the relative strength of observation. For on this definition, despite having been apprehended on the basis of an epistemic instrument, it is the state of affairs that is thrown into doubt itself—because of the absence of the form in which this state of affairs had been previously observed—that generates the *arthâpatti*.

> COMMENTS: The idea seems to be that observation (*darśana*) is a relatively strong and secure epistemic instrument, especially in comparison with absence. In fact Prabhākara and his followers deny that absence is an epistemic instrument. Hence, in order to ensure that *arthâpatti* is an epistemic instrument, it must be demonstrated that the premises from which it starts—in this case, the "trigger" of the postulation—were also apprehended through valid epistemic instruments. Hence some followers of Prabhākara might claim that what sets the process of postulation in motion is not the cognition of "absence from home" itself, but rather the cognition of Devadatta's being alive, which has been rendered doubtful in some way.

There is no contradiction in saying that what generates an inference is an inferential reason that has been ascertained, whereas what generates an *arthâpatti* is a reason that has been seized by doubt. In fact it is for this very reason that it is distinct from inference. It is only when the smoke has been ascertained that it triggers the cognition of fire. Here there is no other thing that puts the smoke in a position of not making sense. Absence from home, by contrast, puts Devadatta's existence into a state of not making sense. His very existence, once it has been brought into a state of not making sense on account of his absence from home—so long as there is no postulation of his relation with an external place—is what causes us to postulate his own relation with an external place.

Therefore *arthâpatti* is different from inference in either case. Either, as in the previous view, it is Devadatta's absence from home, which puts his existence into a state of not making sense, that causes us to postulate his being outside. Or, on this alternative view, it is Devadatta's existence itself, which has been put into a state of not making sense by his absence from home, that causes us to postulate his relation with an external place in order for it to make sense again.

What does not make sense otherwise?

> COMMENTS: On both of the views that Śālikanātha has just sketched, the cognition which "does not make sense" in the absence of a postulation is the cognition of Devadatta's continued existence. He now addresses an opponent who takes the view that what does not make sense otherwise is Devadatta's absence from home. Noteworthy is the fact that Śālikanātha does not even discuss what we take to be the most natural reading of Prabhākara's views on *arthâpatti*, according to which it is the cognition of Devadatta's presence elsewhere that "does not make sense"

otherwise, in the sense that it would never arise were it not for the cognition of his absence from home.

There is someone, however, who believes that it is Devadatta's absence from home which does not make sense, and that this is what triggers the cognition of his being outside. This is wrong. That is to say: what is it about Devadatta's absence from home that does not make sense otherwise?

COMMENTS: Śālikanātha rejects, in sequence, two interpretations according to which Devadatta's absence from home can be said to "not make sense." The first would reduce *arthâpatti* to a particular kind of inference based on negative concomitance (there is no *x* in the absence of *y*), which is itself derived, by means of *arthâpatti*, from a previously-established positive concomitance (where there is *y*, there is *x*). In this first interpretation, "not making sense otherwise" means that one thing is logically impossible without another. In the second interpretation, which Śālikanātha rejects as psychologically implausible, Devadatta's absence from home is said to "not make sense" in that it is subject to doubt.

If, on the one hand, it is his absence apart from a relation with an external place—since the absence from home on the part of someone who is alive cannot occur without that person's relation with an external place—then what we have been calling *arthâpatti* would simply be an inference from negative concomitance, which is characterized by the absence of the inferential reason given the absence of what is to be inferred. And a negative concomitance can only ever be understood through a positive concomitance, which is characterized by the presence of what is to be inferred given the presence of the inferential reason. For it is not possible to ascertain that the inferential reason is necessarily absent from an infinite number of counter-loci—that is, instances where what is to be inferred is absent—until one ascertains that the presence of the inferential reason has a necessary connection with the presence of what is to be inferred. For it is only when that is ascertained that one may conclude, on the basis of *arthâpatti*, a necessary connection of the absence of the inferential reason given the absence of what is to be inferred.

COMMENTS: In the following paragraph Śālikanātha explains how a negative concomitance can be derived from a positive concomitance through *arthâpatti*: if a state of affairs *x* is known to have a positive concomitance with a state of affairs *y*, such that the presence of *y* guarantees the presence of *x*, then *x* cannot possibly be absent unless we postulate that *y* is also absent.

For there are two alternatives: either the inferential reason is present, or it is absent. Among these two, let us first assume that the inferential reason is present. If it is then established that the presence of the inferential reason has a necessary connection with the presence of what is to be inferred, then it will simply never be the case that what is to be inferred is absent. If it were not possible for what is to be inferred to be absent on the other alternative as well, wherein the inferential reason is absent, then it would not make sense at all for what is inferred to be absent. Therefore, on the assumption that the inferential reason is present, once it has been understood that the presence of the inferential reason is necessarily connected with the presence of what is to be inferred, this very necessary connection would put the absence of what is to be inferred in a state of not making sense, so long as we do not postulate that we are actually in the other alternative, wherein the inferential reason is absent. And hence this very necessary connection should cause us to postulate that we are in fact in that other alternative, wherein the inferential reason is absent. Once this is done, however, it stands to reason that the absence of what is to be inferred has a necessary connection with the absence of the inferential reason. Therefore the cognition that something simply does not occur in the absence of what is to be inferred presupposes an understanding of a necessary connection, and therefore does not differ from inference.

If, on the other hand, Devadatta's absence from home does not make sense so long as his relation to an external place is not postulated means that it is actually doubted, then it could never be said to "not make sense."[10] For there is no reason at all why his absence from home would be subject to doubt. We have said, by contrast, that what is rendered doubtful is actually his being alive, since that has always been observed to be related to his home, and what renders it doubtful is his absence from home.

Our position, therefore, is that *arthâpatti*, literally "a sudden occurrence (*āpatti*) related to a state of affairs (*artha*)," is either the state of affairs that renders another one doubtful, or alternatively the state of affairs that is rendered doubtful by it.

Arthâpatti *on the basis of what is heard*

On the topic of *arthâpatti*, some say that the sentence "stout Devadatta does not eat during the day" causes us to postulate the very sentence "he eats at night," since the eating, understood in relation to Devadatta, that is negated in relation to the day and inferred from his being stout, does not make sense.

That, too, is incorrect, because in this case, as well, it is only appropriate to postulate a state of affairs, which in this case is a *meaning*. For something is understood through *arthâpatti* when it would not make sense if that thing were not postulated, and in this case it is Devadatta's eating which does not make sense so long as its connection with the night is not supposed. For it does not make sense because it does not have a relation to another time. And it is precisely a relation with that other time that its not making sense allows us to postulate.

> COMMENTS: Compare the following objection to Kumārila's *Explanation in Verse*, *arthâpatti* section, verse 78*ab* (see p. 81 in this volume), as well as the verses that Śālikanātha had quoted in his *Straightforward and Lucid Gloss* (see above, p. 100), probably from Kumārila's *Long Remarks*.

OBJECTION: We agree that *arthâpatti* starts out in order to postulate a state of affairs. But because that state of affairs is to be known from a conceptual cognition, and because conceptual cognitions are preceded by linguistic expressions, the postulation actually culminates in the preceding linguistic expression, and that linguistic expression, in turn, establishes its proper meaning. And we need not doubt that

---

[10] Reading *anupapattir* instead of *anupapatter*.

every conceptual cognition,
whether inferential or perceptual,
culminates in a linguistic expression by this principle.[11]

Since the sense-faculties and an inferential reason are observed to be capable of producing awareness of a state of affairs at the non-conceptual stage, we assume that, in the conceptual stage as well, they operate with respect to precisely the same object, namely, a state of affairs. Any awareness based on *arthâpatti* on the basis of what is heard, however, cannot possibly be non-conceptual, because it presupposes language acquisition. For only a person who has acquired language, having understood the meaning of a sentence, would ever want to cognize another meaning when the previously-cognized meaning turns out not to make sense.

One might object as follows. In the case of *arthâpatti* on the basis of what is observed, *arthâpatti* is an epistemic instrument for a state of affairs, and hence it ought to be an epistemic instrument for a state of affairs, that is, a *meaning*, in the case of *arthâpatti* on the basis of what is heard as well. But that is not the case. *Arthâpatti* is an epistemic instrument for that upon the understanding of which a condition of not making sense is removed. And in this case, the condition of not making sense is indeed removed as soon as a linguistic expression is understood, so it is not unreasonable for it to be an epistemic instrument for a linguistic expression.

Response: The condition of not making sense lasts as long as the connection between eating and the night-time remains uncognized. Even if the mere form of the linguistic expression were understood, the condition of not making sense would not subside until it was understood, on the basis of that linguistic expression, that eating has a relation with night. For if one has not learned the meanings of the expressions "take meals" and "after dark," then the condition of not making sense related to the meaning of the sentence "stout Devadatta does not eat during the day" will not be resolved just by the mere utterance of the phrase "he takes his meals after dark."

Therefore it is a state of affairs that directly causes the original expression to make sense, and not a linguistic expression. And we have already understood *arthâpatti* to have, as its object, a state of affairs that causes something else to make sense in the case of *arthâpatti* on the basis of what is seen. Hence in no case is it ever an epistemic instrument for a linguistic expression which would, in turn, cause something else to make sense.

What's more, we must accept that a linguistic expression in any other conceptual cognition is the object of memory, and if this is so, then in this case, too, the linguistic expression ought to be the object of memory; it is certainly not the object of an epistemic instrument. Our position, therefore, is that no epistemic instrument—and not even *arthâpatti* on the basis of what is heard—causes us to grasp a linguistic expression, but rather, what it causes us to grasp is a state of affairs that causes something else to make sense.

---

[11] We read this quotation as a (corrupt) *śloka* in support of the objector's position, possibly from Kumārila's *Long Remarks*. Reconstruct as follows: laiṅgikam aindriyakaṃ ca sarvam eva vikalpakaṃ śabda etena nyāyena paryavasyet (maybe *iti sthitam* at the end).

COMMENTS: We follow Rāmānujācārya in his *Secret of the System* (*Tantra-rahasya*) in explaining this brief and difficult passage. The idea seems to be that the followers of Prabhākara do not accept that linguistic expressions in themselves can be valid epistemic instruments, since they are merely provided to us on the basis of associative memories formed from past cognitions, and therefore it does not help the of *arthâpatti* to say that it results in the cognition of a linguistic expression.

REFERENCES

Primary sources

Topical Elaborations [*Prakaraṇa-pañcikā*] (Śālikanātha)
Śāstrī, Subrahmaṇya, ed. (1961), *Prakaraṇapañcikā Mahāmahopadhyāyaśrīmacchālik anāthamiśraviracitā (Prabhākaraprasthānānusāri Mīmāṃsādarśanam) Śrījayapurinā-rāyaṇabhaṭṭavicaritapratyakṣaparicchedāntanyāyasiddhyākhyavyākhyāsaṁvalitā*, Vārāṇasī: Kāśīhindūviśvavidyālaya , 272–81.

Comprehensive Survey of the Epistemic Instruments [*Prāmāṇa-pārāyaṇa*] (Śālikanātha)
See *Commentarial Essays*.

Straightforward and Lucid Gloss [*Ṛjuvimalā Pañcikā*] (Śālikanātha)
Ramanatha Sastri, S. K., ed. part 1 and 2, and S. Subrahmanya Sastri, ed. part 3, 4, and 5 (1934–67), *Bṛhatī of Prabhākara Miśra [on the Mīmāṁsāsūtrabhāṣya of Śabarasvāmin] with the Ṛjuvimalāpañcikā of Śālikanātha*, Madras University Sanskrit Series, Nos. 3.1, 3.2, 24, 25, 26, Madras [Chennai]: University of Madras, 110–17.

Secondary literature

Yoshimizu, K. (1999), "Śrutārthāpatti niyoru ninshiki no taishō ni tsuite," (On the Object of the Cognition by *śrutārthāpatti*), *Bukkyō-gaku. Journal of Buddhist Studies* 40: 1–22.

CHAPTER FOUR

Nārāyaṇa Bhaṭṭa's *Elucidation of Epistemic Instruments and Their Objects*

Translated by MALCOLM KEATING

INTRODUCTION

Not just one, but two authors—Nārāyaṇa Bhaṭṭa and Nārāyaṇa Pāṇḍit—wrote the *Māna-meyôdaya* (MM), a seventeenth-century CE introductory elucidation (*udaya*) of Bhāṭṭa Mīmāṃsā views on epistemic instruments (*mānas*) and objects of knowledge (*meyas*). It is, at some points, an abridged version of the *Appearance of True Principles* (*Nīti-tattvâvirbhāva*) of Cidānanda Muni (*c.* fourteenth century CE), although in other ways, it is an expansion of the same. While the first author, Nārāyaṇa Bhaṭṭa, intended to complete the entire work, he completed only the first part, on epistemic instruments (*pramāṇas*). Nārāyaṇa Pāṇḍita finished the work later. The first Nārāyaṇa was a Kerala-based thinker, famous for his poem about the deity sharing his name, *Nārāyaṇīya* (*On the Lord Nāryāyaṇa*), and his treatise on grammar, the *Prakriyā-sarvasva* (*The Complete Rules of Syntax*), along with many other works. As Raja (1946, 1954) notes, while no precise date has been fixed for the *Elucidation*, the grammatical treatise *Prakriyā-sarvasva* was written in 1616. Several decades later, sometime between 1655 and 1658, under the reign of his patron Mānaveda, the second Nārāyaṇa completed the *Māna-meyôdaya*. The former Nārāyana authored the excerpt included below, part of the *māna* section.

As a Bhāṭṭa Mīmāṃsaka, Nārāyaṇa Bhaṭṭa generally follows Kumārila Bhaṭṭa's exposition of Śabara's *Mīmāṃsā-sūtra-bhāṣya* in the *Śloka-vārttika* and *Tantra-vārttika*, though with some innovations, as we will see. This is in contrast to Prābhākara thinkers, who follow Prabhākara Miśra's *Bṛhatī* and *Ṛju-vimalā* (see Ollett and Freschi in this volume, p. 89). The epistemic instruments section of our text begins with an introduction, setting out the definition of knowledge, "And knowledge (*pramā*) is simply a cognition (*jñāna*) whose object is something true which is previously uncognized" (Raja and Sastri 2004: 2).[1] This definition excludes memory from the scope of epistemic instruments. When remembering an earlier experience or belief, one is merely bringing to mind a previous piece of knowledge, not creating new knowledge, no matter how true the belief or efficacious the memory may be. Within this definition, Nāryāyaṇa explains what has become standard Bhāṭṭa views about all of the epistemic instruments, including *arthâpatti*. In developing his positive view, he argues against two opposing understandings: a Nyāya view which explains *arthâpatti* as *anumāna*, and a Prābhākara view which denies *arthâpatti* is *anumāna* but understands its nature differently than the Bhāṭṭas.

In this short discussion, which consists of twenty-seven verses with interspersed auto-commentary, Nārāyaṇa defines *arthâpatti* in terms of a conflict (*virodha*) between two epistemic instruments, one general (*sādhārana*) and one specific (*asādhāraṇa*). We have seen the general idea of opposition appear in Nyāya analysis, too, when Vātsyāyana (*c.* 450 CE) defines *arthâpatti*'s efficient cause as the presence of an opposition (*pratyanīka-bhāva*), though he takes this opposition as evidence instead that *arthâpatti* is in fact *anumāna*, not something independent (see Keating in this volume, p. 132). An explicit appeal to conflict (*virodha*) is not found in Kumārila's discussion of *arthâpatti*, although Pārthasārathi Miśra interprets Kumārila Bhaṭṭa's discussion (at verse 29) in a manner that suggests some kind of opposition (*pratighātinaḥ*) is involved (see Ollett and Freschi in this volume, p. 57), and Sucarita Miśra uses the term in his commentary. And both Pārthasārathi (middle tenth century CE) and Sucarita (early eleventh century CE) seem to prefer an understanding on which *arthâpatti* avoids a potential conflict, rather than results from an actual conflict (see Ollett and Freschi in this volume, p. 67). Still, as early as Vācaspati (*c.* 900 CE), the idea that there are two conflicting or contradictory (*virodha*) epistemic instruments was explicitly represented as part of the Mīmāṃsaka's view, and rejected by him (see Keating in this volume, pp. 142–3). Arguments against *arthâpatti* on this basis are developed further in Udayana (see Das in this volume, p. 183) and Gaṅgeśa (see Phillips in this volume, p. 202). By the time of this primer's source, the above-mentioned *Appearance* of Cidānanda Muni (fourteenth century) explicitly discusses the presence of a conflict (*virodha*) as the trigger for *arthâpatti*.

Another interesting aspect of Nārāyaṇa's discussion is that it picks up on a topic found as early as Śabara (*ad* MS 4.3.10), but not emphasized in discussion of *arthâpatti* (though it is found in discussion of sentential meaning such as Śālikanātha's *vākyârtha-mātṛka* and in commentaries on Kumārila's ŚV). This is the use of verbal *arthâpatti* to complete syntactically incomplete utterances such as "door, door" which is supposed to convey "Close the door." As presented in the MM, there is a dispute between Prābhākara and Bhāṭṭa Mīmāṃsakas as to whether a fact (*artha*) or a word (*śabda*) is understood by *arthâpatti* to complete the sentence. To whom this Prābhākara position belongs, and how it squares with other aspects of, for instance, Śālikanātha's semantics, is a question worth further inquiry.

[1] Sanskrit: ". . . pramā ca ajñāta-tattvârtha-jñānam eva . . ." The Sanskrit edition referred to in this section is Raja and Sastri (2004) but the translations are mine, unless otherwise noted.

TRANSLATION

> **1.** The *Bhāṣya* characterizes *arthâpatti* in this way: "That which is posited to cause understanding of what would otherwise not make sense is *arthâpatti.*"

And here, what is described by "[does] not make sense" (*anupapatti*) is the conflict between two deliverances of *pramāṇa*s. Therefore, the definition should be taught in this way:

> **2.** Because of the conflict between a general knowledge-cognition and a specific knowledge-cognition when there is an unconflicted element, a cognition of *arthâpatti* is accepted.

> **3.** This is just as when, from the conflict between the knowledge of someone's absence from the house and the knowledge that they are alive, from this conflict, which is the efficient cause, there is posited his being outside of the house.

It is known generally, by *anumāna* based on astrological investigation, that Devadatta is alive somewhere—in his home or else outside. When there is conflict with this *anumāna*, in that he is not in his home, in order to not have conflict it is posited that he is outside. This is the cognition due to *arthâpatti*, whose efficient cause is the conflict between two deliverances of *pramāṇa*s.

COMMENTS: The definition of *arthâpatti* attributed to an earlier commentator (known as the *Vṛtti-kāra*) in Śabara's commentary (*bhāṣya*) is not a direct quotation, which reads instead, "Also *arthâpatti*, that is, the postulation of a thing when another thing that is seen or heard does not make sense otherwise" (see Ollett and Freschi translation in this volume, p. 43). Nārāyaṇa also strays from the traditional Bhāṭṭa understanding in stating that the efficient cause (*karaṇībhūta*) is conflict (*virodha*), since as we have seen earlier, in their discussion on verse 46 of the ŚV, Sucarita and Pārthasārathi think *arthâpatti* avoids a potential conflict, rather than results from an actual conflict (see Ollett and Freschi in this volume, p. 67). Further, for Nārāyaṇa, what does not make sense is the awareness of two cognitions as being in a kind of conflict, rather than the awareness of a single cognition, such as Devadatta's absence.

More precisely, it is because of a conflict between general (*sādhārana*) and specific (*asādhārana*) knowledge-cognitions that we postulate a cognition which is not subject to conflict. (Nārāyaṇa uses the terms *pramāṇa* and *māna* interchangeably here, meaning by them not the epistemic instruments such as *anumāna* and perception, but the veridical cognitions which arise due to such epistemic instruments.) The distinction between general and specific knowledge-cognitions is crucial for Nārāyaṇa Bhaṭṭa's case, as he argues there is a clash between two such cognitions, but not in a way that would lead to the rejection of one or the other.

Citing our classic example of Devadatta who is known to be alive but is observed not to be at home, Nārāyaṇa explains how his understanding of Śabara's definition explains this case. We know—here through astrology, although this detail is not always included—that Devadatta is alive, somewhere. This is our general cognition. It encompasses Devadatta's being alive in his home or outside—it could be either, but we do not know in which place he exists. In contrast, that Devadatta is not at home is a specific cognition, viz, "Devadatta is not alive in his home."

Nārāyaṇa argues that this new cognition does not make sense with the general cognition, in the sense that now Devadatta cannot be alive at his home. However, there is an element which remains "unconflicted" —any place which is not Devadatta's home. The conflict here functions in the sense of excluding one of the candidates for where Devadatta is—we now know that the place Devadatta is alive cannot be his home.

Depending on how we understand "conflict," though, this leads to an immediate objection: a contradiction, for instance, cannot be resolved by adding a further premise. If someone asserts not-*p* and *p*, no further proposition can remove that contradiction. In what sense can a conflict be an instrument for acquiring new knowledge—is it a kind of contradiction? If so, isn't it rather an obstacle to knowing? This is the worry Nāryāyaṇa now raises and attributes to the Naiyāyikas (*tarkika*s).

> 4. However, those who desire that *arthâpatti* belong to the domain of *anumāna*, the *tarkika*s, stubbornly say: "There is no conflict between cognitions of knowledge! And, further, this [*arthâpatti*] is like something already well-established."

Naiyāyikas: First of all, there cannot be conflict between two knowledge-cognitions, such as "This is silver," "This is not silver," because there would be an unwanted consequence, namely, that one of them would lack the property of being knowledge. One might object this way:

Bhāṭṭa Mīmāṃsaka: "Well, even so, the conflict is observed between the two knowledge-cognitions just discussed. That conflict, however, is simply about a part. For here, there are the doubts: 'In the house or outside?' of which just part has the content being the place. An obstacle to knowledge arises because of the knowledge that he is not home. For in this case, an obstacle arises due to doubt about just a part of a place: 'In the house or outside?' qualified by the knowledge that he is absent from the house. Now, through knowledge that he is alive, just his being alive or else his being connected generally to a place is made the content of what is known."

Naiyāyikas Continue: But it can't be that both of these—his living or being connected generally to a place—are "touched" or "smelled" through the knowledge of his absence from the house! Therefore, since there is not, in fact, a conflict between the knowledge-cognitions that he is living and that he is absent from the house, then how is *arthâpatti* said to have that conflict as its efficient cause? And, further,

> 5. Because this kind of conflict is present among well-established *anumāna*s, *arthâpatti* will devour the net of *anumāna* (instead of the reverse).

For, by the knowledge-cognition which grasps this pervasion relationship, "Where there is smoke, there is fire," fire is also understood as being on the mountain. Or else, the smoke being perceived on the mountain signals that fire is its cause. Therefore, by the knowledge-cognition which grasps the pervasion relationship or else through the perception of smoke, it is understood that there is fire somewhere on the mountain. And fire is posited in the lower part because there is a conflict, since fire isn't grasped in the higher part. Therefore (on this implication of the incorrect Bhāṭṭa view), *arthâpatti* is present.

Thus *arthâpatti* should be categorized into the subject of *anumāna*. And so, what is understood by *anumāna* is: Devadatta is outside, when he is living, because he is not at home. That one who is living, not being somewhere, he therefore is elsewhere, just like me. Therefore this supposed "fifth" *pramāṇa* is fraudulent.

COMMENTS: After his initial explanation of this paradigmatic case, Nārāyaṇa argues against the Nyāya position that *arthâpatti* should be understood as *anumāna*. The first argument against *arthâpatti* is that two conflicting cognitions do not result in knowledge, as they would result in the rejection of one or the other. Unless we are prepared to abandon the law of non-contradiction, we do not accept simultaneously that A is *p* and that A is not-*p*. The embedded Bhāṭṭa reply argues that the structure of *arthâpatti* hinges upon a conflict between a general and specific cognition and not two contradictory cognitions. This means that the general cognition is not entirely negated.

The Naiyāyika retorts that even if we restrict the conflict to just an aspect of one of the cognitions, there is still a problem. Suppose that we know Devadatta is alive. From this we know that he is alive somewhere, or else maybe just that he is alive (without characterizing his living as related to a place). Now we learn that Devadatta is not at home. This new cognition is not directly connected to Devadatta's being alive or not. There is thus no conflict between these two cognitions, since one is about being alive and the other is about being at home. As Vācaspati has put it, "there is no contradiction (*avirodha*) between what is delimited and what is not delimited" (see Keating in this volume, p. 142). So, the Naiyāyika concludes, how can we say that *arthâpatti* functions based on a conflict? The only explanation for what is putatively *arthâpatti* is to reduce it to *anumāna*, which is an epistemic instrument already accepted by both Mīmāṃsā and Nyāya (although with some differences). Our Naiyāyika interlocutor here does not identify which kind of *anumāna*: for discussion of this in detail we should look to Udayana (see Das in this volume, p. 183) and Gaṅgeśa (see Phillips in this volume, p. 199).

There is a further worry that the Naiyāyikas raise: if we admit *arthâpatti* in the sense of conflict between two cognitions, then even our paradigmatic case of *anumāna*, the perception of smoke on a mountain giving rise to knowledge that fire is there, would count as an *arthâpatti*. There is first an *anumāna* that leads to the fact that there is fire (somewhere) on the mountain, and subsequently, since we do not see fire on the upper portion on the mountain, we determine through *arthâpatti* that it must be on the lower portion. We see this argument in Udayana (see Das in this volume, p. 194). We get another explanation as to how the smoke–fire case might work as an *arthâpatti* (according to a Naiyāyika) in Cidānanda's NTV: "Thus because of the conflict, which is characterized as the mutually not-making-sense-otherwise between the *pramāṇa* which grasps the pervasion 'that which possesses smoke is that which possesses fire' and the perception of the mountain which has smoke, without the presence of fire on the mountain, there is postulated as well the presence of fire" (Sastri 1953: 159) Here, it doesn't make sense that a mountain has smoke if it is also true that whatever possesses smoke possesses fire, and so from our perception of the smoke and our knowledge of the pervasion relationship, we come to know that the mountain has smoke. However, Nāryāṇa does not take up this option for discussion, only the second option (which Cidānanda also discusses), of the conflict between the observed, fire-free portion of the mountain and the knowledge of fire being present on the mountain.

> 6. *Bhāṭṭa Reply*: That which is taught by us is this: there is indeed a conflict between two knowledge-cognitions; well-established *anumāna* is not split apart, and the case of his being outside is not *anumāna*.

On this point it is stated that, to the extent that there is a conflict between two knowledge-cognitions, it would be that one of the two is not knowledge, as in: "That is silver," "That is not silver." However, it is when both knowledge-cognitions are specific that there is a genuine conflict.

> 7. But when there is a conflict between a knowledge-cognition which is general and one which is specific, because the general knowledge-cognition is very broad, a lack of knowledge does not occur.

Therefore a conflict between two knowledge-cognitions does indeed happen. That which was described earlier on this topic, moreover, is that there is an obstacle (*bādha*) simply with regard to the particular place which is doubted. Therefore, on this point, we say:

> 8. When it is through *anumāna* that Devadatta's being alive is known, his connection to a particular place should be known, as well as the reason which supports his being alive.
>
> 9. In the case at hand, if Devadatta is connected only to the property of being situated generally, then, because he is connected to the property of being situated, a person would be a place, too!
>
> 10. And therefore, what is known would be his being alive, based on place in general, which is unrestricted. About his being alive, it is said, "He is alive, somewhere."
>
> 11. Therefore, although there is the doubt: "At home? Or outside?," that he is alive is known only by grasping his being somewhere specific.
>
> 12. With regard to these cognitions: when one specific content is obstructed before the other one is grasped, the knowledge that he is living would in fact be obstructed, since it wouldn't have any basis.
>
> 13. Thus, the Naiyāyikas speak without knowing that a subtle condition of being obstructed is understood by grasping his absence from the house, before establishing his being outside.

COMMENTS: In response to the Naiyāyika's criticism, Nārāyaṇa reiterates again that the conflict he's describing is not a contradiction between *p* and not-*p*. He now goes further in his response, arguing that it is not possible to reduce the case of Devadatta's absence to *anumāna*. A good *anumāna* requires a pervasion relationship, which describes the invariable relationship between the property S being known through *anumāna* and the property H which signals that S is present in the site in question (such as the mountain). In the case of Devadatta, what is allegedly known through *anumāna* is twofold: he is alive and he is outside of the home. One attempt at such an *anumāna* employs a pervasion relationship between someone's being alive and being situated, generally speaking:

Thesis. There is Devadatta who is alive and outside of the home

Reason. Because Devadatta is alive

Pervasion. And when someone is alive, they are in a place, for instance, myself.

However, there are two problems with this approach. First, we need to have independent reason to think that Devadatta is alive—we cannot use his being alive as the reason without question-begging. Second, in this *anumāna*, we cannot reason based on Pervasion to Thesis, since the thesis is about a specific place, not just generally being located somewhere. Instead, we could only reason this way:

Thesis. There is Devadatta who is in a place

Reason. Because Devadatta is alive

Pervasion. And when someone is alive, they are in a place, for instance, myself.

Yet this *anumāna* falls short of what we attain by *arthâpatti*—that Devadatta is alive in a specific place. Further, Nārāyaṇa argues that we would have an unwanted consequence, that Devadatta is connected to a place, just in general. He says this would mean "That person would be a place, as well." In other words, the *anumāna* above would really be:

Thesis. There is Devadatta who *is a place*

Reason. Because Devadatta is alive

Pervasion. And when someone is alive, they have connection to being situated, generally speaking.

To say that someone has connection to placehood or the property of being situated (*deśatva*) is like saying of something that it has a connection to the property of being a cow (*gotva*). That is another way of saying that someone is that thing—whether a place or a cow. But this is not what we are trying to prove above Devadatta! He has a location, but he does not have the property of being situated, generally—that is what it is for something to be a place.

Additionally, Nārāyaṇa argues that the reason (*hetu*) cannot function, either, since it has an obstacle (*bādha*). An obstacle, or an epistemic defeater, is when an agent comes to know that her initial, apparently veridical, cognition is not veridical, by experiencing a second cognition which obstructs the first. A classic case is of initially seeing "silver" on the ground, but then, in a subsequent

> cognition (such as when one stoops down to pick it up) seeing that the "silver" is a shiny piece of mother-of-pearl. Here, the second cognition is an obstacle to continuing to believe one's apparent perception of silver, as a genuine perception.
>
> In the case of *arthâpatti*, Nāryāyaṇa argues that there is a subtle (*sukṣma*) moment of cognitive obstruction which occurs when perceiving that Devadatta is absent from his home. This obstructs one's initial cognition that he is alive, somewhere. However, this obstruction does not, as in the case of "silver," constitute a complete rejection of the initial cognition. Rather, it leads to the acceptance that Devadatta is alive *outside* as opposed to *in his house*. That is because this obstruction is not a complete rejection of his being alive, but only an obstruction of his being alive in a particular place—his home. However, this is a genuine obstacle, however slight and momentary, which occurs before the cognition that Devadatta is alive and outside. This is what Naiyāyikas miss, according to Nārāyaṇa. Cidānanda's earlier discussion, which Nārāyaṇa is drawing from, develops the idea of obstruction (for him, *pratibandha*) in significant detail. At one point, he compares this kind of obstruction to when there is an obstacle to one seed's growth but the other seeds (presumably in the same field) lack such an obstacle. This, and not a complete obstruction, is what is involved in *arthâpatti*.

Further, what was said with regard to well-established *anumāna*s—that they would also be *arthâpatti*—that is not the case. For, on this point, what causes the ascertainment of fire on a mountain, somewhere, is a general knowledge-cognition. What term should we use for this?

Naiyāyika: It has been said that fire on the mountain is ascertained instead through the knowledge-cognition which causes the grasping of a pervasion relationship.

Bhāṭṭa: Well, now, look at this! What is this prattling by those who kiss the backs of the Prābhākaras?

> **14.** How can one apprehend a mountain as shining with fire when it has not already been observed? Therefore what is thought by the Naiyāyikas is destroyed, even on the topic of *anumāna*.

What was stated earlier was that smoke signals fire, which is its cause. What does this mean? Well, smoke causes the *anumāna* that there is fire—that is what should be said. And therefore, it is just *anumāna* which causes us to grasp that there is fire on the mountain. On this point, it was described as a general knowledge-cognition. Therefore, (already-accepted) *anumāna*s are not consumed (within *arthâpatti*).

> **15.** With regard to something ascertained above, when there is an obstacle, its being below is posited. This is regarded as by means of *arthâpatti*, in fact, and therefore, there is no problem at all.

Moreover, that *anumāna* which is employed to establish Devadatta's being outside has an unestablished nature for someone who is thought to have long life. This is because it is impossible to ascertain the mere fact of that person's living without any specification. Prior to grasping that someone is outside, it is not possible to recognize his not being in the house and his being alive as being combined. Therefore, because in this case, one cannot understand the nature of an inferential sign (*liṅga*) as comprised by absence from the house qualified by living, this reason (*hetu*) has an unestablished and unknown nature. That is what has been said in the *Bṛhaṭ-ṭīkā*:[2]

> **16.** Therefore, that absence from the house which is understood, being known, that is the reason (*hetu*). It is not grasped without having already grasped his being outside.

Therefore *arthâpatti* is in fact distinct (from *anumāna*).

> COMMENTS: Nāryāṇa rejects both the claim that the classic smoke–fire *anumāna* would turn out to be *arthâpatti* and that the Devadatta case should be analyzed in terms of *anumāna*. He likens the Nyāya position to a Prābhākara one, which he has discussed (and rejected) in the *anumāna* chapter. There he is explicit that, according to Prabhākara, the fact of fire on the mountain is not something new which we learn, but is already part of our knowledge of the pervasion between smoke and fire (Raja and Śāstri 1933: 52–3). Understood as an *arthâpatti*, the fact that there is an absence of fire in the visible part of the mountain comes into conflict with the pervasion between smoke and fire, so that we posit fire in the unseen part of the mountain. However, this is—analogous with the case of Devadatta—only to reassert something already known in some general manner. But in the case at hand, we do not already have general knowledge about the mountain we are observing (say, Everest), like we did about Devadatta (his being alive, somewhere). So we cannot, through *arthâpatti*, have a cognition about Everest's possessing fire on its unseen parts. We must, according to Nāryāyaṇa, come to have some new knowledge about Everest, knowledge which, he argues in the *anumāna* section, must be dependent on our new observation that Everest has smoke billowing out of it. See Raja and Sastri (1933: 52–3).
>
> Returning to the claim that Devadatta's being alive and outside could be known by *anumāna*, Nāryāyaṇa reiterates the familiar Mīmāṃsā claim that this cannot occur because of the fallacy of an unestablished reason (*hetv-asiddha*). This line of reasoning is also found in Kumārila (see Ollett and Freschi in this volume, p. 74),Vācaspati's Mīmāṃsaka interlocutor (see Keating in this volume, p. 142), and Jayanta Bhaṭṭa (see Graheli in this volume, p. 156). Since we have to know that someone lives somewhere, specifically, once we have the subtle moment of obstruction that results from seeing Devadatta is not at home, we cannot use his being alive as grounds for reasoning to his being alive and outside. At this point, satisfied with his rejoinders to the Naiyāyikas, Nāryāyaṇa turns to the Prābhākaras who, though they also reject the reduction to *anumāna*, do so in a different manner.

17. However, there is this prattling on by the one who does not know such a form of destroying the Naiyāyikas, the Guru: "There is doubt here regarding his being alive."

[2] This is a work of Kumārila Bhaṭṭa which is now lost.

18. "It is known already that he is definitely alive, through his connection with his dwelling-place. Therefore, there would be doubt about his being alive from not observing him in his dwelling place."

19. "Now, that doubt about his being alive causes a cognition of his being outside. This is the strength of *arthâpatti*: something which, though it is doubtful, is able to cause knowledge."

20. "Thus, when there is doubt about living, the inferential sign would have doubtful qualification. Therefore, refuting *arthâpatti*'s nature as being inferential is made easy for us."

These remarks are laughable. For things are this way:

21. If his being alive is doubtful because of seeing that he is not at home, then certainty about his being alive should be regained by such means as authoritative testimony,

22. or by observing a sign, like his wife's neck still bearing a marriage thread.

But this is not in any way investigated. Therefore, there is not really a doubt.

23. And how is it that his being outside is not grasped from his being alive? Moreover, when there is doubt about his being dead, how is there the knowledge that he is outside?

24. Who but the Guru has the capacity to make this *arthâpatti*: "since he is alive or he is not alive, then he exists outside"?

25. Everything would be possible through the strength of *arthâpatti* in this way, for where one has a doubt that anything is lost, when it is unobserved,

26. having then become certain that it is elsewhere, let the mind be satisfied! In this way, then, doubt is definitely not the efficient cause of *arthâpatti*.

Therefore *arthâpatti* is known as it has been described by us.

Comments: While they agree with Bhāṭṭa thinkers that *arthâpatti* is not *anumāna*, Prābhākara Mīmāṃsakas reject this conflict-centered analysis of *arthâpatti*, and Nārāyaṇa, having characterized the cognitive phenomenology involved as "subtle" (*sūkṣma*), pokes fun at their inability to apprehend what's really going on. Their "prattle," Nārāyaṇa says, is focused erroneously on doubting that Devadatta is alive. But, Nārāyaṇa argues in a sarcastic vein, doubt can't be the basis for knowledge—what an amazingly great epistemic instrument *arthâpatti* would be, in that case!

His argument against Prābhākara here is both practical and theoretical. On the one hand, if we were really in doubt about Devadatta's being alive, we would act differently—go inquire from friends, or look for a tell-tale thread on his wife's neck (which functions like a wedding band in other cultures—a widow would have removed it). Further, Nārāyaṇa argues that from doubt about whether someone is dead, we should not be able to draw a conclusion about where they are—outside or at home. However, unlike earlier Bhāṭṭa Mīmāṃsakas, who do not accept that there is any experienced doubt, Nāryāyaṇa seems to come closer to the Prābhākara view, by admitting some genuine conflict, and some resulting obstruction and a kind of doubt (verse 10). The doubt is importantly different: it is a doubt as to whether he is alive at home or outside, rather than a doubt about whether he is alive or not. However, it is still a doubt, not merely the possibility, as earlier Bhāṭṭa thinkers maintained. Still, it is the conflict (*virodha*) and not doubt (*sandeha*) which counts as the efficient cause or "trigger" of *arthâpatti* for Nārāyaṇa, and thus he distinguishes his view from the Prābhākaras. One other difference with his Mīmāṃsaka interlocutors is the topic of the final section.

Further, *arthâpatti* has two kinds: experiential *arthâpatti* (*dṛṣṭârthâpatti*) and verbal *arthâpatti* (*śrutârthâpatti*). Experiential *arthâpatti* has been described.

27. But when words are brought in so as to establish linguistic connection in an incomplete sentence, verbal *arthâpatti* is accepted.

This is just as in the case of "the door, the door," where the general knowledge-cognition is that there must be a meaning to establish connection in the sentence through another meaning, such as *closing*, understood through a word. When, since no heard word is ascertained, there is a conflict with that [cognition], a meaning such as *closing* is to be posited as being understood from an unheard word. And in this case, someone engaged in positing a meaning such as *closing* along with a word, because it is parsimonious to understand a meaning from a word alone, posits just a word. What has this word-positing character is *śrutârthâpatti*.

In contrast, the Guru says that this is not *śrutârthâpatti* because there isn't the positing of a word, as what is posited is simply the meaning *closing*. But he has been made mute already because it has been already demonstrated that the effective means of connection can only be what is gotten from words.

Guru: And if a meaning alone is posited to complete a sentence, then in the case of "Being pleasing, I offer to Sūrya (the sun deity)," what is to be modified is only the meaning, in the form of *Sūrya*. In contrast, the words "to Sūrya" would not be posited.

Bhāṭṭa: Now, in the archetypal sacrifice, it is observed that this element, the archetype, is only transferred by a word. Thus, in the ectype, too, a word is posited.

Guru: This is not so. For in the ectype, particular characteristics are not drawn into it simply through their being observed (in the archetype), but rather by force of a purpose.

Bhāṭṭa: But for you there is no purpose whatsoever for the element as understood through a word, as connection is established in another way. And if the meaning "threshed" is ascertained merely by its being observed, since an analogically related preparation is observed, then the threshing would have to be performed in the case of golden grains, too. Therefore, it is established that modification is, in fact, *śrutârthâpatti*. Let this be the conclusion.

Comments: Nārāyaṇa is not finished criticizing Prabhākara, the Guru. Bhāṭṭa thinkers accept two varieties of postulation: *śrutârthâpatti* or verbal *arthâpatti*, which works on the basis of what is heard; and *dṛṣṭârthâpatti*, or experiential *arthâpatti*, which works on the basis of what is observed. Verbal *arthâpatti* results in the *arthâpatti* of a linguistic expression, whereas experiential *arthâpatti* results in the *arthâpatti* of an *artha*, a word which is used for both "meaning" and "object." Experiential *arthâpatti* yields a proposition or a state of affairs (*artha*), whereas verbal *arthâpatti* yields a sentence or expression—something linguistic (*śabda*). In contrast, Prabhākara, in his commentary on Śabara, claims that the phrase "experienced or heard," used by him to characterize the input for *arthâpatti*, is an idiom which means "apprehended" (see Ollett and Freschi in this volume, p. 92). Thus for him, there is no difference in kind between so-called verbal and experiential *arthâpatti*. In fact, both putative kinds of *arthâpatti* have as their result an *artha*, whether the epistemic instrument is perception or testimony or anything else.

In response, Nārāyaṇa argues that *arthâpatti* is crucial for modification (*ūha*) of Vedic *mantra*s in new contexts, and that it is also used for completion of incomplete sentences like "the door, the door." The latter case is also mentioned in Nārāyaṇa's discussion of testimony (*śabda*) elsewhere in the MM. These cases require linguistic content, not merely cognition of a fact or a meaning (*artha*). Thus while the Prābhākaras wish to argue from parsimony that linguistic content is unnecessary—as the incongruity is only resolved by the meaning and not the word itself—Nārāyaṇa argues that in the case of Vedic *mantra*s, the presence of a word is crucial. The case treated here is a *mantra* or fragment of Vedic verse which accompanies ritual performances. This particular sentence, "I offer what is pleasing to Sūrya (*sūryāya juṣṭaṃ nirvapāmi*)" is the result of modification of the sentence, "I offer what is pleasing to Agni (*agnaye tvā juṣṭaṃ nirvapāmi*)."

Modification involves changes to the *mantra* based on their use in new ritual contexts. In the example above, the deity receiving the offerings is no longer Sūrya (the sun) but Agni (fire). Thus *sūryāya* ("to Sūrya") is replaced with *agnaye* ("to Agni")—which requires declining the new noun in the dative case, but differently. Kumārila Bhaṭṭa discusses modification in the *Tantra-vārttika*, arguing that grammar, along with ordinary linguistic use (*vyavahāra*), can be authoritative in understanding the correct use of words in the Vedas. Here, Nārāyaṇa does not develop the relationship between grammar and *arthâpatti*. While clearly one must know something about grammar in order to decline the deity's name correctly, we must also take other features, such as the purpose of the ritual, into account, in order to know what deity is appropriate, what part of the *mantra* should be modified, and so on.

The Guru, or Prabhākara himself, accepts this, but he rejects the Bhāṭṭa claim that the word (*śabda*) is also understood by *arthâpatti*. It's enough to change the meaning of the *mantra*. However, Nārāyaṇa's point is that when the archetypal ritual is a pattern for other rituals (ectypes), we understand what elements must be present by carefully matching features from the archetype to the ectype. In this new ritual context, where (due to the time of day) we must be offering to a different deity, the ritual participants understand this through the words of the *mantra* which should be uttered. In the archetype, the words include the vocative "to Agni," so in the ectype, the words should include the vocative "to Sūrya." We can't simply change the meaning *to Sūrya* without also changing the expression.

The Guru responds, according to Nārāyaṇa, by appealing to purpose (*prayojana*). He objects that the principle of analogy between the archetype and the ectype is constrained by purpose. In other words, what ritual elements from the archetype are "drawn into" (*ākṛṣyante*) the ectype is determined by the purpose of the ritual. Not every aspect is copied, but only those which align with the goal of the ectype. Implicitly, the conclusion is that the *arthâpatti* of an expression is not so aligned.

Nārāyaṇa points out that, on the Prābhākara view, in which only a meaning is postulated, this principle would be violated. The reason is that on the Prābhākara view, the effective means of linguistic connection (*anvaya*) is the meanings of words and not the words themselves. This section of the dialectic is very compressed, and it is difficult to see precisely what Nārāyaṇa takes the Prābhākara argument to be. The difficulty is that, in one place, the Guru is arguing that the expression "to Sūrya" is not posited. This could be read in two ways: first, that the expression is not present at all (due to not being posited) or, second, that the expression is present, but not due to the process of *arthâpatti*. If the first reading, then either the *mantra* remains unchanged with the words "to Agni," or those words are merely dropped. The response, that an expression is posited (*padaṃ kalpyam*) retains the same ambivalence.

Since it is possible to have such connection without the words, there is no purpose for the words "to Sūrya." However, in the new ritual context, one is supposed to utter the *mantra* with these words, "to Sūrya," which means that this part of the ritual would be purposeless. A conclusion on which Vedic sentences are purposeless is a conclusion that no Mīmāṃsāka would accept, Prābhākara or Bhāṭṭa. More broadly, the philosophical point is that words are uttered for a reason, which ordinarily is to contribute to our understanding of the sentence meaning. With this, the discussion of *arthâpatti* concludes.

REFERENCES

Primary sources

Raja, C. K., and S. S. Sastri, eds. and trans. (1933), *Mānameyodaya: An Elementary Treatise on the Mīmāṃsā by* Nāryāṇa, Adyar: Theosophical Publishing House.

Sastri, P. K. N., ed. (1953), *Nītitattvāvirbhāva of Cidānda*, Trivandrum Sanskrit Series 168, Trivandrum: University of Travancore Press.

Secondary literature

Keating, M. (2017), "(Close) the Door; the King (is Going): The Development of Elliptical Resolution in Bhāṭṭa Mīmāṃsā," *Journal of Indian Philosophy* 45, no. 5: 911–38.

Raja, K. K. (1946), "The Date of Narāyaṇa Bhaṭṭa," in *Proceedings of the All-India Oriental Conference*, 183–6.

Raja, K. K. (1954–5), "The Date of Narāyaṇa Bhaṭṭa," *Annals of the Bhandarkar Oriental Research Institute.*

SECTION TWO

CHAPTER FIVE

Akṣapāda Gautama's *Nyāya-sūtra* with Early Commentaries

Translated by MALCOLM KEATING

INTRODUCTION

Traditionally ascribed to a person named "Akṣapāda Gautama," the *Nyāya-sūtra* (NS) is likely a compilation of an earlier, orally transmitted collection of short statements (*sūtra*s).[1] Its date of collection is a matter of debate, though it was probably 150 CE or earlier when the 528 *sūtra*s were put into writing. As with other *sūtra* texts, the NS forms the textual basis for a self-identified tradition: here, Nyāya. Our excerpts are from three early commentaries: Vātsyāyana's *Extensive Commentary on Nyāya* (*Nyāya-bhāṣya*) (*c.* 450 CE), Uddyotakara's *Explanation of the Nyāya System* (*Nyāya-vārttika*) (*c.* 550 CE), and Vācaspati Miśra's *Notes on the Meaning of the Explanation of the Nyāya System* (*Nyāya-vārttika-tātparya-ṭīkā*) (*c.* 900 CE). Often, though not always, Uddyotakara and Vācaspati take their cues from Vātsyāyana, elaborating on what he has said before. Later Naiyāyikas such as Jayanta Bhaṭṭa (see Graheli in this volume, p. 145), Udayana (see Das in this volume, p. 183), and Gaṅgeśa (see Phillips in this volume, p. 199), even if they are not directly commenting upon the NS, frequently cite from or refer to it. Though Vātsyāyana and Uddyotakara's commentaries have been translated before, most notably in Jha (1984), Vācaspati's commentary has been translated only in small pieces, and this section practically not at all, save for a few footnotes in Jha's translation.

Discussion of *arthâpatti* comes at NS 2.2.1, well after Gautama (in 1.1.3) has stated that the number of *pramāṇa*s is four: perception (*pratyakṣa*), *anumāna*, comparison (*upamāna*), and testimony (*āgama*). Throughout 2.1.1–68 he has given an account of their natures as knowledge-conducive epistemic instruments. Now, Gautama has an opponent raise a doubt about the number of *pramāṇa*s. The opponent argues that

[1] I am grateful to Stephen Phillips, with whom I discussed portions of Vācaspati's commentary. I also read these texts with Matthew Dasti, and his comments were extremely helpful. Of course, neither should be held responsible for any errors in my translation.

Naiyāyikas ought to include additional *pramāṇa*s, of which *arthâpatti* is one. In this section, we will also see an unnamed skeptic argue that *arthâpatti* is not a *pramāṇa* (2.2.3), a view which does not belong to our Naiyāyikas, since they would argue instead that *arthâpatti* is reducible to an existing *pramāṇa*, that is, *anumāna*. Who this skeptic is, if they represent a historical perspective at all, is unknown.

In what follows, the *sūtra* text is presented in bold when quoted, followed by selections from the commentaries identified by their author (e.g. "Vātsyāyana"). Where it is clear to whom the commentator is referring, I have inserted the name in place of pronouns and completed verbs with implicit subjects, even if Vācaspati does not state "Uddyotakara says." While some of the commentarial material is repetitive on the surface, quoting a previous commentator's words and then restating them in a slightly different manner, I have retained the entire section for the sake of completeness and to give readers a sense of the commentarial style, which is to unpack what is implicit in the previous texts. After all, just what is implicit, and how it can be unpacked, is a point of discussion here, not only in terms of why the discussion of *arthâpatti* comes as it does (see Vācaspati at 2.2.1), but also in terms of *arthâpatti* itself, which is, according to our Naiyāyikas, a way of knowing implicit meanings on the basis of explicit ones.

VĀTSYĀYANA

Thinking that the enumeration of *pramāṇa*s is incorrect, the opponent says:

NS 2.2.1. *Opponent*: The number of *pramāṇa*s (epistemic instruments) is not four because tradition, *arthâpatti*, inclusion, and knowledge of absence are *pramāṇa*s.

Opponent: There are not just four kinds of *pramāṇa*s. But instead, tradition (*aitihya*), *arthâpatti*, inclusion (*saṃbhava*), and cognition of absence (*abhāva*) are also *pramāṇa*s. Why haven't these been discussed? Tradition is a report such as "'Things are like this,' he said," passed down through successive generations, whose original speaker is uknown. *Arthâpatti* is the obtaining (*āpatti*) of something from a fact (*artha*). "The obtaining" is something which follows that immediately understood fact. When a fact is being communicated, the *arthâpatti* is that other fact which follows, as for instance, "When there are no clouds, there is no rain." When this is said, what follows in this case? "When there are (clouds, there is rain)." What is called "inclusion" is grasping the existence of another thing from grasping the existence of something which is invariably present with it. For instance, from grasping the existence of one *droṇa*, there is grasped the existence of one *āḍaka* (one-quarter of a *droṇa*), and from grasping the existence of one *āḍaka* there is one *prastha* (one-quarter of an *āḍaka*). Cognition of absence is "something not present which is in opposition with something that is present . . ."[2] Rain's activity not being present causes the understanding that wind and clouds are present together. For, when the presence of wind and clouds together suspend them, waterdrops don't fall down from their weight.

[2] Quotation is from the *Vaiśeṣika-sūtra*, 3.1.11.

Nyāya Reply: True, these are *pramāṇa*s, but they are not distinct *pramāṇa*s. And an objection is stated to the thought that these are distinct *pramāṇa*s.

UDDYOTAKARA

"Perception, *anumāna*, comparison, and testimony are *pramāṇas*," according to the *sūtra* (1.1.3). With regard to this, it is said, **"There are not just four kinds of *pramāṇa*s because tradition, *arthâpatti*, inclusion, and knowledge of absence are *pramāṇa*s (2.2.1)."**

Its meaning is: This "enumeration of *pramāṇa*s is incorrect. There are not just four kinds of *pramāṇa*s. Tradition (*aitihya*), *arthâpatti*, inclusion (*saṃbhava*), and cognition of absence (*abhāva*) are also *pramāṇa*s" (Vātsyāyana).

Alternately, after having been introduced, tradition and etc. are objected to, for the purpose of dispelling doubt: "And perception and etc. are *pramāṇas*. And tradition etc.," this is what is thought by some. On this topic there could be doubt among those who hear the *sūtra*: "Why have those genuinely existing (*pramāṇa*s) like tradition etc. not been stated? Or are they not genuinely existing *pramāṇa*s?"

Or the discussion's aim is to defend against the deficiency of the teaching (*vidhi*). Since genuinely existing *pramāṇa*s, tradition etc., have not been stated, it could be that the treatise is missing teachings.

Or, because there have not been any statements about the flaws of things which are flawed, it could be that the treatise is overlooking flaws. Therefore, having been enumerated, they are being defended against (flaws). What possesses flaws is tradition and etc., and these have not been stated. If there is a flaw, it should be spoken of. Therefore, as a flaw has not been stated, the treatise is overlooking flaws. It is explained that the section's meaning is the defense against this.

Or, the aim is to point out that these *pramāṇa*s are incorporated within perception and etc. Given that tradition and etc. are to be subsumed within perception, etc., the section's meaning is to show, among these *pramāṇa*s, within which *pramāṇa*s they are to be subsumed.

Objection: This is not undertaken because it has been accomplished already. After all, this meaning, that the *pramāṇa*s are of only four kinds, has been established in the *sūtra* that enumerates into distinct categories—thus because it has been accomplished already, a repetition is not undertaken.

Reply: No—what is understood has the purpose of accurately discerning what has been established. That reasoning that truly settles *pramāṇa*s as fourfold is the reasoning explained in this section. Therefore, it certainly is to be undertaken.

What is it that is called "tradition"? "An unknown original speaker whose report is passed down through successive generations, 'Things are like this,' he said" (Vātsyāyana) which old people report.

"*Arthâpatti* is the obtaining (*āpatti*) of something from a fact (*artha*). 'The obtaining' is something that follows which is immediately gotten" (Vātsyāyana). In case of a sentence, from a fact being communicated "the *arthâpatti* is that other fact which follows. For instance, 'When there are no clouds, there is no rain.' When this is said, what follows in this case? 'When there are (clouds, there is rain)'" (Vātsyāyana).

What is called "inclusion" is knowing (*vjñāna*) the existence of another thing from grasping the material category (*padârtha*) invariably present with it. "For instance, from grasping the existence of one *droṇa*, there is grasped the existence of one *āḍaka*" (Vātsyāyana).

Cognition of absence is the grasping of an opposite from the grasping of an opposition. For instance, "when the presence of wind and clouds together suspend them, waterdrops don't fall down from their weight." By the non-falling of the rain, the "presence of wind and clouds together," (Vātsyāyana) which is an opposition, is understood.

VĀCASPATI

"Incorrect," states Vātsyāyana's *Commentary*. "What is incorrect is the enumeration into distinct categories on the part of the *pramāṇa*s. With regard to this, the *vārttika*-maker, Uddyotakara, explains, 'Perception, *anumāna*, comparison, and testimony are *pramāṇa*s,' according to the *sūtra*" (1.1.3).

"There are not just four kinds of *pramāṇa*s. But instead, tradition (*aitihya)*, *arthâpatti*, inclusion (*saṃbhava*), and cognition of absence (*abhāva*) are also *pramāṇa*s . . ." (Vātsyāyana) Thus "with regard to this," there is a higher number [of *pramāṇa*s]. Having explained how the *Commentary* understands the *sūtra*, Uddyotakara also explains it differently: "Alternately, the meaning" of the section "is to dispel doubts." But the *sūtra* has as its meaning a doubt: It is not possible to be certain that there are four (*pramāṇa*s). Why? Because it is accepted by others that tradition, *arthâpatti*, inclusion, cognition of absence have the nature of *pramāṇa*s, a doubt therefore arises for us—this is the *sūtra*'s meaning. Uddyotakara states a different purpose: "Or the discussion's aim is to defend against the deficiency of the teaching (*vidhi*)." There is an enumeration into distinct categories and a later denial of the surplus [categories], so on this understanding, the incorrect thing is the enumeration of *pramānas*, and these two should be explained earlier. But now, this is the beginning of a different teaching on perception and etc.

"Perception, *anumāna*, comparison, and testimony are *pramāṇa*s" (Uddyotakara). Now, the subsequent denial has this meaning: the position which, having been supported, is now stated—that is a repetition. Uddyotakara states a different purpose: "Or, because there have not been any statements about the flaws of things which are flawed, it could be that the treatise is overlooking flaws." He states another purpose: "Or, the aim is to point out that they are incorporated within perception and etc." Because meaning of the section aims at inclusion, the correctness of the enumeration into distinct categories has already been established—this is the meaning.

It is pointed out: "Because it has been accomplished already, this is not undertaken" (Uddyotakara). For it is not true that everything hinted at by the *sūtra*-maker should be brought out explicitly, by the commentary-maker and others, too because it settles what has been made explicit—this is the idea. Uddyotakara replies: "No"—the rejection of different *pramāṇa*s "has the purpose of accurately discerning." That which, though unstated, can be grasped from a mere hint, is not described by the *sūtra*-maker. But that which, though hinted at, is like something concealed, must be exposed by the *sūtra*-maker. The idea is that with regard to what is hinted at, there is no certainty that the commentary-maker and others state our thoughts and not something else.

"What is that . . . meaning which follows?" this is the question. Later, "When there are clouds, there is rain" (Vātsyāyana).

(Uddyotakara says) ". . . from the grasping of an opposition." From having grasped the not-falling of the rain, which is in opposition to falling, there is the grasping of the presence of wind and clouds together, "which are opposed to that" (Uddyotakara), namely, which are opposed to rain—this is the *pramāṇa* called "cognition of absence," in fact. For what is known is that wind and clouds are together, though clouds are present, since there is an absence of rain falling.

COMMENTS: While Vātsyāyana is content to focus on explaining the opponent's objection about the number of *pramāṇa*s, both Uddyotakara and Vācaspati focus on the question of why the *sūtra*-maker (the person who compiles the text) has put the discussion of these four purportedly different *pramāṇa*s at this point, rather than at the introduction of *pramāṇa*s at NS 1.1.3. Uddyotakara's final explanation, likely the one he prefers, is that it makes explicit what Gautama meant when he says there are four *pramāṇa*s, in a way which really settles the issue. Vācaspati, in his remarks here, draws a contrast between different principles for what should be made explicit by the writer of a *sūtra* and subsequent commentators. The opponent in Uddyotakara's *Explanation* argues that this discussion can't be undertaking an explanation which already came before, because it would be needless repetition. But Vācaspati, while he agrees that there is no need to make everything explicit, points out that that there is a difference between things which we can understand easily without their being made explicit, and those things which need some explication. Since the number of *pramāṇa*s and their relationship to these purported *pramāṇa*s is difficult to understand if left unsaid, we should take the discussion here as clarifying 1.1.3.

Speaking of making the implicit explicit, note that later, in his comments at 2.2.4, Uddyotakara also makes explicit what Vātsyāyana leaves implicit in his original presentation of *arthâpatti*. What is obtained from "When there are no clouds, there is no rain" is the inverse, "Where there are clouds there is rain." If we understand the first sentence as a material conditional ($\neg p \supset \neg q$), then *arthâpatti* delivers us a non-equivalent sentence ($p \supset q$)—hardly desirable for a supposed *pramāṇa*. However, if instead, the relationship between rain and clouds is understood to be biconditional, then "Where there are clouds there is rain" is the contrapositive of the converse conditional ("Where there is not rain, there are no clouds" or $\neg q \supset \neg p$).

Aware of the puzzling nature of the relationship between these two sentences, in what follows, the Naiyāyikas will address possible objections to this as a case of genuine knowledge (after all, sometimes there are clouds and no rain). Ultimately, they will argue that it should be understood as *anumāna*. All the other putative *pramāṇa*s, save for tradition, will be dealt with as cases of *anumāna*, even though our opponent finds them distinct, not only from the four originally adduced, but from each other. Tradition is explained as reducible to testimony.

VĀTSYĀYANA

That objection is this:

NS 2.2.2, *Nyāya Reply*: This is not an objection because tradition is subsumed into testimony and *arthâpatti*, inclusion, and cognition of absence are subsumed into *anumāna*.

This objection is untenable. Why? "Testimony is a trustworthy authority's assertion" (NS 1.1.7). Therefore, the definition of testimony is not distinguished from that of tradition. Due to their common character, this distinction is collapsed. *Anumāna* is the understanding of an imperceptible thing which is closely connected to a perceptible thing. And it is likewise for *arthâpatti*, inclusion, and cognition of absence. *Arthâpatti* is the grasping of an undenoted meaning on the basis of opposition (*pratyanīka*), through the correct understanding of a sentence meaning—this is just *anumāna*. Inclusion is the grasping of the rest of a totality, from the close connection between the totality and its parts, through the operation of inseparable presence (*avinâbhāva*). And that is just *anumāna*, too. When the contradiction (*virodha*) "When this thing is, that does not occur" is established, the obstruction of the cause is understood through *anumāna* because the effect does not arise. This is the enumeration of *pramāṇas* which is in fact correct.

UDDYOTAKARA

Those things that are this way, that is, tradition, etc., are subsumed into these very things (testimony and *anumāna*) because of a non-difference in their definitions.[3] And therefore they have not been described as separate. And (they have not been described as separate) because that is not the topic. For the topic of tradition, etc. as a distinct *pramāṇa* from perception, etc. is not possible. And therefore, they are not different *pramāṇas*. But you think the *pramāṇas* are different due to differences in purpose. If so, then you should reject their being eight. What is accepted (by you), that is, having eight *pramāṇas*, that should be rejected, since (you think) "Because of the difference in purposes, different *pramāṇas* are accepted." And we observe different purposes based on a single instrument, so there would be more than one *pramāṇa*: just like a single visual faculty has its purposes in grasping different colors, such as blue, which are multiple. Or there would be more than one sense faculty. Now, because of the difference in purpose, do you think there is a difference? A single sense-organ gets at multiple objects. But there is a single sense-organ because there is no differentiation among common content. The (following) objection then is not correct: **"There are not just four kinds of *pramāṇas*, because tradition (*aitihya*), *arthâpatti*, inclusion (*saṃbhava*), and cognition of absence (*abhāva*) are also *pramāṇas*" (NS 2.2.1).** If these *pramāṇas* are not different *pramāṇas*, then within which are they subsumed? This should be stated. The *sūtra* has its purpose in pointing out this subsumption.

There is the subsuming of tradition into testimony (*śabda*) because they have the same definition. The definition of testimony does not exclude tradition: "Due to

[3] Reading *lakṣaṇâbhedād*, Dube (1907) rather than *lakṣaṇa-bhedād*, Thakur (1997).

their common character, this distinction is collapsed" (Vātsyāyana). There is the subsuming of *arthâpatti*, inclusion, and cognition of absence into *anumāna*, because they have the same definition. How is *arthâpatti* collapsed into *anumāna*? Because its content is the acceptance of the second of two things, when there is the denial of the first of the two. Wherever one of a pair of things is denied, in such a case, the acceptance of the second is observed. This is just as when from the statement "He does not eat at daytime," there is understood "he eats at night."

But some say that this is not *arthâpatti*: "He does not eat at night." Here there are two things which can possibly be ascertained: "He does not just *eat* during the day," and "He does not eat just *during the day*." Given that both are understood, it cannot be stated that he eats at night.

However, this is not a proper interpretation, because it is not possible. The meaning, "He does not just *eat* during the day," is rejected since it is impossible. For there is not anyone who just eats during the day. Further, someone who is eating "does not just *eat*," let alone someone who is not eating. Therefore, because this meaning is rejected due to being impossible, there is the denial of the time by this sentence "He does not eat at daytime." Otherwise it would be meaningless. Since the rejection of another action is rejected because of its impossibility, and because you do not accept the denial of a time, the statement is meaningless.

Opponent: Let it be meaningless, what is the problem for us?

Reply: How is it not a problem? What you have accepted is rejected.

Opponent: And what is it that is accepted?

Reply: That this is a negation of another action, and it is not a negation of the time. This is not meaningless. Therefore, when there is the negation of one of both things which are equally understood, because there is the acceptance of the second, *arthâpatti* is simply *anumāna*.

Opponent: What kind of *anumāna*?

Reply: It is generalization based on observation (*sāmānyato-dṛṣṭa*). This analysis holds for inclusion and cognition of absence. Inclusion is *anumāna*. And cognition of absence, as well, is understood this way. And this has been explained. As well, both of these two are subsumed within generalization based on observation, therefore. Thus, it is because of their being subsumed that these have not been mentioned independently.

VĀCASPATI

The final position says: "Those things that are this way, that is, tradition and etc., are subsumed into just these things (testimony and *anumāna*) because of a non-difference in their definitions" (Uddyotakara).

Opponent: Were this the case, this topic of the previously stated definition of *pramāṇa*s would not be within the scope of *pramāṇa*s, and tradition etc. would exist as distinct *pramāṇa*s.

Reply: Therefore, Uddyotakara says, "And (they have not been described as separate) because that is not the topic (*viṣaya*)." He urges, "But because of differences in purpose you think the *pramāṇas* are different." He shows this is flawed because it brings about an undesirable over-extension in the definition: "If so, then their being eight is rejected." They should not be rejected since, to the extent that purposes have common contents, *pramāṇas*, possessing purposes, would be mutually distinguished by these common contents. But, rather, what should be said is that they are distinguished on the basis of their being different. And in this way, because there would be an undesirable over-extension of the definition, the enumeration of eight is rejected—this is the meaning.

"But there is a single sense-organ because there is no differentiation among common content" (Uddyotakara). Its "common content," having color, and etc., whenever it has its own particulars, it is undifferentiated and therefore it is is singular—this is the meaning. Uddyotakara objects:[4] "The (following) objection then is not correct," since there are four distinguishers of common content: a single nature lacking obstructing conditions and the triple of bringing about pervasion (*vyāpakatva*), being syntactically connected (*anvitatva*) and having a name (*saṃjñitva*), therefore the denial of (*pramāṇas*) being of four kinds is not correct—this is the idea.[5]

"If these *pramāṇas* are not different *pramāṇas*, then within which are they subsumed?" (Vātsyāyana). If tradition etc. are *pramāṇas*, within which, that is, among perception etc., are they, that is tradition etc., subsumed? "The subsumption of a *pramāṇa* into a non-*pramāṇa* is not possible" therefore "*pramāṇas*" is mentioned.[6] Indeed, for tradition, whose "An unknown original speaker whose report is passed down through successive generations," it might be that the author has not been discerned to be an authoritative speaker (*āpta*). Thus, that would not really be a *pramāṇa*, and therefore it has been said "if . . ."

"This is not an objection because tradition is subsumed into testimony and *arthâpatti*, inclusion, and cognition of absence are subsumed into *anumāna* (NS 2.2.2)." Now, successive syllables that are understood, where there is the instruction of an authoritative speaker, that is testimony—this definition does not range too broadly. That has been stated here, "because of their having the same definition" (Uddyotakara). Uddyotakara asks, "How is *arthâpatti* collapsed into *anumāna*?"

[4] Thakur (1996: 389) reads *nirokaroti*, which I emend to *nirākaroti*.

[5] I especially thank Stephen Phillips and Matthew Dasti for discussion of this sentence. There is a textual variant here which might impact the reading. Thakur (1996) notes that one manuscript lacks the "and" (Sanskrit: *ca*). Without this, one might read the sentence instead as "There is a single nature lacking obstructing conditions in the triple of bringing about pervasion (*vyāpakatva*), being syntactically connected (*anvitatva*) and having a name (*saṃjñitva*). Thus the four (genuine *pramāṇas*) are distinguished by having common content. Therefore the denial of (*pramāṇas*) being of four kinds is not correct—this is the idea." Thus without the "and" there could be three conditions for each genuine *pramāṇa*, excluding perception, each condition being characterized as "a single nature lacking obstructing conditions." Including the "and," there are four conditions, one for each genuine *pramāṇa*: perception (single nature lacking obstructing conditions), inference (pervasion), testimony (syntactic connection), and comparison (having a name).

[6] Correcting to *apramāṇasya pramāṇa-antarbhāvo na bhavati pramāṇa-antar-bhāva* on the basis of Tarkatirtha et al. (1936–44).

"When there are no clouds, there is no rain" (Vātsyāyana). When this is said, what follows in this case? "When there are (clouds, there is rain)" (Vātsyāyana). This is *arthâpatti*. How is it collapsed by definition into *anumāṇa*? It is stated (by Uddyotakara), "Wherever one of a pair of things is denied . . ." On this topic, he states an example: "Wherever one of a pair of things is denied, in such a case, the acceptance of the second is discovered." He brings up the example's (supposed) deficiency with regard to what is being demonstrated: "But some say that this is not *arthâpatti*." If it is "He does not eat just *during the day*," then the denial of the specific time should be understood. Therefore he eats at night, and then what is understood is his action at a different time. But there is no certainty that what is denied is the specific time. This is because there is no implication of eating at night in "He does not just *eat* during the day," since what is denied by this denial is the action, that is, eating, by which there are other actions such as lying down. "He does not eat just *during the day*"—were this the single meaning, then what is understood would be "He eats at night." And when what is understood is the (opponent's) denial of the denial of a different action, there could not be stated "He eats at night," this is the idea.

That has this flaw: "However, this is not a proper interpretation . . ." (Vātsyāyana). For things which are previously accepted are denied. And it is not the case that there is no other action for either someone who eats or does not eat. What follows from this lack of another action is that what is denied cannot be only his eating: "Further, someone who is eating 'does not just *eat*,' let alone someone who is not eating" (Vātsyāyana). But it is not the eating which is not considered only, because there there are other actions as well, since there is an endless number of things (he could be doing other than eating). Whenever there is someone who is doing something, he is not doing other things, too. Would this make him not a doer? For one who is not engaged in other actions still acts—this is the idea. Uddyotakara concludes, "since . . . There is the denial of the time" in the sentence "He does not eat at daytime, *only*," this is what is denied—this is the idea. "since the rejection of another action is rejected because of its impossibility," (Vātsyāyana) because this cannot be understood, it is denied—this is the sense. In "that this is a negation of another action" (Vātsyāyana), the word "another" expresses difference. By it, the actions of eating are what is distinguished as "other." There is the negation of this: the action's being free from another action, that is, (there is the negation of) "eating *only*"—that is the idea. [The sentence] "It is generalization based on observation (*sāmānyato-dṛṣṭa*)" means that what has the relationship of indicated and indicator is not an effect and a cause, but instead what is observed as being in common.

COMMENTS: Here Vātsyāyana argues that, contrary to the opponent's attempt to make fine-grained distinctions, there is a common character between the already-accepted four *pramāṇa*s and the supposedly independent *pramāṇa*s. What characterizes *arthâpatti*, inclusion, and cognition of absence as being *anumāna* is that they all bring about knowledge of something imperceptible on the basis of something that is perceptible and which has a close connection to the imperceptible thing. For *anumāna*, that close connection is a pervasion relationship (*vyāpti*) which guarantees that the perceptible thing, smoke on the hill, can play the role of an inferential mark for the presence of fire on the hill. Vātsyāyana characterizes the paradigm cases of the putatively independent *pramāṇa*s in such a way as to show they have the same structure. We can represent the parallels in Table 1. In what follows, he will explain the opposition involved in *arthâpatti*.

Uddyotakara's comments on this *sūtra*, although they resonate with the idea of contradiction that Vātsyāyana introduces, nowhere uses the term "opposition" (*pratyanīka*). Rather, he talks about the denial (*pratiṣedha*) of one of two things (the term here, *vastu*, could mean facts broadly or the referents of words specifically). When one of two things is denied, the other is accepted. This principle constitutes the general pervasion relationship for *arthâpatti*. Of course, such a principle can only hold with the presupposition that one of the two things must be true, in order to avoid false dichotomizing. Perhaps for this reason, Uddyotakara has an opponent object to the paradigm example, "He does not eat at daytime," arguing (somewhat implausibly) that the negation (Sanskrit *na*, English "not") can take scope over the verb as well as the time. With such an ambiguity, we are not forced into a necesssary entailment that the person eats at night, since the denial could then be that the person eats, and not that they eat during the day. His analysis of *arthâpatti* is that it is a kind of *anumāna* known as *sāmānyato-dṛṣṭa* (described at NS 1.1.5), which Vācaspati will explain in more detail as a kind of *anumāna* in which the indicator and indicated (typically smoke and fire) are not related by cause and effect.

Vācaspati also focuses on the question of how to individuate *pramāṇa*s, a difficult problem which Uddyotakara's opponent has raised. Vācaspati argues that there is some kind of common content (*viṣaya-sāmānya*) which *pramāṇa*s have, so that, for instance, perception has content of things like color and so on. He identifies either three or four differentiators of this common content, depending on how one construes the Sanskrit syntax. Certainly there are three: content that brings about pervasion belongs to *anumāna*; content that is syntactically connected belongs to testimony; and content which bears a name belongs to comparison. Perception may be characterized as having a single nature lacking obstructing conditions, or perhaps this term refers to just the three previous *pramāṇa*s, with perception omitted since it is not typically taken to be reducible.

TABLE 1: Vātsyāyana's Analysis of *Pramāṇas*

Pramāṇa	*Imperceptible*	*Perceptible*	*Instrument*
Anumāna	fire	smoke	pervasion relationship (*vyāpati*)
Arthâpatti	undenoted meaning	sentence meaning	opposition (*pratyanīka-bhāva*)
Inclusion	part	whole	inseparable presence (*avinâbhāva*)
Absence	obstruction of cause	the effect's not occuring	an established contradiction (*virodha-prasiddha*)

VĀTSYĀYANA

It has been said, "True, these are *pramāṇa*s. But they are not distinct *pramāṇa*s" (Vātsyāyana). On this point, what is accepted as a *pramāṇa*, that is, *arthâpatti*, is not suitable (to be accepted as a *pramāṇa*). For thus this is said:

NS 2.2.3 (Opponent) *arthâpatti* is not a *pramāṇa* because of its deviating nature.

Opponent: "When there are not clouds, there is not rain," from that meaning, this is obtained: "When there are clouds, there is rain." However, when there are clouds, sometimes there is not rain. This is the deviating nature of *arthâpatti* which, therefore, is not a *pramāṇa*.

Reply: *Arthâpatti* does not have a deviating nature.

UDDYOTAKARA

This is said (by the objector as stated in Vātsyāyana's commentary): "True, these are *pramāṇa*s, but they are not distinct *pramāṇa*s. On this point, what is accepted as a *pramāṇa*, that is, *arthâpatti,* is not suitable (to be accepted as a *pramāṇa*)." For thus this is said, **"*arthâpatti* is not a *pramāṇa* because of its deviating nature (NS 2.2.3)."** That *arthâpatti* which is understood by you to be a *pramāṇa*, that is not a *pramāṇa*. That it is "not a *pramāṇa*" means that its object is not always caused to be understood. This is just as in the example, "When there are not clouds, there is not rain," from that meaning, this is obtained: "When there are clouds, there is rain . . . when there are clouds, sometimes there is not rain" (Vātsyāyana). Therefore, *arthâpatti* has a deviating nature.

Assuming that the inferential subject (*pakṣī-karaṇa*) is *arthâpatti* in general, then there is a deviating nature, that is a failure to have a pervasion relationship. If you make your objection about *arthâpatti* in general, then the deviating nature of *arthâpatti* is unable to be shown. But if just that which is deviating is made your inferential subject, then we agree. We say, also, that something which deviates is not a *pramāṇa*. And there is no inferential reason (*hetu*), because the reason is specified in the thesis to be proven (*pratijñā*). "That which is deviating, that cannot be a *pramāṇa*"—this is the thesis. There is no inferential reason for this thesis. And this meaning cannot be what is to be proven (*sādhya*) as there is a lack of a reason. And it cannot be what is to be proven because it would be accepting an inconsistency. By saying "A deviating *arthâpatti* is not a *pramāṇa*," what is accepted is "That which is non-deviating is a *pramāṇa*." And this is a pointless statement. That *arthâpatti* which is deviating is not a *pramāṇa*.

VĀCASPATI

"True, these are . . ." says the *Commentary*. This is its meaning: True, tradition and etc. are *pramāṇas*. "But they are not distinct *pramāṇa*s," which says they are not really distinct from *pramāṇa*s such as *anumāṇa* and so on. But these do not have the nature of *pramāṇa*. We will not put up with this—this is the idea.

Opponent: ***Arthâpatti* is not a *pramāṇa* because of its deviating nature (NS 2.2.3).** "If you make your objection about *arthâpatti* in general, then the deviating nature of *arthâpatti* is unable to be shown" (Uddyotakara's NV *ad* 2.2.3). This is because of *arthâpatti* having a non-deviating nature, for instance in cases like "He does not eat during the day."

2.2.4, *Reply*: Because what is thought of as *arthâpatti* is not *arthâpatti*.

VĀTSYĀYANA

"When there is no cause, the effect does not occur." The meaning gotten from this sentence is an opposition (*pratyanīka*). From that meaning, what is obtained is: "When there is a cause, the effect does occur." For the opposite of something's presence is its absence. What is being obtained from the meaning is that "There is an effect produced when there is a cause" and the production of this effect does not waver (*vyabhicarati*) from the presence of the cause. Now, when there is not a cause, the effect is not produced—therefore, there is no deviation.

But that effect which does not occur even when there is a cause, due to the obstruction of the causal basis, as this is a property of causes, that is not the object known by *arthâpatti*. Then what is its object? It is that "When there is a cause, the effect is produced." The effect produced does not waver from the presence of the cause. That is the object known by *arthâpatti*. So, this being the case, the objection was stated having made the supposition of *arthâpatti* in a case where there is not *arthâpatti*. And the property of causes has been observed, and this cannot be denied.

UDDYOTAKARA

That which is thought to be a deviating *arthâpatti* is not deviating, "**Because what is thought of as *arthâpatti* is not *arthâpatti*" (2.2.4)**. This is not a deviating *arthâpatti*. And the *arthâpatti* "When there are clouds, there is rain," how can this be deviating? It is not that when there are clouds, there is always rain, but rather there are always clouds when there is rain. But that—when there are clouds, and there is not rain—this is an obstruction of the cause. "This obstruction is not the object known by *arthâpatti*" (Vātsyāyana). What else is its object? It is that "When there is a cause, there is an effect." How could it be that this is deviating? If, although there is not a cause, the effect is produced. But that is not observed. Therefore, it is never deviating.

VĀCASPATI

Having pointed out there is a flaw by the opponent's own lights, Udayana's commentary on the *sūtra* states what is flawed: "That which is thought to be a deviating *arthâpatti* is not deviating." The meaning is not "When there are clouds, there is rain," by which a wavering might be observed. But, rather, it is "When there are not clouds, there is not rain." And in this way, there is not wavering. This is the meaning.

Comments: In NS 2.2.3 to 2.2.4, the *sūtra*-maker has an opponent object to *arthâpatti* as a *pramāṇa* on the grounds that it has the fault known as "deviation" (*anaikāntika*): sometimes *arthâpatti* may yield a true cognition, but sometimes it does not. But as a *pramāṇa* ought to invariably, or unwaveringly (without *vyabhicāra*), give rise to such cognitions, on pain of being a pseudo- or counterfeit *pramāṇa*, then *arthâpatti* cannot be accepted as a *pramāṇa*. The reason for its deviating nature seems to be that the meaning obtained by *arthâpatti* on the basis of an original sentence "When not x, then not y" admits of exceptions. This is because, in our paradigmatic clouds and rain case, if there is high wind, the opposite (*pratyanīka*) does not hold: "When x, then y," where x = clouds, and y = rain. While Vātsyāyana admits this is the case, he argues that everyone recognizes that causes are susceptible to an obstruction in the causal basis. This is, in fact, the sort of situation in which cognition of absence comes into play (see NS 2.2.1–2 above).

It is tempting, in light of contemporary default logics, to read Vātsyāyana as accepting some kind of non-monotonic reasoning here. An exemplar non-monotonic inference is from "All birds fly" to "Tweety flies" on the basis of "Tweety is a bird." However, on learning that Tweety is a penguin, we retract our inference. The inference is more precisely put, "Generally speaking, all birds fly." This kind of reasoning is often characterized in terms of normality conditions—the inferences are good, *ceteris paribus*. In contrast, monotonic inferences are necessarily good if the premises are true and the form is valid. New information might bring us to reflect on whether our premises actually are true, but not to simply retract the conclusion as an exception to the rule.

Some years back, in fact, Oetke (1996) put forward a non-monotonic interpretation of Vāstyāyana and other early Indian philosophers. However, as Taber (2004) points out, despite the apparently default nature of inferences such as "Where there are clouds, there is rain," the requirement of non-deviation (*anaikāntika*) suggests a sense of strong reliability. Vātsyāyana says that the resulting rule, which we get through *arthâpatti*, is without deviation. He does not add that it is without deviation once one adds the exception of lacking high winds. Further, we do not get discussion of the default conditions under which the general causal rule is acceptable.

Uddyotakara here also takes issue with the opponent's reasoning, which we will see further developed in what follows. Suppose the opponent argues, using *anumāna*,

1. Thesis: *arthâpatti* in general (*pakṣa*) is not a *pramāṇa* (*sādhya*).
2. Reason: because *arthâpatti* has deviation
3. Example: since wherever something has deviation it is not a *pramāṇa*, just like "Where there are not clouds, there is not rain," when *arthâpatti* yields "Where there are clouds, there is rain," when sometimes there are clouds without rain.

However, because the example supporting the illustration is faulty, as Uddyotakara and Vātsyāyana will show next, it does not support the claim about *arthâpatti* in general—what the opponent thinks is a deviation is not.

NS 2.2.5: And the objection that *arthâpatti* is not a *pramāṇa* is because of its deviation.

VĀTSYĀYANA

"Because of its deviation, *arthâpatti* is not a *pramāṇa*." This sentence is an objection. By it, *arthâpatti*'s being a *pramāṇa* is objected to, not its existence. Thus the objection is a deviation. Because of the objection's deviation, it is not a *pramāṇa*. By such an objection, nothing can be objected to. Now you think, among meanings with some specific topic, the variability is about its own specific content. And this (objection's) content is not the existence of the objection.

UDDYOTAKARA

That objection you make, that *arthâpatti* is not a *pramāṇa* because of its having a deviating nature, it, too, is a deviation, because it does not deny the existence (of *arthâpatti*). By this denial, the existence of *arthâpatti* is not denied. How is it not denied? Because a specific *arthâpatti* is denied, but not *arthâpatti* in general. Therefore, because its existence is not denied, there is deviation.

VĀCASPATI

But if, relative to a specific topic, *arthâpatti* is non-deviating, and if the opponent were to point out a deviation after having considered another topic, since the topic which (the opponent supposedly) objects to is *arthâpatti*'s being a *prāmāṇa*, then with regard to the other topic—the existence of *arthâpatti*—after we have considered this topic as an objection, we can say that this objection lacks the nature of a *pramāṇa*. And thus, since the (opponent's) objection is not a *pramāṇa*, it is not true that *arthâpatti* is not a *pramāṇa*. Therefore, it is said, "And the objection that *arthâpatti* is not a *pramāṇa* is because of its deviation."

For it would be an undeviating objection if *arthâpatti*'s being a *pramāṇa* and its existence were denied, but because one is not able to deny *arthâpatti*'s existence, the objection's nature is deviating. For it is not true that whatever is deviating fails to be present everywhere. For instance, in the case of something's being knowable (which is a property of all things), when the reason is that it is eternal, this is a deviation because knowability exists everywhere. "Because a specific *arthâpatti* is denied . . ." (What is denied) is a specific *arthâpatti* being a *pramāṇa*, not the existence of *arthâpatti* in general.

Comments: The discussion under 2.2.5 centers on the question of whether the objection to *arthâpatti* is fallacious in a technical sense known as "deviation" (*anaikāntika*). The definition of deviation, which is a fault in *anumāna*, occurs at NS 1.2.5. When the reason given in an *anumāna* has an "indecisive" or "wavering" (*vyabhicāra*) nature, then there is the fallacy of deviation. A simple example is when someone wishes to conclude that there is fire on a mountain because that mountain has the property of being knowable. She might continue, "Whatever is knowable is fiery." In *anumāna*, a positive and negative example are adduced in support of the general pervasion relationship. While we can give a positive example, such as a match, the reason property or our inferential mark is found also in the negative example: a lake which lacks any fire is still knowable. Since the reason does not support the conclusion, it deviates.

Vācaspati's contribution to this discussion is to make the opponent's assumptions more explicit. They identify a case of purported *arthâpatti* which turns out to not be *arthâpatti*. From this, they conclude that *arthâpatti* is deviating. But just because not all supposed *arthâpatti* instances are *arthâpatti* does not mean that *arthâpatti* itself does not exist. Vācaspati seems to think that the opponent reasons from the absence, in all putative cases, of the property being-an-*arthâpatti* to deviation, and vice versa. But it isn't the case that something which is deviating always fails to be present everywhere (as *arthâpatti* is supposed to, in this case). He cites knowability as a counter-example. Returning to the argument at hand, the point seems to be that even if some cases of *arthâpatti* don't count as *arthâpatti* (and so retracting the defense of that particular case of cause and effect), this is not sufficient to prove deviation. And, as it turns out, the opponent's case of reasoning is itself a case of deviation!

2.2.6: Or assuming the objection is a valid one (a *pramāṇa*), even then it is not the case that *arthâpatti* is not a *pramāṇa*.

VĀTSYĀYANA

Thus we say, then, further, *arthâpatti*'s content is: the presence of a cause does not waver with the production of an effect. And the content is not the property of causes, which is that an effect fails to be produced because of an obstruction in the causal basis.

UDDYOTAKARA

Now you think, "The content of our denial is not its existence, but rather its being a *pramāṇa*. Then this denial, being concerned with its own specific content, is not capable of deviating, because what is called 'deviation' is that which is understood to occur with its own content and others which are similar. And there is nothing deviating about the denial of *arthâpatti*'s nature as a *pramāṇa*. Therefore the objection is not a deviation."

"And the objection that *arthâpatti* is not a *pramāṇa* is because of its deviation (2.2.5)." If you think that deviation occurs with its own content or others which are similar, then *arthâpatti* is not deviating, either, for when there is no cause, an effect's being produced is never observed. That is the meaning of this *sūtra*, to point out an inconsistent statement. What you have said: "because of its own specific content there is no deviation occurring about anything else," and "*arthâpatti* is deviating"—these are inconsistent.

Or (the meaning of *sūtra* 2.2.5 is) ignorance. But, not having understood the workings of non-deviation and deviation, this has been said: "*arthâpatti* is not a *pramāṇa* because of its having a deviating nature." That should be ignored. The statements of an insane person are not able to be set straight.

VĀCASPATI

If the opponent thinks this way, "The denial of *arthâpatti*'s being a *pramāṇa* is not subject to the fallacy of deviation" then (we reply), **"Or assuming the objection is a valid one (a *pramāṇa*), even then it is not the case that *arthâpatti* is not a *pramāṇa*" (NS 2.26).**

Uddyotakara states that the the opponent's denial, whether a misapprehension or non-apprehension, is a clincher (*nigraha-sthāna*)—this is the meaning. Moreover, what the author of the *Commentary on Mīmāṃsā* gives as an example of *arthâpatti* is just *anumāna*: "And, for living Caitra, by observing his absence from his home, there is the positing (*kalpanā*) of his unobserved presence outside."[7] After all, when he is not in one place, he is in another place. Or when something to be proven (*vyāpaka*) is found in one place, he is not in another place. This pervasion relationship is easily understood simply from one's own body. And therefore, the discovery that a living person is outside by means of the mark (*liṅga*) of absence from the house is *anumāna*.

Opponent: But by his being alive, his absence from the house is not able to be refuted, since in virtue of his being alive, his absence from the house is unestablished (*asiddha*) and it would not constitute a reason (*hetu*). Or, by his absence from the house, his being alive is refuted, since in virtue of his absence from the house, his really being alive is unsettled and is not able to independently establish him as being outside. For this is to to say that the mere fact of Caitra's being alive is contradicted (*virudhyate*) due to his absence from the house. Or else, to the extent that he is alive somewhere, there is no contradiction, because not being alive and being in the house do not have the same scope. However, since the place is in common, there is implication (*ākṣepa*) of the house as within the scope (of Caitra's being alive), and therefore there is a contradiction with the same scope.

Reply: No. The refutation is inappropriate, due to doubt about whether we definitely have a *pramāṇa* (about his being alive or not). Further, on the alternative that his being not alive has been definitely ascertained by a *pramāṇa*, that *pramāṇa* does not refute his being in the house. Moreover, it is correct to say that this *pramāṇa* is not able to to reject his being alive or to remove its being doubtful. Since his absence is delimited (*avacchinna*) by the house, his being alive in the house is negated, because of its being contradicted. But the mere fact of his being alive is not negated, because in this case is it is inconclusive.

Therefore, since his absence from the house is established, his being alive somewhere outside is to be inferred—this is the correct position. By this, we have repudiated the content of *arthâpatti* as that content which is understood from the uncontradicted results of two contradictory *pramāṇa*s, since there is no contradiction (*avirodha*) between what is delimited and what is not delimited. Therefore it is established that *arthâpatti* is not a distinct *pramāṇa*, because it is the *pramāṇa* of *anumāna*.

---

[7] This quote is directly from Śabara's *Commentary* on Jaimini's *Mīmāṃsa-sūtra*, although Vācaspati does replace the original "Devadatta" with "Caitra."

COMMENTS: The opponent has earlier objected that *arthâpatti* is not a *pramāṇa* at all, as it does not result in knowledge. The *sūtra* text criticizes the arguments in support of this objection as being fallacious, since they target only some putative cases of *arthâpatti*, not all of them. Uddyotakara, in his comments at this point argues that, even if the opponent's view is not fallacious in the sense of deviation, *arthâpatti* is still a *pramāṇa*. Vācaspati does not rehearse these arguments, but agrees with Uddyotakara in dismissing the skeptical opponent as an ignoramus. He then moves on to a different opponent, the Mīmāṃsaka Śabara. Whether Vācaspati has other Mīmāṃsakas in mind than Śabara is not explicit. By quoting Śabara he could include both Bhāṭṭas and Prābhākaras within his sights. Udayana, in his commentary on the NVTṬ, merely says that the opponent belongs to "old" Mīmāṃsā (*jaran-mīmāṃsā*), adding that Jayanta Bhaṭṭa's *Nyāya-kusumâñjali* explains this topic further.[8] According to Vācaspati, the pervasion relationship in this case, which forms the basis for *anumāna* is:

$$\neg P_1(C) \rightarrow P_2(C)$$

When one place (P_1) is not qualified by Caitra (C), then another place (P_2) is qualified by Caitra's presence (C). Vācaspati observes that this kind of pervasion relationship is one that people know about their own selves—our spatio-temporally limited bodies obviously cannot be in more than one place at a time.

Vācaspati then raises the Mīmāṃsaka's objection, discussed in Kumārila Bhaṭṭa's *Explanation in Verse* 19–25 (see Ollett and Freschi in this volume, p. 152), that the inferential mark for *anumāna* cannot be Caitra's absence from the house. The argument is that, if we know that Caitra is alive, then we cannot establish that Caitra is absent, and so we could not use it as a reason (*hetu*) to ascertain his being outside: "And this is not the case: by his being alive, his absence from the house is able to be refuted (as an inferential mark), since in virtue of his being alive, his absence from the house is unestablished and it would not constitute a reason (*hetu*)." Another potential problem is that, assuming we can demonstrate Caitra's absence, we thereby go too far, showing that possibly he is not alive at all: "Nor is it the case that, by his absence from the house, his being alive is refuted (as an inferential mark), since in virtue of his absence from the house, his really being alive is inconclusive and is not able to independently establish him as being outside." This position is not found in the early Mīmāṃsakas, although Śālikanātha (see Ollett and Freschi in this volume, p. 97) argues that Caitra's being alive is doubted (*sandeha*), or at least amenable to doubt, because of his being absent from the home. However, a doubt or the possibility of one is not yet a contradiction. By the time of Nārāyaṇa Bhaṭṭa's seventeenth-century *Elucidation of Epistemic Instruments and their Objects* (see Keating in this volume, p. 111), the idea of at least partial contradiction or conflict (*virodha*) has been incorporated into Bhāṭṭa Mīmāṃsā objections against Prābhākaras, originating even earlier in Cidānanda's fourteenth-century *Nīti-tattvâvirâbhāva*. Regardless of who originated the point about contradiction, Vācaspati replies by arguing that there

[8] See Thakur (1996: 391).

is no direct contradiction between someone's being not living in one place and their being alive in general, just somewhere else.

The Mīmāṃsaka proponent of a contradiction might wish to argue that, while it is not directly stated, we can understand Caitra's being alive as implicitly involving only his being alive in the house. In that case, there would be a direct contradiction between "Caitra is alive in the house" and "Caitra is absent from the house." But there are two problems with this construal. First, Vācaspati reminds us that the Mīmāṃsaka opponent hasn't admitted that we can know Caitra's absence from the house. Second, even if we do know he is absent, there is nothing that this knowledge can do to confirm or deny whether he is alive. The house acts as a delimitor, or specifier (*avacchinna*), of where Caitra is absent. We can deny Caitra's being alive only within those boundaries. Thus, Vācaspati concludes that *arthâpatti* should be understood as *anumāna*, and we should not understand it as involving contradiction.

REFERENCES

Primary sources

Nyāya-sūtra (Akṣapāda Gautama)

Tarkatirtha, A.M. T. Nyayatarkatirtha, and H. K. Tarkatirtha, eds. (1936–44; reprint 2003: Munshiram Manoharlal), *Nyāyadarśanam*, Calcutta Sanskrit Series 18, Calcutta: Metropolitan Printing and Publishing House.

Thakur, A. ed. (1997), *Gautamīyanyāyadarśana with Bhāṣya of Vātsyāyana*, Nyāyacaturgranthikā, Vol 1, New Delhi: Indian Council of Philosophical Research.

Extensive Commentary on Logic [*Nyāya-bhāṣya*] (Vātsyāyana)

See *Nyāya-sūtra.*

Explanation of the Nyāya System [*Nyāya-vārttika*] (Uddyotakara)

Dvivedī, V. P. and V. P. Dube, eds. (1907), *Nyāyavārttikaṁ by Uddyotakara Miśra, Pāśupatācārya*, Calcutta: Asiatic Society of Bengal.

Thakur, A. ed. (1997), *Nyāyabhāṣyavārttika*, Nyāyacaturgranthikā, Vol. 2, New Delhi: Indian Council of Philosophical Research.

Notes on the Meaning of the Explanation of the Nyāya System [*Nyāya-vārttika-tātparya-ṭīkā*] (Vācaspati)

Thakur, A. ed. (1996), *Nyāyavārttikatātparyaṭīkā of Vācaspati Miśra*, Nyāyacaturgranthikā, Vol. 3, New Delhi: Indian Council of Philosophical Research.

Nyāya-vārttika-tātparya-pariśuddhi (Udayana)

Thakur, A. ed. (1996), *Nyāyavārttikatātparyapariśuddhi of Udayanācārya*, Nyāyacaturgranthikā, Vol. 4, New Delhi: Indian Council of Philosophical Research.

Secondary literature

Jha, G., ed and trans. (1984), *The Nyāya-sūtras of Gautama with the Bhāṣya of Vātsyāyana and the Vārtika of Uddyotakara*, Delhi: Motilal Banarsidass.

CHAPTER SIX

Jayanta Bhaṭṭa's *Flowers of Reasoning*

Translated by ALESSANDRO GRAHELI

Jayanta's discussion of *arthâpatti* occurs in the first chapter of his *Flowers of Reasoning* (*Nyāya-mañjarī*) (NM, I.94–130). The context is his general definition of a genuine source of knowledge, or "epistemic instrument," to use a term conceptually closer to the Sanskrit word *pramāṇa*. In Jayanta's own tradition, Nyāya, four epistemic instruments are accepted, namely perception (*pratyakṣa*), inference (*anumāna*), comparison (*upamāna*), and testimony (*śabda*).[1] Jayanta is now scrutinizing the arguments in favor of other epistemic instruments in addition to the four accepted ones. *Arthâpatti*, accepted by both Bhāṭṭa and Prābhākara authors of the Mīmāṃsā school, is the first among the possible candidates.

As usual, Jayanta systematically treats the topic in a typically well-structured sequence of theses, antitheses, and syntheses. The first two sections contain the Bhāṭṭa defense of two main types of *arthâpatti*: "*arthâpatti* on the basis of what is known," in short "objective *arthâpatti*" (*dṛṣṭârthâpatti*); and "*arthâpatti* on the basis of what is heard," in short "verbal *arthâpatti*" (*śrutârthâpatti*). The third section is the Nyāya reduction of "objective *arthâpatti*" to inference. Within this section, the Prābhākara reasons in favor of *arthâpatti* are also dealt with. The fourth section is the Nyāya reduction to inference of "verbal *arthâpatti*." The fifth section, surprisingly, is the Prābhākara refutation of the Bhāṭṭa "verbal *arthâpatti*," which the Prābhākara considers a feature of language, i.e., of verbal testimony. The sixth section, which wraps up the discussion, concerns poetic meanings, here associated with verbal *arthâpatti* because they are similarly considered implicatures that convey a non-spoken and yet vivid message.

The following pages contain a complete translation of NM, āhnika 1, I.94–130. A paraphrastic English translation of this portion of the NM, without annotations or any detailed analyses and yet insightful and thought-provoking, can be found in Bhattacharyya (1978: 69–102).

---

[1] For practical reasons I'm rendering *anumāna* as "inference," and for consistency purposes I'm translating terms derived from the verbal root *anu-mā-* (*anumeya*, *anumīti*, etc.) on the basis of "to infer." This choice suits the Naiyāyika position well, because *arthâpatti* is indeed subsumed under *anumāna*, as a type of inference. From the Mīmāṃsaka viewpoint, by contrast, here "inference" should be understood as distinct from *arthâpatti*.

Relevant extracts from Cakradhara's scholarly commentary (GBh, 19–34) are provided in the indented comments, where quotes from Jayanta's text are in bold. The text of the printed editions of both the NM and the GBh have been checked and improved in the light of the readings of the important manuscripts, BORI 390 and MDUC 2606.[2]

BHĀṬṬA: OBJECTIVE *ARTHÂPATTI*

Bhāṭṭa authors explain *arthâpatti* as follows:[3] "*arthâpatti* is the hypothesis (*kalpanā*) of an object (*artha*) in the form 'this object, observed or heard, is otherwise incongruous (*anupapanna*).'"

> COMMENTS: This is the formulation as found in ŚBh, ad sūtra 1.1.5, p. 38,1–2. Varadacarya (NM, āhnika 1, I.94) aptly notes that since this is the definition found in the ŚBh, it is actually shared by both the Bhāṭṭas and the Prābhākara, though he continues by anachronistically stating that Jayanta is refuting the view of Pārthasārathi and others. Jayanta, however, here is showing the Bhāṭṭa interpretation of this line, and particularly of the clause "observed or heard."

The observed object is apprehended by means of one among the five epistemic instruments of perception, inference, comparison, *arthâpatti*, and non-apprehension. The heard object is known from a statement, in the form of either the vernacular or the Vedic language. *Arthâpatti* is defined as the hypothesis of an additional entity (the *consequent*) based on the prior knowledge of these two types of otherwise incongruous objects (the *antecedent*).[4]

> COMMENTS: The Bhāṭṭas interpret Śabara's "observed" as "apprehended" (*upalabdha*) by means of any epistemic instrument, and not just "perceived," as the word *dṛṣṭa* would rather suggest.
>
> At first sight the sentence "the heard object is known from a statement, in the form of either the vernacular or the Vedic language" is misleading, because it seems to state that *śruta* is the object known from an utterance, i.e., the *signified*. From the following, however, it is clear that this *śruta* object, in the Bhāṭṭa view, is the completion of an elliptic statement, directly known from the elliptic statement itself, i.e., the missing part of the *signifier*.
>
> In this translation I'm using the two terms "antecedent" and "consequent" to respectively indicate the known fact, the basis of *arthâpatti*, and the hypothetical

[2] A study of the genealogy of the NM can be found in Graheli 2015, chapter 5, where the historical and stemmatic centrality of these manuscripts is researched and justified. For a description of these manuscripts, see Graheli 2015, 38–40, 45–9, 56–9.

[3] NM, I.94,9.

[4] Varadacarya, the editor of NM, glosses *tataḥ* with *śrutād*; Varadacarya understands this last sentence as explaining specifically verbal *arthâpatti*, while I'm interpreting it as a general statement valid for both types of *arthâpatti*. In this regard, there is a crucial textual variant. Varadacarya does not have the *arthād* reading, which is found in BORI 390, 27v3. The complete sentence reads tato'nyathânupapadyamānād arthād arthântara-kalpanā arthâpattiḥ in BORI 390, 27v3, with a stress on *arthāt*, and tato'nyathânupapadyamā nârthāntara-kalpanā arthâpattiḥ in NM, with a stress on *tataḥ*.

object which proves the congruity of the known fact, i.e., the output of *arthâpatti*. This epistemological process thus involves an antecedent (*k*) and an hypothetical consequent (*h*). Following the letter of Jayanta's presentation of the Bhāṭṭa thesis, *h* should be considered the output of the *arthâpatti* (*apannârtha*), i.e., its epistemic object (*prameya*).

As such, since each of these six types of *arthâpatti* is respectively empowered by one of the six epistemic instruments, *arthâpatti* ends up being of six kinds.[5] The verbal *arthâpatti*, however, is separately classified, because even if it shares the property of being based on a known object—which is how the word "observed' is taken here—it is quite distinct from the five types of objective *arthâpatti*: the output of these is an epistemic object (*prameya*), while the peculiar output of this sixth type of *arthâpatti* is an epistemic instrument.[6]

COMMENTS: In the objective *arthâpatti* there is a known fact, e.g., "the living Caitra is not visible," which is incongruous without an hypothetical fact. This hypothetical fact becomes the epistemic object proven by *arthâpatti*. In verbal *arthâpatti*, instead, the incongruous object is an elliptic sentence, while the hypothetical object is the completion of that sentence, which in turn becomes part of the epistemic cause, i.e., part of the complete sentence, which then conveys the sentence meaning.

Perception-based, inference-based, and comparison-based arthâpatti

Of the five types of objective *arthâpatti*, an example of the first, perception-based *arthâpatti*, is the hypothesis of the burning power (*śakti*) of fire, because the fact that fire burns, as known from [tactile] perception, would be otherwise incongruous.

COMMENTS: The observed fact (*k*) is that fire burns; the hypothesis is a burning force inherent in fire (*y*); *y* must be true, because otherwise *k* cannot be explained.

An example of inference-based *arthâpatti* is the hypothesis of the kinetic power of the sun. Its movement is inferred through the inferential mark (*liṅga*) of its changed position in the sky, and such an inferred movement would otherwise be incongruous.

COMMENTS: The inferred fact (*k*) is that the sun has moved. The hypothesis is that the sun has an inherent kinetic power (*y*): *y* must be true, because otherwise *k* cannot be explained.

Arthâpatti based on comparison is the hypothesis of the power of an object, e.g., a particular cow, of resembling the wild animal called "zebu." Without this resembling

---

[5] NM, I.95.

[6] Bhattacharyya (1978: 70) vaguely translates: "Why has the first one been treated separately? Its separate treatment suggests that presumption in this case solves apparent contradictions which is noticed in the matter brought in only by the verbal testimony." The important reason for the distinction, however, is the output of the *arthâpatti*: in one case it is an epistemic object, in the other an epistemic instrument, namely the missing piece of verbal testimony.

capacity, the epistemic output of comparison—a cow is qualified by resemblance in relation to a zebu—would be incongruous.[7]

> COMMENTS: The fact *k*, that is known by comparison, is that a cow resembles a zebu ("comparison" here means the sentence uttered by an expert, "a zebu looks like a cow"). The hypothesis *y* is that a cow has the capacity of resembling a zebu: *y* must be true, because *k* cannot be explained otherwise.

These first three kinds of *arthâpatti* must all be instances of a *sui generis* epistemic instrument, since their epistemic object is an unperceivable power.[8] Since a power is not perceivable, it is not even inferable, because the necessary correlation on which an inference is based requires something perceivable.

> Because the positive and negative correlations (*anvaya-vyatireka*) apply to substances.[9]
> By contrast, the power of substances is intangible, so it cannot be known through these two methods.

As for testimony and comparison, they do not stand a chance to prove the existence of powers. Such powers, therefore, are necessarily known through *arthâpatti*.

> COMMENTS: Here and in the following Jayanta endorses an inference requiring both a positive and negative correlation of the properties of the subject. This type of inference is accepted by every school. Such inferences are based on a necessary relation between two terms, which is learned through the repeated observation of the positive correlation of the property expressed by the probans (*sādhana*) and of the property expressed by the probandum (*sādhya*) in other similar subjects, as well as of the negative correlation of these respective properties in other, dissimilar subjects. Such a repeated observation requires the perceptibility of the subject and of its properties. In the context of *arthâpatti*, the *kevala-vyatirekin* inference, which is purely based on a negative correlation, without a positive correlation, is also relevant. According to Matilal (1998: 117), from Uddyotakara onwards this negative inference is accepted in Nyāya. Jayanta, however, accepts it only because a negative correlation is based on an implicit positive correlation.
>
> With "probandum" I'm here rendering *sādhya*. The probandum, i.e., the thing to be proven, is the property-bearer specified by a property, and not the bare property. As Jayanta explains elsewhere, "the possessor of the inferential mark, a property-bearer specified by a property, is the thing to be proven; not the bare

---

[7] In the text (NM, āhnika 1, I.95,10–11), Varadacharya reverses *gavaya* and *go-piṇḍa*. Since what is qualified by similarity is the cow, however, his emendation is not accepted here. Furthermore, Varadacharya glosses the compound *upamāna-jñānâvagata-go-piṅḍâdi-sārūpya-viśiṣṭa-gavayâdi-prameya-*, explaining the phrase *upamāna-jñānâvagata-* in concordance with *go-piṅḍâdi-sārūpya*. In my version, *upamāna-jñānâvagata-gavaya-sārūpya-viśiṣṭa-go-piṇḍâdi-prameya-*, I rather understand *upamāna-jñānâvagata-* in concordance with *-gavayâdi-prameya-*.

[8] NM, I.96.

[9] Bhattacharyya (1978), among others, renders *anvaya-vyatireka* with "agreement and difference." On the similarity with Mill's method of agreement and difference used to build inductive reasonings, as well as on translating *anvaya* and *vyatireka* with these equivalents, see Matilal (2001: 200).

property-bearer, because property-bearers such as the mountain are already proven, and not even the bare property, because the existence of fire, somewhere in the world, is also already proven."[10]

Arthâpatti-*based* arthâpatti

An example of an *arthâpatti*-based *arthâpatti* (4) is the presumption of the permanence of sound (*śabda*). After postulating the signifying power of a word, through the otherwise incongruous knowledge of the object signified by it, this signifying power would in turn be incongruous without the permanence of that word.[11] We will say more about this *arthâpatti*-based *arthâpatti* in the context of the examination of testimony.

COMMENTS: Jayanta refers to his discussion of postulating the signifying power of words, also called "relation" (*sambandha*), where Jayanta points to the difference between the Bhāṭṭa and Nyāya respective stances. In short, Bhāṭṭa authors argue for three epistemic instruments (*tri-pramāṇakaḥ sambandhaḥ*) to learn a given semantic relation, namely perception, inference, and *arthâpatti*. In Nyāya, instead, perception and inference are considered sufficient (see NM, āhnika 4, I.601,11ff.).

The postulated fact *k* is that a word has the power of signification, without which the observed knowledge of a referent caused by that word would be incongruous; the hypothesis *y* is the permanence of that word: *y* must be true, because otherwise *k* cannot be explained.

Absence-based arthâpatti

An example of the absence-based *arthâpatti* has been provided by the author of the Bhāṣya (ŚBh, ad sūtra 1.1.5, p. 38, 2): "After ascertaining the absence at home of the living Caitra, his presence outside is hypothesized, because this absence of a living Caitra at home would otherwise be incongruous."

COMMENTS: The fact *k* known by non-apprehension (*anupalabdhi* or *abhāva*) is "the living Caitra is absent at home." The hypothesis *y* is that Caitra is present outside: *y* must be true, because otherwise *k* cannot be explained.

OPPONENT: This is just a standard inference: something unperceived is proven by something perceived.[12]

PROPONENT: It is not a standard inference, because it lacks the complete set of inferential conditions (*sāmagrī*). According to the law of logic (*tārkika-sthiti*), inferential knowledge is generated by a specific set of conditions—a property (*dharma*) possessed by a subject (*pakṣa*), etc.—which here is not found.

---

[10] NM, āhnika 2, I.309, 11–310,1: dharma-viśiṣṭo dharmīn sādhyaḥ. sa eva liṅgīti. na dharmi-mātraṃ sādhyam, parvatâdi-dharmiṇaḥ siddhatvāt. na dharma-mātram, agner api yatra tatra siddhatvāt.

[11] For the Nyāya refutation of the permanence of sound, see NM, āhnika 3, I.541ff.

[12] NM, I.97.

COMMENTS: The relation of "possession" between terms has the technical sense of an "occurrence-exacting" relation (*vṛtti-niyamaka*), i.e., it specifies the ontological presence of a property (*dharma*) *on* or *in* another thing, this thing being the subject (*pakṣa*) possessing the property. In the framework of Nyāya ontology, based on the Vaiśeṣika model, such a property does not need to belong to the category "quality," as the word "property' may suggest. In many Nyāya inferences, in fact, the property is ontologically speaking a substance. The crucial aspect is the occurrence-exacting relation of possession.[13]

Arthâpatti *is not an inference, because of the lack of an inferential mark* Let's concede that the probandum *s* is either Caitra qualified by outer presence (*s*1) or the outer presence qualified by Caitra (*s*2). What would then the inferential mark (*liṅga*) be? Would it be Caitra qualified by absence at home (*h*1), or the house qualified by the absence of Caitra (*h*2), or the absence of Caitra in the house (*h*3), or of the non-perception (*adarśana*) of Caitra in the house (*h*4)? None of these meets the requirements to be considered a property of the subject, i.e., of being the inferential mark, because neither the house, Caitra, Caitra's absence, nor Caitra's non-apprehension can be considered a property of either Caitra or his outer presence.

COMMENTS: In *s*1 the property-possessor, i.e., the subject, would be Caitra, and the specifying property (*viśeṣaka dharma*) to be proven would be the outer presence; in *s*2 the property-possessor and property are inverted.

The subject could either be Caitra or the absence. The inferential mark must technically be a property of the subject. The possible candidates are the house, Caitra himself, the absence, the invisibility. But none of these can technically be a property of either Caitra or the absence.

Arthâpatti *is not an inference, because of a circular reasoning*

Moreover, this cannot be an inference also because of the problem of a "circular epistemic object" (*prameyânupraveśa*).[14]

CAKRADHARA COMMENTS:[15] **"Because of the problem of a circular epistemic object."** When it concerns a living being, home-absence is the same as presence-somewhere. This becomes an inferential reason when this home-absence is the property of a property-possessor (namely, Caitra). This home-absence qualified by life cannot possibly exist without outer presence because its existence automatically entails that outer presence. So the circularity of the epistemic object concerns the epistemic object of this inference (the outer presence of the living Caitra), because

---

[13] "Navya-Nyāya logicians define the term 'property' (*dharma*) as the second member (*pratiyogin*) of occurrence-exacting relations which alone are to be denoted by the technical term 'possess' used in inferences. Thus the table *possesses* the book when the book is on the table, and the book is the *property* of the table" (Bhattacharyya 2001: 174). Matilal (2001: 209) proposes a relation of "location" of a "locus" and "locatee" as a solution to the ambiguity generated by the use of the term "property."

[14] Rendered by Bhattacharyya (1978: 73) as "reversal of the order of knowledge."

[15] GBh, 19,6.

it is already apprehended by apprehending the inferential mark: without knowing the inferential object, one cannot know the inferential mark.

First of all, the outer presence of Caitra can be hypothesized because of the absence at the home of Caitra, who is known to be alive from testimony (*āgama*). Otherwise the logical reason would be inconclusive (*anaikāntika*), because it may as well lead to the conclusion that Caitra is dead.

COMMENTS: Without the specification that Caitra is alive, the inferential mark "Caitra's home-absence" may lead not only to the conclusion "Caitra's outer presence," but also to a counter-factual conclusion, "Caitra is dead." The inferential reason would thus be inconclusive. Jayanta cites just testimony (*āgama*) as the evidence for the live status of Caitra. Nonetheless, Bhattacharyya (1978: 72) here translates "From the astrological calculation we learn that Caitra is still alive."

Furthermore, absence may lead to knowledge of the outer presence only after being apprehended, not if it is not yet apprehended, as in the case of an inference of fire from smoke. The apprehension of an absence implies the cessation of the function of other epistemic instruments that may cause the apprehension of present things.[16] Here, however, there is an epistemic instrument that generates knowledge of the living Caitra, because "life" is "presence somewhere." If the epistemic instrument that has caused the apprehension of a present thing has not ceased to operate, how can non-apprehension (*abhāva*) have the freedom to operate? Therefore the epistemic instrument that is now operating must have a distinct epistemic object (*viṣaya*) in the form "his presence outside, but his absence at home." Hence, since the congruity concerns a living being and the apprehension of his absence at home, which is the basis to establish his outer presence, there is a circularity of the epistemic object (*prameyânupraveśa*). In inference, instead, at the time of apprehending an inferential mark such as smoke there is no circularity of the inferential object (*liṅgin*), e.g., fire, which remains just the object of the inference.

COMMENTS: Caitra's living status, i.e., his presence somewhere (s), is already known as the output of testimony, and his absence at home (h) is the output of non-apprehension. An inference using h to infer s begs the question, because s is already known to begin with.

OPPONENT: But why is then this circularity of epistemic objects not a flaw in *arthâpatti*?

PROPONENT: We argue that it is not a flaw. An *arthâpatti* must necessarily take into consideration (*parāmṛśati*) two epistemic objects, in order to enable the absence and presence—conveyed by two distinct epistemic instruments—of a single entity. The reconciliation of these [two epistemic objects] is not possible otherwise.

CAKRADHARA COMMENTS:[17] It "**takes into consideration two epistemic objects,**" the presence and absence related to testimony and non-apprehension, by making

[16] NM, 98.
[17] GBh, 19,12.

> sense of them: the absence is at home, the presence is outside. The reconciliation of these two is not otherwise possible, because there cannot be a convergence of presence and absence in a single entity.

Moreover, the testimonial knowledge "he exists in some unspecified place [i.e., he lives]" has previously occurred;[18] this very knowledge is now accommodated with the knowledge "he is outside" on the basis of the apprehended absence at home.

> *CAKRADHARA* COMMENTS:[19] After showing in this way the operation of *arthâpatti*, in order to show in practice how it culminates in the absence of a restrictive relation, he says, "**Moreover, the testimonial knowledge 'he exists in some unspecified place' has previously occurred.**" But the knowledge "he is outside" must be known through some epistemic instrument, because knowledge of a restricted location does arise. This being the case, even if the outer presence is already entailed when apprehending the absence at home of the living being, still this becomes a distinct epistemic object, because the restriction is previously unknown. The already entailed outer presence culminates in the knowledge of a restriction, "he is outside."

Therefore, because of its distinctive characteristics, *arthâpatti* is not an inference.

> COMMENTS: The circularity of the probandum, which is a flaw in inferential arguments, is the very reason why *arthâpatti* is a distinct epistemic instrument with its special set of conditions that include a preliminary knowledge of the probandum.

Arthâpatti *is not an inference, because a correlation of properties cannot be established* A further reason why *arthâpatti* is not an inference is that the apprehension of the inferential relation is not possible:

> Unlike fire and smoke, presence and absence of something situated in a house and in the outer space cannot simultaneously be known by a single person as being mutually related.
>
> Nonetheless, if the knowledge of their relation is based on this "non-incongruity" (*anyathânupapatti*), then if one wants to call the following process "inference' he may well do so.
>
> *OPPONENT:* Someone standing on the threeshold could grasp this concomitance (*saṅgati*).
>
> *PROPONENT:* But if absence is already ascertained by presence, how could this happen?

> COMMENTS: Here and in the following the discussion concerns the possibility of apprehending an inferential relation between home presence and outer absence

[18] NM, 99.
[19] GBh, 20,1.

> elsewhere, while before the discussion concerned a relation between home absence and outer presence. The presence-absence inversion might be due to an attempt to simplify the problem by starting from a more solid ground, because a presence can be known by perception and does not need the controversial epistemic instrument "non-apprehension" (*abhāva* or *anupalabdhi*).[20]

While the presence of Caitra at home and consequently his non-existence in other locations is known through this "incongruity otherwise" (*anyathânupapatti*), a correlation of properties cannot be apprehended, because of the endless number of possible locations [of the non-existence].[21]

One may argue that this is analogous to the case of smoke ascertained in negative correlation (*vyatireka*) with fire. To this we reply that in such cases the apprehension of negative correlation is not needed, because there is already the apprehension of a positive correlation of smoke and fire. When someone is appeased by the cognition of the probandum (*sādhya*)—made possible by the knowledge of a necessary relation (*niyama*) that is easily apprehended through repeated observation—what is the use of ascertaining the absence of smoke in absence of fire?

In the present situation, by contrast, it was already explained how at the time of apprehending the positive correlation it would be impossible to know the property of the probandum, because such a property would potentially apply to endless locations. One may argue that such an ascertainment could be achieved by non-apprehension (*anupalabdhi*), but this is impossible, because non-apprehension is restricted to a specific location and so it cannot perform the operation of ascertaining the absence of something in a universal ground which excludes the house. One may argue: "I would be able to ascertain this absence by non-apprehension, if I visited all the possible places one by one." Alas, this is also not the case:

> Even if you have checked each of those places, I'm still not sure about Caitra's non-presence:
> might he have reached Kauśāmbī right after your departure?

In sum, for non-omniscient beings such a universal knowledge of absence is impossible, so its ascertainment is a matter of *arthâpatti*.

Opponent: We can ascertain the same epistemic object through inference in the following way: All other places are devoid of Caitra. Because they are distinct (*vyatirikta*) from the place where Caitra is standing, just like the area next to him.

Proponent: This does not work, because your inference is contradicted by this counter-inference: All other places contain Caitra, because they are distinct from the area next to him, just like the place where Caitra stands.

[20] Bhattacharyya (1978: 73) vaguely writes that "In the case of inference the relation of invariable concomitance is grasped by a single means of proof," but his rendition remains obscure because he does not mention *abhāva* and *anupalabdhi*.

[21] NM, I.100.

In conclusion, it is now proven that the body of a sizeable human being, perceived in a given location, can be determined to be absent in all other locations only by means of non-incongruity, through *arthâpatti.*

BHĀṬṬA—VERBAL *ARTHÂPATTI*

From the hanging (*sâkāṅkṣā*) expression "the fat person does not eat at day-time,"[22]
the special knowledge of a part of the sentence is derived. This is called verbal *arthâpatti* (*śrutârthâpatti*).

Upon hearing the elliptic expression the special cognition "eating-at-night" is generated. This cognition is not generated by any other epistemic instrument, because here perception and the other instruments are available (*asannidhānāt*).

Perception cannot convey the cognition of "eating-at-night," which is beyond the reach of the senses (*parokṣa*). Not even inference can provide it, because this "eating-at-night" is known without knowledge of the correlation of properties required in inferences. As for comparison and the others instruments of knowledge, they are out of question here. Therefore the cognition of "eating-at-night' belongs to the domain of verbal testimony.

Verbal arthâpatti *is a necessary aid of testimony*

Here the audible portion of the expression, is not capable of directly conveying the epistemic object "eating-at-night," for three reasons: (1) a single statement cannot convey two distinct meanings in the forms of an assertion (*vidhi*), namely "he eats," and a negation (*niṣedha*), "he does not eat"; (2) the words "night," etc., are not expressed; (3) the sentence meaning cannot possibly include the meaning of absent word-meanings.

Furthermore, from the referents denoted by the audible sentence "He does not eat at day" one cannot derive the meaning "eating-at-night" by assuming that a sentence meaning is an exclusion (*bheda*) from other referents or a mutual specification (*saṃsarga*).

COMMENTS: This last statement is criptic. I'm reading it in the light of Cakradhara's comment.[23] Here *bheda* refers to the idea that every verbal action (*kriyā*) implies all the complements (*kāraka*), and every complement implies every action, and yet, when connected, they mutually exclude every meaning but one. Cakradhara thus seems to intend *bheda* as a sort of exclusion (*vyavṛtti* or *vyatireka*), though it should not be associated with the Buddhist's *apoha* theory. By "association" Cakradhara understands the theory that the sentence meaning consists of the mutual relation of mutually expecting referents. This method of exclusion (*bheda*) is used to describe the process of language acquisition, e.g., apprehending the meaning of "cow" and "bring" by observing the usage of "Bring the cow!," "Tie

---

[22] NM, I.101.

[23] GBh, 20,10.

the cow!," "Bring the horse!," "Tie the horse!," etc. The method of *saṃsarga* evokes the *abhihitânvayavāda* theory, by which the sentence meaning is obtained through the connection of the individual word-referents.

Incidentally, here Cakradhara also points to the one-to-one correspondence between the reality of the external world and the *kāraka* theory of the grammarians, so perhaps *bheda* and *saṃsarga* are just synonyms of the grammarians' *anvaya* and *vyatireka*.

According to Varadacharya, here *bheda* means a particular (*viśeṣa* or *vyakti*). The reflection on *bheda* and *saṃsarga* reminds one of Saussure's discussion of associative and syntagmatic relationships (Bally and Sechehaye 1999: 149):

Therefore, the cognition "eating-at-night' is caused by a hypothetized verbal expression (*āgama*).[24]
The epistemic instrument behind this hypothetical sentence, however, needs to be thoroughly reflected upon.

The unspoken meaning cannot be known from the other sources of knowledge

It cannot be perception, which does not have the power to reach an unmanifested sound.
It is not an inferential mark, because the sentence meaning is ascertained even without apprehending a correlation of properties,
and in some cases, when the expression is invariably unperceivable, the apprehension of a correlation is anyway hardly tenable,
in which cases an injunction (*śruti*) of an applicative type (*viniyoga*) is presumed on the basis of the context (*prakaraṇa*), etc.

COMMENTS: While one might argue for an inductive relation build on the basis of the observation of concomitant states of affairs in the case of common language, in the case of Vedic language the epistemic object is said to be *dharma*, duty, which is by definition beyond the reach of senses.

The *viniyoga* injunction, which is applied according to the hermeneutic criteria of context, etc., is universally accepted by Mīmāṃsākas (*vākyârtha-vit*). As it was stated (TV, 3.3.7.14), "everyone endorses the applicative injunction."

COMMENTS: This passage evokes the six main exegetic principles adopted in Pūrvamīmāṃsā (for further details, see TV, 3.3.7.14): (1) *śruti* (literal assertion); (2) *liṅga* (indication); (3) *vākya* (syntactical relation within the sentence); (4) *prakaraṇa* (extra-sentential context); (5) *sthāna* (hierarchical position or proximity of the statement); (6) *samākhya* (etymological interpretation of a word). These are applied in a descending order of priority (śruti-liṅga-vākya-prakaraṇa-sthāna-samākhyānāṃ samavāye pāradaurbalyam artha-viprakarṣāt).

Since this applicative injunction is invariably unperceivable, its correlation (*pratibandha*) with an inferential mark cannot possibly be apprehended.

---

[24] NM, I.102.

Moreover, the presence of the phrase "eats at night' cannot be inferred. If such a presence is inferred on the basis of a logical reason (*hetu*) qualified by both presence and absence, then it is a flawed reason (*hetvābhāsa*), due to the fallacies of being unfounded (*asiddha*), self-defeating (*viruddha*), and inconclusive (*anaikāntika*).

> COMMENTS: This section addresses the potential objection of a syllogism in the form "The sentence 'he does not eat at day' possesses the words 'he eats at night,' because it possesses the meaning 'eating-at-night.'" The logical reason is flawed, because the subject or property-possessor (the sentence) would contain both an absence (non-eating) and its contrary (eating).

And here a property-possessor (*dharmin*) such as the fire-possessing hill, a necessary ingredient of inferences, is not perceived.

> COMMENTS: What is not perceived is the part of the sentence containing the words "eating at night."

Neither the expression "he does not eat at day," nor its meaning, can become the inferential mark leading to the expression "he eats at night."[25]

> Because, if the expression "he eats at night" is not heard, how can its status of property of the subject (*tad-dharmatā*) be apprehended?
> And if by contrast it is heard, then what is the purpose of reckoning it as a property of a subject?

The referents of the individual words of the expression "fat Devadatta does not eat at day" may serve as an inferential mark, but they cannot convey the knowledge of the expression "he eats at night" through incongruity. This is because the referent of a word, which is typically a generality (*sāmānya*), may be incongruous without the specificity (*viśeṣa*) of the sentence meaning, and not because of the absence of a part of the expression.

> COMMENTS: The referents of the individual words of the spoken part of the sentence are known, so they could serve as an inferential mark. Such referents, however, are by definitions universals, and not particulars, because a particular can be denoted only by a complete sentence and not by an individual word. This argument evokes the Mīmāṃsaka tenet "words refer to universals, sentences to particulars" (*sāmānye hi padaṃ pravartate, viśeṣe vākyam*, see ŚBh, ad sūtra 1.1.24).

In sum, an elliptic expression that as such is not achieving the fulfillment of its operation (*vyāpāra*) of generating a knowledge exempt from expectancy (*ākāṅkṣā*) entails its missing part. This is the process of verbal *arthâpatti*, whose cognitive content is the completing part of the epistemic instrument (i.e., of verbal testimony).

An unknown meaning cannot be inferred from a known one

[OPPONENT] Why is the additional meaning not directly hypothesized (*parikalpyate*) on the basis of the available one?[26]

---

[25] NM, I.103.
[26] NM, I.104.

COMMENTS: This argument invokes a principle of economy. The hypothesis of the phrase missing in the elliptic statement is an additional and superfluous step, because one can directly guess the meaning of the missing referents from the referents of the spoken part, and thus grasp the complete state of affairs.

Fatness is considered the effect of eating, so once perceived it may directly prove its cause, i.e., the act of eating, just as it happens with smoke as the effect of fire. What is denied by the expression "he does not eat" in relation to a specific time (at day) becomes the specific content of the statement in relation to another specific time (at night). What would be the need of inferring an expression (*vacanânumānena*)? Furthermore, this expression does not have an unperceivable meaning, but rather a meaning that leads to another meaning. There would be no flaw in the direct *arthâpatti* of this second meaning (*sākṣād arthasya kalpyamānasya*), unlike with this intermediate step [of postulating a completing expression].

COMMENTS: I understand this passage as suggesting the option of an *arthâpatti* from meaning to meaning, rather than from meaning to expression and back to meaning. And then an *arthâpatti* from meaning to meaning could easily be reduced to an inference, from the effect to the cause. Thus the ambiguous use of *parikalpyate*, *vacanânumānena*, and *kalpyamānasya arthasya* in the same context.

PROPONENT We say:

Child, you are not experienced in the hermeneutics of language.
This [elliptic statement "fat Devadatta does not eat at day time"] generates a cognition of expectancy (*ākāṅkṣā*), so it cannot be an epistemic instrument.
The knowledge generated by perception, etc., may satisfactorily cover even a part of the presented object.
Knowledge from words, instead, does not work like this, because even if the object conveyed by sentence is there, complete with all its parts,
the operation of a sentence is not completed before the cognition of its sentence meaning is acquired.
Speech achieves its status of epistemic instrument only when it conveys such a cognition.
And a sentence is truly considered a sentence only when it conveys its meaning.

COMMENTS: The last line reads *tad-artha-vācakatvāc ca tad vākyaṃ vākyam iṣyate*. The anaphora of *tad* in *tad-vākya* and *tad-artha* could be *prāmāṇya* from the previous line. Unlike in Nyāya, the Bhāṭṭas may call "pramāṇa" both *śabda* and the knowledge of its *artha*. Or, as I understand it, this hemistich shows the correspondence among complete sentences and complete sentence meanings.

Hence, upon hearing an incomplete expression, this must be completed by an hypothetical clause.[27]
Without this preliminary completion, how can there be any knowledge?

[27] NM, I.105.

In general, in relation to injunctions that teach what ought to be done (*kārya*), the Veda is supplemented by verbal *arthâpatti*.
If in those cases the epistemic object (i.e., *dharma*) were directly hypothesized, it would not anymore be the epistemic object of the Veda.

COMMENTS: In order to be the *artha* taught by a Vedic statement, this *artha* must be the meaning of the Vedic statement, not something hypothesized from the observation of objects and on the basis of other epistemic instruments which are not *śabda*, i.e., chiefly the Veda itself in Mīmāṃsā epistemology. The role of the Veda is to teach *dharma*, an unperceivable object. Although the stock example of verbal *arthâpatti* is the lay sentence "Fat Devadatta ...," the main reason for upholding this epistemic instrument is the exegesis of elliptic or apparently contradictory Vedic injunctions.

By *arthâpatti* the injunction of the Eight-day ritual is completed by the invocations (*mantras*), which function as indicators of the purpose (*liṅga*).

COMMENTS: The "Eight-day ritual" (*aṣṭakā*) is a worship to progenitors (*śraddha*), prescribed on the eighth day after the full moon. Further details can be found in MNP, 395. The *liṅga* is the second of the six hermeneutic principles (*pramāṇa*), weaker than the literal meaning (*śruti*), but stronger than the others.

By *arthâpatti* the applicative injunction (*viniyoga-vidhi*) is hypothesized by the indication of purpose (*liṅga*), etc.
By *arthâpatti* the qualification (*adhikāra*) to perform the All-conquering (*viśvajit*) sacrifice is hypothesized on the basis of the duty literally expressed by the injunction.

COMMENTS: The All-conquering ritual is discussed in ŚBh, ad sūtra 4.3.10ff. MNP, 84 writes: "The Mīmāṃsā tradition itself seems doubtful as to what is meant by this rite ..." The point of its reference in this passage of the NM is that the injunction is "One shall sacrifice with the *viśvajit*," but no aim of this sacrifice is directly mentioned, so one must understand it as "One who desires heaven shall sacrifice with the *viśvajit*." The part "who desires heaven" is supplied through verbal *arthâpatti*. The qualification reflects the eligibility to achieve the expected result indicated by the injunction. Cf. MNP, 295, s.v. *viśvajin-nyāya*, "the rule of the *viśvajit* (that when no fruit is assigned to a rite, it shall be understood as heaven)."

By *arthâpatti* the originative injunction (*utpatti-vidhi*) is hypothesized on the basis of the prescription of the qualification (*adhikāra-vidhi*), as in the case of offering to the sun (*Śaurya*).[28]
By *arthâpatti*, in the case of the modification (*vikṛti*) of the offerings to Indra and Agni, from the teaching of the bare duty (*kārya*),[29] its archetypical nature (*prakṛti*) is hypothesized as the end of the injunction (*vidhyanta*).

[28] On the Śaurya rite, cf. MNP, 115.
[29] NM, I.106.

COMMENTS: The procedure (*iti-kartavyatā*) dictates a certain order in the performance of the rite. This order can be altered by stronger principles, such as the hiererchy of predominance (*pradhāna*) of different parts of a rite (see MNP, 126). Accordingly, the end of the injunction is dictated by the stronger principle and not by the weaker one.[30]

Here CAKRADHARA COMMENTS:[31] The end of the injunction is the procedure of the ritual (*vidhyanta iti-kartavyatā*).

In all these cases *arthâpatti* is the first step. Since it is impossible to apprehend an inferential relation,
for the sake of such exegetical operations this verbal *arthâpatti* stands undisputed.
Along with the literal expression, the complete injunction can be postulated by it.
In the theory that the epistemic object is directly postulated from another object, instead, the resulting cognition would not anymore be purely Vedic.
The conclusion is that *arthâpatti*, as explained here, is rightly included in the six epistemic instruments.

NYĀYA—OBJECTIVE *ARTHÂPATTI* IS INFERENCE

If analyzed in this way, *arthâpatti* is not distinct from inference.

Without a relation (*pratibandha*) an entity cannot cause knowledge of another entity.
It is not the case that something is known after knowing any [unrelated] thing.[32]
And even when a real relation is there, it is not a cause of knowledge until it remains unknown.[33]
Such a knowledge of a relation does not occur to newborn babies.

COMMENTS: It is not innate and needs to be learned. This last line may be directed to the notion of "automatic entailment" *ākṣepa*, to which Mīmāṃsakas often resort.

Whenever knowledge of an inferential relation among particulars is not feasible,
there is the possibility of apprehending it in a general form.

COMMENTS: In this introduction of the Nyāya reduction of *arthâpatti* to standard inference, four reasons are adduced by Jayanta: (1) *arthâpatti* cannot function without an established relation, because otherwise anything could cause

---

[30] Further details about these rituals can be found in Bhattacharyya (1978: 78–9).
[31] GBh, 23, 4.
[32] Bhattacharyya (1978: 79) reads the opposite: "No person can know another object on the basis of the knowledge of an object."
[33] NM, I.107.

> knowledge of everything; (2) the relation must be known *a priori*; (3) knowledge of the relation is not innate; and (4) knowledge of a relation between universals is acceptable.

Moreover, *arthâpatti* is said to be an hypothesis in the form "without that, this is incongruous." The very expression "without that, this is incongruous," however, is nothing but the formulation of a negative correlation, and a known negative correlation automatically entails a positive correlation in the form "with that, this is congruous." This positive correlation and negative correlation constitute the very characteristic of an efficient inferential mark, so why would such an *arthâpatti* not be an inference?

In this book we will later explain how an inferential reason characterized by a mere negative correlation is inferentially valid due to its roots in a positive correlation.[34]

Powers are fictional, so the first three types of arthâpatti *are unsound*

As for the three types of *arthâpatti* based on the output of perception, inference, and comparison, which were exemplified as hypotheses of a power, they all lack a cognitive foundation, because these hypothetical and unperceivable powers do not even exist.

> An effect originating from a natural cause (*svarūpa*) enriched by an assisting cause (*saha-kārin*),
> does not justify the hypothesis of an additional, unperceivable power.

> COMMENTS: In the present section the argumentation is based on the metaphysics of Nyāya-Vaiśeṣika, in which six categories are accepted as real and existent: substance, quality, action, universal, particular, inherence (*dravya-guṇa-karma-sāmānya-viśeṣa-samavāya*). Powers are not accepted as a category in this ontology. The essential form (*svarūpa*) is the property (*dharma*) of being one of these categories. Also relevant here is the Nyāya-Vaiśeṣika theory of causation. Jayanta explains causation in terms of a complex of causes, or causal apparatus (*sāmagrī*). What people call "causal power" is nothing but the combined operation (*sannidhāna*) of a substantial cause and other assisting factors (*saha-kārin*). These primary and the assisting factors are all necessary causes, and none is a sufficient cause.[35]

[34] Cf. NM, āhnika 10, II.567,13–568,3, where Jayanta does leaves open the question about the legitimacy of an inference based purely on negative correlation (*kevala-vyatireki anumāna*) (568,19): *ayathā-bhāṣyam api vyākhyānaṃ śreyaḥ*.

[35] A discussion on the concept of the "complex of causes," can be found in NM, āhnika 1, I.35–6: kārakāṇāṃ dharmaḥ sāmagrī, sāmagrī hi saṃhatiḥ.

Objection: without power, a cause is not a cause

OPPONENT: Without a power, a causal factor (*kāraka*) would not be a causal factor. (1) Someone intending to cut a tree, for instance, might as well use his shoe instead of an axe, because if a specific power is not contemplated any effect could in principle be generated by any cause, since the causal nature (*svarūpa*) of a substance (*dravya*) is not specific.[36]

(2) Furthermore,[37] if the power of poison or fire in relation to their respective effects—death or combustion—is not accepted, how can one explain their inefficiency, which is observed when their power is blocked by a magic formula (*mantra*) even while they are still recognized in their unchanged form? The contiguity of the main cause (*svarūpa*) and the possible assisting causes is not prevented by the magic formula, since that contiguity is still observed. Rather, if what is blocked by the magic formula is the power, even the presence of the primary and assisting causes along with the non-production of the effect can be explained.

> COMMENTS: Even without assuming the magic power of incantations to prevent death by poison and burning by fire, one may replace *mantra* with antidotes or fire-retardants, or anything curbing the expected effect of a causal factor. The argument remains the same. In the causal process the primary cause (*svarūpa*) is fire or poison, the effect is burning or death, the assisting causes (*saha-kārin*) are dry wood or a snake bite, and so on. When the magic formula is uttered, the fire, dry wood, poison, snake bite, etc., are still present, and yet the effect is not anymore generated. This argument prevents the Naiyāyika rebuttal, which coincides with Jayanta's own view, that what we call "causal power" is nothing but the combined operation (*sannidhāna*) of multiple factors.

(3) Moreover, even you people have postulated different sorts of unperceivable factors such as moral merit (*dharma*), etc., to explain the diversity of effects [observed in different people] even under the condition of the analogous devotional activities, cultural factors, and so on. Likewise, you may as well accept the existence of unperceivable powers.

> COMMENTS: In the metaphysics of Nyāya and Vaiśeṣika there are several imperceptible entities that are accepted as existent and real. One of these is moral merit, which is listed as one of the qualities of the self. Varadacarya (NM, āhnika 1, I.108fn) provides a different explanation: "As you accept moral merit in conscious beings, you should accept some force leading to effects also in inert things, otherwise you cannot consistently prove merit and its absence."

Reply: a theory of causation does not need postulated powers

PROPONENT: All this is inconsequential. To your argument (1) that without a power there would not be any restriction in the usage of causal factors, we answer as follows.

---

[36] NM, I.108.

[37] Here the sentence begins with *tathā hi*, "This is because," in a continuation of the previous sentence. I'm reading instead *api ca*, with the support of BORI 390 and MDUC 2606, thus beginning a new topic.

We do not need to concoct new causal relations among entities.[38] In practice we act and communicate (*vyava-hṛ-*) according to experience. It is certainly not the case that water mitigates cold, or fire thirst, just because we wish that. In the case of your example, we ascertain the causal efficiency of an axe in relation to the cutting effect on the basis of positive and negative correlations, or by observing the linguistic usage of senior speakers. Therefore, when we want to achieve that result we implement just that specific tool, not shoes or other things.

> COMMENTS: The argument is that whenever we use a tool to generate an effect, we do it either because we have direct experience of its usage, or because we have been told of its efficiency. There is no reason to postulate an invisible power to explain the reason why we use an axe, rather than a shoe, to chop wood. This is also the gist of Varadacarya's gloss in NM, āhnika 1, I.109.

Furthermore, even in the presence of the substance "axe," the effect may still not be generated, because some assisting causes are also required along with the substantial form of the axe, and because the presence of assisting causes is never a sufficient condition.

As for your argument (3) about merit, demerit, etc., these belong to the class of assisting causes, so since the production of the effect requires these assisting causes, how could this effect be invariably produced? Since the diversity of effects in this world is based on merit, demerit, etc., their assumption cannot be avoided. Their imperceptibility is not due to the fact that they are powers; their invisible character is their substantial form, akin to other metaphysical entities such as the internal sense (*manas*) and the atom (*paramâṇu*).

As for your argument (2) about the absence of the effect of poison or fire when a magic formula is used, this phenomenon is not the consequence of an inhibition of a power, but rather of the intervention of a different apparatus of causes.[39]

OPPONENT: What is then the effect of the intervening magic formula?

PROPONENT: There is no effect, except that a different causal apparatus is enabled. In fact, the causes of specific effects are the specific causal apparatuses. You may argue that the essential cause (*svarūpa*) is the only reason for this specification, but then why would poison not be harmful even when not ingested? If you object that contact and other conditions are also required for its effect, then let's consider the absence of the magic formula as an additional condition: the intervening magic formula inhibits the effect of poison or fire just like moral merit (*dharma*) does at the time of undergoing an ordeal (*divya-karaṇa*).

Besides, even conceding the thesis of a power, what would the operation performed by the magic formula exactly be? A magic formula would either destroy the power or inhibit it. As for the first option, there can certainly be no destruction of the power, because once the magic formula has gone the effect reappears. If we

[38] NM, I.109.
[39] NM, I.110.

consider it as a inhibition of the power, it may as well be an impediment of the substance.[40]

What would this inhibiting factor do, respectively, to the essential cause (*svarūpa*) and to the power? If you argue that the inhibition is a detachment from the effect, this explanation suits both our positions. If you argue that the detachment from the effect is only of the substance, because this is what remains visible, then even the power persists, because it can still be inferred through the perception of its effect.[41]

> COMMENTS: The "detachment" explanation implies that the antidote switches off either the substance, according to the Naiyāyika thesis, or the power, according to the Mīmāṃsaka. If they are just detached, it means that the antidote does not destroy them. They continue to exist. Therefore, Jayanta argues, the power postulated by the Mīmāṃsaka should be considered a permanent feature.

Once the power is accepted it should either be considered a permanent category with its own essential form (*svarūpa*), or a contingent product. If it is considered as permanent, then it follows that its effect must permanently be generated. If to avoid this undesirable consequence one specifies that certain assisting conditions are also required, then why not just accept the essential form with the same assisting conditions? What does the power contribute? By contrast, if the power is considered a product, then it must be either an effect of the essential form, i.e., of a category such as a substance, or an effect of a causal apparatus, which includes other assisting conditions.[42]

If it is the effect of the essential form, then there is again the unwanted consequence (*prasaṅga*) of a permanent production of the effect, because since the essential form is permanent its power would be permanently effective. By contrast, if the power is considered the effect of the causal apparatus, then why not say that instead of the effect of a power there is an effect of the causal apparatus? What is the advantage of this intermediate causal power?

> COMMENTS: If the burning power is the effect of the causal apparatus, and combustion is an effect of this power, then we do not need the power to explain the phenomenon. It is more economical to say that burning is the effect of the causal apparatus, without the intermediation of an unseen and hypothetical power.

You may argue that an effect cannot be produced when the causal factor is not empowered. To this we reply that since your power is also an effect there is the consequence of an infinite regress (*anavasthā*), because you need to hypothesize a further power needed to account for the production of this last one.

---

[40] NM, I.111.

[41] Here I'm adopting the reading of BORI 390, 32v16, *svarūpasyaiva, dṛśyamānatvād iti cet*, "If one argues that [the detachment from the effect] belongs only to the substance, because this is what one directly perceives ..." The other witnesses read instead *svarūpam asty eva, dṛśyamānatvād iti cet*, with a subtle change in the argumentative structure.

[42] NM, I.112.

Opponent: We say: The purpose of the hypothesis of an unseen entity is to prove what is seen, not to falsify it. With the hypothesis of a second-degree power the resulting chain of powers weakens the role of the causal factors. Therefore only a single power shall be hypothesized. Then why the infinite regress?

Proponent: We reply: If without an unseen entity what is seen cannot be explained, then indeed something unseen may be hypothesized. But when the production of this entity can be explained even otherwise, why the hypothesis of a power? As shown, this alternative explanation is there. And if something unseen must be hypothesized, then let's do it in a way not vulnerable to charges of an infinite regress, as it is done with moral merit.[43]

> Comments: In the Nyāya-Vaiśeṣika ontology endorsed by Jayanta, "moral merit" (*dharma*) is listed as one of the twenty-four qualities (*guṇa*s), and "quality" in turn is one of the six foundational categories of the system.

Moreover, you Mīmāṃsakas argue in favor of a second unseen factor, besides power (*śakti*), namely "activity' (*vyāpāra*). Since the hypothesis of one of them would be sufficient to explain the production of the effect, why do you load your theory with a double hypothesis? If you argue that a causal factor that has a power but is not active is not a causal factor, then how do we know that it has power to begin with? If you argue that we may know that this causal factor is empowered by observing the effect, then why not say that the effect is simply realized through the activity? If you argue that when a shoe, even if active (when used in the futile attempt of cutting), does not yield the effect of cutting the tree, we reply that such an activity would then be perceivable, not unperceivable, because you would know of the presence of the activity (the shoe hitting wood) even before observing the effect (the cut wood). If the activity is the object of an inference from the effect, then it cannot be known without the effect. And even if the effect is consistent with the hypothesis of one among power and activity, this definitely does not justify the hypothesis of both.[44]

But let's now return to the main topic. Our conclusion is that since an unperceivable power does not exist, the above-listed three types of *arthâpatti* are actually devoid of an epistemic content.

> Comments: This ends the long digression on the fictional nature of powers, which was likely the orthodox Nyāya stance in Jayanta's time. In the following, however, Jayanta concedes the possibility of an existence of powers, but argues that they can be established by inference, without the need of the additional epistemic instrument called *arthâpatti*. After all, *śakti* is a key concept in his own theory of meaning, which is based on the existence of two semantic powers of words, "referentiality" (*abhidhātrī śakti*) and "intentionality" (*tātparya-śakti*).

Or, even if an imperceptible power exists, it is simply the cognitive content of a standard inference, because the relation of pervasion (*vyāpti*) can be apprehended

---

[43] NM, I.113.

[44] NM, I.114.

from the necessary relation of an effect with a cause, and because this causality cannot be attributed to the bare essential form. This surplus is the power.

COMMENTS: The suggested inference of a power seems to involve three arguments: (1) the cutting of the tree has a cause, because it is an effect (pādapa-cchedasya kārana-pūrvakatvam, kāryatvāt. yatra kāryatvam tatra kāraṇa-pūrvakatvam); (2) the axe does not bring forth the effect, because it is the substantial cause (paraśv-ādeḥ kāryânirvahaṇatvam, svarūpa-mātrāt. yatra svarūpa-mātram tatra kāraṇânirvahaṇatvam); (3) the effect is caused by something more than the substantial form, because on its own the bare substance does not produce its effect (svarūpa-mātrâdhika-kārya-nirvahaṇatvam, svarūpa-mātrânirvahaṇatvāt. yatra svarūpa-mātrânirvahaṇatvam tatra svarūpâdhika-nirvahaṇatvam). This "something more" is the power.

Arthâpatti-*based* arthâpatti

As for the *arthâpatti* advanced [by Mīmāṃsakas] as a proof of the permanence of sound (*śabda*),
we will offer our solution in the occasion of the examination of testimony.

COMMENTS: The example of *arthâpatti*-based *arthâpatti*s relates to the permanence of sound, which is the topic of a large part of NM 3 (NM, āhnika 1, I.513–72). The refutation of *arthâpatti* to prove the permanence of words is dealt with in NM, āhnika 1, I.541. In brief, the Mīmāṃsaka contention is that there is a regularity in every listener's understanding of the same meanings (*darśanasya parārthatvāt*) from their respective linguistic sounds, and that this regularity is incongruous without the hypothesis of the stability and regularity of these sounds. Jayanta replies that this regularity is congruous even if sound is considered impermanent, because each linguistic sound is a particular belonging to a class, or universal, such as g-ness, etc.[45]

Reduction of absence-based arthâpatti *to inference*

The correct inference The *arthâpatti* based on absence, however, is nothing but inference, because the outer presence of a living being can be inferred through the absence at home, which is the inferential mark.

COMMENTS: Here BORI 390 reads *abhāva-pūrvikā tu* ... while the other witnesses have *abhāva-pūrvikâpi*. The variant reading is just a single syllable, but while the former reading, which I'm adopting, suggests a partial concession to the Bhāṭṭa position, the latter indicates the more assertive Nyāya stance.

In the prima facie inference refuted by Mīmāṃsakas, the property-possessor (*dharmin* or *pakṣa*) would be the living Caitra: *jīvato caitrasya bahir-bhāvaḥ*.

[45] NM, āhnika 1, I.552,13: gatvâdibhir jātibhir evârtha-sampratyayôpapatteḥ yad-uktaṃ darśanasya parârthatvād ity etad ayuktam.

The subject is Caitra's "home-absence." The probandum is "property-possessor of outside-presence" (P). The inferential reason is "because it possesses home-absence-ness of a living human being" (S). The example is "as in previously experienced such absences at home."[46]

This argument is similar to the one in which smoke is the property-possessor, "possessing fire" is the probandum, and the logical reason is "because it has smokeness," like previously observed cases of smoke.

> COMMENTS: This same inference, not to be confused with the commonly found inference of fire from smoke, is also used by Jayanta in NM, āhnika 3, I.405,11–406,3, during his refutation of the Buddhist's reduction of testimony to inference (Graheli 2017, 203): *dhūmo vahnimān, dhūmatvāt*. Analogously, here "home-absence" is the subject and "home-absence-ness" is the inferential mark.

Hence your arguments denying the status of inferential mark (*liṅga*) to the house, etc., are just attempts to blur the picture.

About the circularity of the epistemic object As for your criticism of a "circular probandum" (*prameyânupraveśa*), this is not a sound argument. In your opinion, what exactly would the epistemic object of *arthâpatti* be? The unspecified existence (*sattā*) of a living being? Or rather an existing thing (*sattva*) qualified by an outer location? If you mean the epistemic object to be the bare existence of a living being, this is already known from testimony.

> COMMENTS: From testimony, according to Varadacarya (NM, I.115), means either from astrological sources, or from a reliable speaker. Also Bhattacharyya (1978: 86) here translates *āgama* with "astrological science," probably from Varadacarya's note. But in fact none of the early authors mentions astrology in relation to *arthâpatti*.

So there is no basis for considering this the epistemic object of another instrument of knowledge. As for an existing entity specified by the outer location, it is indeed the epistemic object. At this point, however, why would there be a circularity (*anupraveśa*) of this epistemic object? The epistemic instrument that produces knowledge of the home-absence does exclude the possibility of another epistemic instrument that grasps something present at home, but it does not concern what exists or does not exist outside.

> COMMENTS: In Nyāya this home-absence would be the epistemic object of perception, and in Bhāṭṭa Mīmāṃsā that of non-apprehension (*abhāva* or *anupalabdhi*). Outside-presence would be the epistemic object of inference or *arthâpatti*, which is a second and separate cognitive act. The *prameyânupraveśa* describes the circularity of epistemic objects known at the same time, involved in the same act of cognition. The gist here is that the cognition of a living being's home-absence (the epistemic object of perception) would be in conflict with his home-presence, not with his outside-presence (the epistemic object of testimony).

---

[46] NM, I.115.

Of a dead one or alive? Far away or in the backyard?
No specificity is yet known, while perceiving this home-absence.

This home-absence becomes an inferential mark when it is apprehended with the qualification "of a living being," because the defect of ambiguity (*vyabhicāra*) is then avoided.[47] And the apprehension of a qualifier is not the apprehension of the epistemic object. One thing is the living status, another is the epistemic object that we are calling "outside-presence."

Opponent: The cognition "outside-presence" is nothing but the cognition "home-absence qualified by life."

Proponent: It is not so, because the cognition "outside-presence" *is caused* by the cognition "home-absence qualified by a living status." It is not the case that this cognition is itself the cognition of "outside-presence." For instance, it is not the case that the cognition of smoke in the subject of fire is itself the cognition of fire.

> Comments: In the inference "the hill possesses fire, because it possesses smoke," the cognition "hill possesses smoke" is not identical to the cognition "fire," but rather the former is the cause of the latter. Similarly, in the inference "Caitra's home-absence possesses a living being's outside-presence, because it possesses a living being's home-absence," the inferential object is not the same as the inferential reason. Otherwise it would be a blatant case of begging the question, and indeed a *prameyânupraveśa*.

Opponent: But fire is a different entity than smoke [while the living Caitra is the same subject, whether present or absent].

Proponent: Also here "outside-presence' is clearly different from both "home-absence" and "living status." Since the hill and fire are already proven, the new (*apūrva*) epistemic object of the exemplified inference is their relation of possessorship. Similarly, even here the new object of inference is simply the connection to the outer space.

> Comments: The possessor (*tadvān*) is the Caitra's home-absence, and the probandum, i.e., the epistemic object of the inference, is the outside-presence possessed by the home-absence. Cf. the sentence at the beginning of the paragraph, *caitrasya gṛhâbhāvo bahir-bhāvena tadvān, jīvan-manuṣya-gṛhâbhāvatvāt.*

If instead you do not accept this additional epistemic object, then your *arthâpatti* is futile, because both the home-absence and the living status are already ascertained through their respective epistemic instruments.

> Comments: The home-absence would be known through perception (Nyāya) or non-apprehension (Mīmāṃsā), and the living status by testimony. There would be no need of *arthâpatti* to ascertain these two facts.

---

[47] NM, I.116.

Therefore the flaw of circularity of the epistemic object is not there, because the inference has a distinct epistemic object, unknown at the time of knowing the first one.[48]

Moreover, this flaw would apply to *arthâpatti* as well, because even *arthâpatti* is considered a hypothesis of an object on the basis of another object. This is exactly what was committed into writing (by Śabara, ŚBh, ad sūtra 1.1.5, p. 38,1–2), "the hypothesis of an object in the form 'this object, observed or heard, is otherwise incongruous.'" Whenever the expression "the cognition of this is caused by that" is used, there must be this flaw of circularity of that [seen or heard object] in the cognition of this [postulated object]; because just as in the case of the essence of a subject used as the logical reason (*svabhāva-hetu*), the proven knowledge of the epistemic object already contains the proof of the object that you want to postulate. Therefore a further epistemic instrument becomes superfluous.

> CAKRADHARA COMMENTS on *svabhāva-hetu*:[49] In the inference "this is a tree, because it has the property of being an elm," when the extension of the elm-ness is grasped, the extension of tree-ness is automatically grasped. If by apprehending this [elm-ness] that [tree-ness] were not apprehended, this [tree-ness] would not be the essence of that [elm].

Prābhākara—objective arthâpatti *is the reverse of inference*

The Prābhākaras explain the distinction of *arthâpatti* from inference in a different way. In inference the property "otherwise incongruous" is a qualifier of the cause of cognition (*gamaka*). For instance, smoke is incongruous without fire. Here in *arthâpatti*, instead, it is the reverse: the cognizable object is incongruous without the cause of cognition. "Outside-presence" is the cognizable object. This object is incongruous without the home-absence of this living being, therefore this living being who has left the house exists outside.

> COMMENTS: The Prābhākaras have a radically different understanding of *arthâpatti*. Unlike in the Bhāṭṭa version, where the incongruity is a property of the antecedent, i.e., the object known by perception, etc., on which basis the hypothesis is formulated, they consider the incongruity as a property of the hypothesis. In the present case, in the Prābhākara *arthâpatti*, the hypothesis "the living being has outside-presence" is incongruous without the home-absence. In this passage the absence of the word "hypothesis" (*kalpanā*), as well as the presence of the words "cognizable" (*gamya*) and "cause of cognition" (*gamaka*), is particularly important because Prabhākara glosses *kalpayati*, "causing an hypothesis," with *gamayati*, "causing a cognition." Jayanta mirrors his interpretation.

In this way they also explain the *Bhāṣya* formulation "an observed or heard object is the hypothesis of an object" as "it causes the hypothesis of another object."[50] This

---

[48] NM, I.117.
[49] GBh, 23,5.
[50] NM, I.11 8.

is because this hypothesis is otherwise incongruous, through the intermediation of the epistemic object. The meaning is that the hypothetical object is otherwise incongruous.

COMMENTS: In light of Cakradhara's gloss (GBh, 23,8), *prameya-dvārikā* (*prameyaḥ dvāro yasya sā*) means that although in the *Śābara-bhāṣya* the grammatical subject of *upapadyate* is 'hypothesis' (*kalpanā*), what is not congruous is the epistemic object of the hypothesis, and only indirectly the hypothesis." The grammatical problem is that the "object" (*artha*) is embedded in a compound-word in which "hypothesis" is the predominant term to be construed with the verb *upapadyate*. This is an instance of "depending compound" (*sâpekṣa-samāsa*), where technically speaking the first term of the compound, "object," cannot be taken as the agent of the verb.

To sum up, this *arthâpatti* is a different epistemic instrument, in respect to inference, because of the reverse direction of incongruity between the object and the cause of the cognition. The outer presence, which is otherwise incongruous, is the cognizable object.

Nyāya—the prābhākara's objective arthâpatti *is a defective inference*

Even this explanation looks like a justification of the inconsistency in the original formulation of Śabara, rather than the ingenious discovery of a new distinction [of *arthâpatti* from inference].

First of all, if the cognizable object is not yet apprehended, how can one possibly determine its incongruity? If instead it is already apprehended, what is the purpose of the apprehension of any incongruity, when the probandum (*sādhya*) is already proven? To this you may object that what is already apprehended is more specifically the property "otherwise incongruous" (rather than simply "incongruous"). Now we wonder: how is this different from inference? You are saying that what is already apprehended is a mutual relation [of probandum and probans]. Furthermore,[51] by saying that there is an incongruity of that outside-presence in absence of this home-absence you entail that there is a congruity of that in presence of this.

COMMENTS: If there is no congruity of p without q, then there is congruity of p with q; $\neg \neg (Cp \wedge q) = Cp \wedge q$

Now, in this specific case, what exactly is this "congruity" (*upapatti*)? Is it production (*utpatti*) or rather causation of knowledge (*jñapti*)? If it is causation of knowledge, than this is the same process of inference: there is no congruity of the object without the cause of knowledge; conversely, if a cause of knowledge is there then the object of knowledge is congruous.

COMMENTS: The verbal root *upa-pad-* may mean both "to cause' and "to prove true." One could still argue in favor of a difference between *arthâpatti* and inference if this *upapatti* in *anyathânupapatti* meant the former and not the latter.

---

[51] NM, I.119.

The production of outside-presence, from home-absence, is not tenable:
home-absence would already be accomplished, and outside-presence would come forth in the subsequent moment.
For only an existing cause can produce an effect.
So there would be a moment when he, although alive, would neither be at home, nor elsewhere.

COMMENTS: If home-absence generates outer presence, there is a first instant when home-absence exists and outer presence does not. In the second instant outer presence is produced. But then, at the time of the first instant, the living Caitra would not be at home, because of his absence, and neither elsewhere, because his outer presence has not yet been produced.

This argument also addresses someone else's attempt to exploit the different character of cognitive and ontological causation and affirm that fire is simply known through smoke, while the outside-presence is produced by the absence at home.

The correlation of properties can be apprehended To say that in this absence-based *arthâpatti* the inferential relation cannot be apprehended is also an unsound proposition, because this apprehension of a relation is plausible from the viewpoint of someone standing at the door:

They raised the issue themselves, but did not solve it.[52]
They showed one more example, but just in reverse order.

COMMENTS: The example in reverse order is the perception of presence at home, leading to the *arthâpatti* of outer absence. Kumārila's idea, perhaps originally intended as a *reductio ad absurdum*, is that even while perceiving the home-presence of Caitra from the threshold one cannot apprehend a universal correlation with his outer absence.

CAKRADHARA[53] here cites Kumārila's verse (ŚV, *arthâpatti* 24), gṛha-dvāri sthito yas tu bahir-bhāvaṃ prakalpayet| yadā tasminn ayaṃ deśe na tadânyatra vidyate ‖ (see Ollett and Freschi in this volume, p. 54).

In relation to this hypothesis of the outer absence through the presence at home, we shall say the following.

This is certainly not an absence-based *arthâpatti*. Your claim is for six types of *arthâpatti*, and yet you have deserted this sixth absence-based *arthâpatti* with callous indifference, like a terrified doe at the mercy of the enraged Naiyāyika lion. This is a mean beahavior, befitting lowly people.[54]

You were this girl's only shelter, deserted her and went away.
What shall other ladies think now, when you'll look at them?

---

[52] NM, I.120.
[53] GBh, 23,16–17.
[54] The word "rage" (*utkopa*), attested in BORI 390 and MDUC 2606, was changed into *uktvā upa-*, of dubious meaning, in the editions.

COMMENTS: The "deserted girl" is the absence-based *arthâpatti*, and the "other girls" are the other five types of *arthâpatti*. Bhattacharyya (1978: 89) translates: "If you desert this young lady (in the shape of the former illustration of presumption) who absolutely depends upon you for her protection then how will the other ladies (the other illustrations of presumption) count upon your protection with confidence?"

The hypothesis of an absence through a presence, in any case, would be a perception-based *arthâpatti*. But even here the inferential relation is not difficult to apprehend, because one can easily determine that a non-omnipresent substance, present in a precise location, is not present in a different place. For instance, what is your take on smoke, which is certainly known to never be present without fire? This situation is analogous to the presently discussed one.

One may argue that in the case of the smoke–fire relation we can rely just on the positive correlation, which is apprehended by repeated observation:[55]

> For us, by contrast, this negative correlation serves the purpose of ascertaining, without perceiving it, the concomitant (*saha-cārin*) (of smoke, i.e., fire).[56]

CAKRADHARA COMMENTS:[57] The first half of Kumārila's passage reads "this defect applies to those who want to know the absence of a different object." This is the purport: For the Buddhist opponent, the absence of another object, characterized by an exclusion of what is not fire, is knowable through inference. But the Buddhist incurs in the defect of not being able to know the absence in any specific place. In other words, until one does not know each and every place from which fire is excluded, the apprehension of the negative correlation cannot be exhaustive. One may object that even in absence of fire the negative correlation of smoke ...[58] cannot be proven. Because, if there are cases of non-grasped absence of fire, how can one grasp the distinction from those? And if [this exclusion] is not grasped, how can there be the apprehension of an inferential relation? But in my theory (Kumārila says), on the strength of the repeated observation of the non-presence of smoke with fire in some dissimilar subject (*vipakṣa*), there is no need to grasp exclusions in every possible dissimilar subject, because of a specific application to this [positive knowledge of fire].

But this is not correct, because a probandum cannot be ascertained without the negative correlation, as we will show later.[59] The negative correlation of the properties of the subject, just like their positive correlation, cannot help an inference until the correlation is apprehended. Your demonstration of the outer absence is thus just the formulation (*prayoga*) of an inference.

---

[55] The following hemistich is a quotation from Kumārila (ŚV, *arthâpatti* 40cd). The first half of the verse was a later addition, as per MDUC 2606 and BORI 390, though in this second witness it is added in margin on the basis of Cakradhara's commentary.

[56] NM, I.121.

[57] GBh, 25,3.

[58] Translator's note: there are some illegible words here.

[59] See NM, āhnika 10, I.562,4, *kevalânvayī hetur nāsty eva*.

COMMENTS: There is the outside-absence of Caitra, because of his home-presence. What possesses home-presence, possesses outside-absence. What does not possesses outside-absence, does not possess home-presence.

The reverse formulation of the inference ends up in a defective inferential reason (*hetvâbhāsa*), because the inferential reason is defeated (*viruddha*) by perception, etc. But now enough with this digression.

NYĀYA—VERBAL *ARTHÂPATTI* AS INFERENCE

An inference from fatness to eating

Even the worthless "verbal *arthâpatti*" does not distinguish itself from inference, for two reasons, (1) the hypothesis of the completion of a statement is implausible, and (2) its object can be known through an effect used as an inferential mark. Once you have perceived smoke on the top of a hill, you can infer its cause, namely fire. Similarly, once you have known from testimony the effect called "fatness" you can also infer its cause, namely "eating." What would be so special here, since this fatness is known as the effect of that eating through repeated observation? Just as in some cases the inferential mark is apprehended through perception, in others it can be known from testimony, but this is not a substantial difference.

Expectancy is a property of things, not of words or of cognitions

OPPONENT: But an incomplete expression cannot convey an adequate cognition.[60]

PROPONENT: Isn't there the cognition of "fatness," caused by the statement "fat Devadatta does not eat at day"?

OPPONENT: It is there, but it is accompanied by expectancy (*ākāṅkṣā*). Something that generates a cognition marked by expectancy is not characterized by epistemic validity (*prāmāṇya*), so it must be first completed.

PROPONENT: This is not true. Whose expectancy are we discussing? Is it the expression's (*śabda*), the meant object's (*artha*), or rather its cognition's? The expression does not possess any expectancy independently of its object, as evident with indistinct sounds. As for the object, if it has expectancy, then it may directly lead to the other expected object, without the need of an hypothesis of a completing statement. As for the cognition, it may have expectancy only when its content is the object, not when its content is just the expression, which is known through the ear-organ. Therefore, even the fulfillment of the expectancy of a cognition would definitely be linked to the hypothesis of the object.[61] Since the hypothesis of the completing statement has only the purpose of leading to the cognition of the object, let's directly have the hypothesis of that object. Why the additional step?

---

[60] NM, I.122.
[61] NM, I.123.

An hypothetical part of the sentence would be non-Vedic

As for the argument that an hypothetical object would be non-Vedic, in your theory of an hypothetical statement the derived object would be even less Vedic, because such an hypothetical statement is obviously different from the Veda.

If you argue that the Veda is of two types, heard and inferred, then let's rather say that the object meant by the Veda is of two types, the one derived from hearing and the one inferred from the one derived from hearing. Why the step of a hypothetical statement? An object should be considered as having a Vedic status only under the conditions of being directly conveyed by an audible statement of the Veda. From whatever angle we may look at it, an *arthâpatti* having the content of the missing part of the statement is not a better solution.

A relation between general meanings can be apprehended

This refutation of the theory (*pakṣa*) of the hypothesis of a partial statement disproves even the argument that the apprehension of an inferential relation is impossible (*aghaṭamāna*) because that [missing part of the statement] would be beyond perception. By adopting this theory of an inference of the object, instead, the apprehension of a relation with a general referent (*sāmānya*) is easily justified. For instance, an example is the referent of the verbal root "to sacrifice' (*yaj-*), which has a necessary relation with the eligibility (*adhikāra*) to sacrifice.

COMMENTS: The context of this paragraph seems to be inference, and not semantics, so the relation under discussion should be an inferential correlation between general terms. This is also how Varadacarya understands it (NM, I.124). But the purport could also be that the referent of *yaj-*, a universal, when combined with another universal referent, "eligibility," it denotes a particular (*viśeṣa*). This explanation would presuppose the *abhihitânvaya* theory of compositionality, according to which the cognition of a sentence meaning is a two-step process: first, individual word referents are known, and the correlation of these referents leads to knowledge of the sentence meaning. This theory is endorsed by the Bhāṭṭas, and partially adopted by Naiyāyikas, but not by the Prābhākaras.

PRĀBHĀKARA—"VERBAL *ARTHÂPATTI*" AS A FUNCTION OF LANGUAGE

The Prābhākaras,[62] by contrast, reject verbal *arthâpatti* by interpreting the Bhāṣya passage "seen or heard" as an idiomatic way of expressing any type of perception. Maintaining that only an audible expression can be causally efficient in relation to its meaning, they state the thesis that this meaning is directly derived from words.

---

[62] NM, I.124.

The causal power belongs to words

Concerning the cognition of the sentence meaning—consisting of a duty (*kārya*) influenced by a group of multiple causes (*kāraka*) of secondary and non secondary activities, etc., remotely and proximately situated—the sentence has a farther and farther reaching activity (*vyāpāra*), like an arrow's.

> COMMENTS: This "etc." (*ādi*) in "secondary activities, etc." is not quite clear. According to CAKRADHARA,[63] it includes the ingredients, the god invoked in the ritual, the qualities of the ingredients, and so on. The arrow analogy, suggesting how the piercing effect of an arrow depends on contingent conditions such as sharpness, speed, material of the target, etc., may be Jayanta's own creation, as I could not trace it in any pre-Jayanta source. It is later found in the writings of Abhinavagupta, Bhoja, and others. Bhattacharyya (1978: 93–4) translates: "As an arrow has a short or long process, i.e., it hits a near or a remote object or it pierces and passes through a thin or thick object quickly or slowly, so a sentence quickly or slowly conveys its meaning since the knowledge of the complete meaning depends upon a group of factors viz. the knowledge of the meanings of words denoting qualities, substances, action, etc."

Such a cognition can arise only if words have not ceased to operate, because once their operativity has stopped there are no other known causes of its production. While learning the correct use of language from the communication among competent speakers, one will observe such speakers using such sorts of sentences, and will accordingly ascertain the capacity of a given sentence in relation to its sentence meaning. The words present in that sentence are the necessary causes (*nimitta*) in respect to the effect (*naimittika*, i.e., knowledge of the sentence meaning).

> *CAKRADHARA* COMMENTS:[64] **"The words present in that sentence are the necessary causes (*nimitta*) in respect to the effect (*naimittika*, i.e., knowledge of the sentence meaning,"** This is the purpose of this statement: if the sentence meaning were determined to be linked to something else but the causal efficacy (*sāmarthya*) of words, then the cognition of the sentence meaning would also conform to that. Instead, when after learning the sentence meaning in its form of duty (*kārya*), on the basis of the usage of competent speakers constituted of activity and non-activity, a correspondence of the causality of words respectively inserted and extracted is also learned. Then, according to the causality learned through this process, one adopts a conforming causality of words. In this sense the necessary causation (*nimittatva*) is different from the signification (*vācakatva*): while signification, in relation to the cognition of the sentence meaning, depends on the apprehension of a [signifier–signified] relation, causation does not. Otherwise [if there were no signification], upon hearing a sentence for the first time there could not be any cognition of the sentence meaning.

[63] GBh, 25,18.
[64] GBh, 26,1.

The assessment of the conditions is done through the observation of what is conducive to the effect.[65] In some cases even unheard words are considered to be necessary causes, for instance the words "he who desires heaven" in the Viśvajit ritual.

CAKRADHARA COMMENTS:[66] **In some cases even unheard words are considered to be necessary causes.** The effect (*naimittika*) is the predisposition towards the execution of the command (*niyoga*), because the realization of the command occurs on the condition of the presence of the eligible executor (*adhikārin*).

COMMENTS: The command can make sense only if it is known whom the command is directed to, i.e., who is the person qualified to execute the command, in this case he who desires heaven. Hence, the words "he who desires heaven" are understood, even if not present in the injunction of the Viśvajit ritual.

In some cases even heard words may relinquish their causal status, because they are not conducive to that effect, as with the word "double" in "he whose double oblation leads to distress" (*yasyôbhayaṃ havir ārttim ārcched*).

COMMENTS: ŚBh, 6.4.22–31. In this case the word "double," even if uttered, is not reflected in the sentence meaning.

Sometimes, even if found in a certain sequential structure, words are differently construed, in compliance with what ought to be done, as in "One should sprinkle the oblation by means of what is left of the main sacrifice (*prayāja*)" (*prayāja-śeṣeṇa havīṃṣy abhighārayati*).

CAKRADHARA COMMENTS:[67] "**Sometimes, even if found in a certain sequential structure, words are differently construed.**" "One should sprinkle the oblation by means of what is left of the main sacrifice." Here the expression "what is left" cannot be secondary in respect to another ritual action within the main sacrifice, because even the remainder of what was intended for the main sacrifice is intended for the main sacrifice. Therefore, since it is impossible to use butter for its purpose, the purpose should be interpreted. In the interpretation, what is to be interpreted is "what is left of the main sacrifice," which since it is predominant should be indicated by the second ending (the accusative ending). As for the oblation, one should intend the seventh ending (the locative) because it is the substratum, as it happens with the horns of the black antelope in the *catvāla* injunction. "He should throw the grass to the horns of the black antelope." Hence, by interpretation, the proper syntax conforming to the meaning of the sentence, is "One should sprinke what is left of the main sacrifice on the oblation."

Therefore, since the causation of present or absent words is established according to the sentence meaning, which is known as a compact unit, and since the cognition of

---

[65] NM, I.125.
[66] GBh, 26,8.
[67] GBh, 27,4.

the complete sentence meaning can already be generated by a partial sentence, what is the purpose of verbal *arthâpatti*? Only with our method is the verbal derivation of the sentence meaning not mediated by this additional step, because it is directly accomplished.

> *Cakradhara* comments:[68] The **additional step** would be verbal *arthâpatti*.

Causes are assessed from their effect, so unspoken words can be such causes

Opponent: One may object: If the necessary conditions, i.e., the words, are not heard, what causes then the cognition of their referents? And if we do not know their referents, what is the effect (*naimittika*) that we are taking into consideration?

Proponent: We answer: even the causation of the audible words is not hypothesized on the basis of their own power, but rather through their relation to the effect.[69] The same will apply to unheard words. In fact, we do not hear the instrumental ending in the root *yaj-*, neither the accusative ending in the word *svarga*, nor the zero suffix (*kvip*) in the word *agnicit*, nor the nominal stem in the indeclinable word *adhunā*,[70] nor the respective endings of words in compounds and of secondarily-derived nouns (*taddhita*). And yet we do understand these meanings.

> *Cakradhara* comments:[71] **In fact, we do not hear the instrumental ending in the root** ***yaj-*****.** One hears just *svarga-kāmo yajeta*, not "*yāga* is the instrument," "*svarga* is the result, etc." Even then, this is the actual sense of these two expressions, as resulting from the efficacy of the command, i.e., the sentence meaning. The person desiring heaven is commanded to perform a sacrifice, but how could he act accordingly, if he desired something else or acted otherwise. Moreover, the command is not realized if the sacrifice is not performed, so the very command, for the sake of its own realization, establishes the instrumental nature of the sacrifice and the teleological nature of heaven. The relation with these two aspects is not conveyed by the audible parts of these expressions.

Analogously, we will understand the meanings "he who desires heaven," etc., also in the case of the verb *yajeta*, "one should sacrifice," applied to the Viśvajit ritual, on the strength of the very effect, i.e., the sentence meaning.

And since the applicative rules (*viniyoga*) are intrinsically commands (*niyoga*), even the hermeneutic rules (*liṅga*, etc.), become applicative rules in relation to the concrete reality (*vastu*) that is apprehended through the operation of the command, even without the hypothesis of any unheard words.

---

[68] GBh, 27,16.

[69] NM, I.126.

[70] Cf. *Kāśikā*, *ad* 5.3.17: *adhuneti nipatyate. idamo'śbhāvo dhunā ca pratyayaḥ*. In the Pāṇinian analysis, here the nominal stem is *idam*, replaced by *aŚ*, followed by the suffix *dhunā*.

[71] GBh, 27,18.

The diversified causation of words

OPPONENT: If this were the case, the operation of words would be all-pervasive,
so the primary meaning (*mukhya*) would be the same as the secondary (*gauṇa*) or
the indicative (*lākṣaṇika*) meaning.[72]
And in cases of conflict between the hermeneutic rules (*pramāṇa*), such as the
letter of the word (*śruti*), the indication of the purpose (*liṅga*), and so on,
how could the principle "the previous one is stronger than the following" ever
apply?

PROPONENT: We say: Even conceding that the operativity of language is all-pervasive, such a problem does not ensue, because this is explained by the different types of that operativity of language. The cognition of the effect does not eclipse (*upa-plu-*) the causality of words, even after this causality is fully effected. And since this is never relinquished, their substantial diversity follows through (*anuvartate*).

One thing is the referent "lion," the lioness's offspring,
another is the one transferred to Devadatta.
The semantic role of "Ganges," in "he dives in the Ganges,"
is not the same as in "herdsmen who live on the Ganges."

COMMENTS: The examples of direct reference are, respectively, "This is a lion" and "He dives in the Ganges." The figurative examples are "Devadatta is a lion," meaning that he has the qualities of a lion, and "These herdsmen settle on the Ganges" (*gaṅgāyāṃ ghoṣaḥ vasati*), meaning that they live on the bank of the Ganges. Due to the presence in Jayanta's verse of the verb *vasati* ("reside," "settle'), the usual translation "The village on the Ganges," for *gaṅgāyāṃ ghoṣaḥ*, does not quite work here.

Even in the application of the hermeneutic criteria—(1) literal statement (*śruti*), (2) indication of purpose or object (*liṅga*), (3) syntactic interconnection of words (*vākya*), (4) context (*prakaraṇa*), (5) position in a sequence (*sthāna*), (6) etymological considerations (*samākhyā*)—there certainly is a specific proximity or distance from the ultimate meaning, i.e., the effect. Therefore, even in the application of such criteria the issue of a conflict among equally applicable rules does not occur.

COMMENTS: This is the beginning of a technical section on the exegesis of rituals. The purpose is to show, from a Prābhākara standpoint, that verbal *arthâpatti* is not needed to explain apparent inconsistencies or contradictions in Vedic injunctions of rituals, because there are already well-established exegetic principles to deal with such apparent conflicts. The interested reader will benefit from a comparison with the corresponding translation of Bhattacharyya (1978: 98–101).

---

[72] NM, I.127.

When the application is construed by *śruti*, *liṅga*, etc.,
why would one encounter any conflict caused by equally applicable rules?
Even in the *arthâpatti* theory, these are distant or proximate.[73]
The hermeneutic criteria relate to the meaning. Why then the hypothesis of the unspoken words?

Cakradhara comments:[74] **"When the application is construed by *śruti*, *liṅga*, etc."** The *liṅga* automatically presumes the *śruti*, and the *vākya* in turn presumes the *liṅga*. Without assuming the power of denotation the hypothesis of an unspoken part of the sentence is not feasible. This is the principle of distance and proximity, which was clarified before.

Comments: In other words, the third principle, the syntactical relation in the sentence, presupposes the indication of purpose, which presupposes the verbatim form of the sentence.

In the derived rituals (*vikṛti*), such as the oblation to Indra and Agni (*aindrāgna*), it is not the case that the expressive force (*vidhy-anta-vacana*) of the archetypical ritual (*prakṛti*) is inferred. It is rather obtained through the very force of the transferring rule (*codaka*). The transferring rule is this sort of expectancy to a transformed injunction.

Cakradhara comments:[75] **"The transferring rule is this sort of expectancy to a transformed injunction."** This is enabled (*sampannam*) by the archetypical injunction (*prākṛta-vidhi*) assisted by perceivable and unperceivable assisting factors. This expectancy is a transferring rule, i.e., a word referent (*padârtha*) that causes the entailment (*ākṣepa*) of duty (*dharma*), in the form "I'm also an injunction, so by me, assisted by perceivable and unperceivable means, something ought to be enabled."

Opponent: With this explanation, since that [*vidhy-anta-vacana*] is not distinctly recognized in these two [archetype and derived ritual, since both are individually just injunctions], what is the specification offered of the two types of injunction, direct rule (*upadeśa*) and transferred rule (*atideśa*)?

Proponent: There is no specification in the cognition of the command itself. The specification is that in the case of the direct rule the duty (*kārya*) conforms to the direct statement, while in the case of the transferred rule the direct rule conforms to the action to be done.

Opponent: If the direct rule conforms to the action to be done, then there cannot be a standing (*prāpti*) of an injunction such as "one should husk," in reference to an object such as "golden coins" (*kṛṣṇalacaru*), so what would then be the purpose of blocking such an inapplicable rule?

---

[73] NM, I.128.
[74] GBh, 28,27.
[75] GBh, 30,13.

Proponent: This does not happen, because the enabling (*prāpti*) of an injunction governing the whole circle (*akhaṇḍa-maṇḍala*) occurs at the very last step (*vidhy-anta-kāṇḍa*).[76] This is because the transferring rule does not work as the part of a composite whole.

But enough with this extensive digression, which was presented in the light of another discipline.

Comments: Here Jayanta confirms that he is still arguing from the standpoint of Prābhākara Mīmāṃsā, purportedly to defend the Nyāya tenets. He adopts the same strategy elsewhere as well, for instance in NM, āhnika 4, I.624,11, *etac ca śāstrântare vistareṇâbhiyuktaiḥ yuktibhir upapāditam*, or in NM, āhnika 5, II.69,2, *śāstrântare vistarataḥ praṇītam*.

The Mīmāṃsaka view has been briefly discussed in some specific application (*prasaṅga*).
But who are we to mark the limits of its correctness or incorrectness?
We have proven the vulnerability of *arthâpatti* to critique.
This critique can be done either through the method explained above (the Nyāya method), or through this latter path (of the Prābhākaras).

Comments: As I understand it, here Jayanta refers to the refutation of verbal *arthâpatti* as a distinct epistemic instrument, that can be accomplished either in the Nyāya way, by reducing the "Fat Devadatta" example to a case of inference, or in the Prābhākara way, by appealing to well-established hermeneutic principles. Bhattacharyya (1978: 101) interprets this last line more specifically, by relating it to the two distinct theories of sentence meaning of Bhāṭṭa and Prābhākara Mīmāṃsā: "The hypothesis of presumption based upon the verbal testimony is only open to serious objection. Any one of the two hypotheses, viz. (i) both given and silent words determine the meaning of a sentence and (ii) the words of a sentence by means of their different intrinsic power of quickly or slowly conveying their objects express the meaning of a sentence without assuming other sentences or clauses."

OF POETICAL MEANINGS

This mighty capacity of words averts something else as well,
namely some sort of "*dhvani*" taught by a self-fancied scholar:
From an injunction comes the cognition of a prohibition,
from a prohibition the cognition of an injunction.

Cakradhara comments:[77] **"By a self-fancied scholar."** Here Jayanta refers to the master Ānandavardhana, author of the *dhvani*. He is the one who labeled as *dhvani* (lit. "sound") that type of poetry in which signifier and signified, with the help of the context, etc., convey a suggested meaning that transcends denotation, because it is the true object of the hearer's cognition (*pratīyamāna*), being the

[76] NM, I.129.
[77] GBh, 32,1.

predominant aspect of a poetical composition. The word *dhvani* had already been used by the grammarians—who are considered the archetypical scholars because grammar is the root of all sciences—because immanent speech (*sphoṭa*) manifests when phonemes resound. Similarly, also Ānandavardhana used the word *dhvani* to denote a particular type of poetry, because it has in common the character of manifestation from sounds.

For instance,

As in "Go freely, gentle monk" and "Do not enter this house, traveller."
While signifying things delimited through other instruments of knowledge, words have this capacity, specifically and diversely applied.
Or, discussing this with poets is not even proper,[78] when even true scholars are perplexed in the unfathomable path (*adhvani*) of sentences and their meanings.

COMMENTS: This passage is also translated by McCrea (2008: 216–17): "In each case, it is the capacity of words—which indicate the form of things which are qualified by some other means of knowledge [i.e. inference]—which functions in this way. In any case, this discussion with poets is not appropriate; even learned people become confused in this difficult path of sentence meaning." Bhattacharyya (1978: 101) has "The second hypothesis that the words of a sentence by means of their intrinsic power completely express the meaning of a sentence is refuted by the hypothesis of the proud rhetoricians that a word, apart from its primary or secondary meaning, conveys a distinct meaning ... They say that a positive sentence suggests a negative meaning and that a negative sentence suggests a positive meaning ... Jayanta joins issue with the rhetoricians and holds that the words only by means of their power of expressing either primary or secondary meaning convey the final meaning of the sentence." Bhattacharyya rightly connects this passage to Jayanta's own theory of sentence meaning (NM, āhnika 6), so his interpretation is worthy of consideration, apart from the misleading notion of Jayanta joining the rhetoricians' view.

CAKRADHARA COMMENTS:[79] **"Do not enter this house, traveler."** "I'm a lonely girl here, together with a deaf and dumb mother-in-law, and my husband is long gone." This line, **"do not enter my house, traveler,"** is part of such a stanza. This is refuted by him [Jayanta] with the line **"This mighty capacity of words averts something else as well,"** above. This is the gist: In the Veda, since the *artha* is directly generated by statements, the meaning does correspond to *śabda*. In common language, however, one uses words to convey something additional, even after the *artha* is known. This knowledge, then, comes from another epistemic instrument, not from testimony. This thing (*vastu*) known through such uses of language, if it is not defeated by another epistemic instrument, may be taken as apprehended from testimony, but not if it is defeated. It should thus

[78] NM, I.130.
[79] GBh, 33,6.

be judged according to its absence or presence of conflict with other epistemic instruments. For instance, in the metonymy "the village on the Ganges" the operation of the words culminates in the communication of the bank of the river, according to another epistemic instrument, because the characteristic of the substratum is not compatible with the meaning "river stream." And in the figurative usage "the lion-boy," the communicative capacity of the word "lion" connotes a specific quality, namely "hubris," because the correlation of two conflicting universals is not possible. Analogous to these two cases, although the power of referentiality culminates in the positive prescription, since there is no plausible construal (*anvaya*) of the referents, the prohibition "do not walk!" flashes as the sentence meaning. In this sentence the activity of walking is enjoined on the basis of a removal of fear of the dog, who has purportedly been killed. And yet, obviously the prescription of "walking" is not the complete sentence meaning, because of the apprehension generated by a conflicting cause of fear, the raging lion. Thus a prohibition of the walking activity emerges and it becomes the true sentence meaning ... Furthermore, from such sentences a cognition of the effect appears at the very outset. As this cognition is there, one needs to plausibly account for the causes of the effect. Having exactly this in mind, Jayanta uses the pronoun *etena*, in *etena paṇḍitaṃ-manyaḥ*. It is also appropriate that the cognition of the suggested meaning (*pratīyamāna*) remains a verbal cognition, because otherwise, after knowing the meaning, the knower would have an awareness such as "I have conjectured this meaning," rather than "I have known this from words." ... In this way, in such sentences, the linguistic usage is not based on the bare substance (*svarūpa*) of the causes, because the causality of the causes is established after the cognition of the effect ... The suggested meaning is always considered to be the sentence meaning, achieved through the intentionality (*tātparya-śakti*) of the sentence. The sentence meaning of "Traveler! Do not enter my house" is thus the prescription: the cause implied by the prohibition is contradicted and so the injunction is rather established ... "**specially applied**," i.e., to cases of indication (*lakṣaṇā*) and so on, and "**diversely**," i.e., by resorting to the functions consisting of indication and so on.

But enough with this lengthy digression, befitting true scholars.
In the view of logicians, this convoluted argument is unsound.
We can now repeat the original claim: In respect to inference,
arthâpatti is not distinct at all. *Quod erat demonstrandum*.

REFERENCES

Abbreviations

ŚV Dvārikādāsa Ś., ed. (1978), *Ślokavārttika of Śrī Kumārila Bhaṭṭa with the Commentary Nyāyaratnākara of Śrī Pārthasārathi Miśra*, Prāchyabhārati Series 10, Varanasi: Tara Publications.

MNP Edgerton, F. (1929). *Mīmāṃsānyāyaprakāśa of Āpadeva*, Introduction, Sanskrit Text, English Translation, Glossary, and Notes, New Haven, CT: Yale University Press.

GBR Shah, N. J., ed. (1972), *Cakradhara's Nyāyamañjarī-granthibhaṅga*, Lalbhai Dalpatbhai series 35, Ahmedabad: L.D. Institute of Indology.

Kāśikā Shobhitamishra, P., ed. (1952), *Kāśikāvṛtti*, 2 vols., Varanasi: Chaukhamba Sanskrit Pustakalaya.

ŚBh Subbāśāstrī, ed., (1929a–34), *Śābarabhāṣya of Śabara, Vol. 6 of Śrīmajjaiminipraṇītaṃ Mīmāṃsādarśanam*, Anandashrama Sanskrit Series 97, St. Petersburg: Anandasramamudranalayah.

TV Subbāśāstrī, ed., (1929b–34), *Tantravārttikam of Kumārila. Vol. 6 of Śrīmajjaiminipraṇītaṃ Mīmāṃsādarśanam.* Anandashrama Sanskrit Series 97, St. Petersburg: Anandasramamudranalayah.

NM Varadacharya, K. S., ed. (1969–83), *Nyāyamañjarī of Jayantabhaṭṭa: With Ṭippaṇī Nyāyasaurabha*, 2 vols., Mysore: Oriental Research Institute.

Secondary literature

Bally, C. and A. Sechehaye, eds. (1999), *Corso di linguistica generale. Introduzione, traduzione e commento di Tullio De Mauro*, ed. and trans. into Italian, Rome and Bari: Laterza.

Bhattacharyya, J. V. (1978), *Jayanta Bhaṭṭa's Nyāyamañjarī: The Compendium of Indian Speculative Logic*, trans. into English (āhnikas 1 to 6), Delhi: Motilal Banarsidass.

Bhattacharyya, S. (2001), "Some Aspects of the Navya-Nyāya Theory of Inference," in J. Ganeri (ed.), *Indian Logic: A Reader*, 162–82, Richmond, Surrey: Curzon Press 2001.

Ganeri, J., ed. (2001), *Indian Logic: A Reader*, Richmond, Surrey: Curzon Press.

Graheli, A. (2015), *History and Transmission of the Nyāyamañjarī: Critical Edition of the Section on the* Sphoṭa, Vienna: Verlag der Österreichischen Akademie der Wissenschaften.

Graheli, A. (2017), "Bhaṭṭa Jayanta: Comprehension, Knowledge, and the Reduction of Testimony to Inference," *Kervan: International Journal of Afro-Asiatic Studies* 21: 175–226.

Matilal, B. K. (1998), *The Character of Logic in India*, ed. J. Ganeri and H. Tiwari, Albany: State University of New York Press.

Matilal, B. K. (2001), "Introducing Indian Logic," in J. Ganeri (ed.), *Indian Logic: A Reader*, 183–215, Richmond, Surrey: Curzon Press 2001.

McCrea, Lawrence J. (2008), *The Teleology of Poetics in Medieval Kashmir*, Harvard Oriental Series 71, Cambridge, MA: Department of Sanskrit / Indian Studies, Harvard University.

CHAPTER SEVEN

Udayana's *The Flower-Offering of Reason*

Translated by NILANJAN DAS

INTRODUCTION

Udayana, active in the late tenth or early eleventh century CE, was an important transitional figure in the history of Nyāya.[1] Even though he remained deeply entrenched in the earlier Nyāya text tradition, his work influenced later Naiyāyikas like Gaṅgeśa Upādhyāya. Seven of his philosophical works are known to us. Three of these are commentaries. *The Purification of Meaning* (*Tātparya-pariśuddhi*) is an explanation of Vācaspati Miśra's sub-commentary on the *Nyāya-sūtra*, *Notes on the Meaning of the Explanation of the Nyāya System* (*Nyāya-vārttika-tātparya-ṭīkā*). *The Appendix of the Nyāya System* (*Nyāya-pariśiṣṭa*) is a commentary on the fifth chapter of Gautama Akṣapāda's *Aphorisms of Logic* (*Nyāya-sūtra*). *The Row of Rays* (*Kiraṇâvalī*) is a gloss on Praśastapāda's commentary on the *Vaiśeṣika-sūtra*, *A Compendium of the Properties of the Categories* (*Padârtha-dharma-saṃgraha*). Two of his non-commentarial works, *The Garland of Definitions* (*Lakṣaṇa-mālā*) and *The Row of Definitions* (*Lakṣaṇâvalī*), are summaries of Vaiśeṣika commitments about ontology. The other two works offer elaborate and highly original defenses of Nyāya views about the self and Īśvara. *The Discrimination of the Truth About the Self* (*Ātma-tattva-viveka*) defends the existence of a substantially real enduring self against Buddhist arguments. *The Flower-Offering of Reason* (*Nyāya-kusumâñjali*) attempts to save theism from arguments given by Buddhists, Mīmāṃsakas, and Cārvākas. It is this last text that shall be our focus.

In the third chapter or *bouquet* (*stavaka*) of *The Flower-Offering of Reason*, Udayana wants to show that there is no good argument against theism, i.e., the claim that Īśvara, an omniscient creator god, exists. In verse 3.18, he considers a Mīmāṃsaka view on which *arthâpatti* can show that Īśvara doesn't exist. Here, the Mīmāṃsaka's argument goes like this: "If a benevolent Īśvara who desires humankind to adopt the path of *dharma* were to exist, then the existence of the Veda—which informs us about *dharma*—would be incongruous. For, in order to motivate people to adopt the path

[1] I am grateful to Malcolm Keating and an anonymous reviewer for comments on this translation.

of *dharma*, Īśvara wouldn't need to create the Veda." In other words, the existence of the Veda is incongruous without the non-existence of Īśvara. Udayana rejects this argument. He claims that a benevolent Īśvara who wants human beings to adopt the path of *dharma* cannot motivate human beings to do so without producing in them the knowledge of what *dharma* consists in. But since this knowledge of *dharma* cannot arise out of empirical investigation alone, testimony is required. That is why Īśvara had to create the Veda which, for the Naiyāyikas since Jayanta and Vācaspati (both active in the ninth century CE) at least, is Īśvara's testimony on *dharma*.

Udayana follows this claim up with a completely general argument for reductionism about *arthâpatti*, i.e., the thesis that *arthâpatti* isn't an independent epistemic instrument. His aim, in this part of his argument, is to show that *arthâpatti* is just a kind of *anumāna*. Earlier in the same chapter, Udayana had argued that *anumāna* cannot refute the existence of Īśvara. It follows from Udayana's argument, therefore, that it is a mistake on the part of the Mīmāṃsaka to appeal to *arthâpatti* as an independent source of counter-evidence against theism.

Udayana's strategy for defending reductionism about *arthâpatti* is this. Suppose *arthâpatti* is just a kind of *anumāna*. Since *anumāna* requires prior empirical knowledge of pervasion (*vyāpti*), then this means an agent engaging in *arthâpatti* must proceed from such knowledge. The Mīmāṃsakas typically resist this claim by arguing that no such empirical knowledge of a generalization is required for *arthâpatti*. What produces *arthâpatti*-based knowledge is something else: what they called *incongruity-otherwise* (*anyathânupapatti*) (see Ollett and Freschi in this volume, p. 44–45). In *The Flower-Offering of Reason* (*Nyāya-kusumâñjali*), Udayana explains why the Mīmāṃsakas' conceptions of incongruity-otherwise cannot help them reject a reductionist view about *arthâpatti*. Udayana deals with three distinct ways of defending an anti-reductionist view about *arthâpatti*. On the first view, instances of *arthâpatti*-based knowledge are based on an awareness of a certain relation of metaphysical dependence between two entities. Udayana argues that the relevant relation of metaphysical dependence is just a relation of pervasion. On the second view, instances of *arthâpatti*-based knowledge are based on the conflict between two epistemic instruments. Udayana shows that either this view is incoherent or leads to a problem of overgeneration. On the third view, instances of *arthâpatti*-based knowledge are produced by what the Nyāya philosophers called negative-only *anumānas*, but these inferences[2] aren't genuine *anumānas* at all. Udayana argues that these inferences are indeed *anumānas*.

TRANSLATION

The opening verse

And *arthâpatti* is not distinct from *anumāna*, since there are no pure examples of *arthâpatti* available in common experience, and there is no *arthâpatti* that is of a different kind from *anumāna*. That is to say:

[2] The term "inference" is used in this translation to refer to any episode of reasoning, so it will not only cover *anumānas* but also instances of inductive or abductive reasoning that cannot properly be treated as kinds of *anumāna*.

3.19ab. That which cannot be regulated (*aniyamya*) cannot be incongruous; neither can that which doesn't regulate (*aniyantā*) make anything congruous.

3.19cd. Nor is there a conflict between two epistemic instruments. Otherwise, this would be the same even in well-known cases of *anumāna*.

COMMENTS: In this passage, Udayana offers two distinct arguments for why *arthâpatti* is not an independent epistemic instrument. The first argument is just that there are no pure or unmixed (*asaṃkīrṇa*) examples of *arthâpatti*-based knowledge available in common experience. For many Naiyāyikas (though it's not clear whether Udayana agrees), instances of knowledge that are produced by distinct epistemic instruments form distinct natural kinds and therefore instantiate distinct natural kind properties (*jāti*). Therefore, if *arthâpatti* and *anumāna* were distinct epistemic instruments, then instances of *anumiti* and instances of *arthâpatti*-generated knowledge would form distinct natural kinds and would instantiate distinct natural kind properties. Moreover, Udayana thinks that natural kinds can't cross-cut each other: there cannot be two natural kinds K1 and K2 such that (i) there are instances of K1 that aren't instances of K2, (ii) there are instances of K2 that aren't instances of K1, and (iii) there are instances of K1 that are instances of K2.[3]

The second argument is that there is no difference in kind between *arthâpatti* and *anumāna*. As Udayana's commentators, Varadarāja and Vardhamāna, note, *arthâpatti* can be distinct from *anumāna* in kind (*prakāra*) only if it differs from *anumāna* either with respect to the causal factors (*sāmagrī*) or the causal operation (*vyāpāra*) by which it gives rise to knowledge, or with respect to the effect (*phala*)—i.e., the knowledge—that it produces.

Despite the Mīmāṃsaka's traditional appeal to incongruity-otherwise (*anyathânupapatti*) (see Ollett and Freschi in this volume, p. 44–45), Udayana argues that it cannot distinguish between *arthâpatti* and *anumāna* in the relevant way. There are two conceptions of incongruity-otherwise: metaphysical and epistemological. On the metaphysical conception, incongruity-otherwise consists in a relation of metaphysical dependence; on the epistemological conception, it consists in a conflict between two epistemic instruments. 3.19ab targets the metaphysical conception of incongruity-otherwise. It says that if incongruity-otherwise consists in a relation of metaphysical dependence, then that which is incongruous must be something that is regulated—i.e., pervaded—by that which makes it congruous. So, incongruity-otherwise is just a relation of pervasion. 3.19cd targets the epistemological conception of incongruity-otherwise. The claim is that there cannot be any conflict between two epistemic instruments as the Mīmāṃsaka suggests. If there were such a conflict, then even well-known instances of *anumāna* would have to be treated as cases of *arthâpatti*. The upshot then is that there is no good way for the Mīmāmsaka to show that there are pure

[3] See his discussion of cross-cutting (*sāṃkarya*) as a constraint on natural kind properties (*jāti-bādhaka*) in *The Row of Rays* in J. S. Jetly (ed.), *Praśastapādabhāṣyam* (Baroda: Oriental Institute, 1971), 23.

examples of *arthâpatti*-based knowledge or that there is a difference in kind between *arthâpatti* and *anumāna*. The rest of Udayana's discussion is an elaboration of this argument.

The argument against incongruity-otherwise

They [the Bhāṭṭa Mīmāṃsakas] offer an example: "That living Caitra isn't at home is incongruous without his presence outside, and therefore implies his presence outside."

With respect to that example, the following is being considered. What is it about the absence of a living person from his house that is incongruous? A non-regulable entity cannot simply be incongruous without something that doesn't regulate. For, otherwise, there would be a problem of overgeneration.

The Bhāṭṭa Mīmāṃsaka: The very nature of a living person's absence from his home is incongruous. First of all, the living person's absence at his home isn't brought about by his presence outside, since it isn't an effect of his presence outside. The nature of a living person's absence from his home is such that it wouldn't obtain unless he were present outside his home.

The Naiyāyika: If this is correct, then a living person's absence from his home, by nature, is indeed something that is regulated by that person's presence outside his home. This is because "incongruity" there just refers to a relation of pervasion determined on the basis of absence (*vyatireka-mukha-nirūpyā*). How else could the living person's presence outside his home make his absence from his home congruous? That which doesn't regulate cannot make congruous that which isn't regulated by it. For, otherwise, there would indeed be a problem of overgeneration (*atiprasaṅga*).

The Bhāṭṭa Mīmāṃsaka: The nature of this absence is such that it obtains insofar as it involves that person's presence elsewhere.

The Naiyāyika: Then, this very same relation of pervasion which is determined on the basis of presence (*anvaya-mukha-nirūpyā*) is called "incongruity."

Comments: In verse 3.19ab, Udayana's target is the metaphysical conception of incongruity-otherwise. He says: "That which cannot be regulated cannot be incongruous; neither can that which cannot regulate make anything congruous." Udayana explains the thought as follows. In any case of incongruity-otherwise, there is some object X that is incongruous (*anupapanna*) and needs to be made congruous (*upapādya*), and there is some other entity Y without which X is incongruous and which makes X congruous (*upapādaka*). In the Devadatta example, the property of being alive but absent from home is incongruous and needs to be made congruous. By contrast, the property of being outside one's home is that without which the property of being alive but absent from home is incongruous and which, therefore, makes this property congruous.

The passage under consideration is intended to be a commentary on 3.19ab. In this passage, Udayana makes two claims. The first is that unless there is a relation of pervasion that connects X with Y, X cannot be incongruous without Y.

Udayana puts this point in terms of regulation (*niyama*): X is regulated by Y if and only if there is a relation of (positive or negative) pervasion between X and Y, i.e., either X is regularly accompanied by Y or the absence of Y is regularly accompanied by the absence of X. Udayana claims that unless X is regulated in this sense by Y, X cannot be incongruous without Y. Why? There is a quick argument right at the beginning of the passage: if a relation of pervasion weren't necessary for X to be incongruous without Y, then anything would be incongruous without everything else. Thus, there would be a problem of overgeneration.

However, this doesn't show that incongruity actually consists in such a relation of pervasion. So, Udayana goes on to make a second, stronger claim: namely, that incongruity of this kind must consist in a relation of pervasion. For any two properties X and Y, the incongruity of X without Y must consist in either

i. X's being caused by Y, or
ii. the nature of X being such that either (a) X wouldn't be instantiated by an object unless Y were also instantiated by it, or (b) whenever X is instantiated by an object, Y is also instantiated by it.

Then, the claim is that (i) cannot be what incongruity-otherwise consists in. In cases where Devadatta's presence is inferred from his being alive and his absence from home, Devadatta's property of being alive but absent from home isn't obviously caused by his being outside. Moreover, if this proposal about incongruity-otherwise were correct, then even prototypical *anumāna*s like the one from smoke to fire could be treated as cases of *arthâpatti*. For, there too, smoke, insofar as it is caused by fire, would be incongruous without fire.

This leaves us with (ii). Here, once again, there are two possibilities. Consider (a): suppose the incongruity of X without Y consists in the nature of X being such that X wouldn't be instantiated by an object unless Y were also instantiated by it. In the Devadatta example, this would mean that the property of being alive but absent from home has a nature such that it wouldn't be instantiated by a person unless that person also instantiated the property of being outside his home. This, according to Udayana, is just a relation of pervasion determined on the basis of absence (*vyatireka-mukha-nirūpyā vyāptiḥ*). Udayana's commentators, Varadarāja and Vardhamāna, take this to be a relation of negative pervasion (*vyatireka-vyāpti*): whenever a person is not present outside his home, he is either not living or not absent from his home.[4] But, on another interpretation, it could be a relation of pervasion that is determined on the basis of negative correlation (*vyatireka-sahacāra*), i.e., by observing cases where both the property to be proven and the reason are absent.[5]

Similarly, if (b) were right, then the incongruity of X without Y would consist in X's having a nature such that X obtains only if Y also obtains. In the

[4] See Upādhyāya and Śāstrī (1957: 419–20).

[5] In his *Tātparya-pariśuddhi*, Udayana himself uses the term *vyatireka-mukhena* in this way at several places: see especially his explanation of the term in the context of his discussion of negative-only *anumāna* (1996: 214).

Devadatta example, this would mean that the property of being alive but absent from home has a nature such that it is instantiated by a person only if that person also instantiates the property of being outside his home. This, according to Udayana, is equivalent to the claim that, between those two properties, there is a relation of pervasion that is determined on the basis of presence (*anvaya-mukha-nirūpyā vyāptiḥ*). On the interpretation favored by Udayana's commentators, this is a relation of positive pervasion: whenever a person is alive and absent from his home, that person is also present outside his home. But it could also be a relation of pervasion determined on the basis of positive correlation (*anvaya-sahacāra*), that is, by observing cases where both the reason and the property to be proven are present. If Udayana's argument succeeds, then incongruity-otherwise consists of some relation of pervasion, positive or negative. This, in turn, will lend support to the hypothesis that instances of *arthâpatti*-based knowledge are just instances of *anumiti* that are based on the agent's prior knowledge of a generalization. Udayana next addresses three objections.

First Bhāṭṭa objection: no need for awareness of incongruity

The Bhāṭṭa Mīmāṃsaka: We don't deny that some kind of pervasion is present in cases of *arthâpatti*; rather, we deny that an awareness of such pervasion is present. However, a relation of pervasion cannot, in virtue of its existence alone, make the inference an *anumāna*.

The Naiyāyika: No. For in cases of *arthâpatti*, the awareness of incongruity-otherwise has to be admitted. For, otherwise, there would be a problem of overgeneration (*atiprasaṅga*) and there would be no room for pseudo-*arthâpatti*. One falls into an error of this sort only when one takes something that is congruous otherwise to be incongruous otherwise; in other cases, there is no such error.

Comments: The Bhāṭṭa objects that it is incongruity-otherwise that yields *arthâpatti*-based knowledge; the awareness of such incongruity may not be necessary. By contrast, in order to gain knowledge by *anumāna*, not only does there have to be a relation of pervasion between the reason and the property to be proven, but the agent must also have a recollective awareness of that pervasion. So, the Bhāṭṭa could just grant that the incongruity-otherwise consists in a relation of pervasion, but deny that an agent requires an awareness of that pervasion in order to gain *arthâpatti*-based knowledge.

Udayana's reply is that if the Bhāṭṭas don't take awareness of incongruity-otherwise to be necessary for *arthâpatti*, there will be two problems. The first is a problem of overgeneration: the proposal will predict that there is *arthâpatti*-based knowledge in cases where there isn't any. For instance, suppose you don't think that the property of being alive but absent from home is incongruous without one's presence outside, but you just judge (on the basis of guesswork) that Devadatta is outside after learning that he's alive and absent from home. This view will predict that your judgment is an instance of *arthâpatti*-based knowledge. For the property of being alive but absent from home is in fact incongruous without the property of being outside one's home. The second problem for the

Bhāṭṭas revolves around cases of pseudo-*arthâpatti*, where people make judgments by *arthâpatti*-like reasoning because they falsely think that one property is incongruous without another. For example, even though Devadatta is dead, you might judge that he's outside his home after not finding him at home, because you falsely think that the property of being absent from home is incongruous without the property of being outside. Such episodes of pseudo-*arthâpatti* are possible, precisely because it is possible for agents like us to make inferences which internally resemble good cases of *arthâpatti* in virtue of involving the same steps of reasoning, but which, unlike good cases of *arthâpatti*, crucially involve a false awareness of incongruity-otherwise. But if an awareness of incongruity-otherwise weren't necessary for *arthâpatti*, such cases of pseudo-*arthâpatti* would be hard to accommodate. Next, Udayana addresses a second Bhāṭṭa objection.

The second objection: the relation of pervasion cannot be apprehended

The Mīmāṃsaka: Even so, how is the relation of pervasion apprehended in this case?

The Naiyāyika: This is established by everyone's perceptual experience: "When I am here, then I am not elsewhere; when I am elsewhere, then I am not here." Why should there even be a "how"-question here? It's also not true that since not all regions of space are perceptible, it is impossible to ascertain the absence of a thing from those regions. For, in one's own case, one can rule out the possibility that one is in contact with any of those other regions of space.

The Mīmāṃsaka: How can one perceive that one is not in contact with imperceptible things?

The Naiyāyika: If one perceives that one object is not related to the other, then one can know by *anumāna* that the former is not related to any of the parts of the latter. However, the same isn't true of things that are not parts of anything. For instance, it is impossible to ascertain that an object is not related to certain atoms unless those atoms are material causes of composite objects (i.e., parts of composite objects).

Comments: How can one know, in the Devadatta example, that there is a relation of pervasion between the reason and the property to be proven? Udayana's answer is that one learns this just as one learns that fire pervades smoke by observing that smoke is correlated in certain ways to fire. In cases of positive correlation (*anvaya-sahacāra*), smoke is present along with fire. In cases of negative correlation (*vyatireka-sahacāra*), fire is absent, and so is smoke. As Udayana seems to suggest, it is not difficult to observe these kinds of correlation in the Devadatta example.

In that example, the putative reason is the property of being alive but absent from one's home, and the putative property to be proven is the property of being outside one's home. Imagine that I am located inside my home. So, I might observe, "When I am here (i.e., inside my house), I am not elsewhere (i.e., outside the house)." This judgment shows that I am able to observe cases of negative correlation between the reason and the property to be proven, i.e., cases where a living person *is not* absent from home and at the same time *is not* present outside their home. Moreover, I might also recall previous experiences, where I was not inside my house and was present elsewhere. So, I might think, "When I am not here (i.e., inside my house), I am present elsewhere (i.e., outside the house)." The second judgment (if correct) demonstrates that I have observed cases of positive correlation, i.e., cases where a living person is absent from home but also is present outside. However, in order to know by perception that I am here at home and not elsewhere, I must perceive in myself the absence of contact with all other regions of space except my home. Here, the Mīmāṃsaka might point out that the Naiyāyikas themselves are committed to the principle that an agent can perceive the absence of an entity *e* only if *e* itself is perceptible. In the example mentioned above, I am supposed to perceive myself as not being in contact with all regions of space outside my home. But contact with all regions of space outside my home is not a perceptible property, since not all regions of space are simultaneously perceptible (at least to an ordinary human being). So, in order to accommodate his view, Udayana must explain how we can perceive one thing as characterized by the absence of another imperceptible thing.

In response, Udayana adopts a subtle strategy. He points out that some perceptible objects have imperceptible parts: for example, a perceptible middle-sized object might be composed of atoms that are themselves imperceptible. Now, it is possible for us to perceive that one middle-sized object, e.g., a pot, isn't in contact with another middle-sized object, e.g., a cloth. From this, Udayana claims, it is possible for me to infer that the pot isn't in contact with the atoms that the cloth is composed of. The same goes for space and its regions. So, Udayana's claim is that even if I cannot perceive myself as not being in contact with all regions of space outside my home, it is still possible for me to perceive myself as not being in contact with the perceptible composite region of space outside my home, and infer from that that I am not in contact with all regions of space outside my home. Therefore, even though it may not be possible to directly observe the negative correlation between the property of being alive and absent from home and the property of being outside home, it may still be possible to know by inference that there are such cases. However, such an inference isn't available for things that aren't parts (or material causes) of other perceptible composite things: for instance, I cannot know by a similar inference that a pot isn't in contact with atoms that aren't parts of any perceptible middle-sized objects. Udayana now considers a last objection to his view.

The third objection: the presence of the ground in the site cannot be known by perception

The Naiyāyika continues: Moreover, it is also unreasonable to say that even though *arthâpatti* brings about knowledge of the property to be proven through the mediation of the agent's certainty about a relation of pervasion, it doesn't require the presence of the reason in the subject. For, if that were so, we would end up with the undesirable consequence that the presence of the reason in the subject is causally unnecessary for *arthâpatti*-based knowledge. But there is no difference between *arthâpatti* and *anumāna* in this respect. And one cannot ascertain that there obtains a relation of pervasion between the reason and the property to be proven unless they are present in the same loci. If the reason and the property to be proven weren't present in the same loci (i.e., at the same place, time, etc.), we would not be able to ascertain a relation of pervasion expressible in the form, "That which possesses smoke possesses fire," or in the form, "Wherever there is smoke there is fire," or in the form "Whenever there is smoke there is fire."

COMMENTS: Kumārila argues that in the Devadatta example, you can't know by perception that the reason is present in the subject.[6] There are two possibilities: either (i) the subject is Devadatta and the property to be proven is the property of being present outside, or (ii) the subject is the property of being present outside and the property to be proven is Devadatta himself. Now, what then is the reason? There are four possibilities: either (a) it is Devadatta himself characterized by his absence from home, (b) it could be the house characterized by Devadatta's absence, (c) it could be the absence of Devadatta from home, or (d) it could be the non-observation of Devadatta's absence. But none of these entities reside either in Devadatta or in his property of being outside his home. So, the reason isn't present in the subject at all.

However, the Naiyāyika would argue there is indeed a subject—namely, Devadatta—and a reason—the property of being alive but absent from home—in this scenario such that the reason is present in the subject. Udayana goes on to point out that if the Mīmāṃsaka were to argue that *arthâpatti* does not involve the presence of the reason in the subject, then the presence of the reason in the subject would be causally unnecessary for *arthâpatti*. Udayana replies that the same could be said about cases of *anumāna*, because (if Udayana's arguments so far are sound) there is no other relevant difference between the two epistemic instruments. So, the presence of the reason in the subject would also be causally unnecessary for *anumāna*. That's a bad result by everyone's lights. Second, it is impossible to ascertain that a reason is related to a property to be proven by a relation of pervasion, unless the two occur in the same loci. This is because the relation of pervasion between a reason and property to be proven consists in the invariable occurrence of the property to be proven in any object or at any spatio-temporal location where the reason occurs. That is why statements of such relations of pervasion involve quantifiers like "wherever," "whenever," and so on.

Udayana's argument so far has only targeted the metaphysical conception of incongruity-otherwise. What about the epistemological conception? On this view, for any two properties X and Y, Y is incongruous without X if and only if, given that the presence of Y in an object o is known by some epistemic instrument, if X weren't posited, then the epistemic instrument by which the presence of Y in o is known would conflict with some other epistemic instrument. Udayana next turns to this topic.

[6] See Ollett and Freschi in this volume, p. 48. Verses 10–18 in the *Arthâpatti-pariccheda* in Śāstrī (1978: 321–2).

The argument against incongruity-otherwise from the sameness of object requirement

The Mīmāṃsaka: When two epistemic instruments conflict with each other, *arthâpatti* is what demonstrates that there is no such conflict (*avirodhôpapādika*). But, *anumāna* isn't like this.

The Naiyāyika: If there were indeed a conflict between two epistemic instruments, one of them would simply be rebutted just as in the case of the rope and the snake. But both couldn't have the status of an epistemic instrument. Alternatively, if both were to have the status of an epistemic instrument, then there wouldn't be a conflict, either (i) because the properties that they ascribe to the same object can be present together just as in the case of an awareness-event of the form "This middle-sized thing is one," or (ii) because they are about distinct objects just as in the case of an awareness-event of the form, "This is Caitra, but this is Maitra."

Comments: As Udayana notes, it's not clear how one epistemic instrument can conflict with another. First, if there is a genuine conflict between two epistemic instruments, then one epistemic instrument could rebut another. In a case where you misperceive a piece of rope as a snake, your awareness-event (*jñāna*) has the content, "That's a snake." As you come closer, you see that it's only a piece of rope, and the content of your perceptual awareness-event is, "That's a piece of rope." The two awareness-events conflict with each other. Since your second perceptual awareness-event has the status of knowledge, it rebuts the means by which the earlier awareness-event arose. Udayana's claim is that, similarly, if one epistemic instrument were to conflict with another, then one would rebut the other.

Second, Udayana endorses the principle that two epistemic instruments can conflict with each other only if they ascribe incompatible properties to the same object. Udayana's claim is that two epistemic instruments cannot satisfy this requirement of conflict. The awareness-event produced by any epistemic instrument is always true. If two epistemic instruments were to conflict with each other, then, by this requirement of conflict, the contents of the awareness-events they produce couldn't be true together.

Typically, in cases of apparent conflict between two epistemic instruments, one of the two conditions for epistemic conflict fails—either their being about the same object, or the properties being genuinely incompatible. In the case where the agent undergoes an awareness-event of the form, "This is Caitra, but this is Maitra," Caitra and Maitra are distinct persons, so the property of being Caitra cannot be instantiated together with the property of being Maitra. But since the two occurrences of the demonstrative "this" pick out two distinct objects, there is no conflict between the two epistemic instruments. In the other case, the agent undergoes an awareness-event of the form, "This middle-sized thing is one." Even though "this" picks out just one object, e.g., a pot, middle-sizedness and oneness can be instantiated together, so there is no epistemic conflict. The implicit claim here is that in the Devadatta example, the agent undergoes two awareness-events of the form, "Devadatta exists somewhere" and "Devadatta isn't at home."

Even though the awareness-events are of the same object, the property of being absent from home isn't incompatible with the property of being present somewhere. By the aforementioned requirement of conflict, therefore, there cannot be any conflict between the two relevant epistemic instruments.

A response

THE MĪMĀṂSAKA: In the relevant scenario, the house enters into the extension of "some place" in the awareness-event of the form "There is some place where he exists," due to its generality. So, in this case too, there is sameness of objects.

THE NAIYĀYIKA: If this is so, there is no conflict here, just as there is no conflict between two awareness-events of the form, "There is some place where he exists" and "There is some place where he doesn't exist."

THE MĪMĀṂSAKA: In this scenario, too, there indeed is a conflict.

THE NAIYĀYIKA: Then, the agent should hold on to only one of these awareness-events.

THE MĪMĀṂSAKA: The agent needn't hold on to only one of these awareness-events, since *arthâpatti* makes both congruous.

THE NAIYĀYIKA: What then is incongruous?

THE MĪMĀṂSAKA: The conflict, which is itself incongruous otherwise, establishes the two awareness-events as being about different objects.

THE NAIYĀYIKA: Why does it not at all establish the awareness-events as being about the same object?

THE MĪMĀṂSAKA: Here, establishing involves showing that there is no conflict. The conflict between these two awareness-events arises insofar as they are about the same object. How can it be resolved in virtue of that very property of the two awareness-events? It is not the case that someone who is rendered unconscious by some poison can be revived by means of that very poison.

THE NAIYĀYIKA: How does one know that the two awareness-events conflict in virtue of having the same object?

THE MĪMĀṂSAKA: The nature of every object is found to be such that it is located at distinct places (i.e., it is never present at one place but also absent from it).

THE NAIYĀYIKA: Well, this is just a kind of pervasion. And in that case, you end up in the proverbial predicament of a daybreak at the tax booth.

COMMENTS: In response to Udayana's objection, the Bhāṭṭa Mīmāṃsakas might try to show there is indeed a conflict between the two epistemic instruments in the Devadatta example. They might say that, when an agent undergoes an awareness-event of the form "Devadatta is alive," the content of this awareness-event can be understood as, "There is some place where Devadatta exists." The existential quantifier "some place" ranges over all possible places, so it covers

Devadatta's house. In this sense, this awareness ascribes to Devadatta's house the presence of Devadatta. When the agent then notices Devadatta's absence at his house, she undergoes an awareness-event of the form, "Devadatta's house is a place where he doesn't exist." This awareness ascribes to Devadatta's house the absence of Devadatta. Thus, the two awareness-events ascribe two incompatible properties to the same object, i.e., Devadatta's house. Hence, as the Mīmāṃsaka notes, there is sameness of objects in this case. Since the two conditions laid down by the aforementioned requirement of conflict are satisfied, a conflict between the two epistemic instruments can arise.

Udayana argues that, if this is right, then there would be a conflict between the epistemic instrument that gives rise to an awareness-event of the form "There is some place where Devadatta exists" and an epistemic instrument that gives rise to the awareness-event of the form "There is some place where Devadatta doesn't exist." By the Mīmāṃsaka's own reasoning, the quantifier "some place" in both awareness-events ranges over Devadatta's house. So, the two awareness-events ascribe two incompatible properties to the same object—, i.e., Devadatta's house. But Udayana thinks that there is no such conflict here.

As Udayana is quick to notice, the Mīmāṃsaka could indeed bite the bullet and argue that there is indeed a conflict between the two epistemic instruments, which the agent is able to resolve by positing that the place where Devadatta is present is distinct from the place from he is absent. This would show that these two awareness-events are in fact about distinct places, so there is no conflict. As a result, the agent would be able to accept the contents of both these awareness-events as true.

Anticipating this move, Udayana goes on to ask how, in this case, an agent can know that there is a conflict between the two epistemic instruments. Note that the conflict arises only if one takes "some place" in both awareness-events to mean the same place. But in order to recognize that there is a conflict in this way, the agent must know that, if someone exists at a certain place, then that person isn't absent from it. But this is just a relation of pervasion. Thus, the agent's knowledge of incongruity-otherwise—insofar as it consists in her knowledge of the conflict between two epistemic instruments—is nothing but knowledge of a certain relation of pervasion. Udayana here compares the Mīmāṃsaka to a thief who wants to evade taxes on stolen goods: in order to cross the river without paying taxes, he sets out in the dark of the night, but is ultimately caught by the tax-collector when day breaks near a tax booth (*ghaṭṭa-kuṭī*) on the riverside.

The argument from overgeneration

The Naiyāyika continues: Alternatively, smoke too would make known the presence of fire in virtue of being incongruous. For it is indeed not congruous without fire. Moreover, there could be a conflict of the following kind: "Since there is smoke, there must be fire (on the hill), and since fire isn't observed, it must be absent." Here, *arthâpatti* helps us establish that non-observation of fire pertains to the front part of the hill, and that smoke has as its object the presence of some fire that is unobservable due to distance. Why would this be a case of *anumāna*?

THE MĪMĀṂSAKA: The agent's awareness of the form "This possesses fire" arises out of an *anumāna* which is based on a relation of pervasion. Otherwise, if there were no *anumāna*, there would be no conflict. However, the awareness of the form "There is fire on the other side of the hill"—which arises due to the conflict with the non-observation of fire on the front part of the hill—is indeed derived from an *arthâpatti*.

THE NAIYĀYIKA: No. The conflict in question has been formulated with respect to the epistemic instrument by which the agent apprehends the relevant relation of pervasion. Furthermore, the latter epistemic instrument (which establishes that there is fire on the other side of the hill) is also not *arthâpatti*. Otherwise, *arthâpatti* would also establish the presence of chaff fire on the basis of a conflict between whiteness and the property of not being produced from chaff.

THE MĪMĀṂSAKA: This is not so, because there is a relation of pervasion between white smoke and chaff fire.

THE NAIYĀYIKA: If this is correct, then how can the previous example be a case of *arthâpatti*? For there is a relation of pervasion between smoke that is characterized by unobserved fire on the front part of the hill and fire that is present on the other side of the hill. So, the two cases are similar.

COMMENTS: Udayana now arrives at the objection that he raises in 3.19cd against the claim that incongruity-otherwise consists in a conflict between two epistemic instruments. His worry is that if incongruity-otherwise just consists the conflict between two epistemic instruments as Bhāṭṭa Mīmāṃsakas think, then certain well-known cases of *anumāna* would have to be treated as instances of *arthâpatti*.

Udayana points out that, in the standard *anumāna* from smoke to fire, smoke could be treated as incongruous without fire, so this *anumāna* could be treated as an *arthâpatti*. This is not convincing: while this could be true on the metaphysical conception of incongruity-otherwise, it's not obvious that there is a conflict between two epistemic instruments in this case. Anticipating this worry, Udayana describes another example involving an agent who doesn't see any fire on the front part of the hill but, on seeing some smoke coming out of the other side of the hill, infers the presence of fire on that side. Udayana wants to say that this is a case of *anumāna*. The hill is the subject of the *anumāna*, and the property to be proven is the property of having fire on the other side. The reason is the property of no fire on the front part but having smoke. However, Udayana points out that the Bhāṭṭa Mīmāṃsaka would have to treat this case as a case of *arthâpatti*. On one reconstruction of the case, this is exactly like the Devadatta example: there are two epistemic instruments, namely non-perception (*anupalabdhi*) and *anumāna*. By non-perception of fire on the front side of the hill, the agent arrives at an awareness-event of the form "That place contains no fire." Then, by *anumāna*, the agent arrives at an awareness-event that is verbalizable as, "That place contains fire." By the requirement of conflict mentioned earlier, these two awareness-events could conflict with each other if "that place" referred to the same place, e.g., the hill. But, by *arthâpatti*, the agent could resolve this conflict by determining that "that place" refers to different parts of the hill in the two awareness-events. As a result, she could thereby come to know that there is fire on the other side of the hill. This, then, would be a case of *arthâpatti*; there won't be any need for appealing to an *anumāna*.

In response, the Mīmāṃsaka might point out that we have to appeal to *anumāna* in order to generate the conflict between the two epistemic instruments, since *anumāna* is one of the epistemic instruments here. However, the final awareness that there is fire on the other side of the hill could still be a product of *arthâpatti*. But, as Udayana notes, even that is not necessary. There is a different epistemic instrument here: namely, the epistemic instrument by which the agent learnt that there is a relation of pervasion between fire and smoke. This produces the knowledge that all places that contain smoke must also contain fire. The quantifier "all places that contain smoke" ranges over the hill which is a place that contains smoke. Now, if "that place" in the previous sentence refers to the hill, there could be a conflict here due to the aforementioned requirement of conflict. So, the conflict can be generated without appealing to any *anumāna*.

In response, the Mīmāṃsaka could just admit that this is a case of *arthâpatti* which doesn't involve any *anumāna*. But this response would only work if this case were an isolated case. There are other such cases, such as the one involving white smoke and chaff fire. This is a straightforward case of *anumāna*. But Udayana thinks that the Bhāṭṭa Mīmāṃsaka can be forced to say that this is a case of *arthâpatti*. Suppose, in that case, the agent first learns by *anumāna* that there is *some kind* of fire on the hill (where the quantifier "some kind of fire" ranges over chaff as well as non-chaff fire), but then notices that the smoke on the hill is white. Since she knows that all places that contain white smoke contain chaff fire, this generates a conflict between the two epistemic instruments with respect to the particular hill. In order to resolve this conflict, the agent would have to posit that the hill contains only chaff fire. Moreover, as Udayana goes on to say, if the Mīmāṃsaka tries to say that this is not a case of *arthâpatti* (since it requires the agent to know that there is a relation of pervasion between white smoke and chaff fire), the same could be said about the earlier case. For there too the agent must know that the property of containing smoke without containing fire on the front part is pervaded by the property of containing fire on the other side.

The Mīmāṃsaka now raises a final worry about the reductionist view.

The final objection and Udayana's response

The Mīmāṃsaka: *Arthâpatti* is what others recognize as negative-only *anumāna*. For, in such cases, there is an absence of positive correlation.

The Naiyāyika: We will not object to the application of the label "*arthâpatti*" to particular varieties of *anumāna*.

The Mīmāṃsaka: Why should they be called "*anumāna*"?

The Naiyāyika: Because they arise out of a reason that doesn't obtain without the property to be proven. The property of not obtaining without a property to be proven is common to reasons of both positive-only and negative-only varieties. And the ascertainment of this property is either due to the observation of both positive and negative correlations, or instances of either. Hence, it is correct to say that the expression "*arthâpatti*" is just a synonym of "*anumāna*," or refers to a particular variety of *anumāna*, like the expression "*pūrvavat*," (i.e., *anumāna* from cause to effect), etc.

COMMENTS: At least in some cases of *arthâpatti*, no positive correlation between the reason and the property to be proven is observed.[7] In such cases, an agent can only know the relevant relation of pervasion by observing a negative correlation between the two. If that is correct, then, for a Naiyāyika who accepts reductionism about *arthâpatti*, any such instance of *arthâpatti*-based knowledge must be produced by an *anumāna* of the negative-only variety. Udayana's imagined Mīmāṃsaka generalizes this claim and says that all instances of *arthâpatti*-based knowledge might indeed be produced by what the Naiyāyikas call an *anumāna* of the negative-only variety.

Udayana points out that the Naiyāyikas may indeed be happy with this view. For *arthâpatti* would just be a kind of *anumāna*.[8] However, the Bhaṭṭas don't recognize inferences of this kind as *anumāna*s. Kumārila argues that inferences of this kind are defective, since the reason in inferences of this sort suffers from a defect known as uncommonness (*asādhāraṇatva*), i.e., it isn't known to be present anywhere apart from the subject.[9] But in order to arrive at an *anumiti*, the agent must antecedently know, and therefore be certain, that there is no place where the reason is present but the property to be proven absent. In order to gain such certainty, the agent must observe both positive and negative correlations between the reason and the property to be proven. Merely observing cases of this second kind cannot help us rule out this possibility. For this leaves open the possibility that there are unobserved cases (including the subject) where the property to be proven is absent and the reason is present.[10] So, we cannot arrive at an *anumiti* by observing a negative correlation between the reason and the property to be proven.

---

[7] See Ollett and Freschi in this volume, p. 61. Sanskrit: verses 35–46 of his *Chapter on arthâpatti*.

[8] Udayana himself defends the necessity of negative-only *anumāna*s in *A Row of Rays*. The argument is basically that a chief function of any definition (*lakṣaṇa*) is to lay down a property by which one can distinguish instances of a kind K from things that don't belong to that kind K. Udayana argues that the defining property that is common to all and only instances of K can only do so by becoming the reason of an *anumāna* like "Earth is different from what is not earth, because it has earthhood." But here the reason—earthhood—is present only in the subject, so there is no object—other than the subject—where the reason and the property to be proven are both present. Hence, this has to be a negative-only *anumāna*. For the relevant passages, see Jetly (1971: 29).

[9] See verses 86–88 in the *Anumāna-pariccheda* in Śāstrī (1978: 266–7).

[10] It is unclear why this is true. Even though Kumārila doesn't explain this, the same issue is discussed by Buddhist epistemologists such as Diṅnāga and Dharmakīrti. At *Pramāṇa-vārttika* III.11–13, Dharmakīrti discusses a *śeṣavat anumāna*, i.e., an *anumāna* that proceeds from an effect to a cause "All living beings have attachment, etc., because they have bodies." Here, the body is supposed to be the effect of attachment, etc. Here, the subject includes all living beings: hence, there is no place—other than the subject—where the reason and the property to be proven are present together. Hence, there are no cases of positive correlation. Dharmakīrti argues that an agent cannot ascertain that the presence of a body is pervaded by attachment, etc., merely because she doesn't observe any cases where a person with a body lacks attachment, etc. For the absence of counter-evidence cannot be sufficient to generate the certainty that this relation of pervasion holds. Dharmakīrti compares this to a case where a person concludes that there is no uncooked rice on a plate because she doesn't observe any uncooked rice. See Gnoli (1960: 8–10).

Here Udayana repeats the standard Nyāya response to this concern. If an agent is to know by *anumāna* the presence of a property to be proven in a subject from her observation of a reason, then she must know that the reason doesn't deviate from the property to be proven, i.e., isn't present at a place from which the property to be proven is absent. This feature of the reason, according to Udayana, can be known not only by observing its positive correlation with the property to be proven, but also by observing its negative correlation with that property, or both positive and negative correlations. So, *arthâpatti* ends up being synonymous with, or just a variety of, *anumāna*.

REFERENCES

Jetly, J. S., ed. (1971), *Praśastapādabhāṣyam: With the Commentary Kiraṇāvalī of Udayanācārya*, Baroda: Oriental Institute.

Gnoli, R., ed. (1960), *The Pramānavārttikam of Dharmakīrti: The First Chapter With the Autocommentary*, Rome: Instituto italiano per il medio ed estremo oriente.

Goswami, M., ed. (1972), *Nyāyakusumāñjali of Udayanācārya with the Commentaries Āmoda, Viveka, Bodhanī* and *Parimala*, Darbhanga: Mithila Research Institute.

Śāstrī, D. D., ed. (1978), *Ślokavārttikam Kumārilabhaṭṭapādaviracitam*, Varanasi: Tara Publications.

Ṭhakur, A., ed. (1966), *Nyāyavārttikatātparyapariśuddhiḥ*, New Delhi: Indian Council of Philosophical Research.

Ṭhakur, A., ed. (1997), *Nyāyabhāṣyavārttikam*, New Delhi: Indian Council of Philosophical Research.

Upādhyāya, P. and D. Śāstri, eds. (1957), *The Nyāyakusumāñjali of Śrī Udayanācārya with Four Commentaries: The Bodhinī, Prakāśa, Prakāśikā (Jalada) and Makaranda by Varadarāja, Varddhamānopādhyāya, Mecha Thakkura and Rucidattopādhyāya and with Notes by Śrī Dharmadatta (Bachchā Jhā)*, Benares: Chowkhamba Sanskrit Series.

Varadācārya, K. S., ed. (1983), *Nyāya-mañjarī of Jayanta Bhaṭṭa with Ṭippaṇi Nyāya-saurabha by the Editor*, Vol. 2, Mysore: Mysore Oriental Research Institute.

CHAPTER EIGHT

Gaṅgeśa's *Jewel of Reflection on the Truth about Epistemology*

Translated by STEPHEN PHILLIPS

INTRODUCTION

Not much is known about our author, Gaṅgeśa. From his traditional designation (*mahôpādhyāya*) we know he was a professional teacher. And we can infer a good deal from his *Jewel* (*maṇi*) as his great work of Nyāya philosophy, the *Jewel of Reflection on the Truth about Epistemology* (*Tattva-cintā-maṇi*), came to be called. Clearly Gaṅgeśa was familiar with most earlier Nyāya literature as well as that of its sister school, Vaiśeṣika, along with some of that of the other classical schools. Outside of Nyāya, his best familiarity is with Mīmāṃsā, but he also knew quite a bit of Vedānta and Buddhist philosophy. And he would have learned the standard curricula in the grammarian literature, the epic poems, etc., some of which he occasionally cites, for example, the *Bhagavad Gītā*.

Dinesh Bhattacharya (1958) collects data from literary and other sources, and in about a dozen pages devoted to Gaṅgeśa (96–109) provides *termini a quo et ad quem* definitively and conclusively (1300 CE and 1350 CE for his period of flourishing) from the evidence he cites, which has not been challenged or corrected to date. Bhattacharya's exposition is followed and cited in, for example, Karl Potter's volume of the *Encyclopedia of Indian Philosophies* that covers Gaṅgeśa (vol. 6, 1992), and there has been little to correct or add. Some details are as follows.

Genealogical records kept in the town where Gaṅgeśa lived, Mithilā, suggest that the philosopher had a wife and three sons and a daughter. One son was the famous Nyāya author, Vardhamāna. Family further removed is apparently unimportant or at least impossible to trace other than through the son of the daughter who is listed as marrying into an important family and having a son, Ratnākāra, who became the head of one of the richest families in the area. Despite the unremarkable birth, Gaṅgeśa achieved quite some fame during his own lifetime, as we can tell from traditional titles he held such as *jagad-guru*, which would be the rough equivalent of "Distinguished University Professor" for the educational institutions of his era. He himself tells us confidently that he was *siddhânta-dīkṣā-*

guru, "Presiding Professor of Philosophical Conclusions," to use Bhattacharya's rendering (1958: 96).

About Gaṅgeśa the person there is little more to say apart from laying out his views. About his reputation, let us look at a few salient judgments of Bhattacharya (1958: 109): "The work of Gaṅgeśa became highly popular very soon and was studied and commented upon in various centers of culture of India. It not only cast the works of the old school of logic into oblivion but the neo-logical works of his predecessors also faded into insignificance and were gradually forgotten due to its overwhelming popularity and all-embracing character." In particular, concerning the part on inference (*anumāna*), the learned Sanskritist writes (107–8):

> The second part on Anumāna (Inference) is by far the most popular, though the most intricate of the whole book . . . The latest phase of Navyanyāya studies in India for about two centuries flowed through a large number of channels cut by single sentences or phrases of this part of Gaṅgeśa's work and by far the widest channel emerged from the general definition of Fallacy. It has now assumed proportions through the efforts of all the best Indian brains in Navyanyāya, which is a world's wonder in the field of intellectual feats, though to the uninitiated it is only "a vast mass of perverted ingenuity."

Obliquely, Bhattacharya refers to A. B. Keith who was the leading American scholar of classical Indian philosophy from the 1920s to the 1940s, who unfortunately knew practically nothing about the later periods.

Gaṅgeśa's reputation got a boost among later Western experts through the work of Daniel Ingalls in his *Materials for the Study of Navya Nyāya* (1951). Until the work of Bimal Matilal (1968) and Jiten Mohanty (1966), however, most of the *Jewel* remained inaccessible not only to non-Sanskritists but also to Sanskritists and indeed specialists in Indian philosophy who did not have the necessary logical tools or patience with Gaṅgeśa's densely packed style.

The *Jewel*'s section on *arthâpatti* occurs in about the middle of a long chapter on inference as a knowledge source (*pramāṇa*). The mainstream Nyāya view is that what Mīmāṃsakas and others regard as a knowledge source of a different character than inference, namely, *arthâpatti*, is indeed a knowledge-generator but is not different from inference, specifically of the negative-only variety. As is explained in the *Jewel*'s immediately preceding section, negative-only inference[1] works based solely on negative correlations. For a given inferential subject (*pakṣa*) which we will call *a*, we are able to prove it is S (the *sādhya* or probandum) given that *a* is H (the *hetu* or prover) and also given that correlations between things not-S and not-H are known without a counter-example. Gaṅgeśa opens the section by asserting this reductive theory.

For a stock Mīmāṃsā case taken up by our philosopher at the end of the section, the two analyses are approximately as follows. First, disregarding for the moment the differences between the Bhāṭṭa and the Prābhākara factions, the Mīmāṃsaka would say that once apprised of the information that Devadatta does not eat during

[1] Editor's note: the term "inference" in this chapter refers only to *anumāna* unless otherwise noted.

the day we presume that he eats at night; that is to say, we arrive at the knowledge that he eats at night by *arthâpatti*. The Naiyāyika view, in contrast, is that "Fat Devadatta does not eat during the day, therefore he eats at night" is an inference: where H = "is fat and does not eat during the day" and S = "eats at night," whoever is H, that person is S; what is not so (¬S) is not so (¬H), like Maitra (who is known not to eat at night and is known to be either not fat or to eat during the day). This would be a negative-only inference so long as there is no one else known to be like Devadatta in being fat and eating only at night. We do know that he eats at night (although this has not been observed); that is, we know by inference, and our inductive base is comprised only of negative correlations.

Also encompassing from the Nyāya perspective the Mīmāṃsaka's putatively additional source in some cases are (the problematic) *sāmānyato-dṛṣṭa* type of inference and hypothetical reasoning (*tarka*). Unlike a few of his Nyāya predecessors—Uddyotakara and Jayanta Bhaṭṭa in particular—Gaṅgeśa does not appear to view the former as the same as negative-only inference, while—in one of Gaṅgeśa's great themes—use of the latter does not amount to admission of another *pramāṇa*. These positions will be elaborated in comments below.

We may note that for Nyāya the issue of *arthâpatti* as a knowledge source is taken up as early as the *Nyāya-sūtra*, which also rejects it as a *pramāṇa* different from inference (NS 2.2.2–6). Uddyotakara views it as the same as *sāmānyato-dṛṣṭa* inference. Unfortunately, the *Nyāya-sūtra* commentaries on this type of inference are not particularly clear, as Jayanta Bhaṭṭa complains, joining and expanding on Uddyotakara, from very early (Sukla 1971: 119 and 274). Rejecting the *Nyāya-sūtra*'s division of inference into three types, Jayanta understands the *sāmānyato-dṛṣṭa* to involve an imperceptible object inferred on the basis of a relation between universals (Sukla 1971: 120 and 277). One of the examples he gives is inference to the existence of the supersensuous organ of hearing. There is a pervasion relationship between (H) the general character of an act such as hearing and (S) the existence of at least one instrument for the act, as an axe for the felling of a tree. Since hearing is an act, it has to have an instrument, and so we presume there is an organ of hearing. Gaṅgeśa seems to have a similar understanding of this type of inference, and despite his opening statement here rejecting it, whether he views it as invariably the same as negative-only inference is a little problematic, considering the whole of the *Jewel*, since he employs it in dozens of places.

WITHIN THE *TATTVA-CINTĀ-MAṆI*, IN THE INFERENCE CHAPTER

Now the section on arthâpatti

GAṄGEŚA: Given that knowledge comes about through negative-only inference (*kevala-vyatireka*), *arthâpatti* is not another knowledge source. For, the things that *arthâpatti* would make known are made known just by negative-only inference.

COMMENTS: After stating the mainstream Nyāya view, Gaṅgeśa invents a Mīmāṃsaka *pūrva-pakṣin* ("opponent") who presents a stock example, one similar to—though Gaṅgeśa fills it out with more detail—a case discussed by Kumārila Bhaṭṭa at the opening of his long section on *arthâpatti* where he defends *arthâpatti* as a separate *pramāṇa* (Sastri 1978: 320–5; Jha 1908: 230–43, see p. 47 in this volume). But probably we should think of the objector as intended by Gaṅgeśa to be a Prābhākara, as will be explained. In any case, a *pūrva-pakṣin* opens by asking us to consider a case that shows that *arthâpatti* should be regarded as an additional knowledge source distinct from inference because the knowledge generated is generated by a causal complex distinct from that of knowledge by inference.

PŪRVA-PAKṢIN: That may be. (But consider the following.) Either from astrological science or from an inferential mark to the same effect, someone (M) understands that Devadatta will live to be a hundred years old. There is the principle, confirmed by perception, that hundred-year-old-persons (Devadatta is, we are to assume, now about ninety-nine) at the end stay at home, while later his absence from his house becomes certain (to M) by means of non-perception of something fit to be perceived. Thus doubt is generated by the two sources of knowledge, the rule about the life (of the very old) and the direct grasping (of Devadatta's absence), with no determination of which is the stronger or weaker. In the moment of doubt, there is no thought that he may be outside. Doubt arises about which of the two rules is correct (that he will live to be a hundred or that the very old stay at home). Having arrived at the doubt, "Is he alive or not?" M (the subject) would think that he has gone outside, as a way of holding onto the idea of his being alive (as attested by the one source), in order to remove doubt about his living. (Assume that it is true that Devadatta has indeed gone outside.) Right after the causal complex is in place as described, M knows that Devadatta is outside. Through the instrumentality of doubt here in this case, as is shown (through other cases) by positive and negative correlation (*anvaya-vyatireka*), (certainty about) his absence from the house or doubt about which of the two rules should generate (cognition here in this instance) would be the trigger (of the knowledge).

Alternatively, doubt about whether he was alive (would trigger the knowledge) in that there is no rule (as you Naiyāyikas think) that a trigger has to be put into operation (as an axe has to be put into operation to fell a tree). Cognition of opposition between the two knowledge sources would be the trigger, according to some (i.e, through the operation), through the instrumentality of the doubt conceived because of that opposition. In this case, because of the impossibility of inference in that the requirement of the inferential mark's qualifying the inferential subject is dubious—that is, his being alive is dubious—*arthâpatti* is another knowledge source.

COMMENTS: Both major subschools of Mīmāṃsā, the Bhāṭṭa and the Prābhākara, recognize *arthâpatti* as a separate *pramāṇa* but view its workings a little differently. The Bhāṭṭa views presumptive knowledge as arising from an appreciation of "inexplicability otherwise," *anyathânupapatti*, whereas the Prābhākara sees it as arising from doubt generated by cognitions containing conflicting information (Śālikanātha 1961: 272–81; Padurangi 2004: 241–67; see Ollett and Freschi in this volume, p. 96). Furthermore, the Prābhākara does not admit non-perception (*anupalabdhi*) as a separate knowledge source, unlike the Bhāṭṭa, but sees perception as capable of generating knowledge of an absence so long as the counterpositive is fit to be perceived. Thus Gaṅgeśa's intention appears to be that we take the current opponent to be a Prābhākara.

The *pūrva-pakṣin*'s argument is clear: the supposition that Devadatta is outside is not inference because the causal complex sufficient for it is different from that for inference. The supposition is knowledge nonetheless, and thus must have a source that is distinct from inference.

Next, we are treated to a series of mainly Naiyāyika but also Bhāṭṭa objections to the Prābhākara and the Prābhākara's responses. The idea that *arthâpatti* works by imagination or supposition (*kalpanā*) resolving an incompatibility is the heart of the Prābhākara position.

OBJECTION (AGAINST THE PŪRVA-PAKṢIN): If doubt is to cause supposition, the unfortunate consequence would be that even from (genuine) doubt (e.g.) whether (something in the distance is) a post or a person there would be supposition settling on one of the options (whereas often doubt cannot be resolved). Furthermore, doubt about something known does not inform supposition (*kalpanā*).

Then if Devadatta's being alive or not were something known, the difficulty would be that there would be no doubt. And if there is to be certainty about his being alive or not, then it would be from inference alone that there is certainty that he is outside.

Moreover, in some cases when something comes to be known, the supposition would be for a while to have doubt about it, before (e.g.) the thing is known as a person.

Furthermore, there would be nothing triggering an inference that he has gone outside, because of (the logical rule of) counter-example, since doubt about his being alive or not would be found also if he were dead.

PŪRVA-PAKṢIN: No. The doubt that originates the causal complex (sufficient to produce M's knowledge) as described does inform the supposition. Just for this reason, certainty about someone who is dead being absent from the house, or about the someone, that is, who is about to be born, does not result in the difficulty about doubt that you describe. Therefore, it is not a causal factor for M's knowledge that he is outside. And absence from the house, which is certain (to M) because of non-perception of something fit to be perceived, does not (generally) make for doubt (but only in the circumstance of two bits of knowledge with incompatible contents, as indicated).

COMMENTS: Incompatible certainties do occur. We can even have simultaneous bits of occurrent knowledge, according to the Prābhākara. Furthermore, the *pūrva-pakṣin* does not see all doubt as generating knowledge, but rather, in this and like cases, only doubt that has itself been generated by incompatible "certainties." The objector overlooks the restriction. Śālikanātha (1961: 273–4; see Freschi and Ollett in this volume, p. 106) considers the opponent's charge and responds in much the same way as our *pūrva-pakṣin*.

Objection (against the pūrva-pakṣin): Well, if the two knowledge sources, the rule about a living (very old) person and the grasping (an absence by non-perception of something fit to be perceived) are understood as equal in strength, where then would there be supposition that he is outside? For there is no experience of the particular (namely, Devadatta). Or there would be two suppositions: like the being outside resolved upon by his being alive being known, there would also be his death resolved upon by the rule about (very old people not leaving) the house, which would be expressed. There would be that supposition, too. For there would be no difference (favoring the one or the other) in the doubts about his being alive or being dead.

Then, of the two, one might be stronger, the other weak. In that case, one would simply be defeated by the other. Thus there would be no doubt.

Therefore, where it has been understood that Devadatta will live a hundred years along with his absence from the house, there will be supposition that he is outside, which has nothing to do with doubt whether he is alive. And so Devadatta's being outside given that he is alive follows from his being the counterpositive of an absolute absence located in the house (i.e., Devadatta's not being in the house). Here it is by *arthâpatti* that there would be knowledge that he is outside, knowledge based on negative correlations (what is not in a house, that is outside the house), because of which there would be no "supposition" that he is outside in response to doubt whether he is living as the qualifying mark.

Moreover, it would not be appropriate to hold that the certainty about his absence from the house—having generated doubt about the particular object that would be known by the pair of knowledge sources—would make M suppose that Devadatta is outside, M having presumed doubt about his being alive. For, it is not the case that from doubt about x from some reason, just there it would make for certainty about x, because such a rule would extend too far.

> Comments: According to this objector, some doubts last and are not resolved. A viable alternative may be to live with a doubt, at least until the time and situation is right for resolving it. The objector seems to be a Naiyāyika who is making the issue how much work a bit of certainty can do. Doesn't the *pūrva-pakṣin* presume *too much* from (albeit) the certainty that Devadatta is not at home?

Pūrva-pakṣin: Don't think like that. Someone (M) having doubt which has been generated by a collection of causal factors as described would be compelled to reason thus: Devadatta's absence from the house has been grasped through non-perception of something fit to be perceived. The certainty about this is very firm. One of two cognitive instigators (complete with evidence), Devadatta's being alive or the rule (about the very old not leaving their houses), is to be defeated, since the two as opposed (to one another) are not (to be regarded as) knowledge sources.

So here M, supposing Devadatta's being dead, would think that the instigator of cognition of his being alive is defeated, that it ought to be let go. Alternatively, M, supposing Devadatta is outside, would think that the rule about the house (and the very old) as cognitive instigator is defeated, that it ought to be let go: the absence would be the defeater precisely of the rule about the house as cognitive instigator if M supposes Devadatta is outside. But on the supposition that he has died, the pair of rules that Devadatta will live to be a hundred years old and as a living hundred-year-old person he would always stay at home would be defeated (as a pair) as well.

Thus it is said: "Because dropping the rule about it would be necessary, (the idea of) his being alive would be defeated."

Moreover, "Today you live, tomorrow you'll wish you were alive" and the like capture how life happens, namely, as lawfully connected to—to consider the attribute of time—a few hours, (days), etc., (all) as the briefest of moments as backed up by much more (positive evidence than the other way around, e.g., someone living a hundred years). To rule this out (namely, that Devadatta is alive): there is (a record of) defeating that correlates much more thoroughly (with crushed hopes through life being short). The correlation of Devadatta, all the parts of him (self, mind, and body), and staying at home (as a very old person) is comparatively slight (we should add, since if he died, he would be "outside" in a sense). Thus, with respect to his dying which would be by its very nature an absence (of him as a whole person, and not just a self, in the house), his being outside (in the broadest sense including his dying as well as his being alive and outside), as an entity (a whole person), is the simpler position, easier to accept. And if (on the other hand) the meaning of the word "outside" is to be taken as there being a locus of the conjunction (between self and body, also mind, namely, Devadatta as a living person), a locus in a relationship of mutual exclusion with the house, then compared with this, his being outside (as a whole person), his being dead is the easier position (easier to take), although compared with his being dead simply his being alive is right (we presume that a person is alive unless we have heard otherwise or know by perception). Therefore, it alone is the one appropriate to suppose.

From this (it follows that) that he is alive (and outside) is known, is supposed through *arthâpatti*. The knowledge that Devadatta is outside, although it could come from inference, too, does come to be (in this way where resolution of doubt is crucial). Doubt, whose origins are the complex of factors explained, aided by hypothetical reasoning (*tarka*) of the sort laid out above, makes M suppose that Devadatta is outside.

Objection: This is the mere appearance of hypothetical reasoning in considering wrong and inconclusive cases. Furthermore, M might wish to infer just this being outside, making an inference aided (indeed) by such hypothetical reasoning such that in consideration of its conclusive determination it would be just this (bit of knowledge, namely, that Devadatta is outside).

Pūrva-pakṣin: That should not be alleged. Bits of hypothetical reasoning of these sorts (as above) of comparative ease or difficulty of acceptance, where we do take up wrong and inconclusive cases (i.e., a complex of considerations, some mutually opposed) are indeed aids to the operation of a knowledge source (and thus genuine, no mere appearance). Just for this reason, the hypothetical reasoning here is an aid, as it would be, too, in support of something known by perception or testimony or in another manner.

And in this situation (as described, featuring doubt as trigger) there is not another way M would know this. Therefore, the hypothetical reasoning is an aid to (a genuine knowledge source, the source we call) *arthâpatti*.

COMMENTS: Here a more natural term for "cognitive instigator" (*grāhaka*) would be "evidence," that is, when we are concerned with inference based on induction. "Cognitive instigation" is broader than "inferential evidence" in that, for example, the operation of a sensory organ could be the instigator of a bit of perceptual knowledge.

Let us remind ourselves that the current *pūrva-pakṣin* is quite sophisticated, and a construct, not an historical figure. Clearly Gaṅgeśa has studied both Kumārila and Prabhākara or at least Prabhākara's primary classical interpreter, Śālikanātha, and the current quotation ("Because dropping the rule about it would be necessary, (the idea of) his being alive would be defeated"), while not from Kumārila, expresses a view Kumārila asserts (ŚV verses 21–4: 1961: 323–4; Jha 1908: 232–3; see Freschi and Ollett in this volume, p. 53). However, the quotation is not necessarily to be taken as from a Bhāṭṭa. There is, after all, only subtle disagreement historically between the Prābhākara and the Bhāṭṭa on the present topic, with many shared views. Nevertheless, the classical commentators tell us that it is a Prābhākara that Gaṅgeśa is constructing as his *pūrva-pakṣin*.

OBJECTION: If doubt as described, complemented by hypothetical reasoning about the individual and his intrinsic capacities, brings about knowledge of Devadatta's being outside, then, whether he is dead or whether he is in the house, whatever the supposition (i.e., whether a lucky guess or justified) that, too, would be knowledge (*pramā*).

PŪRVA-PAKṢIN: Wrong. For, as there can be errors of the sense organs, which are nevertheless knowledge-producers, in other words (so-called) sensory errors—because the illuminating power of the knowledge gets eclipsed through a flaw (*doṣa*)—so likewise there is the possibility of error regarding the above-described doubt, too. The error takes the form of a non-grasping.

Because of this (i.e., because of the success of this explanation), the rule stands concerning conformity (of cognition and object), that is, concerning correctness, given the non-departure (from the truth) of generated knowledge. The principle holds (as well) for bits of knowledge of things unexperienced (just as we have with knowledge by *arthâpatti*). If this is right, then it holds in the present case, too, because of the possibility that the two knowledge sources—the rule and the cognitive instigator to the effect that Devadatta is living and that he is not in the house—could be, the one or other, not a mere semblance or just a semblance.

Alternatively, we should say that the doubt as described, aided by an absence of flaws (*doṣa*), produces the knowledge that he is outside.

COMMENTS: The *pūrva-pakṣin*'s position here on the possibility of error is like his position on perceptual error, e.g., identifying silver when the thing is really tin. A non-grasping of the difference between a veridical memory of silver—"This is *silver*"—and a veridical perception of tin, the thing meant by "this," would be responsible for the action of speech, "This is silver" (when the thing is really tin). Both the perceiving and the remembering would be bits of occurrent knowledge, according to the Prābhākara's *akhyāti* ("failure to grasp") explanation of what others call illusion. The difference between the two is not grasped, and this failure sparks the erroneous statement. Thus cognition in itself is always knowledge, *pace* the Naiyāyika, always capturing the truth, although sometimes we fail to know a situation thoroughly. Here ends the section devoted to views that Gaṅgeśa will proceed to refute. Now what follows are his own views and a *siddhânta* section.

GAṄGEŚA: We answer. One of the two has to be ruled out, defeated, since the two would cognitively instigate things that are mutually opposed. Thus it is just from inference "based on particulars experienced as of a kind" (*sāmānyato-dṛṣṭa*), aided by hypothetical reasoning, that the cognitive instigator of (i.e., the evidence for) the rule about the house (and the very old staying at home) is defeated, and Devadatta's being outside is proved. That is to say, it would be known from an inference given certainty about his being alive as the qualifier (of the inferential subject) which would be the inferential mark. In other words, if the source of M's knowledge of Devadatta's being alive were defeated, then the two putative (*abhimata*) knowledge sources would also be defeated by the force of an inference to Devadatta's death by means of an inferential mark made prominent by the knowledge source which would be the rule about the house (and the very old staying at home). And if the "source" that cognitively instigates the rule about the house (and the very old staying at home) were defeated, the knowledge source showing that he is alive would be unopposed: given certainty about his being alive, that would be the qualifier (of the inferential subject) serving as (part of) the inferential mark in an inference to his being outside, ruling out one (putative) knowledge source alone. The inference would be aided by such hypothetical reasoning as we have seen. It would be of the *sāmānyato-dṛṣṭa* variety. By its force alone, one of the two (putative) knowledge sources would be ruled out, defeated. Inferential knowledge of his (i.e., being dead) about to be (re) born would take as its object that which would make M know, successively, that he is dead, and, in contrast, there would not be a knowledge source showing that he is alive, proving, successively, that he is outside.

And so what's the use of *arthâpatti*, since it would be exclusively from an inference of the *sāmānyato-dṛṣṭa* variety, from this inference alone, that M would know that Devadatta is outside? That is, it would be so given defeat for the cognitive instigation of (i.e., the evidence for) the rule about the house (and the very old) by the force of the knowledge source about his being alive such that M is certain about his being alive: his being-alive can serve as the qualifier (of the inferential subject), as the inferential mark (in the inference to his being outside).

COMMENTS: The *sāmānyato-dṛṣṭa* type of inference would not in this instance be to a supersensuous inferential subject, unlike the example Jayanta gives of the organ of hearing inferred as the instrument of hearing. Devadatta's being outside could be known by perception, and would be, were M to go out of the house and find him. Later, Gaṅgeśa appears to say that the *sāmānyato-dṛṣṭa* type of inference is restricted to the formation of general knowledge and that it takes *tarka* to apply it to an individual.

The crucial inference would take Devadatta as the *pakṣa* (inferential subject), his being a living person coupled with his not being in the house as the *hetu* (prover), and his being outside as the *sādhya* (probandum): whatever is a living person and not in a house is outside that house, *like* Caitra.

OBJECTION (BY OBJECTOR 1): Without knowledge of Devadatta's being outside, (the rule) "A living (very old person) stays always at home," is impossible to defeat even by Brahman the Absolute! From this it follows that the knowledge of his being outside has to come first. It cannot come (as you say) immediately after the defeat of the cognitively instigated rule about the house (and the very old) which (you say) would permit the inference given certainty about his being alive because the cognitive instigation (the evidence) for his living would be without opposition. (And) there can be no knowledge, at first, of his being outside without *arthâpatti*.

OBJECTION (BY OBJECTOR 2 TO OBJECTOR 1): The cognitive instigation (the evidence) for the rule about the house (and the very old) is neutralized if one is attentive (alert, i.e., M weighing the evidence correctly). So how is M to have knowledge of Devadatta's being outside even by *arthâpatti*?

ANSWER (BY OBJECTOR 1): That should not be asked. The *arthâpatti* supplemented by hypothetical reasoning, *tarka*, would be more forceful. M's knowledge of Devadatta's being outside would be produced because the source of the cognitive instigation (the overall evidence) would be defeated.

GAṄGEŚA: Wrong. Inference of the *sāmānyato-dṛṣṭa* variety along with hypothetical reasoning, *tarka*, would be more forceful inasmuch as the rule about the house (and the very old) would be susceptible to defeat in (its evidence base, i.e.) its cognitive instigation. Therefore, on an occasion of doubt as described, if Devadatta is not alive, then necessarily the rule(s) in its support would be defeated in fact (i.e., would be wrong). This is another case of hypothetical reasoning (*tarka*). It is uncontroversial that immediately after it there would be knowledge (on M's part) of Devadatta's being outside (given that the rules are not wrong, as we would realize through the *tarka*). Hypothetical reasoning is not in this scenario an aid to *doubt*, not to the doubt described where there would be no generator of the imagined (knowledge), because that is (epistemically) uneconomical (*gaurava*, compared to our view). Rather, by means of the defeating of the cognitive instigation (i.e., evidence base) of the rule (about the house and the very old) M comes to infer that Devadatta is outside in an inference of the *sāmānyato-dṛṣṭa* type, which works stepwise, because this is the economical position.

COMMENTS: Two rules were mentioned in support of the proposition that Devadatta is alive: one, an astrological prediction with which the section began; and, two, the normal assumption that a familiar acquaintance is alive unless we know by testimony or otherwise that he or she is dead.

Here we learn that the *sāmānyato-dṛṣṭa* type of inference works stepwise, although whether this is in general a differentiating characteristic is unclear. In any case, M, in the scenario presented, would indeed first have to rule out the rule about the house and the very old for the knowledge-forming inference to be triggered by perception of the absence of a *living* Devadatta in the house.

Mathurānātha glosses *kalpanīya-pramāṇâbhāve* as *kalpanīya-pramiti-janakatākâbhāve* (Calcutta 662), "no generator of the imagined (knowledge)."

OBJECTION: ***Even with inference of the** sāmānyato-dṛṣṭa* type coming on the scene, it does not render here (the conclusion you want, namely, that M knows that Devadatta is outside).

GAṄGEŚA: That should not be alleged. For, given that the one rule has been defeated with respect to an unsettled scenario, hypothetical reasoning is capable of determining which of two alternatives is to be supposed in conformity with the defeating of the other. And this would not obtain without *sāmānyato-dṛṣṭa* inference.

Furthermore, if right after cognition of the opposition the thought does not occur that one (of the two) is not a knowledge source, then there would be no doubt about the truth. And if there were no such doubt, then doubt about Devadatta's being alive (would not occur), since both his being alive and his being dead would be taken as matters of certainty (which is absurd).

COMMENTS: The second part of Gaṅgeśa's reply consists of a bit of hypothetical reasoning, which is here of the *reductio ad absurdum* variety, since no one would think that Devadatta is both alive and dead. Thus M would be aware of the fact that the one or the other is not a veritable knowledge source.

The reason that the *tarka* requires the inference is that no *tarka* working on its own is capable of generating knowledge. Hypothetical reasoning has to work in tandem with one or more knowledge sources if knowledge is to be produced as opposed to speculation.

OBJECTION: Because inference of the *sāmānyato-dṛṣṭa* type, having generated the knowledge that one of the two is not a knowledge source, would have settled the matter, the knowledge being produced that he is outside would place causality in the doubt; right after the doubt about Devadatta's being alive, which is implicit in the doubt generated by that (inference)—doubt concerning the pair of rules—there would be knowledge that he is outside, given entry of hypothetical reasoning.

GAṄGEŚA: No. For the very thing that would make M grasp that there are opposed claims—apart from the hypothetical reasoning—would have generated the inferential knowledge that one of the rules, unverified, is wrong. Well, that same thing (that same consideration, according to your line of thought)—supplemented by hypothetical reasoning—would generate, being applied again, an inference (mysteriously) in conformity with the knowledge that he is outside, the inference, namely, that there is a knowledge source that makes M grasp the rule about the house. For (on your theory), just one (consideration), through a variety of supplementations, would result in various effects. And it is not the case that immediately after doubt about Devadatta's being alive there would be such application, which is unproved. For the difficulty would be that without the cognitive instigation of the rule about the house (and the very old) making M grasp that there is a claim opposed to the cognitive instigation for Devadatta's being alive, there would be no defeating even if it were supposed (as a lucky guess) that he is outside.

COMMENTS: Gaṅgeśa brings out the comparative lack of economy of the Prābhākara view, which has doubt as the trigger of presumptive knowledge. But not only is the view uneconomical, it does not come up with the right result. M would not know that Devadatta is outside, because the same consideration could produce different conclusions in the hands of the Prābhākara. Doubt alone could be the basis for concluding that Devadatta is dead.

OBJECTION: Suppose a knowledge source that has done its job generated another effect in being applied again because of a (different and) particular aid. In that case the self would be proved by a negative-only inference, only after the inference to desire's residing in a substance that the self is accomplished, given the defeat of the thesis that it rests in any of the eight substances (earth and the rest). The inference would be of the *sāmānyato-dṛṣṭa* type: "Desire resides in a substance, *since* it is an effect."[2] For, there its proof is from the *sāmānyato-dṛṣṭa* inference alone, which is again being applied, aided by the defeat of the thesis of resting in any of the eight substances.

GAṄGEŚA: No. By the rule that a bit of inferential knowledge has its predication content (*prakāra*) specified by whatever is the pervader ("*a* is S," the probandum, S = the pervader), the knowledge's having that predication content is established by a negative-only inference. For, by restriction, too, of the capability of negative-only inference to something other (than what the first inference is capable of), there is no fault belonging to the second means.

Furthermore, the *sāmānyato-dṛṣṭa* inference, "Devadatta is the relatum (*pratiyogin*) of one or the other, living or dying, *since* he is a creature with breath, *like* myself," has as its (intentional) object—because of the aid of (hypothetical reasoning of the kind) economy ("lightness," *lāghava*)—being the relatum of living.

And likewise the proof of Devadatta's being outside is just from inference because of the certainty of the inferential mark as a qualifier of the inferential subject.

COMMENTS: In the immediately preceding section on negative-only inference, Gaṅgeśa has reformulated Uddyotakara's inference to the self as the locus of desire and examined it extensively (in the section of the *Jewel* on "negative-only" inference). Uddyotakara takes it to appear in the *Nyāya-sūtra*, and it is discussed in many subsequent Nyāya treatises.

Here the *sāmānyato-dṛṣṭa* type of inference appears to hinge on very general knowledge indeed, such as what might in the West be called *analytic*, at least given certain background knowledge in biology: "A creature with breath is either alive or dead."

OBJECTION: Because of the advice and support of conceptual economy, the *sāmānyato-dṛṣṭa* inference, too, has the particular as its object. Thus along with an inference to Devadatta's having died, whose inferential mark would have been made prominent by the knowledge source that makes us grasp the rule (about the very old

---

[2] Instances of *anumāna* in standard form are marked with italics: "Property P is found in subject S, *since* S has property H, *like* example E."

staying at home), there is a counter-inference just to the effect of making M know that he is living. This is because even a lot of evidence can be countered by just one counter-example.

And it is not the case that because of the hypothetical reasoning (*tarka*) the *sāmānyato-dṛṣṭa* inference would win out. For (the two requirements for inference, knowledge of) pervasion and (knowledge of) the prover's being a property of the inferential subject constitute the weight, and that would be known simply as equalized; that which makes M know the pervasion is equalized by the fact that the hypothetical reasoning called simplicity (*lāghava*, "economy of conception") would be conclusive only with respect to the particular (viz., Devadatta and his being outside).

GAṄGEŚA: In that case, by force of the requirement of the prover's qualifying the inferential subject, why wouldn't the particular (and its disputed property) be proved? For in every case (of *sāmānyato-dṛṣṭa* inference)—to consider the knowledge source which operates at the level of generality—there is the possibility of counter-inference insofar as a property is shared with the counterpart with respect to drawing a conclusion about a particular. Because the cognitive instigation of the rule (about the very old not leaving home) is inadequate, there is no equalization (as you claim) in a counter-inference showing the opposite, since there is inadequate motivation (for the pervasion on which it would rely). But the cognitive instigation for the thesis about living, which is an inference of the *sāmānyato-dṛṣṭa* type supported by astrological science, is perfectly correct. There is (adequate) cognitive instigation for the pervasion (on which it relies), which blocks and defeats the counter-position. Therefore, genuine counter-inference works through a knowledge source that makes us grasp some particular as different with respect to a (first) inference which is focused on the (same) particular (as the second), since a (knowledge source) operating at the level of generality by rule needs aid (to be applied to a particular).

COMMENTS: No general principle can be applied to a particular without supplementary premises. It is a truism in philosophy of science that all experimental predictions rely on measurements, specification of laboratory conditions, etc., as well as on scientific laws. The point here seems to be similar.

Noteworthy is Gaṅgeśa's view expressed here that the *sāmānyato-dṛṣṭa* type of inference requires supplementation to be applied to particulars. This seems to be for Gaṅgeśa its characteristic mark, differentiating it from negative-only inference, which of course can make a particular known as qualified by a probandum. Note that Devadatta in our scenario is not known by perception—unlike the mountain in the stock example—but rather his absence. There is perceptual knowledge of an absence; absence itself, *pace* the Bhāṭṭa, is not a knowledge source. He is not observed, although he is not, *pace* Jayanta, unobservable.

OBJECTION: The hypothetical reasoning (in support of what you say is the winning inference) is not (in this case) an aid, because of opposition from a knowledge source.

Gaṅgeśa: That should not be said. For there is no opposition in the absence of conclusions about particulars where hypothetical reasoning does not enter. When it is used, it is just to bring additional weight to that (source which it supports). Otherwise, where hypothetical reasoning has not made an appearance, (admission of) the truth of a counter-inference could not be withheld even when hypothetical reasoning does enter. Moreover, if it were the way you claim, there could be no aid (in hypothetical reasoning) even when there is *arthâpatti*, because of opposition there would be to it.

Objection: What we assert is that on the supposition that Devadatta has died, made on the basis of the rule, "A living person whose years are a hundred would always stay at home," there would be a defeating of it as well (as presumptive knowledge that he is outside). In this case, the defeating would be of (a claim about) the entity (as bearing properties, i.e.) as qualified. It is false that there would be a defeating of (a claim about) the entity (as property-bearer, i.e.) as qualificandum (*viśeṣya*) from which it would be concluded, "A living person, although dead, remains at home," since there is no defeating of (a claim about) the entity as property-bearer. Rather, the defeating is of the qualifier (*viśeṣana*). And (here) it is restricted to his being alive at a hundred years. (It follows that the claim about the entity as qualified is also defeated on the principle:) "That which is endowed with an absence of a qualifier amounts as well to an absence of the entity as qualified."

Gaṅgeśa: Wrong. We do not accept that there is an additional entity as qualified which would be something over and above (the thing as qualificandum together with its qualifiers), such that (somehow) there would belong to something, the thing which has a qualificandum, an absence of the entity as qualified (which is absurd), solely on the basis of a qualifier's absence.

> Comments: On the principle that the absence or addition of a qualifier makes a new entity, the Buddhists Dharmakīrti and company would prove universal momentariness: since things are changing all the time, nothing lasts more than an instant. To reject that principle is a project that lies at the core of Nyāya metaphysics. Gaṅgeśa touches that core here in his rejection of the principle. An entity as qualified consists of a qualificandum together with its qualifiers, also called properties. The qualificandum (*viśeṣya*) is the same thing as a property-bearer (*dharmin*)—these notions being abstractions (useful for certain purposes) from the thing as qualified, which is what we talk about and experience except in a very technical sense. An entity as qualified does not *have* a qualificandum, but rather *consists of* a qualificandum and its properties. Otherwise, there would be a bloating of Nyāya's ontology.

Gaṅgeśa: But others (say the following).

Mīmāṃsā faction: As a living person a hundred years old, Devadatta, the person, would always be at home. Among the knowledge sources, the one (perception, or non-perception) informing M that he is not at home would not be opposed if taken as a pair (with the astrological prediction), but if taken with this third (about the very old staying at home) would be in opposition. From doubt about his being alive embedded in doubt about the knowledge-source status generated by cognition of the opposition, there would be produced (awareness of) lack of opposition of two (of the three putative) knowledge sources. (Then) that he is outside would be supposed as in opposition to the one that is not a knowledge source.

This alone is the essence of the doubt as described: that which thing-wise (i.e., to consider things as they really are) is thought of as opposed to that which is not a knowledge source. The choice between the two options is just to recognize the non-knowledge-source status (or falsity) of that which makes for the oppositional factor, thing-wise.

GAṄGEŚA: That is an empty proposal. From cognition of what is not a knowledge source as a knowledge source, knowledge that Devadatta is outside would not be produced immediately following doubt as has been described, unless there were discoveries about the particular by means of hypothetical reasoning or the like. Therefore, to consider the result, there would be no such suppositional knowledge through *arthâpatti*.

Furthermore, just from such doubt as to whether Devadatta is dead, or whether he is in the house, or whether he is outside, his being outside, or his being in the house, or his having died might be supposed by someone or other, in some circumstances or other, according to how things are. And in this way, there would not be even the appearance of *arthâpatti*.

COMMENTS: Rucidatta, a sixteenth-century commentator, identifies the "others" as a faction of Mīmāṃsakas in his *Prakāśa* commentary (Tirupati 529). What practically all Mīmāṃsakas identify as presumptive knowledge is usually indeed knowledge in Naiyāyikas' estimation. But different scenarios and the reasoning it takes to figure them out require careful analysis considering the operation of knowledge sources supplemented by bits of, as the case requires, hypothetical reasoning. The fact remains that such careful analysis reveals inference as the only *pramāṇa* required to understand the generation of the various bits of knowledge, at least for the examples considered so far.

(NEW) PŪRVAPAKṢIN: That may be. Let us admit that doubt is not the trigger (of knowledge in the scenario described). It is, rather, for presumptive knowledge, inexplicability (*anupapatti*). For example, immediately after the knowledge, "Alive, Devadatta is not in his house," there is the thought that he is outside. The trigger of this knowledge is, by the method of positive and negative correlation, cognition of inexplicability.

OBJECTION (TO THE NEW PŪRVAPAKṢIN): "Devadatta is outside, *since*, given that he exists, he is not in the house, *like* a pot"; this [reasoning] is from inference, given something that exists, if it is not in whatever location, then it is in another location, as, for example, a house, precisely (as in the case discussed). Alternatively, there could be an inference based on an overextension of the rule: "If I am not in the corner, then I'm situated in the middle of the room." Either way, that he is outside would be (considered) proved. So what would be the use of *arthâpatti*?

PŪRVAPAKṢIN: That should not be asked. On an occasion when there is no knowledge of the correlation of an inferential sign and probandum, there can be knowledge that Devadatta is outside if there is inexplicability nonetheless. And the pervasion cannot pull enough together in general for inference. Therefore, the proof that he is in some other place is simply by *arthâpatti*.

> COMMENTS: The new *pūrvapakṣin* appears to speak for the Bhāṭṭa position, championing Kumārila's idea that the additional source, properly called "inexplicability otherwise" (*anyathânupapatti*), is responsible for M's knowledge.
>
> Let us pause to appreciate the cogency of the Bhāṭṭa's point that there is insufficient evidence here for proper inference. Many of the examples cited of inference—not just in this section or in Gaṅgeśa's work but throughout Nyāya literature—seem abductive in character, "reasoning to the best explanation," e.g., from a swollen river to rain upstream or, indeed, from something's smokiness as perceived by M to that same thing's fieriness in fact. The deep question is the sufficiency of inductive evidence for the various generalizations our philosophers would defend, generalizations required by the Nyāya account of inference. The Bhāṭṭa view, in contrast, would vindicate the educated guess, and thus arguably come closer to certain everyday practices (*vyavahāra*).

OBJECTION (TO THE PŪRVAPAKṢIN): When you say that existence outside the house of someone living (albeit very old) is (known as) inexplicable, (1) is it so unless Devadatta is outside is presumed, or (2) is it so unless being outside holds in general (for anyone living and not inside)?

It is not the former option. At first, Devadatta is not thought of as outside. If from that lack of knowledge it is thought that it would all be inexplicable unless he is, then what would be the point of *arthâpatti*? If it is simply from *arthâpatti* that it is to be known, then we have the fallacy of mutual dependence (*anyônyâśraya*). This has been said about being other than something for which there is proof: "Well, later on, it is still not proved."

It is not the latter option. Since there would be no inexplicability unless there were knowledge of the being-outside of simply any person, the proof would be of being-outside holding in general. Although this may be so, *Devadatta's* being outside would not be proved.

PŪRVAPAKṢIN: Wrong. For, without the general form, cognition of inexplicability is the cause of presumptive knowledge, albeit through the form of the general there does result knowledge of the particular. For example, "Unless a person who is living is outside, his not being in the house is inexplicable" is presumptive knowledge. For the one whose absence in a house would be inexplicable, existence outside for him is supposed, and this one is no other than Devadatta. Thus Devadatta's existence outside is definitely presumed.

But the supposition is not in that form (that you allege). Nor is it that without him (without *his* being supposed) knowledge of inexplicability would be the cause of presumptive knowledge. This is like (the predication rule for inference): because of smoke being pervaded by fire in general, there is proof of fire on the mountain. But its proof would not be from smoke taken just as being-on-a-mountain, because the pervading factor (fieriness) is not grasped in that form.

OBJECTION (BY OBJECTOR 1 TO THE PŪRVAPAKṢIN): "Inexplicability" is a rule about the absence of something to be known belonging to something lacking that which would make us know it. But it is not absence in general, because that idea would extend too far. And so what is the use of *arthâpatti*? For the probandum would be proved just by means of the inferential stamp (*mudrā*) in a negative inference, where the absence in general would be a pervasion of the negative variety, thus from (an absence of) that which is to be shown. For example, there is Devadatta as outside (S), *since*, given that he is alive (H1), he is not in the house (H2). What is not so (¬S), that is not so, *like* a dead person (¬H1), alternatively, someone in the house (¬H2).

Furthermore, the rule does not extend too far to establish one thing by means of a pervasion relationship with something else. For the rule concerns the counterpositive in relation to an absence whose pervading is by an absence of the probandum.

Objection (to Objector 1 by Objector 2): The pervasion there by its very nature would be a mark of *arthâpatti*, not inference.

Reply (by Objector 1): That should not be alleged. Unless there is knowledge of inexplicability, the supposition would not arise. Moreover, there is no room for a case of non-genuine *arthâpatti*.

Pūrva-pakṣin: Don't think like that. For in this case there is pervasion, which is of the negative variety. (And) there is the inferential mark's being a property of the inferential subject to take (the inferential terms in) the positive-inference fashion. (But) M's knowledge that Devadatta is outside, although generated by the thought that there is pervasion, is not inferential knowledge, because inferential knowledge by its rule-bound nature is generated by knowledge of the inferential mark's being a property of the inferential subject (and there is no subject in this case) as well as of the mark's being pervaded (by the probandum).

Objection: There is knowledge of the inferential mark's being a property of the inferential subject inasmuch as it is the counterpositive of an absence that pervades an absence of the probandum. This instigates inference, and it is present here in this case.

Pūrva-pakṣin: That should not be said. That is not possible for an inference of the positive-only variety (*kevalânvaya*), and, compared with your conception, knowledge of being pervaded by the probandum is simpler.

> Comments: Although, in a reversal of the normal order of qualification, a prover can be said to be qualified by the inferential subject—smoke, in the stock example, having the property of being-on-a-mountain and many others—the only relevant property for the purpose of determination of a mountain as fiery is that of smoke as qualified by being-pervaded-by-being-fiery. The same predication rule holds for *arthâpatti*, according to the Bhāṭṭa *pūrva-pakṣin* here, accounting for some of the confusion in the discussion of the case of Devadatta known as outside. In other words, there are conversions of terms, but Devadatta as an individual is the subject of the presumptive knowledge.

Objection: A pervasion is found to occur just from an inferential mark where the correlation is of the negative variety. And so from correlation, whether positive or negative or both, there is a triad of types of inference, given that there are three ways a pervasion is grasped. Just for this reason, smoke, on some particular occasion, may trigger a positive inference, a negative inference, or a positive-and-negative inference (depending on how the pervasion would be known to a particular subject M).

PŪRVA-PAKṢIN: First of all, let inference be so (understood). Nevertheless, the absence of the living Devadatta in the house, while persisting, does not become an inferential sign for (M to infer) his being outside, since it does not occur *on* Devadatta (who is rather its counterpositive). The being-outside and the absence located in the house, these two do not have the same locus (*adhikaraṇa*).

Furthermore, there is no pervasion in the form of two things related by rule in the same thing, in the same locus (in this case). For there is the inference, "The sun is above the earth, *since* it emits light," along with others, where it is the being-the-sun that occurs together with being-above-the-earth.

Nor is the correlation with being-the-counterpositive-to-an-absence-located-in-the-house, because it would be a property of Devadatta to be the absence's counterpositive whereas that could not be known by perception: there could be no sensory connection to it.

Just for this reason, that is, because there is no sensory connection to the qualificandum, it would also not be by perception that the triple consideration of the inferential mark (that triggers inference) would occur.

OBJECTION: Knowledge of a negative pervasion as well as of an absence located in the house could be produced just by the mind (by the *manas*, the internal organ), to consider the auxiliary causes (and so there would be a sensory connection).

PŪRVA-PAKṢIN: That should not be alleged. For in considering auxiliary causes, the difficulty (for you) would be admission of an additional knowledge source (which is our position).

OBJECTION: Right after knowledge of pervasion, how is there to be inferential knowledge from the smoke being remembered? By the analysis (*nyāya*) that has been given, there would be no consideration (*parāmarśa*) of the inferential mark (a factor necessary for inference) there too (with an apparent inference from smoke to fire).

PŪRVA-PAKṢIN: Not in any way whatsoever. How, then, is there to be knowledge of fire? Well, grasp this: "Unless there is fire, there is no smoke," from such knowledge of inexplicability, aided by memory of smoke as a property qualifying the inferential subject, there would be knowledge of fire.

Just for this reason, if the following were known—"The smoke being experienced would be inexplicable without fire." If this were known, it would be just *arthâpatti*. But if without knowledge of inexplicability there were comprehended the thing as pervaded, then there would be inference. According to you, too, there are (possible) here three kinds of inference, and the absence of a living Devadatta in the house (you say) would make M suppose, relying on a pervasion of the negative variety, that he is outside.

COMMENTS: Gaṅgeśa accepts the threefold division of inference into the positive-only, negative-only, and positive-and-negative. Inference of the *sāmānyato-dṛṣṭa* type—which we may take to contrast with inference to something about an observed particular, whereas *sāmānyato-dṛṣṭa* inference has an unobserved subject—seems to belong simply to a different classification, and could be of any of the three inductive types.

The Bhāṭṭa *pūrva-pakṣin* does not endorse the (laughable) position that would reduce inference to *arthâpatti*, but rather champions inexplicability-otherwise as differentiating the two knowledge sources. However, it seems that just about any inference could be reformulated to hinge on inexplicability. For example: There is fire on the mountain, *since* there there is "otherwise-inexplicable" smoke. It seems he would see such knowledge as presumptive, and it also seems that he sees the difference between the two knowledge sources as slight. The Naiyāyika, too, finds only a slight difference here in identifying the case as one of negative-only inference as opposed to the other varieties.

GAṄGEŚA: We reply. Although Devadatta would not be in sensory connection (with M, our subject), his being the counterpositive of an absence located in the house would be grasped by perception (by M). The definition of the absential counterpositive covers Devadatta as part of an absence known by perception, for example, "In the house there is an absence of Devadatta." The meaning of the genitive ("of Devadatta") is connected to the absence. He would be one of the two relatees comprising the intentionality (objecthood, *viṣayatva*) of a bit of relational knowledge in that an absence has the same relationality as its counterpositive. And given that his being the counterpositive of an absence located in the house is set in awareness by perception, the relationality to a remembered pervasion would also be easy to grasp.

OBJECTION: There is no knowledge of counterpositiveness to an absence situated in a house (for example) as pervaded by being-outside where Devadatta would be the qualificandum.

GAṄGEŚA: That should not be alleged. Consideration (*parāmarśa*) of the inferential sign as occurring on the inferential subject, consideration of that sign alone produces inferential knowledge. More than this is to be rejected as uneconomical.

Alternatively, the consideration has a remembered Devadatta as qualificandum, the consideration, that is, that for a third time focuses on the inferential mark (and produces inferential knowledge), which would be by the mind alone (not working through sensory connections) by force of aids (such as hypothetical reasoning, *tarka*) not having unwanted consequences. And the position that an aid is not an additional knowledge source has already been explained.

COMMENTS: Gaṅgeśa applies here his theory of absence, which was worked out in the previous chapter of the *Jewel*. Absences constitute an acceptable ontological category. That they have a relational nature, dragging along in their wake, so to say, the relata of both the location and counterpositive, in no way hinders them from standing as terms in a pervasion relationship that permits inference.

The theory of the "triple perception of the inferential mark" is developed by Uddyotakara under the inference sūtra, *Nyāya-sūtra* 1.1.5. One sees smoke, and then sees it *as* pervaded by fire. The third "perception" is mental, called "reflection" or "consideration" (*parāmarśa*), which triggers the occurrence of inferential knowledge by putting all the information—the pervasion and the qualification by the mark or prover of the inferential subject—together in the right way.

Objection (to Gaṅgeśa by Objector 1): Immediately following the bit of knowledge, "The peacock does not dance on anything other than a mountain, and he is dancing," there is the (further) knowledge that the peacock is dancing on a mountain. And this is not possible from inference based on negative correlations.

Objection (to Objector 1 by Objector 2): How, too, is it *arthâpatti*?

Reply (by Objector 1): That should not be asked, given that without it the dancing on the mountain would be unknown and there would also be no comprehension of inexplicability. Without the locus (*adhikaraṇa*) being realized as inexplicable, the dance, aided by blocking of other well-known (possible) loci, would make M (our subject) suppose that its locus is other than those that are well known.

Gaṅgeśa: Wrong. It would be by an inference of the *sāmānyato-dṛṣṭa* type, "The peacock's dance has a locus, *since* it is a dance," that the mountain—one's taking it to be the locus—would generate the (new) knowledge of the dance (namely, that it is on it). The mountain is other than those discussed loci, the mountain taken in general (*sāmānyato-dṛṣṭa*), aided by blockings of the discussed loci.

Alternatively, it would be known by means of testimony, "The peacock does not dance on anything other than a mountain." Testimony would make it known that the testimonial knowledge being produced—right on the heels of thinking that there is some lack of dance—"The peacock is dancing" would come to include the dance being *on a mountain* within its scope. The rule is that it is by concerning ourselves with the particular locus that we have a knowledge source that generates the knowledge, that is to say, by concerning ourselves with the mountain that is other than those loci that have been identified by us, we have a source generating the knowledge in general aided by exclusion of those particulars that are well known.

Just for this reason, our teacher (Udayana) holds that in the case of the inference about earth and the like (requiring an agential cause) it is right after having ruled out the thesis that the (guiding) knowledge (required) could be non-eternal, proving that they are brought about (in part) by knowledge, that there is the proof, through concerning ourselves with eternality.

"The peacock's dance has the mountain as its locus, *since*, given that things other than the mountain are not its locus, it has a locus, *like* the mountain (itself, which is located in its atoms)." The inference is known through positive and negative correlations.

Alternatively, "What (F) does not occur on this or that thing that is other than something (G) that is supposed or conjectured (*sambhāvita*), that thing (F), existing, does not occur on something different from it (G); it (the F) occurs on it (the G)"—it is by means of a pervasion including such a meaning in its general form (*sāmānyena*) that the occurrence (on the mountain) of the dance is proved.

In this way, "Fat Devadatta does not eat during the day" is a bit of (inferential) knowledge of fatness with respect to an unknown probandum of eating at night that is proved by taking to mind night-time eating.

OBJECTION (BY OBJECTOR 1, A BHĀṬṬA): As in the case of "There is someone who does not eat who is fat," where there is knowledge of a violation of semantic fitness (*yogyatā*), so, too, with "That fat person does not eat during the day," there is a violation because eating during the day is ruled out while the factor that would sustain the semantic fitness (*yogyatā*), eating at night, is not (expressly) cognized. Therefore, unless that factor sustaining semantic fitness is supplied to consciousness, this statement will not have its unity experienced. Supposing that the statement amounts to "He eats at night," such that it communicates the night-time eating as the factor securing semantic fitness, with it (i.e., with the supplying of the factor), M (our subject) is made to know the sentential unity. (Thus the knowledge is a matter of testimonial or verbal *arthâpatti*, not inference.)

OBJECTION (BY OBJECTOR 2 AGAINST OBJECTOR 1): So it is simpler to suppose just the night-time eating.

REPLY (BY OBJECTOR 1, THE BHĀṬṬA): Wrong. By the maxim, "For, a verbal expectation can be satisfied only by something verbal," it is something verbal that makes M know the sentential unity, M for whom it is by something verbal that the night-time eating is brought to mind.

And in this way, the making M understand the overall unity of words he is hearing is accomplished through something verbal which brings the factor sustaining the overall unity into consciousness. Unless it is supplied, M would suppose that it (the statement) was inexplicable. Where such an understanding of sentential unity brings about knowledge, there we have the workings of "verbal *arthâpatti*" (*śrutârthâpatti*).

> COMMENTS: "sentential unity," *anvaya*, slightly under-translates the current use of the Sanskrit word, which is the overall semantic and syntactic connection of the words in a sentence. This is a central topic of the final chapter, on testimony.
>
> Prābhākaras reject *śrutârthâpatti*, "*arthâpatti* founded on what has been heard," a good example of which is ellipsis (*lopa*). Several examples of ellipsis are focal in the testimony chapter. Given a situation with several people in a room where the door is open, when someone says, "the door," we presume, says the Bhāṭṭa, the word "close."
>
> The Bhāṭṭa's challenge to Gaṅgeśa here seems cogent. This may be why our Naiyāyika proposes here that testimony could include the unexpressed as part of its surface semantics, e.g., the bit about it being on a mountain where a peacock is dancing. After all, the counterpositive of an absence is taken by Naiyāyikas to be referred to in absential statements such as, "There is no pot on the floor" (the floor as qualified by pot-absence). However, in the next and final passage of the section, Gaṅgeśa expressly repudiates the Bhāṭṭa view.

BHĀṬṬA: To suppose (as we do, supplying) the word "close" with respect to utterances such as " . . . the door," well, this is simply "verbal *arthâpatti*," *śrutârthâpatti*. And if the word that is being heard is in some way checked (*bādhita*, in its meaning), it is still supposed to have purpose (i.e., meaning). The situation is like that on the Guru's view (the Prābhākara view) with "Who desires heaven should sacrifice": If understanding of a direct means (to the production of the fruit of a sacrifice) is blocked, the intermediate factor (intermediate to the performance of the sacrifice and its fruit or result, e.g., going to heaven) will not (on the surface) be set in mind. Because there would be no semantic fit (but there has to be since the Vedic injunction is meaningful), the inexplicability otherwise of (the meaning of) well-known words used in the same case (the word for the subject, the person addressed as the one who should act, and the word for the act referred to being expressed by words in grammatical agreement). Thus knowledge of semantic fitness makes *apūrva* the factor serving as intermediate means, which M (our subject) supposes is what is meant by the optative affix (used injunctively), etc. Hence, the knowledge that the sacrifice (i.e., the Jyotiṣṭoma) is the means to heaven is born. Otherwise, *apūrva*, too, would not be expressed.

GAṄGEŚA: We answer. Semantic fitness is either the absence of a knowledge source that would block (a hearer's understanding a statement) or an absence of anything in the form of opposition to the overall unity of a statement. Thus concerning not eating during the day, although night-time eating is not (expressly) cognized, the thought (that there is nighttime eating) is produced from the words, "He does not eat during the day," *since* being fat is brought about by eating—which is not a case of the inexplicability of the thought. Rather, night-time eating is supposed (i.e., inferred) *because of* the inexplicability of what's known. Just for this reason, *apūrva* is also not meant (in a Vedic injunction where the optative affix is used in an injunctive sense)—I'll talk about this later. Therefore, *arthâpatti* is not something over and above inference.

COMMENTS: The Mīmāṃsaka notion of *apūrva*, "that which has not been known previously (to hearing a Vedic injunction)" is understood as the causal intermediary connecting sacrifice and result. The term as used in Nyāya means basically "karma" as popularly understood. The role of *apūrva* in understanding Vedic injunctions is taken up by Gaṅgeśa in a difficult section of the chapter on testimony. There his effort is to show that it is subsumed in the broader notion of karma, also known as *adṛṣṭa*, "Unseen Force," which is generated by all the actions of a person's life, not just the performance of Vedic rituals. For the Mīmāṃsaka, the concept of *apūrva* appears to be something like the novelist's "*deus ex machina*," since it is used to patch over several difficulties, especially, as mentioned, that of the postponed result of performance of a sacrifice or ritual, but also, as we shall see, certain issues about language and verbal intelligibility. For present purposes, it may be taken as the connection between ritual performance and result, e.g., going to heaven, a connection that is not observed, and so *apūrva* has to be either postulated or presumed (the Bhāṭṭa view) or taken to be the sense of the Vedic injunctive use of the optative affix (the Prābhākara position).

We may also note that, according to Mīmāṃsā theory of language, statements indicate actions that have purposes. So if a purpose, its instrumentation, or its method, which are required for understanding an injunction to perform a certain sacrifice, are not satisfactorily conveyed—for example, what specific sacrifice is to be performed to fulfill the purpose of the Vedic statement, "Who desires heaven should sacrifice"—then something suitable has to be presumed. Or, alternatively, there is taken to be a special sense of a Vedic usage of an inflected verb. Gaṅgeśa opposes both Mīmāṃsaka camps on sentential meaning in the Veda, although he tends to side with the Bhāṭṭa on the more central issues about meaning and language. In any case, we can tell from what he says here that he opposes the Bhāṭṭa on what is to be presumed in order to understand Vedic injunctions. His resistance to even verbal *arthâpatti* as a separate source of knowledge presents a problem for part of his defense of testimony as itself a separate knowledge source not reducible to inference. With secondary, indirect meaning (*lakṣaṇā*, "secondary meaning") in particular, an inferentialist account—which Gaṅgeśa resists in line with defending testimony as a separate *pramāṇa*—seems attractive, since an inferential act, a "consideration" or "reflection," appears required to pass from understanding an expressed, literal meaning to understanding what a speaker intends. (Testimony works by either of two "modes" of meaning, reference and *lakṣaṇā*, "indirect indication," the latter in particular a dominant topic throughout the testimony chapter.)

A long discussion of *lakṣaṇā* and inference threads through the *Jewel*'s last chapter. And several further observations about the Mīmāṃsaka understanding of *arthâpatti* are made in the course of complex argumentation. Indeed, *arthâpatti* is often proffered as a candidate for resolution of problems about meaning and modes of meaning. But it is already easy to see the larger issue and tension in Gaṅgeśa's view with his temptation to have it both ways with the question of *arthâpatti* as a separate knowledge source, which it isn't, he says, but then there is testimony, which is.

REFERENCES

Primary sources

Jayanta, Bhaṭṭa (1971), *Nyāya-mañjarī*, ed. Surya Narayana Sukla, trans. J. V. Bhattacharyya Kashi Sanksrit Series 106, Varanasi: Chowkhamba Sanskrit Series Office.

Jayanta, Bhaṭṭa (1978), *Jayanta Bhaṭṭa's Nyāya-mañjarī*, Delhi: Motilal Banarsidass.

Kumārila (1978), *Śloka-vārttika* (commentary on part of the *Mīmāṃsā-sūtra*), ed. Dvarikadas Sastri, trans. John Taber (the perception chapter), Varanasi: Tara Publications.

Kumārila (2005), *A Hindu Critique of Buddhist Epistemology: The "Determination of Perception" Chapter of Kumārila Bhaṭṭa's Śloka-vārttikā*, London: Routledge. (Other chapters: Ganganatha Jha (1900, 1908), *Slokavartika.*, reprint, Delhi: Sri Satguru Publications.)

Gautama. *NyS. Nyāya-sūtra.* (1) Ed. A.M. Tarkatirtha, Taranatha Nyayatarkatirtha, and H.K. Tarkatirtha. 1936–1944 (reprint 1985). *Nyāyadarśanam* (*Nyāya-sūtra* with four commentaries, the *Nyāya-sūtra-bhāṣya* of Vātsyāyana, the *Nyāya-vārttika* of Uddyotakara, the *Nyāya-vārttika-tātpārya-ṭīkā* of Vācaspati Miśra, and the *Vṛtti* of Viśvanātha). Calcutta Sanskrit Series 18. (2) Ed. Anantalal Thakur. 1997. *Gautamīyanyāyadarśana with Bhāṣya of Vātsyāyana*. New Delhi: Indian Council of Philosophical Research. Translation: (1) Ganganatha Jha. 1919. With Vātsyāyana's and Uddyotakara's commentaries. *The Nyāyasūtras of Gautama with the Bhāṣya of Vātsyāyana and the Vārttika of Uddyotakara*. 4 vols. Reprint. Delhi: Motilal

Banarsidass. (2) Mrinalkanti Gangopadhyay. 1982. With Vātsyāyana's commentary. *Nyāya-Sūtra with Vātsyāyana's Commentary*. Calcutta: Indian Studies. (3) Michel Angot. 2009. *Le Nyāya-sūtra de Gautama Akṣapāda, le Nyāya-Bhāṣya d'Akṣapāda Pakṣilasvāmin: l'Art de Conduire la Pensée en Inde Ancienne*; Édition, Traduction et Présentation. Paris: Les Belles Lettres.

Gaṅgeśa. *Tattva-cintā-maṇi*, the "*Jewel*," inference chapter: (1) Ed. N.S. Ramanuja Tatacharya. 1982 and 1999. With the *Prakāśa* commentary by Rucidatta Miśra and a subcommentary by Dharmarājādhvarin. 2 vols. Kendriya Sanskrit Vidyapeetha Series 33. Tirupati. (2) Ed. Kamakhyanath Tarkavagish. 1884–1901 (reprint 1991). With the commentary of Mathurānātha. 2 vols. Calcutta: Asiatic Society. Perception chapter translated: S. H. Phillips and N. S. Ramanuja Tatacharya. 2004. *Epistemology of Perception*. New York: American Institute of Buddhist Studies.

Śalikanātha Miśra. *Prakaraṇa-pañcikā*. Ed. A. Subrahmanya Sastri. 1961. Banaras Hindu University Darśana Series 4. Varanasi. Partially translated: K.T. Pandurangi. 2004. New Delhi: Indian Council of Philosophical Research.

Secondary literature

Bhattacharya, D. C. (1958), *History of Navya-nyāya in Mithilā*, Darbhanga: Mithila Institute.

Ingalls, D. H. H. (1951), *Materials for the Study of Navya-Nyāya Logic*, Cambridge, MA: Harvard University Press.

Matilal, B. K. (1968), *The Navya-Nyāya Doctrine of Negation*, Cambridge, MA: Harvard University Press.

Matilal, B. K. (1998), *The Character of Logic in India*, ed. J. Ganeri and H. Tiwari, Albany: State University of New York Press.

Mohanty, Jitendranath (1966), *Gaṅgeśa's Theory of Truth*, reprint, Delhi: Motilal Banarsidass.

Phillips, S. (2012), *Epistemology in Classical India: The Knowledge Sources of the Nyāya School*, New York and London: Routledge.

Potter, K. H., ed. (1977), *Encyclopedia of Indian Philosophies*, vol. 2: *Nyāya-Vaiśeṣika up to Gaṅgeśa*, Delhi: Motilal Banarsidass.

Potter, K. H. and S. Bhattacharyya, eds. (1993), *Encyclopedia of Indian Philosophies*, vol. 6: *Indian Philosophical Analysis: Nyāya-Vaiśeṣika from Gaṅgeśa to Raghunātha Śiromaṇi*, Delhi: Motilal Banarsidass.

SECTION THREE

CHAPTER NINE

The Physical Existence of a Living Being and Kumārila's Theory of *Arthâpatti*

KIYOTAKA YOSHIMIZU

0. INTRODUCTION

0.1. *Is arthâpatti a sort of abductive reasoning?*

Suppose that we have a friend, Caitra, who is a so-called *otaku* obsessed with playing PC games at home. We regularly visit Caitra at home, but on one occasion, contrary to our expectations, we cannot find him there. Surprised by his absence, we begin to search for him, believing that he must be somewhere outside. After several failed attempts, we finally find him in a distant café playing a PC game on a brand-new laptop. Feeling relieved, we have learned that even Caitra sometimes goes outside . . .

Looking back on this series of events, we might think that we first hypothesized that Caitra was outside and later confirmed this hypothesis by finding him in a café. In other words, we might be tempted to regard our reasoning as an example of abduction. Alternatively, despite Caitra's absence from home, suppose that we were able to confirm that his heart was beating thanks to a micro-transmitter implanted in his heart. Then, we might regard our reasoning as an example of "Inference to the Best Explanation" (IBE), holding the probability of other competing hypotheses accounting for his absence from home to be comparatively low (for instance, that he was dead but the micro-transmitter was dispatching a false reading due to a malfunction or having been transplanted into someone else's heart).

We should be cautious, however, in believing that the idea of abduction or IBE is shared by Mīmāṃsakas, especially Kumārila Bhaṭṭa (*c.* 560–620),[1] when they argue about *arthâpatti*, which is represented by this kind of reasoning, as a kind of epistemic instrument (*pramāṇa*). According to them, a *pramāṇa* provides decisive knowledge that does not need to be confirmed afterward (*svataḥ-prāmāṇya*). As aptly formulated

[1] For Kumārila's chronological dates, see Yoshimizu (2015: footnote 1).

by John Taber (1992: 219), Kumārila can be said to claim that "a cognition is valid unless and until it is contradicted," because he allows for the possibility that a preceding cognition loses its convincing force once its counter-evidence is discovered.[2] In spite of its apparent validity, the perception of a piece of silver turns out to be false if one takes the object in one's hand and finds it to be a shell instead;[3] a statement by a seemingly reliable speaker turns out to be false if it is determined that the speaker attempted to hide the truth from the hearer.[4] Kumārila can surely be said to propound fallibilism in epistemology. Nevertheless, according to Kumārila, the cognition of Caitra's being outside, postulated on the basis of his absence from home, would not be a fallible hypothesis that is accepted as true for the time being, but rather a piece of established knowledge acquired through a *pramāṇa* called *arthâpatti*.

Naiyāyikas call the postulation of the most plausible hypothesis *tarka* (hypothetical reasoning)[5] and characterize *tarka* as a means to acquire true knowledge (*tattva-jñānârtha*) while denying that *tarka* itself is true knowledge (*tattva-jñāna*). It is through *tarka* that one of the two incompatible theses is approved (*[abhy]anujñā*) on account of a certain reason being feasible (*kāraṇôpapatti*) but not definitively settled yet (*anavadhāraṇa*).[6] To establish publicly what they have approved, Naiyāyikas conduct a debate with an opposing party, which results in one thesis being dismissed (*nivṛtti*) and the remaining one settled with certainty (*nirṇaya*).[7] Therefore, we may rightfully regard Naiyāyika's *tarka* as a certain kind of abduction or IBE.[8] Kumārila maintains, however, that the information acquired through *arthâpatti* is to be accepted as valid because the Mīmāṃsakas' main purpose in applying *arthâpatti* is to find what is implied in a statement of Vedic scriptures, which they claim to be valid beyond empirical confirmation.

0.2. *Methodological remarks*

In the Anumāna-pariccheda of the *Śloka-vārttika* (ŚV-Anu), Kumārila, in spite of his religious antagonism toward Buddhism, fully adopts and elucidates Diṅnāga's theory of inference (*anumāna*) in great detail, whereas in the Arthâpatti-pariccheda (ŚV-Ar), he demonstrates that *arthâpatti* cannot be reduced to an *anumāna*. Therefore, it is worth examining how Kumārila characterizes *arthâpatti* as an alternative form of logical reasoning.

---

[2] *Śloka-vārttika* (ŚV), Codanā-sūtra, v. 53; Taber (1992: 211–12).

[3] ŚV, Pratyakṣa-pariccheda, v. 39ab.

[4] ŚV, Codanā-sūtra, v. 160.

[5] *Nyāya-sūtra* (NS) 1.1.40: avijñāta-tattve 'rthe kāraṇôpapattitas tattva-jñānârtham ūhas tarkaḥ. "*Tarka* is reasoning that proceeds by considering what is consistent with knowledge sources in order to know the truth about something that is not definitively known" (trans. Dasti and Phillips 2017: 44).

[6] *Nyāya-bhāṣya* (NBh) 36,12–37,6 (on NS 1.1.40).

[7] NBh 37,14–15 (on NS 1.1.41: vimṛśya pakṣa-pratipakṣābhyām arthâvadhāraṇaṃ nirṇayaḥ).

[8] Guha (2016: 765–6) characterizes *arthâpatti*, which he renders as "postulation," in comparison with *tarka* and abduction as follows: "(1) Postulation is an epistemic instrument whereas *tarka* and abduction are not. The role of postulation is informative. But the role of the other two is evaluative. (2) *Tarka* and abduction depend on background knowledge based on observation. But postulation does not require any background knowledge, although it may be triggered by experience. (3) *Tarka* and abduction are accepted on probation. But the acceptance of postulation is non-probationary." I basically concur with Guha in this comparison as far as Kumārila is concerned. See footnotes 24, 26, and 35.

Among the three basic types of logical reasoning generally accepted today, namely, deduction, induction, and abduction (including IBE), it would be out of the question for Kumārila to consider his *arthâpatti* concerning Caitra's whereabouts—henceforth, I call this "the Caitra-*arthâpatti*"—as induction, because one does not argue how many people one needs to find outside in order to prove a universal conditional statement that all those who are alive and absent from home are outside. Abduction would also not be the candidate to explain the Caitra-*arthâpatti*, because Kumārila explicitly states that the nature of *arthâpatti* is to draw out the conclusion that is entailed by its preconditions.[9] Therefore, by process of elimination, deduction alone remains viable. Kumārila, however, merely presents the starting-point and the goal of the Caitra-*arthâpatti* without clarifying how the reasoning proceeds in between. Therefore, if we are to call Kumārila's *arthâpatti* "deductive reasoning" or even merely the "vague idea of deductive reasoning,"[10] we have to be able to prove the formal validity of this reasoning. In other words, we have to pursue its deductive process step by step on Kumārila's behalf, by filling in the logical gaps he left between the starting-point and the goal.

The basic system of deductive reasoning is classified in term, propositional, and predicate logic in terms of the unity of operation; the latter two are further classified into axiomatic systems and natural deduction in terms of whether the system of derivation is mainly (even if not exclusively) characterized by axioms or inferential rules. With his rejection of reducing the Caitra-*arthâpatti* to an *anumāna*, Kumārila declares that the *arthâpatti* does not proceed according to term logic. Axiomatic systems would also be unsuitable because Kumārila does not present any formalized statement that can be seen as an axiom. As a result, there remains one possibility: the application of a system of natural deduction, so long as the system uses only inferential rules to which Kumārila expresses no objection. Staal (1962: 645) and Barlingay (1976: 21) consider the Caitra-*arthâpatti* to be an applied sequent of disjunctive syllogism without presenting its proof.[11] Kanaujia (1992: 175) describes the deductive process of its proof, but he does not take "inexplicability otherwise" (*anyathânupapatti*) into account. I concur with them in regarding the Caitra-*arthâpatti* as an example of deductive reasoning, but I further believe it necessary to present how *anyathânupapatti* operates in the process of reasoning insofar as Kumārila makes it an indispensable

---

[9] See section 1.4 of the present chapter on ŚV-Ar, v. 29.

[10] I made this characterization in Yoshimizu 2007: 321, which is an enlarged English version of Yoshimizu 1999. In the present chapter I retain the following three characteristics of Kumārila's Caitra-*arthâpatti* (Yoshimizu 2007: 321–4):

(i) Throughout the whole process of this *arthâpatti*, the unit of operation is always a sentence (proposition) that has the same subject, Caitra. Unlike Diṅnāga's *anumāna* in term logic, *arthâpatti* does not resort to the universal conditional statement that all those that have a certain property (*dharma*) have another property.

(ii) The conclusion of an *arthâpatti* is necessarily involved in the aggregate of its preconditions and is drawn on the grounds that they would not stand to reason if the conclusion were negated, in other words, by "inexplicability otherwise" (*anyathânupapatti*).

(iii) Kumārila approves the inseparability (*avinā-bhāva*) of the reason "being absent from home" from the property to be proven (*sādhya*) "being outside" in the domain of all living beings. According to him, however, this inseparability comes to be known after the *arthâpatti*.

[11] See footnote 37.

part of the definition of *arthâpatti*.[12] The proofs given in this chapter follow E. J. Lemmon's method of natural deduction according to the ten inferential rules presented in his manual, *Beginning Logic* (Lemmon 1972/1965).[13]

Kumārila's *anyathânupapatti* corresponds to *modus tollens* (or *modus tollendo tollens*), which is formulated as "P→Q, ¬Q; therefore ¬P." Accordingly, in order to prove the validity of the Caitra-*arthâpatti*, it is necessary to choose a system that includes *modus tollens* among its inferential rules. However, the number and the content of inferential rules vary among different systems of natural deduction. In particular, because *modus tollens* is a theorem that can be derived concisely by means of *reduction to absurdity*,[14] many logicians who developed systems of natural deduction (such as Jaśkowski, Gentzen, and Suppes) do not adopt *modus tollens* as an inferential rule for the sake of parsimony.[15] Even Lemmon excludes *modus tollens* from his system of natural deduction, system L, which consists of the remaining nine rules.[16] In his *Beginning Logic*, however, he seems to have adopted it because the book is intended to be an elementary manual for beginners. Moreover, Lemmon's system has no axioms presupposed in derivations, and to the best of my knowledge, Kumārila articulates no objections to Lemmon's remaining rules.[17]

---

[12] See section 1.2 of the present chapter on ŚV-Ar, v. 1.

[13] The following ten rules are listed by Lemmon (1972/1965: 39–40):

1. *rule of assumptions* (alias *assumption introduction*): "Any proposition may be introduced at any stage of a proof."
2. *modus ponens* (alias *conditional elimination* or *affirming the antecedent*): "Given A and A→B, we may derive B as conclusion."
3. *modus tollens* (alias *negating the consequent*): "Given ¬B and A→B, we may derive ¬A as conclusion."
4. *double negation* (alias *negation elimination*): "Given A, we may derive ¬¬A as conclusion, and vice versa."
5. *conditional proof* (alias *conditional introduction* or *deduction rule*): "Given a proof of B from A as assumption, we may derive A→B as conclusion on the remaining assumptions (if any)."
6. *and-introduction* (alias *conjunction introduction*): "Given A and B, we may derive A∧B as conclusion."
7. *and-elimination* (alias *conjunction elimination*): "Given A∧B, we may derive either A or B separately."
8. *or-introduction* (alias *disjunction introduction*): "Given either A or B separately, we may derive A∨B as conclusion."
9. *or-elimination* (alias *disjunction elimination*): "Given A∨B, together with a proof of C from A as assumption and a proof of C from B as assumption, we may derive C as conclusion."
10. *reduction to absurdity* (alias *negation introduction*): "Given a proof of B∧¬B from A as assumption, we may derive ¬A as conclusion on the remaining assumptions (if any)."

In addition to the *rule of assumptions* and *modus tollens*, this list consists of the pairs of introduction and elimination of four logical connectives, →, ∧, ∨, and ¬. In proofs 1 to 6 of the present chapter, *or-introduction* and *or-elimination* are never used. In the proofs given below, I follow the style of Noya (1997/1994): In each line, the line number comes first, then the sequent at issue, then the line number(s) of the required assumption(s) in brackets, and finally, the description of the operation.

[14] See footnote 47.

[15] Cf. Pelletier (1999: 3–9, 21–3). Lemmon owes the proof-style of his system L to Suppes (Pelletier 1999: 7).

[16] See https://www.newworldencyclopedia.org/entry/Deduction (accessed September 13, 2019).

[17] Kumārila substantially approves *modus ponens* in ŚV-Anu, vv. 12–13ab (see footnote 37), and *elimination of double negation* in ŚV, Apoha-vāda, v. 1. For *reduction to absurdity*, see section 1.5 of the present chapter.

1. *ARTHÂPATTI* FROM CAITRA'S ABSENCE FROM HOME TO HIS PRESENCE OUTSIDE

1.1. *Vṛtti-kāra's formulation*

Śabarasvāmin (*c.* 500), the author of the earliest extant commentary on the *Mīmāṃsā-sūtra* (MS), quotes a large fragment of another preceding commentary (*Vṛtti*) that gives a basic definition to each *pramāṇa*. The author of this commentary, the Vṛtti-kāra, gives an example of *arthâpatti*: "For the reason that Devadatta, who is alive, is observed being absent from home, one postulates his being outside, which has not been observed."[18] In this example, Devadatta is qualified as being alive (*jīvant*). Devadatta's being alive is an assumption necessary to make sure that he is outside when observing his absence from home because without this assumption, the possibility is not excluded that one cannot find Devadatta at home because he is not alive.[19]

1.2. *Modus tollens applied in the Caitra*-arthâpatti

At the outset of the *Arthâpatti-pariccheda*, Kumārila presents the definition of *arthâpatti*:

> ŚV-Ar, v. 1: A thing that is known from one of the six kinds of epistemic instrument may let one postulate something else that is not known, if the former would not stand to reason otherwise (i.e., unless one postulates the latter). This is *arthâpatti*, the examples of which are adduced [in the following].[20]

If this definition is applied to the present case, Caitra's absence from home (*gṛhâbhāva*) corresponds to the thing that is known (*vijñāta*) from one of the six kinds of *pramāṇa*; in this case, the *pramāṇa* called "non-existence" (*abhāva*) by Kumārila.[21] Caitra's presence outside (*bahir-bhāva*) corresponds to something that is not known (*adṛṣṭa*). With the phrase "would not stand to reason otherwise" (*nânyathā bhavet*), which is another way of saying "inexplicable otherwise" (*anyathânupapanna*) or "otherwise (*anyathā*) inexplicable (*anupapanna*)," it is stated that the former (the observed absence of Caitra from home) would not stand to reason if the latter (his presence outside) were negated. Caitra's absence from home would not stand to reason

---

[18] Śābara-bhāṣya on Mīmāṃsā-sūtra 1.1.1–5 (ŚBh(F)) 32,7–8: jīvato devadattasya gṛhâbhāva-darśanena bahir-bhāvasya adṛṣṭasya kalpanā.

[19] At the end of chapter 2 of the *Pramāṇa-samuccaya*, Diṅnāga quotes the Mīmāṃsā view of *pramāṇa*s held by an older Vṛtti-kāra including the reasoning of one's being outside simply from one's absence from home, under the name "non-existence" (*abhāva*). After declaring that a conclusive (*mthaḥ cig tu ṅes pa/ mthaḥ cig pa*) *arthâpatti* is nothing but *anumāna*, Diṅnāga rejects this reasoning as inconclusive on account of the possibility that one does not exist and therefore is absent not only from home, but also from outside. See Frauwallner 1968: 90,15–92,7 (trans. Vasudharakṣita); 90,32–92,21 (trans. Kanakavarman). The new Vṛtti-kāra quoted by Śabarasvāmin may have intended to overcome the inconclusiveness of this reasoning by characterizing Devadatta as alive.

[20] pramāṇa-ṣaṭka-vijñāto yatrârtho nânyathā bhavet | adṛṣṭaṃ kalpayed anyaṃ sârthâpattir udāhṛtā || In the present chapter, I adopt E. Freschi and A. Ollett's translation of the ŚV-Ar in the present volume, pp. 43ff, with partial modifications.

[21] ŚV-Ar, v. 8.

because it is contradicted by his presence at home,[22] which would follow from the assumption of his absence outside. Considering Caitra's life as a homebody, one habitually expects his presence at home. His observed absence from home contradicts this expectation. Therefore, one can see *modus tollens* being applied in this way: "If Caitra were not outside (P), then he would be at home (Q). However, he is not, in fact, at home ($\neg Q$). Therefore, he is outside ($\neg P$)."

Caitra's absence from home, however, does not necessarily imply his presence outside: if he is not alive, we would not find him wherever we searched.[23] Like the Vṛtti-kāra quoted by Śabarasvāmin, Kumārila holds it necessary to qualify Caitra as being alive in order to derive his being outside from his absence from home.[24]

> ŚV-Ar, v. 22: This cognition of an absence from home, if conjoined with being alive, leads to the conclusion that Caitra, being excluded from home, must exist outside.[25]

Let us take the sentence "Caitra is at home" as A, "Caitra is outside" as B, and "Caitra is alive" as C. Then, Kumārila's statement in v. 22 can be rendered as "$(C \land \neg A) \rightarrow B$," in which C is conjoined with $\neg A$ in order to imply B. In other words, "Caitra is alive" (C) is said to be the sufficient condition for making the conditional "If Caitra is absent from home, he exists outside" ($\neg A \rightarrow B$) true. In fact, Kumārila presents "C" as a single precondition that sufficiently leads to the conditional "$\neg A \rightarrow B$" in the following:

> ŚV-Ar, v. 24: When [Caitra's] existence has been taken for granted, the cognition of his absence from home leads to the conclusion that his existence, being excluded from home, must be located outside.[26]

---

[22] In the Arthâpatti-pariccheda, Kumārila gives no specific term for contradiction ($A \land \neg A$) except for "*pratighātin*," a variant reading in v. 29d (see footnote 44). Including contradiction under "incompatibility" (*virodha*), however, he articulates the law of non-contradiction ($\neg(A \land \neg A)$) concerning the existence (*sad-bhāva*) and non-existence (*asad-bhāva*) of one and the same thing (*artha/vastu*) in ŚV, Pratyakṣa-sūtra, v. 221ab: sad-asad-bhāvayor arthe virodhitvād asambhavaḥ; Sambandhâkṣepa-parihāra, v. 34ab: viruddhau sad-asad-bhāvau na syātām eka-vastuni. For Dharmakīrti's differentiation between contradiction and another type of incompatibility, i.e., the contrariety (cf. Lemmon 1972/1965: 69) of two different things such as heat and coldness ($\neg(A \land B)$), see *Nyāya-bindu* (NB) 3.72–5; Yoshimizu (2007: footnotes 44 and 46).

[23] ŚV-Ar, v. 21.

[24] Kumārila takes Caitra's being alive for granted without explaining how to prove it, whereas Nārāyaṇa, the author of the *Māna-meyôdaya* [MM], infers it on the basis of an astrological treatise (MM 121,1: *gaṇitâgama-mūlena anumānena*). Nārāyaṇa holds the inexplicability (*anupapatti*) at issue to be the seeming incompatibility (*virodha*) between general and specific *pramāṇa*s, i.e., the astrological prediction of Caitra's existence and the observation of his absence from home (MM 120,4–7; 121,2–4; cf. *Śāstra-dīpikā* [ŚD] 221,4–6; Jha 1978/1911: 71). If Caitra is known to be alive on the basis of astrology, one who has observed Caitra's absence from home may suspect that he is possibly not alive even if it is unlikely because astrology provides fallible knowledge, at least for modern people. Although Nārāyaṇa holds Caitra's being alive to be indubitable (MM 129,7–10), medieval scholars' attempts to clarify the means of knowing whether Caitra is alive may have led modern scholars to suppose that *arthâpatti* is a sort of abductive reasoning. See also Yoshimizu (forthcoming: footnote 67).

[25] vidyamānatva-saṃsṛṣṭa-gṛhâbhāva-dhiyānayā | gehād utkālitaś caitro vidyate bahir eva hi ||

[26] siddhe sad-bhāva-vijñāne gehâbhāva-dhiyātra tu | gehād utkālitā sattā bahir eva avatiṣṭhate || If Kumārila were to consider this *arthâpatti* as a sort of abductive reasoning, it would become inexplicable that he takes Caitra's existence (*sad-bhāva*) for granted (*siddha*). With "*siddhe sad-bhāva-vijñāne*," Kumārila does not say that Caitra's non-existence is less probable. Instead, he asserts that it is not to be taken into account.

This statement can be rendered as "$C \rightarrow (\neg A \rightarrow B)$," which is logically equivalent to "$(C \wedge \neg A) \rightarrow B$."[27] However, because "inexplicability otherwise" (*anyathânupapatti*) is declared to be indispensable for *arthâpatti* in the first verse of the *Arthâpatti-pariccheda*, we should not consider "$\neg A \rightarrow B$" to be directly derived from the precondition C, according to Kumārila's way of thinking. Rather, Kumārila supposes the conditional "If Caitra is not outside, he is at home" ($\neg B \rightarrow A$) on the basis of "Caitra is alive" (C), then sublates the consequent "A" with the observation of Caitra's absence from home ($\neg A$), then negates the antecedent "$\neg B$" by applying *modus tollens*, and finally affirms B by eliminating the double negation. Therefore, "$\neg A \rightarrow B$" stated in verse 24 is to be considered as presenting the final phase of the application of *modus tollens*.

Kumārila, however, does not explicitly explain why the conditional "Caitra is outside if he is absent from home" ($\neg A \rightarrow B$) ultimately comes to be established under the precondition "Caitra is alive" (C). Because A, B, and C are three different propositions, "$\neg A \rightarrow B$" cannot be derived from "C" alone; in other words, "$C \rightarrow (\neg A \rightarrow B)$" as well as "$(C \wedge \neg A) \rightarrow B$" is "invalid" in terms of logical form.[28] What then is required to derive them?

1.3. *The body as a sufficient condition for the physical existence of a living being*

Kumārila asserts that the self (*ātman*) is eternal and omnipresent,[29] but as a Mīmāṃsaka who insists upon the indispensability of the physical performance of Vedic sacrifice for wellbeing, he also stresses that the self is inseparable from its body in the present life. Because a body moves under the self's control (*adhiṣṭhāna*), the self can be said to be the agent (*kartṛ*) of the action performed by the body.[30] In other words, the self is the promoter (*prayojaka*) that makes the body perform each action in accordance with the self's intention.[31] Owing to the mutual inseparability of the self and its body in the present life, the property of a body, such as "bearing sacrificial utensils" (*yajñâyudhin*) and so on, is rhetorically transferred to the self by metonymical expression (*lakṣaṇā-vṛtti*) in Vedic phrases[32] such as, "This very sacrificer who bears sacrificial utensils straightforwardly goes to the heavenly world."[33]

Accordingly, we can safely say that Kumārila takes it for granted that a living being has a body insofar as it is alive, and a body, like any other physical entity such as stone, always exists somewhere in the physical world, even if it changes its location as time passes. Then, in the present *arthâpatti*, we can say that it is taken for granted

---

27 Cf. Lemmon (1972/1965), proof 13 "$(P \wedge Q) \rightarrow R \vdash P \rightarrow (Q \rightarrow R)$" and proof 16 "$P \rightarrow (Q \rightarrow R) \vdash (P \wedge Q) \rightarrow R$."

28 In truth-value analysis, "$C \rightarrow (\neg A \rightarrow B)$" as well as "$(C \wedge \neg A) \rightarrow B$" is not tautological because they become false if both A and B are false but C is true.

29 ŚV, Ātma-vāda, v. 20a; *Tantra-vārttika* (TV) 400,28–401,6 (on MS 2.1.5).

30 ŚV, Ātma-vāda, vv. 76–7.

31 ŚV, Ātma-vāda, vv. 83–4.

32 ŚV, Ātma-vāda, vv. 1–2. For Kumārila's differentiation of metaphor (*gauṇī-vṛtti*) from metonymy (*lakṣaṇā*), see TV 354,16–22 (on MS 1.4.23).

33 ŚBh(F) 50,1–2 "sa eṣa yajñâyudhī yajamāno'ñjasā svargaṃ lokaṃ yāti," quoted from Śata-patha-brāhmaṇa (Mādhyandina recension) 12.5.2.8 with modifications. This is a part of the description of a dead householder at cremation; the sacrificial utensils he used during his lifetime are put on his various organs.

that Caitra is at home or outside insofar as he is alive (C→(A∨B)) because all places in the world can be dichotomized into Caitra's home and other places. Due to this spatial dichotomy, Caitra's assumed existence turns out to occur outside necessarily, if it is excluded from home.

> ŚV-Ar, v. 26: Therefore, when the house is cognized through perception, and Caitra's absence is cognized through absence, the cognition of his existence necessarily occurs outside.[34]

From this statement, we can infer that Kumārila accepts only two alternative possibilities: if Caitra exists, his existence is cognized either at home or outside. He does not consider the third possibility that Caitra is neither at home nor outside, although he is alive. Pārthasārathimiśra explicitly declares that it is indubitable that one who is alive must be at home or outside.[35]

1.4. *Disjunctive syllogism through modus tollens*

In the preceding sections (1.2 and 1.3), we examined how the Caitra-*arthâpatti* begins and ends: The reasoning begins with the premise that Caitra is at home or outside insofar as he is alive (C→(A∨B)) and an assumption that he is actually alive (C). Of the inferential rules of propositional logic, *modus ponens* (or *modus ponendo ponens*) is formulated as "P→Q, P; therefore Q." By the application of *modus ponens* to "C→(A∨B), C,"[36] it is derived that Caitra is actually at home or outside (A∨B). In the final phase of reasoning, granting the conditional statement that Caitra is at home if he is not outside (¬B→A), the reasoning reckons with the observation that he is absent from home (¬A), then negates the antecedent of the conditional (¬B) by applying *modus tollens*, resulting in the affirmation that Caitra is outside (B).

Concerning the intermediate phase between the application of *modus ponens* and that of *modus tollens*, neither Kumārila nor his commentators explain how the disjunction "Caitra is at home or outside" (A∨B) is modified into the conditional "If Caitra is not outside, he is at home" (¬B→A). This modification, however, can be proved valid by means of a few rules accepted in natural deduction. The whole procedure of proof can be demonstrated as follows, in Table 2.

---

[34] tasmāt pratyakṣato gehe caitrâbhāve hy abhāvataḥ | jñāte yat sattva-vijñānaṃ tad eva idaṃ bahiḥ-sthitam ||

[35] ŚD 218,9–10: jīvatā hy avaśyaṃ gṛhe vā bahir vā sthātavyam ity asaṃdigdham. For an existentially quantified version of this premise uttered by Śālikanātha, see footnote 57.

To regard this *arthâpatti* as an example of IBE, one might postulate a third (less probable) possibility that Caitra is, in fact, an extraterrestrial who has the surprising ability to be neither at home nor outside at the same time, in other words, nowhere in the physical world. However, because there is no evidence that Kumārila conceives of such a living being, this is nothing but a redundant postulation (*kalpanā-gaurava*) for explaining Kumārila's thought.

[36] Kumārila distinguishes the pervasion (*vyāpti*) between two universals (*sāmānyas*) from that between two particulars (*viśeṣas*) and adduces an example of the latter, saying that one knows the approaching of Aldebaran (*rohiṇī*) after observing the Pleiads (*kṛttikā*) in the night sky (ŚV-Anu, vv. 12b–13ab). Following the astronomical law that *rohiṇī* appears after the appearance of *kṛttikā* (P→Q) without the intervention of other constellations, the approach of *rohiṇī* (Q) can be inferred from the actual appearance of *kṛttikā* (P). We can say that *modus ponens* is applied in this reasoning, which is also mentioned in TV 139,9 (on MS 1.2.26). Kanaujia (1992: 175, vi) also remarks that the process of *arthâpatti* involves *modus ponens*.

TABLE 2: Proof 1, $((C \to (A \vee B)) \to ((C \wedge \neg A) \to B)$[37]

1	$C \to (A \vee B)$	[1] *assumption* (premise) "If Caitra is alive, he is at home or outside." (i.e., "Caitra is at home or outside insofar as he is alive.")
2	$C \wedge \neg A$	[2] *assumption*
3	C	[2] 2, *and-elimination* "Caitra is alive."
4	$\neg A$	[2] 2, *and-elimination* "Caitra is absent from home."
5	$A \vee B$	[1, 2] 1, 3, *modus ponens*
5.1	$(A \vee B) \to \neg(\neg A \wedge \neg B)$	substitution of P and Q in *the law of de Morgan* "$(P \vee Q) \leftrightarrow \neg(\neg P \wedge \neg Q)$"[38] with A and B
5.2	$\neg(\neg A \wedge \neg B)$	[1, 2] 5, 5.1, *modus ponens*
5.3	$\neg(\neg B \wedge \neg A)$	[1,2] 5.2, commutative law for conjunction
5.4	$\neg(\neg B \wedge \neg A) \to (\neg B \to A)$	substitution of P and Q in material implication "$\neg(P \wedge \neg Q) \to (P \to Q)$"[39] with $\neg B$ and A
6	$\neg B \to A$	[1,2] 5.3, 5.4, *modus ponens* "If Caitra is not outside, he is at home."
7	$\neg\neg B$	[1,2] 4,6, *modus tollens*
8	B	[1,2] 7, *elimination of double negation* "Caitra is outside."
9	$(C \wedge \neg A) \to B$	[1] 2,8, *conditional proof*
10	$((C \to (A \vee B)) \to ((C \wedge \neg A) \to B)$	1,9, *conditional proof* "Under the premise that Caitra is at home or outside insofar as he is alive, if he is alive and absent from home, then he is outside."

[37] This sequent can be used for proving "$((C \to (A \vee B)) \wedge (C \wedge \neg A)) \to B$" (cf. Yoshimizu 2007: Proof 4), which Staal and Barlingay suggest with different expressions applying disjunctive syllogism. See Staal (1962: 645): $A \to (B \vee C)$, A, $\sim B \vdash C$; Barlingay (1976: 21): $[p.\{(p \supset ((q \vee r).\sim q)) \supset r\}] \supset r$.

[38] Lemmon (1972/1965: proof 36(a) using *or-elimination*).

[39] Lemmon (1972/1965: proof 35(b)). S. Schayer (2001: 28) points out that "the definition of implication" (i.e., material implication), "$(P \to Q) \leftrightarrow \neg(P \wedge \neg Q)$," was known to the author of the *Kathā-vatthu* (KV). Cf. KV 1.1.1: 2,9–16.

Proof 1 incorporates what is called a "disjunctive syllogism" in classical logic, "A∨B (line 5), ¬A (line 4); therefore B (line 8),"[40] and demonstrates that the conclusion "Caitra is outside" (B) is deductively drawn from the conjunction of the two assumptions that he is alive and absent from home (C∧¬A) under the premise that he is at home or outside insofar as he is alive (C→(A∨B)).[41] In addition to these two assumptions and one premise, no other empirical information is needed to derive the conclusion.

In the *Arthâpatti-pariccheda*, Kumārila begins to criticize the opponent's attempt to reduce the Caitra-*arthâpatti* to an *anumāna* as follows. In this purported *anumāna*, one has to confirm the three characteristics (*trai-rūpya*) of logical reason (*hetu*), but one would immediately have difficulty confirming the first characteristic, that is, logical reason being a property of the subject of inference (*pakṣa-dharmatā*). Inasmuch as "being alive" is an indispensable part of logical reason, it must first be confirmed to be a property of the subject of inference, but this confirmation can be made only after Caitra is found outside. Since Caitra's being outside must be the conclusion to be proved by the purported inference, the logical error of circularity (*anyonyâśraya*) between reason and conclusion is inevitable.[42]

By contrast, *arthâpatti* is exempt from circularity.

> ŚV-Ar, v. 29: When [the preconditions of a reasoning] would be otherwise inexplicable, however, it does not appear to us to be a fault that the conclusion has already entered into [the preconditions][43] because of the cognition having precisely that form.[44]

In this verse, Kumārila proclaims that the task of *arthâpatti* is to draw out the conclusion that is entailed by the aggregate of its preconditions by means of the device called "inexplicability otherwise" (*anyathânupapatti*). Using Peirce's terminology, we can say that *arthâpatti* is a sort of the explicative (explicatory) reasoning used in deduction, but not the sort of ampliative reasoning used in induction and abduction[45] because ampliative reasonings "conclude something not implied in the premises" (CP 6.40). I called this deductive feature of *arthâpatti* characteristic (ii) in Yoshimizu (2007: 322–3).

---

[40] In disjunctive syllogism, alias *modus tollendo ponens*, the major premise is a disjunction (A∨B), the minor premise is the negation of one member of the disjunction (¬A or ¬B), and the conclusion is the affirmation of the other member (B or A). Cf. Lemmon (1972/1965: proof 52).

[41] In the case that both A and B are false but C is true, "(C∧¬A)→B" becomes false (see footnote 28); but only in this case, "C→(A∨B)" also becomes false. Therefore, "((C→(A∨B))→ ((C∧¬A)→B)" is a tautology.

[42] ŚV-Ar, v. 28.

[43] Cf. *Śloka-vārttika-tātparya-ṭīkā* (ŚVT) 394,16: bahirbhāvâkhya-prameyânupraveśa iti na doṣaḥ; Nyāya-ratnâkara (NR) 324,30–31: yo 'yaṃ vidyamānatva-saṃsṛṣṭa-gehâbhāva-buddhāv eva prameyasya bahirbhāvasyânupraveśaḥ sa na doṣaḥ.

[44] anyathânupapattau tu prameyânupraveśitā | tādrūpyeṇaiva vijñānān na doṣaḥ pratibhāti naḥ || pratibhāti naḥ ŚV in *Ślokavārttika-kāśikā* (ŚVK) and NR; *pratighātinaḥ* ŚV in ŚVT.

If "*pratighātinaḥ*" in *pāda* d is adopted, this verse may be translated as "When [the preconditions of a reasoning] would be otherwise inexplicable, however, it is not a fault that the conclusion has already entered into [the preconditions] because that which is clashing [against Caitra's expected presence at home] (i.e., Caitra's observed absence from home) is precisely cognized in that form (i.e., his being outside)." Pārthasārathi comments on the verse adopting "*pratighātinaḥ*" (NR 324,31–325,1).

[45] Cf. The Collected Papers of Charles Sanders Peirce (CP) 4.43, 85, 5.176.

1.5. *Is "inexplicability otherwise" (*anyathânupapatti*) modus tollens or reduction to absurdity?*

The inferential rule "*reduction to absurdity*" means that when an assumption "P" leads to a contradiction "Q∧¬Q," one may derive the negation of that assumption, "¬P," as a conclusion. That is to say, if both "P→Q" and "P→¬Q" would result, one may derive "¬P." In this respect, *reduction to absurdity* seems to be unsuitable for the Caitra-*arthâpatti* because Caitra's absence from home (¬A), one member of the contradictory conjunction, does not rely on the assumption that he is not outside (¬B) but has independently been introduced by observation. Proof 1, therefore, after deriving conditional "¬B→A" from the disjunction "A∨B," applies *modus tollens* to this conditional on the grounds that ¬A is observed.

In natural deduction, however, the application of a *reduction to absurdity* is permitted for a contradictory consequent that has appeared as a result of an assumption, even if additionally resorting to other assumptions.[46] *Modus tollens* itself is a theorem that can be derived by means of a *reduction to absurdity* with the help of other assumptions.[47] In the present case, Caitra's absence outside can be assumed for the purpose of a *reduction to absurdity*, and this assumption leads to the contradiction with his observed absence from home; this contradiction is then removed by denying the assumption of his absence outside, and Caitra's presence outside is finally affirmed. We will see an example of this process in an alternative proof (Proof 2, lines 7–15).[48]

2. RELATION BETWEEN "BEING ABSENT FROM HOME" AND "BEING OUTSIDE" EXPRESSED BY THE QUANTIFICATION OF LOCATION

2.1. *Propositional derivation*

In Proof 1, one may notice that at every step, the proof proceeds by applying an inferential rule to a combination of at most three propositions, that is, sentences that

[46] Cf. Lemmon (1972/1965: 26): "Now suppose that from an assumption A, together perhaps with other assumptions, we can derive a contradiction as a conclusion; then RAA (*reductio ad absurdum*) permits us to derive ¬A as a conclusion from those other assumptions (if any)."

[47] Lemmon (1972/1965: 62) presents the following proof of *modus tollens*:

Proof 55: P→Q, ¬Q ⊦ ¬P

1	P→Q	[1] *assumption*
2	¬Q	[2] *assumption*
3	P	[3] assumption for reduction to absurdity
4	Q	[1,3] 1,3, *modus ponens*
5	Q∧¬Q	[1,2,3] 2,4, *and-introduction*
6	¬P	[1,2] 3,5, reduction to absurdity

[48] In Yoshimizu 2007, I presented "Proof 2," which proves the same sequent as that proved in Proof 1 of the present chapter, "((C→(A∨B))→((C∧¬A)→B)," by applying *reduction to absurdity*. In that previous proof, I posited "(A∨B)∧¬A" at line 6 by combining "A∨B" and "¬A"; I then proved the sequent "((A∨B)∧¬A)→B," which is nothing other than a disjunctive syllogism, in another proof, "Proof 3," applying *reduction to absurdity* (line 13). However, to arrive at "A," which contradicts "¬A," I had to make a detour due to the elimination of the disjunctive "A∨B." In addition, "∧-elimination" in line 9 of Proof 6 (p. 328) is to be corrected to "∨-elimination."

are either true or false. In the case of the *arthâpatti* that proves Caitra's being outside, propositions A, B, and C have different predicates, "being at home," "being outside," and "being alive" respectively, while having the same subject, Caitra. In the whole procedure of the proof, it is never mentioned whether anyone other than Caitra is at home, outside, or alive. Therefore, this proof comes to be completed within the range of propositional logic (sentential logic) and has no need to be involved in the universal quantification of one who is at home, outside, or alive. In Yoshimizu 2007: 321–2, I called this feature of *arthâpatti* characteristic (i) and rendered "*arthâpatti*" as "propositional derivation."

According to Kumārila, every single noun denotes a universal (*sāmānya*), a natural kind property (*jāti*) that commonly inheres in every individual (*vyakti*) of a particular group.[49] One cannot say whether or not a universal exists because it is permanent;[50] only an individual comes to being and perishes. The affirmation or negation of existence is possible only in a sentence because a sentence composed of words can refer (*lakṣ*) to an individual, affirming or negating its existence.[51]

The sentences that form an *anumāna*, however, are not concerned with the existence of an object but make it known in its relation to two separate properties. In the conclusion of an *anumāna*, the subject (*pakṣa*), for example, a mountain, is cognized as a substrate (*dharmin*) qualified by a property (*dharma*), fire.[52] Before being cognized as such, the mountain must have already been cognized as a substrate of the logical reason (*hetu*), namely, smoke, another property that has no epistemic dependence (*adhīna*)[53] on fire because of its own distribution, which is pervaded (*vyāpta*) by fire among the individual substrates that form a domain of discourse.

In *arthâpatti*, however, the situation is different.

> ŚV-Ar, v. 64: In this case (i.e., *arthâpatti*), we do not cognize an object of inference, namely, a previously established and independent substrate qualified by a property (i.e., the logical reason),[54] as a thing that is qualified by [another] independent (property) [to be proven].[55]

In Proof 1, *anyathânupapatti* is applied as *modus tollens*. In the formula of *modus tollens*, "P→Q, ¬Q; therefore ¬P," the conclusion "¬P" negates "P," which is the antecedent of the first assumption (P→Q), as a result of the syntactical relation between two propositions (P→Q and ¬Q) without considering the pervasion between the predicates of P and Q in a domain of discourse. To show the soundness of reasoning via *modus tollens*, "it suffices to consider the propositions as units without looking inside them. The propositional calculus reveals validity when this depends on propositional structure *alone*" (Lemmon 1972/1965: 93).

---

[49] ŚV, Ākṛty-adhikaraṇa, v. 18; ŚV, Vākyâdhikaraṇa, vv. 309cd–310ab.

[50] ŚV, Vākyâdhikaraṇa, vv. 310cd–311c.

[51] ŚV, Vākyâdhikaraṇa, v. 311cd.

[52] ŚV-Anu, vv. 27ab and 47cd.

[53] ŚV-Ar, v. 20.

[54] dharmī dharma-viśiṣṭo ŚV in ŚVK; dharmâdharma-viśiṣṭo ŚV in ŚVT and NR.

[55] pūrva-siddhaḥ svatantro 'rthaḥ svatantreṇa viśeṣitaḥ | dharmī dharma-viśiṣṭo 'tra nânumeyaḥ pratīyate || What is directly addressed in this context is another example of *arthâpatti* (*śrutârthâpatti*): "Devadatta is corpulent and is said not to eat during daytime; therefore, he eats at night."

According to ŚV-Ar, v. 64, the property "being absent from home" is epistemically not independent (*svatantra*) of another property, "being outside"; in other words, they are not separate. In the conclusion drawn through *arthâpatti*, the subject "Caitra" is connected with the predicate "being outside," but this connection is not brought about by the fact that "being absent from home" has its own distribution pervaded (*vyāpta*) by "being outside" in the domain of living beings. As far as the domain of living beings is concerned, they are like two sides of the same coin because "being absent from home" is nothing but the negation of "being at home," which means existence in the only location excluded from "outside." Kumārila, however, does not clarify how these two properties are related to each other. How is this relation to be considered?

2.2. *Quantification of location as a variable for deriving Caitra's presence*

The predicate "being" in the sense of "being located (spatially situated) at" is binomial (or dyadic); that is, it requires two terms to be predicated: what is located and at what location. The property (*dharma*) expressed by this predicate is not the attribute of a substrate (*dharmin*), a being, but its relation with another substrate, which is here a location. In the sentence "Caitra is outside," not only is Caitra predicated as being outside, but also a certain place outside of Caitra's home is predicated as the location where he is. What is referred to as "outside of Caitra's home" is the spatial complementary to Caitra's home. All locations in the physical world can be called "outside" except for Caitra's home, in the same way that all species of animal can be called "non-cow" except for cows. Therefore, taking all locations in the world as a domain of discourse,[56] one can formulate another proof of the Caitra-*arthâpatti* without using the two predicates "being absent from home" and "being outside," by reducing them to the same predicate, "being located," in the negative connection with a certain location, Caitra's home, and in the affirmative connection with one of the other locations, respectively.

If we use "L" for the binomial predicate "being located," "c" for Caitra, and "h" for Caitra's home, then "Caitra is at home" can be rendered as "Lch," and "Caitra is absent from home" as "$\neg$Lch." Expressing any location in the world with the variable "x," we can render "Caitra is somewhere" as "$\exists$xLcx," which states that there is a location where Caitra exists. Then, "Caitra is outside" can be rendered as "$\exists$x(Lcx$\wedge\neg$(h=x))," which states that there is a location where Caitra exists and which is not his home. Because all locations in the world are demarcated into Caitra's home and other places, the premise of Proof 1, "Caitra is at home or outside insofar as he is alive," is tantamount to "Caitra is somewhere insofar as he is alive" or "If Caitra is alive, he is somewhere."[57] Using "A" for the predicate "being alive," we can render this existentially quantified premise as "Ac$\rightarrow\exists$xLcx." Then, we can rewrite Proof 1, made by propositional logic, into the proof in Table 3 by predicate logic.

---

[56] For the idea that location is a variable, I am indebted to the text prepared by Elisa Freschi and Andrew Ollett for the present volume (commentary on ŚV-Ar, vv. 44–5, see p. 66).

[57] Śālikanātha explicitly posits this premise in *Ṛju-vimalā-pañcikā* (ṚP) 114, 9: ato'rthâpattau jīvanasya deśena saha sambandha-mātra-jñānam avagaty-aṅgam. "Therefore, in *arthâpatti*, what is required for the understanding is the cognition of a mere relation between being alive and a place" (trans. Freschi and Ollett in the present volume, p. 92).

TABLE 3: Proof 2: $(Ac \to \exists xLcx) \to ((Ac \land \neg Lch) \to \exists x(Lcx \land \neg(h=x)))$

1	$Ac \to \exists xLcx$	[1] *assumption* (premise) "If Caitra is alive, he is somewhere." (i.e., "Caitra is somewhere insofar as he is alive")
2	$Ac \land \neg Lch$	[2] *assumption*
3	Ac	[2] 2, *and-elimination* "Caitra is alive."
4	$\neg Lch$	[2] 2, *and-elimination* "Caitra is absent from home."
5	$\exists xLcx$	[1, 2] 1, 3, *modus ponens*
6	$Lc\alpha$	[6(α)] *assumption* for *∃-elimination* "Caitra is at location α."[58]
7	$\forall x \neg(Lcx \land \neg(h=x))$	[7] *assumption* for *modus tollens*
8	$\forall x \neg(Lcx \land \neg(h=x)) \to \forall x(Lcx \to (h=x))$	substitution of Fx and Gx in the theorem "$\forall x \neg(Fx \land \neg Gx) \to \forall x(Fx \to Gx)$"[59] with Lcx and (h=x)
9	$\forall x(Lcx \to (h=x))$	[7] 7, 8, *modus ponens*
10	$Lc\alpha \to (h=\alpha)$	[7] 9, *∀-elimination*[60] "If Caitra is at location α, α is his home."
11	$h=\alpha$	[6(α), 7] 6, 10, *modus ponens*
12	$(h=\alpha) \land Lc\alpha$	[6(α), 7] 6, 11, *and-introduction*
13	Lch	[6(α), 7] 12, *substitution rule* "$\forall x \forall y(((x=y) \land Fx) \to Fy)$"[61]
14	$\forall x \neg(Lcx \land \neg(h=x)) \to Lch$	[6(α)] 7, 13, *conditional proof* "If Caitra is nowhere outside, he is at home."
15	$\neg \forall x \neg(Lcx \land \neg(h=x))$	[2, 6(α)] 4, 14, *modus tollens* "It is not the case that Caitra is nowhere outside."
16	$Lc\alpha \to \neg \forall x \neg(Lcx \land \neg(h=x))$	[2] 6, 15, *conditional proof*
17	$\neg \forall x \neg(Lcx \land \neg(h=x))$	[1, 2] 5, 16, *∃-elimination*[62]

[58] When the Greek letter α expresses an arbitrary example of an existentially quantified statement, (α) is added to the line number of the assumption in square brackets insofar as the assumption of α is required (Noya 1997: 113; Pelletier 1999: 22).

[59] $\forall x \neg(Fx \land \neg Gx) \to \forall x(Fx \to Gx)$

1 $\forall x \neg(Fx \land \neg Gx)$ [1] *assumption*
2 $\neg(Fa \land \neg Ga)$ [1] *∀-elimination* (cf. Lemmon 1972/1965: 104–6)
3 $\neg(Fa \land \neg Ga) \to (Fa \to Ga)$ substitution of P and Q in material implication "$\neg(P \land \neg Q) \to (P \to Q)$" (see footnote 39) with Fa and Ga
4 $Fa \to Ga$ [1] 2, 3, *modus ponens*
5 $\forall x(Fx \to Gx)$ [1] 4, *∀-introduction* (see section 3.3 of the present chapter)
6 $\forall x \neg(Fx \land \neg Gx) \to \forall x(Fx \to Gx)$ 1, 5, *conditional proof*

[60] Cf. Lemmon (1972/1965: 104–6).

[61] Cf. Lemmon (1972/1965: 161).

[62] Cf. Lemmon (1972/1965: 112–13).

18	$\exists x \neg\neg (Lcx \wedge \neg(h=x))$	[1, 2] 17, *the law of de Morgan* (predicate logic) "$\neg \forall x Fx \leftrightarrow \exists x \neg Fx$"[63]
19	$\exists x(Lcx \wedge \neg(h=x))$	[1, 2] 18, *elimination* of *double negation* "Caitra is somewhere outside."
20	$(Ac \wedge \neg Lch) \rightarrow \exists x(Lcx \wedge \neg(h=x))$	[1] 2, 19, *conditional proof*
21	$(Ac \rightarrow \exists x Lcx) \rightarrow ((Ac \wedge \neg Lch) \rightarrow \exists x(Lcx \wedge \neg (h=x)))$	1, 20, *conditional proof*

TABLE 4: Comparison of Proofs 1 and 2

	Proof 1	*Proof 2*
assumption (premise)	1 $C \rightarrow (A \vee B)$	1 $Ac \rightarrow \exists x Lcx$
assumption	3 C	3 Ac
assumption	4 $\neg A$	4 $\neg Lch$
modus ponens	5 $A \vee B$	5 $\exists x Lcx$
modification of 5	6 $\neg B \rightarrow A$	14 $\forall x \neg(Lcx \wedge \neg(h=x)) \rightarrow Lch$
modus tollens	7 $\neg\neg B$	15 $\neg \forall x \neg(Lcx \wedge \neg(h=x))$
double negation	8 B	19 $\exists x(Lcx \wedge \neg(h=x))$

Comparing Proofs 1 and 2 in Table **4**, one can see that both closely parallel each other in deriving a conclusion through *modus tollens*.

As in Proof 1, *modus tollens* in Proof 2 derives its conclusion "$\exists x(Lcx \wedge \neg(h=x))$" (line 19) from the negation of the proposition that has appeared as the antecedent of the conditional, "$\forall x \neg(Lcx \wedge \neg(h=x)) \rightarrow Lch$" (line 14). This proposition "$\forall x \neg(Lcx \wedge \neg(h=x))$" universally quantifies only the location where Caitra exists, not the being who exists at a location. Therefore, although Proof 2 adopts the quantification of the location where Caitra exists, it always refers to Caitra alone and does not owe its conclusion to the pervasion (*vyāpti*) of the property "absence from home" by another property, "being outside," because the domain of discourse for this pervasion consists of those who exist somewhere. Therefore, characteristic (i) is shared by Proofs 1 and 2.

3. INSEPARABILITY (*AVINĀ-BHĀVA*) ASCERTAINED AFTER *ARTHÂPATTI*

3.1. *Kumārila's allusion to universal quantification*

Before refuting the purported *anumāna* of Caitra's being outside in view of the remaining characteristic of logical reason (*hetu*) (namely, its correlation (*anvaya-vyatireka*) with the property to be proven), Kumārila states the following:

[63] Cf. Lemmon (1972/1965), proof 114(a)(b) $\forall Fx \leftrightarrow \neg\exists\neg Fx$; Noya (1997: 233–4, proofs 55(2) and 56(2) $\neg\forall x Fx \leftrightarrow \exists x \neg Fx$).

> ŚV-Ar, v. 30: A relationship of inseparability in the case under consideration may be postulated only at that point. It is not ascertained before. Therefore, although this is present,[64] it cannot be a cause [for the cognition of Caitra's being outside].[65]

Here Kumārila accepts that in the domain of all living beings, the property "being absent from home" is inseparable (*avinā-bhāvin*) from another property, "being outside." With this acceptance (*evaṃ saty api*), however, he does not agree with the logicians of other schools who claim that *arthâpatti* can be reduced to *anumāna*. Rather, Kumārila denies their view that the cognition of Caitra's being outside is caused by this inseparability (*na kāraṇam*). Moreover, he declares that this inseparability is not ascertained in advance (*na prāg-avadhṛtā*); rather, it is postulated only at that point (*tadâiva parikalpyate*). That is to say, only after Caitra has been proved to be outside by means of *arthâpatti* can it be proved that all those who are alive and absent from home (i.e., their own houses) are invariably somewhere outside. This epistemic posteriority of *avinā-bhāva* to *arthâpatti* is what I called characteristic (iii) in Yoshimizu 2007: 323–4.

Kumārila's claim here may appear to commit a fallacy of overgeneralization. How is it possible to generalize the behavior of all people from that of a particular person, Caitra? After this allusion to universal quantification (vv. 30–3), Kumārila begins to refute the possibility of empirically confirming the inseparability of "being absent from home" from "being outside," but he does not go so far as to clarify how to ascertain this inseparability on the grounds of *arthâpatti*. In the following sections (3.2 and 3.3), I will explain how Kumārila's allusion to universal quantification is justifiable in view of formal logic.

3.2. *The limits of truth-value analysis*

The final proposition derived at line 21 in Proof 2, "$(Ac \rightarrow \exists xLcx) \rightarrow ((Ac \wedge \neg Lch) \rightarrow \exists x(Lcx \wedge \neg(h=x)))$," consists of the premise "$Ac \rightarrow \exists xLcx$" (line 1) and the proposition to be proved "$(Ac \wedge \neg Lch) \rightarrow \exists x(Lcx \wedge \neg(h=x))$" (line 20). In Table 5 we can analyze this final proposition into its components and check their truth-values, which depend on whether three propositions, "Caitra is alive" (Ac), "Caitra is at home" (Lch), and "Caitra is somewhere outside" ($\exists x(Lcx \wedge \neg(h=x))$), are true (T) or false (F).[66]

This truth table shows that the proposition to be proved, "$(Ac \wedge \neg Lch) \rightarrow \exists x(Lcx \wedge \neg(h=x))$," remains true except in the unrealistic case that Caitra is neither at home nor outside although he is alive (column viii, line 4). In this case, however, the antecedent, "If Caitra is alive, he is somewhere" ($Ac \rightarrow \exists xLcx$), also becomes false (column ii, line 4). Thus, there is no case in which the antecedent (column ii) is true but the consequent (column viii) is false, including this unrealistic case. A

[64] *saty apy eṣā* ŚV in NR and ŚVT; *anyathâiṣā* ŚV in ŚVK. If "*anyathâiṣā*" is adopted, v. 30cd may be rendered as, "Because [the relationship of inseparability] is not ascertained before, this cannot be a cause [for the cognition] otherwise (i.e., unless it is ascertained before)."

[65] avinābhāvitā câtra tadâiva parikalpyate | na prāg-avadhṛtêty evaṃ saty apy eṣā na kāraṇam.

[66] "Caitra is somewhere" (column iii) is logically equivalent to "Caitra is at home or outside."

TABLE 5: Caitra-arthâpatti Truth Table

			i	*ii*	*iii*	*iv*	*v*	*vi*	*vii*	*viii*	*ix*
	Ac	Lch	$(Ac$	$\rightarrow$	$\exists xLcx)$	$\rightarrow$	$((Ac$	$\wedge$	$\neg Lch)$	$\rightarrow$	$\exists x(Lcx \wedge \neg(h=x)))$
	C *is alive*	C *is at home*	C *is alive*	*if*	C *is somewhere*	*if*	C *is alive*	*and*	C *is absent from home*	*if*	C *is somewhere outside*
1	T	T	T	T	T	T	T	F	F	T	T
2	T	T	T	T	T	T	T	F	F	T	F
3	T	F	T	T	T	T	T	T	T	T	T
4	T	F	T	F	F	T	T	T	T	F	F
5	F	T	F	T	T	T	F	F	F	T	T
6	F	T	F	T	T	T	F	F	F	T	F
7	F	F	F	T	T	T	F	F	T	T	T
8	F	F	F	T	F	T	F	F	T	T	F

conditional proposition becomes true if the antecedent is false regardless of whether the consequent is true or false.[67] Therefore, the whole conditional proposition "$(Ac \rightarrow \exists xLcx) \rightarrow ((Ac \wedge \neg Lch) \rightarrow \exists x(Lcx \wedge \neg(h=x)))$" is always true (column iv); in other words, it is a tautology.[68]

Being a tautology, this whole conditional proposition remains true even if "c" (Caitra) is substituted with another name such as "d" (Devadatta), regardless of where Devadatta is or whether he is alive. Repeating this substitution many times, we can generalize this proposition insofar as the number of living beings at issue is finite because the process of substitution comes to an end when the truth of this proposition is confirmed for the last living being. However, if the number of living beings at issue is infinite, then the mechanical truth-value analysis in a truth table becomes insufficient because the substitution never comes to the end.[69] If one intends to derive a universal proposition about the infinite number of all living beings from the proposition about Caitra proved in Proof 2, "$(Ac \wedge \neg Lch) \rightarrow \exists x(Lcx \wedge \neg(h=x))$," one has to prove that it is logically legitimate to apply a rule of predicate logic, "the introduction of a universal quantifier" (abbreviated as ∀I or UI), to this proposition.

3.3. *Universal quantification of "one who is at a location"*

In the natural deduction of predicate logic, it is permissible to derive "∀xFx" from a proposition "Ft" by introducing a universal quantifier only if "t" is arbitrary in

[67] See footnote 39; cf. Noya (1997/1994: 219, theorem 10).
[68] See footnote 41.
[69] Cf. Lemmon (1972/1965: 157).

"Ft," that is, only if "Ft" does not rest on any special assumption concerning "t."[70] If "Ft" rests on a certain special assumption concerning "t," deducing "∀xFx" from "Ft" commits a logical fallacy of overgeneralization because, thereby, even those that do not satisfy the assumption are predicated by "F."

In Proof 2, all assumptions about "c" posited in the course of the proof (lines 2 and 7) change their truth-value according to the case. The assumption "Ac" is true when Caitra is alive but becomes false when he is not alive; the assumption "¬Lch" is true when Caitra is not at home but false when he is at home; and the assumption "∀x¬(Lcx∧¬(h=x))" (line 7) is true when Caitra is not outside but false when he is somewhere outside. By contrast, the proposition that appears at line 1 of Proof 2, "Ac→∃xLcx," always remains true in reality. The case in which this conditional becomes false would be expressed as "Although Caitra is alive, he is not anywhere," but this can never be true because Caitra has a physical body insofar as he is alive. This proposition is posited as an infallible premise at the outset of the proof, unlike the fallible assumptions posited in the course of the proof about how Caitra is or what Caitra is doing in the world. Based on this infallibility, we can think of the proposition "Ac→∃xLcx" as a result of applying "the elimination of a universal quantifier" (abbreviated as ∀E or UE)[71] to a more fundamental premise.

If we use the variable "x" for one who is at a location and "y" for a location, then the fundamental premise that precedes "Ac→∃xLcx" in Proof 2 can be expressed as "∀x∃y(Ax→Lxy)," which means "Anyone who is alive is somewhere." Applying ∀E to this premise by substituting "x" with "c," we can render the second line as "Ac→∃yLcy," calling an arbitrary example of person *x* in this premise "Caitra." Thereafter, we can assume that Caitra is alive and absent from home in the third line. We can transform Proof 2 into the proof in Table 6, starting with the fundamental premise ∀x∃y(Ax→Lxy).

In Proof 3, lines 8 to 14 of Proof 2 each increases their number by one, while retaining exactly the same operation they had in Proof 2. Thus, line 14 of Proof 2, "∀x¬(Lcx∧¬(h=x))→Lch [6(α)] 7,13, *conditional proof*," is transformed into line

TABLE 6: Proof 3, ∀x∃y(Ax→Lxy)→∀x∃y((Ax∧¬Lxh)→(Lxy∧¬(h=y)))

1	∀x∃y(Ax→Lxy)	[1] *assumption* (premise) "Anyone who is alive is somewhere."
2	Ac→∃yLcy	[1] 1, *∀-elimination*
3	Ac∧¬Lch	[3] *assumption*
4	Ac	[3] 3, *and-elimination*
5	¬Lch	[3] 3, *and-elimination*
6	∃yLcy	[1, 3] 2, 4, *modus ponens*
7	Lcα	[7(α)] *assumption* for *∃-elimination*
8	∀y¬(Lcy∧¬(h=y))	[8] *assumption* for *modus tollens*
		(continued)

[70] Cf. Lemmon (1972/1965: 108–9): "suppose that . . . given that *Aa, Ra→Ta*. . . . we have no right to pass from the conclusion *Ra→Ta* to *∀x(Rx→Tx)*, just because that conclusion rests on the *special assumption concerning a that Aa* . . . before we apply UI, we should make sure that '*a*' does not appear in any of the assumptions on which the conclusion rests."

[71] Cf. Lemmon (1972/1965: 104–6).

15 of Proof 3, "$\forall y\neg(Lcy\wedge\neg(h=y))\rightarrow Lch$ [7(α)] 8,14, *conditional proof.*" We can then resume Proof 3 as in Table 7.

With line 21 "$(Ac\wedge\neg Lch)\rightarrow\exists y(Lcy\wedge\neg(h=y))$," which corresponds to line 20 of Proof 2, Proof 3 derives the proposition to be proved by the *arthâpatti*, "If Caitra is alive and absent from home, then he is somewhere outside." The assumption made about "c" at line 3 (line 2 of Proof 2), that is, "Caitra is alive and absent from home," is discharged at line 21 (20 of Proof 2) by *conditional proof.* Another assumption made about "c" at line 8 (7 of Proof 2), that is, "Caitra is nowhere outside," has already disappeared when line 21 appears because it was discharged at line 15 (14 of Proof 2) by *conditional proof.* By contrast, the premise posited at line 1, "Anyone who is alive is somewhere," remains at line 21 and is not yet discharged, but this premise does not contain any special assumption about Caitra. The "c" in line 21 occurs perfectly arbitrarily in the same manner that "c" in line 2 appears as an arbitrary name by applying ∀E to line 1. Accordingly, we can legitimately apply ∀I to line 21 and derive a proposition in which one who is at a location is universally quantified.

The inseparability (*avinā-bhāva*) of "being absent from home" from "being outside" in the domain of all living beings is expressed in line 22, "$\forall x\exists y((Ax\wedge\neg Lxh)\rightarrow(Lxy\wedge\neg(h=y)))$." Under the premise that anyone who is alive is somewhere (line 1), it becomes possible to derive Caitra's being outside from the assumption that he is alive and absent from home (line 21). However, this does not mean that this derivation is ascertained by the inseparability of "being absent from home" from "being outside." On the contrary, that inseparability is ascertained in line 22 (see Table 8) on the grounds that the conclusion of the *arthâpatti* "$(Ac\wedge\neg Lch)\rightarrow\exists y(Lcy\wedge\neg(h=y))$" (line 21) contains no assumption about Caitra.

TABLE 7: Proof 3, Part 2

16	$\neg\forall y\neg(Lcy\wedge\neg(h=y))$	[3, 7(α)] 5,15, *modus tollens*
17	$Lc\alpha\rightarrow\neg\forall y\neg(Lcy\wedge\neg(h=y))$	[3] 7, 16, *conditional proof*
18	$\neg\forall y\neg(Lcy\wedge\neg(h=y))$	[1, 3] 6, 17, *∃-elimination*
19	$\exists y\neg\neg(Lcy\wedge\neg(h=y))$	[1, 3] 18, *the law of de Morgan* (predicate logic) "$\neg\forall xFx\leftrightarrow\exists x\neg Fx$"
20	$\exists y(Lcy\wedge\neg(h=y))$	[1, 3] 19, elimination of *double negation*
21	$(Ac\wedge\neg Lch)\rightarrow\exists y(Lcy\wedge\neg(h=y))$	[1] 3, 20, *conditional proof* (continued)

TABLE 8: Proof 3, Concluded

22	$\forall x\exists y((Ax\wedge\neg Lxh)\rightarrow(Lxy\wedge\neg(h=y)))$	[1] 21, *∀-introduction* "Anyone who is alive and absent from home is somewhere outside."
23	$\forall x\exists y(Ax\rightarrow Lxy)\rightarrow\forall x\exists y((Ax\wedge\neg Lxh)\rightarrow(Lxy\wedge\neg(h=y)))$	1, 22, *conditional proof* "Under the premise that anyone who is alive is somewhere, anyone who is alive and absent from home is somewhere outside."
(Q.E.D.)		

4. *ARTHÂPATTI* FROM CAITRA'S PRESENCE SOMEWHERE TO HIS ABSENCE FROM ALL OTHER LOCATIONS

4.1. *Another aspect of the physical existence of a living being*

At the beginning of the debate about the positive and negative correlation (*anvaya-vyatireka*) to be confirmed for the purported *anumāna* of Caitra's being outside, the opponent claims the following. Suppose that we visit someone's house, say, Devadatta's. Standing at the entrance, we first look in and do not find Devadatta inside. We then stand in front of his house looking around the surroundings, and finally find him squatting in a thicket (*romaśā*).[72] We can then infer that Caitra will also be found somewhere outside in the same manner that Devadatta, who is absent from home, is found in a thicket near to his home.[73] Adducing this example, the opponent insists that the positive correlation (*anvaya*) of the logical reason (*hetu*) with the property to be proven (*sādhya*) in the purported *anumāna* can be confirmed inasmuch as it is easy to find an entity that possesses the logical reason, that is, a living being who is absent from home, among the similar instances (*sapakṣa*s), that is, the instances similar to the subject in possessing the property to be proven, that is, existence somewhere outside.

Against this claim, Kumārila figures out another type of reasoning, which proves that if Caitra is present at a particular location, he is absent from all places other than that particular location. Without explicitly referring by name to "missing Caitra" and "Devadatta found in a thicket," Kumārila explains why this second line of reasoning cannot be reduced to an *anumāna* in terms of the confirmation of the positive correlation (*anvaya*) of the logical reason with the property to be proven:

> ŚV-Ar, v. 35: [Proponent:] Even then, one's absence from *every* place is not understood. Nor can there be a pervasion of the logical reason [by the property to be proven] because of one's not being in one place.[74]

Although it is easy to confirm Devadatta as possessing the logical reason inasmuch as he is found at one location, a thicket, he cannot be counted as a similar instance (*sapakṣa*) because one cannot confirm that he possesses the property to be proven, that is, the absence from every location other than the thicket, unless one visits every other place in the world. Even if Devadatta's absence is confirmed at one location, such as

---

[72] ŚVT 395,22: romaśā-vyavasthitaṃ devadattam upalabhya . . . romaśā-vyavasthitena devadatta-bhāvena. This "*romaśā*" ("something shaggy" in the feminine) might mean a piece of ground (*bhūmi*, a feminine noun) used as a toilet in which a male Brahmin should be squatting while relieving himself, including while urinating (cf. *Manusmṛti* 4.47–9). In ŚVK 171,26–172,8, Sucaritamiśra takes Devadatta as a similar instance of the purported *anumāna* of Caitra's absence from all other locations than his present one.

[73] ŚV-Ar, v. 34: gṛha-dvāri-sthito yas tu bahirbhāvaṃ prakalpayet | yadâikasminn ayaṃ deśe na tadânyatra vidyate ‖ "[Opponent:] But one who, standing at the door of [Devadatta's] house, [has found him in a thicket] may postulate that [Caitra, who is absent from home,] is outside [in the same manner as Devadatta, considering:] 'When this (Devadatta) is in one place, he is not somewhere else.'"

[74] tadâpy avidyamānatvaṃ na sarvatra pratīyate | na câikadeśe nâstitvād vyāptir hetor bhaviṣyati ‖.

inside his house, his absence from all the other locations is not yet confirmed because one can deny the existence of something at a particular location only after having arrived there.[75] Therefore, due to the lack of the property to be proven, one cannot count Devadatta as a similar instance; without finding any similar instances, one cannot confirm the positive correlation (*anvaya*) of this second purported *anumāna*.

In the *Anumāna-pariccheda* of the ŚV, Kumārila declares that the statement of pervasion with a similar instance (*sādharmya-dṛṣṭānta*) is indispensable for a syllogism. If this statement is rightfully given conclusively, one does not need to add another statement of pervasion with a dissimilar instance (*vaidharmya-dṛṣṭānta*).[76] The latter statement is to be added if the former is capable of being understood as presenting just a coincidental correlation (*saha-bhāvitva*).[77] Even in this case, though, the statement with a similar instance contributes to the understanding of pervasion.[78] In short, Kumārila is in no position to approve of the *anumāna* with a negative-only reason (*kevala-vyatireki-hetu*) due to the impossibility of confirming its positive correlation (*anvaya*) in similar instances.[79]

After refuting the opponent's attempt to establish the second *anumāna*, Kumārila declares that *arthâpatti* has an advantage over *anumāna* because *arthâpatti* can also operate conclusively in this line of reasoning:

> ŚV-Ar, vv. 46–7ab: However, because the apprehension of a person as a whole in one place would not be established otherwise [i.e., if the person were also somewhere else], this accounts for the person's absence from other places. Therefore, it is based on an *arthâpatti* in the case under consideration.[80]

Here, Kumārila refers to another aspect of physical existence that he did not mention when arguing about Caitra being outside. The place where the body exists, which is metonymically also the location of the self that controls the body,[81] is restricted to only one at any point in time. In other words, the body is subject to the spatiotemporal (*deśa-kāla*) restriction (*niyama*) of its existence.[82] In verse 46, Kumārila states that from this premise, it is derived that one cannot exist simultaneously at different

---

[75] ŚV-Ar, vv. 36–8. This section is followed by vv. 39–42, in which Kumārila finds practical faults with Diṅnāga's system of logic, pointing out that it is impossible to confirm conclusively the negative correlation (*vyatireka*) of the non-existence of the property to be proven with the non-existence of logical reason concerning the innumerable number of the dissimilar instances (*vipakṣa*s), that is, the instances dissimilar to the subject in lacking the property to be proven. However, Diṅnāga, a pure logician, does not care about how to confirm pervasion (*vyāpti*) in the physical world. See Yoshimizu (2017: footnotes 26 and 38).

[76] ŚV-Anu, v. 118ab.

[77] ŚV-Anu, vv. 118cd–120.

[78] ŚV-Anu, v. 121ab. Cf. NR 273,13: na hy asaty anvaye vyatireka-mātrād arthaḥ sidhyati; "Because, if there is no positive correlation, the state of affairs to be proved is not established only through negative correlation."

[79] This is the reason why at the beginning of ŚV-Ar (vv. 3–7), Kumārila includes the reasoning of the existence of various kinds of *śakti*, that is, a potency particular to a kind of thing, into *arthāpattti* (cf. Yoshimizu 2007: 315–16). Kumārila holds *anyathânupapatti* to be based on *pariśeṣa* (TV 164,6–7: *pariśeṣa-siddha*), that is, the elimination of all but one of the exhaustively enumerated alternatives. See Yoshimizu (forthcoming).

[80] puruṣasya tu kārtsnyena yad ekatrôpalambhanam | tasyânyathā na siddhiḥ syād ity anyeṣv asya nāstitā || tenârthâpatti-pūrvatvam atra.

[81] See footnotes 29–32.

[82] ŚV, Śūnya-vāda, vv. 253, 256cd–257. Cf. Yoshimizu 2011: 509.

places because otherwise this premise would not stand to reason. In verse 47a, he asserts that this argument is made by *arthâpatti*, not by *anumāna*.

4.2. *Conjunctive syllogism through modus tollens*

The disjunction "A or B," as a statement in formal logic, excludes the possibility that both A and B are false but does not exclude the possibility that both of them are true.[83] Thus, the statement "Corpulent Devadatta eats during the day or at night" does not exclude the possibility that he might eat not only during the day but also at night. Taking "Caitra is at home" as A and "Caitra is outside" as B, we can exclude the possibility that Caitra is neither at home nor outside by the sequent "$A \vee B$," which states that Caitra is at home or outside, but this sequent itself does not deny that Caitra can simultaneously be at home and outside. In order to express this negation, it is necessary to negate the conjunction of A and B by "$\neg(A \wedge B)$."

Now, assuming that Caitra actually exists at a certain location α, let us take "Caitra is at location α" as A and "Caitra is outside of location α" as B. We can then construct the premise "Caitra cannot simultaneously be at location α and outside of location α" ($\neg(A \wedge B)$). Under this premise, one can derive "Caitra is not outside of location α" ($\neg B$) from the fact that Caitra is at location α (A), applying *modus tollens* as in Table 9:

TABLE 9: Proof 4, $\neg(A \wedge B) \rightarrow (A \rightarrow \neg B)$

1	$\neg(A \wedge B)$	[1] *assumption* (premise)
2	A	[2] *assumption*
3	$\neg(A \wedge B) \rightarrow (B \rightarrow \neg A)$	substitution of P and Q in the theorem "$\neg(P \wedge \neg Q) \rightarrow (\neg Q \rightarrow \neg P)$"[84] with A and $\neg B$
4	$B \rightarrow \neg A$	[1] 1, 3, *modus ponens*
5	$\neg B$	[1, 2] 2, 4, *modus tollens*
6	$A \rightarrow \neg B$	[1] 2, 5, *conditional proof*
7	$\neg(A \wedge B) \rightarrow (A \rightarrow \neg B)$	1, 6, *conditional proof*

Proof 4 incorporates what is called a "conjunctive syllogism" in classical logic: "$\neg(A \wedge B)$ (line 1), A (line 2); therefore $\neg B$ (line 5)."[85] Comparing Proof 4 with Proof 1, which incorporates a disjunctive syllogism, one can see that Proof 4 does not contain C, "Caitra is alive." In Proof 4, Caitra's being alive is implied by "A" because he is assumed to exist at a physical location, α, whereas in Proof 1, Caitra's being alive is not implied by "$\neg A$," the observation of his absence from home.

---

[83] Lemmon (1972/1965: 19): "$P \vee Q$ is understood not to exclude the possibility that both P and Q might be the case."

[84] Cf. Lemmon (1972/1965), proof 35(b), "$\neg(P \wedge \neg Q) \rightarrow (P \rightarrow Q)$," and proof 9, "$(P \rightarrow Q) \rightarrow (\neg Q \rightarrow \neg P)$."

[85] In a conjunctive syllogism (*modus ponendo tollens*) the major premise is the negation of a conjunction ($\neg(A \wedge B)$), the minor premise is one member of the conjunction (A or B), and the conclusion is the negation of the other member ($\neg B$ or $\neg A$). Cf. Lemmon (1972/1965: proof 34).

Yoshimizu (2007: section V and footnote 55) demonstrates that with the inference of non-existence on the basis of the perception of something incompatible [with the property to be negated] itself (*svabhāva-viruddhôpalabdhi*), Dharmakīrti, who keeps silent about whether *arthâpatti* is reduced to *anumāna*, makes a propositional derivation without pervasion (*vyāpti*) by a conjunctive syllogism, "$(\neg(A \wedge B) \wedge A) \rightarrow \neg B$."

4.3. *Quantification of location as a variable for deriving Caitra's absence*

Kumārila criticizes the opponent on the basis that it is impossible to empirically confirm one's absence from any location (*sarvatra*) other than one's present location (ŚV-Ar, v. 35ab) and declares that *arthâpatti* can do so all at once (ŚV-Ar, v. 47a). Because Proof 4 is demonstrated in the form of propositional logic, the derived conclusion "$\neg$B" merely negates Caitra's presence outside of location α as a whole. To negate his presence at every single location other than location α, one has to resort to predicate logic, making all locations in the physical world the domain of discourse, as we did in Proof 2.

Let us use "L" for "being located (spatially situated)," "c" for Caitra, and "α" for the location where Caitra actually is. Then "Caitra is at location α" is rendered as "L$c\alpha$" and the premise declared by Kumārila in v. 46a, "A person is apprehended as a whole in one place" may be rendered in the case of Caitra as "$\forall x(Lcx \rightarrow \forall y(Lcy \rightarrow (x=y)))$,"[86] which states that "Wherever Caitra may be, all locations where he is are the same" or "Caitra as a whole is at exactly one location." Under this premise, "L$c\alpha$" leads to "$\neg\exists y(Lcy \wedge \neg(\alpha=y))$," which states that "Except for location α, there is no other location where Caitra is."

TABLE 10: Proof 5, $\forall x(Lcx \rightarrow \forall y(Lcy \rightarrow (x=y))) \rightarrow (Lc\alpha \rightarrow \neg\exists y(Lcy \wedge \neg(\alpha=y))$

1	$\forall x(Lcx \rightarrow \forall y(Lcy \rightarrow (x=y)))$	[1] *assumption* (premise) "Wherever Caitra may be, all locations where he is are the same," i.e., "Caitra as a whole is at exactly one location."
2	$Lc\alpha$	[2] *assumption* "Caitra is at location α."
3	$\forall x(Lcx \rightarrow \forall y(Lcy \rightarrow (x=y))) \rightarrow \forall x(\neg\forall y(Lcy \rightarrow (x=y)) \rightarrow \neg Lcx)$	substitution of Fx and Gx in the theorem "$\forall x(Fx \rightarrow Gx) \rightarrow \forall x(\neg Gx \rightarrow \neg Fx)$"[87] with Lcx and $\forall y(Lcy \rightarrow (x=y))$
4	$\forall x(\neg\forall y(Lcy \rightarrow (x=y)) \rightarrow \neg Lcx)$	[1] 1, 3, *modus ponens*
5	$\neg\forall y(Lcy \rightarrow (\alpha=y)) \rightarrow \neg Lc\alpha$	[1] 4, $\forall$*-elimination*

(continued)

[86] This sequent uses the analysis of a phrase that contains "*the*" by Russell (1905: 482): "It is not always false of x that 'if y begat Charles II, y is identical with x' is always true of y," which is what is expressed in common language by "Charles II had one father and no more."

To say that exactly one existing thing has F, Lemmon (1972/1965: 165) presents the following three patterns of sequent: (16) $\exists xFx \wedge \forall x\forall y((Fx \wedge Fy) \rightarrow (x=y))$; (17) $\exists x(Fx \wedge \forall y(Fy \rightarrow (x=y)))$; (18) $\exists x(Fx \wedge \neg\exists x(Fx \wedge \neg(x=y)))$. Replacing $\exists xFx$ and $\forall yFy$ in (17) by $\forall xLcx$ and $\forall yLcy$, respectively, one can make $\forall x(Lcx \rightarrow \forall y(Lcy \rightarrow (x=y))$.

[87] $\forall x(Fx \rightarrow Gx) \rightarrow \forall x(\neg Gx \rightarrow \neg Fx)$

1 $\forall x(Fx \rightarrow Gx)$	[1] *assumption*
2 $Fa \rightarrow Ga$	[1] 1, $\forall$*-elimination*
3 $(Fa \rightarrow Ga) \rightarrow (\neg Ga \rightarrow \neg Fa)$	substitution of P and Q in the theorem "$(P \rightarrow Q) \rightarrow (\neg Q \rightarrow \neg P)$" (cf. Lemmon 1972/1965: proof 42) with Fa and Ga
4 $\neg Ga \rightarrow \neg Fa$	[1] 2, 3, *modus ponens*
5 $\forall x(\neg Gx \rightarrow \neg Fx)$	[1] 4, $\forall$*-introduction*
6 $\forall x(Fx \rightarrow Gx) \rightarrow \forall x(\neg Gx \rightarrow \neg Fx)$	1, 5, *conditional proof*

TABLE 10: Continued

6	$\neg\neg\forall y(Lcy\rightarrow(\alpha=y))$	[1, 2] 2, 5, *modus tollens*
7	$\forall y(Lcy\rightarrow(\alpha=y))$	[1, 2] 6, *elimination of double negation*
8	$\forall y(Lcy\rightarrow(\alpha=y))\rightarrow\forall y\neg(Lcy\wedge\neg(\alpha=y))$	substitution of Fx and Gx in the theorem "$\forall x(Fx\rightarrow Gx)\rightarrow\forall x\neg(Fx\wedge\neg Gx)$"[88] with Lcy and $(\alpha=y)$
9	$\forall y\neg(Lcy\wedge\neg(\alpha=y))$	[1, 2] 7, 8, *modus ponens*
10	$\neg\exists y(Lcy\wedge\neg(\alpha=y))$	[1, 2] 9, *the law of de Morgan* (predicate logic) "Caitra is nowhere except for location α."
11	$Lc\alpha\rightarrow\neg\exists y(Lcy\wedge\neg(\alpha=y))$	[1] 2, 10, *conditional proof*
12	$\forall y(Lcy\rightarrow\forall x(Lcx\rightarrow(x=y)))\rightarrow(Lc\alpha\rightarrow\neg\exists y(Lcy\wedge\neg(\alpha=y)))$	1, 11, conditional proof "Under the premise that Caitra as a whole is at exactly one location, if he is at location α, there is no other location where he is."

TABLE 11: Comparison of Proofs 4 and 5

	Proof 4	*Proof 5*
assumption (premise)	1 $\neg(A\wedge B)$	1 $\forall x(Lcx\rightarrow\forall y(Lcy\rightarrow(x=y))$
assumption	2 A	2 $Lc\alpha$
modification of 1	4 $B\rightarrow\neg A$	5 $\neg\forall y(Lcy\rightarrow(\alpha=y))\rightarrow\neg Lc\alpha$
modus tollens	5 $\neg B$	6 $\neg\neg\forall y(Lcy\rightarrow(\alpha=y))$ (10 $\neg\exists y(Lcy\wedge\neg(\alpha=y))$)

Comparing Proofs 4 and 5 in Table 11, one may find that both closely parallel each other in deriving a conclusion through *modus tollens*.

In Proof 5, as in Proof 2, we can affirm the three characteristics of *arthâpatti*, namely: (i) propositional derivation without the quantification of "one who is at a location," (ii) entailment of the conclusion by a set of preconditions, and (iii) universal quantification of "one who is at a location" in the form of inseparability

[88] $\forall x(Fx\rightarrow Gx)\rightarrow\forall x\neg(Fx\wedge\neg Gx)$

1 $\forall x(Fx\rightarrow Gx)$ [1] *assumption*
2 $Fa\rightarrow Ga$ [1] *∀-elimination*
3 $(Fa\rightarrow Ga)\rightarrow\neg(Fa\wedge\neg Ga)$ substitution of P and Q in material implication "$(P\rightarrow Q)\rightarrow\neg(P\wedge\neg Q)$" (cf. Lemmon 1972/1965: proof 35(a)) with Fa and Ga
4 $\neg(Fa\wedge\neg Ga)$ [1] 2, 3, *modus ponens*
5 $\forall x\neg(Fx\wedge\neg Gx)$ [1] 4, *∀-introduction*
6 $\forall x(Fx\rightarrow Gx)\rightarrow\forall x\neg(Fx\wedge\neg Gx)$ 1,5, *conditional proof*

(*avinā-bhāva*), that is, "whoever may be at location α does not exist at any other location than α," is ascertainable after *arthâpatti* has been determined.[89]

CONCLUSION

In Kumārila's two examples of *arthâpatti* concerning Caitra's whereabouts, the four propositions listed in Table 12 are either posited as an assumption or derived as a conclusion.

In Proofs 1 and 2, conclusion (3) is derived from the conjunction of assumption (2) and another assumption that Caitra is alive (C/Ac) under the premise "If Caitra is alive, then he is at home or outside" ($C\rightarrow(A\vee B)$) or "If Caitra is alive, he exists somewhere" ($Ac\rightarrow\exists x(Lcx)$). In Proofs 4 and 5, conclusion (4) is derived from assumption (1) under the premise "Caitra cannot simultaneously be at location α and outside of location α" ($\neg(A\wedge B)$) or "Caitra as a whole is exactly at one location" ($\forall y(Lcy\rightarrow\forall x(Lcx\rightarrow(x=y)))$). Proofs 1 and 4 proceed within the range of propositional logic without quantification. In Proofs 2 and 5, Caitra alone is always predicated as the living being related to a location. The universal conditional statements "Anyone

TABLE 12: Two Versions of the Caitra-arthâpatti

	Proposition (assumption or conclusion)	*Proofs 1 and 4*	*Proofs 2 and 5*
(1)	"Caitra is at location α."	A_4	$Lc\alpha_5$
(2)	"Caitra is absent from home."	$\neg A_1$	$\neg Lch_2$
(3)	"Caitra is somewhere outside of home."	B_1	$\exists x(Lcx\wedge\neg(h=x))_2$
(4)	"Caitra is nowhere except for location α."	$\neg B_4$	$\neg\exists x(Lcx\wedge\neg(\alpha=x))_5$

[89] In the same way that Proof 2 is transformed into Proof 3, Proof 5 is transformed into the following proof that universally quantifies one who is at location α, by applying $\forall$E (line 2) and $\forall$I (line 13).

Proof 6: $\forall x\forall y(Lxy\rightarrow\forall z(Lxz\rightarrow(y=z))\rightarrow\forall x(Lx\alpha\rightarrow\neg\exists z(Lxz\wedge\neg(\alpha=z))$

1 $\forall x\forall y(Lxy\rightarrow\forall z(Lxz\rightarrow(y=z))$ — [1] *assumption* (premise)
2 $\forall y(Lcy\rightarrow\forall z(Lcz\rightarrow(y=z))$ — [1] 1, $\forall$*-elimination*
3 $Lc\alpha$ — [3] *assumption*
4 $\forall y(Lcy\rightarrow\forall z(Lcz\rightarrow(y=z)))\rightarrow\forall y(\neg\forall z(Lcz\rightarrow(y=z))\rightarrow\neg Lcy)$ substitution of Fx and Gx in the theorem "$\forall x(Fx\rightarrow Gx)\rightarrow\forall x(\neg Gx\rightarrow\neg Fx)$" with Lcy and $\forall z(Lcz\rightarrow(y=z))$
5 $\forall y(\neg\forall z(Lcz\rightarrow(y=z))\rightarrow\neg Lcy)$ — [1] 2, 4, *modus ponens*
6 $\neg\forall z(Lcz\rightarrow(\alpha=z))\rightarrow\neg Lc\alpha$ — [1] 5, $\forall$*-elimination*
7 $\neg\neg\forall z(Lcz\rightarrow(\alpha=z))$ — [1, 3] 3, 6, *modus tollens*
8 $\forall z(Lcz\rightarrow(\alpha=z))$ — [1, 3] 7, *elimination of double negation*
9 $\forall z(Lcz\rightarrow(\alpha=z))\rightarrow\forall z\neg(Lcz\wedge\neg(\alpha=z))$ substitution of Fx and Gx in the theorem "$\forall x(Fx\rightarrow Gx)\rightarrow\forall x\neg(Fx\wedge\neg Gx)$" with Lcz and $(\alpha=z)$
10 $\forall z\neg(Lcz\wedge\neg(\alpha=z))$ — [1, 3] 8, 9, *modus ponens*
11 $\neg\exists z(Lcz\wedge\neg(\alpha=z))$ — [1, 3] 10, *the law of de Morgan* (predicate logic)
12 $Lc\alpha\rightarrow\neg\exists z(Lcz\wedge\neg(\alpha=z))$ — [1] 3, 11, *conditional proof*
13 $\forall x(Lx\alpha\rightarrow\neg\exists z(Lxz\wedge\neg(\alpha=z))$ — [1] 12, $\forall$*-introduction*
14 $\forall x\forall y(Lxy\rightarrow\forall z(Lxz\rightarrow(y=z))\rightarrow\forall x(Lx\alpha\rightarrow\neg\exists z(Lxz\wedge\neg(\alpha=z)))$ 1, 13, *conditional proof* "Under the premise that whoever as a whole is at exactly one location, whoever may be at location α does not exist at any location other than α."

who is alive and absent from home is outside" and "Anyone who is at location α does not exist at any other location than α" are not required in the course of Proofs 2 and 5, but can be ascertained thereafter (in Proofs 3 and 6). Therefore, these two examples of *arthâpatti* cannot be reduced to an inference (*anumāna*) in the form of term logic.

Returning to the question posed in the Introduction (0.1) about whether Kumārila's *arthâpatti* is a sort of abduction that postulates a fallible hypothesis, we can say that all of these proofs adopt a deductive approach but not an abductive one. In both examples of the Caitra-*arthâpatti*, Kumārila explicitly asserts that "inexplicability otherwise" (*anyathânupapatti*) works as an indispensable device for *arthâpatti*, although he does not clarify the course of the proof in detail. This *anyathânupapatti* is tantamount to *modus tollens* (i.e., *negating the consequent*, "P→Q, ¬Q; therefore ¬P"). By contrast, abduction including IBE does not definitively lead to its conclusion. Rather, in formal terms, its process is tantamount to a fallacious reasoning called *affirming the consequent* ("P→Q, Q; therefore P"),[90] because in abduction, one who is confronted with a surprising fact Q may set up P as a hypothesis if one has noticed that Q would be a matter of course if P were true.[91] Despite its logical invalidity, however, abduction is ampliative and pragmatically useful as a means for discovery,[92] whereas *arthâpatti* is explicative[93] and operates as a means for interpretation, an epistemic instrument (*pramāṇa*) appropriate for Mīmāṃsā, the school of exegesis.

The reasoning from (2) "Caitra is absent from home" to (3) "Caitra is somewhere outside" might appear to be an example of abduction (or IBE) if one neglects the assumption that Caitra is alive. This line of reasoning, however, does not lead to a fallible hypothesis, because Caitra is explicitly qualified as being alive in Vṛtti-kāra's and Kumārila's explanations.[94] Caitra's being alive is not the object to be known (*prameya*) but an assumption taken for granted in deriving the object to be known, that is, his presence outside. This assumption can be a hypothesis to be confirmed by finding Caitra somewhere outside. If the missing Caitra is unfortunately found dead somewhere, this assumption becomes false, and the conclusion of the *arthâpatti* that he is outside also becomes false. Nevertheless, it remains logically valid to derive this conclusion from the conjunction of this assumption and his observed absence from home under the premise that he is somewhere insofar as he is alive.

By contrast, the reasoning from (1) "Caitra is at location α" to (4) "Caitra is nowhere except for location α" would never be misunderstood as an example of

---

[90] Cf. Plutynski (2011: 234). Because the conditional implied in abductive reasoning, "P→Q," does not entail its inverse, "¬P→¬Q," the observed "Q" incurs no inexplicability due to the contradiction "Q∧¬Q." Therefore, *anyathânupapatti* has no opportunity to work in abductive reasoning. For further details, see Yoshimizu (forthcoming: concluding remarks).

[91] Cf. CP 5.189: "The surprising fact, C, is observed; But if A were true, C would be a matter of course. Hence, there is reason to suspect that A is true."

[92] Cf. Shida (2011: 515 and Appendix).

[93] See section 1.4 of the present chapter on ŚV-Ar, v. 29.

[94] See footnotes 18, 19, 25, and 26. Holding Caitra's being alive to be doubtful at first, and only his absence from home to be the assumption for reasoning, the Prābhākara school opened up an epistemological argument. See chapters 2 and 3 of the present volume. In Kumārila's exposition of *arthâpatti* in his *Arthâpatti-pariccheda*, it is never doubted that Caitra is alive.

abduction because (4) can be derived deductively from (1) without the additional assumption that Caitra is alive. By ignoring this genuine example of *arthâpatti*, modern scholars have failed to notice that Kumārila's theory of *arthâpatti* (propositional derivation) has no room for fallibilism. Because in both versions of the Caitra-*arthâpatti* the conclusion is entailed by the preconditions, the latter would become inexplicable if the former were negated (*anyathânupapatti*). Therefore, there is no fallibility in deriving the conclusion from the preconditions of *arthâpatti*, and Kumārila's theory of *arthâpatti* as an epistemic instrument (*pramāṇa*) has nothing to do with the fallibilism propounded in his epistemology. Insofar as deductive reasoning is thought to be exempt from fallibility, we should not overgeneralize fallibilism in appraising Kumārila's system of philosophy.[95]

ABBREVIATIONS AND REFERENCES

CP *The Collected Papers of Charles Sanders Peirce*, ed. C. Hartshorne, P. Weiss, and A. W. Burks, Cambridge, MA: Harvard University Press, 1931–58. https://colorysemiotica.files.wordpress.com/2014/08/peirce-collectedpapers.pdf (accessed September 13, 2019).

KV *Kathā-vatthu*, ed. A. C. Taylor, vol. 1, Pāli Text Society Text Series 48, 1894.

MM *Mānameyôdaya*, ed. C. Kunhan Raja and S. S. Suryanarayana Sastri, Madras: Adyar Library and Research Centre, 1933, 2nd edn. 1975.

MS *Mīmāṃsā-sūtra*. In TV.

NB *Nyāya-bindu*. In *Dharmottarapradīpa*, ed. P. D. Malvania. Paṭna: Kashiprasad Jayaswal Research Institute, 1955.

NBh *Nyāya-bhāṣya*, ed. Anantalal Thakur, Nyāyacaturgranthikā 1, New Delhi: Indian Council of Philosophical Research, 1997.

NR *Nyāya-ratnâkara*. In ŚV.

NS *Nyāya-sūtra*. In NBh.

ṚP *Ṛjuvimalā-pañcikā*. In *Bṛhatī*, ed. S. K. Ramanatha Sastri, Madras University Sanskrit Series, no. 3, part 1, Madras: The University of Madras, 1931.

ŚBh(F) *Śābara-bhāṣya* on MS 1.1.1–5. In Erich Frauwallner, *Materialien zur ältesten Erkenntnislehre der Karmamīmāṃsā*, Vienna: Kommissionsverlag der österreichischen Akademie der Wissenschaften, 1968.

ŚD *Śāstra-dīpikā*, ed. Laxman Shastri Dravid, Benares: Chowkhamba Sanskrit Series Office, 1916.

ŚV *Śloka-vārttika*, ed. Dvarikadas Sastri, Prāchyabhārati Series 10, Varanasi: Tara Publications, 1978.

ŚV-Anu *Śloka-vārttika*, Anumāna-paricceda. In ŚV.

ŚV-Ar *Śloka-vārttika*, Arthâpatti-paricceda. In ŚV.

ŚVK *Śloka-vārttika-kāśikā*, ed. K. Sambasiva Sastri, part 1, Trivandrum Sanskrit Series 90, Trivandrum: Government Press, 1926; ed. V.A. Ramaswami Sastri,

[95] The term "*arthâpatti*" came to be used in a variety of senses in medieval times, including the supplementation of an elliptical statement in view of its extraneous context (MM 131,6–7). As far as the ŚV is concerned, however, Kumārila uses the term "*arthâpatti*" as a *pramāṇa* only to draw out a proposition entailed by a set of preconditions.

part 3, Trivandrum Sanskrit Series 150, Trivandrum: Government Press, 1943.

ŚVT *Śloka-vārttika-tātparyaṭīkā*, ed. S. K. Ramanatha Sastri, rev. K. Kunjuni Raja and R. Thangaswamy. Madras: University of Madras, 1941. Revised by K. Kunjuni Raja and R. Thangaswamy, 1971.

TV *Tantra-vārttika*. In *Mīmāṃsā-darśanam*, ed. Subbāśāstrī, 1st edn, Ānandāśrama Sanskrit Series 97. Poona: Ānandāśrama Press, 1929–53.

Barlingay, S. S. (1976), *A Modern Introduction to Indian Logic*, New Delhi: National Publishing House.

Dasti, M. and S. Phillips (2017), *The Nyāya-sūtra. Selections with Early Commentaries*, Indianapolis, IN: Hackett Publishing Company.

Frauwallner, E. (1968), *Materialien zur ältesten Erkenntnislehre der Karmamīmāṃsā*, Veröffentlichungen der Kommission für Sprachen und Kulturen Süd- und Ostasiens 6, Vienna: Österreichische Akademie der Wissenschaften.

Guha, N. (2016), "On *Arthâpatti*," *Journal of Indian Philosophy* 44: 757–76.

Jha, G. (1978/1911), *The Prābhākara School of Pūrva Mīmāṃsā*, reprinted Delhi: Motilal Banarsidass.

Kanaujia, T. R. (1992), "Heterogeneity of Arthâpatti," in H. S. Prasad (ed.), *Philosophy, Grammar and Indology: Essays in Honour of Professor Gustav Roth*, 165–84, Delhi: Indian Books Centre.

Lemmon, E. J. (1972/1965), *Beginning Logic*, London: Nelson.

Noya, S. (1997/1994), *Ronrigaku* (Logic: An Introduction), Tokyo: University of Tokyo Press.

Pelletier, F. J. (1999), "A Brief History of Natural Deduction," *History and Philosophy of Logic* 20: 1–31.

Plutynski, A. (2011), "Four Problems of Abduction: A Brief History," *Journal of the International Society for the History of Philosophy of Science* 1, no. 2: 227–48.

Russell, B. (1905), "On Denoting," *Mind*, New Series, 14: 479–93.

Schayer, S. (2001), "Studies on Indian Logic, I," in *Materials of the International Seminar: Argument and Reason in Indian Logic*, 23–33, Warsaw: Warsaw University. Trans. P. Balcerowicz from German original, "Studien zur indischen Logik I," *Bulletin International de l'Academie Polonaise des Sciences et des Lettres, Classe de Philologie*, fasc. 4–6 (1933): 90–6.

Shida, T. (2011), "Hypothesis-Generating Logic in Udayana's Rational Theology," *Journal of Indian Philosophy* 39: 503–20.

Staal, F. (1962), "Contraposition in Indian Logic," in E. Nagel, P. Suppes, and A. Tarski (eds.), *Proceedings of the 1960 International Congress for Logic, Methodology and Philosophy of Science*, 634–49, Stanford, CA: Stanford University Press.

Taber, J. (1992), "What did Kumārila Bhaṭṭa Mean by Svataḥ Prāmāṇya?" *Journal of the American Oriental Society* 112: 204–21.

Yoshimizu, K. (1999), "*arthâpatti* to *anumāna* tono ronrigaku jōno soui ni tsuite" (On the logical difference between *arthâpatti* and *anumāna*), *Hokkaido Journal of Indian Philosophy and Buddhism* 14: 339–55.

Yoshimizu, K. (2007), "Kumārila's Propositional Derivation (*arthâpatti*) without Pervasion (*vyāpti*)," in K. Preisendanz (ed.), *Expanding and Merging Horizons: Contributions to*

South Asian and Cross-Cultural Studies in Commemoration of Wilhelm Halbfass, 315-35, Vienna: Austrian Academy of Sciences Press.

Yoshimizu, K. (2011), "Reconsidering the fragment of the *Bṛhaṭṭīkā* on restriction (*niyama*)," in H. Krasser, H. Lasic, E. Franco, and B. Kellner (eds.), *Religion and Logic in Buddhist Philosophical Analysis: Proceedings of the Fourth International Dharmakīrti Conference*, 507–21, Vienna: Austrian Academy of Sciences Press.

Yoshimizu, K. (2015), "Kumārila's Criticism of Buddhism as a Religious Movement in His Views on the Sources of Dharma," in Akira Saito (ed.), *Buddhism and Debate, Acta Asiatica* 108: 43-62.

Yoshimizu, K. (2017), "How Can the Word 'Cow' Exclude Non-cows? Description of Meaning in Diṅnāga's Theory of Apoha," *Journal of Indian Philosophy* 45: 973–1012.

Yoshimizu, K. (forthcoming), "*Arthâpatti* in Kumārila's *Tantravārttika*," in Peter M. Scharf (ed.), Felicitation volume for Professor George Cardona.

CHAPTER TEN

Raghunātha on *Arthâpatti*

NILANJAN DAS

Classical Indian epistemologists agree on one thing: whenever we know something, there is an epistemic instrument—a *pramāṇa*—which explains how we acquire this knowledge (*pramā*).[1] Suppose I look out of my window and see a white picket fence. If I thereby know that there is a white picket fence outside, perception (*pratyakṣa*) is the epistemic instrument which explains how I acquire this knowledge. If you tell me, "Bob is in his office," and I thereby learn that Bob is in his office, testimony (*śabda*) is the epistemic instrument which explains how I learn this.

For these classical Indian philosophers, an epistemic instrument M *is independent* (*svatantra*) just in case there is no other epistemic instrument M* which explains how we gain knowledge by M. Now, reductionism about any epistemic instrument M is the view that M isn't an independent means of knowing. For example, *a reductionist about testimony* might claim that we can explain how we acquire testimonial knowledge by appealing solely to inference of some sort.

In this chapter, we will focus on a certain kind of reductionism: *reductionism about arthâpatti*. Consider:

> **Absent Devadatta.** You know Devadatta is alive, but you don't see him at home. Therefore, you judge, and therefore come to know, that he's outside.

How do you gain this knowledge? According to one story, you antecedently know a generalization on the basis of empirical investigation, e.g., the generalization that anyone who isn't outside their home must either be dead or present at their home. When you learn that living Devadatta isn't at home, you infer that Devadatta must be outside. On this story, therefore, your knowledge is derived from a form of observation-based inference,[2] which classical Indian epistemologists label *anumāna*. Many Nyāya philosophers—the *Naiyāyikas*—favor this story.

According to another story, your inference isn't based on the prior empirical knowledge of any generalization. On one version of the story, in **Absent Devadatta,** you know that Devadatta is quite old. So, when you don't find him at his home, you suspect that he might not be alive. But you also know that he's alive on the basis of

---

[1] Many thanks to Elisa Freschi, Alessandro Graheli, Malcolm Keating, Andrew Ollett, Stephen Phillips, Mark Siderits, Anand Vaidya, and an anonymous reviewer for comments on earlier drafts of this paper.

[2] The term "inference" is used here to refer to any episode of reasoning. So, the term "inference" will not only cover *anumāna*s but also other kinds of reasoning, e.g., inductive or abductive reasoning, which cannot straightforwardly be treated as kinds of *anumāna*.

an independent source of information. That is why you resolve your doubt by judging that Devadatta must be outside. This is the story that Prābhākara Mīmāṃsakas typically support. On another version of the story, in **Absent Devadatta**, when you learn that Devadatta isn't at home, you realize that Devadatta's being alive is incongruous or inexplicable unless he is present outside. Then you resolve this incongruity or inexplicability by judging that Devadatta must be outside. This is the account that Bhāṭṭa Mīmāṃsakas typically support. On both accounts, you posit Devadatta's existence outside his home in order to resolve either a doubt (*saṃśaya*) or an incongruity (*anupapatti*) pertaining to his being alive, without having recourse to any purely empirically discoverable generalization. For these Mīmāṃsakas, therefore, the relevant epistemic instrument isn't *anumāna*; it's a separate epistemic instrument called *arthâpatti*.

The Naiyāyikas and the Mīmāṃsakas disagree about whether *arthâpatti* is an independent epistemic instrument. The Mīmāṃsakas are anti-reductionists about *arthâpatti*: they say that no other epistemic instrument can explain how we acquire knowledge by *arthâpatti*. In contrast, many Naiyāyikas are *reductionists* about *arthâpatti*: they say that we can explain how we gain *arthâpatti*-based knowledge by appealing to *anumāna*.

Interestingly, however, the unorthodox fifteenth-century Naiyāyika, Raghunātha Śiromaṇi, argued against reductionism about *arthâpatti* in his commentary *Splendor* (*Dīdhiti*, D) on Gaṅgeśa (fourteenth century CE) *The Jewel of Reflection on the Truth* (*Tattva-cintā-maṇi*, TCM). In this chapter, I reconstruct and explain the significance of this argument. I show that Raghunātha's anti-reductionist argument crucially depends on his opposition to a principle about the ontology of absence (*abhāva*) accepted by earlier Nyāya philosophers like Udayana (tenth/eleventh century CE) and Gaṅgeśa. I also argue that Raghunātha's argument poses a serious challenge for the Nyāya reductionists about *arthâpatti*: they cannot resolve the challenge without making implausible psychological claims. This, I think, reveals an instability within the standard Nyāya view about *arthâpatti*.

This chapter is divided into five parts. In §1, I outline the Nyāya reductionist view about *arthâpatti*, and different ways of precisifying it. On a popular precisification of the view, putative instances of *arthâpatti*-based knowledge are based on negative-only *anumāna*s (*kevala-vyatireky-anumāna*). In §2, I discuss how Gaṅgeśa rejects the view that episodes of such reasoning cannot be treated as *anumāna*s because they proceed from an awareness (*jñāna*, sometimes translated as "cognition")[3] of negative pervasion (*vyatireka-vyāpti*). The second of these arguments depends on a principle about the ontology of absence. In §3, I show that Raghunātha rejects this principle,

[3] The translation of the word "*jñāna*" as "cognition" is misleading. There is an open question in contemporary philosophy and psychology of perception about whether there is a distinction between perception and cognition, where cognition only includes mental states, e.g., beliefs and judgments, which can be directly utilized for the purposes of reasoning, verbal reports, and action. Since some Indian philosophers (e.g., Yogācāra Buddhists) think that some *jñāna*s (which are perceptual in character) don't fit this description, it would be a mistake to call them "cognition" in this sense of the term. So, if we want our translational choices to be consonant with contemporary philosophical and psychological terminology, something more neutral like "awareness" or "awareness-event" (which can refer to both perceptual experiences as well as judgments) seems appropriate as a translation for "*jñāna*."

so he has the resources to block Gaṅgeśa's argument. In §4, I explain how Raghunātha defends the claim that an episode of reasoning that proceeds solely from an agent's awareness of negative pervasion cannot be treated as an *anumāna*. In §5, I say why he takes this to support anti-reductionism about *arthâpatti*.

1. NYĀYA REDUCTIONISM

In this section, I outline the basic commitments of Nyāya reductionism about *arthâpatti*. A simple case:

> **Smoke and Fire.** You see smoke coming out of a hill. You had learnt earlier by empirical investigation that wherever there is smoke, there is fire. You recall this. So, you conclude that there is fire on the hill.

Here, your inference establishes the presence of an unobserved property, i.e., the fire. This is the property to be proven (*sādhya*). The place where the fire is established, i.e., the hill, is the subject (*pakṣa*). Finally, the observed property from which the fire is inferred, namely the smoke, is the reason (*hetu*). Suppose you know, in **Smoke and Fire**, that the subject possesses the property to be proven. According to almost all Naiyāyikas after Uddyotakara (sixth century CE), you arrive at your knowledge in three steps, each of which involves an awareness-event about the reason.

> **Step 1.** First, you undergo a perceptual awareness-event, whereby you learn that the reason, i.e., the smoke, is present in the relevant subject, i.e., the hill (what the Naiyāyikas call the awareness of the reason's being a property (*dharma*) of the subject (*pakṣa-dharmatā-jñāna*)).
>
> **Step 2.** Next, you recall that there is a relation of pervasion (*vyāpti*) between the reason and the property to be proven. The reason is pervaded by the property to be proven just in case wherever the reason is present, the property to be proven is also present. In **Smoke and Fire**, you recall what you previously learnt: namely, that wherever there is smoke, there is fire. This is what the Naiyāyikas call the recollection of pervasion (*vyāpti-smṛti*).
>
> **Step 3.** Finally, you undergo an awareness-event where you unify the contents of the previous two awareness-events: you judge that the reason is both pervaded by the property to be proven and a feature of the subject. In **Smoke and Fire**, you judge that the hill possesses smoke which, in turn, is pervaded by fire. This awareness-event is what Naiyāyikas call a subsumptive judgment or consideration (*parāmarśa*).

Immediately after the third step, you judge that the subject possesses the property to be proven. If the judgment constitutes knowledge, the resulting knowledge is called *anumiti*. The epistemic instrument by which this knowledge arises is *anumāna*.

An *anumāna* can be of different kinds, depending on what relation of pervasion underlies the relevant inference, and how the agent apprehends the relevant relation of pervasion. As I said earlier, a property H is pervaded (*vyāpta*) by another object or property S if and only if wherever H is present, there also is S. (This will be made more precise later.) An *anumāna* that proceeds from smoke to fire, for instance, could be based on two generalizations:

1. Wherever there is smoke, there is fire.
2. Wherever there isn't any fire, there isn't any smoke.

The first generalization says that smoke is pervaded (in the specified sense) by fire. The second generalization says that the absence of fire is pervaded by the absence of smoke. The first kind of pervasion is therefore a relation between two positive entities (i.e., entities that aren't themselves absences), while the second is a relation between two negative entities (i.e., entities that are absences). So, the first kind of pervasion is called positive pervasion (*anvaya-vyāpti*), while the second kind is called negative pervasion (*vyatireka-vyāpti*).

We can define these two relations as follows. Let's say that the counterpositive (*pratiyogin*) of an absence is the thing that is absent; for instance, the counterpositive of the absence of a pot is the pot itself. Suppose H is the reason involved in an *anumāna*, and S is the property to be proven. If H bears a relation of positive pervasion to S, then that relation consists in H's being co-instantiated with S such that H is pervaded by S (*hetu-vyāpaka-sādhya-sāmānâdhikaraṇya*). If H bears a relation of negative pervasion to S, then that relation consists in H's being the counterpositive of an absence that pervades the absence of S (*sādhyâbhāva-vyāpakī-bhūtâbhāva-pratiyogitva*). In **Smoke and Fire**, smoke bears relations of both positive and negative pervasion to fire. On the one hand, smoke is co-instantiated with fire which, in turn, pervades it. For fire and smoke occur together such that wherever there is fire, there is smoke. On the other hand, smoke is the counterpositive of an absence that pervades the absence of fire. For, wherever fire is absent, smoke is also absent. Using this distinction amongst the two kinds of pervasion, we can distinguish two types of *anumāna*: the first kind involves a recollective awareness of a relation of positive pervasion between the reason and the property to be proven, while the second kind involves a recollective awareness of a relation of negative pervasion between them.

We can classify *anumāna*s in another way. In **Smoke and Fire**, you had learnt that wherever there is smoke, there is fire. How could you have learnt this? There are two possibilities. You might have observed lots of places where smoke is present, e.g., a kitchen, and noticed that fire is always present in such places. Or you might have observed lots of places where fire is absent, e.g., a cold lake, and noticed that smoke is always absent from such places. Call places where both fire and smoke are present together instances of positive correlation (*anvaya-sahacāra*) between fire and smoke. And call places where both fire and smoke are absent instances of negative correlation (*vyatireka-sahacāra*) between fire and smoke. In general, a relation of pervasion between a reason and a property to be proven can be known in three distinct ways: either (a) by observing only positive correlation, or (b) by observing only negative correlation, or (c) by observing positive as well as negative correlations. An *anumāna* where the relevant relation of pervasion is known (or can only be known) in the first way is called positive-only (*kevalânvayin*). An *anumāna* in which the relevant relation of pervasion is known (or can only be known) in the second way is called negative-only (*kevala-vyatirekin*). Finally, an *anumāna* in which the relevant relation of pervasion is known in the third way is called positive-and-negative (*anvaya-vyatirekin*).[4]

Here are some stock examples that illustrate the distinction.

i. Consider the inference, "This is nameable (*abhidheya*), since it is knowable (*prameya*)." Here, the reason is knowability, and the property to be proven is nameability. For many Naiyāyikas, everything is nameable. So, the only way you could learn that nameability pervades knowability is by observing cases where both nameability and knowability are present. Since the relevant pervasion here is known solely on the basis of positive correlation, this is a positive-only *anumāna.*

ii. Take another inference: "The earth is different from other substances (*itara-bhinna*); for it has smell." Here, the reason is smell, and the property to be proven is difference from substances other than earth. But since the earth is the subject, there is no observed place (other than the subject itself) where the property to be proven is present. So, the only way the agent could learn that there is a relation of pervasion between the reason and the property to be proven is by observing negative correlation between the two. Hence, this is a negative-only *anumāna.*

iii. Finally, in **Smoke and Fire**, you can apprehend the relevant relation of pervasion by observing instances of both positive and negative correlations, i.e., cases where smoke and fire are present together and cases where they are absent together. When that happens, the resulting *anumāna* is positive-and-negative.

Let us now turn to reductionism about *arthâpatti.*

For many Naiyāyikas, all putative instances of *arthâpatti*-based knowledge are produced by *anumānas.*[5] Even before Gaṅgeśa, several Naiyāyikas, e.g., Udayana and Śaśadhara, explicitly considered the view that at least some—if not all—instances of *arthâpatti*-based knowledge have to be produced by negative-only *anumānas.*[6] Here is an example from Kumārila that motivates this view.

Present Devadatta. I learn by perception that Devadatta is standing at this location. So, I conclude that he is absent everywhere else.

---

[4] See Uddyotakara's *Nyāya-vārttika* (NV) on *Nyāya-sūtra* (NS) 1.1.5 and Vācaspati Miśra's *Nyāya-vārttika-tātparya-ṭīkā* (NVTṬ) on it. (NS 144–5.)

[5] See Vātsyāyana's *Nyāya-bhāṣya* (NBh), Uddyotakara's NV, and Vācaspati Miśra's NVTṬ on NS 2.2.2–6 in NS, 575–81. However, Jayanta Bhaṭṭa and Udayana are exceptional amongst early Naiyāyikas for their systematic defenses of reductionism about *arthâpatti*; for these passages, see Jayanta Bhaṭṭa's *Nyāya-mañjarī* (NM, 94–130) and Udayana's *Nyāya-kusumâñjali* (NKA, 419–26).

[6] For a translation of the Udayana passage, see Das. NKA, 425-6: kevala-vyatireky-anumānaṃ parâbhimatam arthâpattir anvayâbhāvād iti cet. evam etāvatā viśeṣeṇânumāne'rthâpatti-vyavahāraṃ na vārayāmaḥ. tatrânumāna-vyavahāraḥ kuta iti cet. avinābhūta-liṅga-samutpannatvāt. sādhya-dharmeṇa vinā hy abhavanam anvayina iva vyatirekiṇo'py aviśiṣṭam, tan-niścayaścânvayavyatirekābhyām anyatareṇa veti. (Editor's note: transliteration in this passage and the following does not break *saṃdhi* at word boundaries where the edition preserves it; for instance, *nâsti* will be retained rather than *na asti*.) Śaśadhara's passage occurs in his *Nyāya-siddhaânta-dīpaḥ* (NSD, 100): "With this, we reject the view that *arthâpatti* is a negative-only proof (*māna*). For even a negative-only proof depends on pervasion and the presence of the reason in the subject. Therefore, this again is nothing but attaching a different label" (etena vyatireki-mānam arthâpattir ity api parāstam. vyatirekiṇo'pi vyāpti-pakṣa-dharmatâdhīnatvāt. tathā ca punar api nāmântara-karaṇam eva).

For Kumārila, this is a case of *arthâpatti*-based knowledge: since Devadatta's being located here is incongruous (*anupapanna*) without his being absent everywhere else, I posit Devadatta's absence everywhere else to resolve that incongruity. Now a reductionist about *arthâpatti* should say that this knowledge is in fact produced by an *anumāna*. The reason for that *anumāna* would have to be the property of being located here (*etad-deśa-sambandhitva*) and the property to be proven would have to be the property of being absent from every other place (*anyatrâbhāva*). In his *Śloka-vārttika* (ŚV), Kumārila says that in this case, a relation of positive pervasion between the reason and the property to be proven cannot be established by observing instances of positive correlation. For in order to know that something is absent everywhere else, one would have to go to those places and check whether the relevant object is present.[7] So, the Naiyāyikas must say that in this scenario, I gain my knowledge by an *anumāna* of the negative-only variety.

This still leaves open some further possibilities. In **Absent Devadatta**, you gain your knowledge by an *anumāna* where the subject is Devadatta, the reason is the property of being alive but absent from home, and the property to be proven is the property of being outside one's home. Now, two different relations of pervasion could hold between the property of being alive but absent from home and the property of being outside one's home. We can express them as follows:

3. Whoever is alive but absent from home is outside their home.
4. Whoever isn't outside their home is either not alive or not absent from their home.

Relation (3) expresses a relation of positive pervasion between the reason and the property to be proven, while (4) expresses a relation of negative pervasion. This means that the Nyāya reductionist view about *arthâpatti* could be sharpened in (at least) two ways.

The Positive Story. In any case of *arthâpatti*-based knowledge, the *anumāna* on the basis of which the agent gains her knowledge involves an awareness of positive pervasion.

The Negative Story. In all cases of *arthâpatti*-based knowledge, the *anumāna* on the basis of which the agent gains her knowledge involves an awareness of negative pervasion.

In the positive story, in **Absent Devadatta**, your reasoning goes like this.

Step 1. First, you perceive that Devadatta who is alive and isn't at home.

Step 2. Then you remember that whoever is alive but absent from home must be outside their home.

Step 3. Next, you make a subsumptive judgment that Devadatta who is alive possesses the property of being absent from home, which is pervaded by the property of being outside one's home.

---

[7] See Ollett and Freschi in the present volume, p. 61. Sanskrit: vv. 35–46 in ŚV, 324–8.

Finally, you conclude that Devadatta isn't at home. In the negative story, you reason as follows.

Step 1. First, you perceive that Devadatta who is alive isn't at home.

Step 2*. Then, you remember the content of (4): namely, that whoever isn't outside their home is either dead or present at their home.

Step 3*. Next, you make a subsumptive judgment that Devadatta who is alive possesses the property of being absent from home, which is the counterpositive of an absence that is pervaded by the absence of being outside one's home.

The difference between the two episodes of reasoning lies in the second and third steps. At Step 2 in the positive story, you recall a relation of positive pervasion between the reason and the property to be proven; at Step 2* in the negative story, you recall a relation of negative pervasion between the two. At Step 3 in the positive story, you undergo what we may call a positive subsumptive judgment (*anvaya-parāmarśa*), i.e., a judgment that the subject possesses the reason which is pervaded by the property to be proven; at Step 3* in the negative story, you undergo what we may call a negative subsumptive judgment (*vyatireka-parāmarśa*), i.e., a judgment that the subject possesses the reason which is the counterpositive of an absence that is pervaded by the absence of the property to be proven.

In both early and later Nyāya, the negative story about *arthâpatti* seems to have been popular. In his *Flowers of Reasoning* (*Nyāya-mañjarī*, NM), Jayanta supports a version of the negative story.[8] Udayana (at least according to his commentators) partially supports the negative story, while Gaṅgeśa mentions it.[9] In his *Collection of Verses* (*Kārikâvalī*, KA), Viśvanātha says, "*Arthâpatti* is not in fact taken to be a distinct means of knowing. For it is successful [in generating knowledge] in virtue of an awareness of negative pervasion."[10] What explains this? First of all, it is sometimes assumed that *anumāna*s of the negative-only variety involve an awareness of negative pervasion, presumably because an agent can only apprehend a relation of negative pervasion between the reason and the property to be proven by observing the correlation between their absences. (We will discuss this point in the next section, but for a representative passage, see the Viśvanātha passage in footnote 30.) Second, some Nyāya writers, including Jayanta and possibly Udayana, thought that the awareness of incongruity-otherwise (*anyathânupapatti*) involved in an *arthâpatti* could be construed as an awareness of negative pervasion. In **Absent Devadatta**, you

[8] See Graheli in this volume, p. 160. NM, 107: api ca tena vinā nôpapadyata iti kalpanam arthâpattiḥ. tena vinā nôpapadyata iti ca vyatireka-bhaṇitir iyam. vyatirekaś ca apratītaḥ tasmin saty upapadyate ity anvayam ākṣipati. anvaya-vyatirekau ca gamakasya liṅgasya dharma iti katham arthâpattiḥ nânumānam kevala-vyatirekī hetur anvaya-mūla eva gamaka iti vakṣyāmaḥ.

[9] For a translation of the Udayana passage, see Das in this volume, p. 186. NKA, 419: sthitir evâsya tena vinā na syādityasya svabhāva iti cet. evaṃ tarhi tan-niyata-svabhāva evâsau. vyāpter eva vyatireka-mukha-nirūpyāyās tathā-vyapadeśāt. For a translation of the Gaṅgeśa passage, see Phillips in this volume, p. 215. TCM, 676–7: atha upapādakâbhāvavaty upapādyâbhāva-niyamo anupapattir na tv abhāva-mātram atiprasaṅgāt. evaṃ ca vyatireka-vyāptimata upapādyād vyatireky-anumāna-mudrayā eva sādhya-siddheḥ kim arthâpattyā. tathā hi devadatto bahiḥ san jīvitve sati gṛhâsattvāt yan na evaṃ tan na evaṃ yathā mṛto gṛha-sthito vā.

[10] KA, 144: arthâpattis tu naiveha pramāṇântaram iṣyate | vyatireka-vyāpti-buddhyā caritārthā hi sā yataḥ ||.

conclude that Devadatta is outside his home, because you judge that if Devadatta weren't outside, his property of being alive but absent from home would be incongruous. For he would either be dead or at home. This judgment, at least on one interpretation, is simply an awareness of a relation of negative pervasion between the property of being alive but absent from home and the property of being outside one's home.

So far, we've seen two things. The first is that Nyāya reductionists about *arthâpatti* treat at least some putative cases of *arthâpatti* as *anumāna*s of the negative-only variety. The second is that, historically, some Nyāya reductionists about *arthâpatti* have thought that putative cases of *arthâpatti* are *anumāna*s that proceed from an awareness of negative pervasion. In the next section, we'll look at Gaṅgeśa's discussion of the view that no putative negative-only *anumāna* can give rise to an *anumiti*, because any such inference proceeds from an awareness of negative pervasion. If this view were true, the agent's reasoning in cases like **Present Devadatta** couldn't be treated as an *anumāna*. That would be bad news for Nyāya reductionists about *arthâpatti*. Gaṅgeśa's refutation of this view will be useful for understanding Raghunātha's strategy for resisting reductionism about *arthâpatti*.

2. GAṆGEŚA ON NEGATIVE-ONLY *ANUMĀNAS*

In the section on negative-only *anumāna*s (i.e., the *Kevala-vyatireki-prakaraṇa*) in *The Jewel of Reflection on Truth*, Gaṅgeśa first defines the notion of a negative-only *anumāna*.

> [The proponent:] That which is negative-only does not have a similar subject (*sapakṣa*), so that the relation of pervasion involved in it is apprehended on the basis of negative correlation.[11]

A similar subject is an observed place other than the subject, where the property to be proven is present. In a negative-only *anumāna* of the form "Earth differs from other substances, because it has odor," there is no observed place (other than the subject, i.e., earth) where the property to be proven is present. So, there is no similar subject. As a result, the agent must apprehend the relevant relation of pervasion solely by observing negative correlation between the reason and the property to be proven.

However, Gaṅgeśa's opponent takes this to be problem: she thinks that an inference where the relevant relation of pervasion is apprehended solely by observing negative correlation cannot yield an *anumiti*. In the rest of this section, I will explain this objection, and then discuss two responses that Gaṅgeśa offers to it.

2.1. An argument against negative-only *anumānas*

The objection is stated as follows.

> [The opponent:] Well, that which is negative-only is not an *anumāna*. For an *anumāna* is caused by an awareness of a pervaded entity as the property of the

[11] TCM, 582: kevala-vyatirekī tv asat-sapakṣo yatra vyatireka-sahacāreṇa vyāpti-grahaḥ.

subject (*vyāpta-pakṣa-dharmatā-jñāna*). In this case, a relation of pervasion is apprehended there on the basis of negative correlation, whereas a positive entity is the property of the subject.[12]

If we follow the commentator Mathurānātha's explanation of the argument, the claim is that an awareness of pervasion that arises from an agent's observation of negative correlation cannot cause an *anumiti*. This is because an *anumiti* has to be caused by a *positive* subsumptive judgment, i.e., a judgment that the reason, which is pervaded by the property to be proven, resides in the subject. However, in a subsumptive judgment that is based solely on an agent's observation of negative correlation, the relevant relation of pervasion is a negative one, i.e., it holds between two absences, but a positive entity, i.e., the reason, appears as the property of the subject.[13] The argument can be reconstructed as follows.

P1. In any putative negative-only *anumāna*, whatever relation of pervasion the agent may apprehend, she does so by only observing instances of negative correlation between the reason and the property to be proven.

---

[12] TCM, 582–4: nanu vyatirekī nânumānam vyāpta-pakṣa-dharmatā-jñānasya tat-kāraṇatvāt atra vyatireka-sahacārāt vyāptīḥ tatra anvayasya pakṣa-dharmatā. The printed text has "vyāpti-pakṣa-dharmatā-jñānasya" instead of "vyāpta-pakṣa-dharmatā-jñānasya"; following Mathurānātha's commentary, I have corrected it. A parallel argument, offered in the voice of a Bhāṭṭa opponent, which occurs in the section on *arthâpatti* (*arthâpatti-prakaraṇa*), also confirms my preferred reading. See Phillips in this volume, p. 215. Sanskrit: TCM, 678: atra hi vyatireka-vyāptir anvayasya pakṣa-dharmatvam iti vyāpti-dhī-janyam api bahis-sattva-jñānaṃ nânumitiḥ tasyā vyāpta-pakṣa-dharmatā-jñāna-janyatā-niyamāt. na ca sādhyâbhāva-vyāpakâbhāva-pratiyogitvena pakṣa-dharmasya jñānam anumiti-prayojakam tac ca iha apy astîti vācyam. kevalânvayini tad-asambhavāt tad-apekṣayā sādhya-vyāpyatva-jñānasya laghutvāc ca.

[13] TCM, 587–8: "'That which is negative-only' stands for an apprehension of pervasion that results from the awareness of negative correlation. 'It is not an *anumāna*': it is not an instrument that gives rise to an *anumiti*. 'The awareness of the pervaded,' etc.: an awareness of something as a property of the subject, where that thing is qualified by positive pervasion, i.e., the relation of being co-located with a property to be proven that pervades the reason. 'In this case': in a subsumptive judgment produced by an awareness of negative correlation. 'On the basis of negative correlation': on the basis of the correlation between the absence of the property to be proven and the absence of the reason. 'There': between the absence of the property to be proven and the absence of the reason. 'Pervasion': the property of being a pervader. 'A positive entity': the reason. Before 'a property of the subject' insert 'is what appears as.' The thought is that, since a subsumptive judgment involving negative pervasion (*vyatireka-vyāpti-parāmarśa*), which is caused by an awareness of negative correlation, isn't a cause of any *anumiti*, an awareness of the relevant sort of pervasion cannot be a cause of any *anumiti*" ('vyatirekī' vyatireka-sahacāra-janya-vyāpti-grahaḥ, 'nânumānaṃ' nânumiti-karaṇam, 'vyapt'eti hetu-vyāpaka-sādhya-sāmānâdhikaraṇya-rūpânvaya-vyāpti-prakāraka-pakṣa-dharmatā-jñānasyety arthaḥ, 'atra' vyatireka-sahacāra-jñāna-janya-parāmarśe 'vyatireka-sahacārāt' sādhyâbhāva-hetv-abhāvayor sahacāra-jñānāt, 'tatra' sādhyâbhāva-hetv-abhāvayor iti yāvat, 'vyāptiḥ' vyāpakatvam, 'anvayasya' hetoḥ pakṣa-dharmatêti bhāsata iti śeṣaḥ. vyatireka-sahacāra-jñāna-janya-vyatireka-vyāpti-parāmarśasya anumity-ajananakatayā tādṛśa-vyāpti-jñānasya nânumiti-kāraṇatvam iti bhāvaḥ.) Mahādeva Puṇatāmakara paraphrases the same objection in the same way. See *Nyāya-kaustubha* (NK, 245): "Well, that which is negative-only is not an *anumāna*. The cause of an *anumiti* is the awareness of that which is characterized by pervasion as a property of the subject. But in the relevant case, on the basis of negative correlation, a relation of pervasion is apprehended in the absence of the property to be proven with respect to the absence of the reason. And the reason is apprehended as a property of the subject. Therefore, an *anumiti* cannot arise, given that its cause is missing" (atha kevala-vyatirekī nânumānaṃ vyāpti-viśiṣṭe pakṣa-dharmatā-jñānam evânumiti-hetuḥ, prakṛte ca vyatireka-sahacāreṇa sādhyâbhave hetv-abhāva-vyāptir gṛhyate hetau ca pakṣa-dharmatā-graha ity anumiti-kāraṇâbhāvenânumiter asambhavāt iti).

P2. By only observing instances of negative correlation between the reason and the property to be proven, an agent can only learn that the absence of the property to be proven is pervaded by the absence of the reason.

P3. An *anumiti* can only be produced by a positive subsumptive judgment, i.e., an awareness of the reason as pervaded by the property to be proven and as present in the subject.

P4. An agent's awareness of negative pervasion between a reason and a property to be proven can only produce a negative subsumptive judgment, not a positive subsumptive judgment.

C. From a putative negative-only *anumāna*, an *anumiti* cannot arise.

If sound, this argument would count against Nyāya reductionism about *arthâpatti*. . But why are the premises true? P1 is obvious: it follows from our definition of a negative-only *anumāna*. In his elaboration of the argument, Gaṅgeśa focuses on P3 and P4. However, P2 can be motivated in light of a remark that Mathurānātha makes.

Suppose we reject P2 and say that by solely observing negative correlation between a reason and a property to be proven, the agent can learn that the reason bears a relation of positive pervasion to the property to be proven. But to learn this is to learn that the reason is co-located with the property to be proven, which, in turn, pervades it. Wouldn't this view lead to a problem of overgeneration? As Mathurānātha explains the worry, "Well, how does the awareness of the correlation between absences give rise to an apprehension of a relation of pervasion between the counterpositives? For there would be a problem of overgeneration if the awareness of the correlation that resides in two things were to cause an apprehension of a relation of pervasion that resides in two other things."[14] Here's a way of putting the point (perhaps anachronistically) with reference to the more contemporary paradox of ravens. Suppose perceiving the correlation between the absence of blackness and the absence of raven-ness in things like a white chalk, a red car, a grey house, etc., can help us learn, or can give us evidence for, the hypothesis that all ravens are black. But intuitively, these things seem *irrelevant* to the hypothesis. So, if the observation of these things could provide evidence for the hypothesis in question, couldn't we learn or gain evidence for just about any such generalization by perceiving correlations between completely unrelated entities? That is the problem of overgeneration that Mathurānātha is talking about.

What about P3 and P4? Gaṅgeśa notes that someone who wishes to reject P3 may claim that a negative subsumptive judgment (produced by an awareness of negative pervasion) can be a promoter (*prayojaka*) of *anumiti*.[15] What is a promoter? A promoter of some effect X is an object that either directly or indirectly causes X.[16] So, the proposal under discussion is this:

[14] TCM, 592: athâbhāvayoḥ sahacāra-jñānāt katham tat-pratiyoginor vyāpti-grahaḥ eka-niṣṭha-sahacāra-jñānenânya-niṣṭha-vyāpti-jñāna-janane'ti-prasaṅgād iti. It's quite clear that, in this passage, the term "*vyāpti*" refers to positive pervasion, since the objection it answers is directed at Gaṅgeśa's view that an awareness of negative correlation suffices to produce an apprehension of positive pervasion.

[15] TCM, 588. For a parallel passage, see Phillips in this volume, p. 215. Sanskrit: TCM, 678: na ca sādhyâbhāva-vyāpakâbhāva-pratiyogitvena pakṣa-dharmasya jñānam anumiti-prayojakam tac ca iha apy astîti vācyam. kevalânvayini tad-asambhavāt tad-apekṣayā sādhya-vyāpyatva-jñānasya laghutvāc ca.

[16] The notion of *prayojaka* is characterized in different ways across different texts. For detailed discussion, see Guha (1979: 67ff.).

OPTION 0. A negative subsumptive judgment is a causally necessary condition for any *anumiti*.

If Option 0 is correct, then P3 is false. However, as Gaṅgeśa notes on behalf of an opponent, this proposal is unnecessarily complex and is in tension with another commitment of the Naiyāyikas. In positive-only *anumāna*s like "The tree is nameable (*abhidheya*), since it is knowable (*prameya*)," the property to be proven (i.e., nameability) is present everywhere. So, its absence (insofar as it doesn't exist) cannot be pervaded by the absence of the reason. In such cases, the reason doesn't bear a relation of negative pervasion to the property to be proven. Therefore, a true negative subsumptive judgment cannot arise in such cases. So, a negative subsumptive judgment cannot be a causally necessary condition for every *anumiti*.

In the section on negative-only *anumāna*s, Gaṅgeśa explains (on behalf of the Mīmāṃsaka opponent) why other proposals that seek to reject P3 cannot easily succeed.[17] Here are some options.

Option 1. The presence of a uniform or non-disjunctive property that characterizes both positive and negative subsumptive judgments—e.g., the property of being an awareness that the subject of the inference possesses a property that is connected to the property to be proven by some relation of pervasion—is a causally necessary condition for any *anumiti*.

Option 2. The presence of either a positive or a negative subsumptive judgment is a causally necessary condition for any *anumiti*.

Option 3. In some cases, the presence of a positive subsumptive judgment is what causes an *anumiti*; in other cases, the negative subsumptive judgment serves as a cause; in some other cases, it is both.

Gaṅgeśa's opponent rules out all these options.[18] Option 1 is ruled out on the grounds that there is no non-disjunctive or uniform property that is shared by both positive and negative subsumptive judgments. Option 2 is dismissed on the grounds that if a disjunctive property could be a necessary condition for an awareness to be instance of a certain epistemic kind, then we could collapse all the different kinds of knowledge—perceptual, inferential, testimonial—into one kind of knowledge by creating a disjunction of the different causal conditions that give rise to these different kinds of knowledge. Option 3 also doesn't work. In this dispute, it is not common ground between both parties that an awareness-event which is based on an awareness of negative pervasion counts as an *anumiti*. This is because a well-established cause of instances of *anumiti*—namely, a positive subsumptive judgment—that both parties agree on goes missing in this case. So, unless there is some further intuitive pressure on us to treat an inferential awareness based on an awareness of negative pervasion as an *anumiti*, Option 3 seems fairly *ad hoc*. This shows that rejecting P3 in the previous argument will be difficult for the Naiyāyikas.

So far, we have only been discussing strategies for rejecting P3. However, a friend of Nyāya reductionism could also try to reject P4; she could argue that an agent's

[17] TCM, 585ff.
[18] TCM, 585ff.

awareness of negative pervasion can produce a positive subsumptive judgment, e.g., by producing an awareness of positive pervasion. However, Gaṅgeśa's imagined opponent gives an argument against this view.

> Suppose you say: "From the fact that something is a counterpositive of an absence that pervades the absence of the property to be proven, it is known by *anumāna* that that thing is pervaded by the property to be proven. What we call an *anumāna* of the negative-only variety just involves a scenario where an *anumiti* arises on the basis of an *anumāna* from negative to positive pervasion."
>
> [We reply:] That's not right. For a relation of positive pervasion is what yields an awareness of the property to be proven, then it will follow that mentioning the relation of negative pervasion (while stating the *anumāna* aloud for others) suffers from the fault of irrelevance (*arthântaratā*). And if the relation of negative pervasion is mentioned as something that is conducive to [the awareness of] the relation of positive pervasion, then there will be a fault of inappropriate occasion (*aprāpta-kālatva*) when the relation of positive pervasion goes unmentioned.[19]

On the view under discussion, there is no *anumāna* of the negative-only variety where an agent makes an inference of the form:

The Simple Inference

P1*. H is absent wherever S is absent.
P2*. The object p possesses H.
C*. The object p possesses S.

Rather, the agent's inference must involve two extra steps:

The Complex Inference

P1*. H is absent wherever S is absent.
P1**. For any two X and Y, if X is absent wherever Y is absent, then X is only present somewhere if Y is present there.
P1***. H is only present somewhere if S is present there.
P2*. The object p possesses H.
C*. The object p possesses S.

Now, the response that Gaṅgeśa offers on behalf of the opponent is this. Sometimes, we state out loud an *anumāna* that is based on our awareness of negative pervasion. In many such cases, we only mention the relation of negative pervasion between the reason and the property to be proven, not the positive pervasion between them. In other words, we don't mention anything like P1** or P1***. But if the positive pervasion is doing all the work in explaining how an *anumiti* arises in such cases, mentioning just the negative pervasion in an explicit statement of the inference would be pragmatically defective. On the one hand, if the positive pervasion is also

---

[19] TCM, 588–91: atha sādhyâbhāva-vyāpakâbhāva-pratiyogitvena sādhya-vyāpyatvam anumīyate. evaṃ vyatireka-vyāptyā'nvaya-vyāptim anumāya yatra anumitiḥ sa eva vyatirekîty ucyata iti. tan na. anvaya-vyāpter gamakatve vyatireka-vyāpty-upanyāsasya arthântaratâpatteḥ anvaya-vyāpty-anukūlatayā ca tad-upanyāse 'nvaya-vyāptim anupanyasya tad-upanyāsasya aprāpta-kālatvād iti.

mentioned, mentioning the negative pervasion is tantamount to providing extra, irrelevant information. On the other hand, if the positive pervasion isn't mentioned, mentioning the negative pervasion is inappropriate (insofar as it is misleading with respect to the true structure of the inference). But intuitively, there is no such pragmatic defect. Hence, the proposal cannot be right.

Ultimately, Gaṅgeśa doesn't think that the objection we have been discussing succeeds. He outlines two responses to it: the first involving rejecting P2, while the second involves rejecting P3.

2.2. *Gaṅgeśa's first response: rejecting P2*

P2 says that by observing instances of negative correlation between the reason and the property to be proven, an agent can only learn that the absence of the property to be proven is pervaded by the absence of the reason. Gaṅgeśa denies this:

> On the basis of negative correlation that is free from inferential undercutting conditions (*upādhi*), one apprehends just a relation of positive pervasion (*anvaya-vyāptir eva)*. For the relation between the counterpositive (*pratiyogin*) and its absence (*anuyogin*) regulates the relevant awareness, just as in the case of a positive-and-negative *anumāna*.[20]

The first claim of the passage is that by observing instances of negative correlation in cases where there is no inferential undercutting condition (i.e., roughly, any condition that guarantees that the property to be proven may be absent from a place where the reason is present),[21] the agent apprehends just a relation of positive pervasion between the reason and the property of property. So, P2 is false. Thus, all cases of negative-only *anumāna* can in fact be based on an awareness of positive pervasion. However, this faces the problem of overgeneration that Mathurānātha highlights: if we reject P2, we may have to countenance cases where an agent apprehends a relation of pervasion between two properties by perceiving the correlation between two completely unrelated properties! The second part of passage answers this worry: "For the relation between counterpositives (*pratiyogin*) and their absences (*anuyogin*) regulates the relevant awareness, just as in the case of a negative-and-positive *anumāna*."

Here's how I understand this reply. Consider a version of **Smoke and Fire**, where the agent only observes that the absence of fire is always accompanied by the absence of smoke. In this awareness of correlation, the absence of fire has fire as its counterpositive, and the absence of smoke has smoke as its counterpositive. Since fire functions as the counterpositive of its absence in virtue of having firehood, firehood is the property that restricts the role of the counterpositive to all and only fires. In that sense, firehood is the delimitor (*avacchedaka*) of the counterpositiveness

[20] TCM, 591: ucyate. nirupādhi-vyatireka-sahacāreṇa anvaya-vyāptir eva gṛhyate pratiyogy-anuyogi-bhâvasya niyāmakatvāt anvaya-vyatirekavat.

[21] Gaṅgeśa's definition of an inferential undercutting condition is given in TCM, 336: "An inferential undercutting condition is that, due to a deviation from which, the reason deviates from the property to be proven. It is defined as a property that pervades the determined (*paryavasita*) property to be proven, but doesn't pervade the reason" (yad-vyabhicāritvena sādhanasya sādhya-vyabhicāritvaṃ sa upādhiḥ, lakṣaṇan tu paryavasita-sādhya-vyāpakatve sati sādhanâvyāpakatvam).

(*pratiyogitā*) determined by the relevant absence. Similarly, since smoke appears in that awareness as the counterpositive of its absence in virtue of being characterized by smokehood, the counterpositiveness that resides in smoke is delimited by smokehood. According to Gaṅgeśa, by observing the correlation between two absences where the delimitors of counterpositiveness are firehood and smokehood respectively, the agent can learn that the locus of smokehood, i.e., smoke, is pervaded by the locus of firehood, i.e., fire. That is how the relation between a counterpositive and its absence regulates the awareness of pervasion. Gaṅgeśa's commentator, Mathurānātha, explains:

> The meaning is this. There is no problem of overgeneration. For the awareness of the correlation between two absences, which are delimited by two specific properties and are grasped as absences delimited by those two specific properties, causes an apprehension of pervasion between the loci of those specific properties, where those properties are grasped as those two properties.[22]

This avoids the problem of overgeneration, because the rule mentioned by Mathurānātha only applies to cases where the apprehended relation of pervasion holds between the loci of the properties that delimit (the counterpositiveness relevant to) the observed absences. This rule, according to Gaṅgeśa, is already quite plausible, since it explains why in positive and negative *anumāna*s, the agent's observation of both positive and negative correlations can help us learn that the reason is pervaded by the property to be proven.

2.3. *Gaṅgeśa's second response: rejecting P3*

Later, Gaṅgeśa goes on to outline an alternative response that involves rejecting P3, i.e., the premise that a negative subsumptive judgment cannot produce an *anumiti*. Unlike the previous response, this reply leaves open the possibility that observing solely negative correlation between a reason and a property to be proven cannot cause an awareness of positive pervasion between the two. But the reply involves the further claim that an awareness of negative pervasion, and therefore a negative subsumptive judgment that arises from it, can give rise to an *anumiti*. Gaṅgeśa says:

> Alternatively, a relation of negative pervasion can be an indicator (*gamaka*) of a positive entity [i.e., the property to be proven]. Since the reason is just the absence of the absence of a property which pervades the absence of the property to be proven, it can establish the presence of the property to be proven which is just the absence of the absence of the property to be proven.[23]

---

[22] TCM, 336: taṭ-tad-dharmâvacchinâbhāvatvena tat-tad-dharmâvacchinâbhāvayoḥ sahacāra-jñānasya tat-tad-dharma-rūpeṇa tat-tad-dharmâśryayayor vyāpti-grahaṃ prati janakatvān nâtiprasaṅga ity arthaḥ. Once again, it's quite clear that, in this passage, the term *vyāpti* refers to positive pervasion, since the objection it answers is directed at Gaṅgeśa's view that an awareness of negative correlation suffices to produce an apprehension of a relation of positive pervasion.

[23] TCM, 593: yad vā vyatireka-vyāpter eva anvayena gamya-gamaka-bhāvaḥ sādhyâbhāva-vyāpaka-sādhanâbhâvâbhāvena sādhanena pakṣe sādhyâbhāvâbhāvasya sādhyasya sādhanāt. vyāpakâbhāvena vyāpyâbhāvâvaśyam-bhāvāt. In my interpretation of this passage, I am relying on Mathurānātha who takes the term *anvaya* to refer to the property to be proven.

The proposal here crucially depends on a principle about the ontology of absence.

In later Nyāya-Vaiśeṣika ontology, absences are a separate category of entities, distinct from any positive entity (*bhāva-padârtha*), i.e., substance (*dravya*), trope or quality (*guṇa*), motion (*kriyā*), natural kind property (*jāti*), differentiator (*viśeṣa*), and the relation of inherence (*samavāya*) by which the last four kinds of properties reside in substances.[24] Absences are taken to be of two kinds: relational absence (*saṃsargâbhāva*) and mutual absence (*anyonyâbhāva*). A mutual absence of an entity X is an absence of identity with X, so it consists in being different from X. A relational absence of an entity X (though often defined as a kind of absence that is distinct from mutual absence) is basically the absence of X in another entity Y. So, when I say, "There is no bottle on this table," I am ascribing to the table a relational absence, but when I say, "This table is not that one," I am ascribing to this table a mutual absence. Relational absences fall into three categories: prior absence (*prāg-abhāva*), posterior absence or destruction (*dhvaṃsa*), and absolute absence (*atyantâbhāva*). The prior absence of a thing is its absence before it is produced. The destruction of a thing is its absence after it has been destroyed. Finally, the absolute absence of a thing from a place is an absence that is located in that place at all the three times, i.e., past, present, and future. Constructions of the form "The bottle is not on the table" are supposed to illustrate this last kind of relational absence.[25]

Focus now on just absolute absences and mutual absences. Following Udayana,[26] Gaṅgeśa thinks that the absolute absence of the absolute absence of an entity X is identical to X, while the absolute absence of a mutual absence of X is identical to a distinctive property of X.

> The absolute absence of an absolute absence is just the counterpositive, while the absence of a mutual absence is a distinctive property (*asādhāraṇa-dharma*) that resides in the counterpositive.[27]

---

[24] Vācaspati Miśra was possibly the first Naiyāyika to lay out the classification of different absences given below in his NVTṬ on NS 2.2.12. On the Vaiśeṣika side, Śivāditya Miśra was possibly the first to treat absence as a separate ontological category (*padârtha*) in his *Sapta-padârthī*.

[25] This is somewhat puzzling, since we might think that even if the bottle isn't on the table now, it may be later on the table. At that later time, we don't apprehend the absolute absence of the bottle on the table. However, the standard solution is that the relation by which any absolute absence resides at its locus is a self-linking relation (*svarūpa-sambandha*). This relation is qualified by a certain time, i.e., the time at which the counterpositive of the absence isn't present in the locus.. This is supposed to explain why, at a time when the counterpositive present in the relevant locus, the absolute absence cannot be apprehended.

[26] NKA 3.2cd, 329: "The counterpositive-ness of an object is the property of being the absence of an absence" (*abhāva-virahâtmatvaṃ vastunaḥ pratiyogitā*). Udayana doesn't specify what kind of absence he is talking about. I have not seen any decisive support for the Principle of Iterated Absence amongst pre-Udayana Nyāya philosophers, though related issues are discussed in both Uddyotakara's NV 1.1.34 and 2.2.10 and Vācaspati Miśra's NVTṬ on it. However, Karl Potter claims (unfortunately without reference) that Vācaspati Miśra endorses the view that the counterpositive of an absence is identical to the absence of that absence; see Potter (1977: 145).

[27] TCM, 565-6: atyantâbhāvâtyantâbhāvaḥ pratiyogy eva anyônyâbhāvâtyantâbhāvas tu pratiyogi-vṛttir asādhāraṇa-dharmaḥ. Elsewhere, Gaṅgeśa explicitly defends this principle again, in the context of giving an alternative definition of counterpositive-ness (*pratiyogitā*) at TCM, 77–8: "Counterpositive-ness doesn't consist in being something that conflicts [with the absence], which is defined as the property of regularly not obtaining together with something else. For the properties of cow-hood and horse-hood aren't counterpositives of each other, and this property of regularly not obtaining together [with the absence]

While commenting on this passage, Raghunātha points out that the distinctive property that Gaṅgeśa refers to is the delimitor of counterpositiveness.[28] Therefore, a pot, which is the counterpositive of an absolute absence of that pot, is identical to the absolute absence of that absence. Similarly, pothood, which is the delimitor of the counterpositiveness that is determined by the mutual absence of a pot, is identical to the absolute absence of that mutual absence. Why does this make sense? Raghunātha and Mathurānātha suggest that the view is motivated by a principle of property individuation: for any two properties P and P*, if P and P* are apprehended in (or ordinarily ascribed to) exactly the same places, then P must be regarded as identical to P*. Since we observe that the absolute absence of the absolute absence of a pot resides in all and only those places where that pot resides, the pot and the absolute absence of its absolute absence are treated as identical. Analogously, since we observe that the absolute absence of a mutual absence of a pot (i.e., the absolute absence of a difference from a pot) resides in all and only instances of pothood (since only that pot isn't different from itself), the absolute absence of a mutual absence of the pot is regarded as identical to pothood.[29]

From this discussion, we get:

> *Gaṅgeśa's Principle of Iterated Absence.* For any entity X, the absolute absence of the absolute absence of X is X itself.

If this is true, when someone learns about the presence of smoke on the hill by perception, she thereby learns that there is an absolute absence of the absolute absence of smoke on the hill. Similarly, if she learns that there is an absolute absence of the absolute absence of fire on the hill, she thereby learns that there is fire on the hill. Henceforth, whenever I say "absence," I will mean absolute absence unless I specify otherwise.

---

doesn't exist in the counterpositive of a difference. Rather, just as there is a particular self-linking relation between an absence and its locus, so also counterpositive-ness and subjunct-ness (*anuyogitva*) are self-linking relations. Alternatively, counterpositivehood is the property of being the absence of an absence" (pratiyogitvaṃ na virodhitvaṃ sahânavasthāna-niyama-lakṣaṇaṃ gotvâśvatvayor atathātvāt, anyônyâbhāva-pratiyoginy asattvāc ca. kintu yathā'bhāvâdhikaraṇayor svarūpa-viśeṣaḥ sambandhaḥ tathā pratiyogitvam anuyogitvam api. abhāva-virahātmatvaṃ vā). For relevant discussion of the Gaṅgeśa passage, see Matilal (1968: 54–5).

28 GA, 1351: asādhāraṇa iti. pratiyogitâvacchedaka iti tu tattvam.

29 For Raghunātha's argument, see GA, 1353: "It is posited that a positive entity is identical to the absence of its absence, solely because, at a place where a positive entity resides, the absence of its absence is apprehended" (bhāva-vati tad-abhāvâbhāva-pratītyā hi bhāvasya svâbhāvâbhāvatvam kalpyate). For Mathurānātha's argument, see R, 33: "This theory is not reasonable, because of the following. When a property of possessing a pot delimited by pot-hood is apprehended, the absolute absence of a pot is not apprehended, so the absence of the absolute absence of a pot is ascribed. Therefore, the absence of the absolute absence of a pot is identical to the pot. Similarly, when the property of possessing the difference from a pot is apprehended, the absolute absence of a difference from a pot is not apprehended, so the absence of the absolute absence of the difference from a pot is ascribed. Therefore, the difference from a pot is just the absence that is delimited by the property of being the absolute absence of the difference from a pot (yathā hi ghatatvâvacchinna-ghatavattā-grahe ghatâtyantâbhāvasyâgrahād ghatâtyantâbhāvâbhāva-vyavahārāc ca ghatâtyantâbhāvâbhāvo ghata-svarūpas tathā ghata-bhedavattā-grahe ghata-bhedâtyantâbhāvâgrahād ghata-bhedâtyantabhāvâbhāva-vyavahārāc ca ghata-bheda eva tad-atyantâbhāvatvâvacchinna-pratiyogikâbhava iti tat-siddhānto na yukti-sahah). For discussion, see Ingalls (1951: 68–9, 102–3).

Now, consider a variant of **Smoke and Fire**, where you know (on the basis of the negative correlation between smoke and fire) that the absence of smoke pervades the absence of fire. According to a simplified version of Gaṅgeśa's definition of pervasion,

> *Pervasion*. For any two entities H and S, S pervades H if and only if two conditions hold:
>
> > *Co-instantiation Condition*. There are some places where both H and S are present together.
> >
> > *Non-deviation Condition*. S is not the counterpositive of an absolute absence which resides at a place where H is present.[30]

So, if you know that the absence of smoke pervades the absence of fire, you know that

> (7) The absence of smoke is not the counterpositive of an absence which resides at a place where the absence of fire is present.

This is equivalent to:

> (8) If the absence of the absence of smoke is present at a place, then the absence of fire is absent from that place.

If you also know that the absence of the absence of smoke is present on the hill, then, by (8), you can infer the absence of the absence of fire on the hill. By Gaṅgeśa's Principle of Iterated Absence, that is simply identical to fire. So, you know that there is fire on the hill. Hence, an awareness of negative pervasion can indeed produce an *anumiti* in this case.

As Gaṅgeśa goes on to explain, the opponent's earlier worries about whether a negative subsumptive judgment can produce an *anumiti* are unjustified.

> Suppose one says, "Well, that [i.e., an awareness that is based on a negative subsumptive judgment] isn't an *anumiti*. For a well-established cause of an *anumiti* goes missing. If things were otherwise [i.e., if a property common to both kinds of subsumptive judgment were to cause an *anumiti*], there would be a problem of non-uniformity."
>
> [We reply:] No. With respect to any *anumiti*, the awareness of pervasion serves as the promoter. This view doesn't result in any problem of overgeneration. Even when the general causal conditions necessary for an *anumiti* are present, a specific kind of *anumiti* doesn't arise unless the specific causal conditions necessary for that kind of *anumiti* obtain. For the general conditions can only produce the relevant effects with the help of the specific conditions. There is simply no

[30] TCM, 100: "Pervasion [of *x* by *y*] is the co-location of *x* with *y* such that *y* is not the counterpositive of an absolute absence which is co-located with *x* but not co-located with its own absence" (pratiyogy-asamānâdhikaraṇa-yat-samānâdhikaraṇātyantâbhāva-pratiyogī yan na bhavati tena saha tasya sāmānâdhikaraṇyaṃ vyāptiḥ).

> collection of causal conditions that includes the specific causal conditions required for both positive-only and negative-only *anumiti*.[31]

Gaṅgeśa here endorses what we earlier called Option 3: namely, that some *anumiti*s are caused by positive subsumptive judgments, while others are caused by negative subsumptive judgments. On this view, any *anumiti* is produced by a general necessary condition: an awareness of pervasion. Since this is what unifies all instances of an *anumiti*, there is no problem of non-uniformity. But, at the same time, this general necessary condition can only produce specific kinds of *anumiti* through the mediation of specific causal conditions. In the case of a positive-only *anumāna*, the specific causal condition is a positive subsumptive judgment. In the case of a negative-only *anumāna*, it is a negative subsumptive judgment. Finally, there is also no problem of overgeneration due to the simultaneous presence of the causal conditions necessary for both positive-only and negative-only *anumāna*s. For those conditions cannot be present together. So, P3 is false.

The lesson is this. Gaṅgeśa thinks that even if (some or all) so-called negative-only *anumāna*s involve an awareness of negative pervasion, that doesn't prevent them from giving rise to *anumiti*s. Thus, this entire discussion gives us two distinct views about the nature of negative-only *anumāna*s. On one view, a negative-only *anumāna* may involve (or perhaps always involves) an awareness of positive pervasion which is based solely on the observation of negative correlation. On the other view, a negative-only *anumāna* involves an awareness of negative pervasion. These two views are reported quite frequently in primers of later Nyāya.[32] The first view is regularly attributed to Udayana, while some later Naiyāyikas, e.g., Mahādeva Puṇatāmakara (seventeenth century CE), suggest that the latter is the view that Gaṅgeśa favors.[33]

3. RAGHUNĀTHA ON GAṄGEŚA'S PRINCIPLE OF ITERATED ABSENCE

In the last section we reconstructed Gaṅgeśa's account of how an awareness of negative pervasion between a reason and a property to be proven can be the basis of

---

[31] TCM, 593: atha evaṃ na sânumitiḥ kḷpta-tad-dhetu-liṅga-parāmarśâbhāvāt, anyathânanugama iti cen, na. anumiti-mātre vyāpti-jñānasya prayojakatvāt. na ca evam ati-prasaṅgaḥ, anumiti-sāmānya-sāmagryāṃ satyām apy anumiti-viśeṣa-sāmagrī-virahād anumity-anutpatteḥ viśeṣa-sāmagrī-sâpekṣāyā eva sāmānya-sāmagryā janakatvāt. anvayi-vyatireki-viśeṣa-dvaya-sāmagrī ca nâsty eva.

[32] A representative statement comes from Viśvanātha, Siddhânta-muktâvalī (SMA), 499–501: "Amongst those [three kinds of *anumāna*], the awareness of a relation of negative pervasion serves as a cause in a negative-only *anumāna* . . . The apprehension of a relation of negative pervasion is caused by the awareness of negative correlation. However, some say, 'On the basis of negative correlation, only a relation of positive pervasion is apprehended. Therefore, the awareness of a relation of negative pervasion doesn't additionally have to be a cause in a negative-only *anumāna*; an *anumāna* in which the relation of pervasion is apprehended on the basis of negative correlation is called negative-only . . .'" (tatra hi vyatirekiṇi vyatireka-vyāpti-jñānaṃ kāraṇaṃ . . . vyatireka-vyāpti-grahe vyatireka-sahacāra-jñānaṃ kāraṇam. kecit tu vyatireka-sahacāra-jñānenânvaya-vyāptir eva gṛhyate na tu vyatireka-vyāpti-jñānam api kāraṇam yatra vyatireka-sahacārād vyāpti-grahas tatra vyatirekīty ucyate . . . iti vadanti). According to Viśvanātha's commentator, Dinakara Bhaṭṭa, Udayana subscribes to the second view (KA, 501). Also, see Jānakīnātha's *Nyāya-siddhânta-mañjarī* (NSM), 112–17, and Puṇatāmakara's NK, 244–5.

[33] NK: 244–5.

an *anumiti* about that property to be proven. A crucial assumption of this account is Gaṅgeśa's Principle of Iterated Absence. In *A Determination of the True Nature of the Categories* (*Padârtha-tattva-nirūpaṇa*), Raghunātha rejects this principle:[34]

> Thus, the absence of the absence of a pot, etc. is also a distinct entity indeed. For there is an unrebutted awareness of absencehood in the form "The absence of a pot, etc., doesn't exist" with respect to a place that contains a pot. It is also not the case that, if this view is true, there is a regress. For there is no contradiction in claiming that a single absence of a pot is identical to the absence of its own absence.[35]

While explaining this passage, Raghudeva claims that Raghunātha is speaking not only about the absolute absence of an absolute absence, but also about the absolute absence of a mutual absence.[36] On this interpretation, contra Gaṅgeśa, Raghunātha is saying that the absolute absence of an absolute absence is not identical to the counterpositive of the latter, and the absolute absence of a mutual absence is not identical to any distinctive property that resides only in the counterpositive of the latter. Both are in fact distinct entities, i.e., separate absences. A part of Raghunātha's reason for rejecting Gaṅgeśa's claims might be that he rejects the principle of property individuation mentioned earlier. For Raghunātha, even though two properties may be seen to reside in all the same things, they could still be distinct. Let me unpack Raghunātha's reasoning.

Suppose you are looking at something before you, and you judge:

(9) This is a pot (*ayaṃ ghaṭaḥ*).

Awareness-events of this kind present an intentional object (or some intentional objects) as characterized by some feature. In this example, for instance, the awareness-event ascribes the property of pothood to the thing before you. Later Naiyāyikas take such awareness-events to have three kinds of intentional object: the qualificand (*viśeṣya*), the qualifier (*viśeṣaṇa* or *prakāra*), and the qualifying relation (*saṃsarga*).

---

[34] Raghunātha discusses and/or rejects similar principles in at least two other places in his commentary *Splendour* on *The Jewel*: in the *Vyāpti-pūrva-pakṣa-prakaraṇa* and the *Kevalânvayi-prakaraṇa* in GA, 281–2; 1351–4). It's unclear whether there are any post-Gaṅgeśa writers before Raghunātha who reject the Principle of Iterated Absence: Raghunātha himself mentions and refutes a view (which Jagadīśa ascribes to some Miśra, possibly Pakṣadhara), according to which the Principle of Iterated Absence is false, since the absolute absence of a mutual or absolute absence is identical to the relation that delimits the counterpositiveness (*pratiyogitâvacchedaka-sambandha*) determined by the relevant mutual or absolute absence. Even after Raghunātha, his views were not popular: Mathuranātha and Jagadīśa defend the Principle of Iterated Absence in their commentaries on *The Jewel*, while Raghunātha's own commentators report extant views that preserve it. For Mathurānātha's passage, see footnote 29; for Jagadīśa's comments, see TCMM, 42–3; for the commentaries on Raghunātha's passage, see PATN2, 108–12. Matilal claims that the Principle of Iterated Absence is almost universally accepted among later Naiyāyikas; see his, "Double Negation in Navya-Nyāya" in M. Nagatomi, B. K.Matilal, J. M. Masson, and E. C. Dimock (1979: 4).

[35] PATN1, 55.1–4: evaṃ abhāvasyâpy abhāvo'tirikta eva. ghaṭâdimati tad-abhāvo nâstīty abādhitâbhāvatva-pratyayāt. na caivam anavasthā ekasyaiva svâbhāvâbhāva-rūpatve virodhâbhāvāt.

[36] Raghudeva's PATN2, 109: ghaṭâdy-abhāvêti. ghaṭâtyantâbhāvânyônyâbhāvâtyantâbhāva ity arthaḥ.

(i) The object to which the relevant property is ascribed is the qualificand (*viśeṣya*). In this example, the thing before you is the qualificand.

(ii) The property which is ascribed to the qualificand is the qualifier (*viśeṣaṇa* or *prakāra*). In this case, it is pothood.

(iii) The relation in virtue of which the qualifier characterizes the qualifier is the qualifying relation. In this example, the qualifying relation is inherence (*samavāya*), i.e., a relation in virtue of which pothood resides in pots.

Moreover, in any such awareness-event, the qualificand, the qualifier, and the relation between the two are presented under certain modes of thought.[37] These modes of thought are not exactly Fregean senses, but rather properties in virtue of which the agent is able to think about the qualificand, the qualifier, and the qualifying relation. These modes of thought are what the Naiyāyikas call delimitors (*avacchedaka*s), i.e., they delimit exactly which things play which object-role with respect to which awareness-event. In the previous example, the pot is the qualificand, but the mode of thought under which the agent thinks about it is this-ness (*idantva*) or the property of being in front of the agent (*puro-varttitva*). This is what the Naiyāyikas would call a delimitor of qualificandhood (*viśeṣyatâvacchedaka*). The mode under which the agent thinks about the qualifier, i.e, the property of pothood, is pothood-hood (*ghaṭatvatva*). This is the delimitor of qualifierhood (*viśeṣaṇatâvacchedaka* or *prakāratâvacchedaka*). Finally, the mode under which the agent thinks about the qualifying relation, i.e., inherence, is inherencehood (*samavāyatva*). This is the delimitor of relationhood (*saṃsargatâvacchedaka*).

Consider now an awareness-event that can be expressed as:

(10) The absence of a pot doesn't exist on the floor (*bhū-tale ghaṭâbhavo nâsti*).

This awareness-event may be true in a case where there indeed is a pot on the relevant floor. Here, the qualificand is the (absolute) absence of the pot (*ghaṭâbhāva*). The qualifier is non-existence or absence on the floor (*bhū-tala-vṛtty-abhāva*). This, too, is an absolute absence. Finally, the qualifying relation is counterpositiveness (*abhāvīya-pratiyogitva*). For, since the absence of a pot is the counterpositive of an absence (i.e., the absence of the absence of a pot) that resides on the floor (because it is a place where a pot exists), the absence of a pot is connected to the latter absence by a relation of counterpositiveness. The important thing to note here is that there are two properties which together constitute the mode of thought under which the agent thinks about the qualifier in this example: the property of residing on the floor (*bhū-tala-vṛttitva*), and absencehood (*abhāvatva*). Both these properties serve as delimitors of qualifierhood.

Raghunātha's argument against Gaṅgeśa's Principle of Iterated Absence is this: In an awareness-event that is verbalizable as (10), the absence of a pot is taken to be the counterpositive of something that possesses absencehood (*abhāvatva*). Absencehood is not a property that we ordinarily take a positive entity like a pot to possess; in fact,

[37] For the connection between the late Nyāya theory of delimitors (*avacchedaka*) and the theory *of modes of presentations* in Fregean and neo-Fregean theories of content, see Ganeri (1999), chap. 5.

absencehood is often defined as the property of being distinct from a positive entity (*bhāva-bhinnatva*). So, we should think that, in this awareness-event, the absence of the pot appears as the counterpositive of something that possesses absencehood, and therefore is distinct from a positive entity like the pot. And, since the awareness-event in question may not be rebutted by any other means of knowing, we will have to assume that its content is true. Therefore, if the absence of a pot is a counterpositive of an entity X, then X must be distinct from the pot itself. But note that the absolute absence of a pot is the counterpositive of the absolute absence of the absolute absence of the pot. Hence, the absolute absence of the absolute absence of a pot is distinct from the pot. This means that Gaṅgeśa's Principle of Iterated Absence is false. A similar argument can be run against the principle that the absolute absence of the mutual absence of a pot is identical to a distinctive property that resides only in the pot; we only have to consider an awareness-event of the form "The mutual absence of a pot doesn't reside in that pot" (*ghaṭe ghaṭa-bhedo na asti*).[38]

An immediate objection against Raghunātha's argument might be that for any positive entity X, it forces us to posit an infinite hierarchy of distinct entities, i.e., X's absolute absence, the absolute absence of X's absolute absence, and so on. So, there will be an infinite regress. In the last sentence of the quoted passage, Raghunātha explains why he doesn't think this is a problem. He says that if we want to avoid the regress, we can just assume that any absence is identical to the absence of its absence. This would mean that there are only three levels in the relevant hierarchy: positive entities, their absolute absences, and the absolute absences of their absolute absences.

Raghunātha's commentators, Rāmabhadra and Raghudeva, consider another salient objection.[39] Raghunātha's claim basically is that if the absolute absence of an absolute absence of a pot were identical to the pot, then it would not appear, in an awareness-event of this sort, as characterized by absencehood. However, this argument works only if absencehood is construed as a property that doesn't reside in positive entities. Raghunātha's opponent could avoid this problem by positing a property of absencehood (or a property of being an absolute absence), which can reside not only in absences proper (which are distinct from positive entities) but also in positive entities. The response that Rāmabhadra offers on behalf of Raghunātha is that it is simpler just to reject Gaṅgeśa's Principle of Iterated Absence. After all, if we take absencehood to reside in both positive entities and absences proper, how would we distinguish positive entities from absences proper? This view would blur the distinction between positive entities and absences proper.

[38] Raghunātha explicitly rejects two similar principles of iteration about prior absences and posterior absences: the first says that the posterior absence of a prior absence is identical to the counterpositive of the prior absence, and the second says that the prior absence of a posterior absence is identical to the counterpositive of the posterior absence. See PATN1, 56.2–57.1. Interestingly, however, Raghunātha claims that the mutual absence of a mutual absence doesn't have to be a distinct absence; see PATN1, 55.5–56.2.

[39] Rāmabhadra's PATN2, 108: na ca bhāvâbhāva-sādhāraṇam abhāvatvam akhaṇḍôpādhir ity uktau nâyaṃ doṣa iti vācyam. evaṃ sati lāghavād eva ghaṭâbhāvâbhāvasyâtiriktatva-siddheḥ lāghavânādare'bhāva-mātrasyânatiriktatva-prasaṅgād ity ādikam avadheyam. Raghudeva's *Padârtha-tattva-vivecana-prakāśa* in PATN2, 109: pare tu nâsti' iti pratyayo abhāvatvam ālambate param akhaṇḍam atyantâbhāvatvaṃ tac ca bhāvâbhāva-sādhāraṇam abhyupeyatāṃ kṛtam atiriktair abhāvâbhāvaiḥ. 'ghaṭâbhāvâtyantâbhāvo na bhāva' iti ca pratyaya na lokānām iti vadanti.

If Raghunātha's argument succeeds, then Gaṅgesa's account of how an awareness of negative pervasion gives rise to an *anumiti* must fail. For Gaṅgesa cannot explain why learning that there is smoke on the hill amounts to learning that there is an absence of the absence of smoke on the hill, or why learning that there is an absence of the absence of fire on the hill amounts to learning that there is fire on the hill. So, Gaṅgeśa hasn't shown us that a relation of negative pervasion between a reason and a property to be proven can, by itself, give rise to an *anumiti* about the property to be proven.[40]

4. RAGHUNĀTHA'S ARGUMENT

Perhaps this shows that Gaṅgeśa's argument in §2.3 doesn't succeed. But this doesn't rule out the possibility that a relation of negative pervasion between a reason and a property to be proven can, by itself, give rise to an *anumiti* about the property to be proven. In his commentary on the section of *The Jewel* on positive-only *anumāna*s (the *Kevalânvayi-prakaraṇa*), Raghunātha denies precisely this. He argues for:

> *Raghunātha's Thesis.* An agent's awareness of negative pervasion between a reason and a property to be proven cannot *by itself* (i.e., without the mediation of any awareness of positive pervasion) give rise to an *anumiti* about that property to be proven.

Here, I explain his argument for this thesis.

4.1. *Three assumptions*

In his argument, Raghunātha presupposes three principles.

> *Raghunātha's Principle of Iterated Absence.* For any positive entity X, the property of being the absolute absence of the absolute absence of X is distinct from the property of being X.
>
> *The Principle of Deviation.* An agent can acquire knowledge by *anumāna* only if she does not antecedently judge or suspect that the reason *deviates* from the property to be proven (i.e., is present at some place where the property to be proven is absent).

[40] In response, someone like Gaṅgeśa might concede that the absolute absence of an absolute absence is distinct from the counterpositive of the latter absence, but could claim that an agent who understands how the relation between absences and their counterpositives work should know the following principle: For any entity X, the absolute absence of the absolute absence of X is present at a place if and only if X is also present at that place.

So, on observing smoke on hill, such an agent can infer that there is an absence of the absence of smoke on the hill. Similarly, after inferring that there is an absence of the absence of fire on the hill, the agent can infer that there is fire on the hill. However, note that within the Nyāya framework, an agent can only come to know a generalization like this principle by some kind of empirical investigation (which will involve observing correlations between things and the absence of their absences). An agent who doesn't engage in such empirical investigation won't be able to learn this principle. Such an agent won't be able to make the inferences that she is required to make on this revised view.

> *The Principle of Conflict.* Suppose an awareness-event A1 ascribes a property P to an object o1, and an awareness-event A2 ascribes the absence of P to o2. Then, A2 conflicts with A1 only if, in both awareness-events, o1 and o2 are presented under the same mode of thought.

Let me motivate these principles one by one.

Take Raghunātha's Principle of Iterated Absence. If Raghunātha's previous argument against Gaṅgeśa's Principle of Iterated Absence succeeds, then we can show that, for any positive entity X, X isn't identical to the absolute absence of the absolute absence of X. If that is right, then for any positive entity X, the property of being X can't be the same as the property of being the absolute absence of the absolute absence of X. For the first property is instantiated by things that are distinct from the things that instantiate the second. So, this principle follows straightforwardly from what he says against Gaṅgeśa's Principle of Iterated Absence. Moreover, as Jagadīśa notes, we can defend this principle even if Gaṅgeśa's Principle of Iterated Absence is true. If that principle is non-trivially true, we can informatively assert sentences like "The pot is the absolute absence of its absolute absence" (*ghaṭo ghatâtyantâbhāvâtyantâbhāvah*). But an assertion of such a sentence wouldn't be informative (or wouldn't produce a testimonial awareness) unless the delimitor of qualificandhood, i.e., pothood (*ghaṭatva*), were distinct from the delimitor of qualifierhood, i.e., the property of being an absolute absence of the absolute absence of that pot (*ghatâtyantâbhāvâtyantâbhāvatva*). According to a popular principle in later Nyāya, an assertion of the sentence, "The pot is the pot," cannot generate any awareness. For if it did, the delimitor of qualificandhood would be the same as the delimitor of qualifierhood.[41] So, Raghunātha's Principle of Iterated Absence comes out true.

The Principle of Deviation is widely accepted among later Nyāya philosophers.[42] In **Smoke and Fire**, when you infer the presence of fire on the hill after observing smoke on the hill, you are antecedently certain that smoke doesn't deviate from fire, i.e., is never present at a place where fire is absent. In other words, you are antecedently certain that you couldn't have the kind of evidence that forms the basis of your inference unless the conclusion of your inference were true. This is what distinguishes an *anumiti* from other forms of indirect (i.e., non-perceptual) knowledge. For example, in the case of testimonial knowledge, an agent could come

---

[41] The principle is explicitly defended by Gadādadha in his *Vyutpatti-vāda* (VV): "The convention is that an awareness where two objects are semantically combined by a relation of identity can arise only if they are presented differently. For, in the case of sentences like 'The pot is the pot,' 'The stick-bearer is the stick-bearer,' 'He cooks the cooking,' etc., there aren't any awareness-events in which objects that are delimited by pot-hood, stick-bearer-hood, cooking-hood, etc. are semantically combined by a relation of identity with things that are delimited by those very same properties" (abhedânvaya-bodhaś ca virūposthitayor eva iti vyutpattiḥ. "ghaṭo ghaṭaḥ," "daṇḍa-vān daṇḍa-vān," "pākaṃ pacati" ity ādau ghaṭatva-daṇḍavattva-pākatvādy-avacchinne tat-tad-ṛūpâvacchinnasya tathā-vidhânvaya-bodhânudayāt) (VV, 136). The principle is implicit at many places in *The Jewel*, e.g., Gaṅgeśa's discussion of memory demonstratives in the section on qualificative perception (*savikalpaka-vāda*).

[42] For these later Nyāya philosophers, deviation is a defect of a reason (*hetv-ābhāsa*), called *common-ness* (*sādhāraṇatva*). A defect of a reason is some property of the reason the awareness of which prevents an *anumiti* from arising. For definitions of a defect of a reason and common-ness, see TCM, 763–4 and 823.

to judge the content of an utterance to be true, even though she may not have antecedently ruled out the possibility that the sentence in question is never uttered by a certain speaker in a scenario where its content is false.[43]

The Principle of Conflict needs some further motivation.[44] Let's say that an awareness-event *conflicts* with another just in case that, as a matter of rule, the agent never undergoes the two awareness-events at the same time, either because (i) it is psychologically impossible for the agent to undergo both awareness-events at the same time, or (ii) the presence of one awareness-event prevents the other awareness-event from arising or persisting.[45] Suppose an awareness-event A1 ascribes a property P to an object o1, and an awareness-event A2 ascribes the absence of P to o2. According to the principle of conflict, in a normal agent, A2 conflicts with A1 only if, in both awareness-events, o1 and o2 are presented under the same mode of thought. Here's a quick way of seeing why this is plausible. Suppose you know that Caitra is a person. But, then, you see Caitra at a distance, but can't tell that it is Caitra. In fact, the object you see seems a bit like a tree stump to you, so you wonder, "Is that a person, or not?" (*saḥ puruso na vā*) or, perhaps, you judge, "That's not a person" (*so na purusaḥ*). Here, your judgment or suspicion that the object isn't a person doesn't conflict with your judgment that Caitra is a person even though the qualificand is the same in both cases. The only explanation is that the delimitor of qualificandhood, i.e., the mode under which you think about the qualificand, is different in the two cases: in one case, it is Caitrahood (perhaps, all the properties that distinguish Devadatta from other things), and in the other case, it's the indexical property of *that*ness (*tattā*). This supports the Principle of Conflict.

4.2. *The argument*

Now, we are in a position to state Raghunātha's argument for his thesis. In his commentary on the section of *The Jewel* on inferences of the positive-only variety, Raghunātha says:

> In this way, the reason's being the counterpositive of an absence that pervades the absence of the property to be proven is not conducive to an *anumiti*. For this property is complex and doesn't conflict with any awareness of deviation. An awareness-event of the form "The absence of smoke is the counterpositive of an absence that is co-located with the absence of fire" can only sometimes conflict with the awareness of the absence of smoke as co-located with the absence of fire,

[43] The later Naiyāyika, Gadādhara, says in Gādādharī on *Dīdhiti* on *Kevalânvayi-prakaraṇa* of *Tattva-cintā-maṇi* in GA, 1381: "The thought is this. If the set of causal conditions which includes an awareness of deviation can promote an *anumiti*, then testimony, etc., cannot be treated as independent means of knowledge; for the set of causal conditions such as the awareness of expectation (*ākāṅksā*), etc., [which bring about testimonial knowledge] can also involve such awareness of deviation" (vyabhicāra-jñāna-ghaṭita-sāmagryā anumiti-prayojakatve ākāṅkṣâdi-jñāna-ghaṭita-sāmagryā api tathātvâbhāvena śabdâdīnām api svatantra-pramāṇatā-bhaṅga-prasaṅga iti bhāvaḥ).

[44] My explanation here just follows Guha (1979: 208–9).

[45] This relevant notion of conflict or *virodha*—as regularly not obtaining together (*niyata-sahânavasthāna*)—is discussed by Gaṅgesa in his discussion of counterpositiveness. See the passage quoted in footnote 23.

in virtue of attributing the property of being the absence of the absence of smoke but not in virtue of attributing smokehood. For it involves a different qualifier (*prakāra*).[46]

The argument in this passage is this. An agent's awareness of negative pervasion cannot give rise to an *anumiti* for two reasons. First, the relation of negative pervasion is quite complex. Second, this awareness doesn't conflict with any awareness of deviation, i.e., any suspicion or judgment that the reason deviates from the property to be proven. Let's ignore the first worry: as Raghunātha's commentator Jagadīśa notes, there might be a simpler way of stating the relation of negative pervasion (on which a reason is connected to a property to be proven by a relation of negative pervasion if and only if it doesn't reside in anything that lacks the property to be proven (*sādhyâbhāvavad-avṛttitva*)).

The second worry is the interesting one. When an agent comes to know that smoke is connected to fire by a relation of negative pervasion, she knows that the absence of smoke pervades the absence of fire. So, by the definition of pervasion, she knows that:

(11) The absence of smoke is not the counterpositive of an absence which resides at a place where the absence of fire is present (*dhūmâbhāvo vahny-abhāvâdhikaraṇa-vṛtty-abhāvâpratiyogī*).

This is what Raghunātha refers to by the expression "the awareness of the absence of smoke as co-located with the absence of fire." This implies:

(12) The absence of the absence of smoke is absent from any place where the absence of fire resides (*dhūmâbhāvâbhāvo vahny-abhāvâdhikaraṇe na asti*).

In (12), the absence of the absence of smoke is the qualificand, while the absence from any place where the absence of fire resides is the qualifier. The content of this awareness conflicts with:

(13) The absence of the absence of smoke resides at some place where the absence of fire resides (*dhūmâbhāvâbhāvo vahny-abhāvâdhikaraṇa-vṛttiḥ*).

In (13), the absence of the absence of smoke is the qualificand, while the property of residing at a place where the absence of fire resides is the qualifier. Now, notice two things. Here, the qualifiers of the two awareness-events cannot be instantiated together. Moreover, in both cases the qualificand—the absence of the absence of smoke—is presented under the same mode of thought, i.e., the property of being the absence of the absence of smoke (*dhūmâbhāvâbhāvatva*). So, according to the Principle of Conflict, an awareness-event with the content expressed by (13) can indeed conflict with an awareness-event with the content expressed by (12).

[46] GA, 1380: evaṃ sādhyâbhāva-vyāpakâbhāva-pratiyogitvam api na anumity-aupayikaṃ, gauravād vyabhicāra-jñānā-virodhitvāc ca. vahy-abhāva-samānâdhikaraṇâbhava-pratiyogī dhūmâbhāva iti jñānaṃ dhūmâbhāvâbhāvatvena tatra vahny-abhāva-sāmānâdhikaraṇya-buddhiṃ kadācid virundhyāt, na tu dhūmatvena, bhinna-prakārakatvāt.

However, according to Raghunātha, an awareness-event with a content expressed by (12) cannot conflict with an awareness-event with the content expressed by (14):

> (14) Smoke resides at some place where the absence of fire resides (*dhūmo vahny-abhāva-vṛttiḥ*).

In (14), smoke is the qualificand of the relevant awareness, while the property of residing in something that possesses the absence of fire is the qualifier. Here, the delimitor of qualificandhood is smokehood (*dhūmatva*). According to Raghunātha's Principle of Iterated Absence, even if smoke is identical to the absence of the absence of smoke, smokehood and the property of being the absence of the absence of smoke are distinct properties. This, in turn, means that the modes of thought under which the qualificand is presented in (12) and (14) are different. It is this in sense that the two awareness-events involve different *qualifiers* (since the delimitor of the qualificandhood is a qualifier of the qualificand). Here, the principle of conflict entails that the awareness-event with the content expressed by (12) cannot conflict with any awareness-event with the content expressed by (14).

If this argument works, an agent can indeed judge that smoke bears a relation of negative pervasion to fire *and* judge or suspect that smoke deviates from fire. If the agent nevertheless infers the presence of the property to be proven in the subject directly on the basis of her awareness of negative pervasion, then, according to the Principle of Deviation, the knowledge of the property to be proven that the agent gains in such a scenario is not an *anumiti*. This supports Raghunātha's Thesis, i.e., the view that an agent's awareness of negative pervasion cannot generate an *anumiti* by itself.

5. RAGHUNĀTHA'S ANTI-REDUCTIONISM

In response to this argument, someone like Gaṅgeśa might claim that the general causal condition for any *anumiti* is the agent's awareness of *some* relation of pervasion beween the reason and the property to be proven. However, an *anumiti* based on an agent's awareness of positive pervasion differs from one based on an awareness of negative pervasion insofar as they are brought about by different *specific* causal conditions (either by a positive subsumptive judgment or by a negative subsumptive judgment). Thus, even though different *anumiti*s together form a unified epistemic kind, they can be brought about by different sets of causal conditions. Raghunātha addresses this view.

> An awareness-event that arises out of an agent's apprehension of negative pervasion is not an *anumiti*. For it isn't experienced as such, and it is not preceded by one of the well-established causes of an *anumiti*. Moreover, it is permissible to posit that different causal conditions produce awareness-events of the same kind only if these awareness-events are experienced in the same way.[47]

Raghunātha's response proceeds from a principle.

[47] GA, 1380: vyatireka-vyāpti-grahâdhīnā dhīr nânumitis tattvenânanubhavāt. kḷpta-kāraṇâbhāvāt, sāmagrī-bheda-kalpanāyāś cânubhavaikādhīnatvāt.

> *Criterion for Individuating Epistemic Kinds*. Suppose paradigmatic instances of an epistemic kind K are produced by a collection of causal conditions S. Then, awareness-events that are not produced by S can belong to K only if they are systematically experienced (in introspection) as instances of K.

The underlying idea is that unless there is independent reason derived from introspection (or elsewhere), we shouldn't classify awareness-events produced by different causal conditions as instances of the same epistemic kind. Now, suppose all *anumiti*s form a unified epistemic kind. According to the Criterion for Individuating Epistemic Kinds, we should treat an awareness-event produced by a positive subsumptive judgment and an awareness-event produced by a negative subsumptive judgment as *anumiti*s only if there is independent introspective (or any other kind of) evidence for treating them alike. However, according to Raghunātha, when an agent infers a property to be proven by appealing to a relation of negative pervasion between a reason and that property to be proven, two things happen. On the one hand, one of the well-established causes of *anumiti*s—namely, the positive subsumptive judgment—goes missing. On the other hand, she isn't introspectively aware of her final inferential awareness-event as an *anumiti*. Therefore, by the Criterion for Individuating Epistemic Kinds, such awareness-events shouldn't classified as *anumiti*s.

Raghunātha suggests that such awareness-events belong to a distinct epistemic kind.

> Rather, it [i.e., the awareness-event which arises out of an agent's apprehension of negative pervasion] is different in kind from an *anumiti*. *Arthâpatti* is the instrument by means of which it arises.[48]

This is Raghunātha's anti-reductionist view about *arthâpatti*: the awareness-events that are derived solely from an agent's awareness of negative pervasion are produced not by *anumāna* but by *arthâpatti*. His commentator, Jagadīśa, notes that there is in fact introspective evidence in favor of treating these two types of awareness-events as instances of two distinct epistemic kinds: "That there is a distinction in kind is established by means of an (introspective) experience of the form 'I am performing an *arthâpatti*, not making an *anumāna*.'"[49] The lesson: Raghunātha and his commentators seem to think that his argument leads to anti-reductionism about *arthâpatti*.

Raghunātha considers a response to his view. A Naiyāyika could argue that, while an awareness of negative pervasion cannot by itself block a suspicion or judgment that the reason deviates from the property to be proven, the awareness of the

[48] GA, 1380: kintu vijātīyā. tat-karaṇam arthâpattir eva. Raghunātha goes on to point out that in a case where an agent undergoes two subsumptive judgments, positive as well as negative, the resulting awareness will either end up being an *anumiti* or an instance of *arthâpatti*-based knowledge, but not both. This is because, in a case where all the causal conditions necessary for two different kinds of knowledge are present, the causal conditions necessary for one block the production of the other. Things won't be different in this case. He says (GA, 1380): "Moreover, the simultaneous integration of positive and negative properties [with respect to the same reason] is compatible with what happens when two well-established epistemic instruments assemble together" (kḷpta-pramāṇa-dvaya-samāhāra-samaśīlañ ca yugapad-anvavya-vyatireki-dharma-pratisandhānam).

[49] JD, 276: vaijātyam arthâpayāmi nânuminomîty anubhavād eva siddham.

property to be proven that arises from that awareness of negative pervasion may have some other feature that allows us to classify that awareness as an *anumiti*. Note that this move involves rejecting the Principle of Deviation, so it may be costly from the Naiyāyika's perspective. But even if it isn't costly, the Naiyāyika owes us an account of why inferential awareness-events that are based on an awareness of negative pervasion should be treated as *anumiti*s. The answer that Raghunātha explicitly considers is that such inferential awareness-events are caused by *subjecthood* (*pakṣatā*). Let me explain.

In **Smoke and Fire**, the hill is the subject of the inference. What makes it an appropriate subject of that inference? According to earlier Naiyāyikas, it's because the relevant agent is in doubt about whether the property to be proven, i.e., the fire, is present in the hill. So, subjecthood on this view boils down to *having as a property an uncertain property to be proven* (*sandigdha-sādhya-dharmatva*). This was taken to be a necessary causal condition for any *anumiti*. However, later Naiyāyikas like Gaṅgeśa pointed out that there are contexts in which an agent may arrive at an *anumiti* despite having previously learnt (either by an *anumāna* or by some other epistemic instrument) that the property to be proven is present in the subject. In such cases, an *anumiti* is possible because the relevant agent has the desire to establish the presence of the property to be proven in the subject. So, Gaṅgeśa revises the definition of subjecthood: for him, it is the absence of an epistemic instrument which establishes the property to be proven in the subject, such that this instrument is accompanied by an absence of a desire to establish the property to be proven in the subject (*siṣādhayiṣā-viraha-sahakṛta-sādhaka-pramāṇâbhāva*).[50] More simply, an object, e.g., the hill in **Smoke and Fire**, possesses subjecthood if and only if either (i) the reason to be proven hasn't been shown by an epistemic instrument to be present in that object, or (ii) the relevant agent still desires to establish that it exists in that object. Gaṅgeśa and many other later Naiyāyikas think that subjecthood is a necessary causal condition for any *anumiti*.

The rationale behind the objection that Raghunātha considers is that any inferential awareness-event that is derived from an awareness of negative pervasion is produced by the relevant sort of subjecthood, so, such an awareness-event had better be an *anumiti*.

> Suppose you say, "Well, with respect to that which has been ascertained, there arises no *arthâpatti*-based awareness without a desire to establish it. Given that it too is produced by subjecthood, such knowledge is also an *anumiti*. This is because, for reasons of simplicity, the property of being produced by subjecthood is the only promoter of *anumiti*hood . . ."[51]

---

[50] See TCM, 431–2.

[51] GA, 1383: atha nirṇīte vina siddhîcchām arthâpatter anutpādāt pakṣatā-janyatvāt sā'py anumitir lāghavena pakṣatā-janyatvasyaivânumititve prayojakatvāt. The opponent goes on to explain why the view doesn't lead to any undesirable consequences at GA, 280–3: "It is not the case that if this view is true, a perceptual awareness of subjecthood would end up being an *anumiti*. For subjecthood is imperceptible. It has a counterpositive that involves the imperceptible property of being present at a particular time (*eka-kālīnatva*) among other things, since the desire to prove—even when it is present—is absent at other times and other places" (na caivaṃ pakṣatā-pratyakṣasyâpi tathātvâpattiḥ, icchā-sattve'pi kālântare deśântare vā tad-viraha-sattvenaika-kālīnatvâdy-atīndriya-ghaṭita-pratiyogitvena tasyā atīndriyatvād).

Here, given the context, the term "*arthâpatti*-based awareness" just refers to any inferential awareness-event that is based on an awareness of negative pervasion. So, the claim that since being produced by subjecthood is a promoter of *anumiti*hood, any such awareness-event must also be an *anumiti*.

Elsewhere in his commentary on *The Jewel*, Raghunātha expresses that there is no uniform (*anugata*) property of subjecthood that can be treated as a cause of *anumitis*.[52] He repeats that point.

> [We reply:] No. For we have indeed repudiated the view that subjecthood is the cause of any *anumiti*. For subjecthood is non-uniform due to the variation of reasons to be proven, etc., and the property of being produced by subjecthood isn't a promoter of *anumiti*hood. Promoterhood is neither (i) the property of being a cause, because that is impossible, nor (ii) the property of being pervaded by that which it promotes, because there is no evidence for this. This view has been stated more than once. Thus, we also refute the view that the property of being produced by an awareness of pervasion is a promoter of *anumiti*hood.[53]

Here, Raghunātha wants to deny that subjecthood is a cause of every *anumiti*. He offers two reasons for this.

First of all, the claim is that subjecthood will vary from one case to another, depending on what the relevant property to be proven is. This makes it non-uniform. In other words, it is a long disjunction of different conditions rather than a condition that is uniformly present in every case of *anumiti*. Since such disjunctive entities cannot be treated as a cause, subjecthood cannot be treated as a cause of *anumiti*. Raghunātha's commentator, Jagadīśa, sharpens this point in a different way. Raghunātha's opponent intends to give the following argument: "Any awareness that is produced by an awareness of negative pervasion is an *anumiti*, because it is produced by subjecthood, just like an *anumiti* that is produced by an awareness of positive pervasion" (*vyatireka-vyāpti-jñāna-janya-jñānam anumitiḥ pakṣatā-janyatvāt, anvaya-vyāpti-jñāna-janyânumitivat*). The subject of this *anumāna* is any awareness that is produced by an awareness of negative pervasion. The property to be proven is *anumiti*hood. The reason is the property of being produced by subjecthood. The confirming instance (*dṛṣṭânta*), which provides evidence for the relation of pervasion between the reason and the property to be proven, is an *anumiti* that is produced by an awareness of positive pervasion. Jagadīśa poses a dilemma for Raghunātha's opponent.[54] The notion of subjecthood at play in the

---

[52] See the discussion in GA, 1159.

[53] D, 1159: na. anumitāv eva pakṣatāyā hetutvasya nirastatvāt, sādhyâdi-bhedenâṇanugatatvāt taj-janyatvasyâprayojakatvāt. prayojakatvañ ca na janakatvam asambhavāt na vyāpyatvaṃ māṇâbhāvād ityâder asakṛd āveditatvāc ca. etena vyāpti-jñānâdi-janyatvam anumitive prayojakam ity api parāstam.

[54] JD, 284–5: "Therefore, the thought is this. Just as subjecthood varies depending on the property to be proven, etc., so also does it vary depending on whether the relevant desire to establish the property to be proven has, as its qualifier, *anumiti*hood or the property of being *arthâpatti*-based knowledge. If the promoter of *anumiti*-hood is the property of being produced by a kind of subjecthood which involves the absence of a desire that has *anumiti*hood its qualifier, then there will be a fault of being unestablished by nature due to the absence of the reason from cases of *arthâpatti*-based knowledge. And if the promoter of *anumiti*hood is the property of being produced by a kind of subjecthood which involves the absence of a

opponent's argument is ambiguous: subjecthood could involve either the absence of a desire to establish the property to be proven by *anumāna* or the absence of a desire to establish it by *arthâpatti*. If it is the former, then the reason of the inference will be absent from the subject, because the subject may be some case of *arthâpatti*-based knowledge which is produced by the agent's desire to establish something by *arthâpatti*. The reason therefore will suffer from the defect of being unestablished by nature (*svarūpâsiddhi*). If it is the latter, then the reason won't be present in the example that the opponent cites, namely an *anumiti* which is produced by an awareness of positive pervasion. For such an *anumiti* is caused by the kind of subjecthood that involves the absence of a desire to establish the property to be proven by *anumāna* (and not *arthâpatti*). This gives rise to the fault of being unestablished in the confirming instance (*dṛṣṭântâsiddhi*).

Raghunātha's second argument is that the notion of a promoter or *prayojaka* that his opponent invokes is somewhat murky. The property of being caused by subjecthood cannot be a promoter of *anumiti*hood in the strong sense of being a cause of *anumiti*hood. For that is impossible: *anumiti*hood, for the Nyāya philosopher, is a natural kind property (*jāti*), and natural kind properties (in virtue of being eternal) don't have causes. Moreover, the property of being caused by subjecthood cannot be a promoter of *anumiti*hood in the weaker sense of being pervaded by *anumiti*hood. For there is no evidence for it. The reason presumably is that Raghunātha's opponent cannot rule out the possibility that the property of being caused by subjecthood deviates from *anumiti*hood. This is because an anti-reductionist about *arthâpatti* could argue that instances of *arthâpatti* are produced by a distinctive kind of subjecthood which involves the absence of a desire to establish the property to be proven by *arthâpatti*. Since such subjecthood doesn't cause prototypical *anumiti*s, Raghunātha's opponent cannot appeal to prototypical *anumiti*s in order to rule out the possibility that the property of being caused by subjecthood isn't present in inferential awareness-events other than *anumiti*s. So, given that Raghunātha's opponent cannot rule out the possibility that the property of being caused by subjecthood deviates from *anumiti*hood, she hasn't shown us that *anumiti*hood pervades the property of being caused by subjecthood.

Raghunātha ends by noting that his strategy generalizes. For example, if an opponent argues that the promoter of *anumiti*hood is just the property of being produced by an awareness of either positive or negative pervasion, the same arguments from non-uniformity, etc., could be marshaled in favor of Raghunātha's view.

Despite these arguments, Raghunātha's conclusion might seem too hasty: it's not clear that his argument succeeds in dismantling all possible reductionist views about *arthâpatti*. Raghunātha himself seems to recognize this.

---

desire that has the property of being *arthâpatti*-based knowledge, etc. as its qualifier, then there will be a fault of being unestablished in the confirming instance, i.e., the *anumiti*" (tathā ca sādhyâdi-bhedād iva anumititvârthāpattitvâdi-prakāraka-siṣādhayiṣāyā bhedād api pakṣatā-bhedāt anumititvâdi-prakārakêcchā-viraha-ghaṭita-pakṣatā-janyatvaṃ yadi prayojakaṃ tadā hetv-abhāvād arthâpattau svarūpâsiddhiḥ, arthâpattitvâdi-prakārakêcchā-viraha-ghaṭita-janyatvasya prayojakatve ca anumitau dṛṣṭântâsiddhir iti bhāvaḥ).

> Some also say that when the relevant property to be proven is already known, an *anumiti* arises on the basis of another *anumāna* that proceeds from the fact that *the reason is a property which is the counterpositive of an absence that pervades the absence of the property to be proven* to the conclusion that *the reason is pervaded by the property to be proven.*[55] (italics mine)

This proposal is in effect a version of the view (rejected earlier by Gaṅgeśa) that an agent's awareness of negative pervasion can produce an *anumiti* through the mediation of an awareness of positive pervasion. As Jagadīśa points out, Raghunatha doesn't like this view, though he doesn't explain why. However, we may be able to supply a reason. In this view, in order to move from an awareness of negative pervasion to an awareness of positive pervasion, the agent would have to know the further generalization that any two entities X and Y that are connected by a relation of negative pervasion are also connected by a relation of positive pervasion. On the Nyāya view, learning such a generalization will require further empirical investigation. An agent who hasn't engaged in any such empirical investigation won't be able to make any inference on the basis of her awareness of negative pervasion. However, it seems intuitively plausible that an agent who doesn't know such a generalization can still make the inference that we see in **Absent Devadatta.** This puts some pressure on us to reject this story.

In fact, a general challenge for the Nyāya reductionist about *arthâpatti* emerges from this discussion. If such reductionism is true, many instances of *arthâpatti*-based knowledge must be based on negative-only *anumāna*s, i.e., *anumāna*s where the relevant subject apprehends the relation of pervasion by only observing instances of negative correlation. Either such *anumāna*s always involve an awareness of positive pervasion or they don't. Now, to say that such *anumāna*s always involve an awareness of positive pervasion is to say that there are no *anumāna*s that take the form of the **Simple Inference** in §2.1. This seems like a psychological generalization that requires much more evidence than the Nyāya reductionist has given us. Without evidence, it is implausible. So, consider the other option: sometimes, in putative negative-only *anumāna*s, people arrive at their conclusions simply on the basis of their awareness of negative pervasion. Raghunātha has argued that such reasoning cannot yield any *anumiti*; in fact, it is a distinct source of knowledge, namely *arthâpatti*. This supports anti-reductionism about *arthâpatti.*

6. CONCLUSION

In this chapter, I have reconstructed Raghunātha's argument for anti-reductionism about *arthâpatti*. If Raghunātha is right, once we have accepted Raghunātha's Principle of Iterated Absence, Nyāya reductionism about *arthâpatti* is straightforwardly in tension with certain commitments that most later Naiyāyikas share. It remains mysterious, to me at least, how these Naiyāyikas could embrace reductionism about *arthâpatti* without either rejecting the Raghunātha's Principle of Iterated Absence or jettisoning some of their commitments.

[55] GA, 1383: sādhyâbhava-vyāpakâbhāva-pratiyogi-dharmatvena sādhya-vyāpyatvânumāmāt prasiddha-sādhyakaivânumitir ity api kecit.

ABBREVIATIONS AND REFERENCES

D	*Dīdhiti* in GA
GA	*Gādâdharī* of Raghunātha Śiromaṇi in *The Gādādharī: A Commentary on Dīdhiti, the Commentary by Śri Raghunātha Śiromaṇi on the Tattvacintāmaṇi of Śrī Gaṅgeśa Upādhyāya (with texts)*, ed. V.P. Divivedī et al, vols. 1 and 2, Varanasi: Chowkhamba Sanskrit Series Office, 1970.
KA	*Kārikâvali* of Viśvanātha in *Kārikāvali of Viśvanātha Nyāyapañcānana Bhaṭṭacārya: With the Commentaries Siddhāntamuktāvalī, Dinakarī, Rāmarudrī*, ed. A. Jere, New Delhi: Rashtriya Sanskrit Sansthan, 2002.
NBh	*Nyāya-bhāṣya* of Vātsyayana in ND
NK	*Nyāya-kaustubhaḥ* of Mahādeva Puṇatāmakara in *Mahādevapuṇatāmakaraviracito Nyāyakaustubhaḥ: Anumāna-khaṇḍātmako dvitīyo bhāga*, ed. D. Gosvāmī, Varanasi: Vārāṇaseya Saṃskṛta Viśva-vidyālaya, 1967.
NKA	*Nyāya-kusumâñjali* of Udayana in *The Nyāyakusumāñjali of Śrī Udayanācārya with Four Commentaries: The Bodhinī, Prakāśa, Prakāśikā (Jalada) and Makaranda by Varadarāja, Varddhamānopādhyāya, Mecha Thakkura and Rucidattopādhyāya and with Notes by Śrī Dharmadatta (Bachchā Jhā)*, eds. P. Upādhyāya and D. Śāstri, Varanasi: Chowkhamba Sanskrit Series, 1957.
NM	*Nyāya-mañjarī* of Jayanta Bhaṭṭa in *Nyāyamañjarī of Jayanta Bhaṭṭa with Ṭippanī- Nyāyasaurabha of the Editor*, Ed. K.S. Varadacharya, vol. 1, Mysore: Oriental Research Institute, 1969.
NS	*Nyāya-sūtra* of Akṣapāda Gautama in *Nyāyadarśanam: With Vātsyāyana's Bhāṣya, Uddyotkara's Vārttika, Vācaspati Miśra's Tātparyaṭīkā & Viśvanātha's Vṛtti*, eds. T. Tarkatīrtha and A. Tarkatīrtha, New Delhi: Munshiram Manoharlal, 1985.
NSD	*Nyāya-siddhaânta-dīpaḥ* of Śaśadhara in *Nyāyasiddhāntadīpaḥ*, ed. B.K. Matilal, Ahmedabad: L. D. Institute of Indology, 1976.
NSM	*Nyāya-siddhânta-mañjarī* of Bhaṭṭa Ācārya Cūdāmaṇi in *Nyāyasiddhântamañjarī with Nīlakaṇṭha Dīkṣīta's Dīpikātarkaprakāśa*, ed. G. Sastri, Delhi: Satguru Publications, 1990.
NV	*Nyāya-vārttika* of Uddyotakara in ND
NVTṬ	*Nyāya-vārttika-tātparya-ṭīkā* of Vācaspati Miśra in ND
PATN1	*Padârtha-tattva-nirūpaṇam* of Raghunātha Śiromaṇi in *Padârthatattvanirūpaṇam of Raghunātha Śiromaṇi: A Demonstration of the True Nature of the Things to Which Words Refer*, ed. and transl. Karl H. Potter, Cambridge, MA: Distributed for the Harvard-Yennching Institute by Harvard University Press, 1957.
PATN2	*Padârtha-tattva-nirūpaṇam* of Raghunātha Śiromaṇi in *Padārthatattvanirūpaṇam* of Raghunātha Śiromaṇi in Rajpal, A. (2008), *Padârtha-tattva-nirūpaṇam Tīkā-trayopetam*, Delhi: Amara Grantha Publications.
R	*Rahasya* of Mathurānātha Tarkavāgīśa in TCM.

ŚBh *Śābara-bhāṣya* of Śabara in *Śābarabhāṣyam*, ed. G.S. Musalagaonkar , Vārāṇasī: Chowkhambha Sanskrit Series Office, 2004.

SMA *Siddhântamuktâvalī* of Viśvanātha in *Kārikāvali* of Viśvanātha in *Kārikāvali of Viśvanātha Nyāyapañcānana Bhaṭṭacārya: With the Commentaries Siddhāntamuktāvalī, Dinakarī, Rāmarudrī*, ed. A. Jere, New Delhi: Rashtriya Sanskrit Sansthan, 2002.

ŚV *Śloka-vārttika* of Kumārila Bhaṭṭa in *Ślokavārttikam Kumārilabhaṭṭapādaviracitam*, ed. D. Śāstrī, Varanasi: Tara Publications, 1978.

TCM *Tattva-cintâmaṇi* of Gaṅgeśa in *The Tattvacintāmaṇi of Gaṅgeśa Upādhyāya: Anumityādi-bādhānta Anumāna-khaṇda with the Commentary "Rahasya" by Mathurānātha Tarkavāgīśa*, vol. 2, part 1 (Delhi: Chaukhambha Sanskrit Pratishthan, 1990),

JD *Jāgadīśī* of Jagadiśa Tarkalaṁkāra in *Tattvacintāmaṇi* of Gaṅgeśa in *Śrīman-mahāmahopādhyāya-gaṅgeśopādhyāya-viracitaṃ Kevalānvayīprakaraṇam*, ed. V. Bhaṭṭācārya, Varanasi: Motilal Banarasidass, 1955.

TCMM *Tattva-cintāmaṇi-mayūkha by Jagadīśa Tarkālaṅkāra*, ed. G. Sastri, Calcutta: Sanskrit Sahitya Parishat, 1980.

TSDP *The Tarka-saṇgraha-dīpikā-prakāśikā* of Cinnambhaṭṭa in *The Tarkasaṇgraha-dīpikā-prakāśikā with the commentaries Bālapriyā and Prasāraṇa*, ed. N. Veezhinathan, Chennai: Sri Sri Sri Manalakshmi-Mathrubhutheswarar Trust, 2008.

VV *Vyutpatti-vādaḥ* of Gadādhara. *Gadādhara's Vyutpatti-vādaḥ: Abhedānvaya-prakaraṇam. A Critical Edition of the Text with Seven Commentaries*, ed. A. Dash, Delhi: New Bharatiya Book Corporation, 2004.

Ganeri, J. (1999), *Semantic Powers: Meaning and the Means of Knowing in Classical Indian Philosoph*, Oxford: Clarendon Press.

Guha, D. C. (1979), *Navya Nyāya System of Logic*, New Delhi: Motilal Banarasidass.

Ingalls, D. H. H. (1951), *Materials for the Study of Navya-nyāya Logic*, Cambridge, MA: Harvard University Press.

Matilal, B. K. (1968), *The Navya-Nyāya Doctrine of Negation: The Semantics and Ontology of Negative Statements in Navy-ayāya Philosophy*, Cambridge, MA: Harvard University Press.

Matilal, B. K. (1979), "Double Negation in Navya-Nyāya," in M. Nagatomi, B. K. Matilal, J. M. Masson, and E. C. Dimock (eds.), *Sanskrit and Indian Studies*, Dordrecht: Springer.

Potter, K. H., ed. (1977), *The Encyclopedia of Indian Philosophies*, vol. 2: *Indian Metaphysics and Epistemology: The Tradition of Nyaya-Vaiśeṣika Up to Gaṅgeśa*, Princeton, NJ: Princeton University Press.

CHAPTER ELEVEN

Against Reducing *Arthâpatti*

MARK SIDERITS

In *Tattva-saṅgraha* (TS) and *Tattva-saṅgraha-pañjikā* (TSP) vv. 1587–1647, the Buddhist philosophers Śāntarakṣita and Kamalaśīla examine and reject the claim of Mīmāāṃsakas that *arthâpatti* is a distinct epistemic instrument (*pramāṇa*). In much of my writing I have defended Buddhist authors against objections raised by Brahmanical philosophers. Here I shall be doing something a little different. There is much to be said for including *arthâpatti* under the category of inference, if that category is construed broadly enough. But if, as is usually done in discussions of classical Indian theories of the epistemic instruments, we were to reserve the term "inference" for the epistemic instrument of *anumāna*, with the latter understood along the lines laid out by Diṅnāga and Dharmakīrti, then we should not call *arthâpatti* an inference, for it is an epistemic instrument distinct from *anumāna*. Or so I shall argue. I shall then go on to consider what Buddhists might gain by adding *arthâpatti* to their list of epistemic instruments, alongside perception and *anumāna*.

This chapter has three parts. In the first, I try to sort out some of the terminological complications that arise when one attempts to make debates among classical Indian epistemologists accessible to a wider audience. In explaining the key terms of the debate over *arthâpatti*, I also indicate what I take to be some of the distinctive features of the Indian approach to doing epistemology. The second section examines the debate over the status of *arthâpatti* between Śāntarakṣita and Kamalaśīla on the one hand and the Bhāṭṭa Mīmāṃsakas on the other. There I examine the arguments of Śāntarakṣita and Kamalaśīla against *arthâpatti* being an autonomous epistemic instrument distinct from *anumāna*. I claim that these arguments fail and explore what this might tell us about *arthâpatti*. In the third section, I discuss why at least certain Buddhist philosophers might welcome this result. While many Buddhists agree with Śāntarakṣita and Kamalaśīla that there are just two epistemic instruments, perception and *anumāna*, that position leads to difficulties in accounting for the possibility of meta-cognition. Embracing the claim that *arthâpatti* is a distinct epistemic instrument opens up the possibility that Kumārila (the founder of the Bhāṭṭa Mīmāṃsā school) was right: cognitions are cognized through *arthâpatti*, understood as postulation or inference to the best explanation. I shall argue that such an account of meta-cognition accords better with the core Buddhist tenet of non-self than the reflexivist account of how cognitions are cognized that is favored by Śāntarakṣita and Kamalaśīla.

1. THE TERMINOLOGY

From what was said above concerning how we should construe "inference," it will be clear that there is room for terminological confusion here. For instance, *anumāna* is commonly translated as "inference." At the same time, *arthâpatti* is sometimes called "abductive inference" or "inference to the best explanation." Adopting those translation conventions would seem to give Śāntarakṣita and Kamalaśīla an undeserved victory, for *arthâpatti* would then turn out to be a variety of *anumāna*. In order to avoid begging any substantive questions, I will stipulate that for the purposes of this essay some key terms we will use to discuss the debate be understood in the following way. First, the term "epistemic instrument" (*pramāṇa*) will be understood to mean an epistemic procedure, implementation of which causes a veridical cognition.[1] I shall use the term "inference" to refer to a cognitive procedure whereby the subject comes to accept some statement on the basis of evidence that they already possess and take to have evidentiary value.[2] An inference is a variety of thought-transition, a process whereby thoughts trigger further thoughts. Not all thought-transitions involve evidential relations: wool-gathering, wordplay and free association all involve thought-transitions that are not ordinarily subjected to epistemic assessment. Inferences are the thought-transitions that are governed by norms of epistemic evaluation. Clearly, when inferences are so characterized, some will be epistemically better than others. Viewed from the perspective of logic, the best inferences are those that instantiate the form of a deductively valid argument. I will reserve the term "argument" for any set of propositions where one (the conclusion) is claimed to follow from the others (the premises).[3] A deductively valid argument is one whose corresponding conditional—the conditional whose antecedent is the conjunction of the premises and whose consequent is the conclusion—is true in virtue of its logical form alone.

[1] Two points are worth bearing in mind. First, when we think of Indian theories of epistemic instruments as theories of knowledge, by "knowledge" is here meant cognitive episodes of a certain sort. On what difference it might make to epistemology to take an episodic as opposed to a dispositional approach to knowledge, see Matilal (1986: 97–135). Second, while Indian theories of the epistemic instruments are epistemological externalist insofar as the cognizer's having knowledge need not involve their being able to show that all the factors of the epistemic instrument have been implemented, this is not a reliabilist externalism. For the Indian theorists, a procedure is not an epistemic instrument unless it (not just reliably but) invariably causes true cognitions.

[2] Of course inferences may also be used to attempt to persuade others to accept some statement. This is the point of the distinction drawn between *anumāna* "for one's own sake" (*svârthânumāna*) and "for the sake of another" (*parârthânumāna*). But since I know of no logical issues relevant to the subject of this essay that turn on that difference, I shall speak throughout of just the first-person case.

[3] I distinguish between statements—the constituents of inferences—and propositions—the constituents of arguments. By a statement I mean an assertoric sentence (a syntactically complete string of words) of some natural language. By a proposition I mean the abstract or third-realm entity that is expressed by a statement. To say that "snow is white" and "*Schnee ist weiss*" have the same meaning is to say that both express the same proposition.

I think we should resist translating *anumāna* as "inference"[4] because even those inferences that instantiate deductively valid arguments may have false conclusions. Only sound inferences, those that instantiate deductively valid arguments and also contain only true premises, are guaranteed to have true conclusions. No *anumāna*, however, has a false conclusion. As it happens, I think that *anumānas* instantiate deductively valid arguments and one might suspect that this lies behind the claim that no *anumāna* ever leads us to falsity. But there is a different reason at work here: an *anumāna* is an epistemic instrument (*pramāṇa*), and epistemic instruments are processes that cause veridical cognitions. The truth of a cognition formed through the *anumāna* procedure follows straightforwardly from its being defined as resulting from the exercise of an epistemic instrument. The same holds for *arthâpatti* as well, whether it is reducible to *anumāna* or is instead a separate epistemic instrument. Any cognition formed through this procedure is veridical. When a cognition produced through what we think is an *anumāna*- or *arthâpatti*-process turns out to be false, this is because the prescribed procedure did not actually occur. What we take to have been an *anumāna* or an *arthâpatti* was in fact a pseudo-*anumāna* or pseudo-*arthâpatti*.

In the case of *anumāna*, this can be seen from its being understood as an inference having a reason (*hetu*) that meets three conditions: that the reason is seen to be present in the locus of investigation, that it is present in everything in which the target property (*sādhya*) is present, and that it is absent in everything lacking the target property.[5] If these three conditions are met then the cognition resulting from the inferential procedure must be true. If that really is smoke one sees on the hill, and it is also true that wherever there is smoke there is fire (that smoke is pervaded by fire), then it must be true that there is fire on the hill. An inference that follows this pattern but contains a reason failing to meet one or more of these conditions is deemed a mere pseudo-*anumāna*. Of course, much has been made of the fact that in time the doctrine of the reason with three conditions (*trai-rūpya-hetu*) came to be understood as really involving just two conditions: presence of the reason property in the locus and pervasion of the target property by the reason property.[6] This allegedly logical difference between Diṅnāga's and Dharmakīrti's accounts is, however, merely a difference in perspective. That Diṅnāga's formulation involves the two separate steps of citing both positive evidence of pervasion (smoke and fire are co-present in the kitchen) and also evidence of lack of counter-examples (the white stuff rising from the lake is not smoke but mist) reflects his concern with the

[4] That an *anumāna* is not an argument follows from the fact that an argument consists of propositions. No classical Indian philosopher recognizes anything like (Fregean) propositions.

[5] Granoff (2018) discusses the common skeptical challenge to this characterization of *anumāna*: the case where a hill is qualified by fire and smoke, but fire is inferred from seeing not smoke but mist that is mistaken for smoke. In fact, this challenge fails: the agent of the inference lacks epistemically significant causal contact with the hill's being qualified by smoke.

[6] The claim that there is a radical rupture between an "inductivist" Diṅnāgan understanding of the *anumāna* and a "deductivist" Dharmakrtian reading was strongly championed by Oetke. For discussion, see, e.g., Tillemans (2005). My response is in Siderits (2003). See also Balcerowicz (2003: 361): "The mere fact that Indian models of inference in general, it seems, resorted to empirical exemplification and left no scope for deductive reasoning would rather speak against ascribing a deductive character to Indian logic. In Indian logic we link not ideas or propositions, but events. That is why the inductive–deductive distinction seems not at all applicable to the realm of *anumāna*."

epistemic situation of the cognizing subject. Not only does the cognizer not initially know whether the locus has the target property, but if they did, then there would be no incentive to infer in the first place. They also do not typically know if concomitance of the reason and the target property holds in all other cases besides that of the locus; instances of smoke and fire being endless, one could not possibly survey them all. Hence the injunction both to seek supportive instances and also to make a principled search for counter-examples (cases like the lake that, being known to lack fire, may appear to nonetheless have smoke). When we shift over to how things actually are in the world, however, then either pervasion does hold or else it does not. Pervasion's holding can be expressed either as every locus of smoke being a locus of fire or as every locus lacking fire also lacking smoke. But pervasion's holding, together with the hill's being a locus of smoke, is enough to guarantee that there is fire on the hill.

What makes this difficult to grasp is, I believe, a failure to recognize the role of universal fallibilism in classical Indian epistemology.[7] Universal fallibilism makes epistemic luck ineliminable. For an epistemological externalist this is hardly surprising. That a cognition's counting as a knowledge episode or event may depend in part on factors outside the subject's ken is just what externalists claim. This is not to say that knowledge is all a matter of guesswork. While a lucky guess does yield a veridical cognition (that's what makes it a *lucky* guess), guessing cannot be relied on to cause veridical cognitions. Those seeking knowledge should instead follow the procedures laid out in the correct account of valid epistemic instruments. But trying to follow those procedures is never a guarantee that the resulting cognition is true. What looks like smoke rising from the mountain may instead be a swarm of midges. Or it might have been a cosmic coincidence that smoke has so far always been accompanied by fire, but that long run is now over. A bit of luck helps. When we're lucky, our cognitions count as knowledge. But we may not always know this. One need not know that one knows in order to have knowledge (provided one has done one's epistemic duty.)

This in turn makes it clear why it matters whether *arthâpatti* is reducible to *anumāna*. The task of classical Indian epistemology is to determine the number and nature of valid epistemic instruments. If, as the Bhāṭṭas claim, *arthâpatti* and *anumāna* are distinct epistemic instruments, this will be reflected in there being distinct procedures that cognizers must follow in order to obtain veridical cognitions through inference. Responsible epistemic agents try to improve their luck by following accredited procedures. If there is a difference between the procedures for *arthâpatti* and *anumāna*, knowing this would be important for responsible knowers.

All this has been an attempt to sort out the terminological complexities involved in this discussion. As indicated earlier, I shall use "inference" to mean a cognitive procedure whereby the subject comes to accept some statement on the basis of evidence that the subject already possesses. By *anumāna* I shall mean an inference that is sound in virtue of its having a reason meeting the three conditions. By

[7] See Phillips (2017) for a discussion of universal fallibilism in Nyāya.

arthâpatti I shall mean those inferences that are classified as such by the Mīmāṃsakas.[8] By "abductive inference," I shall mean an ampliative inference that supplies an explanation for some puzzling phenomenon. Being ampliative, an abductive inference does not instantiate a valid argument form, and so is not sound.[9] Our question is then whether all *arthâpatti* are *anumāna*. Śāntarakṣita and Kamalaśīla claim they are. I shall claim instead that they are abductive inferences.

2. THE DEBATE

We begin with the debate between those, like the Bhāṭṭas, who defend the claim that *arthâpatti* is a distinct epistemic instrument, and Śāntarakṣita and Kamalaśīla, who hold that it is reducible to *anumāna*. The presentation in TS and TSP includes three examples of inferences understood by the Bhāṭṭas as applications of *arthâpatti*: 1) the case of fire's being known to have the power to consume its fuel; 2) the case of Devadatta's being known to eat unobserved at night from his being corpulent and yet not observed to eat during the day; and 3) the case of Caitra's being known to be elsewhere from his not being at home.

2.1. *Fire's power to burn*

At TS 1588, the opponent lists power (*śakti*) as one type of object known by *arthâpatti*. The illustrative example is fire's power to burn, which is inferred from seeing the consumption of fuel in the presence of fire. Śāntarakṣita's response (1607–8) is that there is no need for a distinct power over and above the fire, since it is precisely the fire that is acknowledged as what burns. This is the reply one would expect, given the position of Yogācāra-Sautrāntika (the school whose views Śāntarakṣita expounds in TS) that powers do not exist over and above the entities thought of as having them.[10] To this, the Mīmāṃsaka might respond that not all fire burns. The body, for example, does not burn due to the presence of the fire in the

[8] Mīmāṃsā takes "inexplicability otherwise" (*anythânupapatti*) to be the mark of *arthâpatti*. Jainas move in the opposite direction, taking "inexplicability otherwise" to be the defining characteristic of all inference. See TS 1389–92; see also Balcerowicz (2003). The fire-on-the hill inference can be understood to have this feature: the conjunction of the occurrence of smoke on the hill and smoke's being pervaded by fire is inexplicable if there is not fire on the hill. The Mīmāṃsā stance is that a more fine-grained distinction is called for with respect to inference understood as epistemic instrument: between those inferences having a reason with the three marks, and those having only the feature of "inexplicabililty otherwise."

[9] Here it is important to keep three points in mind: that one may have knowledge without knowing that one knows; that abductive inference is also known as "inference to the *best* explanation"; and that a cognition produced by an epistemic instrument is true by definition. If what is posited in an abductive inference truly yields the best explanation of an otherwise inexplicable state of affairs, then the conclusion reached will indeed be true—even if one does not know that the posited explanation is the best. That abductive inferences do not instantiate deductively valid arguments is no bar to *arthâpatti* being an abductive inference.

[10] This follows from the point Dharmakīrti makes at PVSV *ad* PV1.75, to the effect that ultimately a property is not distinct from the property-possessor. But it also follows from momentariness when conjoined with the denial of the eternalism of Sarvāstivāda. Yogācāra-Sautrāntika's purely trope-theoretic ontology is part of its inheritance from Sautrāntika. Mīmāṃsā has a far more capacious categorial scheme, one having room for a separate category of powers.

belly (*jaṭharâgni*) that is thought to be responsible for digestion. This would mean that some non-evident power must be posited in order to explain those cases where fire does burn.

Buddhists do recognize the necessity of this sort of posit in some cases. For instance, in AKBh Chapter 9, Vasubandhu listed the faculties of sight, hearing, and so on as ultimately real objects that are cognized only by *anumāna*. And sense faculties are, of course, kinds of powers. So at least in this case a power is accepted as something distinct from the organ that we think of as its possessor (e.g., in the case of hearing, the ear). Vasubandhu formulates the inference as follows:

> There being the cause [of sensory cognition], it is known that the effect does not exist when the auxiliary conditions are absent, but does exist when they are present, as with the sprout [that arises from the seed only when soil, moisture, and warmth are present, not when they are absent]. And in the presence of the cause—an object suitable for appearing, and attention—it is known that (1) there is no apprehension of the object, and (2) there is apprehension of the object, in the case of the blind and deaf, etc., and the sighted and hearing, etc., respectively. It is thus ascertained that there is here the absence and the presence, respectively, of an auxiliary cause. And so there is the inference that this auxiliary cause is the sense faculty.
>
> —AKBh 9, LVP1 461

The Mīmāṃsā opponent, in defense of their claim that powers are cognized only by *arthâpatti* and not by *anumāna*, responding (TS 1590–1) to the example of the sense faculties says that even here, since powers are themselves imperceptible (at least in the case of hearing and the like), there is no prior cognition of co-occurrence of a power and its effects, as there is in the case of fire and smoke. This means that there is no evidence that the reason property is pervaded by the target property. Neither is there cognition of the power at the time of the inference, since it is the point of the inference to establish the existence of that power. Thus, there can be no establishing of the pervasion necessary for a valid *anumāna*. The opponent also asks why Śāntarakṣita should now (TS 1616) say that the existence of the faculty of hearing is "arrived at" (*gamyate*), when he said earlier that its existence is "proven" (*sādhyate*). Kamalaśīla responds:

> What is established is that auditory cognition, etc., as subject (*dharmin*), depends on another cause, for there can be absence of auditory cognition even when such other causes of auditory cognition etc. as attention etc. are present. Here is the argument: When something arises only sometimes, there is dependence of that on another cause, just as the sprout that appears only sometimes when there is soil, etc. And there is auditory cognition etc. only sometimes when attention, etc., occur. This is a reason from intrinsic nature (*svabhāva*). This dependence on another cause having been established, this other cause is what is generally known (*prasiddha*) as the faculty of hearing etc., in this way it is said that existence is arrived at, the alleged fault does not arise.
>
> —TSP *ad* TS1617, K 463

This looks like no more than a recapitulation of Vasubandhu's reasoning, but there are two important differences. First, he adds that the faculty of hearing is "generally known" and so is available to fill the explanatory gap left by the failure of the assemblage of perceptible cause and conditions to be invariably succeeded by the effect. And second, while Vasubandhu's inference turned on the presence or absence of the "additional factors" of soil, moisture, and warmth, Kamalśīla's involves cases where a sprout fails to arise even when the additional factors are present. Concerning the first point, how exactly is the existence of such a faculty "generally known"? Such "general knowledge" would seem to depend on precisely the postulation of a hidden cause that accounts for the variation in the occurrence of auditory cognition. The inference that both Vasubandhu and Kamalaśīla claim explains our knowing that there is such a thing as a hearing faculty looks like a *post hoc* reconstruction. It may explain how someone might learn from others what is meant by "auditory faculty," but it does not explain how an auditory faculty first came to be posited. Their inference relies on the principle that an explanatory gap may be accounted for by positing something unobserved. But in a valid *anumāna*, the cognizer must have evidence that the principle being utilized holds—that the reason property is pervaded by the property to be proven. Where was this evidence obtained? Certainly not from observation of the co-occurrence of otherwise inexplicable phenomena and hidden explainers. There is no such thing as observation of hidden explainers.[11]

This point is bolstered by the second difference. Vasubandhu's defense of the inference to the existence of sense faculties involves the differing results obtained due to the seed's being in the presence or absence of soil and so on; these "additional factors" are observable. Kamalaśīla's defense turns on the point that even when those additional factors are present, the seed may fail to germinate. This brings the seed example closer to the target inference of sense faculties. What one infers in the case of the seed is that there must be some hidden defect in the non-germinating seeds that explains their failure to produce a sprout even in the presence of the additional factors of soil and so on. Modern botanists can tell through close inspection whether or not a seed has the capacity to germinate. But for Śāntarakṣita and Kamalaśīla, the positing of such a capacity would have been a shot in the dark.

It may be worthwhile to consider the metaphysics underlying this dispute. First, we have seen that while in the case of fire Kamalaśīla explicitly rejects the positing of a power as something existing over and above the fire that is said to possess it, he sides with Vasubandhu in positing an auditory faculty as something distinct from the hearing organ. This is odd considering Dharmakīrti's categorical rejection of powers from his ultimate ontology. Momentariness plays a role in that rejection, but so too does the "Humean" view of causation that is first articulated by Vasubandhu. Ābhidharmikas may have felt compelled to include the sense faculties in their lists of ultimately real entities because the Buddha mentioned them in his account of the arising of cognition. Yogācāra-Sautrāntika, though, is much more parsimonious in its ontology. To claim that the sense faculties can only be known through inference is to concede that faculties occupy a distinct ontological niche. Why not simply hold that

[11] Just to reiterate, the point here is not that pervasion of the reason property by the property to be proven must be known with apodictic certainty. The point is rather that in an *anumāna* the cognizer must have some grounds for thinking that pervasion holds. Otherwise their thought-transition might be no more than a lucky guess.

the variation in occurrence of auditory cognition is due to some (as yet) unmanifest factor present in the hearing but absent in the deaf? To call this factor a faculty, and thus a kind of power, is to fall into the trap of reintroducing the discredited notion of a necessary connection between cause and effect.[12]

Mīmāṃsakas were happy to make room for powers in their ontology. On this point, I think later Buddhists' general bias against powers is more supportable.[13] Nevertheless, there is still something to be said for the Mīmāṃsā position. What we now know to be missing in the deaf and present in the hearing are the right physical and neural connections among the parts of the auditory apparatus. Since classical Indian philosophers lacked the technologies we now use to detect those features, it is not surprising that they should have stopped with the posit of a faculty. There is, though, something to be said for understanding this positing as the result of *arthâpatti* and not *anumāna*. Understood in the first way, it might be seen as an invitation for further empirical inquiry. The second route leads to the termination of inquiry; if the auditory faculty is something that can only be cognized through *anumāna*, and perception and *anumāna* have non-overlapping domains,[14] then empirical investigation is pointless. Indeed, further empirical inquiry has revealed not only that there is such a thing as the auditory faculty, but also that it is multiply realizable: it is normally realized in the collective functioning of parts of the ear and brain, but can also be realized in a cochlear implant as well. When the positing of a power is treated not as terminating inquiry but as inviting further empirical investigation, this can result in the discovery of an underlying mechanism. That in turn can reveal other ways in which the same function might be performed.

A similar point could be made about the case for positing a power to burn in fire. Since we are unlikely to take seriously the case for variation supposedly posed by "fire in the belly," the claim that fire possesses a power to burn looks rather like the sort of thing Moliere lampoons (in "The Imaginary Invalid") when he has a physician explain the efficacy of a sleeping draught by claiming it has a "dormitive virtue." But the further empirical investigation spurred by positing a power to burn has yielded important results. Among other things, it has shown that the same mechanism at work in the combustion of wood in the stove is also responsible for the heat generated by the digestion of food in the belly (and elsewhere in the body). Of course, we no longer think of digestion as a case of fire. But then the same investigation also shows that "fire" is not a natural-kind term. What we call "fire" is a sufficiently rapid and sustained process of combustion, and there can be no answer to the question just how rapid and sustained this must be to count as fire. To stop at the positing of a

---

[12] Candrakīrti has much to say about this in MAV 6.56–66.

[13] The bias against real powers is at least more supportable as a principle governing what goes into our ultimate ontology, the base that grounds our conventional ways of talking and thinking about the world. The positing of powers, though, may prove useful at the higher levels. We discuss below how this could impact Madhyamaka.

[14] The claim that perception and *anumāna* take radically distinct kinds of object (the *svalakṣaṇa* or unique particular, and the *sāmānya-lakṣaṇa* or object-in-general) is foundational for Yogācāra-Sautrāntika epistemology. Diṅnāga's argument for this claim is at PS 1.2. Mīmāṃsā follows Nyāya in holding that the cognitive instruments have overlapping domains; a given object may be cognized by two or more distinct epistemic instruments.

power may seem metaphysically extravagant, but if such a posit triggers further empirical inquiry, postulating a combustive virtue may be its own reward.[15]

2.2. *Devadatta*

The case of the Devadatta inference may be understood in one of two ways. It can be understood as proceeding from someone's testimony that the corpulent Devadatta does not eat during the day or as proceeding from the cognizer's own observations and non-observations. Let us consider the first, as resulting from testimony. As is well known, Buddhist epistemologists try to reduce the case of testimonial knowledge to an *anumāna* inference to the speaker's intention. As we will see below, the Bhāṭṭa account of meta-cognition gives us some reason to wonder just how a speaker's intentions are known if not by *arthâpatti*. But even if we were to waive this difficulty, special problems arise in cases of conversational implicature, which is how the Devadatta testimonial inference must be construed. Śāntarakṣita and Kamalaśīla wish to construe it in this way:

> Alternatively, the sentence "Fat Devadatta does not eat during the day," taken literally (*anvaya-vākya*), as an effect-reason (*kārya-hetu*), bringing about the inference of a particular intention to speak as cause, by inference from a property of the sign, because of the capacity of something modified like wood in the case of smoke, the implicated sentence "He eats at night" is also obtained, but not directly, as he (Śāntarakṣita) says,
>
> > 1631: Or the speaker's intention to reveal a second sentence is inferred,
> >
> > And by means of this, from the literal sentence the implicated (*vyatireka*) [sentence] is obtained.
>
> "by means of this" = but not directly by means of inference from the reason property. For such a desire to speak, inferred from the literal sentence, also manifests an implicated sentence within itself. Otherwise, if nocturnal eating were not meant to be brought up, and what was wished to be communicated was only the denial of eating, then "Devadatta does not eat" would just be said; nothing about the day and being fat. [This is how] the implicated sentence is obtained.
>
> —TSP *ad* TS 1630–1, K 466–7

The reference to wood's being modified in the case of the fire inference concerns the fact that, according to their conception, smoke is caused by fire only when the fuel is wet. The inference of fire on the hill consequently supplies additional information about the hill: that the fire located there burns wet wood. The "modification" in the testimony concerning Devadatta is the speaker's mentioning of Devadatta's corpulence and their specifying that the non-observation of eating only pertains to what is observed "during the day." From this, one might reasonably infer that the

---

[15] As is well known from the history of science, sometimes a positing will pan out, other times it does not. Consider the postulation of phlogiston. The "dark energy" currently posited in astrophysics in order to explain otherwise inexplicable facts about the expansion of the universe is a case where the jury is still out.

speaker intends to communicate not only that Devadatta is not seen to eat, but also that Devadatta is a stealth eater, that he indulges in unobserved eating at night. It would be reasonable to attribute this intention to the speaker given the assumption that they abide by the Gricean maxims of conversation. Otherwise their speech act is simply too verbose.

While it would be reasonable to attribute this communicative intention to the speaker, the attribution is defeasible. The speaker may, after all, just be verbose. The inference involved in a conversational implicature is always ampliative; the information contained in the conclusion exceeds that in the premises. Of course any inference concerning a speaker's intention is risky. The speaker may be using a bizarre idiolect, may (like a parrot) lack any intention at all in uttering the words, or may simply misspeak. Still, suppose someone were to utter the following: "There is smoke on the hill, and wherever there is smoke there is fire." It would be distinctly uncharitable to deny that the speaker intended to communicate that there is fire on the hill, and far less so to deny that the speaker of the Devadatta sentence intended to communicate that Devadatta eats at night. For consider that one might say, "While the corpulent Devadatta does not eat during the day, I am not sure he eats at night either." But something akin to Moore's Paradox would result if one were to say, "While smoke is universally pervaded by fire, and there is smoke on the hill, I am not sure there is fire on the hill."[16] Kamalaśīla's appeal to conversational implicature backfires; it strengthens the case for the Devadatta inference being abductive.

What happens when we take the Devadatta inference as one's own thought-transition and thereby leave questions of the speaker's intention out of the picture? Here the case for the reduction of *arthâpatti* to *anumāna* might seem stronger. That Devadatta must have eaten to stay corpulent seems like a reasonable assumption. Granted, the connection between eating and staying fat is not airtight: consider the secret imbiber, or Bibendum ("Michelin Man"). But these could be easily dismissed as cooked-up counter-examples, so let us grant the connection. The question remains of how it is that we have come to believe that unobserved eating must be posited in order to explain Devadatta's continuing obesity. Our evidence for a connection stems from observed cases: the correlation of continued corpulence with observed eating and loss of corpulence with observed non-eating. What we lack is evidence of a correlation between continued corpulence and only unobserved eating. Current knowledge of the facts of nutrition and human metabolism may convince us that there is such a connection. The theories in play here may well be correct. The point, though, is that it is these theories, and not direct observations, that lead to our confident postulation of Devadatta's nocturnal eating. The Sanskrit term for this activity of postulating, *kalpanā*, ordinarily means "imagining" or "fabricating." While the fire on the hill cognized through *anumāna* is unseen and so in a sense may be said to be imagined, one must have seen fires (in connection with smoke) in order to perform the inference. One never experiences unobserved eating; it is something one can only imagine. This is the hallmark of *arthâpatti*.

---

[16] Moore's Paradox concerns the fact that while sentences of the form "*p*, but X does not believe that *p*" may often hold, they necessarily fail in the first-person case. One cannot assert "*p*, but I do not believe that *p*."

2.3. *Caitra*

We come now to the most difficult case, that of the Caitra inference. Here, I want to do two things. First, I shall look at what Śāntarakṣīta and Kamalaśīla have to say specifically about this inference, comparing their case for reducing it to *anumāna* to Kumārila's case for taking it to represent a distinct form of inference. Then I want to stand back from the specific details of the dispute and ask why it might be important to distinguish between the two as different epistemic instruments. As we will see, Kumārila's strategy in defending the Caitra inference as an *arthâpatti* is to argue that there is no way to establish the additional premise that would be needed to give the inference the form of a logically valid argument. Yet when we reconstruct the reasoning that we think is involved in the Caitra inference, it certainly appears sound. What might resolve the tension in this otherwise inexplicable conjunction?

There is a lack of clarity concerning exactly what form the Caitra inference takes. This much is clear: on cognizing that Caitra is not at home, one infers that he is elsewhere. What is not clear is whether Caitra is already known to be alive when one performs the inference. On some later formulations of the inference, it is said that one knows that he is alive through testimony. Indeed, if the evidence of Caitra's absence were itself obtained through testimony, one might take the testifier's use of the name "Caitra" as evidence that Caitra is alive. But Kumārila himself does not include Caitra's living as part of the evidence base for the inference. In fact, he says that when one knows of Caitra's absence from the house, to know as well that he is alive is tantamount to knowing he is elsewhere, so all reason for inferring his being somewhere else would be missing were one to know both things (ŚV AP 28). Still, it is clear that the success of the *arthâpatti* depends on Caitra's being alive, for his absence from home might equally be explained by his being dead. But this seeming disparity may be due to the fact that there can be a gap between one's evidence base and what must in fact obtain for there to be epistemic success. In the case of the fire *anumāna*, one could never cognize smoke's being universally pervaded by fire because no one could ever inspect all instances of smoke, past, present, and future. Yet the successful performance of this inference, *qua anumāna*, depends on the pervasion actually holding. It's the same in the case of the Caitra inference. Where Caitra is indeed alive, one who correctly postulates his being out on the basis of his not being home but without first ascertaining that he is indeed alive can still be said to have a veridical cognition that is caused in the right way. There is luck involved here because Caitra's absence from the house might instead have been the consequence of his untimely demise. But there is also luck involved in accepting the pervasion of smoke by fire, given the limited sample on which that acceptance is based.

Let us now look at what Śāntarakṣita and Kamalaśīla have to say about the Caitra inference. Regarding TS 1645, Kamalaśīla comments as follows:

> This [verse shows that *arthâpatti*] is another form of *anumāna*. For here Caitra is the locus (*pakṣa*), being outside is the target property (*sādhya*), and being alive but not in the house is an effect-reason (*hetu*). A man standing outside the house is the similar example, but one inside the house is the dissimilar example. This is ascertained just from the examples. And the reason is not unestablished. For

> being unconnected with the house is ascertained by means of non-apprehension of what is perceptible, but being alive is established by consent of the other. Ultimately, however, the reason is doubtful. For there is no epistemic instrument of any sort that ascertains his being alive. "But it was said that there are such [epistemic instruments as] testimony and the like." In that case his being outside is ascertained due to the epistemic instruments of testimony, etc., why bother with performing an *arthâpatti*? Thus, it follows from what the opponent affirms that the reason is proven whereby *arthâpatti* is shown to be subsumed under *anumāna*.
>
> —TSP 1645, K 470

This describes two different ways of understanding the inference as an *anumāna*: without and with knowledge, respectively, of Caitra's being alive. On the first reading, Caitra's being alive is not independently known, but is merely assumed (i.e., "by consent of the other"; why, after all, would one be looking for Caitra at home if one didn't take it as given that he is alive?) Kamalaśīla says this inference fails on the grounds that the alleged reason property, being alive but not in the house, is open to doubt, which is a generally acknowledged defect in reason-properties. If we doubted that it was smoke over the hill, and not mist or a cloud of midges, we would not infer that there is fire on the hill.[17]

Some later Bhāṭṭas seek to resolve this issue by introducing the claim that Caitra is known by testimony to be alive (e.g., by the words of a reliable astrologer). Kamalaśīla responds that in this case Caitra is known to be outside by means of testimony, so that this example gives us no reason to posit *arthâpatti* as a distinct epistemic instrument. But there is a difficulty here too. As mentioned above (in connection with the Devadatta inference), for Yogācāra-Sautrāntikas (like Śāntarakṣita), knowledge obtained by testimony is through an inference to a speaker's intention. And as we shall soon see, there is some reason to think that mental states such as intentions can only be known by *arthâpatti*. If so, then this strategy would fail to show that the Caitra inference does not involve *arthâpatti*.

Once again, let us waive this point however. Construed as an *anumāna*, the Caitra inference would then look like this:

1. Caitra is elsewhere
2. because Caitra is alive but not at home,
3. and everyone who is alive but not at home is elsewhere.

The question is how (3) is known. Here is an immediate difficulty: one never has evidence both of someone's being alive but not at home and of their being somewhere else. When we observe (the living) Caitra's absence from his home, we do not simultaneously observe his being elsewhere. When we observe (the living) Caitra's presence away from home, we do not simultaneously observe his absence from

[17] Śālikanātha would add that Caitra cannot serve as locus insofar as he is not cognized at the time of performing the inference. But we forgo discussion of the question of what could count as the locus of the inference if it were construed as an *anumāna*.

home. (3) could only be obtained from the more general principle, (4) Every living person is located at one and only one place at a time. Or perhaps from the even more general principle, (4a) Every existing physical object is located at one and only one place at a time.

But how might (4a) be known? We might be tempted to suppose that it is known *a priori* in virtue of its being analytic. But not only is the notion of the *a priori* unknown to Indian epistemologists,[18] we also now know just how deeply problematic the idea of analyticity is.[19] Take the statement "Nothing is both red and green all over," which is supposedly known *a priori*. We accept the statement as true. Is this something that we take to be true in virtue of our knowledge of the meanings of "red" and "green"? We know that something that is red all over can also be vermillion all over, so why not green? The difficulty at the heart of analyticity is that it is not at all clear where the meanings of words leave off and empirical knowledge about the referents begins. This is the difficulty that haunts all attempts to explain just what a concept is, and it should be no surprise that the same difficulty infects the notion of analytic truth; they are one and the same problem.

We can likewise discard the idea that (4a) is known *a priori* in virtue of its being logically true. Water is physical, yet water is present at distinct places simultaneously. It might be objected that while water is physical, it is not properly thought of as a physical *object* but rather as a physical substance; "water" is a mass noun. Perhaps, it might be said, it is *a priori* that every physical object (a category that includes persons such as Caitra) is located either here or somewhere else. But this raises the question of how we come to apply the distinct categories *physical object* and *physical substance* to physical things. How do we know to assign rocks, cows, and persons to the first category, and water, air, and soil to the second?

Here there may be a lesson to be extracted from the distinct but related question of how children come to learn the principles of conservation we routinely apply to physical objects. Consider the child who first observes a toy duck, then does not see a duck (it being occluded by a screen), then once again observes a toy duck on the other side of the screen. As Millikan (2011) points out, the child must learn to describe their observations as first "duck" and then "more duck," before they can conceptualize what they see as first "duck" and then "the same duck." That physical objects are substances that can persist through change of location is a bit of "common knowledge" that the child must acquire. Conservation principles like this play a fundamental role in our conceptual scheme, and this may help account for the intuition that they are known *a priori*. But the child's mastery is an achievement, not something preordained. The metaphysics developed by Buddhist momentarists in

[18] Part of the difficulty here stems from the fact that modern epistemology treats knowledge as a disposition, whereas classical Indian epistemology is concerned with particular knowledge episodes. It makes little sense to say that one knows that 2+2=4 before a first case of counting if "know" is taken in the episodic sense. But there is also the fact that Indian epistemologists generally impose a "new knowledge" requirement: if one has already seen the fire on the hill, then inferring its occurrence would not count as a case of a knowledge episode.

[19] That is, the idea that some statements are known to be true just in virtue of the meanings of the constituent words.

conjunction with their mereological nihilism reveals that the concept of persisting physical objects is but one of a number of different ways in which we might organize our sensory experience so as to make it more tractable. The object at one moment is, the Buddhist metaphysician claims, a bundle of tropes. The object that persists over time is a sequence of such bundles, a sequence that obeys certain replacement rules. The synchronic and diachronic bundling are done (by us) to lighten the cognitive load when trying to anticipate future experience. Once we have adopted the scheme that features persisting physical objects, the relevant conservation principles will seem to be known *a priori*. But the scheme is optional.

This point may help clarify the otherwise puzzling Bhāṭṭa claim that one only knows that the sun moves by performing an *arthâpatti*. One sees the sun in the east at dawn, then overhead at midday, and infers that the sun has moved during the morning. Although some might balk at the general Mīmāṃsā position that actions are never cognized by perception (the position that motivates their view about meta-cognition, that cognitions are never directly cognized), it makes a certain amount of sense in the case of the sun's movement. The displacement is simply too gradual to be noticeable by direct observation. But why should this be a case of *arthâpatti* and not *anumāna*? The answer is that for it to be the latter, we must be able to establish pervasion between what is observed (the two positions at different times) and what is unobserved (motion), something we now know we cannot do. We must also be able to confirm that the sun we see at midday is the same object we saw at dawn. And how is that to be done, given the possibility that the momentarist thesis is true: that at each instant there is a new entity? To assert diachronic identity between the two seen objects is precisely to affirm that what we saw at dawn has since moved. This echoes Kumārila's remark that to know Caitra is alive is precisely to know that he is elsewhere. Apparently in the case of *arthâpatti*, the transition from the puzzling phenomena to the postulation of something that resolves the puzzle is a direct one and not via a covering law or general principle.

Up to this point, we have discussed the part of common sense that derives from the conservation principles for physical objects. The localization principles behind (4a) are distinct from the conservation principles involved in our notion of persisting objects. But we know that the part of our conceptual scheme behind (4a) is likewise optional; certain quantum phenomena violate (4a). Moreover, we might have stipulated that location is among the identity conditions for physical objects, so that when the living Caitra is absent from the house (i.e., when the house is qualified by the absence of Caitra), it is not Caitra but Caitra* who is located elsewhere. To make such a scheme workable, we might also stipulate that there may be temporal gaps in the existence of persisting physical objects. This is clearly not our way of organizing the phenomena, but it is a possible way of doing so. (4a) is not known *a priori*. And since (3) cannot be known through observation alone but would instead require the support of some more general principle, it follows that the Caitra inference cannot be an *anumāna*.

These considerations shed some light on what *arthâpatti* is. Datta (1997: 205) suggested that *arthâpatti* has important affinities with Kant's account of how synthetic *a priori* propositions are known. This goes too far. Synthetic *a priori* propositions are said to be true by necessity, and there is no such thing as logical necessity in classical Indian philosophy. The idea, though, of states of affairs that hold in virtue of our using a certain conceptual scheme may be on the right track. We are told that once one has performed the relevant *arthâpatti*, the result grounds knowledge of the pervasion necessary if one is to perform an *anumāna*. This suggests that it is through *arthâpatti* that we acquire the cognitive habits that reflect the conceptual schemes constituting "common sense." These in turn inform our inferential practices, so that it will seem in retrospect as though general principles like (4a) have the right sort of epistemic pedigree.

One difficulty of this interpretation derives from Mīmāṃsā's metaphysical realism. It is important to the Mīmāṃsā project that the object cognized by a valid epistemic instrument be real in an ontologically robust sense. In the Mīmāṃsā scheme, such epistemic instruments as testimony and *arthâpatti* are capable of giving us epistemic access to states of affairs that, while not empirically accessible, are nonetheless just as real as the entities cognized through perception. Buddhists, by contrast, hold that at least some epistemic instruments take as objects entities that are mere conceptual constructions. This may help explain Śāntarakṣīta's and Kamalaśīla's resistance to the view that *arthâpatti* is distinct from and not reducible to *anumāna*. The Yogācāra-Sautrāntika view is that there are just two epistemic instruments: perception and *anumāna*. This is said to follow from the fact that there are just two kinds of object of cognition: the unique particular (the object of perception) and the object-in-general (the object of *anumāna*). The fire one would perceive were one on the hill is a robustly real particular; the fire one infers from seeing smoke over the hill is not. The latter is, instead, the conceptually constructed representation of what is common to the robustly real particular occurrences of fire. The enduring person Caitra and the motion of the sun are prime examples of what most Buddhists would call mere conceptual constructions, that is, products of a conceptual scheme that proves useful for creatures like us, but still not to be found in an inventory of how things are *anyway*, i.e., independently of the concepts that we happen to use.

There are, however, Buddhists who do not draw this distinction between ultimately real entities and mere conceptual constructions. Mādhyamikas claim that the project of serious ontology is seriously misguided. For them, to ask whether something exists is not to ask whether it is table-poundingly real, but rather to ask whether positing it is useful given our going theories. Mīmāṃsakas may take offense at the Madhyamaka claim that everything real is conceptually constructed. However, Madhyamaka drops the invidious "mere" from the claim, so that for them what is postulated through *arthâpatti* would be no less real than what is cognized in perception. That *arthâpatti* is, according to this interpretation, an ampliative inference would thus be no bar to its being a valid epistemic instrument.

3. META-COGNITION

I first became interested in the subject of *arthâpatti* when I encountered Kumārila's argument for the other-illumination (*para-prakāśa*) position on meta-cognition. His view is that one cognizes one's own cognition of an object (such as a pot) by performing an inference based on the fact that the object has the property of cognizedness (ŚV *Śūnya-vāda* 190–1). His theory is an instance of what is now known as a higher-order thought (HOT) account of meta-cognition. That is, cognition of one's own cognitions is not achieved reflexively, by the very cognition that cognizes the object, nor by a distinct act of introspection or "looking within" (as in a "higher-order perception" (HOP) account). Instead, one infers the occurrence of the cognition from the fact that the object's cognizedness would otherwise be inexplicable. This account runs counter to what Carruthers (2011) calls the transparency thesis. The transparency thesis is the widely shared view that each subject has privileged access to their own conscious mental states. Kumārila's response to the transparency thesis is that one's own conscious mental states should be no more transparent to oneself than are the mental states of other subjects. His point can be seen by considering the consensus view that the attribution of conscious states to others involves an inference from their behavior (including their verbal behavior). This means that such other-attributions involve criteria for application of the predicate "conscious." According to the transparency thesis, though, there are no criteria involved in the self-attribution of this predicate. Solipsism would then follow, since differences in criteria of application entail differences in the concepts being applied, i.e., what I take to be going on in the minds of others when I say that they are conscious would not be what I find in my own case. Since solipsism is absurd, the transparency thesis must be false. Cognition of one's own cognition must proceed in the same way as does the cognition of others' cognitions. And since on this view one never cognizes the co-occurrence of cognizedness and cognition (since one never cognizes cognition), the inference of the latter from an occurrence of the former must be a matter of *arthâpatti*.

Śāntarakṣita and Kamalaśīla themselves accept Diṅnāga's reflexivist account of meta-cognition (the *svasaṃvedana* thesis), and so are committed to the transparency thesis. But while Dharmakīrti strove mightily to show that solipsism does not follow from the reflexivity thesis, Ratnakīrti argues persuasively that *svasaṃvedana* does have this consequence. The basic difficulty here is that if cognitions are understood to be self-luminous or self-disclosing, and this disclosure is not a matter of the content being given to a subject (which it cannot be on a non-egological Buddhist account), then any establishment of the occurrence of cognition in distinct mental streams (*santāna*s) requires one to establish pervasion across distinct mental streams. The establishment of pervasion is required because for the followers of Diṅnāga *arthâpatti* reduces to *anumāna*, and there is no other epistemic instrument available, and the distinctness or otherness of mental streams is simply not given in experience. The argument here is reminiscent of the one attributed to Wittgenstein in the Appendix of Kripke (1982). On Kripke's telling, Wittgenstein's concern is that in the absence of a self to serve as subject of experience, to say what it is like for another to have the experience of, say, seeing blue, one must somehow subtract the element of first-person givenness that the transparency theorist builds into their account of one's own mental states. The difficulty is that the content of the state (the blue aspect) and first-person givenness (the noetic aspect) are inseparable. We have no idea what it would be like for blue to appear without its seeming to appear *for me* (or *in here*). Diṅnāga was right about this much: if cognitions are ownerless and reflexively aware, the grasped and grasping aspects of cognitions are ultimately non-distinct. But that in turn means that what we attribute to others when we say that they are conscious is something quite different from what we take ourselves to undergo in our own experiential lives.

Of course, we sometimes say that the mental states of others are also transparent to us. When someone announces they are leaving the room and then reaches for the doorknob, we immediately think of them as perceiving the doorknob and intending to grasp and turn it. Likewise, when we see someone grimace, we might even say that we feel their pain. This is, though, a response that is based on an interpretation of their behavior. Mind-reading may be so rapid as to feel direct, but only where the situation is stereotyped. We observe some physical objects in our environment behaving in ways that appear to be best explained by the hypothesis that they possess inner states that serve to control their behavior. When such hypotheses turn out to help us predict others' behavior, we come to supply them habitually. According to Kumārila's opacity thesis, the same holds for self-attributing cases of meta-cognition. Later Bhāṭṭas unpack what Kumārila calls the cognizedness of the object as availability for speech and action.[20] (The resulting view of consciousness anticipates what is nowadays called the "global availability" thesis.) The *arthâpatti* involved in meta-cognition works from my awareness of my uttering or thinking "There is the doorknob," or my reaching for the doorknob, to the hypothesis that a visual cognition brought it about that the doorknob came to be available as a target of my behavior. As with those other physical objects that we take to be sentient beings, in the case of self-attribution as well, the transition from observation to hypothesis proceeds from the point that the behavior of this physical object is otherwise inexplicable. And since supplying such an explanation enhances the valuable properties of self-monitoring, self-control, and self-revision, it also becomes habitual. We thus come to see ourselves as having rich mental lives to which we have privileged access.[21]

The key point about the sort of inference involved in the opacity-thesis account of meta-cognition is that it cannot be construed as involving an awareness that the property to be proved (there being a cognition of the object) is pervaded by the reason property (cognizedness of the object). If the argument that the reflexivity thesis leads to solipsism is right, then one is never directly aware of cognitions. Thus, there cannot be a class of observed instances of concomitance between cognizing an object on the one hand, and speech or action with respect to that object on the other.

---

[20] Unlike the Bhāṭṭas and like the Yogācāra-Sautrāntikas, the Prābhākara Mīmāṃsakas hold that cognition is self-illuminating and hence self-cognizing. Pārthasārathi, in dialogue with the Prābhākaras, grants that illumination is the intrinsic nature of cognition, and that the cognized object and cognizer are only illuminated through connection to cognition (ŚD 205). But insofar as cognitions are actions, which Mīmāṃsā holds are not perceptible (see the example of the motion of the sun), they can only be cognized through their effects. Since speech and action are only possible with respect to an object that is illuminated (ŚD 203), it follows that cognitions are to be cognized by means of the postulation of that which illuminates, namely cognition.

[21] There is now considerable empirical evidence to support the opacity thesis. A useful survey is Carruthers (2011). For discussion of support derived specifically from developmental cognitive psychology, see Bogdan (2010). On the connection between self-attribution and other-attribution, see also Graziano (2013).

The opponent might invoke the *kevala-vyatirekin* ("only negative") strategy as a way of maintaining that cognitions are cognized through an *anumāna*. If pervasion is invariable concomitance, then it can be known through the absence of the target property wherever the reason property is absent. But if we cannot directly cognize cognition, how are we to know that entities that neither speak of nor act with regard to objects also lack cognition? And if there can be no grounds for accepting pervasion, the inference cannot be an *anumāna*. It must instead be an abductive inference, an inference to the best explanation of an otherwise puzzling phenomenon.

One can understand the appeal of the reflexivist account of meta-cognition to Buddhists like Diṅnāga, given their non-self thesis. What else, in the absence of a self understood as cognitive agent, could serve to illuminate the occurrence of cognition? Given the additional Buddhist thesis of momentariness, it cannot be a subsequent introspective cognition. For, as Diṅnāga saw, a subsequent cognition can take an earlier cognition as its target object only by means of memory, and one does not remember what was not experienced earlier.[22] This difficulty, claim Yogācāra-Sautrāntikas, is resolved only by supposing that the target cognition experienced (i.e., cognized) itself. Support for the reflexivist view is only heightened when we add representationalism to the mix of Buddhist non-self, momentariness, and mereological nihilism. Central to the account of cognition in Yogācāra-Sautrāntrika is the claim that for a cognition to cognize its object is for it to take on the form of that object, e.g., the cognizing of blue color is just the occurrence of a cognition that represents blue by taking its form. In the absence of anything distinct from cognition that might serve as cognizing agent, it seems that seeing blue can only be the cognizing of this representation by the very cognition that bears the form. To see blue is for there to be the self-illumination of a blue mental image.

While this position has struck many as plausible, it has its own difficulties. First, the reflexivist account violates the well-attested principle of irreflexivity, to the effect that an entity cannot operate on itself, e.g., a fingertip cannot touch itself, a knife cannot cut itself, etc. The proposed counter-example, the light that illuminates itself as well as other things, is challenged on the grounds that a light could be said to be illuminated only if it were the sort of thing that might also exist in the unilluminated state; "illuminated" is a contrast term. In the absence of a valid counter-example to irreflexivity, it is difficult to see how it can be maintained that a cognition might cognize itself while also cognizing its intentional object.[23] A second difficulty is that the argument from memory fails to rule out a Kumārila-style HOT account of meta-cognition. On such an account, we explain the ability to remember a past experience not by appeal to some direct cognizing of the target cognition, but instead by positing an earlier cognition as what best explains our subsequent behavior, including the remembering itself. This is precisely Prajñākaramati's response to the objection that Śāntideva's rejection of reflexivism deprives him of the ability to account for meta-cognition. In fact, in giving his response to the argument from memory, Prajñākaramati

[22] Diṅnāga's argument is at PSV 11d, Dharmakīrti's is at PVin 1.40,11–41,13 *ad* 1.54cd.

[23] Buddhist mereological nihilism rules out such potential counter-examples to irreflexivity as the self-driving car. For discussion, see Siderits (2015: 97–126).

even uses language strikingly similar to the standard "inexplicable otherwise" of the Bhāṭṭa *arthâpatti* account. He says that "there would be absurd consequences otherwise" (*anyatra prasaṅga syād*), i.e., if cognition were not posited as the source of veridical episodic memory (*Pañjika ad* BCA 9.24cd).

Prajñākaramati is a Mādhyamika Buddhist, not an adherent of Diṅnāga's Yogācāra-Sautrāntika school. Other Mādhyamikas, such as Candrakīrti, acknowledge additional epistemic instruments beyond the two, perception and *anumāna*, accepted by Diṅnāga (see PP, LVP2 p. 75). *Arthâpatti* is not among the added epistemic instruments, but perhaps it should be. While Kumārila no doubt understood *arthâpatti* as committing one to the ultimate reality of whatever entities are posited in explaining the phenomenon in question, it need not be construed in this way. *Arthâpatti* instead might be construed as ontologically non-committal. Since Madhyamaka questions the coherence of anything other than purely provisional ontological commitments, such a feature would make *arthâpatti* more acceptable to Mādhyamikas. Perhaps the greatest challenge facing the Madhyamaka form of global anti-realism is to show how the rejection of the very idea of ultimate truth does not lead to a facile form of truth-relativism. How, for instance, is the rejection of the idea of mind-independent natures to be reconciled with the success of scientific reduction? If there can be no final way that things are *anyway*, how can one way of conceptualizing the world be better than another? Acknowledging an ontologically non-committal *arthâpatti* would help by showing how, at a certain stage of inquiry, one might postulate an as-yet unobserved entity, such as a sense faculty, in order to explain what is observed. That the entity in question is merely postulated will spur further inquiry, which may in turn lead to discovery of an underlying mechanism. Exploration of this deeper level may raise new questions, requiring further acts of postulation, and so on. One need not suppose that this process will terminate.

One might wonder whether this "provisional commitment" reading of *arthâpatti* leaves intact its status as an epistemic instrument. If further inquiry should reveal that, say, there is ultimately no such thing as an auditory faculty (due to its being multiply realized), would this not render the inference that led to its positing a mere pseudo-*arthâpatti*? An inference leading to a false judgment cannot be an epistemic instrument, and in this case the judgment that there is an auditory faculty would turn out to have been, strictly speaking, false. But a Mādhyamika can reply that the *arthâpatti* leading to this judgment is valid at the level of analysis at which it is conducted. And Madhyamaka's global anti-realism renders moot the question whether it is ultimately ("strictly speaking") valid. Recognizing *arthâpatti* as a distinct cognitive instrument would enable Madhyamaka to explain away the idealist's (as well as the dualist's) table-pounding insistence that mental states are ultimately real.

This leads to a final reason for a Buddhist to embrace an *arthâpatti*-based opacity account of meta-cognition, one that appeals to their soteriological aims. Buddhists claim that liberation from existential suffering is attained by coming to see what they call the "I"-sense (the sense of an inner subjective realm) as illusory. Reflexivist accounts of meta-cognition, particularly when joined with the subjective idealism of Yogācāra, tend to have the unfortunate side-effect of valorizing the "I"-sense. An *arthâpatti*-based opacity account, by contrast, allows one to explain the widely shared intuition that there is an inner subjective realm—positing cognition turns out to be a useful way to enhance self-control and promote social coordination—while at the same time avoiding hypostatization of the attribution of mental states.

Here is one last point concerning the opacity thesis. In their discussions of the Devadatta and Caitra inferences, Śāntarakṣita and Kamalaśīla raise the question of whether these are to be understood as involving testimony or instead as inferences one performs for oneself. The first possibility brings in their view that what one comes to know through testimony is not the state of affairs denoted by a statement, but rather the intention of the speaker to assert that this state of affairs obtains. But we can now ask how one learns to attribute a certain assertoric intention to a speaker who utters certain words. We could all agree that one is never directly aware of the communicative intentions of others. Do we learn to associate utterances with communicative intentions from correlations between the two in our own case? If the opacity thesis is true, then one is never directly aware of one's own communicative intentions either. Access to communicative intentions, it seems, is acquired through *arthâpatti*. The view of testimonial knowledge that Śāntarakṣita and Kamalśīla use to reduce the Devadatta and Caitra inferences to *anumāna* turns out to require the use of *arthâpatti*. The reduction fails.

4. CONCLUSION

I have said little about the difference between *arthâpatti* and *anumāna* that was not already said by Datta (1997). He also makes an important point about what follows from *arthâpatti*'s being an epistemic instrument. He says that when an abductive inference fails to deliver what is in fact the best explanation, this does not "prove that the principle of *arthâpatti* is defective . . . it shows only a defect in the practical application of the principle" (1997: 205–6). When we explain the otherwise inexplicable by positing something that does not in fact obtain, our failure simply shows our procedure to have been a mere pseudo-*arthâpatti*. If there is anything here that is genuinely new, it is only my attempt to explain the temptation to reduce *arthâpatti* to *anumāna*. We learned from Frege not to psychologize logic, and surely he was right to insist that logic is a purely formal science. But when the bias against empirical psychology extends to the theory of inference understood as an epistemic achievement, the lesson may have been taken too far. That cases of *arthâpatti* can be reconstructed as instantiating valid arguments does not validate their reduction to *anumāna*s. In epistemology, we must also consider the situation of the epistemic agent.

Śāntarakṣita and Kamalaśīla see *arthâpatti* as a variant formulation of *anumāna*, something with the form of a deductively valid argument. The other point that might be worth emphasizing here is that strictly formal considerations also warn against trying to understand *arthâpatti* as distinct from *anumāna* but also, like the latter, a form of inference that instantiates a formally valid argument scheme. I believe the Bhāṭṭas are right to claim that there is no way to establish pervasion between an observed property and an unobserved property. Without knowledge of pervasion, one could never establish the universally quantified conditional (or the disjunction) needed to arrive at new knowledge. And the unquantified conditional (or disjunction) cannot be established as a premise without either begging the question or appealing to the problematic notion of *a priori* knowledge. Inferences of such forms as, for instance, "$p \wedge q \vdash p$" do instantiate logically valid argument forms, and here the premise can be established without reliance on knowledge of pervasion. But inferences of this sort do not deliver what would count as new knowledge. The prospects for finding a deductively valid alternative to *anumāna* strike me as dim. But once again, that is not an obstacle to counting *arthâpatti* as a distinct epistemic instrument.

ABBREVIATIONS AND REFERENCES

AKBh	*Abhidharma-kośa-bhāṣya* of Vasubandhu. LVP1 = *L'Abhidharmakośa de Vasubandhu*, ed. Louis de La Vallée Poussin, Louvain: Istas, 1923–31 (Société Belge d'Études orientales).
MAV	*Madhyamakâvatāra-kārikā*, ed. L. Xuezhu, chap., 6 *Journal of Indian Philosophy* 43 (2015): 1–30.
PP	*Prasanna-padā* of Candrakīrti. LVP2 = *Mūlamadhyamakakārikās (Mādhyamikasūtras) de Nāgārjuna avec la Prasannapdā Commentaire de Candrakīrti*, ed. Louis de la Vallée Poussin, Osnabrück: Biblio Verlag, 1970.
PS	*Pramāṇa-samuccaya*. In *Dignāga's Pramāṇasamuccaya, Chapter 1: A hypothetical reconstruction* by Ernst Steinkellner, https://www.oeaw.ac.at/fileadmin/Institute/IKGA/PDF/forschung/buddhismuskunde/dignaga_PS_1.pdf.
PV	*Pramāṇa-vārttika*, ed. Raniero Gnoli, Rome: Istituto Italiano per il Medio od Estremo Oriente, 1960.
PVin	*Pramāṇa-viniścaya*. In *Dharmakīrti's Pramāṇaviniścaya. Chapters 1 and 2*, ed. E. Steinkellner, Beijing and Vienna: China Tibetology Publishing House, 2007.
ŚD	*Śāstra-dīpikā*, ed. Śāstri, Kashi: Bidyabilas, Press, 1975.
ŚV	*Śloka-vārttika*, ed. Dvarikadas Sastri, Prāchyabhārati Series 10, Varanasi: n.p., 1978.
TS/TSP	*Tattva-saṃgraha* (= TS), *ed. with the Pañjikā* (= TSP) by Embar Krishnamacharya, Baroda: Oriental Institute, 1984 (= K).

Balcerowicz, P. (2003), "Is 'Inexplicability Otherwise' (*anyathânupapatti*) Otherwise Inexplicable?" *Journal of Indian Philosophy* 31: 343–80.

Bogdan, R. J. (2010), *Our Own Minds: Sociocultural Grounds for Self-consciousness*, Cambridge, MA: MIT Press.

Carruthers, P. (2011), *The Opacity of Mind*, Oxford: Oxford University Press.

Datta, D. M. (1932), *The Six Ways of Knowing: A Critical Study of the Advaita Theory of Knowledge*, Kolkata: University of Calcutta Press.

Granoff, P. (2018), "Chance and Causality: Of Crows, Palm Trees, God and Salvation," *Journal of Indian Philosophy* 46: 399–418.

Graziano, M. (2013), *Consciousness and the Social Brain*, Oxford: Oxford University Press.

Kripke, S. (1982), *Wittgenstein on Rules and Private Language*, Cambridge, MA: Harvard University Press.

Matilal, B. K. (1986), *Perception: An Essay on Classical Indian Theories of Knowledge*, Oxford: Oxford University Press.

Millikan, R. (1998), "A common structure for concepts for individuals, stuffs and real kinds: more mama, more milk and more mouse," *Behavioral and Brain Science* 21: 55–65.

Phillips, S. H. (2017), "Fallacies and Defeaters in Early Navya Nyāya," in J. Tuske (ed.), *Indian Epistemology and Metaphysics*, 33–52, London: Bloomsbury Academic.

Siderits, M. (2003), "Deductive, Inductive, Both or Neither?" *Journal of Indian Philosophy* 31: 303–21.

Siderits, M. (2015), *Personal Identity and Buddhist Philosophy: Empty Persons*, 2nd edn, Farnham, Surrey: Ashgate.

Tillemans, T. (2005), "The Slow Death of the *trairūpya* in Buddhist Logic: *A propos* of Saskya Pandita," *Vergleichende Studien zur japanischen Kultur* 11: 83–93.

CHAPTER TWELVE

Arthâpatti: An Anglo-Indo-Analytic Attempt at Cross-Cultural Conceptual Engineering

ANAND VAIDYA

1. CROSS-CULTURAL CONCEPTUAL ENGINEERING

In a series of papers (2010, 2012, and 2015) I have articulated and defended a philosophical methodology called **ACE**. On this approach to philosophy one uses analytical, experimental, and cross-cultural methods in combination with one another, to provide the non-academic public with a comprehensive understanding of a phenomenon in the human condition, such as the nature of knowledge. The central thesis of the method is the following:

> **ACE**: A combination of analytical, experimental, and cross-cultural approaches to philosophy is superior to any one of these philosophical approaches alone when the purpose of the philosophical engagement is to deliver to a reasonably informed audience a comprehensive understanding of a phenomenon.

The combinatorial claim used in ACE holds that if analytical, experimental, and cross-cultural methods are each independently good for exploring a phenomenon, then, assuming their combination causes no problems, the joint use of them yields a more robust understanding of the phenomenon than any of the methods alone. However, ACE can be used for purposes other than generating a comprehensive understanding of a pre-given phenomenon. The *constructive* use of ACE I call "cross-cultural conceptual engineering," **CCCE**. My account of CCCE builds on work by David Chalmers, who has emphasized the need for philosophers to engage in conceptual engineering as a philosophical enterprise of value over the more traditional project of conceptual analysis. Moreover, philosophical methodology can move away from analysis and towards engineering.

On the picture I favor, instead of asking "what is X," one should focus on the roles one wants X to play and see what can play that role. The roles in question

> here may in principle be properties of all sorts: so, one focuses on the properties one wants X to have, and figures out what has those properties. But very frequently, they will be causal roles, normative roles, and explanatory roles.
>
> —Chalmers, 2011: 563

For example, within the project of conceptual analysis, philosophers have asked, what is knowledge? And sought to provide an analysis of knowledge, such as through the tripartite analysis of knowledge as justified true belief. Within this program the primary task of philosophers is to debate whether an analysis of a concept is correct across all cases. By contrast, in conceptual engineering, philosophers seek to answer the question: What epistemic concept can we make or identify that fits certain roles in certain domains, given other concepts we have and the goals we want to achieve? In other words, rather than trying to find out what a given epistemic concept is either through *a priori analytic* analysis or *a posteriori experimental* analysis, we seek to engineer a concept for a certain use.

In what follows, I will be engaging in cross-cultural conceptual engineering, a variant of conceptual engineering that engages cross-cultural philosophy for the purposes of conceptual engineering. CCCE can be done in two ways. On *the uni-directional* approach, one exports concepts and debates from tradition A to B for the purposes of conceptual engineering within B. On the *bi-directional* approach, one takes concepts and debates from A and B in order to engineer a concept that can bring forward discussion across traditions, or serve a new role not yet explored by either tradition. In what follows I will use bi-directional cross-cultural conceptual engineering to lay the foundation for engineering an epistemic relation that I call "epistemic grounding." This relation is similar to the contemporary Western analytical distinction between the *ground* and the *grounded* and the classical Indian distinction between *ādhāra* and *ādheya*. Those distinctions, however, operate in the field of metaphysics. Here, I aim to engineer grounding for the purposes of epistemology. I will apply CCCE to the classical Indian debate over whether *arthâpatti* is an epistemic means for acquiring knowledge independently from *anumāna* and the contemporary analytic debate over whether inference to the best explanation is epistemically reducible to enumerative induction. From there I will move into a first attempt at the conceptual engineering of "epistemic grounding."

2. THE DEBATE ON *ARTHÂPATTI*

One of the central debates in classical Indian epistemology concerns the following question: what are the valid instruments for acquiring knowledge? Following Dunne (2004: 15–20), I will refer to these as *pramāṇa* debates. The central instruments of knowledge debated are perception (*pratyakṣa*), testimony (*śabda*), inference (*anumāna*), comparison (*upamāna*), yogic perception (*yoga-ja-pratyakṣa*), and postulation (*arthâpatti*).

Within the *pramāṇa* debates, there is a specific debate as to whether *arthâpatti* is a means of knowledge independent from that of (ia) inference alone, (iia) inference in combination with another instrument, or whether it is epistemically reducible to (ib) inference alone or (iib) inference in combination with another instrument. Many classical Indian philosophers, such as Kumārila, Gaṅgeśa, Cidānanda, Śālikanātha, and Jayanta discuss a variety of examples of *arthâpatti*. Some examples are frequently discussed, while others are seldom mentioned. Three of the main examples are the following:

Absent Caitra
One knows Caitra is not at home and thereby postulates that Caitra is outside.

Fat Caitra
One hears the sentence "Fat Caitra does not eat during the day" and thereby postulates either the sentence "He eats at night," or the fact that Caitra eats at night.

Fire
One perceives that fire burns and thereby postulates that fire has a capacity for burning.

One question in the classical and contemporary literature on this topic is: how should these examples be classified? For example, in the classical literature there is a classification according to the distinction between *śrutârthâpatti*, or *arthâpatti* on the basis of what is heard, and *dṛṣṭârthâpatti*, or *arthâpatti* on the basis of what is seen. According to this classification scheme, Fat Caitra involves a kind of *arthâpatti* distinct from what is found in the cases of Absent Caitra and Fire because of the difference between hearing and seeing. By contrast, in the contemporary literature, Kanaujia (1992: 166–7) claims that the examples should not be classified according to whether they are linguistic or non-linguistic (using sight for example, as opposed to sound). Rather, they should be classified by the difference between *arthâpatti* based on "linguistic unintelligibility," *arthâpatti* based on "factual unintelligibility," and *arthâpatti* based on "the unintelligibility of a contradiction." For our purposes here, we will not be concerned with which taxonomy is better. Rather, the point of displaying the examples and the different systems for distinguishing them is to show that the classical and contemporary theorists are concerned with answering the question: what exactly is the phenomenon in question?

3. THE ISSUE OF INFERENCE

In this section we will focus on the following question: what is inference, such that we can debate whether *arthâpatti* is independent of it? This question can be answered through two methods.

According to the "intra-framework approach," the question of independence is debatable only within the framework of classical Indian debates about instruments, and thus we cannot and should not engage it outside of Indian philosophy. On this view, it makes no sense to bring classical Indian philosophers and contemporary analytic philosophers into contact with each other if they don't share a common theory of inference.

According to the "inter-framework approach," the question of independence should be engaged across the two traditions because we can, through careful historical work, take account of background assumptions about "inference," which lead to important insights that feed bi-directional cross-cultural conceptual engineering. For the purposes of my project, I will be taking the inter-theoretic approach. It requires that we start with the question: Is "inference" a good translation of "*anumāna*"? Speaking to the question raised, both Siderits and Yoshimizu, in their contributions to this volume, provide critical considerations about the issue.

Siderits (this volume, p. 289) argues that the epistemic differences between *anumāna* and inference make "inference" a poor translation of "*anumāna*." On my account his argument is the following:

1. An inference, from the perspective of contemporary logic, can be deductively valid even if the conclusion is *false*.
2. An *anumāna*, from the perspective of classical Indian *pramāṇa* debates, cannot have a false conclusion.
3. When the logical and epistemic properties of terms from different languages are sufficiently different, it is not good to translate the terms as being equivalent across all contexts. In this case they are sufficiently different.

   ∴

4. For the purposes of epistemology, "inference" is not a good translation of "*anumāna*."

While Siderits' analysis is accurate, it is does not impede the inter-framework approach. Rather, it provides a point of departure for a deeper understanding of what issues are at play in the cognitive-epistemic environments in which we find discussions of inference and *anumāna*.

First, while Siderits' argument shows that *anumāna* is not an exact translation of the technical sense of "inference" used in logic, it does not show that "*anumāna*" is beyond the semantic range of the ordinary language use of "inference." The term "inference" is a common-sense notion. It is made technical and precise within a specific logical system by logicians. We should note that the contrast between *anumāna* and inference regarding the possibility of a false conclusion might be an advantage of the classical Indian conception, and something that ought to make us critically reflect on whether the Western logician's conception is useful in contexts where we have epistemic concerns. Importantly, we learn something powerful by bringing these distinct notions into contact with each other.

Second, there is enough "role similarity" between the two notions at the level of mental state transitions. It is not as if classical Indian epistemologists are talking about mind wandering, and contemporary Western epistemologists are talking only about deductive validity. Rather, both traditions are talking about human reasoning and offering accounts of what the goal of it is, and what makes an instance of human reasoning good.

In contrast to Siderits' epistemic considerations about translating "*anumāna*" as "inference," Yoshimizu (this volume, p. 225) points out some important logical considerations concerning Kumārila's account of the difference between *arthâpatti* and *anumāna*. These logical considerations provide insight into the difference between some classical Indian discussions of *arthâpatti* and *anumāna* in relation to how "inference" is used by Western logicians. On my account, Yoshimizu argues for the following points about Kumārila's view of *arthâpatti* and *anumāna*:

1. Throughout the whole process of *arthâpatti*, the unit of operation is always a sentence (proposition) that has the same subject, Caitra. Unlike Dignāga's *anumāna*, which makes use of a term logic, *arthâpatti* does not resort to the universal conditional statement that all those that have a certain property (*dharma*) have another property.
2. The conclusion of an *arthâpatti* is necessarily involved in the aggregate of its preconditions and is drawn on the grounds that they would not stand to reason if the conclusion were negated, in other words, by "not being possible otherwise" / "inexplicability otherwise" (*anyathânupapatti*).

From Yoshimizu's first observation, we can generate an insightful contrast between Kumārila's account of *arthâpatti* and typical discussions of "inference" by Western logicians.

If Kumārila is correct and *arthâpatti* applies to sentences while *anumāna* applies to terms, then we might ask, from the inter-theoretic framework: does Kumārila's account of *arthâpatti* differ from *anumāna* only because of the relata of those two systems, i.e., sentences vs. terms? If they differ only in virtue of their relata, this feature will not be sufficient to distinguish them as *two different ways of knowing* from the perspective of contemporary analytic epistemological discussions of logic. For example, in analytic epistemology, propositional logic and predicate logic are not taken to be distinct ways of knowing simply because of the structure of the logic of each. The fact that they are different because one is sub-sentential (predicate logic) and the other is sentential (propositional logic) and the rules of inference in predicate and propositional logic are different is not sufficient to lay claim to the view that they are two different ways of knowing. In the case of [if P, then Q; P; therefore Q], and in the case of [for all *x*, F*x*, then G*x*; F*x*; therefore G*x*], one knows by inference. Differences in inferential structure do not yield to differences in the way something is known. Rather, differences in inferential structure help determine whether the inference is good. However, where two inferences are good, and differ only in their structure, one still knows only by inference.

Yoshimizu's second observation forces us to go deeper into the background conditions that are in effect across classical Indian philosophy and contemporary analytic philosophy.

To start, if Kumārila is correct and *arthâpatti* is non-ampliative because the conclusion is contained in the premises and follows by necessity, then from the inter-theoretic framework it would be inappropriate to think that knowledge acquired by *arthâpatti* is either inductive or abductive. It would appear that *arthâpatti* is deductive and *anumāna* is something else. But if the former is deductive, what could the latter be? Let's look at the classic case of *anumāna* and see how it provides a taxonomical problem for Western logic.

It is well known that the classical account of *anumāna* presented by the founding father of the Nyāya school, Gautama Akṣapāda, holds that there are five steps in a good *anumāna*:

1. Thesis: There is a fire on the hill over there (not directly perceived).
2. Reason: There is smoke on the hill over there (directly perceived).

3. Pervasion: Wherever there is smoke there is fire, like in a kitchen when one is cooking and observes fire and smoke, and unlike on a lake where one never observes either fire or smoke.
4. Application: The case of smoke and fire is like the case of what is experienced in the kitchen.
5. Conclusion: There is a fire on the hill over there (not directly perceived).

Colonialist commentators on the Fire-Syllogism often negatively criticized it as a mixture of inductive and deductive reasoning. For example, A. H. Ritter (in 1838) wrote:

> One point alone appears certain, and that is, that they [the Nyāya] can lay but slight claims to accuracy of exposition. This is proved clearly enough by the form of their syllogism, which is made to consist of five instead of three parts. Two of these are manifestly superfluous, *while by the introduction of an example in the third the universality of the conclusion is vitiated.*
>
> —Ganeri 2001: 9, *emphasis added*

Ritter's critique is that step (3) introduces an example, which draws into question the nature of the claim in (3). For example, were the premise simply (3a) "Wherever there is smoke, there is fire," the argument would look more like a deductive one, where the conclusion, "There is fire on the hill over there," is correctly derived. However, by introducing the example, it seems as if step (3) is problematic, since it now looks as if the universal claim, "Wherever there is smoke, there is fire" is supported by an instance, which is *inductively* insufficient to support the universal claim. So, what is the correct classification of *anumāna* according to the distinction between ampliative and non-ampliative reasoning found in the West? If *arthâpatti* is deductive, thus non-ampliative, because the conclusion is contained in the premises, what is *anumāna*? Let me explore three options from the inter-theoretic frame.

The *rejection* option holds that it is neither, and not even a good way of arguing because it confuses ampliative and non-ampliative reasoning. The *mixed* option holds that it falls into more than one category or that it falls into neither category. Unlike the *rejection* option, the *mixed* option tries to save *anumāna* as a viable account of reasoning within the classic distinction between ampliative and non-ampliative reasoning. In contrast to these two options, the *confrontation* option holds that the standard form of *anumāna* as presented by Gautama challenges the adequacy or completeness of the Western distinction between ampliative and non-ampliative reasoning. That is, on Yoshimizu's reading of Kumārila, where *arthâpatti* is a form of reasoning involving sentences and *anumāna* is a form of reasoning focusing on terms, we are in a position to critically examine the Western philosophical view held by logicians, statisticians, and educators that maintains that the distinction between ampliative and non-ampliative reasoning is basic.

The alternative conception of how to carve up the space denies that the distinction between ampliative and non-ampliative is the basic distinction. Rather, the distinction between *anumāna* and *arthâpatti* is fundamental, because what one reasons upon, sentences vs. terms, is more fundamental than the kind of reasoning they engage in, ampliative vs. non-ampliative. One reason for adopting this view maintains that good reasoning requires both deductive and inductive support. Inductive support aims to captures which generalities we are to reason from. Deductive support helps us discover what follows from the generalizations. Moreover, a piece of reasoning is good only when it has both parts. What separates kinds of reasoning is what one is reasoning with: terms vs. sentences.

Let me now articulate four issues about inference that we must turn to in order to effectively use the inter-theoretic framework. The first issue concerns the metaphysics of inference itself. Is a theory of inference a theory of a specific kind of transition between mental states for a kind of agent in an environment or is it simply a theory of an abstract relation between sets of propositions or sentences which can be used to represent and talk about the normativity of inference with respect to what counts as a good or bad inference? As I will use the term, a "separatist" on this issue holds that a theory of inference is only concerned with answering one of these questions, but not both. By contrast, a "unionist" holds that both questions are part of a theory of inference. A unionist accepts that there is a relationship between them, where a satisfactory answer to either needs to integrate with and complement the answer to the other.

The second issue derives from the first, and involves drawing a distinction between the logical representation of an inference and the mental realization of one. The logical representation of an inference is an abstract formal representation of an inference within a logical system, such as first-order classical logic. The mental realization of an inference is an actual inference made by a specific kind of cognitive agent in a reasonably well-defined type of environment, where the inference is for some purpose. In addition, whether the inference needs to be made consciously is dependent on the cognitive situation and the goal in question. For example, in the debate on expert cognition, some, such as Hubert and Stuart Dreyfus (1980), argue that an instance of expert cognition, such as in a lightning chess game, is non-conceptual and non-inferential. One core issue at play in that debate is whether inferences are (a) conceptual or non-conceptual, (b) consciously and deliberatively made or non-consciously and non-deliberatively made, and (c) how much duration is necessary for a mental state transition to count as inferential. Moreover, there are various parameters that we can apply to a theory of inference when considering it in a given cognitive environment, with respect to a specific domain, and in light of an agent's skill level and goal.

The third issue concerns the location of a theory of inference within the broad categories of ontology, logic, social debate theory, philosophy of mind, and epistemology. Here one asks: To which field(s) does a theory of inference properly belong? As I use the term, a "singularist" on this issue would claim that a theory of inference belongs to one of these categories primarily and to others only derivatively, if at all. A "pluralist" would argue that a theory of inference belongs to two or more of these primarily, but not to all. Siderits' observation that *anumāna* as a *pramāṇa* cannot lead to a false cognition trades on the fact that classical Indian philosophers see the debate over how *anumāna* works as being part of the debates over which instruments are valid instruments of knowing (i.e., *pramāṇa* debates). In modern terms one might say that classical Indian philosophy takes human reasoning to be in the service of epistemology.

The fourth issue concerns the debate over logical monism. Logical monism—which has been the default view concerning logic in Western debates for centuries—holds that there is only one true logic. Logical monists give an account of (a) why there is only one true logic, and (b) which logic is the one true logic. Logical pluralists, such as Beal and Restall (2005) and Bueno and Shalkowski (2009), hold that there is more than one true logic. Pluralists try to give an account of (c) why there is more than one true logic, and (d) which logics are contained within the set of true logics. The main logics considered by pluralists include the classic trinity of classical, intuitionistic, and paraconsistent logic. The question they engage is: How should we understand the notions of "logical consequence" and "validity" so that the trinity of logics are all a kind of logic?

All four of these points speak to the questions: (1) How should one pursue the inter-framework approach? and (2) What are the core benefits one derives from consideration of these issues? Let me now apply these points so as to answer (1) and (2).

Using logical pluralism as a background for the inter-theoretic framework, the following argument sets up an answer to (1).

The argument from logical pluralism

1. Either logical pluralism or logical monism is true.
2. If logical pluralism is true, then there is more than one correct formal system of reasoning.
3. Logical Pluralism is true.

∴

4. There is more than one correct formal system of reasoning.
5. The question of whether *arthâpatti* is independent of inference depends on which system of inference we are talking about. For example, it could be dependent on system L_1 while being independent of L_2. And debates over whether it is dependent on L_1 can be engaged without consideration of the question of dependency with respect to some other L_i.

∴

6. Whether or not *arthâpatti* is dependent on or independent of inference rests on which system, L_i, we are talking about.

As an initial response to question (2) we can say the following. We need not debate whether the form of classical Indian *anumāna*, provided by the well-known *Fire-Syllogism* is in fact correct or superior to other forms of inference found in the West, such as Aristotle's categorical syllogism. Second, we need not limit the historical debate as to whether *arthâpatti* is independent of *anumāna* to the framework of classical Indian philosophy, a project pursued by Das (this volume, p. 255) and Yoshimizu (this volume, p. 225). Third, we can make room for the idea that even if *arthâpatti* is dependent on one kind of formal system, that does not preclude it from being independent of another formal system. We can now apply these points to show what value they have in the context of the debate over whether *arthâpatti* is independent of *anumāna*.

Suppose that Ram hears (Utterance 1) "Caitra is alive, but not at home," and transitions to (Thought 2) "Caitra is outside." Yoshimizu (this volume, p. 233) shows that Ram's thought transitions allow for a deductive proof in propositional logic of the sentence "Caitra is outside," and a deductive proof in predicate logic of the sentence "There is some place such that Caitra is at that place, but that place is not home."

For Proof 1, let: C = Caitra is alive, A = Caitra is at home, and B = Caitra is outside. For Proof 2, let A*x* = *x* is alive, L*yx* = *y* is located at *x*, c = *Caitra*, and h = home. Both Proof 1 and 2 are elaborated in much greater detail in Yoshimizu (this volume, p. 233). For the points I will be making, the shortened versions of the proofs will be sufficient. It is important to note that the steps in Yoshimizu's proofs are *intended* to align with *Kumārila's* explicit claims in his account of *arthâpatti*.

Proof 1	
1. $C \rightarrow (A \vee B)$	Assumption
2. C	Assumption
3. $\neg A$	Assumption
4. $A \vee B$	1, 2 MP
5. $\neg B \rightarrow A$	4, IMP
6. $\neg\neg B$	3, 4 MT
7. B	6 DN

Proof 2	
1. $Ac \rightarrow \exists x Lcx$	Assumption
2. Ac	Assumption
3. $\neg Lch$	Assumption
4. $\exists x Lcx$	1, 2 MP
5. $\forall x \neg (Lcx \wedge \neg (h=x)) \rightarrow Lch$	Assumption
6. $\neg \forall x \neg (Lcx \wedge \neg (h=x))$	3, 5, MT
7. $\exists x (Lcx \wedge \neg (h=x))$	6 $\neg\forall x\neg / \exists x$

My commentary on these proofs will use the four issues about inference I listed above. I will start with the fourth point and work backward to the first.

Since logical pluralism is assumed, we can immediately note that these proofs constitute ways in which the relevant claims can be proved. The fact that we can represent Ram's thought transitions in first-order classical logic does not mean that the representation in that system is either correct or the only useful one. For example, we know that the argument expressed by the English compound sentence "All men are mortal, Socrates is a man; therefore Socrates is mortal" can be represented in propositional logic as P, Q, / R, where each letter stands for one atomic sentence in the argument. We are permitted to do this since there are no operators (such as "and") in any of the premises. More importantly, there are no quantifier symbols in propositional logic that can be used to capture the quantificational facts of the argument given by "all" and "some." In terms of propositional logic, the inference captured as P, Q, / R is *invalid*. When we move to quantificational logic, we get a better representation. Where "a" is a name for Socrates, "F" a predicate for "*x* is a man," and "G" a predicate for "*x* is mortal," we can symbolize the argument as: $\forall x\ (Fx \rightarrow Gx)$, F*a* / G*a*. In this translation we can recover the intuition that the inference is *valid.* So, even if Yoshimizu's representations in first-order logic capture an intuition about Ram's thought transition (i.e. that it is valid or good), it does not follow that we need to hold to the view that it is the only representation that can express the intuition that the inference is good. Importantly, we cannot prove Caitra is outside in either propositional intuitionistic logic or predicate intuitionistic logic, since disjunctive syllogism is not permitted in those systems. So, if the thought transition essentially depends on disjunctive syllogism, then intuitionistic logic cannot be a method of proof for Ram's thought transitions. This point shows why the provability of Caitra's location, as elegantly and rigorously provided by Yoshimizu, is important. Kumārila could not have accepted *both* intuitionistic logic *and* thought that Ram's thought transitions are an instance of *arthâpatti*, where it is understood as a non-ampliative inference.

Taking a step backwards, we ought to keep in mind two things: (a) the relation between logic and epistemology in classical Indian philosophy, and (b) the domain in which this inference is supposed to be operating. Concerning (a), as I noted earlier, for classical Indian philosophers human reasoning is in the service of epistemology. This view of the relation could be considered a failing of classical Indian philosophy by those that hold that logic is the pure science of logical consequence, and that the absence of a distinction between logic and epistemology reveals an "immaturity" in their development of a theory of reasoning. This account of the situation is not necessary. First, from the fact that they were primarily interested in another topic—sources of knowledge—it does not follow that they *could not* have developed a theory of the abstract patterns of reasoning and the relations between them. Second, it is perhaps a virtue, rather than a flaw, of their engagement with logic that it is articulated within the framework of their epistemology. In this way, logic is presented as a tool that aims at some end. The aim of logic is knowledge. It is not just truth and the relations that hold between abstract patterns, where the notion of a good argument derives from its *form* being such that it is *impossible* for the premises to be true and the conclusion false.

Stepping backwards again, to an even broader perspective, we need to note that there is a reasonable distinction to be made between the logical representation of an inference and the mental realization of one. As already noted, Yoshimizu could be correct in the way he has represented the logical inference, at least in the sense that he has given us a rendering of it in first-order logic. The fact that it is a plausible logical representation of the inference within a system, however, does not mean it is mentally realized in that way. For example, suppose Ram has a mental transition from a thought produced by hearing (Utterance 1) "Caitra is alive, but not in his house" to (Thought 2) "Caitra is outside." Now Ram could have had a mental transition from (Utterance 1) via steps (1) to (6), culminating in inferring (7). However, he need not. Our question should be the following: For a subject that does not mentally realize the transition from (Utterance 1) to (Thought 2) via (1) to (6) followed by inferring (7), what is the status of their mental state transitions? Are they good? We need not decide whether it is an inference in the narrow sense of fitting into some logical system of inference. Instead, we can say that it is an inference in the broad sense, where we are simply interested in whether one ought to believe (Thought 2) on the basis of (Utterance 1) in a way that respects the environmental conditions under which the utterance and thought were generated. We need to note that both logical representations of inferences and mental realizations (i.e., the actual mental transitions that a cognitive agent undergoes) are of equal value in epistemology. This takes us to our final, and since we are moving backwards, our first point.

What is a theory of inference a theory of? In particular, what were classical Indian philosophers thinking about when they were theorizing about *anumāna*? One thing is quite clear, and strikingly in contrast with the bulk of contemporary Western philosophy of logic: classical Indian philosophers were interested in a *causal theory of inference* because they were interested in human reasoning for the purposes of knowledge acquisition. In the case of inference, a conceivable problem that would arise from the Western philosophical point of view is that the focus on a causal theory of inference leads to the view that classical Indian philosophers were unconcerned with or unable to comprehend the idea of a normative theory of inference. What is the difference? The simple contrast comes from two distinct questions. For a causal account the central question is: How do we in fact reason? For a normative account the central question is: How ought we to reason? Those that advocate a normative account often maintain that a focus on causation misses the point of logic. We draw conclusions; that is, we make all kinds of inferences, in all sorts of ways. Given a specific cognitive end, such as the truth, some of these ways are good, and some are bad. A theory of inference should guide us to which ways of reasoning are productive relative to a given constraint, such as truth or knowledge.

Taking the unionist approach I mentioned earlier, my position is that a theory of inference should be concerned with what sorts of mental realizations cognitive agents experience and the kinds of causal processes involved, as well as how they ought to go about reasoning. We cannot really investigate how one ought to reason unless we are also concerned with how they can and cannot reason. The strong divide between causal accounts and normative accounts is a false dichotomy.

For example, suppose at t_1 someone hits me on the head with a cricket bat, and at t_2 I announce, "Given that there are clouds in the sky and the pavement is wet it is probably raining." Furthermore, it is in fact raining, and I am looking out at the sky and the pavement. A theory of inference should be able to tell us that this series of mental state transitions (assuming that the t_1 event is in the set of proximal causes of the t_2 event) is not a good one. The fact that what I announce counts as a good probabilistic argument isn't enough to tell us why the mental state at t_2 is not a good mental state given the t_1 event. We ought not to believe that it is raining when the set of proximal causes for the belief involves both a thump on the head and a good inductive argument. There is a clear sense in which we can mix *because* and *should* in this case. I should not believe that it is raining, when the cause of that belief involves a thump on the head, regardless of the inferential credentials of the pattern of reasoning that can be abstracted from my mental state transitions. A *unionist* holds that this kind of back and forth between normativity and causal pathways is necessary for a comprehensive theory of inference.

4. THE ISSUE OF REDUCTION

Given that we are exploring the question of whether *arthâpatti* is independent of *anumāna*, we need to discuss not only the nature of inference, but also what it means to say that an instrument is *independent* of other instruments. Das (this volume, p. 255) offers a useful gloss on the classical Indian conception of an independent means of knowing: "For . . . classical Indian philosophers, an epistemic instrument M is *independent* (*svatantra*) just in case there is no other epistemic instrument, M*, which explains how we gain knowledge by M."

Using the inter-framework approach, it will be useful to engage both the debate over "basic sources" in analytic philosophy and the "independent means debate" in classical Indian philosophy, so as to observe the differences. In Table 13, I offer an account of some of the differences.

The table shows that classical Indian philosophers debated whether *arthâpatti* is an independent means of knowledge. They were not debating whether *arthâpatti* is a basic source of knowledge. By contrast, contemporary analytic philosophers are debating whether a source is basic or derivative. However, because we are engaged in cross-cultural conceptual engineering we should ask: how can we bring these debates together to generate new ideas? One way to do so is by looking at recent work within analytic epistemology as to whether inference to the best explanation is reducible to some set of epistemic tools. This question is relevant because, at least in some cases, *arthâpatti* has been identified with a kind of inference to the best explanation. Keating (2013) offers a partial defense, Guha (2016) a critique, Yoshimizu (this volume, p. 225) a further critique.

TABLE 13: Basic Sources and Independent Means Debate

Debate	*Characterization*	*Differentiation*	*Arthâpatti*
Independent Epistemic Instrument Debate in Classical Indian Philosophy	*I* is an independent epistemic instrument of knowledge only if what *I* gives one access to is such that there is no other *I** that can give one access to what *I* does.	Inference is an independent source of knowledge because even though it takes perceptual states as inputs, it yields knowledge that perception cannot yield.	Could be an independent source of knowledge because even though it can take input from other sources, it might still yield knowledge that one cannot acquire through other means.
Basic Sources of Knowledge Debate in Contemporary Analytic Philosophy	*S* is a basic source of knowledge only if *S* does not depend on any other source of knowledge *S** for its deliverances.	Inference is not a basic source of knowledge, since inference takes perceptual input.	Cannot be a basic source of knowledge, since it positively depends on input from other sources, such as perception.

Argument for reduction of *arthâpatti* to inference and perception

1. Some cases of *arthâpatti* involve what might be called "power *arthâpatti*." For example, in the Fire case one postulates the unobservable capacity of fire to burn, based on either a single observation of a burning fire or after repeated observations of burning fire.
2. In cases of power *arthâpatti*, we reason by way of inference to the best explanation.
3. Inference to the best explanation is reducible to enumerative induction combined with perceptual acquaintance.

∴

4. Cases of power *arthâpatti* are reducible to induction combined with perceptual acquaintance.

The crucial premise in the reduction argument above is (3), and Fumerton (2018) provides us with a defense of (3). Not only is his argument important for our investigation of power *arthâpatti*, but the epistemological overlay that he provides for inference to the best explanation (hereafter "IBE") is instructive. The epistemological overlay allows for a contrastive understanding of the classical Indian debate about epistemic instrument reducibility in relation to the Western epistemological debate about source reducibility. What then is the epistemological overlay?

Fumerton maintains a position called "inferential internalism." A consequence of this view is that inference to the best explanation can help solve an epistemological problem for a subject *only if* it has the following form, and the subject has justification for believing both premises.

1. O has occurred.
2. E is the best explanation of O.

∴

3. E.

With respect to the question of whether IBE is reducible to induction, Fumerton (2018: 6) is most interested in examining the question within the framework of *special powers*: "The question . . .I want to ask, is whether these forms of reasoning are *sui generis* kinds of reasoning that do not owe their epistemic power to other more fundamental kinds of reasoning." He offers us an illustrative example:

> If I know what usually causes that distinctive sound I associate with thunder, then I can certainly use the fact that I heard that sound as part of my enthymematic reasoning to reach the conclusion that lightning just struck. But if the causal hypothesis appears as a *premise*, there is no reason yet to suppose that the *reasoning* is anything other than a more mundane sort of statistical reasoning. I antecedently know that this sort of sound is *usually* produced by lightning, I can inductively infer from my awareness of the sound, and my knowledge of its usual source, that in all probability lightning occurred. This is just classic enumerative induction where the correlation described in the premises involves causes and effects.
>
> —Fumerton 2018: 7

Importantly, he characterizes the relationship between conscious awareness and background principles in a way that bridges the gap between internalism and externalism about justification in analytic epistemology.

> We may not bring to the fore of consciousness all that we rely upon in forming beliefs based on what others tell us, but the relevant beliefs are there lurking in the background, and it doesn't take much to remind ourselves that we are critically relying upon them. Furthermore, even as they hovered in the background as non-occurrent beliefs, or even merely beliefs we would form were we prompted in the right way, it is not clear that the ground of those dispositional beliefs isn't active in producing a prodigious array of output beliefs. And in so far as they are active, it seems to me that they would themselves need to be justified.
>
> —Fumerton 2018: 7

His basic argument against IBE having special and distinct powers is the following.

1. There are two cases in which inference to the best explanation is claimed to be used: old cases and novel cases.
2. Both cases can be explained by induction without there being any special powers that attach to inference to the best explanation.

∴

3. IBE has no special powers for arriving at knowledge over and above that of induction alone or induction in combination with perception.

He considers two cases of IBE. The first concerns prior experience cases. Here he discusses the case of testing acidity through litmus paper. The second concerns novel experiences. Here he discusses the case of a gorilla being dissected for the first time.

The Litmus paper case: Suppose we dip litmus paper in a liquid, and it turns red. We infer that it is an acid. In that case, Fumerton argues that even if it looks like we are reasoning to the best explanation, the epistemic powers of our reasoning actually come from standard induction where a causal relation holds between litmus paper turning a certain color and a solution being acidic. He denies that there are any special rules, such as "litmus paper" rules, that we specially employ when we make the inference. Rather, the litmus paper case is simply an instance of general inductive reasoning.

The Gorilla case: Suppose we have never dissected a gorilla. Can we expect to find a heart and a kidney? Recounting the relatively late discovery of gorillas by Europeans, Fumerton argues that we can expect to find a heart and a kidney. The mere fact that gorillas have not been dissected is not sufficient to show that there is nothing from which we can reason. Gorillas are animals of a certain kind, mammals. They have externally identifiable characteristics that allow for them to be classified in this way. Consequently, we can reason via induction, as opposed to IBE.

The basic point of the argument underlying these two cases is that IBE is reducible to induction because the epistemic powers come from induction and not from anything distinctive about IBE. The novel cases are the ones he thinks are significant. His view is that although we might think that we are required to use IBE in a novel case, since there is nothing prior to go on, we are in fact wrong. Often enough, novel cases really are subsumable under larger categories from which we can reason. In effect, there are no true novel cases that would require IBE having special powers.

For the purposes of cross-cultural conceptual engineering, we should note that there are three ways in which Fumerton's argument for the reduction of IBE *does not* align with the classical Indian investigation into whether *arthâpatti* is an independent means of knowledge.

First, Fumerton couches his argument within the framework of justification and belief that one finds in the analysis of knowledge debates following the work of Gettier (1963), where justified true belief is not sufficient for knowledge. However, Karl Potter (1984) and Purushottama Bilimoria (1985) have debated the question of whether classical Indian philosophers even think of knowledge within the paradigm of justified true belief. There are two open questions. On the one hand, if classical Indian philosophers think of knowledge as involving belief and justification, do the Sanskrit equivalents of those terms operate in exactly the same way or do they differ? On the other hand, perhaps classical Indian philosophers, do not begin their epistemic investigation with a compositional account of knowledge, where it has parts. For example, Bilimoria (1985) holds that many Indian philosophers think of knowledge as an episodic mental state as opposed to a static state that persists. In addition, *arthâpatti* is debated as an epistemic instrument independent of inference with respect to knowledge acquisition, and not mere justified belief.

Second, although Fumerton tries to resolve a tension between internalism and externalism about justification in analytic epistemology, he adopts an overarching internalist framework for presenting an account of IBE. On this conception, conscious access to reasons are essential to justification for a belief. By contrast, the dominant conception of knowledge explored in classical Indian philosophy is externalist. On this conception, conscious access to reasons is not essential to knowledge acquisition. As a consequence, there is a partial misalignment. Moreover, can Fumerton's internalist account of justification be used to make sense of *arthâpatti* as a source of knowledge?

Third, *arthâpatti* is debated in classical Indian philosophy as an epistemic instrument for gaining knowledge in a case where *no other means are possible*. However, Fumerton's argument simply shows that in the cases he has considered one can use induction instead of IBE and that the epistemic powers of IBE in those cases are due to induction. From that result, *it does not follow* that *there are no* cases where IBE delivers knowledge that is *not* accessible by other means, even if induction were used. For example, what if there really are novel cases where reasoning via other categories does not lead us to any valuable insights about the target which we are reasoning about. Should we be using induction to show that every argument is either inductive or deductive?

Moving away from cross-cultural comparative philosophy within the inter-theoretic framework approach, it is time to turn to conceptual engineering. Here I want to ask: Is there a way to make progress beyond these two debates by conceptually engineering a new concept for cross-cultural epistemology? I believe this can be done by looking to metaphysics for an alternative account of what could be at issue in epistemic instrument independence and epistemic reduction.

5. ENGINEERING EPISTEMIC GROUNDING

Jonathan Schaffer (2009) offers an account of a kind of metaphysical inquiry based on "metaphysical grounding" within neo-Aristotelian metaphysics. His view is opposed to ontological conceptions of metaphysics, where the central question is: "What exists?" By contrast, he argues:

> The neo-Aristotelian will begin from a *hierarchy view of reality* ordered by priority in nature. The primary entities form the sparse structure of being, while the grounding relations generate an abundant superstructure of posterior entities. The primary is (as it were) all God would need to create the posterior is grounded in, dependent on, and derivative from it. The task of metaphysics is to limn [delineate] the structure.
>
> —Schaffer, 2009: 351

Building on Schaffer's work on metaphysical grounding, we can introduce a notion of "epistemological grounding" into the territory of reduction and independence. A theory of epistemic grounding should tell us (a) which instruments are more fundamental than others, and (b) why certain instruments might be more appropriate for a given domain. By moving away from the notions of reduction and independence and toward the notion of grounding, we invite a new debate on *arthâpatti*, as well as other epistemic instruments.

The following analogy between metaphysical grounding and epistemological grounding is useful for the conceptual engineering of the latter. Within debates on metaphysical grounding, the following inference patterns are discussed. Where T is a table and $P_1 \ldots P_n$ are its proper parts, we get:

General Claim	*Example*
1. X is metaphysically grounded in Y.	T is grounded in its parts $P_1 \ldots P_n$.
∴	
2. Y is more fundamental than X.	$P_1 \ldots P_n$ are more fundamental than T.
3. X is not real, but Y is.	T is not real, but $P_1 \ldots P_n$ is.
4. X is real, but less real than Y.	T is real, but less real than $P_1 \ldots P_n$.

One of the core debates is about what follows from (1). All proponents take it that (2) follows, since grounding is a relation concerning fundamentality; but they differ over whether (3) or (4) follows. Some proponents, such as Schaffer (2009) and Audi (2012), take it that (3) does not follow, but that (4) follows. Replacing, "metaphysical ground" with "epistemic ground," and "real" with "instrument" or "less fundamental," and holding R as a variable ranging over epistemic instruments, we get the following arrangement.

General Claim	*Example*
1. X is epistemically grounded in Y.	*IBE* is epistemically grounded in R.
∴	
2. Y is more fundamental than X.	R is more fundamental than IBE.

General Claim	*Example*
3. *X* is not an instrument, but *Y* is.	*IBE* is not an instrument, but *R* is.
4. *X* is an instrument, but less fundamental than *Y*.	*IBE* is an instrument, but less fundamental than *R*.

Nevertheless, one might ask, what are the advantages of dropping the debate over epistemic reduction and epistemic independence and moving to a debate over epistemic grounding? There are three central advantages.

First, in terms of breathing life into an old debate by bringing it into contact with a contemporary discussion we can manufacture a new debate for philosophers of mind, cognitive scientists, and historians to engage in. Instead of simply asking whether *I* is an epistemic instrument, we can also ask whether *I* is a fundamental epistemic instrument. Although classical Indian philosophers were not in fact discussing epistemic grounding, we can take their work on epistemically independent means as a starting-point for a debate on how to think about epistemic grounding. Importantly, being historically accurate about what they were debating lays a proper foundation for helping us to determine why epistemic grounding might be a more valuable topic of discussion than epistemic independence or epistemic reduction.

Second, we can acknowledge that the rational foundations of an epistemic instrument might be laid out in one way while the cognitive processes that bring about the product of the epistemic instrument are explained in another way. For example, Fumerton could be correct that IBE is not *rationally* fundamental because its rational foundation is best captured by acquaintance and enumerative induction, not by any special powers that IBE has. However, that would not validate an inference to the claim that there *isn't* some context in which IBE is a more accurate description *of the causal processes* that bring about a justified belief in a claim. The only thing that is validated by the fact that the epistemic powers of IBE are present *in virtue of* other rational procedures, such as induction, is that IBE is *not* as fundamental as induction with respect to rational powers. In other words, IBE is less fundamental than induction because it can be adequately explained by other rational procedures. Nevertheless, we need not conclude from its being less fundamental *that it is not an independent epistemic instrument in some contexts*.

Third, there is an obvious constraint on actual exercises of reasoning that supports the drawing of a distinction between *context-sensitive rationality* that is less fundamental than *absolute rationality*. The constraint concerns time-sensitivity with respect to cognitive goals that require conscious decision-making. Human agents make decisions in time. And time is a constraint on rationality. We can model rationality both in terms of an infinite amount of time and a finite amount of time, or without taking time into consideration at all. Given that reasoning takes time, a decision that is rational under n amount of time, might be irrational under $n + m$ amount of time, where either new information is introduced or the connections between pieces of information are further reviewed for error detection. Temporally bounded rationality has been a research program in economics, decision-theory, and psychology for at least fifty years. Herbert Simon, who pioneered the move away *from* abstract time-independent accounts of cognitive agents with perfect rationality *to* time-bound real agents, said this about the research program of "bounded rationality":

> Broadly stated, the task is to replace the global rationality of economic man with the kind of rational behavior that is compatible with the access to information and the computational capacities that are actually possessed by organisms, including man, in the kinds of environments in which such organisms exist.
>
> —Simon 1955: 99

By acknowledging time-sensitivity as a factor on rationality, we can acknowledge that the pattern of reasoning from (1) to (2) still allows for (3) to hold true.

1. *X* is epistemically grounded in *Y*.

∴

2. *X* is a less fundamental epistemic instrument than *Y*.
3. However, *X* can be used as an epistemic instrument in context *C* with respect to goal *G*, where its mental realization is independent of *Y*.

We can take our discussion of *arthâpatti* as an example.

1. *Arthâpatti* is epistemically grounded in *anumāna*.

∴

2. *Arthâpatti* is a less fundamental epistemic instrument than *anumāna*.
3. However, *arthâpatti* can be used as an epistemic instrument in context *C* with respect to goal *G*, where its mental realization is independent of *anumāna*.

In addition, many schools of Indian philosophy hold that *anumāna* depends on *pratyakṣa*. Consequently, the pattern relating *arthâpatti* to *anumāna* can usefully be compared to the pattern relating *pratyakṣa* to *anumāna*.

1. *Anumāna* is epistemically grounded in *pratyakṣa*.

∴

2. *Anumāna* is less fundamental than *pratyakṣa*.
3. However, *anumāna* can be used in context *C* with respect to goal *G* where its mental realization is independent of *pratyakṣa*.

What is the difference between the two cases?

In the case of *pratyakṣa* and *anumāna*, claim (1) is false. The relation that governs how *anumāna* is related to *pratyakṣa* is the relation of epistemic input to epistemic processes, which does yield a dependency relation, if the input always has to come from a given source, such as *pratyakṣa*. Reconsider the classic Fire-Syllogism.

1. Thesis: There is a fire on the hill over there (not perceived directly).
2. Reason: There is smoke on the hill over there (perceived directly).
3. Pervasion: Wherever there is smoke there is fire, like in a kitchen when one is cooking and observes fire and smoke, and unlike on a lake where one never observes either fire or smoke.
4. Application: The case of smoke and fire is like the case of what is experienced in the kitchen.
5. Conclusion: There is a fire on the hill over there (not perceived directly).

TABLE 14: Epistemic Grounding vs. Epistemic Fundamentality

Case	*Epistemic Grounding*	*Epistemic Fundamentality*
anumāna/pratyakṣa	Partial epistemic grounding, since perception merely provides an input to inference, which means that part of the epistemic powers of inference depend on the epistemic powers of perception.	Perception is epistemically more fundamental than inference, since no case of perceptual knowledge depends on inferential knowledge, but all cases of inferential knowledge partially depend on perceptual knowledge for their epistemic powers.
arthâpatti / anumāna	Whole epistemic grounding, since inference provides all the epistemic powers of *arthâpatti*.	Inference is epistemically more fundamental than *arthâpatti*, since no case of inference depends on *arthâpatti*, but all cases of *arthâpatti* derive their epistemic powers from inference. However, *arthâpatti* causally operates independently from inference.

At step (2), we learn that the epistemic support for the reason claim, "that there is smoke on the hill over there," is perception. Therefore, the conclusion of the Fire-Syllogism is *partially* epistemically grounded in perception, but not *wholly* grounded in perception, since the other elements are not perceptual.

By contrast, in the *arthâpatti* and *anumāna* case, the claim is that the epistemic powers of *arthâpatti* are wholly, epistemically grounded in *anumāna*. However, the causal processes that bring about knowledge in the case of *arthâpatti* need not follow the same path as in the case of *anumāna*. Consider Table 14.

The key difference between the two cases concerns the issue of epistemic powers vs. causal pathways. *Anumāna* requires perceptual input, and thus *anumāna* depends on a perceptually acquired input *in all contexts*. Thus, the causal pathway for *anumāna* involves input provided by the causal pathway of *pratyakṣa*. However, in the case of *arthâpatti*, the epistemic powers derive from *anumāna*, but they need not share the same causal pathway. The process of *arthâpatti* takes a causal pathway different from that of *anumāna*. That is, even if the epistemic powers of *arthâpatti* are epistemically grounded in *anumāna*, it will not follow that *arthâpatti* is *not* epistemically independent of *anumāna*. For in some contexts, the causal pathways for *arthâpatti* and *anumāna* will be different.

6. A PATH FORWARD FOR *ARTHÂPATTI*

Bi-directional cross-cultural conceptual engineering is about building concepts for the purposes of a cross-cultural conceptual repertoire. In this effort, I have begun the work necessary to establish *epistemic grounding* as a concept within cross-cultural epistemology. In order to move forward with this project, we should ask ourselves: What purpose does the engineering of epistemic grounding serve for philosophy?

First of all, it alleviates a tension in classical Indian and contemporary analytic debates over the questions of epistemic independence and epistemic reduction. On the one hand, classical Indo-analytic epistemologists are interested in discussing which epistemic instruments are independent of other epistemic instruments. On the other hand, contemporary Anglo-analytic epistemologists are interested in discussing what sources of knowledge are reducible to other sources of knowledge. By engaging with the topic of epistemic grounding, one can address both the issue of instrument independence and epistemic reduction. Furthermore, within the framework of epistemic grounding, one can think about degrees of fundamentality with respect to epistemic powers, but also about how instruments causally operate independently of one another. In general, the account of where the epistemic powers of an instrument rationally derive from is both entangled and separable from the causal pathways in cognition that epistemic instruments take.

Second, the engineered concept opens up room for discussion of the question: what epistemically grounds what? While in the past, we might have debated what sources of knowledge are basic and which instruments are independent of one another, we can now look at how those debates are (a) different, or (b) relevant to a new debate centering on what epistemically grounds what. This makes room for preserving what was at stake historically in the debates, while at the same time allowing for philosophical progress. Just as work on metaphysical grounding makes room for the revitalization of a metaphysical project that focuses on the hierarchy of reality, epistemological grounding transforms two culturally separate debates into a new, third debate. The first debate is exemplified by the exchange between various members of the Nyāya and the Mīmāṃsā tradition over whether *arthâpatti* is an independent instrument from that of *anumāna*. The second debate is exemplified by the question, "Is inference to the best explanation epistemically reducible to induction?"

Finally, the method of bi-directional cross-cultural conceptual engineering I have engaged in here used the classical debate in Indian philosophy over independence and the contemporary analytic debate over epistemic reduction in order to engineer the concept of epistemic grounding. The hope has been that a sufficient amount of groundwork has been laid so as to encourage two things: first, that the method of cross-cultural conceptual engineering is fruitful; and second, that the concept of epistemic grounding can be developed further. The hope here has been that epistemic grounding can serve as a point of departure for an inquiry into what grounds what at the boundary of the mind in relation to ways of knowing. In this inquiry we take seriously the idea that the causal pathways for reasoning in time while constraining rationality partially depart from the way in which we determine whether an instrument is absolutely fundamental from the perspective of temporally unbounded rationality. In a new way we marry the debates between classical Indian philosophers over instrument independence with analytic debates about epistemic reduction.

REFERENCES

Audi, P. (2012), "A Clarification and Defense of the Notion of Grounding," in F. Correia and B. Schneider (eds.), *Grounding and Explanation*, 101–21, Cambridge: Cambridge University Press.

Bilimoria, P. (1985), "*Jñāna* and *Pramā*: The Logic of Knowing—A Critical Appraisal," *Journal of Indian Philosophy* 13, no. 1: 73–102.

Beal, J. C and G. Restall (2005), *Logical Pluralism*, Oxford: Oxford University Press.

Bueno, O. and S. Shalkowski (2009), "Modalism and Logical Pluralism," *Mind* 188, no. 470: 295–321.

Chalmers, D. (2011), "Verbal Disputes," *Philosophical Review* 120, no. 4: 515–56.

Dreyfus, H. and S. Dreyfus (1980), "A Five-Stage Model of the Mental Activities Involved in Directed Skill Acquisition," *Storming Media*, www.stormingmedia.us/15/1554/A155480.html.

Dunne, J. (2004), *Foundations of Dharmakīrti's Philosophy*, Boston: Wisdom Publications, Inc.

Fumerton, R. (2018), "Reasoning to the Best Explanation," in K. McCain and T. Poston (eds.), *Best Explanations: New Essays on Inference to the Best Explanation*, 65–80, Oxford: Oxford University Press.

Ganeri, J. (2001), *Indian Logic: A Reader*, New York: Routledge.

Guha, N. (2016), "On *Arthâpatti*," *Journal of Indian Philosophy* 44, no. 4: 757–76.

Kanauji, T. D. (1992), "Heterogeneity of Arthâpatti," in H. S. Prasad (ed.), *Philosophy, Grammar, and Indology: Essays in Honor of Professor Gustav Roth*, 165–84, Delhi: Indian Books Center Publishing.

Keating, M. (2013), "Mukulabhaṭṭa's defense of *Lakṣanā*: How we use words to mean something else, but not everything else," *Journal of Indian Philosophy* 41, no. 4): 439–61.

Potter, K. (1984), "Does Indian Epistemology Concern Justified True Belief?" *Journal of Indian Philosophy* 12, no. 4: 307–27.

Schaffer, J. (2009), "On What Grounds What," in D. Chalmers, D. Manley, and R. Wasserman (eds.), *Metametaphysics: New Essays on the Foundations of Ontology*, 347–83, Oxford: Oxford University Press.

Siderits, M. (2003), *Personal Identity and Buddhist Philosophy: Empty Persons*, Farnham, UK: Ashgate Publishing.

Simon, H. (1955), "A Behavioral Model of Rational Choice," *Quarterly Journal of Economics* 69, no. 1: 99–118.

Vaidya, A. (2010), "Philosophical Methodology: The Current Debate," *Philosophical Psychology* 23, no. 3: 391–417.

Vaidya, A. (2012), "Intuition and Inquiry," *Essays in Philosophy* 13, no. 1: 284–95.

Vaidya, A. (2015), "Public Philosophy: Cross-Cultural and Multi-Disciplinary," *Journal of Comparative Philosophy* 6, no. 2: 35–57.

TABLE OF IMPORTANT FIGURES, DATES, AND WORKS

Dating figures in Indian philosophy is difficult, and sometimes approximations involve a matter of centuries. The table below should be taken as a helpful guide and not an authoritative position on matters of dating—see introductions to relevant translations for further discussion.

Figure	*Dates*	*Relevant Works*
Jaimini	second to fourth century BCE	MS
Akṣapāda Gautama	first to second century CE	NS
Śabara	fifth century CE	ŚBh
Vātsyāyana	450 CE	NBh
Diṅnāga	fifth to sixth century CE	PS, PSV
Kumārila Bhaṭṭa	sixth to seventh century CE	BT, ŚV, TV
Dharmakīrti	sixth to seventh century CE	PV, PVSV
Prabhākara Miśra	seventh century CE	B
Umbeka Bhaṭṭa	early eighth century CE	TṬ
Śāntarakṣita	725–88 CE	TS
Kamalaśīla	740–95 CE	TSP
Jayanta Bhaṭṭa	ninth century CE	NM
Śālikanātha Miśra	ninth century CE	PP, RP
Vācaspati Miśra	tenth century CE	NVTṬ
Sucarita Miśra	middle tenth century CE	K
Pārthasārathi Miśra	early eleventh century CE	NR
Udayana	eleventh century CE	NK
Gaṅgeśa	early fourteenth century CE	TCM
Raghunātha Śiromaṇi	fifteenth century CE	D, PATN
Nāryāyaṇa Bhaṭṭa	seventeenth century CE	MM

ENGLISH–SANSKRIT GLOSSARY

absence, cognition of absence, non-perception, non-presence, non-apprehension	*abhāva*
actualization, bringing-into-being	*bhāvanā*
arthâpatti of an audible antecedent, *arthâpatti* on the basis of what is heard, verbal *arthâpatti*	*śrutârthâpatti*
being a property of the subject	*pakṣa-dharmatā-jñāna*
cognition, awareness-event	*jñāna*
comparison, analogy	*upamāna*
conflict, contradiction	*virodha*
consideration, subsumptive judgment	*parāmarśa*
counterpositive	*pratiyogin*
delimitor	*avacchedaka*
denotation through what is construed	*anvitâbhidhāna*
deviating, inconclusive	*anaikāntika*
differentiator	*viśeṣa*
dissimilar example, counter-locus	*vipakṣa*
doubt	*saṃśaya*
epistemic instrument	*pramāṇa*
epistemic validity, validity, knowledge-source status, truth	*prāmāṇya*
example, confirming instance	*dṛṣṭânta*
expectancy, verbal expectation, dependency	*ākāṅkṣā*
expression of related word meanings	*anvitâbhidhāna*
fallacy, consequence, undesirable consequence, difficulty	*prasaṅga*
faults of the locus	*pakṣa-doṣa*
hypothetical reasoning	*tarka*
incongruity, inexplicability, not making sense otherwise	*anupapatti*
inexplicability otherwise, does not make sense otherwise, incongruity-otherwise	*anyathânupapatti*
inference	*anumāna*
inferential set of conditions, causal apparatus, inferential complex, causal complex	*sāmāgrī*
invariable concomittance	*avinâbhāva*
knowledge	*pramā*
language, linguistic expression, verbal testimony	*śabda*
mark, indicator, inferential reason	*liṅga*
mutual dependence	*anyônyâśraya*
negative (correlation)	*vyatireka*
negative correlation	*vyatireka-sahacara, -sahacāra*
negative pervasion	*vyatireka-vyāpti*

negative-only	*kevala-vyatireka*
non-apprehension, non-cognition	*anupalabdhi*
object, state of affairs, meaning	*artha*
objective *arthâpatti*, *arthâpatti* on the basis of what is seen	*dṛṣṭârthâpatti*
obtaining, sudden occurrence of, besetting	*āpatti*
perception	*pratyakṣa*
pervasion	*vyāpti*
positive (concomitance, correlation), co-presence	*anvaya*
positive and negative	*anvaya-vyatireka*
positive correlation	*anvaya-sahacara*, -*sahacāra*
positive-only	*kevalânvaya*
positive pervasion	*anvaya-vyāpti*
postulation, positing, hypothesis, imagination, supposition, presumption	*kalpanā*
probandum, object known by *anumāna*	*anumeya*
promoter	*prayojaka*
property	*dharma*
property to be proven, inferred property, probandum	*sādhya*
proximity	*sannidhi*
qualificand	*viśeṣya*
qualifier	*viśeṣaṇa*
reason, inferential reason	*hetu*
regulation	*niyama*
relation of expressed meanings	*abhihitânvaya*
semantic fit, compatibility	*yogyatā*
similar example	*sapakṣa*
subject, locus	*pakṣa*
substance	*dravya*
testimony, statement, Vedic testimony	*āgama*
thesis	*pratijñā*
tradition	*aitihya*
trigger, indicator	*gamaka*
trope, quality, property	*guṇa*
universal, natural kind property	*jāti*
unseen, unobserved	*adṛṣṭa*
unseen force	*apūrva*
wavering, ambiguity, deviation	*vyabhicāra*

SANSKRIT–ENGLISH GLOSSARY

This glossary is organized in order of the Sanskrit alphabet, as listed below.
a ā i ī u ū ṛ ṝ ḷ ḹ e ē ai o au
k kh g gh ṅ c ch j jh ñ ṭ ṭh ḍ ḍh ṇ t th d dh n p ph b bh m y r l v ṣ ś s h

adṛṣṭa	unseen, unobserved
anumāna	inference
anumeya	probandum, object known by *anumāna*
anupapatti	incongruity, inexplicability, not making sense otherwise
anupalabdhi	non-apprehension, non-cognition
anaikāntika	deviating, inconclusive
anyathânupapatti	inexplicability otherwise, does not make sense otherwise, incongruity-otherwise
anyônyâśraya	mutual dependence
anvaya	positive (concomitance, correlation), co-presence
anvaya-vyatireka	positive and negative
anvaya-vyāpti	positive pervasion
anvaya-sahacara, -sahacāra	positive correlation
anvitâbhidhāna	expression of related meanings, denotation through what is construed
apūrva	unseen force
abhāva	absence, cognition of absence, non-perception, non-presence, non-apprehension
abhihitânvaya	relation of expressed word meanings
artha	object, state of affairs, meaning
avacchedaka	delimitor
avinâbhāva	invariable concomittance
ākāṅkṣā	expectancy, verbal expectation, dependency
āgama	testimony, statement, Vedic testimony
āpatti	obtaining, sudden occurrence of, besetting
aitihya	tradition
upamāna	comparison, analogy
kalpanā	postulation, positing, hypothesis, imagination, supposition, presumption
kevalânvaya	positive-only
kevala-vyatireka	negative-only
gamaka	trigger, indicator
guṇa	trope, quality, property

jāti	universal, natural kind property
jñāna	cognition, awareness-event
tarka	hypothetical reasoning
dṛṣṭânta	example, confirming instance
dṛṣṭârthâpatti	objective *arthâpatti*, *arthâpatti* on the basis of what is seen
dravya	substance
dharma	property
niyama	regulation
pakṣa	subject, locus
pakṣa-doṣa	faults of the locus
pakṣa-dharmatā-jñāna	being a property of the subject
parāmarśa	consideration, subsumptive judgment
pratijñā	thesis
pratiyogin	counterpositive
pratyakṣa	perception
pramā	knowledge
pramāṇa	epistemic instrument
prasaṅga	fallacy, consequence, undesirable consequence, difficulty
prayojaka	promoter
prāmāṇya	epistemic validity, validity, knowledge-source status, truth
bhāvanā	actualization, bringing-into-being
yogyatā	semantic fit, compatibility
liṅga	mark, indicator, inferential reason
vipakṣa	dissimilar example, counter-locus
virodha	conflict, contradiction
viśeṣa	differentiator
viśeṣaṇa	qualifier
viśeṣya	qualificand
vyatireka	negative (correlation)
vyatireka-vyāpti	negative pervasion
vyatireka-sahacara, -sahacāra	negative correlation
vyabhicāra	wavering, ambiguity, deviation
vyāpti	pervasion
sapakṣa	similar example
sannidhi	proximity
saṃśaya	doubt
sādhya	property to be proven, inferred property, probandum
sāmāgrī	inferential set of conditions, causal apparatus, inferential complex, causal complex
śabda	language, linguistic expression, verbal testimony
śrutârthâpatti	*arthâpatti* of an audible antecedent, *arthâpatti* on the basis of what is heard, verbal *arthâpatti*
hetu	reason, inferential reason

NAME AND SUBJECT INDEX

Sanskrit words are included within this index, ordered without taking diacritics into account. Please see glossaries for translations of Sanskrit terms. The index does not include a comprehensive listing of each English translation possible.